MARKETING
FOUNDATIONS
AND FUNCTIONS

Jim Burrow, Ph.D.
North Carolina State University

Steve Eggland, Ph.D.
University of Nebraska

SOUTH-WESTERN PUBLISHING CO.

Vice-President/Editor-in-Chief: Dennis M. Kokoruda

Developmental Editor: Nancy Long

Marketing Manager: Larry Qualls

Production Manager: Carol Sturzenberger

Production Editor: Mark Cheatham

Art Director: John Robb

Photo Editor: Linda Ellis

Cover Design: Lisa Acup
Graphica Design and Communications Group

Internal Design: Elaine St. John-Lagenaur,
South-Western Publishing Co.

Internal Electronic Art: Alan Brown, Angela Fisher, Matt Strippelhoff,
Photonics Graphics

ISBN: 0-538-62541-4

Library of Congress Catalog Card Number: 94-066356

1 2 3 4 5 6 7 8 9 0 VH 99 98 97 96 95

Printed in the United States of America

I(T)P

International Thomson Publishing

South-Western Publishing Co. is an ITP company. The ITP trademark is used under license.

PREFACE

What has allowed the U.S. economy to be the most successful in the world? In one word—marketing. Marketing makes it possible for businesses to find customers for their products and services and to sell them at a profit. Marketing helps consumers select the best products and services from all those available in order to satisfy their wants and needs.

We live in a marketing-driven economy that has resulted in one of the highest standards of living in the world. Countries that are struggling to change after years of Communist control and those that are seeking to emerge from "third world" economies look to United States marketers for help.

Marketing and You

Marketing Foundations and Functions has been developed to help you learn about marketing and to develop marketing skills. You will see that marketing is one of the largest and most exciting career areas in business today. It also includes some of the highest paying occupations in business. Marketing is increasingly important to many non-business organizations as well. Even if you do not choose a career in marketing, an understanding of marketing will be very useful in your future. This is true no matter what job you hold or in what organization you work.

Consumers and business people alike are just beginning to understand the value and power of marketing. They realize that it is much more than advertising and selling. Marketing includes a full range of tools, ranging from product and service planning to marketing-information management to financing and distribution.

Coverage of this Text

Marketing Foundations and Functions is divided into two parts. In Part I, Foundations of Marketing, you will study the three important areas fundamental to successful marketing. They are economic foundations, business and marketing foundations, and human resource foundations. The 11 chapters in Part I review principles and concepts you have probably learned in other courses, such as Economics, Algebra, English, and Business Principles. You will see how those principles and concepts support marketing decisions. You will also learn about important marketing concepts, such as target markets, marketing mixes, marketing research, and marketing strategy. You will learn how marketing is used successfully in a variety of United States and international businesses. At the end of Part I, you will be introduced to the most important marketing tool: the marketing plan.

Part II, Functions of Marketing, will help you increase your understanding of all major marketing activities. You will develop useful marketing skills as you review many current business applications of marketing and complete a variety of real-world marketing activities. Part II expands the study of marketing into areas not often covered in marketing textbooks, including important applications of computers and other technology and interesting uses of marketing in sports, entertainment, politics, and international business.

Marketing Foundations and Functions is designed to make your study of marketing both interesting and successful. The basics of marketing are presented early in the text and you use them immediately. You will see how those concepts relate to the knowledge and skills you have already developed in other courses and through your own experience as a consumer and as an employee. Each chapter will expand your knowledge and relate the new information to what you have already learned. You will see that the emphasis is not on memorizing long lists of definitions and facts, but on using marketing knowledge and skills.

Special Features

You will see businesses using marketing in special features in each chapter. The *Newsline* at the beginning of each chapter provides a focus on important topics in a news article format. *Classics and Contemporaries* illustrates how businesses of the past and today have used marketing, both effectively and ineffectively. *A Global Vision* presents examples of marketing in international businesses to illustrate the worldwide applications of marketing principles. *In the Spotlight* features individuals, businesses, and products that have made unique marketing contributions. Finally, *Challenges* raises important issues facing today's marketers, providing the opportunity for you to consider how businesses should address the challenges they face.

End-of-Chapter Activities

The end-of-chapter activities are organized in a very unique way. Rather than completing a series of vocabulary terms and questions, you will apply what you have learned using problems, projects, and creative activities organized within four sections. *Marketing Foundations* reviews new concepts and principles from the chapter. *Marketing Research* presents data for analysis or asks you to gather and review information used by marketers to make decisions. The *Marketing Planning* section includes problems in which you apply new information and develop marketing skills. The final section, *Marketing Management*, lets you think about marketing problems, make the same types of decisions as marketing managers, and integrate the information you have learned in previous chapters.

Supplements to the Text

Several supplementary resources are available with the textbook to add to your knowledge of marketing and to aid in developing marketing skills. You may use some of these within your classroom, individually or as a team. Some may be completed on your own at home to reinforce key concepts.

Student Workbook

The *Student Workbook* provides additional problems and projects to challenge your creativity and decision-making skills. The *Student Workbook* uses the same format as the end-of-chapter activities to build your understanding and skills from foundations to management.

Casebook

Management education programs in colleges, universities, and industry often use case studies to present realistic business situations for analysis. The *Casebook* that accompanies *Marketing Foundations and Functions* includes 24 cases, one case for each chapter. Cases are drawn from businesses around the world. You will analyze the information, make a decision, and defend that decision to your instructor or other class members.

Template Disks

Technology, especially computer technology, has changed the way businesses operate. It will be difficult to be successful in business in the future without well-developed computer skills. Many of the end-of-chapter activities have been designed so you can use typical business computer software applications (word processing, database, spreadsheets, graphics/desktop publishing) to complete them. These are identified with the computer icon shown at left.

In each chapter, one end-of-chapter activity has been developed that can be completed with the use of a supplementary template disk. These have been identified with the diskette icon shown at left. You can use the template developed for each of the problems to create a solution using the computer and a spreadsheet program.

Marketing Planning Guide

A unique resource available with this package is the *Marketing Planning Guide.* A written marketing plan is one of the most important tools available to marketers. Businesses that develop and use marketing plans are typically much more successful than those that do not. However, developing an effective plan is a difficult challenge.

The *Marketing Planning Guide* takes you step-by-step through a marketing plan as you learn about marketing. By gathering information, answering specific questions, and making decisions, you will be able to create an effective marketing plan for a product, service, or business of your choice. The *Marketing Planning Guide* is available in both a workbook format and a word processing template disk.

Enjoy this Text

Marketing is both challenging and interesting. Marketing careers require people who are well educated, creative, and energetic. *Marketing Foundations and Functions* will help you understand marketing and how it is used in businesses and other organizations. Through its use, you will develop the knowledge and skills needed for many exciting careers. Enjoy your study of marketing.

About the Authors

The authors of *Marketing Foundations and Functions* have spent all of their professional lives in marketing and marketing education. Both are nationally known for their work in marketing education and their leadership in professional associations.

Dr. Jim Burrow is an Associate Professor at North Carolina State University. He was a member of the Marketing Strategy Committee that developed the national marketing plan for Marketing Education in 1987. He co-chaired the Curriculum Committee that designed the Curriculum Framework for Marketing Education that is now used nationwide to guide curriculum planning.

Dr. Burrow has served as a board member of the Marketing Education Association for six years and was a member of the National Council for Marketing Education for four years. He is also a member of the American Marketing Association and the American Society for Training and Development. He regularly consults with businesses and other organizations on marketing, marketing planning, and the training of marketing personnel.

Dr. Steven Eggland is a Professor at the University of Nebraska. He was also a member of the Marketing Strategy Committee that developed the national marketing plan for Marketing Education.

Dr. Eggland has been active in many professional marketing associations, including service on the Boards of Directors of the American Vocational Association, the Marketing Education Association, and the Marketing Education Resource Center. Dr. Eggland has also been a contributor to *VocEd*, the journal of the American Vocational Association, and served on the editorial board of *Marketing Educators' Journal*.

Contributors

The authors acknowledge with appreciation the contributions of many others to the development of *Marketing Foundations and Functions*. Many marketers and marketing instructors participated in research and offered ideas and recommendations for the book, as well as reviewed chapters during its development. Cathy Williams, marketing instructor at Apex High School, Apex, North Carolina, deserves special recognition for field testing the initial manuscript with her students. Finally, the authors acknowledge the many businesses and business publications identified in the text. The information from each allowed the authors to present a real-life picture of marketing.

CONTENTS

PART 1   FOUNDATIONS OF MARKETING

PART 2   FUNCTIONS OF MARKETING

UNIT 4   CREATING THE MIX: PRODUCT AND DISTRIBUTION • 340

UNIT 6 MANAGING RISKS, FINANCES, AND INFORMATION • 600

CHAPTER 20 BE AWARE OF RISKS • 602

CHAPTER 21 MARKETING REQUIRES MONEY • 626

CHAPTER 22 MARKETERS NEED INFORMATION • 662

UNIT 7 MANAGING AND IMPROVING MARKETING • 694

PART

1

FOUNDATIONS OF

MARKETING

UNIT
1

Introducing Marketing

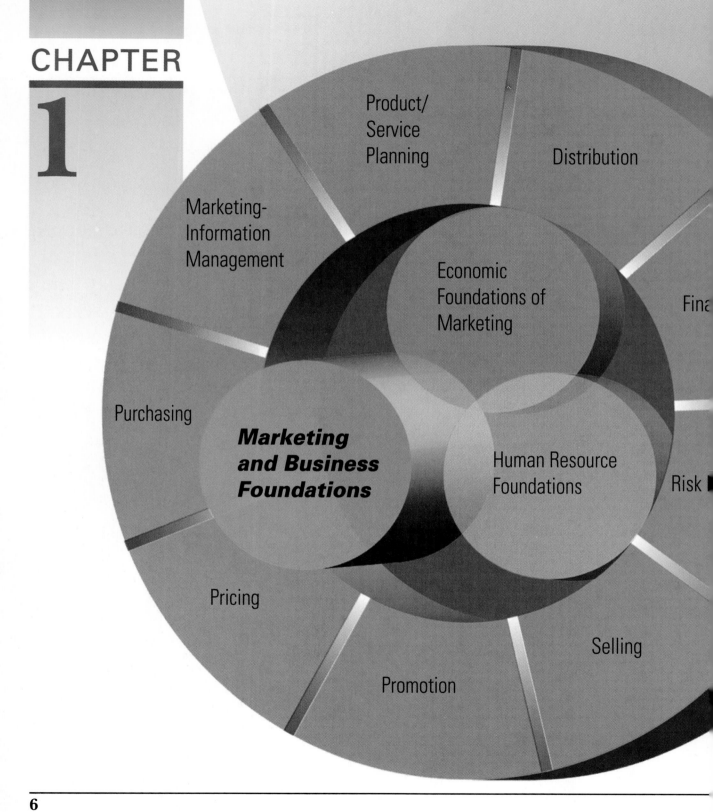

Product/
Service
Planning

Distribution

Marketing-
Information
Management

Economic
Foundations of
Marketing

Fina

Purchasing

*Marketing
and Business
Foundations*

Human Resource
Foundations

Risk

Pricing

Selling

Promotion

Marketing Today

⬤BJECTIVES

1. List several benefits you can obtain from studying marketing.

2. Provide examples of the types of organizations involved in marketing and several marketing activities.

3. Identify and define the nine marketing functions.

4. Present a simple definition of marketing.

5. Explain the importance of the marketing concept.

6. Describe the two steps used to implement the marketing concept.

7. Discuss why marketing is important for businesses.

NEWSLINE

THE UNITED STATES EXPORTS FREE ENTERPRISE EXPERTISE

As the former Soviet Union and eastern European countries continue their difficult transformations from government-controlled to "free-market" economies, the United States is once again demonstrating international leadership. Those nations implementing new economic systems are looking to the United States for expertise in organizing and managing the marketing systems essential to competitive business success.

It became evident long ago in the United States that the capability of producing and manufacturing good products is not enough to guarantee the success of companies. Marketing activities are also necessary. Companies need to be able to identify customers, move products efficiently to those customers, develop effective communications and promotion programs, assist in financing for customers, and help the customer use the products after the sale. These activities must be done in a way that allows the company to make a profit.

In government-controlled economies, individual businesses did not have to be as concerned about profits for each product or as concerned that consumers were necessarily satisfied with each product. Therefore, marketing functions are not well developed in those countries, making it very difficult to implement the changes needed for new economic systems to suceed.

Hundreds of United States marketing experts are now working in the developing countries to help with the changes. People are redesigning transportation systems, looking at processes for handling and storing products, developing the technology for market research,

> **Those nations implementing new economic systems are looking to the United States for expertise in organizing and managing the marketing systems essential to competitive business success.**

establishing credit and financing policies and procedures, and assisting with the many other activities needed for effective marketing. The United States is viewed as a model of marketing effectiveness, and U.S. marketers are in demand to assist with the development of the effective functions and activities required. Marketing expertise has become an important new U.S. export.

WHY STUDY MARKETING?

Marketing is exciting, important, and profitable. Businesses, individual consumers, and our economy benefit from effective marketing. This chapter introduces marketing in a way many people will not recognize. Even though marketing is a well-known word, it is often misused or misunderstood. Marketing has changed a great deal in the past ten to twenty years. Some businesses still do not use marketing effectively.

As you study this chapter you will begin to understand the term marketing and how marketing provides broad benefits when used effectively. You will be able to identify the differences between effective and ineffective marketing. You will see how marketing and marketing activities have changed. Marketing is now an important activity essential not only to the success of manufacturers and retailers, but also to government agencies, hospitals, law offices, schools, and churches. After completing this chapter, you will be able to identify the major functions of marketing and describe examples of those functions as they are performed by businesses. In addition, you will see that successful businesses develop an approach to marketing planning that responds to the needs of customers so that customers will be satisfied with the products and services they purchase.

WHERE DOES MARKETING TAKE PLACE?

Marketing is one of the most visible business activities around you. You do not often see products being manufactured, accountants maintaining the financial records of a business, or human resources managers hiring and training personnel. But you see marketing every day. Marketing includes advertisements on the radio, products being transported by truck, and marketing researchers in shopping malls.

You are involved in marketing. You make marketing decisions regularly. You assist routinely in the effective marketing of products and services. Marketing activities are involved when you select the products or services you intend to purchase. You are involved in marketing activities when you decide to use cash or a credit card. When you pay for the delivery of a bulky product to your home (rather than attempt to transport it yourself), you are involved in marketing activities.

By studying marketing, you will learn how businesses use marketing to increase their effectiveness and the profits they make. You will also improve your personal marketing skills. Those skills are useful to you as a consumer as you make better purchasing decisions. Marketing skills are used as you make an application for college. You use marketing skills when you interview with a potential employer. Marketing skills are used also when you serve as a leader of an organization. And they are the skills needed for many exciting and well-paying careers in the business world.

Every business today is involved in marketing. Over four million firms in the United States have marketing as their primary business activity (see Figure 1-1). Examples of those businesses are advertising agencies, real estate offices, marketing research businesses, finance companies, travel agencies, and retail stores. Most large businesses have marketing departments employing many types of marketing specialists. Even small companies are finding they need to employ people who understand marketing and are able to complete a number of marketing activities.

There are many types of marketing jobs ranging from selling to inventory management. Careers in advertising, sales promotion, customer service, credit, insurance, transportation, and research require preparation in marketing. Marketers work for manufacturers, law offices, hospitals, muse-

All Types of Businesses Use Marketing		
Businesses Directly Involved In Marketing	**Businesses With Major Marketing Activities**	**Businesses With Limited Marketing Role**
advertising agencies	retailers	law offices
marketing research firms	manufacturers	physicians
sales representatives	banks	accounting firms
trucking companies	real estate agencies	government agencies
credit card companies	insurance companies	universities
telemarketing businesses	automobile dealers	construction businesses
travel agencies	farmers and ranchers	public utilities

FIGURE 1-1 ▪ Some businesses are more actively involved in marketing than others, but all businesses complete many marketing activities.

ums, professional sports teams, and symphonies. There are marketing jobs available as you begin your career. These jobs include retail clerk, bank teller, stock person, telemarketing interviewer, and delivery person. You could advance to many marketing management jobs, some requiring a great deal of education and experience. Typically marketing positions can be among the highest paid jobs in most companies. Because of the change and growth that has occurred in marketing, many people view it as the most diverse and exciting career area of the twenty-first century.

WHAT IS MARKETING?

When many people hear the word marketing they only think of advertising and selling. However, many marketing activities need to be completed before a product or service is ever ready to be advertised and sold.

MARKETING FUNCTIONS

Marketing activities can be grouped into nine functions. These functions will be introduced with brief descriptions in the following sections, and they are summarized in Figure 1-2 on the following page. Don't be concerned if you don't completely understand the meaning as you read the descriptions. You will learn more about the functions and how each function is used as a part of effective marketing in later chapters.

1. **Product/Service Planning**—Assisting in the design and development of products and services that will meet the needs of prospective customers.

2. **Purchasing**—Determining the purchasing needs of an organization, identifying the best sources to obtain the needed products and services, and completing the activities necessary to obtain and use them.

3. **Financing**—Budgeting for marketing activities, obtaining the necessary financing, and providing financial assistance to customers to assist them with purchasing the organization's products and services.

4. **Distribution**—Determining the best methods and procedures to be used so prospective customers are able to locate, obtain, and use the products and services of an organization.

5. **Pricing**—Establishing and communicating the value of products and services to prospective customers.

6. **Risk Management**—Providing security and safety for products, personnel, and customers, and reducing the risk associated with marketing decisions and activities.

7. **Marketing-Information Management**—Obtaining, managing, and using market information to improve decision making and the performance of marketing activities.

8. **Promotion**—Communicating information to prospective customers through advertising and other promotional methods to encourage them to purchase the organization's products and services.

9. **Selling**—Direct, personal communications with prospective customers in order to assess needs and satisfy those needs with appropriate products and services.

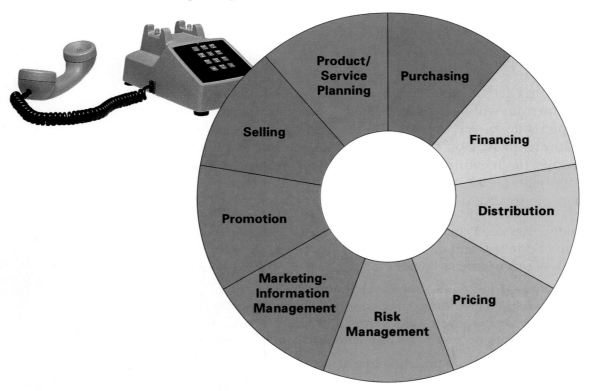

FIGURE 1-2 ■ Marketing activities can be categorized within nine functions.

Each of these functions occurs every time a product or service is developed and sold. The performance of the activities described in the functions is the responsibility of marketers. So you can see that marketing is a very complex part of business and is very important to the success of businesses and to the satisfaction of customers.

COMPANIES USE THE MARKETING FUNCTIONS

If you study businesses carefully, you can identify the marketing functions being performed by companies as they develop new products, improve marketing procedures, and respond to customer needs. For example:

■ The Sony Corporation used *product/service planning* to develop the Video Walkman, which combines a 3-inch television with an 8 mm. videocasette recorder.

■ Wal-Mart uses the *purchasing* function when it develops agreements with U. S. manufacturers to purchase products that other retailers obtain from foreign suppliers in order to promote a "buy American" image.

■ Major automobile manufacturers, such as General Motors, demonstrate the *financing* function when they maintain their own financing organizations (GMAC) to make loans to consumers available at the automobile dealerships.

■ Hertz uses a unique *distribution* strategy as a part its car rental service. Hertz will park a car at the exit of an airport terminal with the engine running, heated in the winter or cooled in the summer, and with all paperwork completed for selected customers to speed their departure from the airport.

■ A company that supplies pastries, cookies, and other snacks to offices uses an "honor system" for *pricing* where customers select the items they want from a self-service display and put the money into a cash box. A representative from the company regularly resupplies the display and collects the money from the cash box.

■ A security tag is used by apparel retailers to reduce shoplifting as part of *risk management*. When a shoplifter attempts to remove the tag from the merchandise, a permanent dye capsule explodes, ruining the material so the apparel is of no value to the shoplifter.

■ The electronic scanners used at checkouts of supermarkets provide information on purchases so managers can instantly determine what is being purchased in order to keep the best assortment of products available for customers. This is an example of the use of *marketing-information management*.

■ Businesses selling expensive products such as ocean-front condominiums prepare high quality video tapes which provide information and promote products using audio and video messages. The video tapes are sent to carefully selected customers to interest them in purchasing a condominium through a unique type of *promotion.*

■ Many professional firms are recognizing the importance of personal *selling* to the success of their practices. Selected executives in law offices, accounting firms, and banks are completing professional sales training in order to effectively develop new clients for the businesses.

DEFINING MARKETING

Because of the many functions and activities that are part of marketing, it is not easy to develop a definition of marketing that effectively describes it in a way that is meaningful to everyone. And, as you will learn in Chapter 2, marketing has changed a great deal in recent years and continues to change. A simple definition was presented in a 1960 book of marketing terms published by the American Marketing Association. Marketing was described as "the performance of business activities that direct the flow of goods and services from producer to consumer or user." As marketing developed and was applied in a broad set of businesses and organizations, definitions became more complex. Marketing now includes customer research and product development activities. It applies to non-profit businesses and to organizations not considered businesses (churches, sororities and fraternities, schools, and libraries). Not only is marketing used for products and services, but for individuals (political candidates, artists, sports stars), and even to promote ideas (stop smoking, recycling, stay in school).

The most recent definition of marketing, accepted by the American Marketing Association in 1985, is very long and complex, but it communicates how marketing has changed over the years. That definition is: *Marketing is the process of planning and executing the conception, pricing, promotion, and distribution of ideas, goods, and services to create exchanges that satisfy individual and organizational objectives.* Because marketing can be applied in very different ways in various businesses and organizations, and because marketing needs to be easily understood, a simplified definition will be used for this book that describes the value marketing offers to those who use it well. *Marketing is the creation and maintenance of satisfying exchange relationships.*

As you think about that definition you need to carefully consider all parts of it in order to understand marketing. *Creation* suggests that marketing is involved from the very beginning as products and services are being developed. *Maintenance* means that marketing must continue to be used as long as a business or organization is operating. *Satisfaction* of both the business and the customer is an important goal of marketing. In other words, when products or services are exchanged, the needs of everyone involved must be met as well as possible. Finally *exchange relationships* applies the definition to any exchange where people are giving and receiving something of value as shown in Figure 1-3. Marketing is needed by, but not limited to, businesses that are selling products and services. The next section will show why a definition that emphasizes "satisfying exchanges" accurately describes effective marketing.

THE MARKETING CONCEPT

Marketing was not always an important part of business. Indeed, marketing was not even a term used in business until the last half of this century. In the early part of the century,

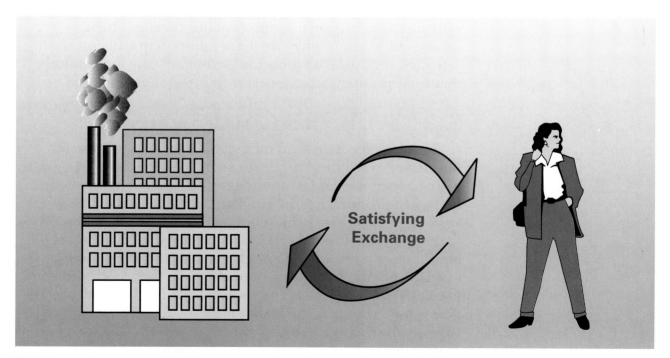

FIGURE 1-3 ■ Marketing creates satisfying exchanges between businesses and consumers.

businesses were concerned about producing products that customers needed and were able to afford. Major efforts that could be considered marketing were directed at getting the products to customers. There were not many choices of transportation methods, and roads and highways were not well developed. The primary way to sell more products was to be able to deliver them to a larger number of customers.

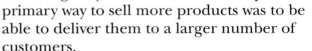

As consumers increased their standard of living and had more money to spend, the demand for newer and better products increased. Demand was usually greater than the available supply of products. Business people concentrated on production and seldom had to worry a great deal about marketing. Customers were often eager to buy new products and would seek out the manufacturer when they heard of a product they wanted.

Over time, however, production processes improved, there was more competition among producers and manufacturers, and consumers had more choices of products and services available. Therefore, businesses had to compete with each other to get customers to buy their products. Businesses began to increase their attention to basic marketing activities, such as advertising and selling, to convince customers that their products were superior to those of competitors.

SATISFYING CUSTOMER NEEDS

As it became more and more difficult and expensive for businesses to sell their products, some business people began to realize an important fact. Businesses could no longer be successful by just producing more products or by increasing the amount of advertising and selling efforts for the products. They had to produce products that customers wanted. The most successful businesses were the ones that considered customers' needs and worked to satisfy those needs as they produced and marketed their products and services. That philosophy of business is now known as the marketing concept. *The marketing concept is using the needs of customers as the primary focus during the planning, production, distribution, and promotion of a product or service.*

Using the marketing concept is not as easy as it might sound. Three activities must be accomplished by businesses if they want to use it successfully. Those three activities are illustrated in Figure 1-4.

Elements of the Marketing Concept

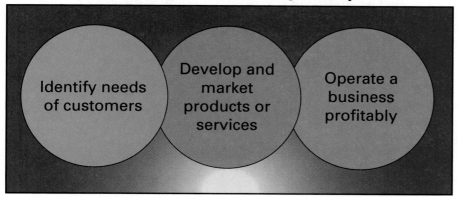

FIGURE 1-4 ▪ Effective marketing emphasizes customers, products, and profits.

▪ First, the business must be able to identify what will satisfy customers' needs.

▪ Second, the business must be able to develop and market products or services that customers consider to be better than other choices.

▪ Third, the business must be able to operate profitably.

You can see many examples of businesses that are successfully identifying and responding to needs of customers. Fast food restaurants provide breakfast menus and late night hours in order to have their products available when customers want them. Many banks now provide services so customers can pay bills, transfer money, and check account balances by using a telephone or a personal computer. Hospitals offer wellness programs, weight loss clinics, and fitness centers to attract additional clients and broaden their image. Colleges offer courses to area high school students to allow college credits to be earned prior to graduation and to interest students in enrolling full time at the college.

THE CONSEQUENCES OF NOT SATISFYING CUSTOMER NEEDS

Businesses that do not use the marketing concept are more concerned about producing products than understanding customer needs. Once products are developed, they rely on marketing activities to try to sell those products. You may be aware of the difficulty some automobile manufac-

CLASSICS AND CONTEMPORARIES

WAL-MART KNOWS MARKETING!

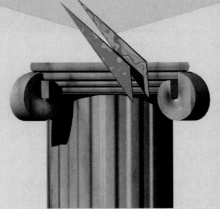

Sam Walton, founder of Wal-Mart Stores, discovered long ago that marketing can be one of the keys to success. He began his business career in the Ben Franklin chain after graduating from the University of Missouri. He spent a great deal of time in other retail stores looking for ways to improve operations. He also regularly talked to customers to determine what products they needed and what they liked and did not like about the store's operations.

One of the things he discovered is that some stores were buying large quantities of certain products and setting very low prices on them. This was one of the first examples of discount marketing. He would often drive long distances to find bargains and bring them back to his store for sale. He was able to increase his profits because of the large quantities sold even though his profit for each item was quite low.

Companies like K-Mart, Woolco, and Ardan found success as large volume discounters in cities. Sam Walton believed the same approach would work in smaller towns that big businesses would not enter. From his beginnings with one store in the 1940's, his company has grown to become the largest retailer in the United States. In 1991, there were nearly 2,000 Wal-Mart stores.

The success of Wal-Mart comes from many different factors, but marketing and the marketing concept played an important role. Effective purchasing, an efficient distribution system, keeping track of inventory, pricing products for quick sale, and an excellent marketing information system are all part of the success. Most importantly, however, is the commitment of all Wal-Mart employees to customer satisfaction. Sam Walton insisted that all employees, known as associates, provide the highest level of customer service possible.

For those who want an example of the marketing orientation in action, Sam Walton's stores are a place to look. They satisfy customer needs with an effective marketing mix while returning a profit to the business.

turers have selling their cars. In some cases the difficulty results because they are not producing the type, style, or quality of cars customers want. The companies then have to use extensive advertising, price reductions, rebates, and pressure selling to convince customers to buy a product that is not really what the customers prefer.

Retail stores sometimes buy products that they believe will sell, but then see that customers are not willing to buy them. The stores then have to cut prices, increase advertising, use special displays, and other strategies to convince customers to buy the products. The extra expenses of marketing products that customers may not have a strong interest in buying can lead to reductions in profit or even losses for the business. Additionally, after purchasing the product, the customer may decide it is not what was wanted and return the product to the business or become very unhappy with both the product and the company that sold it. The customer may be reluctant to buy from that company in the future and may express dissatisfaction to prospective customers, resulting in reduced sales for the company.

IMPLEMENTING THE MARKETING CONCEPT

Companies that believe in the marketing concept operate differently than those who do not. Businesses using the marketing concept follow a two-step process.

IDENTIFY THE MARKET

The first step is to identify the market they want to serve (see Figure 1-5). *A market refers to the description of the prospective customers a business wants to serve and the location of those customers.* An example of a market for a bicycle manufacturer may be people who ride bicycles for health and fitness in the mountains. A potential market for a sports arena may be teenagers within 80 miles of the arena who attend concerts more than two times a year.

DEVELOP A MARKETING MIX

The second step is to develop a marketing mix that will meet the needs of the market and that the business can provide profitably. *A marketing mix is the blending of four marketing ele-*

Identifying a Market

FIGURE 1-5 ▪ The definition of a market includes people and their location.

ments (product, distribution, price, and promotion) by the business. The bicycle manufacturer may decide to offer a mountain bike with three choices of frames and tires; sold through a selected group of bicycle shops in resort towns in Colorado, Wyoming, Utah, and New Mexico; priced in a range from $280–$550; and promoted by advertising in two fitness magazines, a cable sports channel, and by salespeople in the bicycle shops. The sports arena manager could choose a marketing mix for concerts that includes groups that have albums in the top 40 of the pop/rock charts, scheduled on Saturday or

CHALLENGES
MISUSING MARKETING

It is possible that you or people you know do not have a positive image of marketing. There are many examples of marketing practices that take advantage of prospective customers rather than satisfying their needs. That occurs if the person planning the inappropriate marketing activities is only concerned about making a sale, rather than developing a long-term relationship with the customer.

The misuse of marketing often occurs when a business person believes a product or service is not going to be sold and the business is about to lose money. Some recent examples of ways marketing has been misused include:

■ Stating that the price of a product has been reduced by 50 percent when it really was not. The product price was increased briefly to an unrealistically high price and then cut in half to make it look like a sale.

■ Sending a consumer a letter which says the person has won an expensive prize. When the consumer attempts to claim the prize, a large amount of money has to be paid for shipping and handling costs.

■ Showing a picture of a product in a catalog or magazine that is described as a high quality product for sale by mail order. When the customer receives the product after payment, it is of very poor quality and not as pictured or described.

■ A person receives a telephone call to participate in a marketing research survey. After the person answers several personal questions, the person making the call attempts to sell the customer several products.

■ Advertisements for toys, or other products directed at children, show the products being used in ways that are very exciting. When children try to use the products, they are unable to get them to perform in the same way.

■ Advertising products at an extremely low price. When the customer goes to the store to buy the low-priced product, the salesperson tells the customer the product is not worth the low price and attempts to sell another product at a much higher price.

How do you feel (or how do you believe others feel) when you are the customer and marketing is misused to sell you something? If you were a business person trying to satisfy customers through the effective use of marketing, what would you do if you became aware that other business people were misusing marketing?

Sunday evenings, priced at $30 for reserved seating and $22 for open seating, and promoted on the three area FM radio stations with the highest audience ratings for listeners age 15–25.

Each of the elements of the marketing mix shown in Figure 1-6 provides many alternatives from which the business can select in order to better satisfy the market. The development and implementation of the marketing mix will be discussed in detail in other chapters. Basic definitions of each mix element are:

Product is anything offered to a market by the business to satisfy needs, including physical products, services, and ideas. Distribution includes the locations and methods used to make the product available to customers. Price is the actual amount customers pay and the methods of increasing the value of the product to the customers. Promotion includes the methods and information communicated to customers to encourage purchases and increase their satisfaction.

While each of the definitions is written to describe marketing of products by a business, we will learn that mix elements are also part of services and ideas. Non-business organizations and even individuals can effectively develop marketing mixes. The strategies of effective marketing that you will be learning have very broad applications.

MARKETING IS IMPORTANT

You can see that the role of marketing in business today is very complex. Marketing managers are responsible for a large number and variety of activities. They must work with many people inside and outside of a company. Marketing managers are

The Elements of a Marketing Mix

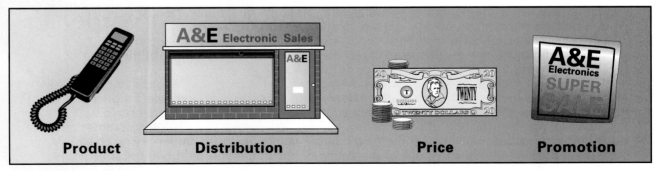

| Product | Distribution | Price | Promotion |

FIGURE 1-6 ■ Businesses use the four elements of the marketing mix to satisfy customer needs.

ultimately responsible for a large part of the company's budget. People involved in marketing need information about customers, competitors, and market conditions. This information helps marketers make decisions that will result in sales and profits for the business. Marketers have varied amounts of experience and education. They work in businesses to complete all of the functions and activities described in this chapter. Marketing is an exciting and challenging career area. If you are interested in marketing you must be willing to develop the needed knowledge and skills. Marketing offers many opportunities for you now and in your future.

REVIEW

Today, marketing is a very important activity in all businesses. In addition, it is valuable for other non-business organizations and individuals and offers many exciting career possibilities. Effective marketing is used to insure that those involved in exchanges of products, services, and even ideas are satisfied with what they receive in the exchange. Businesses that use marketing successfully believe in the marketing concept that bases decisions on the needs of potential customers. To satisfy customer needs profitably, businesses must be able to identify markets and then control the elements of the marketing mix—product, distribution, price, and promotion. A large number of marketing functions and activities are performed each time a product or service is sold to a customer.

MARKETING FOUNDATIONS

1. NINE FUNCTIONS

There are nine marketing functions that describe the major activities of marketing. Those functions are listed on the wheel that follows. Match each function with the correct description from the list.

Description

a. Designing and developing products and services

b. Determining needs of an organization, identifying sources, and completing activities to obtain and use needed products and services

c. Budgeting, obtaining finances, and providing financial assistance to customers

d. Developing procedures so customers are able to locate, obtain, and use products and services

e. Establishing the value of products and services

f. Providing security and safety for products, personnel, and customers

g. Obtaining and using information to improve decision making

h. Communicating information to prospective customers to encourage them to purchase

i. Personal communications with prospective customers to assess and satisfy needs

2. YOUR OWN DEFINITIONS

On a separate sheet of paper, define each of the following marketing terms. Use your own words rather than those in the chapter. Then develop a specific example from your own experience that illustrates the term.

Marketing Terms
Marketing Mix
Market
Product
Distribution
Price
Promotion
Marketing Concept

MARKETING RESEARCH

1. PERCEPTIONS OF MARKETING

Identify 10 people who vary in age, gender, occupation, and other personal characteristics. Ask each person the following three questions. Record their answers:

a. What do you believe the word "marketing" means?

b. When you hear the word "marketing," are your feelings more positive, more negative, or neutral?

c. Do you believe most people involved in marketing are attempting to meet your needs as a customer....Yes or No?

When you have completed the interview, develop a written summary of your findings. Include two graphs illustrating the answers to questions b and c.

2. USING MARKETING FUNCTIONS

Find and clip (or photocopy) an article from a current magazine or newspaper that describes how a company performed a marketing function as it developed a new product or service, improved a marketing procedure, and/or responded to customer needs. Prepare a brief oral report describing the function and how it does or does not illustrate the marketing concept.

MARKETING PLANNING

1. LISTS OF FIVE

 Make some lists of five. Write at least five examples from your own experience for each of the following:

a. Five marketing activities you have seen in the last week.

b. Five businesses in your community that have marketing as an important activity.

c. Five careers in marketing.

d. Five examples of businesses performing marketing functions.

e. Five descriptions of markets.

f. Five ways that marketing can be useful to you now and in the future.

2. AGREE OR DISAGREE

 Think carefully about each of the following ideas presented in the chapter. For each idea, develop a specific written statement of no more than four sentences describing why you agree or disagree with the idea. Make sure your statement includes logical support for your decision. Be prepared to read and justify your statement in class.

a. You see marketing activities every day.

b. You assist in the effective marketing of products and services.

c. Every business today is involved in marketing.

d. Marketing positions are among the most highly paid jobs in many companies.

e. Each marketing function occurs every time a product or service is developed and sold.

f. Marketing is used by politicians, artists, and sports stars.

g. Satisfaction of both the business and the consumer is an important goal of marketing.

h. Companies that believe in the marketing concept operate differently than those who do not.

i Marketing is valuable for non-business organizations and individuals.

MARKETING MANAGEMENT

1. EFFECTS OF PRICE CHANGES

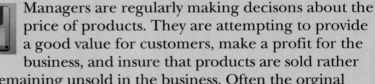

Managers are regularly making decisons about the price of products. They are attempting to provide a good value for customers, make a profit for the business, and insure that products are sold rather than remaining unsold in the business. Often the orginal price charged for a product is not the price at which it is sold.

Collect information on price reductions for at least ten products. You can gather the information from products you, your family, or friends have purchased; by checking prices in stores in your community; or from studying advertisements. Identify the original price and the reduced price for each product. Then complete the following activities.

a. Calculate the amount and percentage of decrease in price for each product. For example, if a compact disc player originally sold for $150 and is on sale for $125, the price reduction is $25 ($150 − $125). The percentage of decrease is the price reduction divided by the original price. For the compact disc player, the percentage of decrease in price is 16.7% ($25 ÷ $150).

b. Assuming the business makes 4% net profit on each sale (this may not be true for many of the products identified), determine how much reduction in profit the store will have for each product. For the CD player, at the orginal price the profit would have been $6 ($150 × 4%); at the reduced price the profit is $5 ($125 × 4%). The reduction in profit is $1.

c. Assuming that the business has a loss on any product that has a price reduction of more than 35% (again this may not be true of some products), identify the products on which losses will occur and the amount of that loss. In the CD example, if the business loses money on any price reduction of more than 35%, the loss will begin when the price is reduced to $97.50 ($150 × 65%).

d. Using the idea of the marketing concept, determine reasons why the manager of the business may have decided to reduce the price for the product you identified. Suggest other things the manager might have been able to do to avoid reducing the product's price.

2. CASE STUDY: PROBLEMS WITH MARKETING RESEARCH

As the manager of a jewelry store, you are committed to employing the marketing concept in your business. You are determined to have the products and services customers want to buy in your store and to develop an effective marketing mix.

You have decided one way to find out about the needs of prospective customers is with a well-planned marketing research effort. Part of that effort involves interviewing shoppers as they enter the mall in which your store is located. You plan to ask your interviewers to politely stop shoppers and ask them a few questions about their preferences for jewelry and what they would like to see jewelry stores do to make shopping more satisfying.

When you propose your research idea to the manager of the mall, she raises several concerns. The manager believes that shoppers don't want to be bothered by interviewers. It could be seen as an intrusion on the shoppers' privacy. Other businesses may believe you are getting an unfair advantage by talking with shoppers. Finally, the manager is concerned about how the information could be used. She is concerned that if the questioning identifies people who purchase a large amount of jewelry, their safety might be threatened if that information got into the hands of the wrong people.

a. How would you respond to the mall manager's concerns?

b. Are there ways to avoid the problems identified and still obtain the information you need?

Product/
Service
Planning

Distribution

Marketing-
Information
Management

Economic
Foundations of
Marketing

Fina

Purchasing

*Marketing
and Business
Foundations*

Human Resource
Foundations

Risk

Pricing

Selling

Promotion

Marketing Supports Business Activities

1. Identify reasons that marketing is important to businesses.

2. List three or more ways that marketing contributed to the development of early businesses.

3. Describe the major functions of business and their contributions.

4. Explain why businesses can be more successful if functions are coordinated with each other.

5. Understand the development of marketing from a production emphasis to a marketing concept emphasis.

6. Explain why the marketing concept has been adopted by businesses and other organizations.

7. Discuss how nonbusiness organizations use marketing to succeed.

nt

NEWSLINE

MARKETING PAVES THE ROAD TO THE TOP

What is the best preparation if you want to be the top executive of a major corporation? Many executives in the past had engineering or production backgrounds. More recently, finance was the route to the top. But surveys of the executives of the largest United States firms have found that marketing now leads other business areas as the area where more executives got their experience.

A study of the 500 top industrial businesses and 300 non-industrial businesses showed that nearly 30 percent of the chief executive officers had a marketing background. That number was followed by 25 percent who had preparation in finance and 19 percent who were from production and operations. A similar study by a management recruiting firm found that over 28 percent of businesses hiring new executives selected people from marketing.

While it might be expected that companies that have marketing as their primary activity would want marketers as managers, other types of businesses are also looking to marketing for leadership.

Manufacturers with marketers in the top position include Brunswick, Colgate-Palmolive, Owens-Corning, and Procter and Gamble. Two of the top computer manufacturers, Apple Computer and IBM, were recently headed by marketers. Food processors Campbell Soup, General Mills, and H. J. Heinz; agricultural products manufacturers John Deere and Snap-On Tools; and consumer appliance manufacturers Whirlpool and Maytag have all been directed by people from marketing.

Understanding marketing is not enough to qualify for the top job in a company. Those who are selected for top positions are also knowledgeable and experienced in many other areas of business in addition to their primary area of marketing. But the background of an increasing number of executives makes an important point. Marketing has become the "way to the top" in American business.

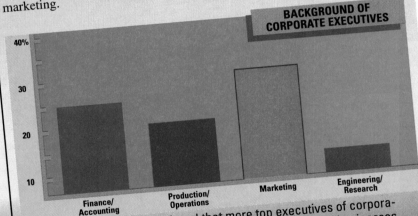

FIGURE 2-1 ■ Studies have found that more top executives of corporations have backgrounds in marketing than in other areas of businesses.

THE NEED FOR MARKETING

Marketing today is quite different than it was many years ago. Ever since the first products were exchanged, there has been a need for marketing. Often, however, marketing was viewed as a simple set of activities that would help a business sell its products to more customers.

As you study this chapter, you will see how marketing activities developed. The very first businesses developed marketing to improve exchanges. You will learn that marketing is just one type of activity that occurs in business. All business activities are important. They all contribute in specific ways to the success of the business. You will be introduced to each of the other major functions that are part of business operations.

Business managers know that marketing must be carefully planned. It must be coordinated with other business activities. This chapter helps you understand why the approach to managing marketing activities changes as businesses and other organizations implement the marketing concept.

Marketing is an important part of business. Some people believe that if a business offers a good product, marketing is not necessary. However, if the customer does not know about the product, does not know where to purchase it, is unable to get to the place where it is sold, cannot afford the price of the product, or does not believe the product is a good value, the product will not be purchased. Marketing is required to provide a variety of activities or services so the customer will be able to purchase the product.

On the other hand, marketing cannot be successful if the product is not what the customer wants or is a poor quality product. While a customer may be encouraged to buy a product through advertising, selling, or a low price, the product must be seen as satisfying a need of the customer. If the customer decides to buy the product, and it does not work the way the customer was led to believe, if it is of poor quality, or if it has a defect, the customer will likely return the product for a refund. Even if the customer does not return a product that was not satisfying, it is unlikely the customer will buy the same product again.

We learned in Chapter 1 that effective marketing is used by businesses and other organizations to provide satisfying exchanges of products and services with customers. The ways marketing is used to provide those exchanges have changed over the years, but the need for marketing has not. From the very beginning of exchanges, we can find examples of marketing. In the next section we will look at the historical development of business and learn how marketing has been an important part of the growth of business activities.

MARKETING AND THE DEVELOPMENT OF BUSINESS

There have been times in history when people were self-sufficient. *Being self-sufficient means you do not rely on others for the things needed in order to survive.* Those people were able to find or produce the food and materials needed for themselves and their families. However, that type of lifestyle required very hard work and was very risky. Self-sufficient people had to have good hunting, fishing, or farming skills to obtain needed food as well as the capability of developing shelter, clothing, and other necessities. Often it was not possible to obtain everything needed to survive because of poor weather, competition with other people, sickness, or lack of skill.

BARTERING

Some people who found they were not successful at being self-sufficient tried to find other ways to survive. They saw that often, when they did not have certain things they needed, other people had those things. If each person had something the other person valued, they were able to exchange so each would be better off than before. *Exchanging products or services with others by agreeing on their values is known as bartering.* A system of bartering was developed so people could exchange with others to obtain the things they needed. For example, in an early bartering system, someone who was a good hunter but was not able to grow grain might exchange products with another person who had extra grain but needed meat. People who had developed skills in weaving cloth might barter with people who raised animals. Exchanges of products through bartering was one of the first examples of marketing.

SPECIALIZATION OF LABOR

People discovered that they had particular interests or skills in certain kinds of work, while they were not as good or were uninterested in other types of work. If they concentrated on the work they did well, they were able to accomplish much more than if they tried to do a variety of things. *Concentrating on one or a few related activities so that they can be completed very well is known as specialization of labor.* Specialization of labor made it possible for people to produce a larger quantity of a product than if they were attempting to produce many different products. Therefore, more of that product would be available to exchange with other people.

MONEY SYSTEMS

As specialization of labor became more common and a greater variety and quantity of products were available, it was not always possible to barter. Not all people needed the products of others and it was not always possible to reach agreement on values of products so they could be exchanged. To assist with the exchange process, a money system was developed. *A money system established the use of currency as a recognized medium of exchange.* With money, people could obtain products even if they did not always have products to exchange. Those with products to sell could obtain money which could then be used for other purchases. The development of a money system was another example of marketing.

CENTRAL MARKETS

With many people producing more types of products and with people having money to purchase the items they needed, the demand for products increased. However it was a difficult process to locate and accumulate all of the products people wanted and needed. A great deal of time was spent traveling to sell and purchase products. To solve that problem, central markets were developed. *A central market is a location where products are brought to be exchanged conveniently.* Central markets were often located at places where many people traveled, such as where rivers or roads met.

Towns and cities developed at those locations and became centers of trade. People brought the products they wanted to sell to the markets. Those people needing to obtain products would also travel to the market to make purchases. Developing locations where products could be bought and sold was another step in the development of marketing. (See Figure 2-2.)

Marketing Through Central Markets

FIGURE 2-2 ▪ Central locations where many people travel provide convenient places for marketing activities to be completed.

OTHER MARKETING ACTIVITIES

As central markets expanded, other types of business services were created to make exchanges easier. It was not always possible for sellers and buyers to travel to the markets at the same time. Therefore, businesses were formed to purchase products from producers and hold them for sale to purchasers. Other businesses were started to loan money to buyers or sell-

CLASSICS AND CONTEMPORARIES

SATURN EMPHASIZES CUSTOMER SATISFACTION

One American industry that has not had a strong reputation for customer service is the auto industry. Many people have charged that automobile manufacturers still maintain a production emphasis: they develop products that they believe are right for the consumer. Others see a strong sales emphasis where high-pressure sales tactics are used to convince people to buy.

A new auto company is changing the way American automobiles are designed, manufactured, and sold. The emphasis is on customer satisfaction. That company is Saturn, a division of General Motors. Saturn started with a new production facility and new management strategies. They encourage employee involvement in manufacturing decisions. The emphasis is on building a quality automobile. Quality is very important. When some new cars were found to have a problem, Saturn replaced the cars for the customers. This kept customers from waiting for a major repair.

Can Saturn maintain that level of quality as more cars are manufactured?

The careful manufacturing process resulted in a product that owners rank near the top of all new automobiles. Saturn rates in the top three in a poll of customer satisfaction. Its customer satisfaction rating was close to that of Lexus and Infiniti. These two brands sell for thousands of dollars more than Saturn models. Can Saturn maintain that level of quality as more cars are manufactured? Can they make a profit? Their first efforts are very promising.

Saturn continues the emphasis on customer satisfaction in the dealerships that sell the automobiles. A new approach to selling and service is used to overcome the negative views customers have of their experiences in buying a car. Salespeople emphasize quality and service and encourage customers to compare Saturn to other brands before making a decision. Prices are set at one level so customers don't feel they have to fight for the lowest price. Finally, after the purchase, the salesperson works with the buyer to ensure that there are no problems or that service is provided quickly and effectively when needed.

The marketing concept provides a new way for businesses to operate. It affects all parts of the business from production to sales. Saturn is demonstrating that the marketing concept can work in the auto industry.

ers, to help with transportation of products, or to locate products that were not available in the market but that customers wanted. Each of those activities resulted in the development of another marketing activity and made the exchange process more effective for those who produced products and those who purchased and consumed the products.

THE FUNCTIONS OF BUSINESS

The previous examples have illustrated how marketing developed to improve the exchange of products between producers and consumers. It is clear that marketing is an important part of business and that businesses cannot be effective without marketing. However, marketing cannot be successful alone; a number of other activities are important to businesses. In this section we will examine the other major functions of business and what they contribute. These functions are summarized in Figure 2-3.

The Other Major Functions of Business

Production

Operations

Accounting and Finance

Management and Administration

FIGURE 2-3 ▪ Marketing must be planned cooperatively with many other activities in a business.

PRODUCTION

The primary reason for a business to exist is to provide products or services to consumers. *The production function creates or obtains products or services for sale.* Think of the variety of products and services available from businesses and you can see that production can take various forms.

Production includes obtaining raw materials for sale to customers. Mining, logging, drilling for oil, and similar activities are examples of this type of production. Other businesses take raw materials and change their form through processing so they can be used in the production of other products or in the operation of businesses or equipment. Examples include oil refining and the production of steel, paper, plastics, food products, and so forth. A third example of production is agriculture where food and other materials are grown for consumption or for processing into a variety of products.

Manufacturing businesses are also involved in production. Those businesses use raw materials and other resources to produce products for sale to consumers or to other businesses. Most of the products consumed by you, your friends, your family and businesses have been produced by manufacturers.

The development of services is also an example of the production function. While a physical product is not provided to the customer, offering a service such as preparing tax returns, cutting hair, providing lawn maintenance services, or performing a concert meets customer needs in the same way that the consumption of products can.

Finally, some businesses do not produce or manufacture products but accumulate products for resale to customers. *Offering products produced or manufactured by others for sale to customers is known as merchandising.* Retailers and wholesalers are examples of merchandising businesses. While merchandising is not production, it makes products available for sale in those businesses in the same way that production and manufacturing do for other businesses.

OPERATIONS

The ongoing activities designed to support the primary function of a business and to keep a business operating efficiently are known as operations. Many things must occur for a business to successfully produce and market products and services. Buildings and equipment must be operated, maintained, and repaired. Products must be obtained, transported, stored, and protected. Paperwork must be completed. Customer questions must be answered and customer services provided. The way operations are completed often means the difference between profit or loss for a business.

ACCOUNTING AND FINANCE

Businesses are very complex with a variety of activities occurring at the same time. A large amount of money is handled by most businesses in many forms including cash, checks, and credit. *The accounting and finance function plans and manages financial resources and maintains the records and information related to the business' finances.*

Finance begins by determining the amount of capital needed for the business and where that capital will be obtained. Budgets must be developed, watched carefully, and updated. Most businesses must regularly borrow money for major purchases as well as for some day-to-day operations. Determining sources for borrowing, interest rates, and loan payback schedules are important responsibilities of accounting and finance personnel. Without careful record keeping and an understanding of the financial situation, managers will be unable to plan the activities of the business. The accounting and finance function provides that type of information and assistance in the business.

MANAGEMENT AND ADMINISTRATION

Even the smallest businesses require that considerable time be spent in planning and organizing activities. Someone must determine what the business will do, how it can best meet the needs of customers, and how to respond to competitors' actions. Problem-solving, managing the work of employees, and evaluating the activities of the business are ongoing responsibilities of managers. *The function of management and administration involves developing, implementing, and evaluating the plans and activities of a business.*

Managers are responsible for everything that occurs in the business including the work of the employees. They must develop plans and objectives, make sure the appropriate resources are available, be responsible for buildings and equipment, and assign responsibilities to others. Managers are held responsible for the performance of the company including whether or not it is profitable.

MARKETING

The focus of this book, marketing, is also an important function of business. All businesses need to complete a variety of activities in order to make their products and services available to consumers and to ensure that effective exchanges occur. As we have already learned, those activities are known as marketing.

COORDINATION OF BUSINESS FUNCTIONS

Each of the functions of business is dependent on the other functions if the business is to be effective. Products can be produced, but if the company is not operated or managed effectively, if adequate records are not maintained, or if marketing is not successful, the products will not be sold at a profit. In the same way, operations, management, and administration are used to coordinate the work of the business. Finance and accounting provide information to the other parts of the business to ensure that a profit is possible.

In the past, some organizations have not tried or have not been successful in coordinating the business functions. The various functions operated independently and often competed with each other. Products were produced that could not be sold; marketing activities were planned with little attention to their costs; managers concentrated on specific activities of the business without considering if their decisions would have negative effects on other functions. The result was that the quality of products and customer service declined while prices increased. Customers became unhappy when they found that products were declining in quality, they could not get the level of service they expected, or prices were increasing rapidly. Competitors who were better organized were able to take advantage of those situations.

Today, most businesses recognize that they must carefully coordinate the functions and activities if they are going to satisfy their customers and make a profit. Managers and employees are trained to work together. A great deal of planning is done to determine how activities should be organized. We will learn in the next section that marketing plays an important role in the successful coordination of business activities.

THE CHANGING ROLE OF MARKETING

While marketing is necessary in all exchanges, businesses have not always believed marketing was important. They expected customers to take most of the responsibility for completing marketing activities. Only recently have many business people realized the value of effective marketing. We will look at several changes in the role that marketing has played in U.S. businesses during this century. The historical development of marketing is summarized in Figure 2-4.

The Historical Development of Marketing		
Production Era	1900s–1920s	Emphasis on producing and distributing new products
Sales Era	1930s–1940s	Emphasis on using advertising and salespeople to convince customers to buy a company's products
Marketing Department Era	1950s–1960s	Emphasis on developing many new marketing activities to sell products
Marketing Concept Era	1970s–today	Emphasis on satisfying customers' needs with a carefully developed marketing mix

FIGURE 2-4 ▪ The philosophy of marketing has changed throughout this century.

THE PRODUCTION EMPHASIS

In the early years of the century (1900–1920), production processes were very simple and few product choices were available. People had limited money to spend on products and much of their purchasing was for basic necessities. Transportation systems were not well developed so it was difficult to get products from where they were manufactured to the many people throughout the United States.

In that environment, businesses believed that if they could produce products, they would be able to sell them. So they concentrated on developing new products and improving the process of production. The only real marketing effort was devoted to distribution, moving products from the producer to the customer.

THE SALES EMPHASIS

During the 1930s and into the 1940s, businesses became more effective at producing products. Efficient methods of producing large numbers of products at a low cost, such as assembly lines, were used. Transportation systems improved including the use of trains, boats, and trucks, making it easier to get products to more customers. At the same time, the standard of living of many Americans was improving, giving them money to spend on more products.

These changes resulted in increased competition among businesses. They could no longer rely on customers buying their products just because they were able to get the products to the customers. Companies began to rely on salespeople to represent their products. The salespeople would attempt to convince customers that their company's products were better than the products of competitors.

THE MARKETING DEPARTMENT EMPHASIS

The sales emphasis continued on until well into the 1950s for many businesses and well beyond that time for others. However, after World War II, the U.S. economy expanded rapidly and wage levels increased for consumers as their hours of work declined. Therefore, they had more money to spend and more time to enjoy the use of many products. Companies increasingly found that consumers were not easily convinced to purchase products when they had many choices available to them. Therefore, the businesses had to find different ways to be sure that consumers purchased their products. The companies began to develop marketing departments that were responsible for developing those new methods.

One of the first efforts of the new marketing department was to expand the use of advertising. Advertising had an important role of informing consumers about a company's products, the reasons to buy the products, and where they could be located. New methods of getting products to customers were developed including catalog sales through the mail and even the use of airplanes to move some products very rapidly. Products were distributed extensively through many retail stores. Customers were offered credit to make purchases more affordable. As companies worked to find additional methods to encourage customers to buy, the marketing department became an important part of the business.

THE MARKETING CONCEPT EMPHASIS

The marketing department emphasis showed that marketing could be a very important tool for businesses. A number of activities were now available that had not been used in the past.

However, just because more activities were used, companies were not always more successful. It was discovered that marketing was becoming quite expensive. Also, since the goal of the marketing department was to sell the products of the company, marketers began to misuse marketing activities. These unethical activities sometimes resulted in sales, but also led to customer complaints. Examples included high-pressure sales, misleading advertising, and customer services that were not provided as promised.

Marketers also discovered that no matter how hard they tried, there were products that customers did not want to buy. If customers did not believe the product would satisfy their needs, marketing was not effective. Yet marketers were not involved in developing the company's products.

In the 1970s, some companies began to realize that they could be more successful if they listened to consumers and considered customer needs as they developed products and services. As we learned in Chapter 1, the marketing concept uses the needs of customers as the primary focus during the planning, production, distribution, and promotion of a product or service.

When the marketing concept was adopted, marketing became more than the work of one department. It was now a major part of the business. Marketing personnel worked closely with people in other parts of the company. Activities were completed with customer satisfaction in mind. By coordinating the efforts of the departments in the company and by focusing on satisfying customers' needs, companies were able to develop and market products that customers wanted and that could be sold at a profit. Those companies were using the marketing concept. Since its first use in the 1970s, the marketing concept has been proven as an effective method and is now used by the majority of businesses and by other organizations.

CHALLENGES
JUST IN TIME—JUST RIGHT!

Have you ever wanted to purchase something from a business only to discover that the product is out of stock and will not be available for several weeks? Or you may have found an item of clothing that is just what you want but all of the items in your size have been sold.

These situations occur frequently in some businesses and cause customers to be upset and dissatisfied. The business is hurt because of the lost sales and the chance that the dissatisfied customers will not shop at that business again. On the other hand, if the business keeps a large quantity of all products in stock, expenses will be much higher and many of the products will have to be sold at a very low price or may remain unsold.

The availability of the right quantity of products at the right time is not just a problem for customers and retail businesses. Manufacturers also want to be sure that the right materials and supplies are available at the time they are needed. Think of the problems and expense a manufacturing business faces if one part is unavailable when it is needed for production. All of the manufacturing activity of the business must stop until the part can be delivered.

One method being used to solve this problem is a Japanese management procedure known as Just In Time (JIT). Managers carefully determine the quantity of each item needed to manufacture a product, when the item is needed, the source of the item, and the amount of time needed to order and deliver it. Then the managers work with each supplier to be sure the items can be delivered exactly when needed.

Retail businesses are also starting to use inventory control methods similar to JIT. By carefully determining the quantity of each item needed and keeping track of inventory levels, managers can decide when items must be reordered so they will always be in stock. Just In Time management is an excellent example of the coordination of business activities. If it is successful, customers should be able to obtain the products they want, where they are needed, at the time they are needed. That is a benefit for customers and businesses and fits the definition of the marketing concept.

THE CHANGING DEFINITION OF MARKETING

The previous sections have shown us that marketing is very different today than it was even just fifteen or twenty years ago. If we look back over the history of business, we can see that marketing has played a role in even the simplest early businesses. But business people have not recognized the full value of marketing as a business tool until recently. We can see in Figure 2-5 how the definition of marketing has changed because of the progression of marketing activities.

The role of marketing in business has changed along with the definition. Previously, marketing was seen as a tool to help the business sell its products and services. It was not needed if sales were high. Today, business people see that marketing contributes in several important ways to the business. It provides information about customers and their needs through market research, which helps businesses plan more effectively. Marketing provides many ways to serve customers better including distribution, pricing, credit, and customer services. Marketing can increase customer satisfaction by solving cus-

The Progression of Marketing

Marketing as a Variety of Activities

Marketing as Promotion

Marketing as Selling

Marketing as Distribution

FIGURE 2-5 ▪ As the activities of marketing have changed, marketing has become more important to businesses.

tomer problems. Finally, marketing can help the business be more profitable by coordinating activities and controlling costs.

MARKETING IN OTHER ORGANIZATIONS

Because of the successful use of marketing in businesses, other organizations now look to marketing for help. Libraries, churches, government agencies, community organizations, and the military are using marketing activities. Some use marketing very well while others do not understand marketing. They may view marketing as advertising or selling only and not as a way of satisfying their customer or client needs.

You can evaluate organizations with which you are familiar to determine if they understand the value of marketing. If they rely on promotion with brochures, advertisements, and public service announcements, they probably view marketing as a way to convince consumers of the value of their organization. Without research to help them understand their clients, they are not able to respond to the clients' needs. On the other hand, if they use marketing to determine what products and services to offer, where to make them available, how to help consumers determine the value of their services, and to communicate effectively with those consumers, they have adopted the marketing concept in their organization. The marketing concept works just as well for those types of organizations as it does for businesses.

REVIEW

Marketing has changed dramatically as a part of business. Previously, it was viewed as a way to sell products if customers did not immediately choose them or if competition increased. Today, the marketing concept suggests that marketing is very important to businesses. As one of several business functions, it offers many activities that can help satisfy customer needs profitably.

Marketing activities have expanded from distribution, selling, and advertising, to a wide range of business activities including market research, product and service planning, pricing, financing, inventory management, and many others. The marketing concept is a new way of thinking about marketing. It helps organizations understand customers' needs and respond with satisfying products and services.

MARKETING FOUNDATIONS

1. DEVELOPING MARKETING UNDERSTANDING

 The two statements below express opinions often held by people who do not understand marketing. For each of the statements, develop a paragraph of at least five sentences that demonstrates why the opinion is not correct.

"My business offers high-quality products, so they do not need marketing."

"Customers have been complaining my products are not as good as they would like. I need to use marketing to be sure those poor products are sold."

2. SATISFYING EXCHANGES

 We learned in Chapter 1 that marketing is defined as *creating and maintaining satisfying exchange relationships.* The following words describe marketing activities of the first businesses. For each word or phrase, provide a definition and then describe how it can accomplish the goal of satisfying exchange relationships.

Marketing Activities: Bartering, specialization of labor, money systems, central markets, retail businesses, banking, transportation of products

MARKETING RESEARCH

1. STUDYING BUSINESS CAREERS

Each of the functions of business described in the chapter provide career opportunities. There are careers available for people who have completed high school and have no experience in the area. Other careers require a college degree and and/or a great deal of experience.

Locate a newspaper, magazine, or other publication that lists job opportunities or contains advertisements for employment. For each of the business functions in the following list, find at least two examples of jobs that have responsibility for that function. One example should be open to people with a high school diploma and little or no experience. The other example should require a college degree and several years of experience. Copy information about the job, including job title, description of duties, qualifications required, and level of pay (if listed).

Business Functions: production, operations, accounting and finance, management and administration, marketing

2. BECOMING AN EXECUTIVE

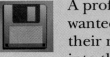 A professional association of business executives wanted to determine the primary areas in which their members worked prior to being promoted into their current positions. They had a copy of each member's resume in their files. After reviewing the resumes they identified the following numbers:

Production	225 members
Accounting	104 members
Finance	160 members
Operations	85 members
Marketing	358 members
Administration	58 members
Management	44 members

There were 32 resumes from which the work areas could not be determined.

Analyze the data for the association by determining the following information:

a. What is the total membership of the organization?

b. For what percentage of the membership were they able to determine the specific area in which the member worked?

c. What percentage of the association membership worked in each of the business areas listed before becoming an executive?

d. What is the combined total of members from accounting and finance backgrounds? What percentage of total membership is that number?

e. Construct a pie chart that illustrates the results of the research.

MARKETING PLANNING

1. DRAW A PICTURE

A business has been operating for the past five years selling handmade, beaded necklaces. The owner had started the business as a hobby and sold the necklaces to friends. The necklaces have become so popular that the owner has a customer list of 1,700 people. Now, much of the owner's time is spent answering telephone calls to take orders, packaging necklaces for sale, and either delivering the necklaces or mailing them to the customers. There is less and less time to produce necklaces, while at the same time demand for the necklaces is increasing.

Pictures can be used to illustrate concepts. Draw a picture that demonstrates how the owner can use the marketing activities of specialization of labor, central markets, and retail businesses to help solve the problem described.

2. WHAT IS THE EMPHASIS?

Read each of the following statements. Then classify each statement according to which business emphases it illustrates.

Business Emphases: production emphasis, sales emphasis, marketing department emphasis, marketing concept emphasis

a. "Our products are not selling. The salespeople must not be doing a good job."

b. "If we could increase our advertising, more people would know about our products."

c. "The important thing is to be able to find a way to deliver the products to people in other states."

d. "We have the best bicycle on the market. I wonder why people are not buying more of them."

e. "Our marketing research shows that our prices are a bit high. Let's see if we can find some ways to reduce prices while still meeting important customer needs."

f. "Our competitors are always coming out with new products before we do. Let's give our engineers more money for product development and see what they can come up with."

g. "We need to think of other things that could help sell our products. What about offering our own credit card to customers?"

h. "We need to improve our level of customer satisfaction. Let's create a team of managers from production, finance, operations, and marketing to plan a new customer service program."

MARKETING MANAGEMENT

1. SOLVING PROBLEMS THROUGH COORDINATION

We learned in this chapter that businesses may have problems when the business functions are not coordinated. An important way to increase customer satisfaction and make a profit is to organize the functions so they cooperate rather than compete. For each of the following sets of functions, identify two specific problems that might result if the functions compete, and two ways that customer satisfaction or company profits could improve if the functions are coordinated.

Business Functions: production and marketing; finance and marketing; operations and production; management and finance

2. CASE STUDY—WHAT DO TEENS WANT?

The DeLong Community Center is a non-profit organization that offers a variety of services to the people in the neighborhood. Those services include a food bank, day care, adult education classes, a visiting nurse for minor health problems, and a recreation program. The center has an extensive program for school-aged children, including a strong teen program. The teen program includes interest clubs like painting, photography, computers; recreation (basketball and volleyball); an after-school tutoring program; and personal and group counseling sessions. Many of the activities are free, but a registration fee of $5–$20 is charged for some of the club activities (to cover the cost of materials) and for team sports.

During the past five years, the numbers of teens using the center has dropped by about 50 percent. Some teens say the center is getting old and doesn't provide a good atmosphere for them. Others say they don't have time for center activities. But no one knows for certain why the number of teens using the center is declining.

The programs and activities for the center are developed by the staff hired to run the center. Most of the teen programs are the same as those offered in other parts of the city where they seem to be more successful.

a. Using your understanding of effective marketing, suggest several reasons why the center programs for teenagers might not be as successful as they were previously.

b. Apply the marketing concept to propose a way the center staff could better serve teenagers. Make sure you discuss customer needs and a marketing mix.

Product/
Service
Planning

Distribution

Marketing-
Information
Management

Economic
Foundations of
Marketing

Fin

Purchasing

**Marketing
and Business
Foundations**

Human Resource
Foundations

Risk

Pricing

Selling

Promotion

What Does Society Expect?

OBJECTIVES

1. Describe the impact of effective marketing on businesses, individuals, and society.

2. Discuss some common criticisms of marketing.

3. Identify ways that marketing is used to help solve problems facing society.

4. Explain how consumerism, government regulations, and business practices improve the social responsibility of businesses.

5. Understand the importance of ethical behavior for marketers.

NEWSLINE

WHO IS RESPONSIBLE?

Remember the new product that made a "splash" on the market? It was a super squirt gun with a water capacity of 2 liters or more and a range of 50–100 feet. When the product was shown to several toy manufacturers by its inventor, they didn't believe it would be successful. It was just another water gun and so big and heavy that most children would not want to carry it around. However, those manufacturers were very wrong!

From the time it was first introduced, it was a big hit. Stores could not keep enough in stock. It was not a product just for children; teenagers and adults bought the super squirt guns. They were used at the beach, in the streets, and

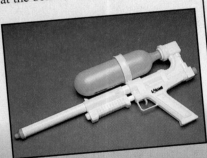

at parties; some even showed up at schools.

What led to problems for this popular product relates to an area of business that is often unrecognized— the business' responsibility to society.

However, just when the success of the new product seemed assured, many stores decided to stop selling it. What led to problems for this popular product relates to an area of business that is often unrecognized—the business' responsibility to society.

While the super squirt gun was fun to use, the force of the water from the gun was great enough that it could be harmful if it was directed at people who were close to the gun or were unaware that they were about to be hit. Stories were heard about people who were bruised by the force of the water and of automobiles involved in accidents when their drivers were hit

by water through an open window.

Some businesses feared that they could be liable for injuries caused by the squirt guns. Several stores decided not to sell them. A few cities passed laws outlawing the sale and use of the squirt guns. Parents learned of the potential problems. They were reluctant to buy the toys for their children.

The super squirt guns continue to be manufactured and sold. However sales are lower than before. Their popularity may increase again. They could be a very successful product in the future. However, the businesses that either manufacture or sell the water guns must determine how the sales will affect the business. Will the business be seen as irresponsible? Will they be involved in lawsuits? Will they lose money if they have a large number of guns for sale and the product is declared illegal? There are many reasons why businesses may decide not to sell a product. A large demand for the product and the possibility of high profits may not overcome social responsibility.

THE IMPACT OF MARKETING

We have seen that marketing is now an important activity for businesses. It is responsible for helping businesses find markets for its products and services and sell them profitably. But many people question the value of marketing. Some see it as adding to the cost of products; others believe it causes people to buy things they otherwise would not want or need. Still others suggest that if businesses produce quality products and services, there is no need for marketing.

It is important to determine if marketing plays a positive or a negative role. What does marketing contribute to businesses, to individuals, and to society? If there are problems with marketing, what can be done to eliminate those problems? This chapter will help you develop answers to those questions.

WHAT IS THE IMPACT OF MARKETING ON BUSINESS?

Marketing is an important business function. Even though businesses have not always understood marketing and used it effectively, we know they could not have existed without marketing. Marketing is responsible for the activities leading to the exchange of a business' products and services for the customer's money. Transportation, financing, promotion, and the other marketing functions are needed for the exchange to occur.

Businesses that use the marketing concept benefit even more from marketing. In those businesses, marketing is responsible for identifying and understanding customers. Through the use of market research and marketing information systems, the business is able to determine customer needs, attitudes, likes, and dislikes. Then the business can carefully develop products and services that meet the needs of the customers and earn a profit.

Manufacturers developing a new brand of toothpaste will make better decisions if they are aware of what consumers like and dislike about the current brand used. The manager of a clothing store will want to know what consumers are expecting in terms of styles and prices before purchasing new items for sale.

Marketing helps businesses satisfy customer wants and needs. This means that customers are more likely to be loyal and continue to purchase from the business. Marketing also helps the business make better decisions about what to sell and how to sell it. Therefore, the business is more likely to operate efficiently. So, effective marketing is important to businesses.

WHAT IS THE IMPACT OF MARKETING ON INDIVIDUALS?

Because marketing improves exchanges between businesses and consumers, individuals benefit from marketing. While many people do not easily recognize those benefits, those who understand marketing can provide examples of its value.

Consider going to a supermarket to purchase supplies for a party. If the store is conveniently located, you will not have to worry about how you will get to and from the store. You want the store to stock your favorite brands of decorations, drinks, and snacks. There should be an adequate supply of the items you need. When you get into the store, the products should be easy to locate. The prices should be clearly marked and affordable. A store employee should be able to answer your questions and help you check out and sack your purchases. The store should allow you to pay for your purchases with cash, check, or credit card.

Each of the activities described for the purchase of your party supplies at the supermarket is an example of marketing. Those activities make it easier for you to shop and help to ensure that you get the items you need for your party, quickly and at a reasonable price. Not only does the business benefit because you purchase the products; you also benefit because the business is able to satisfy your needs.

Marketing provides other contributions to individuals that may not be as obvious. Because marketing is continually determining what consumers like and dislike and what needs are not satisfied, improvements are made to products and services and new products are developed. As a result of marketing activities, more products are available to meet the needs of more customers, which results in higher sales volume. The increase in sales allows businesses to produce products more efficiently and costs can actually decline. This is shown in Figure 3-1.

Consider the first personal computers. They were very basic and not very powerful, but cost several thousand dollars. Today's personal computers are hundreds of times more powerful, have many features to make them easy to use, and can be purchased for under one thousand dollars. This is possible because of improved technology and marketing.

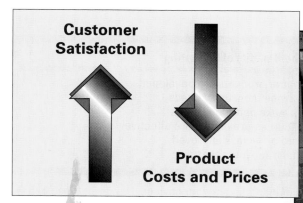

FIGURE 3-1 ■ When the marketing concept is used, customer satisfaction increases, while costs of production and selling prices decrease.

Another contribution of marketing to individuals is a vast area of employment. Between one-fourth and one-third of all jobs in the United States are marketing jobs or have marketing as a major job responsibility. Salespeople, customer service representatives, warehouse managers, inventory specialists, marketing research personnel, and many others have interesting, financially rewarding careers because of marketing.

Finally, marketing skills are valuable to people who are not directly employed in marketing. By understanding the marketing process and using the marketing concept, you will be able to accomplish a number of your goals. Marketing skills can help you get elected to an office in a club, prepare for a job or for college, plan a fund-raising activity for an organization, or start your own business.

Marketing is valuable to individuals. Through marketing, people can choose from a wide variety of products and services, find businesses that respond to their needs, have access to good jobs, and develop a set of skills that help meet many personal goals.

WHAT IS THE IMPACT OF MARKETING ON SOCIETY?

Does society benefit because of marketing? Many people suggest that marketing creates problems for society. We will look at some of those criticisms in a later section, but first we will explore the many positive effects of marketing for society shown in Figure 3-2.

The Benefits of Marketing

New and better products are developed
Businesses meet consumer needs
Consumers make better decisions
Natural resources are used more effectively
The standard of living is improved
International trade increases

FIGURE 3-2 ▪ All of the benefits of marketing are not obvious. However, those benefits are important to consumers, businesses, and society.

In the previous section, we learned that marketing helps to identify new and better products and services for consumers. Many of those products and services are beneficial to society in general. More efficient automobiles use less gasoline and cause less pollution. Biodegradable products reduce the growing need for landfill space. Products like airbags and motorcycle helmets reduce the number and severity of injuries from accidents.

Marketing encourages businesses to provide products and services that consumers want. It also helps consumers make more effective decisions about what to purchase. As a result, the natural resources and raw materials of a country should be used more efficiently rather than being wasted on products consumers will not buy.

Marketing improves the standard of living in a country. The standard of living is based on the products and services available to consumers, the amount of resources consumers have to obtain the products and services, and the quality of life for consumers. Countries that have well-developed marketing systems are able to make more and better products available to consumers. Those countries also have more jobs for their citizens and higher wage scales as a result of marketing.

Marketing has been particularly effective in improving international trade. International trade contributes many benefits to the participating countries and to the consumers in those countries. Think of the number of products you buy that were produced in another country. Just as the United States is a large consumer of foreign products, many businesses in this country sell products internationally. Without marketing, such benefits would not be possible.

Marketing activities are essential for international trade. Marketers help to determine where products can be sold and how to sell them in countries that may have very different business procedures, money systems, and buying practices. Methods of shipping and product handling must be identified or developed. Decisions about customer service must be made. Promotional methods appropriate for the people in each country or region have to be developed to ensure that customers understand the products and their benefits.

CRITICISMS OF MARKETING

Based on the examples above, it would be easy to say that marketing has only positive results. That is not always the case. If not used appropriately, marketing can have negative effects. The misuse of marketing has led to some criticisms and has created a negative image for some marketing activities.

Criticisms of marketing must be taken seriously by business people. Those criticisms often represent the attitudes of many consumers. If consumers have a negative opinion about an important part of a business, it can affect whether they will be customers or not.

Marketers and other business people need to study marketing practices to be sure they result in effective exchanges and customer satisfaction. In the following sections we will examine some specific criticisms of marketing practices and some possible responses.

MARKETING CAUSES PEOPLE TO PURCHASE THINGS THEY OTHERWISE WOULD NOT BUY

Through marketing, consumers have many choices of products available for them to purchase. Those products are readily available in many stores, are displayed in ways that make them easy to purchase, and are attractively packaged to attract attention. Advertising is used extensively to encourage people to consider specific brands of products. Credit and special financing arrangements are available for most expensive products to make them seem more affordable. It is clear that the number of marketing activities and the power of promotion can increase the sales of specific products and services.

Businesses using the marketing concept should carefully consider the potential impact of marketing activities on consumers. While it might seem appropriate to use any tool that will result in more sales of a product, the long-term results of the sale should be considered as well. If a customer buys a product because of marketing rather than because the product is really needed, there is a good chance the customer will be dissatisfied. How many times have you or your friends purchased something and then quickly decided you really didn't want or need the item? What was your response?

Many consumers simply return the item to the business and expect a refund of their money. In that case, the business not only has lost the sale, but now has a product that is worth much less than before and perhaps cannot be resold. Even if the consumers do not return the products, they are likely to be quite dissatisfied. That is particularly true if the product cost a great deal of money. Do you believe the consumers will buy that product again? The business is left with returned merchandise, a dissatisfied customer, and possibly a bad reputation among the customer's friends.

To respond to this criticism, business people must be very sensitive to the needs and experiences of customers. Products and services should be carefully matched to customers' needs. Products that do not sell should be evaluated to determine why they are not wanted by customers. In that way, the business can make better purchasing decisions in the future in order to offer products and services that customers want.

Marketing should start with good products. If a product is not meeting customer needs, business people should avoid using marketing strategies such as promotion and price reductions to try to sell the product. This will often lead to dissatisfaction with the product and the business.

Finally, the business must value long-term relationships with customers. One sale is not enough. The business will be successful when customers return again and again because they are satisfied with the business and believe the business is concerned about their needs.

MARKETING ADDS TO THE COST OF PRODUCTS WITHOUT PROVIDING ANYTHING OF VALUE

On average, the cost of all marketing activities is about 50 percent of the price of products. For some products it is much higher and for others it is a very small percentage. Since many people think of marketing as only advertising and selling, they are upset when they believe those activities double the price of their purchases. (See Figure 3-3.)

In reality, selling and promotion are a small part of the cost of marketing—typically about 5–10 percent of the product's price. And effective selling and promotion do increase the value to the customer. If a salesperson helps you select the best product for your needs rather than selling you something you do not want, you have spent your money more effectively. When advertising provides product information so you can make the best choice, or informs you where a product can be purchased and when it is on

The Typical Costs of Marketing

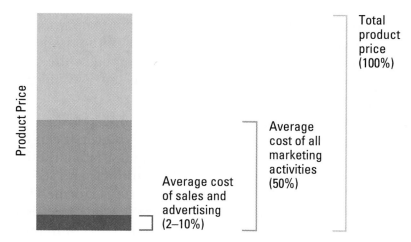

FIGURE 3-3 ■ On average, total marketing expenses are about one-half of a product's price, while sales and advertising costs average about 2–10 percent of the price.

sale, it helps you make better decisions. It can even result in savings because of the information provided.

Economists who study the impact of marketing activities on product prices have demonstrated that marketing actually results in lower prices in the long run. Because products can be sold to more customers, there is greater competition among businesses. When consumers have choices of products, they will usually buy those that are reasonably priced. That encourages businesses to keep prices as low as possible in order to be competitive. According to the economists, increased sales volume and competition result in lower prices for consumers.

QUALITY PRODUCTS AND SERVICES DO NOT NEED MARKETING

There are many examples of businesses that rely on marketing to sell poor quality products. Think of the used automobile with many defects that is sold only because the salesperson convinced the unsuspecting customer that the car was really in good condition. You have probably heard of someone buying land for a home based on information in a brochure or a video tape, only to discover that the land is in a swamp or on the side of a steep mountain. Marketing is certainly misused in those situations to misrepresent poor products.

On the other hand, consider whether or not a high-quality product needs marketing. Without marketing, it would be the responsibility of the consumer to find out that the product exists and to gather information about it. The consumer would have to locate the product, pay cash for it, and transport it from where it was manufactured to where it was to be used. All of the risk in handling and moving the product would be assumed by the customer; if it was damaged, the customer would be responsible.

There are many other marketing activities we could discuss in this example. However, it can be seen clearly from those described, that marketing is important even for quality products and services. Marketing activities must be performed in every exchange. If the business is not responsible for marketing, consumers will have to complete the activities themselves in order to purchase the product or service.

MARKETING SOLVES PROBLEMS

We have seen that marketing, if misused, can have negative results. However, marketing can help to solve important problems and contribute to social improvement. Here are some examples of very positive results when marketing is used effectively.

MARKETING INCREASES PUBLIC AWARENESS

There are many serious problems facing our society. Concerns about health care, crime levels, poverty, diseases, racism, education, unemployment, drug use, the environment, and teenage pregnancy all require the attention of many people if solutions are to be found. Marketing contributes to the solutions in several ways. Through communication, people are more aware of the problems and how they affect individuals and the country. Consider the number of times you have received information on using seat belts, recycling, the dangers of drugs and alcohol, and reasons to stay in school. Marketers have been responsible for developing the advertisements and public service announcements you have seen. Some of these are shown in Figure 3-4.

Marketing has encouraged people to eat low cholesterol products, quit smoking, contribute money to colleges, apply for scholarships, and support research into cures for diseases like AIDS and cancer. Marketing has encouraged people to vote and to avoid drinking and driving. You can think of many important social issues that are now receiving much attention because of effective marketing.

Marketing Increases Public Awareness

FIGURE 3-4 ■ Publicity and advertising are important tools in developing public awareness of issues, problems, and solutions.

MARKETING HELPS MATCH SUPPLY WITH DEMAND

Products and services are not always available where they are most needed by consumers. Marketing activities help to solve that problem. For example, if there is a drought in one part of the country, farmers and ranchers in that area may not have enough hay and grain to feed their livestock. At the same time, there might be an excess supply in other areas. An effective distribution system can move the hay and grain quickly from one part of the country to another, matching supply and demand. See Figure 3-5.

Oil products and gasoline can be distributed throughout the country using an extensive network of pipelines. If a greater supply of natural gas or heating oil is needed in the north during an especially cold winter, it can be routed away from areas that have less demand. These examples (drought and inadequate heating supplies) show that marketing helps to prevent or reduce the impact of problems that could otherwise result in serious problems for society.

Marketing Helps Match Supply and Demand

FIGURE 3-5 ▪ In the private enterprise economy, supply and demand for products and services are not always balanced. Marketing activities are important in making the economic system work.

INCREASING SOCIAL RESPONSIBILITY

Marketers cannot think only about selling products and making a profit. They must be aware of other effects of their activities. Marketing is a powerful tool that can have both positive and negative results. Marketers must be willing to pay attention to society's needs to determine how businesses can contribute to solutions.

The trend in society today is a greater expectation for business to be socially responsible and to aid in solving the problems facing society. *Concern about the consequences of actions on others is social responsibility.* Also, business people recognize that they must make decisions that consider factors beyond what their customers want and what is most profitable for the business. Most business people recognize their businesses cannot be successful in the long run if society is facing major problems.

Increasing the social responsibility of businesses is occurring in three major ways. The growth of consumerism, government regulation, and improving business practices are each playing a role. See Figure 3-6.

Social Responsibility Must Be Shared

FIGURE 3-6 ▪ Consumer groups, government, and business organizations all must play a role in improving society.

THE GROWTH OF CONSUMERISM

Consumerism is the organized actions of groups of consumers seeking to increase their influence on business practices.
Consumers as individuals can have only a small influence on the activities of a business. However, when organized as a group of consumers, they have a much greater impact by speaking out, meeting with business people to recommend changes, and using the money they spend on purchases to influence decisions.

While consumers have always attempted to influence business practices, consumerism became an important influence on business practices in the 1960s when President John F. Kennedy presented the Consumer Bill of Rights. The Consumer Bill of Rights identified four basic rights that all consumers should expect: the right to adequate and accurate information, the right to safe products, the right to product choices, and the right to communicate their ideas and opinions to business and government.

As a result of the attention focused on those rights, consumers have become very active in ensuring that their rights are protected. Some ways used to protect consumer rights are consumer education, consumer information, lobbying, and product boycotts. Consumer groups develop materials and educational programs to be used in schools and in other places to help people become better consumers. You may have used some of those materials to learn how to use banking services, purchase insurance, and apply for loans.

There are a number of consumer organizations that test products to determine whether they are safe and if they provide consumers with a good value for the price. The organizations often publish the results in books and magazines or have a telephone service so people can call for product information before making a purchase. Consumer lobbyists work with national and state legislators to develop laws to protect consumer rights. Some important consumer laws are described in Figure 3-7.

Finally, consumers have found they can influence business practices by the way they spend their money; their consumer vote. If a group of consumers is dissatisfied with the actions or products of a business they can organize a consumer boycott. *A boycott is an organized effort to influence a company by refusing to purchase its products.* Consumer groups also reinforce positive business practices by encouraging their members to purchase products from businesses that respond to consumer needs.

GOVERNMENT REGULATION

The United States government plays an active role in business practices. Many of the laws and regulations of government are designed to improve the social impact of business practices.

Federal Legislation Designed to Improve Business Practices	
Legislation	**Purpose**
Mail Fraud Act, 1872	Protect consumers from businesses using the mail to defraud
Sherman Antitrust Act, 1890	To increase competition among businesses by regulating monopolies
Food and Drug Act, 1906	To control the content and labeling of food and drug products by forming the Food and Drug Administration (FDA)
Federal Trade Commission Act, 1914	To form the Federal Trade Commission (FTC) to protect consumer rights
Robinson-Patman Act, 1936	To protect small businesses from unfair pricing practices between manufacturers and large businesses
Fair Packaging and Labeling Act, 1966	To require packages to be accurately labeled and fairly represent the contents
National Traffic and Motor Vehicle Safety Act, 1966	To set safety requirements for automobiles and automotive products
Consumer Credit Protection Act, 1968	To require accurate disclosure of credit requirements and rates to loan applicants
Consumer Product Safety Act, 1972	To set product safety standards and to form the Consumer Product Safety Commission (CPSC)
Fair Debt Collection Act, 1980	To prevent harassment of people who owe money by debt collectors

FIGURE 3-7 ▪ Federal legislation is one method of increasing the social responsibility of businesses.

Others are specifically developed to protect consumers. Examples of some of the most important laws are highlighted in Figure 3-7.

CLASSICS AND CONTEMPORARIES

BUSINESS LEADERS ARE SOCIAL ACTIVISTS

There is often a perception that businesses are not concerned about the problems facing society. When it comes to choosing between profits and social concerns, many people believe businesses will choose profits. But a group of business people have recently started a process to change that image and to show that businesses can be profitable while demonstrating concern for the environment, employee needs, and community issues.

Businesses for Social Responsibility (BSR) was organized in 1992. At that time, 55 companies pledged to "do the right thing" through individual company actions and to encourage other businesses to adopt new business practices. BSR believes that companies resist changes such as energy-efficient operating procedures, recycling, a safer working environment, and involvement in community improvement. BSR's goal is to show that if businesses do not get involved in social and community changes, those businesses will face economic problems in the future. BSR asks its members as well as other companies to contribute a percentage of profits to community improvement activities and encourages employees to volunteer for those activities.

Among the original companies involved in organizing BSR are Ben & Jerry's Homemade Ice Cream, The Body Shop USA, Crib Diaper Service, Esprit, Just Desserts, Lotus Publishing, Reebok International, Rhino Records, and Stride Rite Shoes. They hope to expand the membership of the organization to over 500 businesses in just a few years.

Some people, including other business owners, look at BSR skeptically. They believe it is a publicity stunt, or will be forgotten if the businesses start to lose money. However, the founding owners say they are committed. They see a new way of doing business in a world that is very different than it was just a short time ago. BSR companies believe businesses must plan for the future. That future will only be successful if the society can meet today's challenges.

IMPROVING BUSINESS PRACTICES

Most businesses recognize their responsibility to consumers and to society. If consumers are dissatisfied with the business' practices, they will soon stop buying the company's products. Social problems often lead to increased regulation of businesses by government or increases in taxes to pay for programs designed to solve the problems. Businesses do not want either increased regulation or increased taxes.

Individual businesses and business organizations are working to improve business practices in several ways. Those ways include codes of ethics, self-regulation, and social action.

Code of Ethics

A code of ethics is a statement of responsibilities for honest and proper conduct. Business people recognize that the inappropriate or illegal behavior of one firm can have a very negative effect on the whole industry. They attempt to influence that behavior by agreeing on standards of conduct. By agreeing to a code of ethics, the business people encourage responsible behavior. In some groups, the codes of ethics are enforced by penalties, established by the industry, that are applied to businesses who violate the standards. A portion of the American Marketing Association's Code of Ethics is summarized in Figure 3-8 on the next page.

Self-regulation

Individual businesses and groups of businesses in the same industry have developed procedures to respond to consumer problems and to encourage customers to work directly with the businesses to solve problems. *Taking personal responsibility for actions is known as self-regulation.* The Better Business Bureau is a consumer protection organization sponsored by businesses. The purpose of the Better Business Bureau is to gather information from consumers about problems, to provide information about improper business practices so consumers can make better decisions, and to attempt to solve problems between businesses and their customers.

Many businesses have consumer service departments that work to solve consumer problems and to provide consumers with information about the company and its products. The General Electric Answer Center offers a 24-hour-a-day, toll-free telephone service that customers can use to get information, register complaints, and make suggestions. Chrysler Motors de-

A Section of the Code of Ethics of the American Marketing Association

RESPONSIBILITIES OF MARKETERS:

In the area of product development and management,
disclosure of all substantial risks associated with product or service usage;
identification of any product component substitution that might materially change the product or impact on the buyer's purchase decision;
identification of extra-cost added features.

In the area of promotions,
avoidance of false and misleading advertising;
rejection of high-pressure manipulations or misleading sales tactics;
avoidance of sales promotions that use deception or manipulation.

In the area of distribution,
not manipulating the availability of a product for purpose of exploitation;
not using coercion in the marketing channel;
not exerting undue influence over the reseller's choice to handle a product.

In the area of pricing,
not engaging in price fixing;
not practicing predatory pricing;
disclosing the full price associated with any purchase.

In the area of marketing research,
prohibiting selling or fundraising under the guise of conducting research;
maintaining research integrity by avoiding misrepresentation and omission of pertinent research data;
treating outside clients and suppliers fairly.

FIGURE 3-8 ▪ Organizations and industries often develop a code of ethics to promote honest and proper standards of conduct.

veloped a Car Buyer's Bill of Rights and added the position of Vice President for Consumer Affairs to ensure those rights are protected.

Some industries, such as home builders, developed procedures that consumers can use to resolve problems with a specific builder. Problems that cannot be resolved between the customer and the business are referred to a panel of business people and consumers who can help determine a fair solution.

Social Action

Business people are concerned about the world in which they live. Many are active in helping to solve some of society's serious problems. They use resources from their businesses to help. Members Only, a clothing manufacturer, spent more than $100 million on advertising messages directed at reducing drug abuse and increasing voter registration. Most recently it is directing its efforts at reducing the homeless problem.

Nike committed about $50 million to a literacy program. McDonalds sponsors Ronald McDonald Houses. These are homes for families with children who are hospitalized with serious illnesses. Each day you see many examples of businesses that are concerned about their communities. They invest time and money to help the community and its people.

ETHICS IN MARKETING

The ethics of business people have received a great deal of attention in the past several years. *Ethics refers to decisions and behavior based on honest and fair standards.* Most business people are ethical in their practices. However, some very visible examples of inappropriate actions by a few, cause people to wonder if ethical behavior is really valued in business.

Marketers deal directly with customers. They ask customers to spend money for products and services intended to satisfy needs and wants. Because of this close relationship, marketers have a special responsibility for ethical behavior.

Each individual, whether in business or not, can decide whether an action is right or wrong. It is difficult to always agree on whether an activity is ethical or unethical. However, people place a high value on ethical behavior in all relationships, including business relations. Business people are expected to be honest and fair in dealings with customers, employees, and other businesses.

The Code of Ethics of the American Marketing Association (see Figure 3-8) describes the specific responsibilities for marketers in the areas of product planning, promotion, pricing, distribution, and marketing research. Those responsibilities are areas where marketers have agreed on ethical and unethical behavior.

Each marketer is responsible for ethical behavior. Decisions made and actions taken should be evaluated to determine if they are honest and fair. It is not always easy to decide whether all actions are ethical or not. Sometimes there will appear to be conflicts in what is best for the business, for the employees of the business, for its customers and competitors, and for society in general. Some people suggest the decision should be based on what is best for the most people. Others believe that ethics is more personal. Whether an action is right or wrong should be determined based on the effects on the people directly involved.

In some cases, it may appear there is no real harm in unethical behavior. If dishonesty results in a customer buying your product rather than your competitor's, or if you can conceal a mistake you made, you may believe that it does not matter. However, marketers must remember that their emphasis must be on what is best for everyone involved in an exchange. Their actions usually affect many other decisions and people, both inside and outside of the business.

In other cases, unethical behavior has very obvious negative consequences for individuals and businesses. Customers can be physically or financially harmed by improper marketing. Society is hurt by businesses that have no concern for the types of products and services they sell or how or to whom they are marketed. Finally, many unethical business practices are also illegal. Those responsible for unethical activities, as well as their businesses, are accountable. People have been fined and even imprisoned as a result of unethical actions.

Some businesses are now developing education programs and operating procedures to help employees understand the importance of ethics and learn how to make ethical decisions. Those businesses want to improve the ethical image of all businesses and to ensure that customers believe they will be treated fairly by every employee.

CHALLENGES

CAN THE SUPPORT OF EDUCATION CREATE PROBLEMS?

Ethical decisions are not always clear cut. What may be viewed as a very effective and needed product or service by some may be seen as inappropriate by others. Those situations offer marketers a real challenge to determine whether to continue to offer the product or withdraw it from the market. That decision was faced by Whittle communications about its current events program for schools.

Channel One is a 12-minute newscast offered each day to students throughout the United States. In 1992, Channel One was viewed by more than 6 million students in nearly 10,000 schools. Expectations are that the numbers will grow to 10 million students in 20,000 schools.

Channel One was developed in response to data showing that students have little understanding of current events. Whittle Communications believed satellite-delivered television offered a solution. A student-oriented news program could be produced and offered to schools at the beginning of each school day. However, in studying the market, Whittle discovered that most schools did not have the needed satellite receiver or televisions. The schools also had budget problems which prevented them from purchasing the program even if they could receive it.

The solution developed was to sell advertising on each program. Four, 30-second commercials would be sold to businesses wanting to reach the large and profitable school-age market. The funds received from advertising would be used to give each school the necessary equipment to show Channel One, to pay for production of the news show, and to provide a profit to Whittle. The solution seemed to benefit everyone concerned. Students would be able to learn about current events, the schools would get new equipment, and advertisers would have another method of getting their messages to an important audience.

However, many teachers, administrators, and parents objected. Some people said that schools and the minds of children should not be bought with advertisers' dollars! Lawsuits were filed in several states to prevent Whittle from putting Channel One into the schools. Some companies, fearing that advertising on Channel One would create a negative image, decided not to continue supporting the program.

Channel One is an example of the type of ethical decision that business people often face. The correct decision is not clear. Whittle is currently successful with Channel One, but will the success last if criticisms of the advertising continue?

REVIEW

While the marketing concept is important, satisfying customer needs and wants is not the only responsibility of businesses. Businesses must be concerned about their impact on society and how they can help solve society's problems and improve the quality of life.

Effective marketing can make important contributions to businesses, individuals, and society. Those benefits are not always apparent, and marketers need to emphasize them in order for people to understand the value and importance of marketing. Some people criticize marketing because of poor marketing practices in the past. Marketers need to understand those criticisms in order to improve marketing and to change people's perceptions.

Several groups are involved in improving the social responsibility of business and marketing. The work of consumer groups, government, and business organizations have had a very positive effect on business-consumer relationships. Ultimately, one of the best ways to improve business and marketing practices is for each person to act ethically. Honest and fair actions will usually be viewed as socially responsible.

MARKETING FOUNDATIONS

1. **YES OR NO?**

   The following statements describe the social responsibility of business. On a separate sheet of paper, answer yes if the statement is true, and no if it is false.

   a. With the use of marketing, businesses are able to produce products and services that consumers need.

b. Only businesses can complete marketing activities; consumers cannot be involved in marketing.

c. If marketing is effective, the costs of products and services can actually decrease rather than increase.

d. An important social problem created by marketing is that it always results in the misuse and waste of raw materials and natural resources.

e. Effective marketing is used to encourage people to buy things they otherwise would not buy.

f. On average, the cost of all marketing activities is about 50 percent of the price of a product.

g. Even when a business has a high-quality product or service, marketing is necessary to sell the product at a profit.

h. Marketing has not been an effective tool in helping society to solve some serious problems.

i. Transporting water to an area where there is a severe drought is an example of a marketing activity.

j. Business people cannot be expected to contribute to solving social problems.

k. Individual consumers can usually be quite effective in influencing the activities of businesses.

l. The Consumer Bill of Rights was part of the original U.S. Constitution.

m. It is illegal for a group of consumers to agree to stop buying a business' product in order to influence the actions of the business.

n. Federal laws to improve business practices and protect consumers have only been in existence since 1960.

o. The Better Business Bureau is an example of businesses working together to improve business practices.

p. For all marketing decisions there is a clear choice of what is ethical or unethical.

2. WHAT IS THE IDEA?

Match each of the following terms in the column on the left with the situation that illustrates the idea in the column on the right.

Term	Situation
Social Responsibility	The Automobile Dealers Association prepares a statement of acceptable and unacceptable sales procedures for its members.
Consumerism	A salesperson who sees that a customer was charged the regular price rather than the sale price decides to return the excess amount to the customer.
Boycott	A restaurant owner must decide whether to support a community campaign to make all public areas of buildings (including businesses) nonsmoking areas.
Code of Ethics	A community action group's members decide to stop shopping at a supermarket chain that charges much higher prices at its inner-city locations than at its suburban stores.
Self-Regulation	A computer manufacturer provides a list of procedures and a telephone number for new customers to use if they have problems with their purchases or with company personnel.
Ethics	The members of a student club meet with a business to encourage it to hire more high school students as part-time employees.

MARKETING RESEARCH

1. MARKETING AFFECTS PRICES

The following four consumer products have undergone significant price decreases from the time they were first sold until now. Those price decreases occurred because of improved technology and effective marketing, which resulted in higher sales. The prices listed for each product are typical of the prices charged when the products were first introduced and more recently.

Product	Introductory Price	Recent Price
Hand-held Scientific Calculator	$ 138	$ 18
Quartz Watch	320	60
Personal Computer	2,800	895
Microwave Oven	860	220

a. For each product, calculate the difference in price and the percentage of price reduction from the introductory price to the recent price.

b. Assume that you planned to buy all four of the items. Calculate the total cost of the purchases if all were purchased at the introductory price. Now calculate the total cost if all were purchased at the recent price. Calculate the percentage of savings to you if you were able to make all purchases at the recent price.

c. List four other products with large price decreases from the time they were first introduced until now.

2. ISSUES IN SOCIAL RESPONSIBILITY

Review five issues in the business section of a newspaper or five issues in a business magazine (*Business Week, Fortune, Money*). Identify all articles that relate to the social responsibility of businesses. For each article determine (a) the primary issue involved; (b) whether the problem is being addressed by consumer groups, government, businesses, or a combination; and (c) the type of action being proposed to solve the problem. After you have collected the information, summarize your findings in a one-page written report.

MARKETING PLANNING

1. PROBLEMS AND RESPONSES

 The following statements describe marketing activities that may result in a problem for society. For each statement, describe a problem that may result from the practice and one way that consumers, government, and businesses could respond.

a. Fast-food restaurants use a large amount of packaging.

b. Credit card companies use advertising to encourage people to use credit for more of their purchases.

c. A hospital cannot afford to admit patients who do not have health insurance.

d. A market research organization asks a large number of personal questions during interviews.

2. USING YOUR EXPERIENCE

a. Three criticisms of marketing were listed in this chapter. Provide specific examples demonstrating that each criticism is not always accurate.

■ Marketing causes people to purchase things they otherwise would not buy.

■ Marketing adds to the cost of products without providing anything of value.

■ Quality products and services do not need marketing.

b. Two positive results of marketing were listed in the chapter. Provide specific examples demonstrating that those contributions do exist.

■ Marketing increases public awareness of problems and solutions.

■ Marketing helps match supply and demand to solve serious problems.

MARKETING MANAGEMENT

1. DEVELOPING A CODE OF ETHICS

Work in small groups of students to prepare a code of ethics for students and teachers. Pattern your code of ethics after the example in the chapter or another code of ethics you can locate. When you are finished, share your group's code of ethics with the other groups. Identify the areas of agreement and disagreement in the various codes of ethics. Discuss how the students in the class could enforce the code of ethics through self-regulation.

2. MAKING SOCIALLY RESPONSIBLE DECISIONS

Both the Newsline on super squirt guns (page 56) and the Challenges discussing Channel One in schools (page 75) present situations in which business people must decide how their decisions can be socially responsible. Choose one and answer the following questions:

a. What is the social responsibility issue presented?

b. Who is affected by the decisions of the business? How is each group affected?

c. What is a possible action that can be taken by a concerned consumer group? government? a group of businesses? the business involved?

d. What do you believe is the most socially responsible action? Why?

UNIT

2

Economic and Business Foundations

83

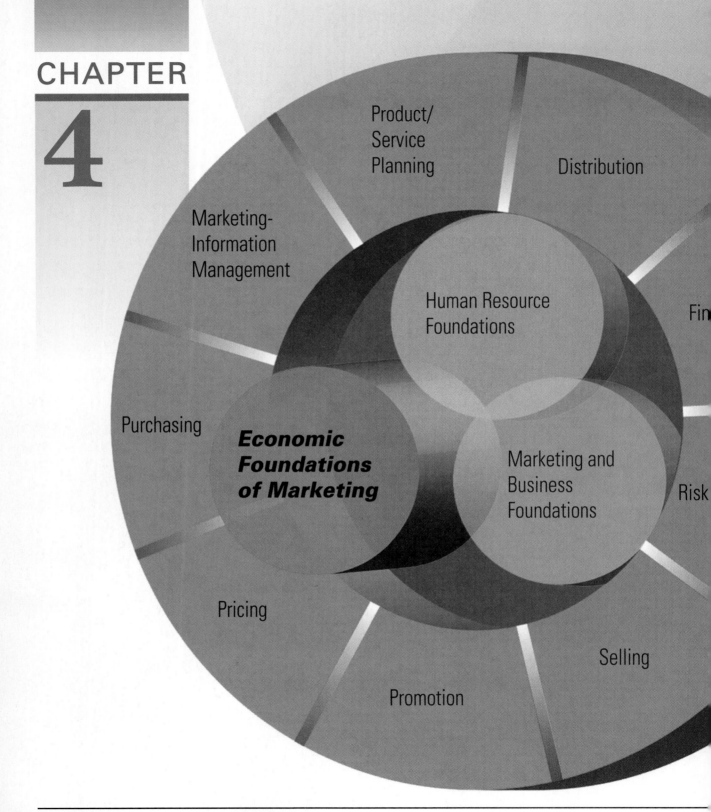

Product/
Service
Planning

Distribution

Marketing-
Information
Management

Human Resource
Foundations

Fin

Purchasing

*Economic
Foundations
of Marketing*

Marketing and
Business
Foundations

Risk

Pricing

Promotion

Selling

Marketing Begins with Economics

OBJECTIVES

1. Identify how marketers can benefit from an understanding of economics.

2. Explain the basic economic problem of scarcity and how societies solve the problem.

3. Describe the characteristics of the U.S. private enterprise economy.

4. Identify the roles of consumers, producers, and government in a private enterprise economy.

5. Discuss why knowledge of microeconomics is an important tool for marketers.

6. Explain the law of demand and the law of supply.

7. Compare the competitive environments faced by businesses operating in pure competition, monopoly, oligopoly, and monopolistic competition.

8. Provide examples of how each of the types of economic utility can be used to improve customer satisfaction.

NEWSLINE

AN ECONOMIC DOGFIGHT

"Fly the friendly skies." "We love to fly and it shows." "Something special in the air." Airlines are fighting for passengers and profits. In addition to extensive advertising, airlines have engaged in price wars by cutting ticket prices and offering discounts for certain flights and travel days. Because of this competition, several major airlines have gone out of business or declared bankruptcy.

In the 1970s, airlines were considered a very profitable business. Many small, regional airlines were expanding into national routes and competing with large airlines. Even small cities had airports that were served regularly by one or more airlines. Today, many cities have lost all air service and even some moderate- to larger-sized cities are served by small, commuter airlines. The larger airlines that remain concentrate their services in "hub" cities, (cities where there is a large amount of passenger traffic and where the airline has a chance to dominate the competition).

Why has an industry gone from being very profitable to unprofitable in about twenty years? Much

Why has an industry gone from being very profitable to unprofitable in about twenty years?

of the reason is based on the role government played and the nature of competition faced by airlines. Due to safety concerns for millions of people who fly, the federal government provides a great amount of regulation for the industry. But in addition to maintaining safety standards, the government also regulated competition. Unprofitable service to smaller cities was subsidized by the government; the numbers of competitors serving various travel routes was controlled. Therefore, profits and service were reasonably protected because of government involvement.

In the 1980s the government reduced its role in, or deregulated, the airline industry. No longer were subsidies provided for unprofitable routes and airlines were generally able to compete with each other for routes and customers. As a result many of the smaller airlines could no longer compete as the larger companies battled for revenues.

Airlines have attempted to show customers how their airlines are different from each other to encourage passenger loyalty. However most customers are concerned about getting to a particular location at a specific time and at a reasonable cost. Many customers do not see important differences among the major competitors.

As a result, airlines have used price competition, heavy advertising, and sales promotion to attract customers. The nature of competition in the airline industry gives each company very little control over the things that allow them to be more profitable. When the government reduced its role, executives had to find a new way of doing business.

THE IMPORTANCE OF ECONOMIC UNDERSTANDING

Many people believe that effective marketing relies on creativity. In their view, people who can create a memorable image for a product or attract the customer's attention will increase sales. Those who understand marketing, however, know that the marketing process is more scientific. Effective marketing relies on the principles and concepts of economics. Knowledge of economics and how economic decisions are made improves marketing decision-making and results in both increased customer satisfaction and profits for the company.

This chapter will introduce the key economic concepts that explain how marketing decisions are made. You will see how the private enterprise economy of the United States has characteristics that do not always result in the best decisions about what to produce and consume. Marketing can provide the means of increasing the effectiveness of the economy.

An understanding of the types of competition businesses face will also contribute to better marketing decisions. We will describe the types of competition and illustrate how marketers can manage within each type. You will learn how to interpret economic information in order to improve marketing decisions. Marketers, as well as all business people, must recognize that the increasing amount of competition facing most businesses places a whole new importance on understanding and using economic information.

THE BASIC ECONOMIC PROBLEM

People's wants and needs are unlimited. We seldom feel like all of our wants and needs are satisfied. However, the availability of resources is limited. There are never enough resources available to meet everyone's wants and needs. For example, producing a car requires a variety of resources including glass, rubber, steel, and plastic. There is a limited supply of each of those resources and they are needed for things other than producing cars. So there may not be enough resources to produce all the automobiles people might want.

Unlimited wants and needs combined with limited resources result in scarcity. Scarcity of resources is the basic economic problem. Because of scarcity, choices must be made. How will limited resources be used to satisfy the wants and needs of society? Because wants and needs will always be greater than the available resources, choices and tradeoffs must be made. The available resources will have to be allocated to satisfy some wants and needs and not others.

Scarcity creates difficult problems for a society. Some needs and wants are satisfied while others are not. Resources are used to produce certain products and services. Other products and services are not produced. What is produced and for whom it is produced must be determined. How those decisions are made indicates the type of economic system a society has.

An economy is designed to facilitate the use of resources. The resources satisfy the individual and group needs of people in the economy. Economies are organized in many ways. The type of economic system determines who owns the resources. It determines how decisions on the use of resources are made. Which needs are satisfied and how resources are distributed depends on the economic system. Even the cost of those resources depends on the economic system.

In systems known as controlled economies, the government attempts to own and control important resources and to make the decisions about what will be produced and consumed. In other economies, known as regulated economies, the resources and decisions are shared between the government and other groups or individuals. Finally, in free economies, all resources are owned by individuals rather than the government, and decisions are made independently with no attempt at regulation or control by the government.

THE UNITED STATES HAS A PRIVATE ENTERPRISE ECONOMY

The United States has many of the characteristics of a free economy. Specifically, the United States is said to have a private enterprise economy. *Private enterprise is based on independent decisions by businesses and consumers with only a limited government role regulating those relationships.*

Business people can decide whether to produce products and services. They can also determine what to produce. Consumers can decide what to purchase to satisfy needs from a variety of choices, or they may decide not to purchase anything.

Government limits its role in regulating what is produced and what is consumed only to those situations where it seems there is a real advantage or disadvantage for businesses or consumers or where the government wants to encourage or discourage some type of production or consumption.

CHARACTERISTICS OF PRIVATE ENTERPRISE

There are several important characteristics that describe a private enterprise economy.

■ Resources of production are owned and controlled by individual producers.

■ Producers use the profit motive in deciding what to produce. *The profit motive is a decision to use resources in a way that results in the greatest profit for the producer.*

■ Decisions about what will be purchased to satisfy needs are made by individual consumers.

■ Consumers use value in deciding what to consume. *Value is a decision to use resources in a way that results in the greatest satisfaction of wants and needs.*

■ The government remains out of exchange activities between producers and consumers unless it is clear that individuals or society are harmed by the decisions.

Because business people have a great deal of independence in a private enterprise economy, the decisions they make can determine whether they will be successful or fail. The activities and interactions of producers, consumers, and government must be understood in order to make effective decisions.

CONSUMERS IN PRIVATE ENTERPRISE

Consumers purchase products and services to satisfy needs. They have limited resources (money) to satisfy their needs. Consumers will select from among those products they believe are able to provide the greatest satisfaction for the price. *The quantity of a product consumers are willing and able to purchase at a specific price is known as demand.*

Consumers gather information about available products and services in order to select those that appear to satisfy their needs. As an example, a basic consumer need is for clothing. Depending on their skills, preferences, and money, some consumers will sew their own clothes. Others will buy basic and inexpensive clothing. Still others will spend a great deal of money on a large and expensive wardrobe.

PRODUCERS IN PRIVATE ENTERPRISE

Producers use the resources they control to develop products and services. They hope to be able to sell the products and services to consumers for a profit. *The quantity of a product that producers are willing and able to provide at a specific price is known as supply.*

Producers gather information on the types of products and services consumers want in order to provide those that are most

likely to be purchased. An example of a producer's decision is the development of a restaurant. We know that many consumers eat a number of their meals outside the home. This presents opportunities for business people to start a business that responds to that need. However, there are many possible choices of types of restaurants, menu items, levels of service, locations, and hours of operation. Individual restaurant owners can determine the type of business they want to operate based on what they believe customers want.

GOVERNMENT IN PRIVATE ENTERPRISE

Under ideal circumstances, government allows consumers and producers to make decisions about demand and supply without any interference. However there are times when it appears that some consumers or producers are at a disadvantage and will not receive fair treatment, or that society will be harmed by the decisions made by producers and consumers. In those situations the government uses its powers through laws and regulations to attempt to help those who are treated unfairly. In Chapter 3, you saw some examples of the laws and government agencies that are used to regulate the exchange of products and services.

Let's look at a simple example of decision-making in a private enterprise economy. One community has a variety of types of entertainment, but does not have a social club for teenagers—a place where teenagers can go to meet each other, dance, eat, play video games, and relax. Many teenagers indicate a need for some type of club and suggest they would visit it and spend money there if one was developed. However, even though it appears that the need for the new type of business exists, there is no requirement that any business person open a teen social club. It will be developed only when someone recognizes the need, determines the club could be opened and operated profitably, wants to operate that type of business, and has the resources to do so.

It may be that members of city government recognize the need for a teen club. They may see teenage crime rates increasing, or had concerns expressed to them by teenagers and their parents, or just want to meet important needs of people living in the city. Based on that concern, the government may encourage the development of a teen club by a business person through tax incentives or other economic assistance. Or they may have the city develop and operate a teen center as a city service.

Typically, in the private enterprise economy, government would not enter into the economic problem described. It would rely on the profit motive to encourage the development of a new business and on consumers expressing their needs to businesses for products and services.

MARKETERS FOCUS ON MICROECONOMICS

Economics attempts to understand and explain how consumers and producers make decisions concerning the allocation of their resources. That understanding helps consumers and producers to use their resources as effectively as they can. It also helps government decision-makers determine if and when they should become involved in the economy as they work to maintain an even balance between producers and consumers and to maintain a strong economy that improves the standard of living for citizens.

Economics operates on two levels, as illustrated in Figure 4-1. *The first level, known as macroeconomics, studies the economic behavior and relationships for the entire society.* Macroeconomics looks at the big picture. It helps to determine if the resources of the entire country are being used as effectively and efficiently as possible. The decisions of all consumers and producers and the effects of those decisions on the economy are studied.

The second level, known as microeconomics, studies the relationships between individual consumers and producers.

Comparing Macroeconomics and Microeconomics

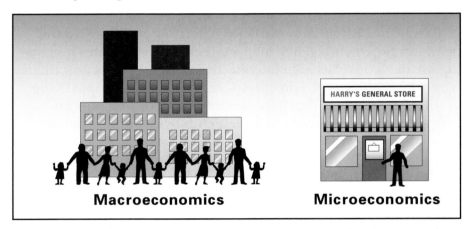

FIGURE 4-1 ■ Macroeconomics studies the whole economy while microeconomics studies the relationships between individual businesses and their consumers.

Microeconomics looks at small parts of the total economy. Microeconomics studies how individuals make decisions about what will be produced and what will be consumed.

While a broad understanding of economics is important to marketers, they are most concerned about microeconomics. You can see that information about how consumers make decisions on what they will purchase and how much they are willing to pay can be very important in selecting target markets and developing effective marketing mixes. It is also important to understand how a business' competitors make decisions about what they will produce and the prices they are likely to charge. Microeconomics looks at supply, demand, and the level of individual product prices. We will now examine the economics of demand and supply and show how this knowledge is an important tool for marketers.

FACTORS AFFECTING DEMAND

Several factors influence the consumer's decision on what to purchase and how much to pay. If a need or want is particularly important or strong, the consumer may be willing to spend more money to satisfy it. For example, if you are at a concert and really like the songs you just heard, obtaining a CD or tape may seem very important to you. You may be willing to pay much more than normal to buy a CD or tape at the concert rather than waiting to make the purchase later.

Another factor that affects consumers' decisions is the available supply of products and services to satisfy their needs. If there is a very large supply of a product, that will usually cause consumers to place a lower value on the product. Consider, walking through a farmers' market where a large number of producers are selling fresh fruits and vegetables. As a consumer, you see there are many choices of sellers and a large quantity of each product available. Therefore, you will probably be careful not to overpay for the fruits or vegetables you want. On the other hand, if a large number of customers are at the market and only a few farmers are there to sell their products, the customers may pay much higher prices to be sure they get the items they need.

A third factor is the choice of alternative products and services consumers believe will satisfy their needs. If consumers believe there is only one product or brand of product that meets their needs, they are willing to pay a higher price. However, if several choices seem to be equally satisfying, consumers are more careful about how much they pay. An example of this factor is your choices of entertainment for an evening. If there are very few choices of things for you and your friends to do, you are willing to pay quite a bit for a specific activity. If you identify several possible choices (movies, bowling, a local sporting event, or renting a video) and each choice seems appropriate, you may consider the cost of each choice more carefully. You might select the one that is inexpensive, but which you and your friends will still enjoy.

ANALYZING DEMAND

Economists try to determine how much consumers are willing and able to pay for various quantities of products or services. *The relationship between price and quantity demanded is often illustrated in a graph known as a demand curve.* Figure 4-2 shows a sample demand curve for movies in a city. As you can see in the graph, as the price of movies is increased, fewer people will buy tickets. As the price decreases, more tickets will be sold. *This relationship is known as the law of demand: When the price of a product is increased, less will be demanded; when the price is decreased, more will be demanded.*

Just as in marketing, economists use the concept of a market. *All of the consumers who will purchase a particular product or service are an economic market.* Economists believe that consumers in an economic market view the relationship of products and prices in the same way.

FACTORS AFFECTING SUPPLY

There are several factors that influence what and how many products or services a business will produce. Factors include the

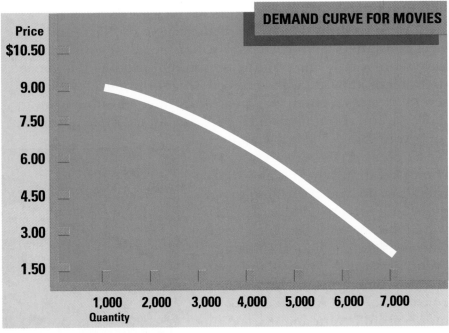

FIGURE 4-2 ▪ As the price of movies increases, the number of consumers willing and able to pay that price decreases.

possibility of profit, the amount of competition, and the capability of developing and marketing the products or services.

One of the most important reasons for businesses to operate in a private enterprise economy is to be able to make a profit. Businesses will try to offer products and services that have a better chance of making a profit rather than those that will have either a small profit or the possibility of a loss. Business managers carefully consider the costs of producing and marketing products and the prices they will be able to charge for the products. That analysis helps in determining the most profitable choices to produce.

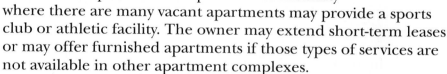

When looking for opportunities, businesses consider the amount and type of competition. When competition is intense (many businesses offering the same types of products or services), there are fewer opportunities for success than when there is little competition. When possible, suppliers may choose to offer products and services that have few competitors. Another choice when facing much competition is to change the product to make it different from those offered by other businesses. For example, an owner of an apartment complex in a community where there are many vacant apartments may provide a sports club or athletic facility. The owner may extend short-term leases or may offer furnished apartments if those types of services are not available in other apartment complexes.

Finally, businesses use the resources available to develop products and services. *Economic resources are classified as natural resources, capital, equipment, and labor.* The specific types of resources a business has available will determine the types of products and services it can develop and sell. Some resources are very flexible so the business can change and offer new products quickly. For example, if the owners of a retail furniture store found that major appliances such as refrigerators and stoves were not profitable, they could quickly change the products sold in that part of the store to some that are more profitable. Other businesses have more difficulty changing products. Companies that own oil wells or coal mines are very limited because the natural resources they own are their products. They have to sell the oil and coal even if those products are not very profitable.

ANALYZING SUPPLY

Economists predict how the quantity of products and services producers will provide changes at various prices. *The graph of the relationship between price and quantity supplied is known as a supply curve.* An example supply curve for watches is shown in Figure 4-3. The graph demonstrates that as

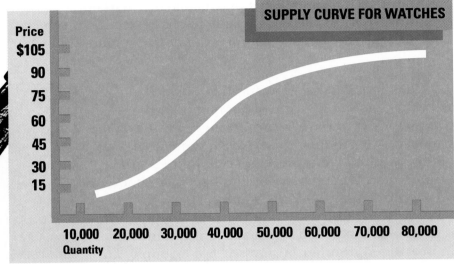

FIGURE 4-3 ▪ As the price for watches decreases, the quantity of watches manufacturers will be willing to supply decreases.

the price increases, producers will manufacture more watches. As the price goes down, fewer will be manufactured. *This relationship is known as the law of supply: when the price of a product is increased, more will be produced; when the price is decreased, less will be produced.* Whenever possible, producers use their resources to provide products and services that receive the highest prices. Just as with demand, economists believe that producers respond in similar ways when determining what to produce. Like consumers, producers see a relationship between products and prices.

SUPPLY AND DEMAND IN PRIVATE ENTERPRISE

We learned earlier that suppliers and consumers make independent decisions. However when all of the decisions of consumers for the same product are combined, they form a demand curve illustrating the quantity of a product or service that will be demanded at various prices. And when all the decisions of suppliers of the same product or service are combined, they form a supply curve. That curve illustrates the quantity of the product that will be supplied at various prices.

Figure 4-4 shows a demand curve and a supply curve for a particular type of notebook computer. The demand curve shows that fewer computers will be purchased as the price increases.

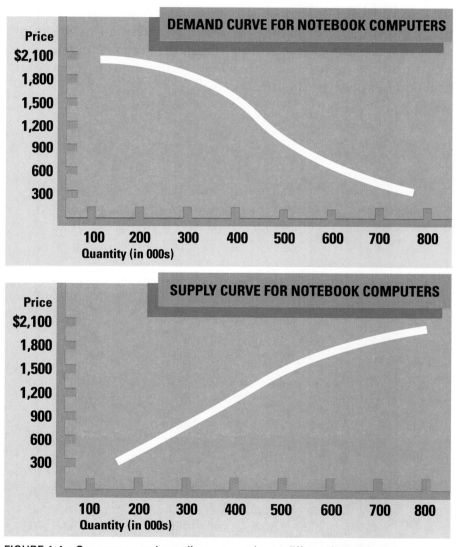

FIGURE 4-4 ▪ Consumers and suppliers respond very differently to price changes. The demand curve illustrates consumers' responses and the supply curve illustrates suppliers' responses.

As expected, computer manufacturers are willing to supply a large number of computers if prices are high, but very few at low prices.

To determine the number of computers that will actually be produced and sold, the two curves must be combined. The combined curves are shown in Figure 4-5. Notice that the two lines cross or intersect at a price of $1,300 and a quantity of 450,000 computers. *The point where supply and demand for a product are equal is known as the market price.* At that price, 450,000 computers will be manufactured and sold.

Each product in a specific market has its own supply and demand curves. And each market has price and quantity relationships that are unique and result in different curves on the graphs. In the next section, we will examine the market conditions that explain those differences.

TYPES OF ECONOMIC COMPETITION

Both consumer and supplier decisions are affected by the type of competition found in the market. We learned earlier that if consumers see a variety of products that seem to be very

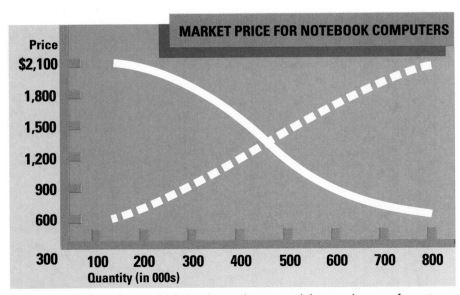

FIGURE 4-5 ■ The point at which the demand curve and the supply curve for notebook computers intersect is the market price.

similar, the consumers will be less willing to pay higher prices. In the same way, if suppliers are in a market with many other businesses offering similar products, they will not be able to easily increase their prices. Business people must be able to determine the type of competition they are facing and the amount of control they have over the prices they can charge in order to make effective production and marketing decisions. Two factors are important in determining the type of economic competition in a specific market:

1. The number of firms competing in the market

2. The amount of similarity between the products of competing businesses

Using those factors, economists have described four forms of economic competition—pure competition, monopoly, oligopoly, and monopolistic competition.

PURE COMPETITION

There are a few markets where there are a large number of suppliers and their products are very similar. In these markets, consumers have a great deal of control over choices and prices. Because the suppliers are unable to offer products that consumers view as unique, they must accept the prices consumers are willing to pay or the consumer will buy from another business. This market condition is known as pure competition. *In pure competition there are a large number of suppliers offering very similar products.*

The traditional examples of industries in pure competition are producers of agricultural products (corn, rice, wheat, livestock). Each producer's products are just like every other producer's. There are many producers so customers have no difficulty finding a business that will sell the products. Because customers have so many choices of suppliers and the products of all suppliers are similar, prices will be very competitive. One supplier will be unable to raise the price. Other examples of markets in which businesses face pure competition are those for many of the low-priced consumer products you purchase—bread, milk, toothpaste, shoelaces, and the like.

An example of the demand curve for a business in a purely competitive market is shown in Figure 4-6. In theory, it is a straight line at one price. This suggests that the supplier will receive the same price no matter how much of the product the supplier is willing to sell. Therefore, businesses have no control over price if they want to sell their products.

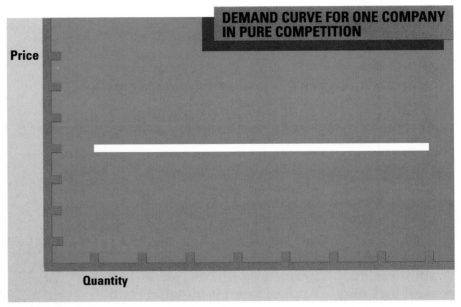

DEMAND CURVE FOR ONE COMPANY IN PURE COMPETITION

FIGURE 4-6 ■ In pure competition, the seller must accept the market price no matter how much of the product is sold.

MONOPOLY

The opposite type of economic competition from pure competition is a monopoly. *A monopoly is a type of market in which there is one supplier offering a unique product.* In this market, the supplier has almost total control and the consumers will have to accept what the supplier offers at the price charged. This occurs because of the lack of competition.

Because of the obvious advantage a business has in monopoly markets, the government attempts to control them so there are few examples of actual monopolies. However, utility companies that supply a community with electricity, gas, or water are typically organized as monopolies. There is only one supplier of each product since it would be very inefficient to have several companies extending gas and water lines or electrical service to every home. Once a home is supplied with the utilities, it would be easy for the company to raise the price. The consumer would have no choice but to pay the higher price or go without the gas, water, or electricity. That is the reason government agencies regulate the prices that can be charged by the utility companies.

Other examples of markets that can operate like a monopoly are cable television, some local telephone services, and businesses that are the only ones of their type in a particular geographic area where consumers have no choices. If you are driving down an interstate highway and there are is only one gasoline station at a particular exit, that business can operate much like a monopoly for those customers who need gasoline or other automotive products. A supermarket or other retail business in an area where there is no other similar business can also operate as a monopoly for those customers who are unable to travel to a competing business.

In theory, the demand curve facing a business that is a monopoly would look like the one in Figure 4-7. There is a fixed demand for the product since there are no other businesses offering a similar product. Therefore, if unregulated, the business can charge any price it chooses. The consumer either pays the price set by the business or goes without.

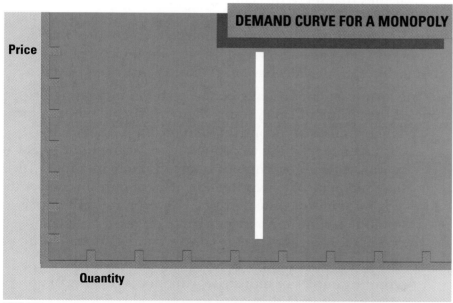

FIGURE 4-7 ■ In theory, a business in a monopoly can charge any price because it is selling a unique product.

OLIGOPOLY

Between the extremes of pure competition and monopoly are two other types of economic competition. The first one we will examine is known as oligopoly. *In an oligopoly a few businesses offer very similar products or services.* As you consider

the difference between an oligopoly and the other two types of markets we have discussed, you might be able to see the problems and advantages facing businesses in this type of market. If the businesses work together, they will be like a monopoly and have a great deal of control in the market. On the other hand, if they are very competitive, the similarity of their products or services will give consumers choices, much like in pure competition. Therefore the consumers will have more control and prices will be lower.

The airline industry that we studied at the beginning of the chapter is an example of an oligopoly. There are only a very few large airlines competing for national travel in the United States. It is difficult to see real important differences between two or three airlines that serve the same cities. Therefore, if one airline wants to increase the number of passengers on its flights, it will often do it by reducing the prices charged. To counter that effort and to keep passengers from flying with the competitor, other airlines will usually have to reduce their prices as well.

One airline will not usually be successful in increasing prices alone. If the airline industry wants higher prices to cover operating expenses and contribute to profit, the competing companies will have to cooperate in raising their prices as well. Again, government agencies often attempt to regulate that type of activity making it illegal for businesses to work together to control prices. However, you will notice that if one airline announces a price increase or decrease, the competing airlines are usually very quick to match the change.

Other examples of industries with characteristics of an oligopoly are automobile manufacturers, oil refineries, computer manufacturers, and telephone companies offering long-distance services. On the local level, some businesses operate as oligopolies because there are only a few businesses offering almost identical products and services to the consumers in that market. Some examples in medium- to large-size communities are taxi services, movie theaters, banks, and hospitals.

The demand curve facing businesses in an oligopoly is difficult to describe. For an individual business, the demand curve will look like the demand in pure competition since one business cannot influence the price it can charge to any great ex-

CHALLENGES
WHEN IS COOPERATIVE PRICING LEGAL?

In some industries, controlling prices is very difficult. That is especially true in an oligopoly. A few large businesses offer products that are very similar. Therefore, it is difficult to attract customers with factors other than price. If a customer wants to purchase an automobile and sees several brands as very similar, the customer will shop among dealers to find the lowest price. Dealers know they must have very competitive prices in order to make a large number of sales.

When business people see that they are competing in an oligopoly, they might be tempted to agree with other businesses to keep prices high. To protect consumers, the federal government makes it illegal for businesses to "fix" prices—cooperating to set the prices that will be charged. It is not unusual to hear of charges being brought against several companies who appear to have violated the law. Recently, several milk producers were charged with fixing prices for the milk they sold to school districts. In another case, companies who sold concrete for government buildings were accused of agreeing in advance on the prices they would use when they bid for the construction contracts.

It is difficult for the government to regulate pricing practices of businesses when a few large firms compete with each other. For example, it is not unusual for an airline to announce a price increase or decrease that will take effect in several weeks. Then competing airlines can determine if they are going to match the price change. Automobile manufacturers typically announce new model prices one or two months in advance of distribution. That gives competing manufacturers time to set their prices. While these pricing practices are not illegal, they have much the same effect as illegal price fixing.

Do you think government should be involved in regulating the prices businesses charge for their products? Do you believe the legal pricing practices described for the airline and auto industry are ethical?

tent. Figure 4-8 shows an example of a demand curve for one company in an oligopoly. The demand curve for all of the businesses combined in an oligopoly will look much like that of a monopoly. Cooperatively, the businesses have a great deal of control over price. Consumers who want the product or service will have to purchase from one of the few companies in the market or go without. An example of a demand curve for the entire industry in an oligopoly is shown in Figure 4-9.

MONOPOLISTIC COMPETITION

By far the most common type of economic competition facing most businesses is monopolistic competition. *In monopolistic competition there are many firms competing with products that are somewhat different.* The fewer the number of competitors and the greater the differences among the competitors' products or services, the greater the control each firm will have in the market. With more competitors and only minor differences, businesses will have very limited control.

There are many examples of businesses in monopolistic competition. Most retail businesses in which you shop face this type of competition. Most of the products or services you buy fit the

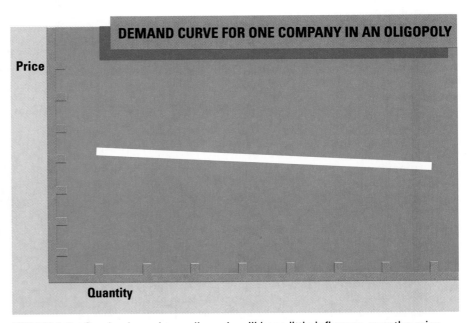

DEMAND CURVE FOR ONE COMPANY IN AN OLIGOPOLY

Price

Quantity

FIGURE 4-8 ▪ One business in an oligopoly will have little influence over the price it can charge.

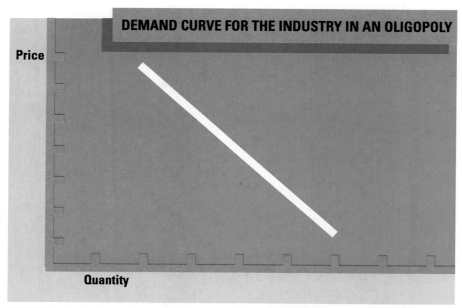

DEMAND CURVE FOR THE INDUSTRY IN AN OLIGOPOLY

Price

Quantity

FIGURE 4-9 ▪ Because there are few firms in an oligopoly, the total industry has much more control over prices.

definition. As a consumer you typically have several choices of businesses or products. Among those choices, you can identify differences. Some differences are very noticeable and important. Other differences are only minor. When you have choices as a consumer, you usually select the one providing the most satisfaction at the best value. Examples of businesses and products in monopolistic competition are clothing, restaurants, stereo equipment, convenience stores, jewelry, and concert promoters.

The demand curve for businesses in monopolistic competition falls between that of pure competition and monopoly. The greater the differences among products and services, the more control the business has. The demand curve is more vertical. If there are few differences, the business has less control. The demand curve is more horizontal. Examples of the differences in demand curves for businesses in monopolistic competition are shown in Figures 4-10 and 4-11 on the next page.

USING INFORMATION ABOUT ECONOMIC COMPETITION

It is important for business people and especially marketers to understand the type of economic competition they face. As

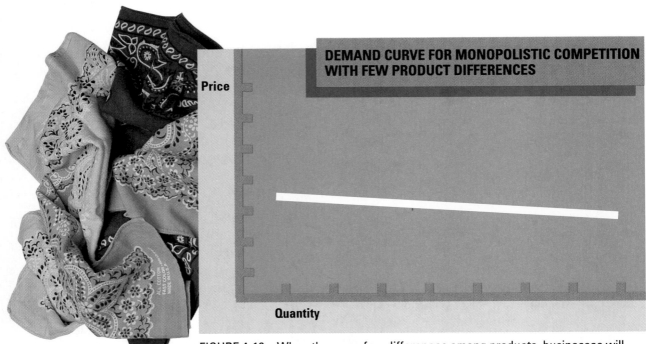

FIGURE 4-10 ▪ When there are few differences among products, businesses will have little price control.

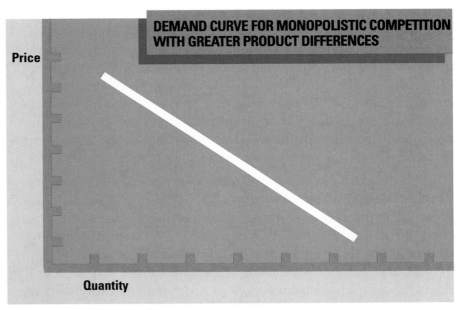

FIGURE 4-11 ▪ With greater product differences, businesses have much more control over prices.

you can see, a business in pure competition will not have much control in the market while one in a monopoly will have almost total control. Businesses in an oligopoly must pay careful attention to the actions of competitors. Finally, for the largest number of businesses in monopolistic competition, the differences between competing products will be very important. If possible, marketers will want to do things that result in products that are different and better than those of competitors. In that way they will have more control in the marketplace.

ECONOMIC UTILITY

How do you decide on the products and services you buy? Most of us would like to purchase many more things than we are able to afford. Because we have limited resources and unlimited needs, we have to choose from among the available products and services. We select those that provide the greatest amount of satisfaction for the amount of money we are able or willing to spend. You may have to choose between attending a concert or purchasing a CD. There may be two or three styles, colors, or brands of jeans you would like, but you can afford only one. Saving for college may be more important than being able to purchase an automobile.

Economists attempt to determine how you will make choices among competing products using the concept of economic utility. *Economic utility is the amount of satisfaction a consumer receives from the consumption of a particular product or service.* Products that provide great satisfaction have a higher economic utility, while those providing less satisfaction have a lower utility.

Business people can use the concept of economic utility to increase the likelihood that consumers will buy their products or services. If a consumer believes that a particular business' product will provide higher utility than other choices, that is one that will likely be purchased. There are four primary ways businesses can increase the economic utility of a product or service. Those ways are changes in form, time, place, and possession.

FORM UTILITY

The actual physical product provided or the service offered is the primary way that consumer needs are satisfied. *Form utility results from changes in the tangible parts of a product or service.* Some products and services are in a more usable form than others. They may be constructed of better or more durable materials. They may be in a quantity or size that is easier or more efficient to use. The product may come with features that consumers want. These are all examples of improving form utility.

TIME UTILITY

Even though a product is in the form a customer wants, it may not be available when the customer is able to obtain or consume the product. *Time utility results from making the product or service available when the customer wants it.*

A bank stays open longer hours in the evening and on Saturday mornings. A theater schedules a show in the early afternoon or later in the evening. An auto dealership keeps its service department open on weekends. A physician's office schedules physical examinations just before an athletic season. Each of these examples illustrates improvements in time utility for a product or service.

PLACE UTILITY

Just as some consumers are concerned about when a product is available, others may want to purchase or consume the product at a particular place. *Making products and services available where the consumer wants them is place utility.*

Convenience stores are successful because they are located in neighborhoods close to where consumers live. Automatic teller machines have made banking easier because they are located in supermarkets, airports, and even on street corners. Businesses that provide mailing, photocopying, and facsimile services are becoming very popular, but they must be located

conveniently to small businesses and individual consumers who need them. A convenient location for products and services is an important utility for people with busy lifestyles.

POSSESSION UTILITY

Possession utility is the most difficult to understand but a very important type of economic utility. A product may be in the form a consumer wants and be available at the right time in the appropriate location. The consumer may still not be able to purchase the product because of a lack of resources. *Possession utility results from the affordability of the product or service.* It is usually not possible for a business to decrease the price just so a product can be sold. The business does not want to sell products at a loss. However there are other ways to make the product more affordable for customers.

Some people today would have a difficult time shopping without a credit card. The use of credit allows people to purchase things for which they do not have enough cash available at the current time. They can then pay for the product when the credit bill is received or gradually with monthly payments. In a similar way, many retail businesses offer layaway services where a person can pay a small amount of the purchase price over several months and own the product after full payment is made.

Few people want to spend the money to purchase a movie just so they can watch it more than once. However, video stores are very successful because they rent rather than sell movies. With low-cost rentals, people can watch movies over and over. Some automobile dealerships now lease more new automobiles than they sell. Leases make it possible for customers to drive new cars without having to make a huge down payment. You or your school will probably rent a cap and gown for your graduation ceremony rather than buy them. Finding ways to finance, rent, or lease products has become an important business activity today and is a valuable way to offer possession utility to customers.

ECONOMIC UTILITY AS A MARKETING TOOL

Business people who use the marketing concept identify customer needs and develop marketing mixes to satisfy those needs. Economic utility supports the marketing concept. It identifies ways to improve customer satisfaction through changes in form, time, place, and possession. Marketers need to determine what changes customers would like to have in products and services in order to develop an effective marketing mix. You can see that there are many possible ways to improve products. Not only can the actual product or service be changed; you can also provide it at a more convenient time or place, or find ways to make it more affordable.

IN THE SPOTLIGHT

MAKING COTTON COMPETITIVE

Can a small cotton farmer with only a few acres of land find a way to compete against large agricultural corporations with thousands of acres of cotton? Sally Fox not only competes effectively, but created an entirely new market with colored cotton.

It is very difficult for small companies to be successful in most agricultural markets. These markets are characterized by pure competition, with many businesses offering similar products and having little or no control over the price received. Think about the cotton from several producers. Would you be able to determine what cotton was supplied by one business and what was supplied by another? The lack of difference puts small producers at a disadvantage. The large cotton producers can usually operate much more efficiently because of large amounts of land and equipment.

To be able to compete, small cotton growers must be able to find a way to make their cotton different and better than that of the other producers. Sally Fox was able to do that with Fox Fibres—cotton that is grown in colors other than white.

In the past, if apparel manufacturers wanted cotton fabric in colors, they had to use dyes. Not only did dyes contribute to some pollution, they often faded rapidly. Some consumers were allergic to the dyes used in clothing. Sally Fox started growing a brown-colored cotton and has since developed a green cotton as well. She is working to develop additional colors including yellow, blue-green, and gray. The cotton grows in the colors so it does not require dye. As cloth from the cotton is washed, the color gets brighter rather than fading.

Many clothing manufacturers who are responding to environmental concerns have become very interested in Fox Fibres. Specifically, Levi Strauss and Esprit are important customers. Sally Fox demonstrates an important economic lesson. Develop a product that is different from the competition and that meets an important customer need and a small company can be successful.

Adapted from an article in VISaVIS, August, 1992.

REVIEW

One of the most important disciplines for marketers to understand is economics. In order to plan and implement marketing activities effectively, you need to understand the private enterprise economy and economic principles. Supply and demand, types of competition, and economic utility are not just theories. They are important tools for marketers. The marketers who understand economics and use it to plan marketing activities have an important advantage. Applying economic concepts in marketing helps you to understand competitors and consumers and make profitable business decisions.

MARKETING FOUNDATIONS

1. **ECONOMIC CONCEPTS IN BUSINESS**
   The following is a list of business examples and a list of economic concepts that were explained in the chapter. For each business example described in A–E, identify the economic concept from the list that best matches it. For each of the remaining economic concepts in the list, develop a business example (like those provided in A–E) that illustrates the concept.

   a. Jan Frantzen just completed cosmetology training and wants to open a hair styling business. Jan has the resources needed to start the business. However, she must first be licensed by the government in order to insure the business will operate safely.

   b. Sonja Frerich is an economic analyst for Group One, a company that advises business executives on economic changes that can affect a business' planning. One of the measures of the economic health of a country is known as the gross domestic product (GDP). The GDP is the total of all goods and services produced in that country. Sonja is the company's expert on how the GDP affects business planning.

c. Torre Johnston normally purchases two bottles of apple juice every day in the school's lunch room. However, the price of apple juice was increased this year by 15 cents a bottle. Torre decides he will purchase only one bottle a day because of the higher price.

d. An Ngyen notices an announcement that people participating in a 600-mile bicycle road trip will be traveling on a road five miles from his home and will pass by in mid-afternoon the next day. An decides to purchase three cases of frozen yogurt cups to sell on the roadside. The day turns out to be very hot and many of the cyclists are willing to pay three and four times as much as the yogurt normally costs since An has the only supply available.

e. The Cramble Company has sold furniture in Harvey City for the past 50 years. Sales have been very low for the past 6 months because of the economic recession that has faced the region. Cramble's owner decides to begin a furniture rental program through which people obtain rooms of furniture for a monthly payment equal to four percent of the total price of the furniture. The furniture can be returned if payments cannot be maintained, but can be purchased at any time by paying the remainder of the full price.

Economic Concepts

controlled economy	law of supply
private enterprise	pure competition
microeconomics	monopoly
macroeconomics	form utility
law of demand	possession utility

2. IS IT ACCURATE?

Each of the following statements describes an economic concept or principle. Decide if the statement is accurate or inaccurate. Rewrite each inaccurate statement to make it accurate.

a. Private enterprise is heavily regulated by government.

b. Economic systems are developed to make decisions about the ownership and control of resources.

c. Consumers have unlimited resources and limited needs.

d. The quantity of a product producers are willing and able to provide at a specific price is known as demand.

e. Microeconomics is used to determine the best economic decisions for an entire country.

f. A large supply of a product will usually cause consumers to place a lower value on the product.

g. When the price of a product is raised, a larger quantity will be demanded.

h. Economic resources are classified as natural resources, capital, equipment, and consumers.

i. In pure competition, there are a large number of suppliers offering very similar products.

j. Businesses in monopolistic competition offer products that have some amount of difference from competitors' products.

k. Economic utility is the amount of profit businesses make from selling a product.

l. Changes in a product's physical features affect the form utility.

m. Locating an automatic teller machine in an airport is an example of improving the possession utility for banking services.

n. Understanding economic utility helps marketers make improvements in the marketing mix.

MARKETING RESEARCH

1. TYPES OF ECONOMIC COMPETITION

Businesses can be classified into the four types of competition—pure competition, monopoly, oligopoly, and monopolistic competition—based on two factors:

- the number of competitors in the market

- the amount of similarity between the products of competing businesses

Use the advertising section of your local telephone directory, a business directory, or copies of newspapers or business magazines to identify as many businesses as you can that fit into each of the four categories listed. Be able to explain each decision based on the two factors listed.

2. CREATING A DEMAND CURVE

 Select a popular food item that is sold through your school's lunch menu or in a vending machine in your school. Determine the current price for the item. Then construct a chart showing the following price increases and decreases for the product: +10%, +25%, +50%, +100%; −10%,−25%,−50%,−90%.

Survey 15 people from your school. Ask each person how many of the items they typically purchase in one week at the current price. Then ask each person how many of the items they would purchase at each of the price increases and decreases. Based on the results, construct a demand curve to illustrate the effect of price changes on demand for the product.

MARKETING PLANNING

1. DETERMINING TOTAL REVENUE

 When a marketer analyzes a demand curve, it is important to determine what effect changes in price and quantity demanded will have on the amount of money the business will receive from selling the product. The amount received is known as the *total revenue* and is determined by multiplying the price by the quantity demanded. For example, if the price of a product is $8.50 and the quantity demanded at that price is 1,550 items, the total revenue would be $13,175 ($8.50 × 1,550). The following information was taken from the demand curves for two different products. Calculate the total revenue for each price listed. Then construct a demand curve for each product.

PRODUCT 1		PRODUCT 2	
Price	Quantity Demanded	Price	Quantity Demanded
$1.00	350,000	$250	1,125
2.50	280,000	325	950
3.25	225,000	400	600
4.00	175,000	500	425
4.75	75,000	850	250
5.50	25,000	1,000	200

2. CREATING AN ECONOMIC SYSTEM

You have been an economist for the United Nations for the past 15 years. Now, in the year 2028, a large industrial colony is being developed on the moon. It will be started by two thousand people initially and there are plans to expand it until nearly a million people are living in the colony by 2050. The United Nations is studying the best form of economic system to develop on the colony.

Prepare a two-page report in which you compare the three types of economies (controlled, regulated, and free). Discuss the advantages and disadvantages of each for consumers, businesses, and the government. Make a recommendation on the most appropriate system for the colony. Consider factors like resources available, supply and demand, the amount of competition, and so forth.

MARKETING MANAGEMENT

1. IMPROVING ECONOMIC UTILITY

The four types of economic utility can be used to improve customer satisfaction for products and services. Marketing managers must be creative in determining ways that products and services can be improved. For each of the following three items, determine changes that could be made in form, time, place, and possession utility. Then recommend the one change for each product that you believe would be the most effective in improving customer satisfaction. Provide a reason for your recommendation.

a. Vending machine selling freshly-popped popcorn

b. Large-screen television

c. College recruiting high school seniors

2. CASE STUDY

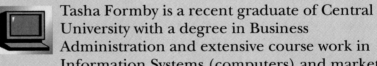

Tasha Formby is a recent graduate of Central University with a degree in Business Administration and extensive course work in Information Systems (computers) and marketing. She completed one summer internship with a computer manufacturer during which she worked in sales. She worked full time during another summer and part time during two school years at a local company that provides commercial printing services to small businesses. She was in charge of design work using computer software.

After interviewing with several companies, Tasha decides to open her own printing business. She decides to locate in the same city in which she attended college. There are three large printing companies in the city including the one she worked for during her college years. Those businesses compete for the printing services of the large and small companies in the area. There are eight other small printing businesses, each of whom serve individual consumers rather than businesses.

Tasha decides to compete with the larger companies for business printing rather than with the small printers. She believes there is more opportunity for larger printing jobs from business and she would like her business to grow as rapidly as possible. She also believes her computer background could help her better serve the businesses' needs.

After operating the business for six months, Tasha is becoming concerned. The prospective customers she contacts are very concerned about the prices of printing rather than the personalized service she provides. The larger printers are usually able to price lower than her business. It also seems like the larger businesses have much more control over the prices they charge, raising prices for some customers and lowering them for others.

a. What type of competitive environment do you believe Tasha's business is facing? What information leads you to that answer?

b. Do you believe she would face the same type of competition if she had chosen to sell to individual consumers? Why or why not?

c. What do you believe Tasha can do to improve the chances of success for her new printing business? What economic concepts support your answer?

Product/
Service
Planning

Distribution

Marketing-
Information
Management

Human Resource
Foundations

Fir

Purchasing

*Economic
Foundations
of Marketing*

Marketing and
Business
Foundations

Risk

Pricing

Selling

Promotion

Moving Into a Global Economy

OBJECTIVES

1. Discuss the impact of international trade on the U.S. economy.

2. Provide examples of products you consume that are produced in other countries.

3. Explain why businesses want to sell their products and services in other countries.

4. Describe five ways businesses can become involved in international markets.

5. Discuss how the marketing concept can be used to identify opportunities in international markets.

6. Identify several categories of information business people need to consider to understand international markets.

7. Describe ways that each of the marketing functions can be designed to meet the needs of international markets.

8. List sources of information and support available to businesses participating in international trade.

NEWSLINE

TRADE AGREEMENTS: BARRIERS OR BRIDGES?

EC, NAFTA, GATT, ECWAS, CACM. Are these the names of new rock groups or characters from a science fiction movie? No, but they may become as important in your life as either music or movies. The acronyms stand for European Community, North American Free Trade Agreement, General Agreement on Tariffs and Trade, Economic Community of West African States, and the Central American Common Market. They represent a few of the many agreements among nations developed to encourage economic cooperation and international business.

In the past businesses found their greatest competition were companies in their own cities and states, and sometimes companies from other parts of their country. Now, the strongest competition for many businesses is coming from countries that may be many thousands of miles away. Our standard of living depends on how successful our country is in the global marketplace. A few countries, such as Japan, Germany, and the United States, have been able to expand their markets outside their own countries and dominate international competition.

To respond, countries with smaller populations and less international experience have developed trade agreements to increase their competitiveness. One example of an international trade agreement is the European Community (EC). The EC started with the Treaty of Rome in 1957, when France, Italy, West Germany, the Netherlands, Belgium, and Luxembourg agreed to form the European Economic Community, better known as the Common Market. Business people and politicians from those countries saw how much the countries depended on each other for products and services. Yet trade among the countries was often difficult because of restrictions such as tariffs, taxes, and licenses. The Treaty of Rome started the process of reducing and removing those barriers so

that products, people, and money could move freely. Since 1957, other European nations have joined the original six and in 1987, a council of representatives from each country began to develop laws, policies, and procedures that would regulate all business transactions. The results even included detailed manufacturing standards for specific products so that products produced in any country would be compatible with those of other countries.

It is too early to determine the real success of the European Community. The unique political systems of individual countries might not allow the close economic cooperation anticipated. As economic power is developed in regional markets like the EC, trade wars between the regions of the world could develop. There is concern that the countries that are not a part of a powerful international economic association will see their economies ruined. It is clear that we are part of a global economy. The decisions of business people in countries around the world are as important to our lives as those made in the United States.

THE EXPANDING WORLD ECONOMY

Can you imagine how big the number "one trillion" is? It is so large that we have a difficult time developing examples that make it meaningful to us. But multiply one trillion by twenty.

Now you have a number that describes the size in dollars of the total world economy in the early 1990s. At that time, the total value of all products and services produced in the world was estimated to be about $20,000,000,000,000.

THE UNITED STATES AND INTERNATIONAL TRADE

The United States is the world's largest producer and economy. In 1990, the Gross Domestic Product (GDP) of the United States was nearly $5.5 billion, which is over one-fourth of the world's production. The United States also consumes about one-fourth of all goods and services produced in the world. Other countries with large economies are shown in Figure 5-1 on the next page.

Most of the products and services produced in the world are still consumed by people in the countries where they are produced. However, nearly one-third of all world production (over $7 trillion) is sold outside of the country in which it is produced. *The sale of products and services to people in other countries is known as international trade.*

It is very easy to find examples of international trade. Spend just one day looking at all the products and services you consume that day to determine where they were produced. You will quickly see that many are not produced in the United States. *Products or services purchased from another country are known as imports.*

You may start your morning with fruit and cereal grown in El Salvador and Argentina and transported here in ships from Panama. The clothes you wear may have been manufactured in Taiwan or China. You may ride to school on a bus that was assembled in Canada or Mexico. Your textbooks may have been published by a company that is part of a larger British corporation. You call your friends after school on a telephone that could have been assembled in Japan. You use a Korean-manufactured computer for homework. That evening you watch a movie that was filmed in Kenya on a video-cassette recorder

The World's Largest Market Economies

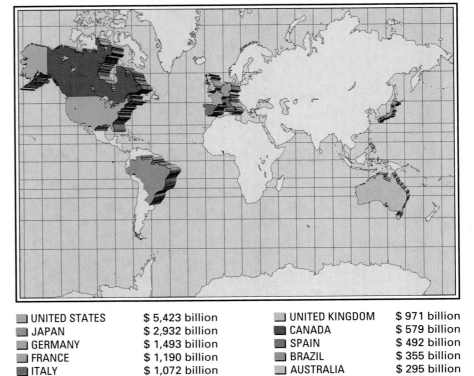

UNITED STATES	$ 5,423 billion	UNITED KINGDOM	$ 971 billion
JAPAN	$ 2,932 billion	CANADA	$ 579 billion
GERMANY	$ 1,493 billion	SPAIN	$ 492 billion
FRANCE	$ 1,190 billion	BRAZIL	$ 355 billion
ITALY	$ 1,072 billion	AUSTRALIA	$ 295 billion

FIGURE 5-1 ▪ The United States is the world's largest producer of goods and services. However, other countries are increasing their production rapidly.

assembled in Poland. Certainly, you will also discover that a large number of the products and services you use were produced in the United States, but you and the people in your community are indeed international consumers.

International business is important to other countries as well. Just as you use products produced in foreign countries, consumers in those countries are important customers for U.S. businesses. *Products and services that are sold to another country are known as exports.* Important consumer products exported from the United States to other countries include music, movies, blue jeans, automobiles, and many types of food products. U.S. manufacturers of airplanes, farm equipment, computers, and communications equipment also have a large number of international customers.

THE TYPES OF PRODUCTS ARE CHANGING

The amount of international trade increases each year. The type of products and services exchanged between countries is changing. In the past, most of the products exchanged were raw materials. Some countries had an abundance of raw materials (timber, coal, iron ore, petroleum). But they had not developed their manufacturing capabilities. Other countries were heavily involved in manufacturing. However, they did not have adequate supplies of needed materials to operate their factories. Therefore, they purchased the raw materials from other countries. Raw materials made up almost all of the products traded between countries. Today, raw materials are only about one-third of the world's exports. The remaining two-thirds is manufactured goods and services.

It may be difficult to identify the types of services that could be exchanged between countries. However, today, services as a part of international trade are growing faster than products. Common types of services exchanged between countries include communications, travel, education, consulting, financial services, and information. One interesting example of the exchange of services is in the area of data management. Banks and other financial institutions in the United States are using companies in Korea and Ireland to complete a large amount of the data processing for their businesses. At the end of the business day in the United States, data is transferred to another country via telephone lines or satellite transmission. The data processors in the other countries complete work on the information, update the customers' accounts, and transfer it back to the U.S. location in time for use the next business day.

WHY ARE BUSINESSES GOING GLOBAL?

Some businesses first decide to market products in other countries out of necessity. They find that competition is very intense in their current markets and that sales and profits are declining. In order to find additional customers to increase sales, those companies begin to look at other countries. When the numbers of babies in the United States declined because of a lower birth rate, several companies that manufactured products for babies (formula, baby food, diapers) looked for markets for those products in other countries. As another example, attendance at movie theaters declined for several years in the United States. Because of that, film distributors increased their efforts to market films abroad.

Other companies consider international markets when they see companies from other countries entering their own markets. Rather than just competing with the foreign companies in their own country, the businesses decide to enter other markets to keep the competition more balanced. In the 1970s, automobile manufacturers from Japan and Germany moved rapidly into the United States market to take advantage of the need for smaller and more fuel-efficient cars. Because of their efforts,

they took a major share of the U.S. automobile market away from American companies. One of the responses of U.S. firms was to increase efforts to sell their brands in other countries.

A third reason for global marketing is the increasing demand for products. Consumers in many countries look to the United States for product and service ideas. As economies expand throughout the world and as standards of living increase, consumers are willing to spend their money for a variety of products. Businesses that recognize the increasing demand attempt to meet it by offering their products for sale wherever customers are willing to buy, including other countries. Manufacturers of products ranging from the latest styles of blue jeans to cassettes, hamburgers, and video games are finding success in world markets.

For some business people the idea of selling products or services in other countries appears to be complicated and difficult. Because of those feelings they may decide not to become involved in international trade. However, with changes and improvements in transportation, communication, and other technologies, it is now often as easy to serve markets in other countries as it is to sell in markets that are several states away.

HOW DO BUSINESSES GET INVOLVED?

We have seen that international trade is a substantial part of the sales of products and services. In the United States, about 20 percent of the total production of businesses is exported. One in every 16 U.S. jobs is directly related to international business.

However, only about ten percent of businesses are involved directly in international trade. Each of those figures is likely to increase. Because of its growing importance, we will examine the ways businesses typically get involved in selling products and services internationally.

EXPORTING

International trade exists in many forms. Most businesses first get involved through exporting or selling existing products in other countries. When businesses have been successful selling products in their own country, they may begin to look for additional markets. Or customers from other countries may become aware of the products and ask to purchase them. In either case, the company begins to sell its existing products in other countries.

Due to lack of experience, a company may first use indirect exporting. *Indirect exporting is the process in which marketing businesses with exporting experience serve as agents for a business and arrange for the sale of its products in other countries.* The company will not be directly involved in exporting activities but will rely on the exporting business to serve the international markets. *With more experience a company may begin direct exporting and take complete responsibility for marketing its products in other countries.*

In 1991, the United States was the world's leading exporter of products, selling $422 billion of products to other countries. That accounted for about 12 percent of the entire world's exports. Germany was second with $402 billion. The United States also led in imports, with $509 billion or nearly 14 percent of the world total in 1991. Again, Germany was second with $309 billion.

Those figures suggest one of the problems countries face concerning international trade. *The difference between the amount of a country's imports and exports is known as its balance of trade.* As you can see from the figures above, in 1991 the United States had a negative balance of trade of $77 billion, while Germany had a positive balance of trade of $93 billion. While in the short run the balance of trade may not have an effect on a country, many economists believe that a continual negative balance can create problems. A negative balance of trade shows that a country is sending more of its resources to other countries through the purchase of products than it is receiving from the sale of products abroad. It also demonstrates that busi-

A GLOBAL VISION

SONY—SO INTERNATIONAL

Televisions, portable cassette and CD players, stereo equipment. Many Sony products are very familiar. They are such a part of most American homes that some people may not even stop to consider that Sony is a Japanese-owned multinational business.

Akio Morita started a small business in Japan because of his fascination with electronic technology. He was always looking for new product ideas for his own use and believed that there was a growing market for consumer electronics. In 1953, he purchased the then-new transistor technology from a U.S. company, Western Electric. Sony entered the international business environment first with transistor radios in 1955 and followed with transistorized televisions in 1959.

Other innovative electronic products developed by Sony include the first solid-state video tape recorder, the Trinitron color television tube, and the Walkman portable tape player. Most recently, Sony introduced a 3-inch optical disk and portable player called the Data Discman that stores full books and even encyclopedias.

While you are familiar with many of Sony's electronic products you may not be aware of some of its other businesses. In the United States, Sony owns Sony Music, (formerly CBS records), Sony Pictures Entertainment (formerly Columbia Pictures), and the Loews theater chain. Sony has developed performance contracts with Michael Jackson and the Rolling Stones. Sony companies are responsible for producing many popular television shows including *Wheel of Fortune* and *Jeopardy*.

The international success of Sony is based on several factors. First, the company is committed to innovative products. It spends almost one billion dollars on research each year. Sony often develops partnerships with other businesses to improve its product development and marketing. In addition, Sony has both strong management and marketing systems that help it to understand the needs of customers throughout the world.

Each year, Sony receives more than 70 percent of its sales from outside of Japan. In 1990, total worldwide sales were over $18 billion with nearly 30 percent earned in the United States. An understanding of global business has allowed Sony to be a very well-known and successful multinational company.

nesses from other countries are satisfying the needs of consumers better than the country's own businesses.

FOREIGN PRODUCTION

Another example of international trade is foreign production. *With foreign production, a company owns and operates production facilities in another country.* Rather than manufacturing a product in one country and then shipping the product to another country, the entire process is completed in the country where the product is to be sold. Nearly $4 trillion of products and services are developed by companies using foreign production each year. Foreign production has advantages over exporting in that the major business activities are performed within the country in which the products will be sold. This reduces the amount of distribution activities and the time needed to move products from one country to another.

People in some countries are becoming concerned about the amount of products being purchased from other countries. For example, some people in the United States believe too many automobiles produced in Japan and Germany are being sold in this country. So manufacturers like Honda, Toyota, and BMW now have automobile assembly plants *in* the United States. The use of foreign production allows those companies to continue to sell their products while responding to the consumer concern about where the products are manufactured.

FOREIGN INVESTMENT

Some companies have identified businesses in other countries that have already developed production or marketing capabilities. Rather than entering the country and starting a new business, the company purchases the existing business. *Owning all or part of an existing business in another country is known as foreign investment.* Through foreign investment, businesses can move more quickly into another country. They can also use the business' past records to determine whether it is a good investment. The new owners may decide to change the business or continue to operate it in the same way as the previous owners. That decision will be based on the past success of the business and the needs of the company making the foreign investment. Figure 5-2 lists some recent examples of companies that have been purchased by organizations from other countries.

Examples of Recent Foreign Investments		
Purchaser	**Investment**	**Type of Business**
Phillip Morris Co, Inc. (United States)	Jacobs Suchard Ltd. (Switzerland)	Chocolate/Coffee
Ford Motor Company (United States)	Jaguar (United Kingdom)	Automobiles
PepsiCo, Inc. (United States)	Empresas Gamesa SA de CV (Mexico)	Snack Foods
Bass PLC (United Kingdom)	Holiday Inns (United States)	Motels
Investcorp International (Bahrain)	Saks Fifth Ave. (United States)	Retailing
Accor SA (France)	Motel 6 (United States)	Motels

FIGURE 5-2 ▪ Many well-known businesses are owned by companies from other countries.

American companies have been active in foreign investments in the past, but in recent years other countries have also increased their investments. In 1960, the United States had half of the world's total foreign investment. While the actual dollars invested in the businesses in other countries has increased from that time, today the United States has only about one-third of the world total. In addition, the United States is an attractive country in which foreign businesses like to invest. Currently it is the leading host country for foreign investments.

Just as the types of exports are changing, so are the types of businesses in which foreign companies invest. At this time about half of all foreign investments are in manufacturing businesses, with 20 percent in mining and oil companies and 30 percent in marketing, finance, and service businesses. The percentage of manufacturing investments is declining while marketing investments are increasing.

JOINT VENTURES

When two or more companies in different countries determine that they have common interests, they may form a joint venture. *In a joint venture, independent companies develop a relationship to participate in common business activities.* The agreement may be in the form of a contract where the companies agree to a specific set of activities for a determined time. Another form of joint venture is where each company actually agrees to purchase a portion of the other company to create joint ownership. They then have a continuing relationship based on that ownership. Recently, three large airlines, Delta, SwissAir, and Singapore Airlines, agreed to purchase five percent of the stock in each of the other airlines in order to develop an international venture. Consider the advantages that type of relationship could offer when the three companies compete with other airlines for international travel. It also creates some problems in managing the three companies since they are still independently operated companies with different markets and customers.

MULTINATIONAL COMPANIES

Some companies have been involved in international business for a long time. They may use several of the strategies described above and sell services and products in a large number of countries throughout the world. They probably are purchasing products and services from companies in many countries to use in production and operations. Businesses that are heavily involved in international business usually develop factories and offices in several countries in order to keep operations closer to the customers. *Businesses that have operations throughout the world and that conduct planning for worldwide markets are multinational companies.* Multinational businesses no longer think of themselves as located in one country selling to customers in other countries. They think globally.

There are many businesses that you may think of as U. S. companies that are really multinational. They operate throughout the world and derive a large part of their sales and profits from countries other than the United States. General Motors is an example of a multinational company. Recently, it earned over 70 percent of its profits from outside the United States. Other examples of well-known multinational companies that started in the U.S. are Coca Cola, Hilton Hotels, John Deere, 3M Corporation, Nike, and IBM. There are also many multinational firms that started in other countries. Some familiar examples are Nestle S.A.,

Mercedes-Benz, Panasonic, Seiko, Hyundai, L'Oreal, and Ciba-Geigy. These are just a few of the growing number of multinational businesses.

Multinational companies hire employees, including managers, from many countries. They expect their employees to be able and willing to work with people from all over the world. Employees often travel and some even relocate and live in other countries while they work for the multinational company. Figure 5-3 shows that there are many employment opportunities in multinational businesses.

Competitors for multinational businesses also come from many different locations. A business may compete with one set of companies in Australia and another in Africa or South America. There may be a few large multinationals that compete for customers in all parts of the world. Thinking globally opens up many opportunities for businesses but also makes business and marketing decisions even more complex.

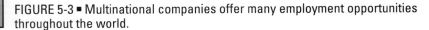

The Largest Worldwide Employers		
Company	Country	Estimated Number of Employees
General Motors (vehicles)	United States	750,000
Coal India (mining)	India	670,000
IRI (metals)	Italy	410,000
Siemens (electronics)	Germany	400,000
Daimler-Benz (vehicles)	Germany	380,000
IBM (computers)	United States	350,000
PepsiCo (food, beverages)	United States	340,000
Ford Motor Co. (vehicles)	United States	330,000
Hitachi (electronics)	Japan	310,000
Unilever (food)	United Kingdom	300,000

FIGURE 5-3 ▪ Multinational companies offer many employment opportunities throughout the world.

UNDERSTANDING INTERNATIONAL MARKETS

The concept of a market in other countries is the same as the definition we used earlier in this book. A market refers to the description of the prospective customers a business wants to serve and the location of those customers. It is important to remember that just as markets are not all alike in your own country, there are differences in markets within other countries as well (see Figure 5-4). Business people should not assume that all people in a country have the same characteristics, needs, and interests.

There is a great deal of similarity but also some differences between marketing internationally and marketing within one country. The idea of identifying markets and developing a marketing mix remains the same. So does the need to complete each of the marketing functions. The characteristics of markets, the information needed and how it is obtained, and the procedures used in developing each of the marketing mix elements will change as companies concentrate on markets in other countries.

THE MARKETING CONCEPT HIGHLIGHTS OPPORTUNITIES

Business people who do not understand the marketing concept may make an important mistake when entering markets in other countries. They may believe that because a product is successful in their country, the same product without any changes can be equally as successful in other countries. They attempt to use the same types of marketing strategies used in the past. This

Information Needed for International Markets

FIGURE 5-4 ▪ Businesses must gather a great deal of information in order to determine if they can successfully market their products and services in another country.

attitude represents the old production philosophy we saw being used in the United States many years ago.

We know that markets can be very different from each other and each market will require changes in the marketing mix. A company that believes in the marketing orientation will carefully study the consumers in each country to determine if appealing markets exist. If so, the company will study the markets to identify unique characteristics. Once markets are identified, the company will then begin to design an appropriate product or service, determine how the product will be distributed, establish a price and pricing policies, and develop promotion strategies that are appropriate for the country and the specific market. You can see that this strategy is likely to result in differences from the way the products are marketed in the original country but will provide the best opportunity for the company to be successful.

CONSUMER CHARACTERISTICS

Information needs to be gathered about the people in a country to determine if there are enough prospective customers, if they have needs for the types of products or services offered by the company, the amount of money they have available to spend, and other characteristics such as age, income, employment, and education. It will also be important to determine where prospective customers are located in the country, where they typically purchase products, the methods of transportation, and the communications media available. This information that helps us identify and locate people is known as demographics. We will take a close look at demographics in Chapter 8.

CULTURE AND CUSTOMS

The culture and customs of a country may determine whether certain products or marketing methods will be appropriate or acceptable. *Culture is the common beliefs and behaviors of a group of people who have a similar heritage and experience.* Family structures, religion, beliefs and values, language, personal habits, and daily activities may be quite different from what the marketers are used to in their own culture. Failure to recognize differences that are important to people from other cultures may result in misunderstanding and mistrust.

For example, certain words when translated into another language may have very different meanings than intended. Specific colors in some countries signify happiness, sadness, birth, or death. The incorrect use of a color on a product or package may cause a product to fail in that market. The meaning of time is often a cultural factor. In some countries it is important to be exactly on time for a meeting or appointment while in other countries people are not concerned if they are quite late for the scheduled time. In some cultures, work stops after lunch for a time and then employees work later into the evening.

The types of communications that are acceptable in business and the meaning of communications are important in international business. Some cultures require a great deal of personal or social conversation preceding the discussion of business, while others are offended by conversations that are too personal. In some countries, a verbal agreement is all that is needed to conduct business while other countries will not complete an agreement without a formal written contract. Other cultural factors include understanding of ethics and values, dress and grooming requirements, male/female relationships, and the importance of social factors such as age, education, and income.

ECONOMIC ENVIRONMENT

The level of economic development of a country and the current condition of the economy must be understood for effective marketing. A country that has a high standard of living will usually manufacture and sell a variety of consumer products and services. That country will offer very different marketing opportunities than a country that is struggling to meet basic consumer needs. Economies of the world's countries can be grouped into three broad categories: preindustrial, industrial, and postindustrial (refer to Figure 5-5).

Preindustrial Economies

The preindustrial economy is based on agriculture and the development of raw materials (mining, oil production, lumber, etc.). Many of the country's citizens are self-sufficient and may have a very low standard of living. The manufacturing, distribution, and retail systems are just beginning to develop. This makes it difficult to produce, distribute, or sell products.

The Three Stages of Economic Development

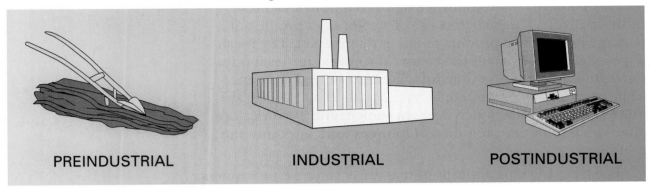

PREINDUSTRIAL   INDUSTRIAL   POSTINDUSTRIAL

FIGURE 5-5 ▪ There are three types of economies in the world's countries. Each economic stage requires a different type of marketing.

Leaders of the countries in the preindustrial stage of economic development recognize the importance of moving to the next stage. They see their natural resources being consumed and few choices of jobs for their citizens. Those countries are unable to participate in the international economy except through the sale of raw materials. The leaders of the countries are looking for help in developing their economies.

Countries with preindustrial economies were once viewed as offering few opportunities for foreign businesses. Some companies purchased raw materials in the countries. Others actually developed mining, lumbering, or oil drilling activities. However, those companies were accused of exploiting the countries. Some companies took natural resources and returned very little to the economies. Today, many preindustrial countries provide opportunities for companies that want to sell manufacturing equipment or cooperate in the development of manufacturing businesses.

Many of the countries also seek assistance in developing their distribution systems. There must be effective methods of getting products to customers. There must be places for the products to be sold. Without distribution systems, businesses will not be successful. Roads, railroads, and airports are needed to distribute products as manufacturing develops. Developing distribution systems as well as organizing wholesale and retail businesses will make it possible to sell the products that are produced.

Industrial Economies

Today, most countries have industrial economies. *In industrial economies, the primary business activity is the manufacturing of products.* Much of the manufacturing in the early stages of an industrial economy is devoted to the production of equipment and materials for businesses and the development of marketing systems. Later, as people work in the factories and other businesses, wages increase and the standard of living improves. There is greater demand for a variety of consumer products, and businesses develop to meet those needs.

There are certainly many opportunities for international businesses in industrial economies. There is demand for industrial and consumer products. Often products and services that are successful in countries with more developed economies can be sold in the industrial economies as those countries develop.

Postindustrial Economies

The largest and most-developed economies in the world have moved into the postindustrial stage. *A postindustrial economy is based on a mix of industrial and consumer products and services produced and marketed using high-technology equipment and methods that are purchased and sold in the global marketplace.* Countries with postindustrial economies have very high standards of living with many opportunities for international business. Most of these countries are developing laws and business procedures that encourage trade with other countries.

People living in postindustrial economies are very aware of products and services available from other countries. They expect the businesses in their country to produce similar products of equal or higher quality at a reasonable price. If the products are not available from businesses in their country, they are very willing to buy from companies from other countries. However, they expect high quality, service, and value before they will buy. We can see examples of that consumer analysis in products such as electronics and automobiles. Those manufacturers compete in a truly global market. There are many opportunities in postindustrial countries but business people must be prepared for the competition of many effective companies from around the world.

Condition of the Economy

The long-term picture of a country's economy is shown by its stage of economic development. However, the short-term condition of the economy is important as well. If a country's economy is growing, its citizens will have more job opportunities and money to spend on products and services. Businesses will have a better chance for sales and profits in a growing economy.

When an economy is not growing or is shrinking, business opportunities decline. Consumers' incomes will not be increasing. In fact, many of them may be unemployed. Therefore they may reduce the amount of money they spend to purchase products and services.

There are several important measures of the condition of a country's economy. One of those measures is the Gross Domestic Product (GDP). As we learned in Chapter 4, the GDP is the total value of the goods and services produced in a country during the year. It is important for a country's GDP to increase in order to have a strong economy.

Another important measure is the standard of living. *The standard of living is the average value of resources produced by a country based on its total population.* The economies of countries with high standards of living are producing a large quantity of goods and services. An increasing standard of living is a sign of a strong economy. The standard of living is influenced by the number and type of jobs available, the wage levels paid, and the success of businesses in producing and marketing goods and services.

A final measure of the condition of a country's economy is purchasing power. *Purchasing power is the amount of goods and services that can be obtained with a specific amount of money.* Purchasing power declines in a weak economy. *That decline may be caused by inflation where prices increase faster than the value of the goods and services. It may also result from a recession—a period of time in which production, employment, and income are declining.*

POLITICAL AND LEGAL STRUCTURE

One of the most important factors that can affect the success of international marketing is the type of political and legal system in a country. The types of political systems range from democratic, in which the citizens of the country control the decisions of the government, to autocratic, where power is in the hands of a very small group of people. In the recent past, one of the major political structures, communism, was rejected in many Eastern European countries and the former Soviet Union. Those countries reorganized their political systems to adopt more democratic principles.

The stability of the political system is important for businesses. If a country is unstable, it is very possible that business ownership and operating procedures may be threatened. There have been many examples of countries in which the government was overthrown and the businesses owned by people from other countries were destroyed or taken over by the new government.

Countries develop laws to regulate business. Many of those laws affect international business operations. Some countries have laws that provide strong support for their businesses in the sale of products and services in other countries or to protect the country's businesses from foreign competition. Because the leaders of industrial economies want the businesses in the country to be successful, they may try to restrict the amount of imports through the use of quotas or tariffs. *Quotas are limits on the numbers of specific types of products foreign companies can sell in the country. Tariffs are taxes placed on imported products to increase the price for which they are sold.* As an example, the United States has laws that regulate the number of trucks and motorcycles that can be imported into the country. Some categories of vehicles are charged an import tax to increase their price. This makes the American vehicle a better value for many consumers, effectively limiting the number of foreign products sold.

Countries may also support their businesses through subsidies. *A subsidy is money provided to a business to assist in the development and sale of its products.* European countries are providing financial support to an airplane manufacturer, Airbus, so it can compete with U.S. manufacturers. The company has signed contracts to produce nearly one-third of all commercial airplane orders in a recent year.

TECHNOLOGY

The technology of business and marketing is changing rapidly. Businesses are adopting new methods of manufacturing, transportation, product handling, and communication. Consumers have access to computers, new types of appliances, and changing technology for work and leisure time.

Once these new technical products are developed in one country they are usually distributed and accepted in many other countries. Businesses cannot assume, though, that the same technology used in their home country is available or used in other countries. Even if the technology is used, there might be important differences in those countries. Even basic technologies that have existed for many years may be different. An excellent example is the metric system. Several years ago, there was an attempt to convert most of the measurement systems in the United States to the metric system, which is widely used throughout the rest of the world. That attempt was not successful although metric measures are used more widely than before. If it is the standard in another country, customers there will expect it to be used on all products. It will affect everything from tools, to container sizes, to measurements for replacement parts. Another example is standard voltage for appliances. In the United States, 110 volts is standard. In other countries, a higher voltage is standard so electrical products have to be redesigned if they are to be sold there.

GATHERING MARKET INFORMATION

We will look carefully at procedures for gathering and analyzing market information in a later chapter. The procedures are quite similar for international markets as those used in the business' home country. The business needs to develop a marketing information system to collect and analyze information. It also needs to complete marketing research or work with

A GLOBAL VISION

CULTURAL DIVERSITY EQUALS MARKET OPPORTUNITY

The United States is the "great melting pot." Its citizens come from many countries and cultures. The United States has greater cultural diversity than any other country. However, businesses usually misinterpret the meaning of "melting pot." They believe that people are different in characteristics such as race, ethnic identity, and religion. Businesses often believe that everyone is similar when it comes to purchasing products. A common business practice is to provide what the majority seems to want. Businesses assume that everyone else will be satisfied as well.

Businesses that began marketing products in other countries soon found that their new customers often have very different expectations than Americans. If they tried to sell the same products without any changes, the businesses would often be unsuccessful. So they began to develop products and services specifically for the new markets.

That experience caused many of the businesses to recognize that American citizens were not all alike and often were not satisfied with the products businesses had developed for the majority of their consumers. You can identify the characteristics of people that make them unique. You may live in a community where English is not the primary language. Your school and even this class may have students of several races and ethnic backgrounds. Your family might have special customs or traditions that are different from those of your friends or neighbors.

Businesses are responding to those types of differences in order to satisfy the unique segments of the U.S. population. Many supermarkets and restaurants now offer a variety of foods to appeal to the cultural tastes of their customers. Music and movie producers and concert promoters are marketing products specifically directed at ethnic audiences. Advertising agencies design advertisements using language, people, and settings that reflect the varied backgrounds of consumers.

International marketing has shown business people that all people do not want the same things. Businesses that respond to cultural and ethnic uniqueness are finding success. Those who continue to believe all people will be satisfied with products and services designed for the majority consumer will have an increasingly difficult time making a profit.

research companies to answer specific questions about customers and competitors.

The characteristics of specific countries require special attention to both marketing information management and marketing research. The sources of information, the types of technology and research capabilities, how people respond to research procedures, and the laws relating to information collection will likely be quite different. For example, in the United States much of the consumer research today is completed using telephone calls. In some countries, technology is not as well developed and fewer people have telephones. In other countries, asking personal questions using the telephone is considered very rude.

Businesses often work with marketers and marketing businesses from the country in which they hope to market products to gather information. This helps to insure that those doing the research have a better understanding of the unique characteristics of the country and that the research will be completed in a way that does not harm the image of the business. Those involved in international business need to listen carefully to people from the countries they want to serve to avoid biases and stereotypes.

INTERNATIONAL MARKETING ACTIVITIES

After business people have gathered the necessary information to understand the new market, they can develop the marketing mix. With this information, the mix can be specifically designed to meet the needs of the international market. Again, the types of marketing activities often will be the same or similar to those previously used by the company. However, there are some important differences in international marketing. We will look at those differences by briefly reviewing each of the functions of marketing. (The marketing functions are summarized in Figure 5-6.)

PRODUCT/SERVICE PLANNING

We know that products and services must be developed to meet the needs of customers. Important activities for interna-

Marketing Functions in International Business

Marketing-Information Management
Product/Service Planning
Distribution
Financing
Risk Management
Selling
Promotion
Pricing
Purchasing

FIGURE 5-6 ▪ The same marketing functions must be completed by businesses whether marketing nationally or internationally. However, there will often be some important differences in each function as well.

tional markets include packaging for protection and for easy use by customers. In addition brand names must be carefully selected to fit the language of the country. Finally, any product information or instructions must be written to meet the laws of the country and to clearly communicate with the customers.

PURCHASING

The procedures used to purchase products or to assist customers in purchasing will need to conform to the country's laws and customs. The types of contracts and forms used, as well as the monetary system, may be different.

FINANCING

In most cases, the business needs to extend credit to wholesalers or retailers who distribute the products in the country. The accepted credit practices for consumers will also have to be considered. While some credit cards are used internationally, they may not be the typical form of payment used by consumers in each country. The business will usually need to develop relationships with banks and other financial organizations in the new country.

DISTRIBUTION

Effective distribution of products to other countries may be the most challenging marketing function. Decisions need to be made on the appropriate shipping method from country to country and within the country of the new markets. Selection of the types of businesses in which the product will be sold is part of distribution. It is important to know the amount of time it will take from processing an order until the product is available to customers. Also, laws regulating distribution including taxes, tariffs, and quotas must be observed. Most countries require an inspection of imported products, which must be arranged either before the product is shipped or when it reaches the country.

PRICING

It is not likely that customers from another country will have the same perception of value as those in the business' home country. Even if that perception is similar, a different monetary system is used and the costs of marketing are often higher. Therefore, prices will have to be changed. The business may have been used to offering discounts or other types of price reductions. The customs of the new country may require a new approach to determining the way prices are set, changed, and communicated to the customer.

RISK MANAGEMENT

Business people with no international experience often believe that risks are higher when selling in other countries. That is not always true and businesses can take steps to reduce risks.

There is specific insurance for products transported on ships. Also the U.S. government has established organizations to help businesses develop overseas markets and to protect those investments. Banking services are available that increase the likelihood that payments will be received from foreign customers in a timely fashion.

MARKETING INFORMATION MANAGEMENT

Earlier, we discussed the importance of marketing information for international markets. Businesses need to identify information needs, create methods of collecting and analyzing that information, and set procedures for ensuring the information is up-to-date. In the United States, the government is an important source of information about many other countries. The United States Foreign Commerce Service is an agency in the Department of Commerce. It collects business information from a large number of international sources that is updated very frequently. The information is available on an electronic database and can be accessed by businesses using CD-ROM technology.

PROMOTION

Promotion is the marketing function where a country's customs and culture are very important. Promotion relies on effective communication. Language and pictures communicate a business' message to customers. There are many examples of promotional mistakes where words were not translated correctly or had very different meanings after translation.

Promotional planning for international markets includes careful selection of the media to be used. Mass media may not be as available in some countries or may not be used for promotion. In many countries, television is not used as extensively for advertising as it is in the United States.

SELLING

Personal contact between a business and its customers is very important in many countries. Once again, customs play an important role in successful selling. Salespeople must be aware of the need to be formal or informal, who initiates conversations, how a business card is presented, and whether it is appropriate to conduct business during a meal. In some cultures, it is expected that salespeople present a gift to a prospective customer; in other countries the gift would be seen as a bribe and would be illegal or offensive.

ASSISTANCE WITH INTERNATIONAL MARKETING

International markets provide important opportunities that most businesses cannot ignore. However, some business people are reluctant to begin international marketing because of a lack of experience and understanding. Every country benefits from international business because of the availability of a greater variety of products and services and the profits available from exporting the country's products. Most governments are developing support for businesses that want to increase the amount of business conducted in other countries.

There are several examples of government support for U.S. businesses. The Department of State maintains embassies in most countries which can help with passports, documents, and laws. The U.S. Department of Commerce maintains the Agency for International Development, which develops new markets and offers financial support to some countries to assist them in working with U.S. companies. The Export/Import Bank provides financing and support to businesses whose foreign competitors receive government subsidies. Even the Small Business Administration has an office to provide international trade assistance for small U.S. businesses wanting to expand into foreign markets. Many states now have trade promotion offices to help local businesses develop markets in other countries.

There is a rapidly growing number of sources for assistance in international business. Professional and industry associations often gather information or employ international business experts. Banks, insurance companies, accounting firms, transportation companies, and advertising agencies recognize the importance of international businesses and may provide assistance to their customers.

REVIEW

You can seldom read a newspaper or magazine or watch television without hearing about the global economy. International markets are important to almost all businesses. If you are going to work in business, you will want to consider the many career opportunities in international business. In the future, business people who are not prepared to work with customers from other countries will have a difficult time being successful.

The marketing concept applies in markets from other countries as it does in the United States. In fact, companies that use the concept successfully have an advantage in international markets. They enter the markets knowing that they must understand customers and their needs before developing a marketing mix. They also recognize the need to study factors such as culture and customs, laws and regulations, economic conditions, technology, and business procedures used in the country.

While the same marketing functions are used in international business, there are differences in the marketing activities from one country to another. Business people often work with marketing experts from the foreign country to be sure that effective procedures are used. The amount of international business ranges from only limited exporting by some companies to large multinational organizations.

MARKETING FOUNDATIONS

1. INTERNATIONAL BUSINESS FACTS

There are often misunderstandings about international businesses. Some of the following statements about international business are true while others are not. Based on information from the chapter, identify the statements that contain accurate facts.

1. The total value of all products and services produced in the world is about $10,000,000,000,000.

2. The United States consumes about one-fourth of all goods and services produced in the world.

3. Nearly one-third of all world production is sold outside of the country in which it is produced.

4. Raw materials make up only about two-thirds of the world's exports.

5. One in every 16 U.S. jobs is directly related to international business.

6. About 50 percent of U.S. businesses are involved directly in international trade.

7. The U.S. leads the world in imports with nearly 14 percent of the world total.

8. In 1991 the United States had a negative balance of trade of $77 billion.

9. The percentage of manufacturing investments in other countries is declining while marketing investments are increasing.

10. Today, most countries have postindustrial economies.

2. BE AN INTERNATIONAL BUSINESS EXPERT

 Demonstrate your understanding of international business by defining the following terms:

international trade	exports	indirect exporting
direct exporting	imports	balance of trade
foreign production	foreign investment	joint venture
multinational companies	quotas	tariffs
subsidy inflation	standard of living	purchasing power
	recession	

1. CALCULATING STANDARDS OF LIVING

The standard of living of a country is calculated by dividing the country's gross domestic product (GDP) by its population. For example, a country with a GDP of $150 billion and a population of 10 million people would have a standard of living of $15,000 ($150,000,000,000/10,000,000).

The following information lists the estimated GDP and population of several countries in a recent year. Calculate the standard of living for each country. Then determine the rank order of each country from highest to lowest based on the standard of living.

Country	GDP (in billions)	Population (in millions)
Australia	$ 301.0	17.3
Austria	164.8	7.8
Bahamas	2.1	.25
Bahrain	4.5	.5
Canada	595.0	26.9
France	1,205.1	56.6
Germany	1,724.2	79.6
Great Britain	1,017.9	57.8
Hong Kong	82.6	5.9
Japan	3,370.1	124.0
Kuwait	10.0	1.2
New Zealand	42.3	3.4
Switzerland	229.6	6.8
United Arab Emirates	31.4	1.8
United States	5,674.2	253.2

2. LEARNING ABOUT PROSPECTIVE INTERNATIONAL MARKETS

It is important to learn as much about a country as possible before making a decision about marketing products and services there. In the chapter, we reviewed several types of information that would help business people understand a country and potential markets in the country. Your task is to develop a market research report about a country.

Select any country you believe might provide potentially attractive markets for U.S. businesses (your teacher might assign a country). Gather facts and information about the country using your school's library, a community library, or other appropriate information sources. Collect information about the following factors: population characteristics, geography, culture, economy, government and politics, and business statistics. If possible, find someone from your school or community who is familiar with the country and interview them.

When you have completed the data collection, prepare a written report describing the country and its potential for international business. Include several tables or figures in your report. Also make sure to use footnotes and attach a bibliography.

MARKETING PLANNING

1. WHAT IS THE ADVANTAGE?

In order to be successful, businesses that sell their products in other countries must be able to offer a product that has advantages compared to the competing products in the country. U.S. consumers usually have choices among products manufactured in several countries.

Look at several products you own and identify five that were manufactured outside the United States. For each product, identify the part of the marketing mix (product, price, distribution, or promotion) that was the most important reason you decided to purchase the product. Then make a recommendation for U.S. manufacturers on how they can improve their marketing mix to be more competitive with foreign manufacturers.

Next, identify five products that were manufactured by U.S. companies. For each product, identify the primary reason why you selected that product rather than one manufactured in another country.

2. CHANGES IN MARKETING FUNCTIONS

Choose one of the following products or services:

a. Large piece of equipment used for road construction

b. Vitamins and minerals for use by consumers in their homes

c. Movie

d. Fresh flowers

Assume you are deciding how to market the product or service to another country. For each of the nine marketing functions, describe a specific marketing activity that must be completed in order to market that product internationally.

MARKETING MANAGEMENT

1. SHOULD GOVERNMENT BE INVOLVED?

The governments of countries have different views of their roles in international business. Some governments are very active in supporting the businesses in their countries. We learned in the chapter that government can use quotas, tariffs, and subsidies to give advantages to their country's businesses. Some even restrict certain products from entering the country so their businesses will have no international competition. In private enterprise economies, governments usually try to remain out of the economy as much as possible. They are reluctant to use the methods discussed above and believe that competition is good for the economy.

While the United States has a private enterprise economy, there is often discussion about whether the government should be more involved in supporting U.S. businesses against foreign competition. Some people argue that U.S. businesses have a disadvantage if other governments offer support for their companies and the U.S. government does not.

Think about the advantages and disadvantages of greater government involvement based on what is best for businesses, consumers, and the economy. Develop a list of reasons to support greater involvement and another list to support limited involvement or no involvement. After you have developed the lists, decide which side you support. Prepare a brief oral report defending your decision. (Your teacher may ask you to participate in a debate on the subject.)

2. ETHICAL ISSUES

In Chapter 3 we studied the social responsibility of business. It is not enough that a business makes a profit and satisfies customer needs. It must also make decisions that are ethical and socially responsible. However, when marketing products internationally, the cultures and values of several countries may conflict with each other. Business people may be criticized for decisions that seem to be positive for their customers and acceptable in another country but are not viewed as appropriate in their home country.

The following scenarios describe ethical decisions faced by United States businesses when marketing in other countries. Read each carefully and consider the effects of the decisions on the company, its customers, and the country in which it plans to market the products. Also consider the business' social responsibility in the U.S. and internationally. Prepare a statement describing how you would respond to the ethical situation facing the company if you were the manager.

A. A furniture manufacturer has built cribs for babies for 80 years and has a very positive image as a quality manufacturer. Customers have been satisfied and several generations of families have purchased the company's baby cribs as they started their families. Because of some injuries and deaths to babies who got their heads trapped between the bars on other companies' cribs, a federal law was passed regulating the space between bars on all cribs. The manufacturer's bed design had spacings that were one-half inch too wide. The company immediately redesigned the beds to meet government requirements but had several thousand of the older model beds in warehouses and retail stores. The company decided they would not sell the beds in the U.S. but could not afford the loss if the old beds were not sold. They considered selling the older styles in other countries that did not have laws regulating the spaces between crib bars.

B. A pipeline manufacturer learned that an Eastern European country was planning to build an oil pipeline across the width of the country to bring heating oil to several major cities. The amount of pipe to be purchased was equal to 25 percent of the pipeline manufacturer's annual sales, so selling the pipe was very important to the company. Upon talking to a government official, the company learned that the price the country was willing to pay was higher than what could be received for a similar sale in the United States. However, the government official also indicated that the company selected to supply the pipe would have to pay several government officials sizable bribes. Even with the bribes, the pipeline manufacturer would still make a nice profit. Since business was slow in the U.S. the company was reluctant to miss out on such a large order.

C. A hotel chain was considering a joint venture with a company in another country. The plan was to build five new hotels in resort areas that were growing rapidly. The businesses already located in the resorts were experiencing a great deal of success and it was clear that other hotels would be built in the resorts as soon as companies could purchase the land and obtain the needed financing. The advantage of the joint venture for the hotel chain is that the company they were working with already owned land in several of the resort areas and had available cash to begin hotel construction while additional financing was being developed.

As the hotel company management was preparing the paperwork to finalize the joint venture, they received a letter from an important civil rights group providing evidence that the company with which they were planning to cooperate had an unwritten but clear policy to discriminate in their hiring practices. A check of the company's employment records showed that the employees were 96 percent white in a country that had a 35 percent non-white population. Also no women had ever been promoted beyond the level of supervisor in the company. The management knew that if the joint venture was not successful, it was unlikely they would be able to find a similar company with which to work.

CHAPTER
6

Product/
Service
Planning

Distribution

Marketing-
Information
Management

Economic
Foundations of
Marketing

Fin

Purchasing

*Marketing
and Business
Foundations*

Human Resource
Foundations

Risk

Pricing

Selling

Promotion

The Basics of Marketing

OBJECTIVES

1. Describe important changes that have occurred in marketing.

2. Explain the influence of the marketing concept on how a business plans and operates.

3. Demonstrate understanding of the elements of a marketing strategy.

4. Outline the steps consumers take when making a purchasing decision.

5. Identify how businesses can effectively respond to competition.

6. Discuss factors that affect the marketing efforts of various types of businesses.

7. Show how marketing can be used successfully in organizations outside the traditional business world.

NEWSLINE

QUALITY SELLS

Disney, Kodak, UPS. What do these companies have in common? They were all recognized in a consumer survey as the top brand names. Respondents believe they offer "extraordinary quality". That image is just what those companies want. They have worked hard to achieve their ranking. Each company works to maintain a quality product. They provide high levels of customer service. Their entire marketing mix is directed at the goal of meeting customer needs.

The survey is completed each year by the Total Research Corporation. It asks 2,000 people, aged 16 and older, to rate nearly 200 brands on a 10-point quality scale. This is an important difference from some research that simply asks participants to *identify* the most memorable brand names. Some of the most popular brands do not receive high quality ratings. The survey clearly shows that brands' ratings go up and down over a period of years as customers see the quality of a brand changing.

Some brands clearly reflect their companies' commitment to quality. Fisher-Price toys, Levi's jeans, and

> **Sometimes factors that are difficult for a company to control account for the decline.**

Chiquita bananas hold top-ten spots in the survey. So does Mercedes, although its ranking is beginning to drop. An automobile brand that didn't even exist a few years ago is making rapid gains. Lexus moved from 56th to 26th place in one year. There are well-known brands that do not do well in the quality survey, such as McDonald's, Diet Coke, and Diet Pepsi. In each case, the ranking may be due to the specific target market to which the company appeals and an image that is not directly focused on quality.

Companies have to be concerned if their brands are declining in the survey ratings. Some interesting examples of companies whose brands have a much lower quality rating than in previous years are Sears, American Express, and Eureka vacuum cleaners. Sometimes factors that are difficult for a company to control account for the

decline. Many Japanese brands dropped in the early 1990s as U.S. customers were encouraged to *buy American*. An example of a company that has worked hard to repair a poor image is Chrysler. A commitment to new product designs, careful manufacturing processes, customer service, and aggressive pricing combined with an extensive promotional campaign to move up Chrysler's quality rating 23 places in one year.

Source: "Upbeat Outlook for U.S. Brands." Marketing News, May 24, 1993.

CHANGES IN TODAY'S MARKETING

Marcus and Camille are waiting for the start of their career seminar. As they look at the course outline, they see that they are beginning a study of marketing today. They begin to talk about their interest in marketing careers.

Camille: Marketing seems to be an area where there are a lot of jobs. You hear about marketing all the time and several of my friends are planning to major in marketing.

Marcus: I'm not sure I'm interested in a marketing job. It seems like you have to be a salesperson and you know what people think of salespeople. It doesn't seem like it takes anything to be a retail salesperson. You know how many people work long hours for no money in retail. What is your image of an automobile salesperson or of the person who calls you on the telephone at home to sell something? Even the good sales jobs in industry require you to travel all of the time. It seems like you have to be able to out-think and out-talk your customers to convince them to buy your products.

Camille: It does seem that way, but there are other marketing jobs. Advertising is a part of marketing. Don't you think it would be exciting to create television commercials? I know some of them are weird or boring, but a lot of the advertisements are really creative and get me interested in the products they are selling.

Marcus: I guess you're right. But still, it seems that marketing is used to get people to buy things they don't really need. I know companies need to sell their products to stay in business, but I'm not sure I want to be the one who has to convince someone to spend their money with my business whether it is with advertising or selling.

Camille: Well, I'm going to be open-minded. I want to work in business and everything I read now says that marketing is one of the fastest-growing and highest-paying career areas in business. I'll be interested to see what types of jobs are available and what it takes to be successful.

Just like Marcus and Camille, you may have started your study of marketing with limited understanding of this important function of business. Much of our understanding comes from experience, and people have not always had positive experiences with marketing. Now that you have begun the study of marketing, you know that marketing is quite different than many consumers and business people realize. There are many marketing activities and many ways that marketing can improve exchanges between businesses and consumers.

Marketing today is quite different from marketing only a few years ago. Understanding those differences will help you use marketing more effectively. Some of the important changes are shown in Figure 6-1.

How Has Marketing Changed?

From a few activities . . . . To a variety of activities

From independent . . . . To integrated

From problem-solver . . . . To opportunity-provider

Income Statement		Balance Sheet

From an expense . . . . To an investment

FIGURE 6-1 ▪ Effective marketing increases a business' chance of being successful in meeting customers' needs.

1. *A change from a few activities to a variety of activities.* The earliest use of marketing was to move products from the producer to the consumer. Over time, it expanded to include a variety of promotional tools. Today, the nine marketing functions include many types of marketing activities ranging from research to purchasing and offering customer credit. Effective marketers understand all of the marketing tools and know when and how to use them.

2. *A change from an independent activity to an integrated activity.* In the past, marketing was not well understood by many business people so they didn't know how to use and support marketing. Marketers often worked by themselves and had little contact with others in the business. Planning for marketing was done after other business planning was complete. Now, marketing is considered an essential part of the business and marketers are involved in all important business decisions. Marketing strategies are developed as a part of the business plans.

3. *A change from a problem-solving tool to an opportunity-creation tool.* Marketers have often been called upon when a company faced a problem. If inventory was too high or competitors were attracting customers away from a business, marketers were asked to increase sales and promotion efforts or to find weaknesses in the competitor's programs. Today's marketers are continuously looking for new markets and for ways to improve a company's offerings in current markets. Businesses cannot afford to wait until problems occur. Marketing is responsible for identifying opportunities and helping a company to plan for those opportunities.

4. *A change from an expense to an investment.* Marketing can be very expensive. When businesses have faced financial problems, some have looked to marketing as a place to reduce costs and save money. Most business people today recognize that companies will not be able to make a profit if products remain unsold. Effective marketing is an investment because it is responsible for matching a company's offerings with market needs. Spending money to improve marketing usually results in increased profits for the company.

Understanding and using marketing is an important business skill. Marketing is a valuable business asset in today's competitive world. People who understand the basics of marketing are in high demand in the business world. Those basics include understanding the marketing concept, planning a marketing strategy, responding to competition, and integrating marketing into the business.

UNDERSTANDING THE MARKETING CONCEPT

The marketing concept has changed the way businesses operate. The marketing concept is much more than a change in the way a business completes marketing activities. It requires a change in the approach to business planning. We learned in Chapter 1 that the marketing concept is *using the needs of customers as the primary focus during the planning, production, distribution, and promotion of a product or service.* That may seem obvious and rather simple to complete, but some examples show how difficult it actually is.

RELIABLE AUTO SERVICE

John has always enjoyed repairing cars. Since he was a teenager, he has bought older cars, fixed them, and resold them at a profit. He studied auto mechanics while in high school and completed a two-year program to become a certified mechanic at a community college. He worked for several years at a franchised auto repair center but was dissatisfied with the center's policy to complete repairs as quickly as possible using inexpensive repair parts rather than those specified by the automobile manufacturer. John preferred to spend time with each car making sure all problems were identified and repaired carefully with the best available parts. Often he spent weeks with the cars and knew that when he had finished, the car would provide reliable transportation for its owner.

John decided to open his own auto repair business and was happy to find a small building he could afford to rent on the edge of a large shopping center only two miles from his home. He opened the Reliable Auto Service and was pleased with the early response. He didn't have a great deal of money to spend on advertising, but the store's signs seemed to be enough to attract the shopping center customers to stop in. Many said they appreciated the convenience of being able to leave their car while they were shopping and had more confidence in a business where the owner worked on their car than in the typical repair center. Now that he owned the business, John knew he would give each car special attention and the best possible service.

However, John soon began to hear complaints from his customers. Many were not pleased when they were asked to leave their cars overnight while John completed the repairs. They were also concerned that the costs of repairs were a great deal higher than they were used to paying at other businesses. When John told them that the price reflected the highest quality parts and that he guaranteed all repairs, customers told him that other businesses also offered guarantees at much lower prices. After several months, John's business was declining. He was disappointed that customers did not seem to recognize the quality of his work.

DEE'S DESIGNS

Dee Sloan turned a hobby into a home business. She had combined her talents in art and clothing construction to work with the community theater. She designed and sewed the costumes for many of the theater's productions. Several of the actors and actresses were so impressed with her unique designs that they asked her to create some items for their personal wardrobes. She enjoyed the work and word-of mouth from her customers soon resulted in more orders than she could fill. Because of that success, Dee decided to hire several people who would help her with the sewing so she could expand into a full-time business. She believed she could sell her products through small businesses who would appreciate the unique designs and use them to compete with larger stores. She contacted several small retail chains hoping to find one who would agree to buy and distribute her fashions.

After three contacts, Dee was discouraged. The responses of the retailers were all quite positive toward her fashions. They indicated the clothing was unique and well-constructed. However, the first retailer felt the fashions did not fit into the image of their stores. The second was willing to buy one or two of the designs but wanted Dee to produce a large volume of a limited number of the fashions in various sizes. Dee preferred to produce a variety of designs and styles. The last contact was willing to display Dee's fashions, but required a full display for each store in the chain and was unwilling to pay until 60 percent of the original order was sold. Dee could not afford that investment.

Dee could not hide her disappointment. It was hard to understand why her current customers could be so excited about her work yet she could not interest people who were in the fashion business.

The experiences of John and Dee illustrate the difficulty of implementing the marketing concept. Both of them had a quality product or service to sell. Initial reactions from customers were positive. Yet they were unable to develop a successful strategy for their businesses. There are several reasons they were unable to be successful.

1. They were concerned only about the product or service in developing the business.
2. They believed that they knew what customers would buy.
3. They did not study the market.
4. They failed to use a variety of marketing tools available to them.

Every day we can see examples of business people just like John and Dee who fail because they do not understand and use the marketing concept. It is not just new or small businesses that do not use marketing effectively. Automobile manufacturers, retailers, restaurants, and movie theaters fail, often after many years of successful operations. A business that is unwilling to study the needs of customers or that does not use customer needs when planning and marketing products and services is taking a big risk. Competitors who understand and use the marketing concept will turn that understanding into an advantage.

PLANNING A MARKETING STRATEGY

Every business decides how it will attempt to achieve its goals. Most businesses use carefully prepared plans to guide their operations. *Planning that identifies how a company expects to achieve its goals is known as a strategy.* The strategy used by a business provides the clearest indication of whether that business understands the marketing concept.

Without the marketing concept, a business will develop a product or service and then decide how to market the product. There will be little consideration of who the customers are or what their needs are until the product is ready to be sold. Marketing planning will occur only after the product has been designed and will typically be done by marketing specialists working apart from others in the company. The business expects that most people are potential customers of the product and that with adequate marketing those customers can be convinced to buy the product.

With the marketing concept, a very different strategy will be used. The company believes it will be most successful if it can respond to needs of customers. It also recognizes that those needs may be different among consumer groups, and that needs can change over time. As shown in Figure 6-2, the company will begin its planning by identifying potential customers and studying the needs of those customers. Marketers will be involved in that study and in using the results to plan the products and services to be developed. The company will attempt to develop products and services that respond to customers' needs rather than what the company thinks should be offered. Marketing and product planning will occur at the same time involving many people in all parts of the company. Marketing will be directed at meeting the identified needs of the customers rather

How Does The Marketing Concept Affect Planning?	
Without the Marketing Concept	**With the Marketing Concept**
1. Develop a product.	1. Conduct research to identify potential customers and their needs.
2. Decide on marketing activities.	2. Develop a marketing mix (product, distribution, price, promotion) that meets specific customer needs.
3. Identify potential customers.	

FIGURE 6-2 ▪ When a firm uses the marketing concept to plan, the marketing mix is based on customers' needs.

than developing ways to convince people to buy something they may not need.

UNDERSTANDING THE CUSTOMER

Consumers have many choices of products and services they can purchase to meet their needs. Today, most consumers are well informed, experienced in gathering information, and compare products and services before they make decisions. Even if a hurried decision is made, if the buyer is dissatisfied with the purchase or finds a better choice later, the buyer will likely return the original product for a refund.

Bringing a new product to the marketplace is very expensive for businesses. It takes time and money to develop, produce, distribute, and promote products. Once in the market, a new product competes with many other products offered by companies who also have invested a great deal and do not want to fail. The competition among products and companies is usually very intense. Companies that are not prepared for that competition have a difficult time staying in the market.

Identifying Customer Needs

Successful companies are usually those that meet customer needs. Consider the products you buy or the businesses you return to time after time. They are usually not your only choices, but have met your needs in specific ways better than the other choices. The reasons may be higher quality, convenience, better prices, or a unique image. Your purchases illustrate the definition of marketing discussed earlier in the text. Satisfying exchanges occur when you spend your money for products and services that meet your needs, and the business is able to make a profit on the sale of its products.

However, meeting customer needs is not easy. First, many customers are not sure of their needs or may have conflicting needs. Second, while consumers have many needs, they typically have limited amounts of money available to satisfy those needs. They may not have enough money to buy a specific product even though they believe it is the one that best meets their needs. Finally, the needs of individuals and groups of consumers can be quite different, and their perceptions of what products or services will meet their needs are also quite different. You need only compare your feelings about specific products or services with your friends, family members, or other people, and you will find that there are often major differences.

Businesses tend to deal with customer needs in one of two ways as shown in Figure 6-3. Some businesses do not see the specific needs of consumers as important. They believe either that consumers don't understand their own needs or that businesses can influence consumer needs with well-designed products and effective prices and promotion. In other words, if they can effectively produce and market products, customers will buy their products. These businesses feel that most consumers are quite similar in terms of their needs and purchase behavior.

Other businesses believe that an understanding of consumer needs is an important part of their business activities. They study needs and attempt to understand how consumers evaluate products and services to make decisions about what to purchase. The businesses recognize that consumer needs can be quite different, so they try to identify groups of consumers who have similar characteristics and needs. They feel that they can do a better job of satisfying customers if they can develop products and services that respond as much as possible to what the consumer wants and expects.

Two Views of Consumers

Customers are all alike and can be influenced to buy what a business offers.

Customers are quite different and they select products and services to meet their unique needs.

FIGURE 6-3 ▪ Businesses need to recognize that consumer needs can be quite different before they can develop products and services to meet those needs.

Satisfying Customer Needs

The business that is concerned about consumer needs believes in the marketing concept. The business' activities begin with a focus on the customer and a belief that if it can satisfy customer needs better than its competitors, it will have the best chance of being successful. The business studies markets

carefully to identify groups of consumers with unsatisfied needs on which it can focus its efforts. Through extensive marketing research, the business gathers consumer information and analyzes that information to categorize customers according to similar characteristics, needs, and purchasing behavior. *Groups of similar consumers within a larger market are known as market segments.*

After segments have been identified, the business analyzes the segments to determine which can be served most effectively and which have the strongest needs, the most resources, the least competition, or other characteristics that provide the business with opportunities for success. *Studying and prioritizing market segments to locate the best potential based on demand and competition is known as market opportunity analysis.* Once segments have been identified and prioritized, the business selects those segments on which it will focus its efforts. The information resulting from the study of those markets will be used to make production and marketing decisions.

PLANNING THE OFFERING

Determining what to sell and how it will be presented to the customer consumes much of the planning efforts of a company. Products and services to be offered need to be identified and developed, and marketing strategies must be planned in order to make the products and services available to customers.

A business that believes in the marketing concept uses a planning process that is based on customer needs. This business knows that product planning and marketing must work hand-in-hand. Therefore it will carefully coordinate the development of the entire marketing mix.

You will recall that the marketing mix is the *blending of product, distribution, price, and promotion by the business.* Many decisions must be made to insure that a satisfying product is made available to the selected markets at the time, in the location, at the price, and with the information that best meets customers' needs. An effective strategy will bring together many complex activities. The business will be able to control a large number of the activities but will usually have to rely on other businesses to help with its plans.

Some of the decisions in the marketing mix are obvious. Some decisions are not. When one decision is made, it affects other decisions. For example, an improvement is made to a product. The company may then need to increase the price. The company may decide to make the product available to the customer in more locations. The business may then need to reduce the number of product options. Developing the best marketing mix requires the cooperation of many people. It requires careful planning and creativity.

A business uses the marketing concept because it believes that the best decisions can be made when the needs of consumers become an important focus of the planning. By combining the planning of product, distribution, pricing, and promotion, as shown in Figure 6-4, the company has the best opportunity to develop a satisfying, competitive, and profitable mix. Business people need to understand each of the mix elements and all of the choices available in order to develop a good marketing mix.

Combining Parts of the Marketing Mix

FIGURE 6-4 ▪ The parts of the marketing mix are combined to satisfy customers.

Product Development

When the term *product* is used, many people think of the basic offering of a company that is similar to the offering of many other competitors, such as an automobile, a chair, a meal at a restaurant, or an insurance policy. But there is much more to the product. Each competitor must make decisions that will make its brand different from and better than those offered by competitors.

Parts of the *product* decision that can improve customer satisfaction are special features such as a unique design, construction, size, color, or operation. Accessories can be added to make the product easier to operate, more efficient, and so on.

Products can be improved with the service available to customers. Services can be provided before or after the sale and can be related to the purchase, delivery, installation, use, or maintenance of the product. Guarantees and warranties should be considered a part of the product because they make customers more confident in the purchase.

Another part of the product decision is the use of the product. Often products have more than one use. Also, customers may be dissatisfied with the product if they are not able to use it in the way they want. Brand name and image can also be important factors consumers consider when making a purchase. Packaging is needed to protect the product, but also it can make the product easier to use and provide customer information.

Distribution Decisions

Distribution is a critical part of a business' decisions. It has an important impact on customer satisfaction by making the product available where and when the customer wants it. You

can probably identify many examples of products that were not available when you needed them or were not found in the businesses where you expected to find them. Products may have been damaged during shipment, poorly packaged, or assembled incorrectly. Each of these examples demonstrates the importance of distribution.

While a few products and services are exchanged directly between the producer and the customer, most businesses must involve others in the distribution process. Manufacturers must rely on wholesalers and retailers to get products to the consumer. In the same way, a retailer must locate sources of the products its customers want and insure that those products can be obtained. Many businesses are usually involved in the production and marketing of a product.

An interesting activity is to try to trace the channel of distribution for products you purchase. Sometimes it is almost impossible to identify the companies involved in some part of the distribution process or even the company that manufactured the product. Even though many of the businesses are not obvious to the consumer, business people recognize the importance of each member of the channel and the importance of the activities they perform to the success of the marketing process. Activities such as order processing, product handling, transportation, and inventory control must be completed well in order for companies to get the product to the customer.

Pricing Products and Services

Price is probably the most difficult marketing decision to understand and plan. Theoretically we know that price is determined from the interaction of supply and demand. That relationship is important in setting the best price. Practically, however, we know that it is almost impossible to set the price of a specific product in a specific business using supply and demand. Businesses must develop specific procedures to set prices that are competitive and allow the business to make a profit.

First the business needs to know its objectives in pricing its products and services. If the goal is to increase the sales volume of a particular product, a different price will be used than if the company is attempting to make the most profit possible on each sale. Many businesses set their prices so they will be the same or slightly lower than their major competitors. That may be necessary in some situations but can also create problems.

Calculating the price to be charged involves several elements. Production, marketing, and operating costs make up a great percentage of the price of most products so the net profit available is very small. If all of the components of a price are not considered, or prices are not calculated carefully, businesses may find that there is no profit available after expenses have been tallied.

Another part of the pricing decision is how price is presented to customers. Normally, retailers use a price tag or sticker and customers pay the price that is marked. Price may be communicated by manufacturers through catalogs or price sheets or by the salesperson representing the product.

A GLOBAL VISION

BACK TO THE BASICS

Dean Foods Co. started as a small dairy in Chicago, but is now a $2.3-billion-a-year business. While the United States studied the North American Free Trade Agreement, Dean was already developing the 90-million-customer market for dairy products and vegetables in Mexico. The demand was huge, but government price controls have removed most of the profit in distributing fresh foods by wholesalers and retailers. Few regulations are in place to enforce quality standards for products. Many homes, as well as the typical small stores where consumers shop, do not have refrigeration.

Those challenges might cause other businesses to ignore the market, but Dean Foods was willing to make changes in the way it markets products. Dean Foods believes the solution is to return to marketing strategies that were used years ago when U.S. markets had similar characteristics. Production and processing facilities can be developed close to the consumer. Smaller containers can be used so products are consumed before they spoil. Distribution can be accomplished through door-to-door delivery by refrigerated trucks. The company can purchase refrigerated cases for stores to maintain the freshness of products.

Other companies are seeing similar challenges and responding by going back to the basics. Campbells has found it increasingly difficult to increase sales of and profits from its canned soups in the United States as it competes with many brands of fresh and frozen foods. The company has set a goal of earning half its revenues from foreign sales by the year 2000, even though they now account for only about one-fourth of the company's total. Cutting back on varieties simplifies the distribution process in other countries. Promotion in many countries focuses on getting consumers to switch from homemade soups to canned soups.

Colgate-Palmolive is a very successful consumer-products manufacturer facing the challenge of developing markets in Eastern Europe. The company's salespeople have had to concentrate on locating businesses who can sell the products, developing transportation and storage systems, and training retailers in methods of display, inventory control, and pricing. Advertising appeals often have to be much more direct, focusing on the use of the product.

Sources: "Marketing Share Con Leche?" Business Week, Special Supplement, Reinventing America 1992; "Colgate-Palmolive Is Really Cleaning Up in Poland," and "Campbell: Now It's M-M-Global." Business Week, March 15, 1993.

It is not an uncommon practice for businesses to offer discounts from their list prices to some or all of their customers. Markdowns, allowances, trade-ins, and coupons are other ways that prices can be changed. Finally credit is commonly used to enable customers to purchase a product without paying the full price at the time they make the purchase.

In pricing products and services, marketers must try to balance the costs of the product with the customer's feelings about the value of the product. The goal is a fair price and a reasonable profit.

Planning Promotion

Businesses need to be careful not to overstate the value of advertising, selling, and other promotional methods. While they are powerful tools if used to support effective marketing programs, they can easily be misused and can have no impact or a negative effect on consumers. Promotion must be planned to communicate the value and benefits of a product or service to consumers to aid them in decision-making.

Think of promotions you believe are particularly effective or ineffective. Now try to determine the impact of a specific promotion on your purchase behavior. It is very difficult to determine the influence of just one promotion on a decision even if you believe it is effective. If you keep track of the promotions you are exposed to in only one day, you will find that there are more messages around you than you can ever notice or to which you can actually respond.

When planning promotion, business people select from a variety of methods. The most common are advertising, personal selling, sales promotion, visual display, and publicity—however other less frequently used methods are available. The selection will be based primarily on the communications objectives the company wants to accomplish and the audience it wants to reach. Each method varies in terms of the cost per person, number of people reached, types of messages carried, and other factors. Careful planning needs to be done to reach the specific audience with an understandable message in a way that helps the consumer make appropriate decisions.

Promotion is a unique type of marketing tool. It doesn't create economic utility by itself. It is used to communicate the value and benefits of other product and marketing decisions to the consumer. Promotion cannot do a great deal to help a company that has a poor product, prices that are too high, or ineffective distribution. However, companies that have otherwise made good decisions need to have an effective promotional plan to help consumers decide from among the many choices available to them.

HELPING CONSUMERS MAKE DECISIONS

Consumer decision-making has been studied extensively by psychologists, sociologists, and marketers. While there are a number of theories about what influences consumers to make decisions, there is general agreement that people follow a sequence of specific decisions when making a commitment to purchase. Some people have a difficult time accepting that they make decisions in the same way. You may have to review several purchase decisions you have made in order to see a pattern. If you make the same decision frequently, you have probably formed a habit and you may not go through all of the steps that you use for a new decision. Many purchase decisions become routine and quite simple when they are repeated again and again.

STAGES IN CONSUMER DECISION-MAKING

Figure 6-5 illustrates the stages in consumer decision-making. The typical purchasing process begins when the consumer recognizes that a need exists. Prior to that time, the consumer may

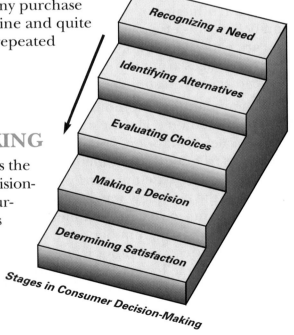

FIGURE 6-5 ■ Consumer decision-making follows a specific sequence of steps.

have been aware of many products and services, but took no action. Once a specific need is identified, the decision-making process begins. If the need is urgent, the process may occur quickly; if not, the consumer may take some time before a decision is made.

Following awareness, the consumer becomes interested in finding a solution to the need. That interest leads to identifying products or services that relate to the need and sources of information that can help the consumer make an effective decision. When the consumer has identified several choices and has information about the choices, the available choices are evaluated. The evaluation is done to see if one or more of the choices seems to be better, more available or affordable, or in other ways meets the consumer's needs better than the others.

Some consumers spend very little time and use a small amount of information to evaluate choices. Some people are very careful and objective while others are much less rational. When the consumer has evaluated the available information, a decision is made. The decision will be to select one of the choices available, to gather more information, or to do nothing at that time. Following the decision, the consumer will determine if the choice was correct or not. If the consumer tried a specific product, the product will be evaluated to see if it satisfied the need. If it did, the decision will likely be repeated the next time the same need occurs. If it did not, the purchase decision will probably not be repeated.

Understanding the decision-making process is a very important marketing skill. Knowing where consumers are in that process helps the marketer provide the right information at the right time. The result should be a more effective exchange.

DECISIONS IMPROVE WITH INFORMATION

Marketers are often described as creative people. Indeed, a great deal of creativity is needed to plan a marketing mix. Developing new product features and uses, preparing promotional activities, and demonstrating value to customers depend on the creativity of the people involved. However, marketing is increasingly becoming a scientific process in which information is gathered to improve decisions and alternative methods are studied to determine which are most effective.

Conducting research is an important marketing activity. Marketers need to be skilled in organizing research and using research results. The most important type of research for most businesses is the study of potential and current customers. Companies need to be able to clearly identify their customers, characteristics that make groups of customers different from others, their important needs, and how they make purchase decisions. Additionally, research about competitors will identify the type of competition and the strengths and weaknesses of competing companies. Finally, businesses study alternative marketing strategies to determine which are most effective and most profitable.

Marketers are using more and more information to make decisions. Most companies are developing marketing information systems which collect and store a variety of information. That information is readily available, often through the use of computers, when decisions need to be made.

USING MARKETING TO RESPOND TO COMPETITION

The private enterprise economy offers many opportunities for businesses. A person who wants to start a business and has the necessary resources can probably do so. Our economy is also good for consumers. Because of the opportunities for people to operate businesses, consumers typically have many available products and services from which to choose.

Even though private enterprise offers many opportunities, it also presents challenges to business people. When there are many businesses in a market, competition is usually very intense. Consumers can select from among a number of products and services. They expect real value from businesses or they will purchase from a competitor. Value may mean higher quality, more service, or lower prices. Businesses that are unable to meet customer expectations better than their competitors may not be able to survive.

In Chapter 4, we learned that there are several types of competition that businesses face. Marketers need to be able to identify the type of competition that a company faces and develop an appropriate marketing strategy. Using the marketing concept provides direction for developing effective strategies.

RESPONDING TO INTENSE COMPETITION

The most difficult type of competition faced by businesses is a market in which businesses compete with others that offer very similar products. One example is pure competition, where there are many businesses offering the same product. Another example is an oligopoly. In this case, there are only a few companies competing in the same market, but they offer products in which consumers see few, if any, differences. Business people can study the customers in the market to determine if there are some groups that are not currently satisfied with the choices available.

In the past, businesses facing intense competition responded by emphasizing price or promotion. When they found that customers saw no important difference among competing products, they believed they had to reduce their prices to make a sale. Those companies that emphasized promotion attempted to convince customers that their products were different from and better than those of competitors. In some cases they created relatively minor differences and promoted those differences as being important to consumers. In other cases, they attempted to create unique brand names and images so customers would remember the brands and select them from among all of the available choices.

With careful study of consumer needs and their experience with available products, businesses may be able to identify ways to change or improve products, features, or the services offered with the products. New product uses might be identified. The goal of any product change is to make the product different from that of competitors and more satisfying to the target market.

There may also be opportunities in other parts of the marketing mix. Distribution can focus on making the product available at better locations and times, with more careful handling, or greater customer service. Pricing can offer alternative methods of payments, greater ease of obtaining credit, extended time for payment, or leasing rather than ownership. Promotion can provide more personalized or detailed information, use non-traditional methods or media, or communicate with the customer after the sale to aid in the use of the product.

RESPONDING TO LIMITED COMPETITION

Some businesses have the advantage of offering a product or service that has little or no direct competition. In economic terms, this is known as a monopoly. Businesses facing limited competition often operate in very different ways than those in intense competition. They do not have to worry as much about price or even promotion since consumers are restricted in their choice of products. Therefore, the business will usually concentrate on maintaining its advantage in the market. It will attempt to keep competing businesses from entering, protect its location, and concentrate on keeping its product or service as unique as possible.

Customers who use the products and services of businesses who have a monopoly often become dissatisfied with their lack of choice. They believe that without competition they pay higher prices, have poorer service, and must deal with a company that has more concern about protecting its market and making a profit than about meeting the needs of consumers.

Consider the only hospital in a community where the next closest hospital is 60 miles away. That hospital would be in a market very much like a monopoly with no direct competition. It would be difficult for consumers to drive the 60 miles every time they needed health care. The hospital administrators would not have to be particularly concerned about the people who need hospital services and could offer the services that provided the highest level of profit. Customers may not be happy, but they would have little choice of an alternative.

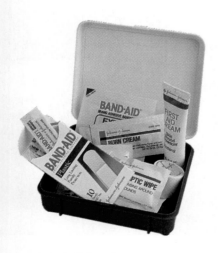

While it may not be as profitable in the short run, the hospital administrators may want to adopt the marketing concept as a way to make operating decisions. As a result, consumers are more likely to use the services of the local hospital and to encourage others to use them, and will be less likely to look for other places and other methods to meet their health care needs.

The same analysis could apply to the only convenience store, supermarket, or other retail business in a neighborhood; the only distributor of fuel and agricultural supplies in an area; or a

CLASSICS AND CONTEMPORARIES

Since the 1800s, J.C Penney has appealed to middle America with apparel, home furnishings, appliances, furniture, and hardware. Generations of families grew up with Penney's brands. But as retailing changed in the 1970s and 80s, so did Penney's traditional customers. There was no longer a "middle America". Some consumers were attracted to national brands, unique designs, and an upscale image. Others were looking for basic quality with limited service at a very low price. So how can a store known for its middle-of-the road image and prices survive in a market that is dividing into two segments?

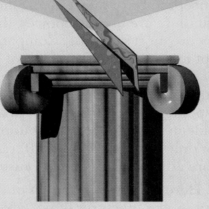

A PENNEY STILL HAS VALUE

chandise to insure that quality standards are maintained. They study the brands that their customers prefer to make sure that Penney's either carries those brands or offers comparable styles.

Initial efforts to redesign the business centered on copying the upscale stores. But customers did not respond. Because the customers had grown up with Penney's, they had a well-established image in their minds of what Penney's was and what it offered.

After considerable study, executives redesigned Penney's strategy again. The consumers Penney's targeted are careful shoppers who have little brand loyalty. They will shop for national brands, but if they find the same or higher quality for less, they will choose the better value. So Penney's had to offer the same styles as the national brands, maintain quality standards, and keep costs low so prices were competitive.

Today, Penney's buyers pay careful attention to the styles offered by stores like The Gap, L.L Bean, and the Limited. They have added a staff of inspectors who work with the manufacturers of Penney's mer-

One of the most effective strategies Penney's has adopted is to offer well-known brands to attract customers into the store. Ads feature Nike, Dockers, and Bali to show customers that they can find their favorite brands in the stores. But Penney's maintains its own labels of comparable merchandise and emphasizes the consistent quality and regular lower price of those brands.

Penney's is now the fourth-largest retailer in the United States and recent years' sales growth and profits have been among the top in the industry. More importantly, Penney's has become a store of choice for a target market. Those customers seeking quality merchandise at a good price once again will shop at Penney's.

Source: "Penney's Rediscovers Its Calling." Business Week, *April 5, 1993.*

government agency or school system. Each has the characteristics of a monopoly and can decide whether to adopt the marketing concept or not.

RESPONDING TO MONOPOLISTIC COMPETITION

Most businesses face competition that is somewhere between monopoly and intense competition. They have many competitors, but customers see some differences among the choices. Therefore, the customers will attempt to determine which of the available products and services best meet their needs. It is important for the companies to have clearly identified differences that result in customers selecting their brands from among all of the available choices.

Companies in monopolistic competition find the marketing concept to be of most value. Since customers already recognize that there are unique choices, they attempt to select the brands that are most satisfying. Companies that use the marketing concept focus on specific groups of customers and attempt to identify their needs. Then they will use the full range of decisions within the marketing mix to develop products and services that respond to those customers. Changes and improvements can be made in the product, distribution, prices, and promotion that not only make the brand different from its competitors but more attractive to potential customers.

Here are some examples of the use of the marketing concept. A manufacturer of portable CD players makes its product smaller, more durable, and offers it in a variety of colors and styles. A day care center keeps children overnight to meet the needs of parents who have evening jobs. A supermarket accepts debit cards from customers who do not want to carry cash. Information about concerts in a local amphitheater is provided through a database that can be accessed by home computer, and orders for tickets can be placed using a computer. In each case, a change is made in the marketing mix that is designed to improve the mix, make it different from the competition, and respond to an important need of the target market.

HOW BUSINESSES USE MARKETING

Marketing activities are performed every time an exchange of products and services occurs, whether it is between businesses, a business and a consumer, or even between consumers. The same basic marketing functions and activities are used in all exchanges. Each exchange involves a supplier, a consumer, and a complete marketing mix. However, there are differences in the ways that various types of businesses use those marketing tools. While the entire marketing mix and all marketing functions are important, each type of business will need to place special emphasis on some marketing decisions.

PRODUCERS AND MANUFACTURERS

The role of producers and manufacturers is to develop the products and services needed by other businesses and by consumers. Because of that role, the product element of the marketing mix receives the most attention. Distribution is also important as the companies develop channels of distribution that will get the products to important markets. Unless direct channels of distribution are used, other businesses have major responsibility for determining the prices consumers pay and for consumer promotion. Manufacturers and producers must respond to the needs of the people who will be the final consumers of their products. However, they must also be able to satisfy the needs of the businesses involved in the marketing channel for the products.

CHANNEL MEMBERS

A channel of distribution is developed in order to move products from the producer to the consumer. Channel members are used to provide many of the marketing functions during the distribution process. For those channel members, less emphasis will be placed on the product element of the marketing mix. Decisions are made about what products and services to offer and then attention is given to the other mix elements. Wholesalers emphasize distribution planning. Many wholesalers help their customers with financing and provide marketing information. Retailers are responsible for most final pricing decisions and use a variety of promotion activities to encourage customers to purchase their products. Channel members must be able to work cooperatively with other businesses involved in the channel while responding to the needs of the customers in their target markets.

SERVICE BUSINESSES

Service businesses face unique marketing challenges. Most service businesses work directly with their consumers rather than through a channel of distribution so they are responsible for the entire marketing mix. Also, services are usually developed and delivered by people, making it more difficult to con-

trol the quality of the service each time it is offered. Because of the characteristics of services, the product mix element is very important. The business must develop procedures to insure that the customer receives the expected quality of service every time. Distribution planning is also important because the service must be available where and when the customer wants it. If there is not a large enough quantity available, sales will be lost. If the business is prepared to offer more services than the customers want, expenses will increase.

Service businesses usually have more control over pricing than businesses that sell products. It is more difficult for customers to determine the appropriate price for a service or to compare the prices of several companies, since each one may offer the service in a different way. Services are quite difficult to promote since the customer may not be able to see or examine the service. Services that customers are not familiar with may require a great deal of promotion.

NEW APPLICATIONS OF MARKETING

The successful use of marketing has moved from the business world to other organizations. Previously many people viewed marketing in limited or negative ways. Because of those views, they were reluctant to use marketing. But today, many consumers are more aware of marketing. They see many businesses use marketing effectively. These businesses have the interests of their customers in mind. They recognize that marketing is an important tool to help organizations achieve their goals.

It is not unusual to see marketing being used by museums, libraries, symphonies, athletic teams, churches, and clubs. Just as businesses have not always understood marketing and have misused it, many organizations have made mistakes as they attempted to develop marketing plans. They often emphasized promotion and treated people as if they all have the same needs and interests. The organizations that believe marketing is simple or that fail to study and understand marketing may be disappointed with the results. However, many organizations seek help from people who understand marketing and know how to use the marketing concept to identify target markets and develop marketing mixes. Those organizations have seen very positive results and now view marketing as an important part of their efforts.

REVIEW

Marketing is a very complex set of activities and yet is, in some ways, quite simple. While there is still a great deal to learn, you now are aware of the basic concepts of effective marketing. Marketing is used to improve the exchange of products and services. Many business people do not see important differences among consumers. Other business people believe in the marketing concept. They believe customers have different needs and that customers choose the products that will best meet their needs. Those business people study the market, identify market segments with unmet needs, and develop marketing mixes specifically for those customers.

The type of competition faced by a business affects the way it operates. If a business is in a market with very intense competition, it needs to make its products and services different from and better than its competitors. When a business has little competition, it has less concern about other businesses, but tries to maintain its position in the market. The effective use of marketing has made important differences in businesses. Often new markets or better ways to produce, distribute, price, or promote products and services are discovered. As businesses have used marketing to improve customer satisfaction, other organizations have seen that marketing can be an important tool.

MARKETING FOUNDATIONS

1. YOU PROVIDE THE REASON

Each of the following statements describes a fact or concept about marketing. Using information from the chapter, write a supporting reason that helps to explain each fact or concept.

a. Marketing is quite different than most people realize.

b. Marketing should be considered an activity that is well-integrated with other business functions.

c. Businesses that are concerned about consumer needs believe in the marketing concept.

d. Product development includes more than just the physical offering of the product.

e. Pricing is probably the most difficult marketing decision to understand and plan.

f. Understanding the consumer decision-making process is very important to marketers.

g. In markets where there is little or no competition, there is little pressure for businesses to find ways to change their marketing mix.

h. Service businesses face unique marketing challenges.

2. **TRUE-FALSE**

Determine if each of the following statements is true or false.

a. Marketing consists of a few basic activities, such as promotion and distribution.

b. In the past, marketing was used basically as a problem-solving tool, such as a way to reduce inventory.

c. Spending money to improve marketing usually results in increased profits for the company.

d. Following the marketing concept requires a total commitment to satisfying customers' needs.

e. Marketing is primarily effective for new or small businesses that can respond quickly to changes in the market or economy.

f. A marketing strategy is defined as how a company expects to achieve its goals.

g. Understanding and meeting consumer needs is relatively easy to do because it is well known that all people have the same needs such as food and shelter.

h. Groups of similar consumers within a larger market are known as market segments.

i. The marketing mix elements all act independently of each other.

j. Distribution can be described as the physical handling and transportation of a product.

k. Because of so many other variables, it is impossible to set a product or service price strictly on the concepts of supply and demand.

l. The promotion element of the marketing mix is the communication link between the seller and the buyer.

m. Because effective marketing requires large amounts of information, most companies are now developing marketing information systems that collect and store information.

n. The most difficult type of competition faced by businesses is a market in which businesses compete with others that offer very similar products.

o. In a limited-competition situation it is not important for marketers to pay attention to the effectiveness of their mix elements.

MARKETING RESEARCH

1. MASS MARKETING VERSUS TARGET MARKETING

Marketing involves understanding customers and their wants and needs. To demonstrate two views on customers, draw two large circles on a piece of paper. Within each circle, create a collage of pictures. One should contain customers that are all alike and would respond to a mass-marketing approach. The other circle should contain pictures of customers who are different and would respond to target marketing.

2. BRAND NAMES MEAN QUALITY

Brand names often have a significant impact on the consmer's perception of quality. In this exercise, you are to survey 10 people to find their perception of the quality of the following brands: Nike, Kenmore, IBM, Redken, and Del Monte. Use a rating scale where 1 is the worst quality and 10 is the highest qualtiy. Record their answers in the following chart and find an average quality rating for each product.

Respondent	Nike	Kenmore	IBM	Redken	Del Monte
1					
2					
3					
4					
5					
6					
7					
8					
9					
10					
Total					
Average Quality Rating					

MARKETING PLANNING

1. DEVELOPING THE APPROPRIATE MARKETING MIX

Develop a marketing mix for a house painting service. Make sure that you consult the chapter to include all of the variables of each mix element.

2. LOCATING NEW MARKETS

 The study of customers and their wants and needs is primary to running a successful business. As the needs and wants of customers change, marketers are able to identify new markets or customer groups for old products or services.

Now it's your turn to identify new markets. Pick-up trucks, vans, and fast food are products that have been on the market for a long time. Recently, marketers have located new markets for them. For each of these products determine the following:

a. Traditional markets

b. New markets

c. Changes in the marketing mix for new markets

MARKETING MANAGEMENT

1. RELIABLE AUTO SERVICE AND DEE'S DESIGNS

Based on the stories in the chapter, how could John and Dee alter their marketing mixes to make their businesses successful? Be specific and complete in answering.

2. MOM'S TAXI SERVICE

A service that is gaining in popularity is shuttle service for children whose parents work. These shuttle services provide rides to and from after-school activities such as dancing, gymnastics, and music lessons. The service is gaining in popularity as more families are unable to transport their children because the activities occur while both parents are still at work.

Regarding this service, what factors would you consider in:

a. Developing a product mix?

b. Planning your distribution?

c. Setting your price?

d. Creating your promotional plan?

Product/
Service
Planning

Distribution

Marketing-
Information
Management

Economic
Foundations of
Marketing

Fir

Purchasing

*Marketing
and Business
Foundations*

Human Resource
Foundations

Risk

Pricing

Selling

Promotion

Get Ready for Competition

1. Explain how markets can be segmented by geographic location, demographic characteristics, psychographics, product usage, and benefits derived.

2. Understand how to evaluate market potential and calculate market share.

3. List at least four bases for marketing positioning.

4. Demonstrate an understanding of two types of competition and how competition benefits consumers.

5. Describe the types and sources of competitive information.

NEWSLINE

SATURN: GM HAS A WINNER

After a slow start, General Motors' import-fighting Saturn is so hot that the Spring Hill, Tennessee factory can't keep up with the demand. Boasting a high-quality product and a revolutionary no-haggle sales force, Saturn dealers have been selling automobiles at twice the rate of the nearest competitor. Saturn's Vice-President for Sales says the rate has far exceeded GM's expectations.

As foreign competitors continue to flood the U.S. market with new models, Saturn is meeting them head-on. Almost overnight, Saturn has become the highest quality American-made brand, with as few defects as the best imports.

General Motors clearly has a winner on its hands. Now Saturn's growth spurt is forcing some tough decisions at General Motor's Detroit headquarters. To keep up with the new division's momentum, General Motors' managers will have to pump more money into Saturn to keep the investment moving. Saturn probably won't turn a profit until the mid- or late-1990's. The reason for this is the tremendous amount of research and development costs that went into the creation of the Saturn automobile.

Automobile Customer Satisfaction Rating*	
Car:	Score:
Saturn	160
Acura	148
Mercedes Benz	145
Toyota	144
Industry Average	129

*Source: J.D. Powers Survey of New Car Buyers

> **Boasting a high-quality product and a revolutionary no-haggle sales force, Saturn dealers have been selling automobiles at twice the rate of the nearest competitor.**

COMPETITION IS EVERYWHERE

Competition is not new to you. You live in a competitive world. You engage in competition every day. In school you compete for grades. Through sports you compete for points. In your personal life you compete for friends and attention. The goal of competition is to win, to be the best.

When you compete, you gather all of your resources and put them together toward a specific goal. When our favorite football team takes the field, they put their best resources together. They hope to produce a winning effort. The same is true in business. Businesses decide on a goal. Then they direct all their resources and efforts toward achieving it.

In this chapter, we are going to learn about competition and the marketing strategies that businesses use to compete for sales dollars, customers, market share, or whatever goal they have set. We will also discuss market segments and the significant role they play in deciding on competition strategies. And finally we will learn about market positioning strategies; that is, the measurement that competing companies use to gauge how they stand in relation to each other.

MARKET SEGMENTATION

A market segment is a group of individuals or organizations within a larger market that share one or more important characteristics. The characteristics of the market segment result in similar product or service needs. Everyone belongs to many segments. You may belong to a segment of the population who own a CD player and enjoy rock music. You might also belong to a segment that drinks a certain brand of cola or prefers to drive a certain type of car. In school, you belong to various segments depending on how you dress, how you spend your leisure time, or even the importance you place on school and grades.

Businesses use market segmentation to focus their marketing efforts. Consumers can be divided into specific, well-defined segments based on geographic location, demographic characteristics, psychographics, product usage, and benefits derived.

GEOGRAPHIC SEGMENTATION

Geographic segmentation refers to dividing consumers into markets based on where they live. These markets might be as large as a country or as small as a ZIP code designation. Remember that companies vary in size and scope and therefore the group of customers they want to reach also varies in size.

Geographic segmentation is based on the concept that for certain products, people who live in the same geographic area might have the same wants and needs. Consumers who live in Minnesota are more likely to have an interest in cold weather sports than people who live in Oklahoma. A member of a state House of Representatives might want to send a newsletter to the constituents in his or her district. This market could easily be segmented by zip codes.

DEMOGRAPHIC CHARACTERISTICS

Demographics refer to the descriptive characteristics of a market such as age, gender, race, income, and educational level. (See Figure 7-1.) Often marketers want to serve a market segment that has similar demographic characteristics. Shavers for women, skin care products for teen-agers, and hair restoration products for balding me are marketed to specific demographic groups. You belong to many demographic marketing segments. Marketers have segmented you according to your age, gender, ethnic group, hair color, and possibly even your height. They have designed products that meet your needs in each of these categories.

PSYCHOGRAPHICS

Psychographics refers to people's interests and values. You are segmented psychographically by the way you spend your time and make your lifestyle choices. Psychographic segmentation is responsible for bowling alleys, sports stores, swimming pools, big screen televisions, and religious book stores. Do you visit arcades, miniature golf, or teen centers? These products are available because business people have found segments with wants and needs that are satisfied by these products and services.

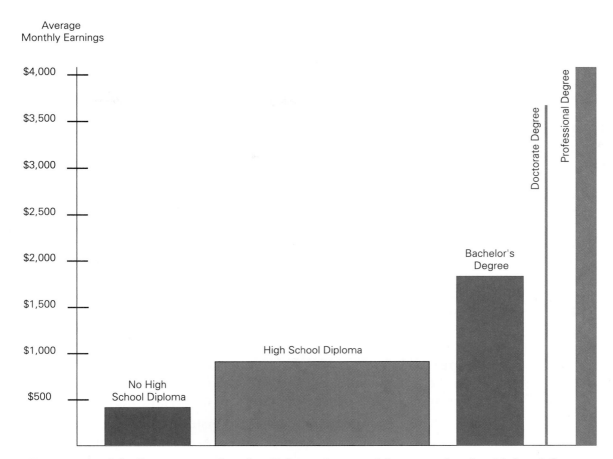

Average Monthly Earnings

- $4,000
- $3,500
- $3,000
- $2,500
- $2,000
- $1,500
- $1,000
- $500

No High School Diploma

High School Diploma

Bachelor's Degree

Doctorate Degree

Professional Degree

Demographic Segmentation by Education and Income in the United States

FIGURE 7-1 ▪ In the U.S. population, the demographic characteristics of education and income are closely linked.

PRODUCT USAGE

Product usage is the frequency that a consumer uses a product. Marketers want to know how frequently people use their products and then divide the population into segments based on frequency of usage. For example, some people drink soft drinks at every meal. There are other people who drink soft drinks once a day, once a week, or not at all. Marketers want to communicate to frequent users that drinking soft drinks often is a great idea and they should continue. Marketers want to communicate to infrequent

users how great it is when they drink the soft drink and perhaps they would like to have the experience more often. By segmenting the market based on usage, business people approach each group differently.

BENEFITS DERIVED

As you learned earlier, each product or service on the market has a value or utility to the consumer. *The benefits derived segmentation technique divides the population into groups depending on the value they receive from the product or service.* An example is shampoo. A visit to your local drug store should convince you that there are many market segments for a product as simple as shampoo. There are segments for consumers with oily hair, dry hair, normal hair, or possibly somewhere in between. There are shampoos for people with dandruff or dry scalps. There are an equal variety of creme rinses on the market and even shampoos with creme rinse added for people who want one-step hair care. Add the number of products on the market to the variety within each product category and you can see the infinite number of segments that are created by benefits derived.

Just as marketers segment the consumer markets, they also segment business markets. Business markets are segmented by geographic location, the size of the business, the key criteria used in making purchasing decisions, or purchasing strategies. The subject of business segmentation and purchasing strategies will be discussed in depth in Chapter 14.

ANALYZING MARKET SEGMENTS

Once market segments have been identified, they must be analyzed. Not all segments present a marketing opportunity. Businesses select market segments that become the focus of their marketing efforts (see Figure 7-2). Market segments should be evaluated on the following criteria:

1. Number of potential consumers
2. Interest in the product or service and other mix elements
3. Money available to make the purchase
4. Ability to communicate with consumers through the promotional mix

Market Segment Analysis

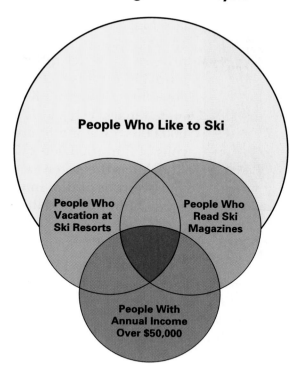

People Who Like to Ski

People Who Vacation at Ski Resorts

People Who Read Ski Magazines

People With Annual Income Over $50,000

FIGURE 7-2 ▪ A company that sells expensive ski equipment through specialty ski shops at ski resorts would be interested in targeting consumers who they can communicate with, who have the income to support the purchase, and who will be shopping at ski resort shops.

Since businesses operate to make a profit, it is important to estimate the value of each market segment. This is called the market potential. *The market potential is the total revenue that can be obtained from the market segment.* Since it is unlikely that one company will attract all customers in a given market, businesses also calculate their market share. *Market share is the portion of the total market potential that each company expects to get in relation to its competitors.* Market share is usually expressed in dollars or percentages.

A typical marketing objective is to increase or maintain its current market share. For example, the total market potential for 35mm film in Boise, Idaho is $3,000,000 per year. Kodak estimates that it can convince 75 percent of the total market to buy its brand. To calculate Kodak's estimated market share in Boise, multiply $3,000,000 x .75 for a figure of $2,250,000.

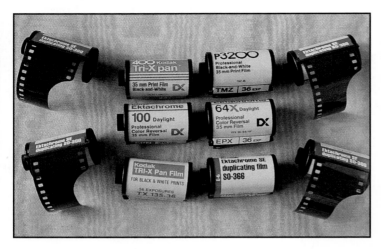

Kodak can also determine the market potential by units instead of dollars. Since the market potential is $3,000,000 and film has an average price of $5.00 per roll, the market potential in units is $3,000,000 ÷ $5 = 600,000 rolls of film. Kodak's estimated market share is 75 percent of 600,000 rolls, for a figure of 450,000 rolls of film (600,000 x .75 = 450,000). Kodak has the potential of selling 450,000 rolls of film in this market segment in Boise, Idaho.

MARKET POSITION

The word *positioning* suggests the relationship among several items. *Market position refers to the unique image of a product or service in a consumer's mind relative to competitive offerings.* Marketers develop specific marketing mix strategies that will influence customers' perceptions of a business' product or service. Businesses know that people usually consider a number of products or services as alternatives when they try to satisfy specific needs.

BASES FOR POSITIONING

Remember that positioning is done to highlight differences between competitors in the mind of the consumer that may influence purchases. What methods can effectively create market positions? Firms use a variety of methods for positioning: attribute, price and quality, use or application, product user, product classification, and competitor (see Figure 7-3).

Attribute

One way of positioning a product is to highlight a product feature or attribute that it possesses. For example, certain toothpastes have ingredients that whiten teeth. The manufacturer says "Our toothpaste does everything every other toothpaste does, and, in addition, it helps make your teeth white." The positioning is accomplished with product characteristics and related promotion.

Market Position		
	Laundry Product A	**Laundry Product B**
Attribute	Cleans quickly and easily	Leaves fresh scent
Price and Quality	Low price, good value	Higher price for highest quality
Use or Application	Use as pre-wash on tough stains	Use for hand-washing sweaters and delicates
Product User	Homemakers' reliable friend	New generation's discovery
Product Classification	Used by Olympic athletes	Used by professional laundries
Competitor	Gets out dirt Product B can't	Gentler on clothing than Product A

FIGURE 7-3 ■ Competitors develop marketing mixes that emphasize the market positions of their products. These laundry products are clearly positioned to appeal to different target markets.

Price and Quality

This position strategy may stress high price as a sign of quality, or emphasize low price as an indication of value. Mercedes Benz doesn't apologize for the high price of its automobiles; instead, it suggests that because they are high-priced they are high-quality. Wal-Mart suggests that its products are as good as, or better than anybody else's plus, they are available for the lowest possible price. Again, the positioning is accomplished by creating the desired level of quality in the product and establishing an appropriate price.

Use or Application

Stressing unique uses or applications can be an effective means of positioning a product with buyers. Arm & Hammer baking soda stresses uses for its products in addition to being an ingredient in baking recipes. Many consumers now believe that Arm & Hammer baking soda is an effective product with uses ranging from deodorizing your refrigerator to brushing your teeth.

Product User

This positioning strategy encourages use of a product or service by associating a personality or type of user with the product. Pepsi Cola, for a time, suggested that Pepsi products were con-

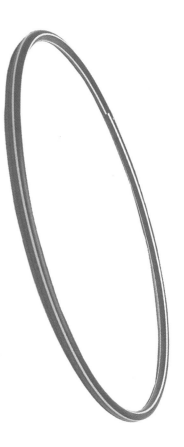

sumed by a "Pepsi Generation," and this generation was portrayed as young and active.

Product Classification

When positioning according to product class, the objective is to associate the product with a particular category of products. Railroads, for example, attempt to imitate the look, service, and scheduling associated with airlines. Pork, as the "other white meat," is positioned with turkey and chicken to create an image of a healthier, leaner product.

Competitor

Sometimes marketers make an effort to demonstrate how they are positioned against competitors that hold a strong market position. Seven-Up's "Uncola Campaign" is a good example of an effort to position its product against cola soft drinks. Anytime you see an advertisement comparing one product against one or more competitor's products or services, you can assume that a competitor positioning strategy is being used.

SELECTING A POSITIONING STRATEGY

All businesses need to develop a positioning strategy. A positioning strategy will outline how a company is going to present its product or service to the consumer and how it will compete in the marketplace. Positioning strategies usually revolve around three major areas:

1. Consumer perceptions

2. Competitors in the marketplace

3. Changes in the business environment

Consumer Perceptions

Consumer perceptions are the images consumers have of competing goods and services in the marketplace. The objective is for marketers to position their products so that they appeal to the desires and perceptions of a target market. A group of consumers that has a distinct idea of the image desired for a product or service might represent a target market. A firm will do well when the attributes of its products are perceived by consumers as being close to the consumers' ideal image. Over the years, Hershey has done an excellent job of responding to consumer perceptions. Hershey produces a product perceived by many consumers as an ideal chocolate bar.

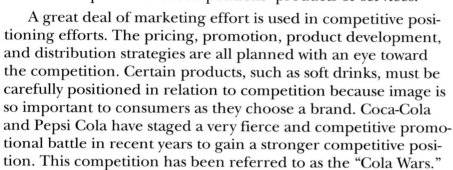

Competition

Businesses are concerned about the perception consumers have of an organization in relation to its competitors. The ideal situation is when consumers perceive a business's products to be superior to its competitions' products or services.

A great deal of marketing effort is used in competitive positioning efforts. The pricing, promotion, product development, and distribution strategies are all planned with an eye toward the competition. Certain products, such as soft drinks, must be carefully positioned in relation to competition because image is so important to consumers as they choose a brand. Coca-Cola and Pepsi Cola have staged a very fierce and competitive promotional battle in recent years to gain a stronger competitive position. This competition has been referred to as the "Cola Wars."

Business Environment

Organizations must be aware of changes in the business environment that might affect the position of its products or services. These environmental elements include new products coming onto the market, changing consumer needs, new technology, negative publicity, and resource availability. Manufacturers of golf clubs have been significantly affected by the introduction of graphite as a material used in shaft construction. Ice cream companies are well aware of the effects of fat in diets. And colleges have discovered that they must respond to the needs of non-traditional students; that is, students over 25 years of age. In each case, these environmental changes can affect the way in which goods and services are positioned.

COMPETING FOR MARKET SEGMENTS

Market segments are important because they contain the potential customers for marketers' products. Competition is the rivalry between two or more businesses to secure a dominant position in a market segment.

As you learned previously, resources are limited. This includes the consumer dollars available to be spent on products or services. Businesses are in competition for these scarce dollars. In order to compete successfully, businesses must develop a product that meets the market segment's wants and needs. They must also develop a marketing mix that fits the unique characteristics of the market segment.

TYPES OF COMPETITION FOR POSITIONING

Just as there are different types of market segments and positioning strategies, there are different types of competition businesses face when positioning their products. Successful competitive strategies rely on the ability of the business to define a market position and reach a market segment. There are two major types of competition: (1) direct versus indirect competition and (2) price versus non-price competition.

Direct versus Indirect Competition

Direct competition is competition in a market segment with businesses that offer the same type of product or service. (See Figure 7-4.) This is a common form of competition. We are all familiar with Holiday Inn and Ramada Inn competing directly with each other. We have also seen laundry detergent advertisements where the two leading brands are compared, by name. This is direct competition.

Businesses which decide to compete directly must first decide who their competition is. For example, McDonald's has obvious competitors such as Hardee's, Burger King, and Wendy's. It also competes against other fast food restaurants such as KFC, Taco Bell, P.D. Quix, and locally-owned fast food restaurants. These are all direct competitors even though they may offer different menu items.

McDonald's competes head-on with these businesses. It tells

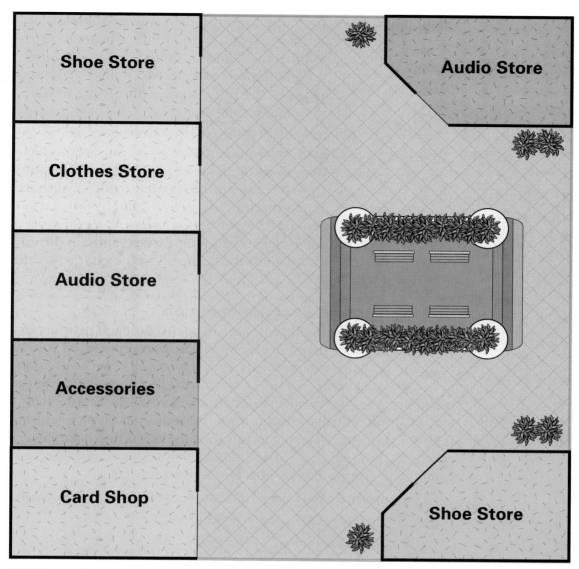

FIGURE 7-4 ▪ Shoe stores compete directly with each other in large malls. At the same time, shoe stores compete indirectly with music stores for consumer dollars.

consumers why Big Macs taste better, are economical, and easily available. McDonald's lets consumers know why they should buy McDonald's products rather than someone else's.

Indirect competition occurs when a business competes with a product that is outside its product classification group. For example, if McDonald's promotes its products as easy and convenient to obtain, then it might be in competition with meals offered at the deli counters of many grocery stores. McDonald's might also find itself competing with microwaveable meals. Remember that you have limited dollars to spend on this meal and you only want to eat lunch one time. How does McDonald's compete with all these similar businesses in the marketplace?

The marketing managers at McDonald's have some important decisions to make. One of the first decisions they must make is what features of their products they wish to highlight or what benefits they wish to emphasize. Remember that each market segment places value on different things and each business must appeal to the characteristics of this segment.

Price versus Non-Price Competition

Since there are limited dollars to spend on each product or service, some marketers decide to emphasize price when they compete. *Rivalry among firms on the basis of price and value is called price competition.* Look in your local newspaper at the various grocery store advertisements and you will see an excellent example of price competition. Restaurants use price competition with their lunch specials. Another example of price competition is air fares. When one airline reduces its prices, usually the competing airlines also lower their fares.

The opposite of price competition is non-price competition. *Non-price competition occurs when businesses decide to emphasize factors of their marketing mix other than price, such as quality, brand, location, or service.* Non-price competition occurs for several reasons. First of all, some businesses have price controls. An insurance company may not be able to compete based on price because prices are regulated by the government. Therefore, they communicate with their customers about non-price issues to increase usage.

Another reason a company might choose to use non-price competition is because its product is higher priced than the competitors. These higher-priced companies will want to communicate to their segment about quality, service, or convenience.

Non-price competition is effective when the market segment values something other than price. The consumers must recognize a unique quality in the product which leads to a product preference regardless of the price. These qualities might be service, quality, credit, location, guarantees, or a unique image.

A GLOBAL VISION

JAPAN'S POSITION IN ASIA

Japan has been a world leader in the development of various forms of electronic technology for the last three decades. Four rapidly growing Asian competitors are challenging Japan in this market: Hong Kong, Singapore, South Korea, and Taiwan. Taiwan's electric appliance maker, Sampo Corporation, turns out everything from refrigerators to washers. With 35,000 employees and $420 million in sales, Sampo dreams of one day becoming the dominant competitor in a global market. However, Sampo has been unable to break into the Japanese market, which is by far Asia's largest. Nor has Sampo been able to break free of dependence on Japanese technology to make such products as TVs and VCRs.

A few years ago experts expected Taiwan and South Korea to give the Japanese a run for their money. Government officials in both countries targeted key industries for development. They supplied companies with capital and shut out competing products from abroad. Exports grew quickly and there were predictions that Taiwan and Korea would bring the competition to Japan's own shores. Japan hasn't let that happen.

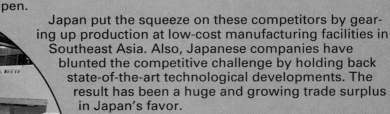

Japan put the squeeze on these competitors by gearing up production at low-cost manufacturing facilities in Southeast Asia. Also, Japanese companies have blunted the competitive challenge by holding back state-of-the-art technological developments. The result has been a huge and growing trade surplus in Japan's favor.

Japan understands the competitive environment in which it is working, and has analyzed the competition within that environment. It has learned a great deal about competing in that environment and is appropriately positioned to remain competitive.

Source: Adapted from "How Japan Keeps the Tigers in a Cage," Business Week, August, 17, 1992. pp. 98 d-h.

BENEFITS OF COMPETITION

There are many benefits of competition. One benefit is that the consumer receives the best price for products available. Competition forces businesses to offer reasonable prices for the products and services that we use. If businesses want to be successful, they must price their products in line with others in the same classification. As a result, the consumer is given the most value for the least amount of money.

A second benefit of competition is that it encourages improvements in products with the addition of unique features and benefits. Each company is looking for a way to make its product distinctive so that it attracts the attention of the market segment. The benefit to the consumer is that we get the very best products.

Another benefit of competition is that businesses are always looking for new and improved products to put into the marketplace to compete with their competitors. Bicycle manufacturers saw a need for a bicycle halfway between a traditional ten speed *English* bicycle, and a mountain bike and created something that has come to be known as a cross-breed bicycle. As consumers we have the advantage of continually having the newest products available to us.

Finally, competition offers consumers the benefit of a wide variety of products from which to choose. The market segments are so diverse that businesses make sure that there are products to meet all our wants and needs. An example of this is the range of television channels available to most viewers. Today, most of us can receive over 30 television channels and soon we will be able to receive over 100. Each channel is competing with the other for viewers. Viewers benefit from having a large selection available to watch.

LEARNING ABOUT THE COMPETITION

In order to compete effectively, it makes sense that a business find out all it can about the competition. Athletic teams have used scouts for many years. These scouts attend the competitor's games to analyze their strategies, tactics, strengths, and weaknesses. This information is used to prepare their teams to be more effective competitors.

The same is true in business. In order to compete effectively, businesses make an effort to learn as much as they can about their competitor's products, services, strengths, weaknesses, competitive strategies, and new product development.

TYPES OF INFORMATION NEEDED

All marketers develop each element of the marketing mix to best meet the wants and needs of their consumers. It is helpful for businesses to know how competitors are developing each element of the marketing mix and what strategies and tactics they are going to implement.

Price

When businesses are in direct competition, they need to know the competitors' pricing strategies. Are they planning a sale or are they going to raise the price and add features, options, or additional services that will benefit the consumer? For example, if Chrysler reduces the price of all of its cars and trucks so there is a significant difference between their prices and the competitors', will that cause the consumer to consistently choose Chrysler brands over other brands? For some people, the answer would be *yes*, because for that segment, price is the most significant factor. For others, the answer would be *no* because there is a value in a variety of automobile features that causes us to buy the competitors' products regardless of price.

Distribution

The second area to gain information about is competitors' distribution systems. Does the competition have wide distribution or selective distribution? Are they planning to change their distribution strategies? Remember we learned that part of satisfying the wants and needs of the consumer is to have the product in the right place when the customer wants to purchase it. If the competition is planning on distribution changes, their products might be more convenient to purchase than yours. It is important to know what distribution strategies your competition is planning.

Product/Service Planning

The third type of information that is helpful to know about when planning a competitive strategy is the product/service planning process. Is your competition planning a new product introduction and do you have a product to compete effectively with it? When Pepsi introduced a clear cola, Coke did not put a comparable product on the market to compete with it. Possibly they decided it was not a significant competitor because the market segment is not large enough, or they believed the product would not succeed. It is important to know what changes and additions your competition is making in their product line.

Promotion

A fourth area that is important to gather competitive information about is promotional strategies. Are they planning a large campaign, planning new tactics, using a new medium, or changing the times they advertise? When Sears puts coupons for carpet cleaning in newspapers, it affects the competition's business. If the competition is aware that Sears is planning this tactic, they can counter with coupons of their own or other offers that will keep them equally competitive.

IN THE SPOTLIGHT

AMERICAN GREETINGS HOLDS ITS OWN

Five years ago, American Greetings Corporation's earnings were being destroyed in a price war with its two major competitors, Hallmark Cards and Gibson Greetings. Since then, American Greetings has turned around its earnings by cutting costs, improving customer service, and avoiding direct competition in the price arena. As a result, earnings have more than doubled in a recent five-year period.

American Greetings is targeting narrow consumer segments, while continuing to improve services to retailers. One move that helped American Greetings beat their competition was the purchase of Custom Expressions Incorporated. Custom Expressions kiosks, called CreateaCard, allow customers to design and print their own cards in minutes. Because of its appeal to non-traditional card buyers, such as men and young people, the company expects CreateaCard to reach $500 million in annual revenue within the next ten years.

The competition in the greeting card industry is fierce. Greeting card manufacturers meet this competition by listening carefully to customers' needs and wants. Recently, American Greetings launched a series of ambitious customer service programs. The goal was to differentiate it from its competitors without cutting prices. For example, the new retail creative services department developed seasonal displays to use throughout stores, not just in the card area. Evidently, it's paying off. In the most recent year reported, American Greetings card sales grew by an industry-leading ten percent.

Source: Adapted from "This Stock Promises Many Happy Returns," Money, December Forecast, 1993, p. 53.

Competitor's Market Position

There are additional factors that affect each business' competitive edge. For example, is the competition planning to enter markets in other countries? Has the competition located a new and unserved market segment? Can your company reach that market segment?

Is the competition in a good financial position? Do they have the funds available to spend on effective promotional strategies? Do they have the money available to develop new products and improve old ones? Do they have the financial flexibility to respond to pricing changes? Have your competitors located new suppliers that will make a significant difference in how their product is produced, how quickly it can be delivered, or how much it costs?

All of these factors significantly affect the competitive position among businesses. They can make the difference between a product or service being successful in the marketplace or failing.

SOURCES OF INFORMATION

Competing companies are not going to willingly exchange this essential, competitive information. Competing businesses must therefore find ways of obtaining information (see Figure 7-5). Sometimes it is fairly easy and sometimes it is difficult. *The process of gaining competitive market information is called marketing intelligence.*

Businesses engage in the following activities to gain information about their competition:

1. Ask salespeople to be alert to information about competitors' products, prices, and anticipated changes.

2. Buy competitors' products. In this way they can examine the products carefully and learn from studying them.

3. Shop in competitors' businesses or hire consultants to shop for them. It is well known that competitors are in and out of one another's businesses frequently, seeking information about pricing, promotion, and other strategies.

4. Subscribe to information services. There are business services that provide information about the activities of companies in an indus-

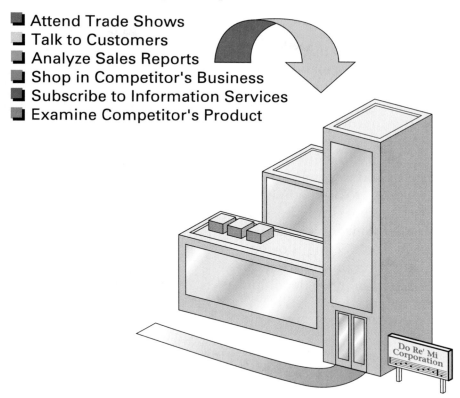

Marketing Intelligence

- Attend Trade Shows
- Talk to Customers
- Analyze Sales Reports
- Shop in Competitor's Business
- Subscribe to Information Services
- Examine Competitor's Product

FIGURE 7-5 ▪ A business gains information about its competitor's strategy in order to compete more effectively and better serve its target market.

try. Trade associations are a good example of this. The National Restaurant Management Association and the National Retail Merchants Association are just two examples of trade associations that offer information services to their members.

5. Study customers. As part of market research efforts, discussed in Chapter 9, a great deal can be learned about competition.

6. Attend trade shows. Trade shows are usually held in conjunction with conventions where vendors show their products. For example, a grocer's convention might have a trade show that includes the latest in freezer units. If you were one of the vendors attending the trade show you would be able to determine what your competitors were displaying.

COLLECTING AND ANALYZING INFORMATION

Businesses do not collect competitive information randomly. Large businesses have staffs of people whose responsibility it is to work with marketing intelligence. Their objectives are to identify the strengths and weaknesses of key competitors, to assess their current marketing strategies, and to predict their future actions. The job of collecting, storing, and analyzing this information is discussed in more detail in later chapters.

REVIEW

Competition is an integral part of the free market system. The benefits that consumers derive from competition are low prices, high quality, innovative products, and product/service variety. In order for businesses to compete effectively, they must know who their customers are and how to segment the market into groups of consumers with similar wants and needs.

To compete in today's markets, businesses must know several things about their own products and services. First, they must know their market position. Second, businesses must know the market potential. Third, they must be able to calculate their individual market shares.

Since consumers have a limited amount of money to spend on products and services, businesses compete with each other for the same consumer dollars. Sometimes they compete with businesses offering the same products and services and sometimes they compete with businesses outside their industry.

After businesses have determined who their competitors are, it is important for them to learn as much as possible about their competitors' products and marketing mix strategies. This information can be obtained by buying competitors' products, asking salespeople, collecting information at trade shows, talking to customers, or purchasing marketing intelligence.

MARKETING FOUNDATIONS

1. **MATCHING**

   a. Benefits derived

   b. Demographics

   c. Geographics

   d. Market potential

e. Market position

f. Market segment

g. Product usage

h. Psychographics

1. A group of individuals or organizations that share one or more important characteristics.

2. The total revenue that can be obtained from the target market.

3. The unique image of a product or service in a consumer's mind relative to the competition.

4. The value a customer receives from a product or service.

5. The frequency that a product is consumed.

6. How people spend their time or what gives value to their lives.

7. The term that refers to the characteristics of a market, such as age, hair color, height, and sex.

8. The term used to divide consumers into groups based on where they live.

2. **TRUE-FALSE**

a. In the business world, organizations always compete for the highest sales dollars.

b. A market segment is always defined by its physical characteristics.

c. Every segment that is identified becomes a potential marketing opportunity for a business.

d. In order to compete effectively with other businesses, marketers must create a unique image of their product or service in the consumer's mind.

e. Market positioning is most effective when it is based on price.

f. Marketers do not need to know how consumers are using their products, as long as they are using them.

g. The business environment is relatively unimportant for marketers because every business operates in the same changing environment.

h. An example of indirect competition would be a bowling alley and a video arcade.

i. The type of competition that stresses convenient location or ample parking is called attribute competition.

j. There are no consumer benefits to competition, only benefits to businesses in terms of larger sales volume.

k. In order to compete effectively, it is important to learn as much as possible about your competitor's marketing strategies.

l. Marketing intelligence is the process of gaining information about the competition.

m. Most marketing intelligence techniques are illegal.

n. A trade publication is an example of an information service that a business could use to gain competitor information.

o. Most businesses schedule information gathering on their competitors in the spring and the fall.

MARKETING RESEARCH

1. CALCULATING MARKET POTENTIAL AND MARKET SHARE

A medium-size city in southern Alabama has three major grocery stores that have 94 percent of the total market. The remaining 6 percent are small, locally-owned stores. It is estimated that the total market potential for this town is $137,500,000. There are approximately 25,000 potential customers in this town.

a. What is the total market potential in dollars for the three major grocery stores?

b. What is the total market potential in dollars for the small, locally-owned stores?

c. What is the market share in dollars for each major grocery store if they all have an equal share of the market?

d. One of the major grocery stores has recently remodeled and expanded, and has begun to stay open 24 hours. As a result of these changes, this store has increased its market share to 45 percent of the total market. What is its new market share in dollars?

e. Assuming the locally-owned stores still have 6 percent of the market, what market share is left for the two major stores (in dollars)?

2. IDENTIFYING COMPETITION

There are several different ways to compete in the marketplace. The method chosen by a business is dependent on the type of business, product or service, and the type and amount of competition.

a. Locate five newspaper advertisements that use price competition and five advertisements that stress non-price competition.

b. Cut and paste the advertisements on separate sheets of paper.

c. How do the businesses using price competition characterize or draw attention to the price? For example, do they claim to have the lowest prices in town?

d. What buyer benefits do the businesses using non-price competition emphasize?

MARKETING PLANNING

1. POSITIONING YOUR PRODUCT OR SERVICE

It is important to position a product or service in relation to your competitors. The objective of positioning is to cause your product or service to occupy a prominent position in your customer's mind in comparison to the competition.

Using the list below, decide which of the six positioning techniques would be most important for each product/ service. After you have made your selection, give a reason why you selected that technique.

- Hospital's emergency services
- Imported perfume
- Office desks
- Welding classes
- Semi trucks
- Household cleaning detergent

2. GATHERING INFORMATION ABOUT YOUR COMPETITION

 An important part of any marketing strategy is knowing what your competition is doing. It is important to understand your competitors' goals and strategies. Using the lists of types of information needed in the section about learning about your competition, determine what type of competitor information would be needed for each of the following businesses. Explain why the information would be important.

- Pizza delivery
- Inter-city bus lines
- Travel agency
- Locally-owned grocery store
- Country radio station in a larger city

MARKETING MANAGEMENT

1. SPEAKING TO SMALL BUSINESS PEOPLE

Borderline, Texas is a city with a population of 120,000 people. There is an association of downtown business people called the Borderline Business Bureau. It is an organization that is interested in learning as much as they can about marketing concepts and practices. They have lunch together once a month and accompanying this lunch is usually a guest speaker.

Assume you have been invited to speak to their organization this month about positioning in the market. Prepare a presentation, including visual aids, for a speech to the Borderline Business Bureau. The talk and discussion are scheduled to last approximately ten minutes.

Your presentation could include a discussion of positioning, the results they could expect with effective positioning, and a discussion and examples of the six positioning techniques. Your visual aides should emphasize any aspect of your speech.

Your presentation should include a portion for audience participation. You might wish to ask your audience to name products or services and then determine the most appropriate basis of positioning for those products and services.

2. A PRICING ENTREPRENEUR

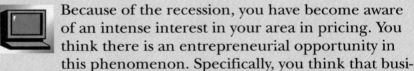

Because of the recession, you have become aware of an intense interest in your area in pricing. You think there is an entrepreneurial opportunity in this phenomenon. Specifically, you think that businesses and organizations in your area would pay for the service of receiving competitive price information. You have decided to open a business with a friend called Partners In Pricing. It is your idea that PIP will use various methods to determine the prices of an assortment of products and services as needed by customers.

You will offer the service of finding out what competitors' current prices are for products and services. You will comparison shop in stores; call for prices on the telephone; read advertisements in newspapers, magazines, and circulars; and visit with business and organization owners directly to acquire this information. In preparing your own promotional material, describe how you would use each of the positioning techniques for PIP. That is, what attributes would you claim to have, what is unique about your price and quality, and how will your customers be able to use the information? Also, who are your competitors, how would you classify yourself in the larger arena of business, and who will be your most prominent users?

Use your answers to these questions to prepare a three-fold brochure describing the services you have to offer that you might mail to all of the members of your local Chamber of Commerce.

Marketing Planning

Product/
Service
Planning

Distribution

Marketing-
Information
Management

Economic
Foundations of
Marketing

Fi

Purchasing

*Marketing
and Business
Foundations*

Human Resource
Foundations

Ris

Pricing

Selling

Promotion

Marketing Begins with Customers

OBJECTIVES

1. Describe the importance of understanding consumer behavior.

2. Demonstrate an understanding of consumer wants and needs.

3. Distinguish between rational, emotional, and patronage buying motives and how they impact consumer and business buying behavior.

4. Review the steps in the consumer decision-making process.

5. Explain how consumers and businesses use routine, limited, and extensive decision-making.

NEWSLINE

SONY GETS CLOSE TO CONSUMERS

To get an insight into consumers' behavior, Sony developed a "playground" for customers. This electronics playground in Chicago provides Sony with an opportunity to observe and listen to their customers.

The two-story showroom is designed to expose customers to Sony's technology in an inviting environment. Customers are not afraid to ask questions or touch the equipment. The gallery is located on Chicago's Michigan Avenue. This is the city's main shopping street for upscale purchasers.

Sony's products are displayed in lifestyle settings, such as a bedroom or a home office. The setting encourages consumers to interact with the products. If consumers can't bear to part with something they have found and liked, they can buy it on the spot.

The showroom employees do not push Sony products. Their main

> **Sony's products are displayed in lifestyle settings, such as a bedroom or a home office.**

responsibility is to keep an eye on which products elicit oohs and aahs and which products are passed over without a fleeting glance. Sony expects to use this information to develop better marketing strategies.

The showroom staff has discovered some interesting things. One of the biggest surprises has been watching consumers discover products that have been on the market for quite awhile. From this Sony

can determine in which markets it is successful in advertising, and which ones it is not.

> **One of the biggest surprises has been watching consumers discover products that have been on the market for quite awhile.**

CONSUMER BEHAVIOR

If there is one idea that is key to understanding marketing it is that marketing begins with customers. The marketing concept states that marketers must be responsive to customers. Successful businesses are those that continually consider the consumers' wants and needs.

This chapter will describe how important it is to understand consumers and their buying behavior. It will suggest ways to analyze customer needs and to use the information to make wise marketing decisions.

You cannot implement the marketing concept without understanding customers. However, understanding customers is not simple. *The study of consumers and how they make decisions is called consumer behavior.* Consumer behavior includes the factors that influence the purchase and use of goods and services.

FINAL CONSUMERS

Most people picture a customer as someone who enters a retail store, purchases a product, takes it home, and uses it. For example, when you buy a notebook, take it to school, and use it in your marketing class, you are a final consumer. *A final consumer buys a product or service for personal use.*

BUSINESS CONSUMERS

A second category of consumers is called the business consumer. *A business consumer buys goods and services to produce and market other goods and services or for resale.* An example of a business consumer is the notebook manufacturer. The manufacturer buys paper, glue, ink, wire and other raw materials to produce the notebook. The manufacturer also purchases cardboard, staples, tape, and ink to produce the packaging. In each case, when the manufacturer purchases materials to manufacture and package notebooks, it is a business consumer.

The notebook manufacturer also buys products and services that are used

in the day-to-day operation of the business. The company purchases paper, pencils, security services, cleaning services, computers, furniture, and all the items needed for business operations. Even though it consumes the products and services, it is still a business consumer.

CONSUMERS' WANTS AND NEEDS

All consumers have wants and needs. *A want is an unfulfilled desire.* Consumers want pizzas, BMWs, vacation trips to France, a different hair color, a new CD player, or tickets to the Super Bowl.

A need is anything you require to live. Needs are considered to be the root of all human behavior. You need nutritious food, a good night's sleep, shelter from the weather, air to breathe, and clean water.

HIERARCHY OF NEEDS

Abraham Maslow's classic work on motivation theory has helped marketers immensely in their study of needs[1]. Maslow, a psychologist, identified five areas of needs that people have (see Figure 8-1). They are physiological, security, social, esteem, and self-actualization.

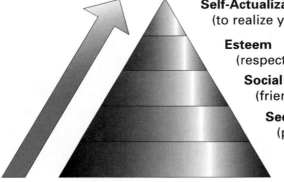

Self-Actualization
(to realize your potential)

Esteem
(respect and recognition)

Social
(friends, love, belonging)

Security
(physical safety and economic security)

Physiological
(food, sleep, water, shelter, air)

FIGURE 8-1 ■ Maslow's hierarchy of needs illustrates the progression people follow in satisfying needs.

[1]Abraham H. Maslow, "A Theory of Human Motivation," *Psychological Review,* Volume 50, (1942), pp. 370–396

Maslow believed that these groups of needs are satisfied in a hierarchy and that the needs of people change as they satisfy the needs at each level. Everyone must satisfy the physiological needs; they are not options. We must eat, sleep, and breathe to exist. After these needs are generally satisfied, a person can start to satisfy security needs. While it's important to be secure, it is only important to be secure after you have satisfied your physiological needs. To go one level higher, our social needs are certainly important, but only after we meet physiological and security needs.

Esteem needs are satisfied by gaining respect and recognition from others. Running for student council might be an attempt to satisfy esteem needs. The need for self-actualization usually involves intellectual growth, creativity, and accomplishment. Attending college or taking music lessons might satisfy needs for self-actualization.

Marketers must recognize that people are at different levels on the hierarchy of needs. Some people are focusing on security needs while others are satisfying esteem needs. Regardless of what the needs individuals are attempting to satisfy, marketers must identify them if they want to satisfy them.

Housing provides a good example of how consumers' needs differ depending on where they are on Maslow's hierarchy of needs. The physiological need for housing is served by a house that provides protection from the weather. The need for security would be provided by a house that is in a fairly safe neighborhood and has a security system. For a family with young children, social needs might be satisfied by a house that is in a neighborhood with lots of young families. A house might satisfy esteem needs if it is well-maintained and the yard is landscaped. Self-actualization needs might be satisfied by a home that is designed and built by the owner.

BUYING MOTIVES

As we decide we want or need products or services, we are motivated by what marketers call buying motives. *Buying motives are the reasons that we buy.* There are three categories of buying motives that drive consumers to purchase products or services or respond to ideas: emotional motives, rational motives, and patronage motives.

EMOTIONAL MOTIVES

Emotional motives are reasons to purchase based on feelings, beliefs, or attitudes. Forces of love, affection, guilt, fear, or passion often compel consumers to buy. Marketers realize that emotional motives are very strong. For example, Hallmark card advertisements encourage us to buy greeting cards because of love and affection. Folger's presents drinking coffee as a relaxing social experience. AT&T uses reach out and touch someone to give emotions to an inanimate object, a telephone.

Fear is also a motivator that is used to encourage us to buy products. We buy security systems because we are motivated by the fear of being robbed. We buy cars with optional air bags because we are motivated by fear of injury. Marketers understand our emotional motivations and use them to present their products to us.

RATIONAL MOTIVES

Sometimes emotional motivation is not appropriate or effective. We are also motivated by rational reasons. *Rational motives are reasons to buy based on facts or logic.* Rational motives include factors such as saving money, durability, and saving time. Often the products or services we purchase with rational motives are expensive. We can be swayed to purchase computer equipment because it is more powerful, faster, has more memory, includes a modem, and has the best graphics. These are all attributes that affect the function of the computer. Automobile purchases are rational decisions when we consider features such as price, gas mileage, warranties, or extended mileage protection packages. However, it is easy to understand how rational motives can

A GLOBAL VISION

REACHING THE MARKET

The Spanish-speaking population of the United States is growing at a steady rate. Does the Hispanic population have special characteristics that require special marketing efforts and approaches? There is no one formula for marketing to Hispanics, a diverse and dynamic cultural group. However, the language, values, lifestyles, and social systems that are shared by the Hispanic culture can influence promotional strategies.

The following suggestions are based on comments from Hispanic respondents in focus groups that tested advertisements for several products and services.

1. Testimonials. Hispanics, like most cultural groups, tend to find testimonials believable when used with settings that Hispanics can identify with in their everyday lives.

2. Happiness. Hispanics tend to enjoy being portrayed as upbeat, colorful, and lively. Music is an excellent vehicle to deliver these characteristics in advertising.

3. Family. Cooking and caring for the home and family remain strong Hispanic values. Advertisements that convey a sense of pride in pleasing and providing the best for families are generally effective.

4. Language. A significant portion of the Hispanic market consists of second- and third-generation family members whose fluency in Spanish has dwindled. Advertising copy that is written in simple, informal, "spoken" Spanish works best.

5. Dubbing. Hispanics generally reject ads that are English-speaking versions with a Spanish translation dubbed in.

Marketers who target Hispanic markets should develop promotional strategies that are responsive to the wants and needs of the consumers. While individual markets will have differences, Hispanics want recognition of their culture and values.

Source: Adapted from "Some Approaches Better Than Others When Targeting Hispanics," Marketing News, *Volume 26, Number 11.*

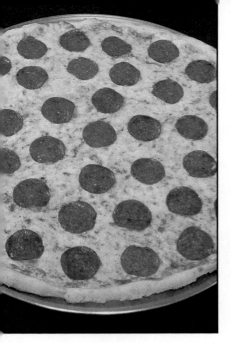

turn into emotional motives when we really want that red Corvette.

Business people try to avoid basing purchases on emotional motives. It does not make good business sense. Business people base their purchasing decisions on rational motives. The best price, fastest delivery, best credit terms, and reliable products are rational motives that appeal to business consumers.

PATRONAGE MOTIVES

The third type of consumer motivation is the patronage motive. *The patronage motive is based on loyalty.* It encourages consumers to purchase at a *particular* business or to buy a *particular* brand. Consumers develop patronage motives for various reasons. They might like the low prices, high quality, friendly staff, great customer service or convenient location. Patronage purchasing is not limited to large, expensive purchases. It can

involve a grocery store, gas station, hair stylist, department store, or brand of vegetables. The important point to remember is that people who are motivated by patronage are very loyal supporters of the product, service, or brand. Businesses encourage and cultivate these patronage motives so they will have less competition.

BUYING BEHAVIOR

Buying behavior describes the decision processes and actions of consumers as they buy and use services and products. Marketers know it is advantageous to understand the process customers go through when selecting goods or services so they can assist the customers in making the best possible decisions.

THE CONSUMER DECISION-MAKING PROCESS

A consumer goes through five steps when making a purchase decision (see Figure 8-2). *The consumer decision-making process is the process by which consumers collect information and make choices among alternatives.* Decision-making, as it applies to a specific purchase, moves through problem recogni-

The Decision-Making Process

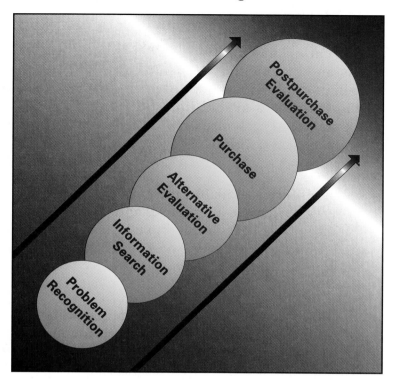

FIGURE 8-2 ■ The consumer decision-making process describes how consumers make purchasing decisions.

tion, information search, alternative evaluation, purchase, and postpurchase evaluation.

Problem Recognition

First the consumer must recognize a need, desire, or problem. For example, in order to play the piano, you recognize the need to find a good piano instructor. Once you recognize the need, you are on the decision-making path to buy a product or service.

Information Search

Next the consumer gathers information about alternative solutions. After you recognize the need to hire a piano instructor, you talk to your parents, teachers, or friends about piano teachers. You might look through the phone book or search the classified section of the newspaper. You might check the bulletin boards at the library. You might ask at a music store or call the music department of the local college.

Evaluation of Alternatives

After gathering information the consumer evaluates the various alternatives to determine which is best. Sometimes this involves summarizing the information, comparing the pros and cons of each choice, making tradeoffs between price and various options, and ranking the alternatives. Evaluating piano instructors might involve determining whom you can afford, what hours the instructor is available, how you will get to the lesson, and the reputation of each instructor. Based on these evaluations, you will make a decision.

Purchase

If a suitable choice is available, the consumer selects the product or service from the alternatives and makes the purchase. At this stage you have decided to take lessons at the local music store for half an hour every week. You call the instructor and register for a convenient time.

Postpurchase Evaluation

At this point the consumer judges the satisfaction or dissatisfaction with the product or service purchased. You have now had several lessons, can play some simple songs, have worked with the instructor, and can tell how lessons are fitting into your schedule. If you are satisfied with your lessons, you will probably continue and may recommend your instructor to your family and friends. If you are dissatisfied, you will probably find a new instructor or quit taking lessons.

Recently, marketers have been paying more attention to postpurchase satisfaction. The use of toll-free telephone numbers for customer service departments lets consumers easily call and ask questions or express concerns on products ranging from toothpaste to vinyl siding. Businesses strive to be responsive to consumer concerns by providing this service. The goal is to resolve customers' concerns and increase their satisfaction.

IN THE SPOTLIGHT

THE SCALES ARE TIPPING

The United States is a nation of dieters. Diet foods, diet books, diet centers, diet therapy, diet clubs, and just plain diets are popular. Spurred by health and vanity motives, we go to great lengths to control the kinds and amounts of food and drink we consume.

There is some evidence that Americans are getting tired of this dieting craze. At a demonstration against dieting, 50 women trashed their bathroom scales while they carried banners that said "Scales Are For Fish, Not Women."

A scientific study carried out at Boston University found that genes and body type, not dieting, are the key to trimness. In another development, a National Institutes of Health panel revealed that most of the people they studied who lost weight through an assortment of diets, regained the weight after five years. Many put it back on within one year.

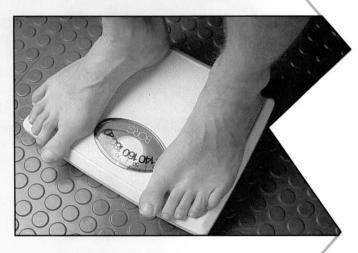

Some marketers face legal consequences for making claims regarding the ability of their products to help consumers shed pounds. Three separate marketers of liquid diet programs reached agreements with the Federal Trade Commission (FTC) to settle charges that they made deceptive and unsubstantiated claims.

This anti-diet movement could have an enormous effect on the diet industry. You can be sure that marketers to the diet-conscious will be carefully watching these developments.

Source:"Anti-diet Forces, Health Report, The Sale of Weight Loss Programs," Marketing News, *Volume 26, Number 11.*

INFLUENCES ON THE CONSUMER DECISION-MAKING PROCESS

Knowing what influences a customer's buying decision is helpful to marketers. As we learned previously, in order to remain profitable, businesses must provide customers with products and services that meet their wants and needs. By understanding what motivates and influences customer purchases, businesses are able to provide the products and services at the right place and the right time.

Many internal and external factors influence our purchase decisions. These factors include personality, social class, cultural environment, and reference group.

Personality

The first influence is personality. *Personalities are well-defined, enduring patterns of behavior.* Personalities influence buying decisions because everyone has individual preferences based on their patterns of behavior. Using the example of a car purchase, personality influences the type of vehicle you prefer. You might be the flashy convertible type, the laid-back pick-up truck type, or the conservative four-door sedan type. Do you prefer a particular style, color, or perhaps a certain wheel cover? All these decisions are influenced by your personality.

Social Class

A second influence is social class. *Social class refers to the lifestyle, values, and beliefs that are common to a group of people.* Often social classes are identified by income level or neighborhood. Your social class affects whether you have the money or available credit to purchase a car at all and whether your choice will be acceptable to those around you. Social class exerts a strong influence on your desire for particular types and brands of goods and services.

Cultural Environment

The third influence is cultural environment. *Culture is a set of beliefs or attitudes that are passed on from generation to generation.* In many parts of the United States, high school students often have a car at their disposal. This would be very different in China, where high school students rarely have access to a car.

Reference Groups

Reference groups are groups or organizations from which you take your values and attitudes. You may currently belong to this group or you aspire to belong to it. In either case, the values of a reference group can exert a strong influence on buying behavior. Reference groups might include church groups, fraternities, work groups, civic organizations, families, or peer groups. In the case of a car purchase, you might be strongly influenced by the people in your peer group when selecting the style, model, or color.

TYPES OF DECISION-MAKING

Consumers spend varying amounts of time and consider different factors when making decisions. It takes different decision-making skills to buy a tube of toothpaste than to buy a computer. There are three types of decision making that consumers go through: routine, limited, and extensive decision-making.

ROUTINE DECISION-MAKING

Routine decision-making is used for purchases that are made frequently and do not require much thought. For routine purchases, the consumer is familiar with the products available, often chooses the same brand repeatedly, or can make an easy substitution if the usual choice is not available. Final consumers use routine decision-making for purchases of chewing gum, personal care products, and regular food purchases.

Businesses use routine decision-making when making regular purchases such as operating supplies. The business will often use one supplier and will reorder from that company whenever necessary.

LIMITED DECISION-MAKING

Limited decision-making takes more time than routine decision-making. Often limited decision-making is associated

with a product that is more expensive or is purchased less frequently. When you go to the mall to buy a pair of jeans, you might try on several styles, compare prices, and consider the fabrics of the selections before you make a decision. This is an example of limited decision-making. You need to evaluate alternatives before making a purchase.

Limited decision-making is not strictly for more expensive items. If you are a Coke drinker and the store you stop at is out of Coke, what do you do? Some people easily choose another brand while others have to stop and evaluate the alternatives. Something as simple as buying a soft drink can involve limited decision-making.

Businesses use limited decision-making for many purchases, such as office equipment, furniture, fixtures, component parts, and others. For routine purchases, such as supplies, limited decision-making might be used if a new supplier offers substantially lower prices or better delivery terms. Limited decision-making may be required while the purchasing agent compares the new information.

EXTENSIVE DECISION-MAKING

The third type of decision-making is called extensive decision-making. Extensive decision-making happens when the consumer methodically goes through all five steps of the decision-making process. Normally, extensive decision-making is for expensive purchases, such as a car or a stereo system. Consumers do not make the decision lightly and spend time and effort evaluating alternatives and arriving at a decision.

Extensive decision-making is used in business when a purchase has not been made before or when it involves a large amount of money. Perhaps a business needs a new mainframe computer or new delivery trucks. The purchasing agent will conduct an extensive search for the best terms before a purchase decision is reached. Information about purchasing decisions in business is detailed further in Chapter 14.

THE MARKETERS' RESPONSE

Why is this information important to marketers? Marketers want the opportunity to explain to consumers the benefits of their products and services and how they can satisfy consumer needs. When consumers stop and consider alternatives, marketers have the opportunity to explain their products through the use of communication channels.

On the other hand, if you consistently buy the same product because you are brand-loyal, marketers want to encourage you to continue to purchase their product. They will work to insure that the product is available to you at the price you expect. They may even provide coupons, rebates, or other incentives to encourage your continued use of their product.

REVIEW

Marketers depend on consumers. Consumers satisfy their wants and needs through the purchase of products and services. If the consumers do not select the products and services of a company, marketing has not been successful. Marketers study the behavior of final customers and business customers to learn how to satisfy their wants and needs.

Consumers have a variety of wants and needs. One method of understanding consumers is Maslow's Hierarchy of Needs. According to that theory, people progress through a series of needs from physiological to security, social, esteem, and finally self-actualization.

Buying motives are the reasons people buy. Motives can be emotional or rational. Some consumers also use patronage motives, in which they are loyal to a particular brand or business.

Decisions to purchase are made in an orderly process. Consumers move through a series of five smaller decisions. That process is influenced by factors such as personality, social class, culture, and reference groups. Consumers make routine decisions quickly and with little thought. Extensive decision-making will be done very carefully using much more time and information.

MARKETING FOUNDATIONS

1. MATCHING

a. Business consumer   f. Final consumer
b. Buying motives   g. Need
c. Consumer behavior   h. Personalities
d. Decision-making process   i. Rational motives
e. Emotional motives   j. Want

1. The study of consumers and how they make decisions.
2. One who buys a product or service for personal use.
3. One who buys goods and services to produce other goods and services or to resell.
4. An unfulfilled desire.
5. Anything you require to live.
6. The reasons that we buy.
7. The forces of love, affection, guilt, fear, or passion that compel consumers to buy.
8. The functional benefits to be derived from a product or service.
9. The process by which consumers collect information and make choices among alternatives.
10. Well-defined enduring patterns of behavior.

2. MULTIPLE CHOICE

1. The marketing concept states that marketing begins with
   a. selling a good product.
   b. understanding customers.
   c. pricing the product correctly.
   d. developing a consumer survey.

2. A dinner in a fancy restaurant, a Sega Genesis, or a portable telephone are usually classified as
   a. wants.
   b. needs.
   c. motives.
   d. buying decisions.

3. Maslow classified esteem needs as
   a. physical and economic safety.
   b. to realize one's potential.
   c. friends, love, and belonging.
   d. respect and recognition.

4. Motivators such as fear and guilt are classified as
   a. emotional motives.
   b. limited motives.
   c. extensive motives.
   d. affection motives.

5. Business people and purchasing agents are usually motivated by
   a. rational motives.
   b. emotional motives.
   c. buying motives.
   d. objective motives.

6. In the decision-making process, when the consumer gathers information about various products or services it is called
   a. problem recognition.
   b. information search.
   c. alternative evaluation.
   d. purchase evaluation.

7. The lifestyle, values, and beliefs that are common to a group of people is called
   a. reference group.
   b. culture.
   c. personality.
   d. social class.

8. A set of beliefs or attitudes that are passed on from generation to generation is called
   a. reference groups.
   b. social class.
   c. personality.
   d. culture.

9. When consumers choose products that they are familiar with and they often buy repeatedly, what type of decision-making do they use?
   a. The decision-making process is not necessary for these products.
   b. Limited decision-making
   c. Routine decision-making
   d. Repeated decision-making

10. When a business investigates new vendors or locates a supplier for a new component part, it uses what type of decision-making?
    a. The decision-making process is not necessary for these products.
    b. Limited decision-making
    c. Extensive decision-making
    d. Repeated decision-making

MARKETING RESEARCH

1. GENERATING CUSTOMER FEEDBACK

In order to learn more about customers many organizations use customer feedback cards. The organizations use that information to improve their products and services and increase customer satisfaction. An example of a customer feedback card used by a restaurant is provided.

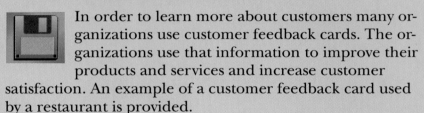

GOOD FOOD RESTAURANT

Tell us how you like us. What did you think of our:

Food? _____

Atmosphere?_____

Service? _____

Cleanliness? _____

Prices? _____

Thank you for sharing your views with us!

In an effort to help your school provide better service, develop a customer feedback card to give to students at your school. The customer feedback card should be designed to find out from students what they like and dislike about your school. You may wish to ask questions about the curriculum, classes, teachers, atmosphere, spirit, extracurricular activities, grades, homework, the building, and any other items relevant to your school. Survey at least 15 students.

After you have completed the survey, tabulate your responses. Then find the mean, median, and mode for each question. Display the survey results in a chart or graph. Compare your results with those of your classmates and make recommendations for improvements.

2. DETERMINING BUYING MOTIVES

Marketers strive to capture your attention with advertisements that use a variety of buying motives. Identify four advertisements from each of the following media: magazines, television, and radio. Two should describe emotional motives and two should describe rational motives. Clip and paste the magazine advertisements on a large piece of paper or posterboard. Prepare a written description of the television ads and radio ads. Classify the type of buying motive used in each advertisement.

MARKETING PLANNING

1. IDENTIFYING FINAL AND BUSINESS CONSUMERS

Some products are sold to both business consumers and final consumers. Name at least one business consumer use and one final consumer use for each of the following items: pencils, balloons, skillet, radio, sofa, fishing lure, raisins, tractor, suitcase, and file folder. Here is an example:

Item	Business Use	Final Consumer Use
banana	restaurant	family lunches

2. VIDEO TELEPHONES

Telephone companies are introducing video telephones into the consumer market. Sales have been slow, because video phones are not a pressing want or need for most consumers.

Assume you are the marketing specialist for a telephone manufacturer. It is your job to develop an advertising strategy to promote video phones. Using the five steps of the decision-making process, write the advertising copy for an ad promoting video phones. After you have finished writing the ad, identify the prominent buying motive you used in the ad. Make sure you focus on an appropriate target market before you begin your work.

MARKETING MANAGEMENT

1. MOTIVATING YOUR SALESPEOPLE

One of the activities of a marketing manager is to encourage the sales people to constantly keep the marketing concept in mind by paying attention to customer needs and wants. Write a letter to your sales people that reminds them of the marketing concept and motivates them to put it into action. Use the following words or phrases in your letter: customers, buying behavior, consumer decision-making process, needs, consumer behavior, wants, and final consumer. Your letter should be logical, upbeat, and convincing.

2. ETHICAL PRACTICES

In the past, the use of buying motives and the consumer decision-making process was considered unethical by some people. What are your thoughts? Is identifying buying motives and using them in a promotional campaign an ethical or unethical use of marketing techniques?

Write a 200-word essay either in support of or against the use of buying motives and the decision-making process. Make sure that you use specific reasons to defend your position.

Product/
Service
Planning

Distribution

Marketing-
Information
Management

Economic
Foundations
of Marketing

Fi

Purchasing

Marketing
and
Business
Foundations

Human
Resource
Foundations

Ris

Pricing

Selling

Promotion

Using Research to Avoid Mistakes

OBJECTIVES

1. Explain why businesses need market information and marketing research.

2. Identify the types of information collected by marketers to improve decision-making.

3. Discuss the importance of developing a marketing information system.

4. Describe the way marketing research is used to solve problems.

5. Explain the three methods of primary data collection: survey, observation, and experimentation.

6. Decide when marketing research should be used.

NEWSLINE

RESTAURANTS FIND A NICHE

It's hot, it's fast, and it's competitive! On average, Americans eat between 30 and 50 percent of their meals outside the home. A large percentage of those meals are purchased from fast food or casual dining restaurants. For many years, the chain restaurants had a cookie cutter image; that is, they all looked the same with very similar menus and service. However, casual dining is changing, as noted by the success of specialty and ethnic chains.

General Mills had success with the introduction of the Red Lobster restaurants. Building on that success, General Mills conducted research in the area of ethnic menus. The researchers discovered that many people were looking for a convenient, comfortable, sit-down restaurant where families could go for a unique menu at a reasonable price. The restaurants had to offer good food with efficient service and an ethnic atmosphere that complemented the menu.

After five years and nearly $30 million of research, General Mills completed the planning for the Olive Garden restaurants that fea-

tured an Italian menu, comfortable atmosphere, and affordable prices. Now General Mills is doing the same careful planning for a Chinese-menu restaurant called China Coast.

What does it take to be successful in fast food? The major chains (McDonald's, Burger King, and Wendy's) compete with expanded menus, healthier sandwiches, salads, and more customer service. However, a new group of businesses are experiencing rapid growth by returning to the concept of "fast food." Some customers still want a basic menu of hamburgers and drinks. They want cheap prices and quick service. Businesses like

Rally's, Checkers, and Daddy-O's respond to those needs. They offer only the basic menu items at very low prices. The restaurants are located where it is easy to drive in and out. They emphasize fast service with two drive-up lanes. They meet the needs of customers who want food, no frills, and the lowest cost.

The success of these two categories of restaurants demonstrates the importance of understanding customers and responding to their needs with a unique marketing mix. All restaurants do not have to be the same. In fact, there is probably a niche no one has tried to serve. What ideas do you have?

WHY DO BUSINESSES NEED MARKET INFORMATION?

People who understand the marketing concept understand why market information is important. When businesses use the production philosophy, they make all of the decisions based on their experience and their ideas about what is needed. As you can see in Figure 9-1, the marketing concept is based on satisfying customer needs. In order to meet those needs, business people must understand customers. Therefore, market information is necessary to understand market segments, the global market, competition, and change in the marketplace.

MARKET SEGMENTS

Most businesses today do not try to satisfy the needs and wants of all possible consumers. They recognize that groups of consumers have very different needs and wants and may view product and service choices quite differently. Businesses gather specific information to determine the differences among market segments and how to best meet the unique needs and wants of each segment.

How Businesses Make Decisions

"Here's what I think our customers will buy."

Businesses that use the Production Emphasis

"What can we provide that will meet your needs as our customers?"

Businesses that use the Marketing Concept

FIGURE 9-1 ▪ Business people that believe in the production emphasis rely on experience; business people that believe in the marketing concept base their decisions on an understanding of customers and their needs.

THE GLOBAL MARKET

As businesses develop an international focus, the possible market segments and the differences among customer groups can become even greater. Even if we believe we understand the consumers in our own country quite well, we will not have as much confidence about new consumer groups in other countries. Gathering information about the country and its people can help us determine how to become effective global business people.

COMPETITION

Competition is becoming much more intense for most businesses. It is more difficult to make decisions that will ensure customers will prefer one company's products over those of other companies. Gathering information about competitors' products and marketing activities in order to determine their strengths and weaknesses will help businesses to be more competitive.

THE CHANGING MARKETPLACE

We learned a great deal about customer needs in Chapter 8. We know that customer needs and their choices in satisfying those needs are changing. Many consumers are able to satisfy their basic needs much more easily than was possible in the past. Therefore they have moved beyond those basic needs to satisfy their wants. They have many choices and much more information about those choices so their decisions are much more informed. In order to develop a marketing mix that will satisfy consumer wants, businesses must have a clear understanding of these changing consumer needs.

As consumers' wants and needs have expanded, products and services have changed as well. In the past, products may have been quite basic with few additional features or options available for consumers. Because of those limited differences, businesses often competed for sales by emphasizing such things as their location, reputation, or price. Businesses can now compete by emphasizing differences resulting from product development and technology. However, such changes can be expensive and may not always meet customer needs. The correct decisions can be very profitable, but the wrong choices can result in losses for the company. Decision makers want information so that the best and most profitable product and service improvements can be made.

You can see that there are many reasons for businesses to collect information. However, all the reasons can be summarized in two statements: (1) effective marketing information improves the decisions of businesses and (2) effective marketing information reduces the risk of decision-making. If a business can make better decisions that have a greater likelihood of resulting in a profit, the time and money spent gathering information will be a good investment.

THE EFFECT OF RESEARCH ON PLANNING

J'Borg Apparel is deciding on next year's designs for its lines of shirts and shorts. The members of the design team meet and share their ideas about possible changes. Several of the designers suggest that J'Borg should keep its basic designs from this year and simply develop new colors and some additional accessories. Another group of designers believes that customers are moving away from the baggy cuts and will want shorter and more tailored styles. They argue that entirely new designs for its lines of apparel should be developed.

J'Borg's primary competitor is Dominique Designs. The designers at Dominique are also meeting to consider changes in product lines for the new season. However, before the meeting, they request information from the company's marketing manager. The marketing department provides records on each of the company's products. Those records identify the quantity sold by size and color for each week of the year. They also show the region of the country and the retail store in which sales were made. Original prices of products sold, markdowns, and the number of items returned or unsold are also recorded.

The marketing manager also provides a report that was purchased from a national apparel manufacturing association. It presents information on total consumer apparel purchases in the United States for each of the past five years for ten major categories of apparel. Sales are identified within four geographic regions of the country and are categorized by age and gender of consumers and by type of retail store where the products are sold. The report identifies the top six brands of apparel and shows the percentage of the total sales each of the brands has achieved during the five-year period. The final section of the report discusses the anticipated changes in the economy and in customer expenditures for apparel for the next year.

The final information supplied by marketing is the result of a marketing research study completed during the past month. Four groups of consumers from across the country were invited to a meeting to discuss their attitudes about apparel and their ideas about planned purchases. The groups discussed ten questions about designs, brands, and value. The results of the discussions are summarized in the research report. All of the designers for Dominique have carefully studied the market information and they discuss it thoroughly before deciding on next year's designs.

How will each of the companies decide whether to make design changes and the types of designs to use for the next year? Which of the companies do you believe will make decisions that are most likely to be successful? What is the biggest difference in the way Dominique makes decisions compared to J'Borg?

WHAT TYPES OF INFORMATION ARE NEEDED?

Put yourself in the position of the marketing manager for a national chain of yogurt stores. It is your responsibility to collect information to help store managers decide what they can do to increase sales and profits. What information do you believe is needed? It seems like the possibilities are unlimited.

A yogurt business is different from a ranch, a hospital, or an airplane manufacturer. Each type of business needs specific information, but there are some general categories of information that all businesses should consider. Those categories are customer information, marketing mix information, and information about the business environment.

Figure 9-2 provides examples of specific types of information in each of the three categories that will be helpful in making good marketing decisions.

Types of Information Needed for Effective Marketing Decisions		
Consumers	**Marketing Mix**	**Business Environment**
age	basic products	type of competition
gender	product features	competitors' strengths
income	services	competitors' strategies
education	product packaging	economic conditions
family size	guarantees	government regulations
home ownership	repairs	new technology
address	product price	consumer protection
occupation	credit choices	ethical issues
how money is spent	discounts	tax policies
attitudes	location of sale	proposed laws
primary needs	type of store used	international markets
product purchases	display procedures	
purchase frequency	use of salespeople	
brand preferences	promotion methods	
information needs	promotional message	
media preferences	promotional media	
shopping behavior		

FIGURE 9-2 ■ Marketers study information to help them make the best decisions.

As the marketing manager of the yogurt stores, you will need information from each of the categories. You will want to help store managers determine who their customers are, where they live, how much they spend on desserts, how they make decisions on what and when to purchase, and how they feel about your store's brand of yogurt. You also will want to know what new flavors to add, if other food products should be sold, whether specific locations or certain store layouts are more effective, the prices to charge, and the most effective promotional messages and methods. A study of internal operations such as costs of operations, training requirements for employees, and management methods may help determine the best ways to operate the stores. Your store managers will want to know if the economy will improve in the next year, if there will be new competitors or if current competitors are making important changes, if taxes or government regulations will increase, and even such specific information as whether the city is planning to make street improvements in front of a store.

HOW IS MARKETING INFORMATION MANAGED?

One of the functions of marketing is marketing information management. In Chapter 1, marketing information management was defined as obtaining, managing, and using market information to improve decision-making and the performance of marketing activities. Certainly businesses need a great deal of information to operate successfully. With all of the information needed, business people could spend most of their time gathering and studying information. In order to use information effectively, businesses develop a marketing information system. *A marketing information system (MkIS) is an organized method of collecting, storing, analyzing, and retrieving information to improve the effectiveness and efficiency of marketing decisions.*

Each business develops its own marketing information system. In some new, small businesses, the MkIS (pronounced M-K-I-S) may be as simple as a filing cabinet in which the owner collects, organizes, and stores customer information, business records, and other information important to the business. In large businesses, the MkIS may be an important part of the company with a computer system and a staff of people who collect and analyze information and prepare reports.

All effective marketing information systems contain five elements. Those elements are input, storage, analysis, output, and decision-making. Those elements are illustrated in Figure 9-3.

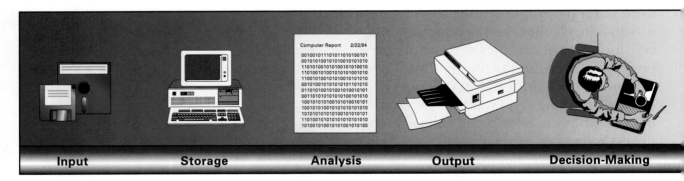

| Input | Storage | Analysis | Output | Decision-Making |

Elements of a Marketing Information System (MkIS)

FIGURE 9-3 ▪ An example of an MkIS using a computer system.

Input is the information that goes into the system. It can include company records, reports, or information on competitors and customers. *Storage is the resources used to maintain the information so that it can be used when needed.* For example, computers use floppy and hard disks, and magnetic tape to store information. *Analysis is the way in which information is studied so decisions can be made.* Programs are written for computer systems that organize and analyze information. *Output is the results of the analysis and the ways it is presented to the people who need the information.* Usually reports are prepared in which information is summarized for managers to use in making decisions. The final element of the MkIS is the decision. Because information is collected, stored, and analyzed, decisions should be better and decision-making should be faster.

Marketing managers carefully plan the marketing information system used in their businesses. It is important to have a system that will help them use important information to make decisions. It must be able to provide needed information quickly, but it must also be accurate. Because marketing information management is such an important part of today's marketing, it will be discussed in detail in Chapter 22.

HOW IS MARKETING RESEARCH USED TO SOLVE PROBLEMS?

A marketing information system should provide the information needed for marketers to make regular and routine decisions. However, there are many decisions that must be made that relate to a specific problem or a new situation. A business may be considering entering a new market in which it has no previous experience. The company's engineers may have suggested a modification in the product that is totally new. The company's MkIS may not have all of the needed information for the marketers to make a good decision in those situations. In order to gather the additional information, the company uses marketing research.

Marketing research is a procedure to identify solutions to a specific marketing problem through the use of scientific problem-solving. You have probably studied and used scientific problem-solving in many other classes. If you have, you already know the steps in scientific problem-solving. Those steps are shown in Figure 9-4. The scientific method is used to ensure that a careful and objective procedure is followed in order to develop the best possible solution.

Implementing a Marketing Research Study

5. Propose a Solution

4. Gather and Study Information

3. Develop a Data-Collection Procedure

2. Analyze the Situation

1. Define the Problem

FIGURE 9-4 ▪ A good marketing researcher plans a study by following the steps in scientific decision-making.

DEFINE THE PROBLEM

Marketing research is used when a business needs to solve a specific problem. Therefore, the first step in the process is to be certain that the problem is clearly and carefully defined. That is not always an easy step. Sometimes the problem is very clear—identify the characteristics of a market *or* select a new advertising medium. In other cases, you may not know the real problem. If sales are declining, the problem might be that customers are dissatisfied with some part of the marketing mix or a competitor may have introduced a new product choice. Consumers may believe the economy is not strong and are less willing to spend money. You may have to gather some specific information before the problem is clear.

It is important to state the problem clearly and have several people review it to make sure it is understandable. The problem should be specific enough that researchers know what to study, who to involve in the study, and the types of solutions or results that might be appropriate for the problem.

ANALYZE THE SITUATION

An important part of scientific decision-making is to understand the problem well enough to determine how to solve it. Analyzing the situation allows the researcher to identify what is al-

ready known about the problem, the information currently available, and the possible solutions that have already been attempted.

This step is completed by reviewing available information and talking to people who might have ideas or additional information. Reviewing similar problems or other studies that have previously been completed can help the researcher decide how to study the current problem.

It is possible that a careful situation analysis may result in the identification of a solution. If the decision-maker is confident in the proposed solution and has limited time or money to study the problem further, the marketing research process will come to an end. A good marketing information system will frequently provide the necessary information so that further study is not needed.

DEVELOP A DATA-COLLECTION PROCEDURE

After thoroughly reviewing the situation and the available information, the researcher decides what additional information is needed and how it should be collected. In this step the actual marketing research study is planned. The researcher needs to know where to obtain information and the best and most efficient ways to obtain the information.

There are two types of data that can be collected—secondary data and primary data. *Secondary data is information already collected for another purpose that can be used to solve the current problem.* Examples of secondary data include company records, government reports, studies completed by colleges and universities, information from trade associations and other business groups, and research reported in magazines.

Primary data is information collected for the first time to solve the problem being studied. It is the result of a study designed specifically in response to current needs of the company. Because primary data collection is such an important part of marketing research we will discuss methods used to collect primary data later in the chapter.

GATHER AND STUDY INFORMATION

Have you ever participated in a marketing research study? A great deal of information is collected through questionnaires mailed to your home, telephone interviews, or by stopping people in shopping malls to ask questions. No matter what method is used to gather the information, procedures must be carefully developed and followed to be sure the results are accurate.

Selecting the Participants

The selection of participants in marketing research is one of the most important decisions to be made. In most situations, there are many more potential customers than a company can afford to involve in the research. Researchers usually collect information from a small group of people. That smaller group must be representative so its members will give responses that are similar to those of the larger group if the research is to be useful. A company could have serious problems if it made decisions from information that did not reflect the attitudes or behavior of its customers.

Researchers use several terms to describe the people who are the focus of study. *All of the people in the group the company is interested in studying are known as the population. A smaller group selected from the population is a sample.* When selecting a sample, the researcher usually wants to be sure the small group is representative of the larger group. *To do that, the researcher will use random sampling, a procedure in which everyone in the population has an equal chance of being selected in the sample.*

Collecting the Data

Procedures should be identified in advance to ensure that all useful information is reviewed and that the people reviewing the information are objective in their work. Procedures for primary data collection are particularly important. When gathering information directly from other people, researchers must be careful to maintain the privacy of the individual and treat the person ethically. A great deal of consumer research is conducted by telephone calls to people's homes. The number of calls and the time of day when people are called may be upsetting to many people. A few unethical businesses tell consumers they are conducting a research study when they are really collecting personal information or attempting to sell a product or service.

Analyzing the Data

Once information is collected, it needs to be reviewed to determine whether it can aid in developing a solution to the problem. For small amounts of information or simple studies, the information may not be difficult to review. However, most marketing research studies collect a large amount of information that requires a great deal of analysis. Therefore, most research is analyzed using computers and statistical programs in order to increase the speed and accuracy of obtaining the results.

After the study is complete, the researchers examine the information collected. That information may be in the form of answers to surveys, observations that have been recorded, or data collected from an experiment. The information needs to be organized so that it is meaningful and easy to study in order to solve the problem for which the research was conducted.

Numerical data is the easiest to organize. Researchers total the number of responses to each question or for each factor being observed. When more than one group is involved in the research, it is typical to compare the responses of the groups. The simplest form of comparison is done by calculating the percentage of responses or average response (mean, median) of each group. Advanced levels of comparison can be made to determine the relationships between two or more variables. For example, the researcher may want to study the relationship between the number of times an advertisement is run on a television station and the number of customers who call a business seeking information about a product. Another comparison could be to determine if there is a relationship between the price of a product and the level of customer satisfaction identified through a survey of recent purchasers.

Some research information is not numerical, so it is much more difficult to analyze. When customers respond to open-ended questions or observers describe how a consumer acted in a specific situation, there is not a common set of specific answers recorded. There are special methods for people trained to analyze that type of information. Results can be classified into broad categories that are identified before the information is collected or categories that are determined by looking for similar ideas from the responses.

The results of the study are usually organized into tables and graphs. This makes it easier to analyze a great deal of information in a brief time and to make comparisons of information from different groups. Some examples of the visuals often used to report research results are shown in Figure 9-5.

The results of the research are often summarized and analyzed in several ways. This allows marketers to consider several possible solutions. Studying and analyzing marketing research is an important marketing skill. Marketing research departments and companies employ research analysts to complete these tasks.

Visual Summaries of Marketing Information

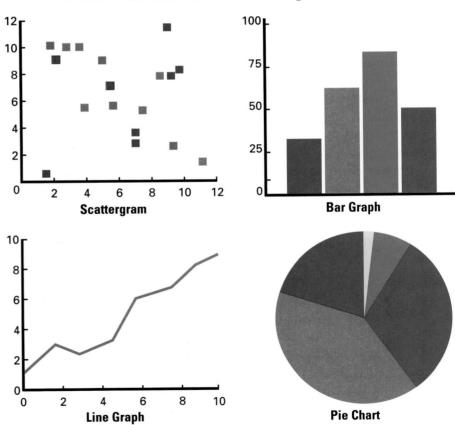

FIGURE 9-5 ■ There are several common methods of summarizing marketing research information including tables, charts, and graphs.

PROPOSE A SOLUTION

The purpose of marketing research is to identify strategies for the company to follow in implementing and improving marketing activities. Scientific decision-making often begins with the development of a hypothesis (or possible solution) to the problem. After the research results have been organized, they need to be studied to determine if the findings support the proposed solution or suggest an alternative solution.

In most cases, market researchers do not make decisions about solutions. They prepare a report of the research results. The report is presented to managers. The marketing managers carefully study the report. They use the results to help them with decision making. It is important that results are accurate and clearly communicated in a research report.

Marketing research reports can be presented in writing or orally. In both cases, the report should describe the study and its results in detail. Effective communication is an important skill for all marketers, especially market researchers.

When preparing a report, two items are very important. First, the person preparing the report must know who will be receiving and studying the report. Just as a marketing mix should respond to the needs of customers, the research report must be prepared to meet the needs of its consumers. Second, the report must clearly describe the purpose of the study and the research procedures followed to collect the information in the report. Without an understanding of the problem being studied and the methods used, those receiving the report may misunderstand or misinterpret the results.

A research report, whether written or oral, is usually organized just like the study. An outline that could be used to develop a report is shown in Figure 9-6. A research report begins with a statement of the problem or the purpose of the research and includes a brief discussion of why the study was needed. Then it summarizes the secondary information that was collected.

Sections of a Research Report

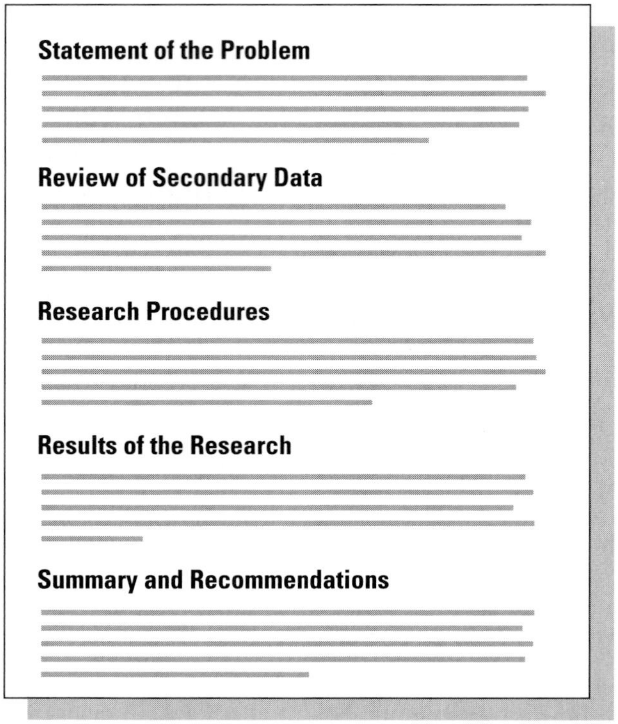

Statement of the Problem

Review of Secondary Data

Research Procedures

Results of the Research

Summary and Recommendations

FIGURE 9-6 ▪ A research report is carefully organized and clearly written in order to communicate the results to managers.

The third part of the report is a description of the procedures used in the study. This includes the population studied and the way a sample was obtained. It will also describe the method used to collect information including surveys, observations, or experiments.

The most important part of the report is the presentation of the results of the research. In a written report, the results are presented in the form of tables and graphs with brief written explanations. When making an oral presentation, the results are also presented using visuals. Visuals are charts, transparencies shown on an overhead projector, slides, or computer graphics displayed on a computer screen or projected onto a wall screen. The presenter provides explanations of the visuals.

Finally, the research report concludes with a summary that emphasizes the most important information from the study. It may also contain recommendations for solutions if they have been requested. Sometimes the research will not completely demonstrate that a solution will be successful. Marketers will need to decide if they have enough information or if they need to continue to study the problem.

A GLOBAL VISION

AN INTERNATIONAL DIET

Will the new tastes in America sell in Europe? Yes and no. Nothing is as American as Coke and Pepsi. Both companies have found that people throughout the world want American soft drinks. Both have successfully marketed their major brands using the same strategies developed for American markets. The taste, package, and even the advertisements are often the same no matter in what country the products are marketed.

Now a difference has been created. Many American soft drink consumers have become health conscious and are switching to diet brands. Diet Coke and Diet Pepsi are competing for nearly one-third of the total soft drink market in the United States. However, less than five percent of the international sales come from diet brands. What makes the difference?

Market research was used to discover if diet drinks could be marketed outside the United States. The research found that an increasing number of people world-wide were concerned about their health and that a low-calorie drink would be accepted. However, the use of the term *diet* on the product created problems. The people studied believed a diet drink would not taste good. European consumers felt that diet products were only for sick people.

PepsiCo has been looking for a way to match the success it has in the United States in international markets. Until recently, its sales outside the United States were only one-fourth the amount of Coca Cola's. After several years of consumer research and testing of various recipes for its diet cola, PepsiCo finally came up with a combination that received high ratings when tested in international markets. It has one calorie like Diet Pepsi. To avoid the negative image associated with a diet drink both the package and name were redesigned. Pepsi Max in a bright blue and red can is the first soft drink that a U.S. company developed specifically for an international market. Pepsi Max does not sound like a diet drink and does not leave an aftertaste. Do you think it would sell in America?

Source: Adapted from "Eurofizz" Fortune, March 22, 1993, p. 15.

METHODS OF PRIMARY DATA COLLECTION

If you need information from a group of people in your community, what method would you use to gather it? If you are completing a marketing study, you would decide on the method by considering the type of information needed. If you want to know how people shop for a specific type of product you might use a different method than if you want to know how they use that product. It would take a different method to determine consumer attitudes toward advertising than to identify the quantity of a specific type of product they consumed during the year. There are three methods of collecting primary data as part of a marketing research study. Those methods are surveys, observation, and experimentation.

SURVEYS

A survey is a planned set of questions to which individuals or groups of people respond. The survey can be completed in writing or orally. People can be surveyed in person, through the mail, or by telephone. Some companies even survey people using computers or interactive television. With these methods, consumers are presented questions on the computer or television screen. They respond to the questions by keying responses on the computer, pushing buttons on a special key pad provided by the researcher, or entering information on a touch-tone telephone that is transferred by telephone lines to a computer.

Most surveys use closed-ended questions. *Closed-ended questions offer two or more choices from which respondents can select one answer.* Examples of closed-ended choices are yes-no; do you agree or disagree; select a, b, c, or d; or rate this item on a scale of 1–10.

Occasionally, researchers will use open-ended questions. *Open-ended questions allow respondents to develop their own answers without information about possible choices.* Examples of open-ended questions include, "What are the most important features of this product?"; "How does the durability of brand A compare to brand B?";

or "How did you feel about your shopping experience in Z-Mart?"

Open-ended questions are often used while researchers are attempting to identify the problem or are completing a situation analysis. They may not be certain about the alternatives to include in a closed-ended survey. In that case, researchers may discuss the problems with some consumers using open-ended questions in order to get more specific information.

One of the popular research methods used to gather specific information is a focus group. *A focus group is a small number of people brought together to discuss identified elements of an issue or problem.* Focus group participants are selected carefully because they are representative of a larger group of people or because they are experts in the topic being studied. A skilled moderator uses a set of open-ended questions to guide the discussion and gather ideas.

It is important that survey questions are carefully written. They need to collect information that will help to solve the problem. They must be written in such a way that the respondent understands what is being asked, is encouraged to respond honestly, and is not directed toward one answer so that the results are biased. Questions should be short, clear, and simple. Each question should deal with only one concept and use language that is easily understood by the respondent.

The survey should be organized in a way that makes it as easy as possible to complete. Directions should be given so the respondent knows how to record answers and what to do with the survey when finished. The respondent should be assured that the answers will be treated confidentially.

Surveys should only ask questions that are needed to accomplish the objectives of the research. Surveys that appear to be long or complex will not be answered by many people. Gathering unneeded information can be both misleading and, in some cases, unethical. It may also provide confusion in solving the marketing problem by introducing information that is not relevant.

OBSERVATION

A second method of gathering research information is observation. *Observation collects information by recording actions without interacting or communicating with the participant.* The purpose of observation research is to see the actions of the participant rather than to have the person recall or predict their actions. This usually results in greater accuracy and objectivity. However, using observations to gather data normally requires greater time and expense than if surveys are

CHALLENGES
DOES THIS BOTHER YOU?

Your family is just sitting down for your evening meal when the telephone rings. It is a marketing research firm that wants to ask a few questions. Ten minutes later, the phone rings again. Another person with more questions. This time, however, the person is not really doing marketing research but tries to sell some magazines. Finally, just as the family gets back to the meal, the doorbell rings. If you answer the survey questions, your family has the chance to win a vacation.

These situations are becoming more frequent and cause consumers and business people to question marketing research practices. Here are some other examples of questionable research practices:

■ Using a computer to call every telephone number in a directory. When the telephone is answered, a recorded script asks the person several questions which are answered using a touch-tone phone.

■ Using one-way mirrors in businesses to observe how customers complete certain purchasing activities. The customers are not aware they are being observed and might be embarrassed if they knew.

■ Disguising the purpose of a questionnaire. Respondents think they are answering questions about one topic when the researcher is really interested in topics that are hidden in the questions.

■ Providing incorrect or negative information about competitor's products as part of a research activity.

■ Excluding people from research because of factors such as age, race, or education even though the people are customers of the business.

■ Paying research participants large sums of money or giving expensive gifts in return for their opinions.

People are upset with the disruption created by businesses who *say* they are doing research. When people are mislead they not only have a negative opinion of the business but also begin to distrust other businesses and any type of research activity. Many people are refusing to participate in surveys.

What is the responsibility of businesses to solve this problem? Is it enough for ethical businesses to use appropriate methods? Should businesses attempt to change the practices of unethical businesses?

used. It is difficult to gather information from a large number of participants using observation.

Observations must be carefully planned in order to keep from changing the participants' actions as a result of the observation. If people know they are being watched, they may do things very differently. Trained observers typically know what to observe and how to record information quickly and accurately. In some situations, observations can be made mechanically with television cameras, audio tape recording, or with other types of equipment designed to gather information about the actions of people. A common example of the use of equipment is the bar code scanners used at the checkout counters of many retail stores. They can record the types and quantities of products purchased, the timing of purchases, how payment was made, whether coupons or other promotions were used, and what items were purchased at the same time. A great deal can be learned about purchasing behavior in that way without asking the consumer any questions.

Another unique equipment-based observation method is the use of eye-tracking photography. A discount store or supermarket may be interested in how customers examine displays. Through the use of close-up photography, researchers record where the eyes look first, how long the customer focuses on certain products, how they search the entire display, and what they look at when making a product choice. This information can be very helpful in organizing displays and placing specific brands in the displays. The same type of equipment is used to study how consumers read magazine and newspaper advertisements.

Some observations are made without the consumer even being aware that they are being observed. Researchers are interested in learning how participants behave in normal situations. In other cases, researchers may ask people to participate in a preplanned situation. In these cases, the researcher wants to learn how people respond to specific, controlled activities. For example, a business might want to know how customers would react if a different type of sales presentation is used. Another example would be to study consumer responses to a new piece of equipment such as an automatic teller machine in a bank.

EXPERIMENTS

The most precise and objective information is obtained through experimentation. *Experiments are tightly controlled situations in which all important factors are the same except the one being studied.* Scientific research is done by planning and implementing experiments and then recording and analyzing the data obtained. The researcher wants to determine the result, if any, of the change. Experiments are not used as often in marketing research as surveys or observations. That may be because it is difficult to manage a large number of marketing activities at the same time. It also takes a great deal of time to organize an experiment and operate it for a long enough time to determine if differences occur. It is likely, however, that many researchers do not recognize the real benefits of carefully planned experiments in marketing.

Implementing the marketing concept provides many opportunities for research to determine the best market segments to serve and the appropriate mix elements to provide. A business may want to determine if a customer's geographic location makes a difference in purchasing behavior. In that case, an experiment in which two groups of customers from different areas are provided the same marketing mix may help to answer the question. A business may be uncertain about the effect of a price increase on sales volume. An experiment can be developed in which everything except the price is held the same for two groups of customers. One group is given a 10 percent-off coupon while the other is not given a discount. The experiment can demonstrate the amount of sales change that results from the price difference.

Other examples of possible marketing experiments are a test of two different locations for a product in a store, determining whether a radio or television commercial is more effective in maintaining customers' memory of a product, and analyzing the effect on customer satisfaction of follow-up calls from salespeople after the purchase of an automobile. Experiments may be quite difficult to implement successfully.

However, you can see that these types of experiments can provide very important information to marketers if they are done well.

Test Markets

Because of the need for control over important conditions, experiments are difficult to manage. Some companies have developed test markets. *Test markets are specific cities or geographic areas in which marketing experiments are conducted.* To prepare for a test market, companies gather a great deal of information about consumers, competitors, and past marketing activities. The companies try new product ideas or make marketing changes in the test markets. They collect data on the product performance for a period of several months and compare it with previously-gathered information. In this way they can attempt to predict the performance in their total market based on the results in the test market.

Simulations

When experiments are not possible in actual markets, companies may develop simulations. *Simulations are experiments operated in laboratories where researchers create the situation to be studied.* For example, a business may want to see how children respond when playing with a new toy. Rather than observing children playing in their homes or schools, the business may organize a play center in a laboratory. Then they bring groups of children into the center and observe them under more carefully controlled circumstances. An automobile company studying the layout of the driver's seat area does not have to build an entire new car. It can build a small area that duplicates the front seat of a car. Changing the positions of the seat and controls allows the company to determine which is most satisfying to the driver.

Some simulations are now done on computers. Computer graphics can be created to allow research participants to visualize a change and react to it. Architects can use computer software to develop a complete external view of a proposed building from all sides. The software allows the viewer to enter all doors and immediately see the interior of a room. The software could be used to test consumers' attitudes about various changes in the architectural plans of the building before final design decisions are made.

WHEN SHOULD MARKETING RESEARCH BE USED?

Some business people seldom use marketing research. They believe it is too expensive or requires too much time. They want to make decisions quickly and believe they have the necessary knowledge and experience to make good decisions. Companies that have a production philosophy do not believe in marketing research.

Other business people have found that marketing research is very valuable. Marketing is expensive and marketing mistakes can cause serious problems for a business. Business people who understand the marketing concept believe that the cost and time needed for research are worthwhile if it means that correct marketing decisions will be made and customers will be satisfied.

The decision whether to use research or not is based on how risky a decision is and how much it will cost to gather information. If there is little risk, there is no need to do research. On the other hand, if a business is considering investing several hundred thousand dollars in a new product or a new distribution system, they may want to collect information to determine if it will be successful. Marketing research can reduce the risk of important decisions.

REVIEW

In the past, business people often felt they could dictate what their customers would buy. Today business is much more complicated. Changing customer needs, the global marketplace, and increasing competition require that business people make careful decisions.

Business decisions are based on an understanding of a variety of information. That information includes customers' needs and attitudes, competitors' activities, and marketing mix choices. Much of that information will be obtained from marketing research.

Marketing research procedures follow the scientific decision-making process. Several methods can be used to complete a study. These methods include surveys, observation, and experiments. Researchers need to select participants who will provide accurate and honest information.

Once the research is completed, the information must be summarized and studied. A well-organized research report is developed. The report communicates the results of the research so managers can make good decisions.

Marketing research can be both expensive and time consuming. But business people are willing to invest in research because they know it is an important way to improve their decisions and reduce mistakes.

MARKETING FOUNDATIONS

1. YOU PROVIDE THE REASONS

 Each of the following statements describes a fact or concept about marketing research. Using information from the chapter, write a supporting reason that helps to explain each fact or concept.

Example: Marketing information is needed by businesses that believe in the marketing orientation.

Supporting Reason: Businesses using a marketing orientation need to study information about customers in order to satisfy their needs.

a. Marketing research helps businesses that are involved in international competition.

b. Businesses that have a good marketing information system also need to use marketing research.

c. Marketing research follows the steps of scientific problem-solving.

d. Marketing researchers need to maintain the privacy of individuals and treat them ethically.

d. Researchers usually collect information from a small group of people.

f. Open-ended questions are often used while researchers are attempting to identify the problem or are completing a situation analysis.

g. Surveys should only ask questions that are needed to accomplish the objectives of the research.

h. A great deal can be learned about purchase behavior by observing the consumer rather than asking questions.

i. The most precise and objective information is obtained through experimentation.

j. After a study has been completed, the researcher needs to organize the information.

k. Effective communication is an important skill for people involved in marketing research.

l. Whether to use marketing research is based on the risk involved in decision-making.

2. **MAKE THE MATCH**

Match the definitions with the correct marketing research terms.

Marketing Research Terms	Definitions
1. Primary data collection	a. Experiments operated in laboratories where researchers create the situation to be studied
2. Marketing information system	

3. Test market

4. Experiments

5. Observation

6. Marketing research

7. Simulations

8. Focus group

9. Population

10. Survey

b. A small number of people brought together to discuss identified elements of an issue or problem

c. A planned set of questions to which individuals or groups of people respond

d. All of the people in the group the company is interested in studying

e. An organized method of collecting, storing, analyzing, and retrieving information to improve the effectiveness and efficiency of marketing decisions

f. Tightly controlled situations in which all important factors are the same except one being studied

g. Specific cities or geographic areas in which marketing experiments are conducted

h. Information collected for the first time to solve the problem being studied

i. A procedure to identify solutions to a specific marketing problem through the use of scientific problem-solving

j. Collecting information by recording actions with-out interacting or communicating with the participant

MARKETING RESEARCH

1. DEALING WITH DATA

An important part of the marketing research process is to summarize and analyze the data after the surveys, observations, or experiments have been completed. The following chart shows the data collected from a study of store and brand choices for four age groups of consumers. A total of 1,000 people were surveyed and each respondent indicated his/her preferred store and preferred brand.

Age	Store Preference			Brand Preference		
	Bardoes	**Kelvins**	**1-2-3**	**Motif**	**Astra**	**France**
16–20	38	82	130	80	106	76
21–25	56	20	174	156	90	18
26–30	110	64	76	104	98	60
31–35	44	120	86	54	30	128

Calculate the following information from the data and develop tables, charts, or graphs to illustrate the results.

a. Determine the total number of participants who prefer each store and each brand. (To determine the total, add the numbers in each column of the table.)

b. Using the totals from a, calculate the percentage of the total number of participants who prefer each store and each brand. (To calculate the percentage, divide the total of each column by the total number of participants, 1,000.)

c. For each of the age categories calculate the percentage of respondents who prefer each store and each brand. (Divide the number of respondents in each preference category by the total number of participants in that age category.)

d. Illustrate the rank order of stores and the rank order of brands for each age category. (Rank order shows the store and brand which is most preferred, next most preferred, and so on.) Then illustrate the rank order of stores and brands when the responses of all age categories are combined.

e. Using the information you have summarized for a through d, develop two specific conclusions about store and brand preferences for the sample surveyed.

2. RIGHT TO THE SOURCE

Marketing researchers need to be aware of important sources of information that help solve problems and provide guidance in decision-making. Important categories of information include business data, consumer information, information on the economy, government data, and information about specific industries or types of businesses.

Go to your library and become familiar with the reference materials that list sources of business information. Then identify two specific information sources for each of the five categories of information listed above. For each of the information sources, prepare a note card that describes the name of the publication, the publisher, copyright date or frequency of publication, and the type of information that is included in the publication.

If you can obtain a copy of the publication, select a small sample of the information it contains and summarize it on your note card.

MARKETING PLANNING

1. UNDERSTANDING SCIENTIFIC DECISION-MAKING

Identify which of the five steps in scientific decision making is described by each of the following marketing research activities.

a. After receiving the surveys from the respondents, the analyst tabulates the results and prepares charts illustrating the survey results.

b. The manager reviews sales records for the past five years to see if there have been changes in the geographic location of customers during that time.

c. After considering several methods to collect information, the researchers decide to organize two test markets in which they can use different distribution methods to determine which is most effective.

d. The managers listened to the report of the research results and decided to implement the top three recommendations of the research team.

e. In a discussion with salespeople, the marketing manager agrees that there has been an increase in the number of customer complaints about the cost of repair parts for the product.

2. DESIGNING AN MkIS

We know a marketing information system (MkIS) is an organized method of collecting, storing, analyzing, and retrieving information to improve the effectiveness and efficiency of marketing decisions. We also know that an MkIS has five components: input, storage, analysis, output, and decision-making. The idea of an MkIS has many different applications but each should have the five components listed. You want to get a high grade on your next marketing test so you decide to develop an effective system to organize and review the information you are learning. Plan a realistic MkIS you could use. Using pictures or brief descriptions, identify your a) inputs, b) storage, c) analysis, d) output, and e) decision-making that will result in a high grade on your test.

MARKETING MANAGEMENT

1. USING SCIENTIFIC DECISION-MAKING

 For each of the situations listed, describe how you would follow each of the steps in scientific decision-making to solve the problem.

a. You are planning your schedule for your senior year in

high school. You want to be sure you complete all of the requirements for graduation, meet the admissions requirements for one of your state's universities, and take several electives that will help you prepare for your current career choice.

b. You are driving down the street on your way home from school and your car's engine stalls. You are able to pull off on the side of the road and park safely.

c. You are the shift manager of the shoe department in a department store. You have one full-time and three part-time employees who work in the department; two of the employees work with you each day but it is not always the same two. During the past three weeks, the amount of receipts in the cash register at the end of the shift has not matched the total sales on five days. The amount of shortage has been as little as $6 and as high as $55.

d. As the transportation manager for a computer software business you want to find the best way to ship packages of software to customers. The method needs to be rapid, reliable, and not too expensive. You know that you have several choices of air, parcel services, truck, and the U.S. postal system.

2. DESIGNING A MARKETING RESEARCH STUDY

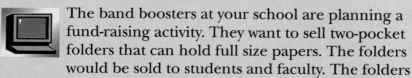 The band boosters at your school are planning a fund-raising activity. They want to sell two-pocket folders that can hold full size papers. The folders would be sold to students and faculty. The folders would be printed and assembled by a local printing company. They want your help in determining a design for the folder, the price to charge, and the best ways to promote the folder in the school to achieve a high sales volume. Prepare a 3–5 page proposal describing a marketing research study that will help the boosters answer their questions. Include the following sections in your proposal: identify the problem, design the research method, select the participants, analyze the data, report the research results.

The proposal should identify ways that all three types of data collection could be used—survey, observation, and experiment.

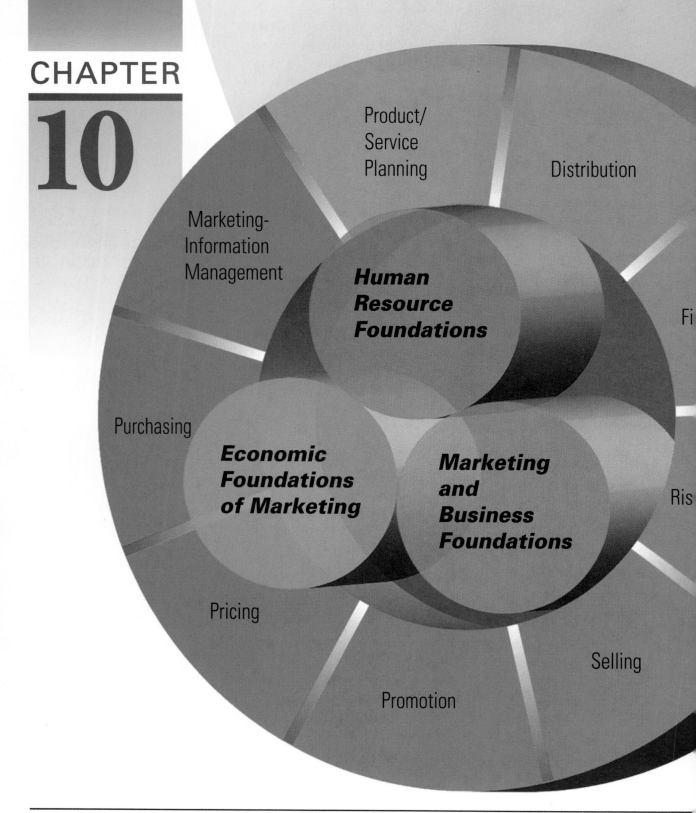

Product/
Service
Planning

Distribution

Marketing-
Information
Management

**Human
Resource
Foundations**

Fi

Purchasing

**Economic
Foundations
of Marketing**

**Marketing
and
Business
Foundations**

Ris

Pricing

Selling

Promotion

Start with a Marketing Strategy

OBJECTIVES

1. Defend the need for a marketing strategy.

2. Explain how a marketing orientation changes the procedure for planning a marketing strategy.

3. Describe the components of a marketing strategy.

4. Identify ways that marketers can change each of the marketing mix elements.

5. Use life cycle analysis and product/service purchase classifications to plan a marketing strategy.

6. Develop criteria for determining if a marketing strategy is effective.

NEWSLINE

DEBIT OR CREDIT?

You have been waiting for months to buy a leather coat. The coat costs $450. Finally it is reduced to $250. You have the last one in the store in your hands. But you don't have enough cash with you. You used the last check in your checkbook this morning. You don't have a credit card yet. What will you do?

The newest method of payment is the debit card. Debit cards look like a credit card but work like a check. When you present the debit card for payment, the amount of the purchase is automatically subtracted from your bank account. Debit cards have been around for many years but have not been widely accepted. *Business Week* reports that cash is currently used for over 80 percent of all purchases at retail businesses. Credit cards are used for just over 10 percent of purchases and checks for just under 10 percent. Debit cards account for less than 1 percent of those purchases.

Why have debit cards been so slow to catch on? They would seem to be a useful product for customers, retailers, and banks. Customers would no longer have the risk of carrying cash and it should be easier to maintain a checkbook. Retailers get payment immediately and banks do not have

> ### Debit cards look like a credit card but work like a check.

to worry about collecting on charge accounts. However, debit cards require special computer equipment in each business and access to the computer system of each bank that offers the debit card. With only a few banks offering the debit cards, there has not been enough demand from consumers or retailers to use them.

Things may begin to change, however. The large credit card companies, MasterCard and Visa,

> ### However, debit cards require special computer equipment in each business and access to the computer system of each bank that offers the debit card.

have decided to enter the debit card business. They are working hard to sign up banks and businesses and to promote the use of debit cards to consumers. Since both companies operate nationally and internationally, the market could develop rapidly. Also since more and more consumers are getting used to using automatic teller machines, the idea of a debit card is no longer new. Most people are comfortable with the product and the technology needed to use it.

Source: Business Week, "The Dawn of the Credit Card. Well, Maybe," September 21, 1992, p. 79.

PUTTING IT ALL TOGETHER

Marketing is much more complex than most people realize. We have seen that marketing includes four mix elements—product, distribution, price, and promotion. Nine marketing functions are involved: product/ service planning, purchasing, financing, distribution, pricing, risk management, marketing information management, promotion, and selling. The many activities occurring within marketing must be coordinated to reach a specific market. Finally, marketing cannot be effective unless it works hand-in-hand with other business activities such as production and finance.

Let's look at an example to show why coordination is so important. At the beginning of the year, a computer manufacturer realizes that several of its competitors are experiencing rapid increases in the sales of their personal computers. The manufacturer wants to enter the market in May but its personal computer models will not be ready for distribution to retail stores until November at the earliest. The marketing department feels that many consumers will be willing to delay their purchases of new computers if they are aware that a better product will be available soon at a reasonable price. Therefore, marketing wants to complete the planning for the product's introduction as soon as possible so that it can begin a communications and promotion program for those consumers.

Initially, the company has to determine for whom the new computer is being developed. Some personal computers sell well to individuals and families as home computers; others are purchased for use by people in their small businesses; still others are purchased as part of a large computer order by businesses, schools, or government agencies. In each case the type of computer needed, the software and other supporting products (such as modems, printers, and carrying cases), and the required level of customer support will be very different.

The type of customers and their needs will affect where and how the computers will be sold. Should they be sold directly to customers using the manufacturer's own salespeople, or would it be better to sell through retail stores? If retail stores are used, should business products stores be used or should the computers be sold through department and discount stores? Currently the manufacturer uses its own salespeople to call on large businesses that purchase over 200 computers each year. The remaining customers are served by salespeople who work for office products wholesalers.

In order to announce the new personal computers, the marketing department needs to know how much the products will cost. Since all of the development and testing is incomplete, it is difficult to set a final retail price at this time. Accounting is still working to estimate many of the projected costs including warranty work, transportation, and unsold or damaged products. If retail stores will be used, prices need to be set that will allow both the manufacturer and retailer to earn a profit.

Production managers are planning the assembly procedure for the personal computers. Designing the work, obtaining necessary materials, and training the work force are all part of their responsibilities. The production department will need to determine how long it will take after final design and testing to start full production of the new computers. They also must be able to predict how many units can be produced once assembly begins.

You have seen just some of the many important decisions that must be made and coordinated if a new product is going to be successful. Marketing is an important part of that process. Marketing decisions cannot be made alone and they cannot wait until the product is ready to be sold. In this chapter we will study procedures for marketers to use in marketing planning. We will learn how to determine the characteristics of target markets that can be served well. We will examine each of the marketing mix elements to determine how each can be developed effectively. Finally, we will learn how to use important marketing tools to select effective markets and make good marketing mix decisions.

DEVELOPING A MARKETING STRATEGY

Throughout this book we have learned how to identify effective marketing. It is more than advertising and selling. It is even more than the nine marketing functions. Effective marketing develops satisfying exchange relationships. In order to accomplish that goal, businesses need to develop a marketing strategy. *A marketing strategy can be defined as the way marketing activities are planned and coordinated to achieve the goals of an organization.* An organization that believes in the marketing concept develops marketing strategies that satisfy customer needs. We learned in Chapter 1 that those organizations follow a two-step process. That process is shown in Figure 10-1.

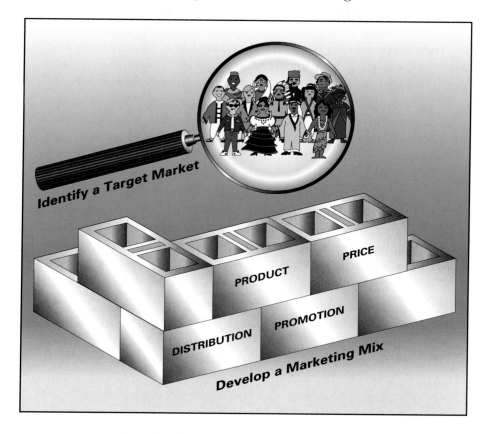

Developing a Marketing Strategy

FIGURE 10-1 ■ Businesses that believe in the marketing concept use a two-step process to develop a marketing strategy.

IDENTIFY A TARGET MARKET

A market includes all of the consumers a business would like to serve. It is almost impossible for a business to serve all customers well. What if a business came into your classroom to sell items for students who will be graduating next spring. It's likely that not everyone in the room is a senior, so some would automatically not be customers. Each person has different plans for graduation. Some students have not even considered their plans and will not do so for several months. Others probably have made plans as early as last summer and may have already purchased many of the things they will need. In some families, high school graduation ceremonies are an important tradition with specific procedures to be followed. In other families, it is up to each graduate to determine the plans.

Your class is a very small market. It is likely the business that visits your class will be interested in all of the prospective graduates from your school and from other high schools in your city

and state. They might want to serve graduating seniors from colleges and universities. Some companies offer products for graduates from adult education programs, junior high schools, and even the "graduates" from preschools. However, it is not likely that all of those graduates want the same things. The differences among all of the people who might buy graduation products will affect what they want to buy, where and when they want to purchase, the prices they are willing and able to pay, and the type and source of information they need to make decisions.

Markets are made up of many segments. *Segments are components of a market in which people have one or more similar characteristics.* The most important characteristics of a market are the needs and wants of consumers. While needs and wants are quite different from person to person, segments of a market can be identified that have one or more strong needs or wants in common. A second way of identifying market segments is through demographic characteristics such as age, income, location, and educational level. Markets can also be described by psychographic or lifestyle characteristics including activities, attitudes, customs, and traditions. The attitudes of potential consumers are important in segmenting markets (see Figure 10-2). How do consumers feel about the type of products and specific brands of the products?

Another way to segment is by identifying the way consumers make their purchase decisions. These factors could include their previous experience with products, what sources of information they use, whether decisions are more rational or emotional, and how much time they take in gathering and evaluating information before a decision is made. Marketing information systems and marketing research are used to gather information in order to divide markets into segments.

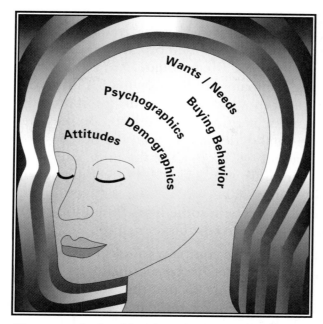

Characteristics Used to Segment a Market

FIGURE 10-2 ▪ In order to identify unique segments of a market, businesses must gather a variety of consumer information.

In order to develop an effective marketing strategy, a business should concentrate its attention on a specific market. In marketing, that is known as selecting a target market. *A target market is a clearly identified segment of the market to which the company wants to appeal.* In order to be an effective target market, it must meet four criteria:

1. The people in the target market must have common important needs and respond in a similar way to marketing activities designed to satisfy those needs.

2. The people outside of the target market should have enough differences from those in the market that they will not find the marketing activities satisfying.

3. There should be adequate information about the people in the target market so they can be identified and located.

4. There should be enough information about the consumers' needs and how they make purchasing decisions that an effective marketing mix can be developed.

In the example given earlier of the firm that offers graduation products, all of the students who will be graduating should be studied. Segments can then be identified based on the type of school, its location, and when the graduation will occur. Other segments could be based on factors such as the age, gender, or even income of the graduate. After identifying several segments, the company would study needs, attitudes, and family customs to see if they are similar or different among various segments. Also, information will be collected to see when and how each segment makes decisions about the purchase of products related to graduation. From all of the information collected, the business will identify which segment offers the best marketing opportunity. That will become the target market. Later in this chapter we will work with some marketing tools that will be helpful in selecting the best target market.

It is possible for the company to select more than one segment for a target market. To be successful, the segments must have enough common needs that they respond in the same way to marketing efforts. For example males and females from the same school may be a part of one target market. Or all graduating seniors from high schools in the Midwest may be similar enough to be considered one target market. Larger companies often work with several target markets at the same time. However, each target market will require different marketing activities because of its differences with other markets.

DEVELOP A MARKETING MIX

The most important work of marketers is to design and implement the marketing mix. The marketing mix includes all of the marketing activities the business will use to satisfy the target market. The marketing mix is the combination of the four marketing elements—product, distribution, price, and promotion.

Businesses that do not use the marketing concept develop their marketing mixes without studying the market. They do not have a specific target market so they must try to satisfy a large group of customers who will likely have very different needs. Since the only customer information they have is based on their past experience, they rely on their own ideas to design marketing activities.

Using the marketing concept provides a real advantage to marketers. Remember that the first step is to identify target markets. Because of the information collected in that step, the marketing mix can be developed based on that information. A complete study of the market will tell you who your prospective customers are, where they live, what their needs and attitudes are, what they are willing to spend, where they prefer to purchase, and the information they need to make a decision. That information will be very helpful to you as you plan product, distribution, price, and promotion activities.

Consider a situation in which you must make marketing decisions. Assume that you work for a furniture rental store. It is located in a city of 300,000 people. You decide what types of furniture, appliances, and other home furnishings to purchase. You also decide how to market rental furniture. Without information about the types of people in the city, who rents furniture, and what types of furniture they rent, it is difficult to develop the marketing mix. But you must make those decisions or the business will not be successful. The wrong decisions may cause the business to buy too much of some items and not enough of others. The business may not have the correct prices or rental terms for customers. The advertising and promotion may be misdirected so prospective customers have difficulty gathering information about the business. What is the marketing mix you would recommend?

With target market information, you would know that your primary target market is made up of college students and young single workers. They live in five major apartment complexes in the city. All but one of those complexes are located in the southeast part of the city within five miles of the local college. You have research on the types of home furnishings usually purchased and leased by people fitting your target market characteristics. You also have a government report that identifies the average amount spent each month for various personal purchases, including home furnishings.

Using information supplied by a media research service, you can identify which radio and television stations are most popular in your target market and the level of newspaper readership. You are aware of a research report that concludes people aged 16–29 are most influenced in purchase decisions by their close friends. You also have a buyer behavior study that suggests young people are more likely to buy used furniture than to rent or buy new furniture and that the typical consumer makes purchase or rental decisions within three days of signing a lease agreement on an apartment. The average consumer calls or visits at least two businesses before deciding on their purchases of home furnishings.

You can see how a specific definition of your target market and the type of information described can be very valuable in developing a marketing mix. With that information, what type of mix would you recommend for the rental business?

IDENTIFYING MARKETING MIX ALTERNATIVES

Have you had the experience of shopping for an item and finding that you have very few choices? While there may be two or three brands available, each of the brands is almost identical to the others. This is a common problem when businesses attempt to sell products to a large market. They attempt to meet the needs of the *average* consumer. If you are not *average* you may find that there is little available that is particularly appealing to you.

We learned in Chapter 4 that it is very difficult to compete when a business' products are almost identical to those of its competitors. Those businesses are in a competitive market that is close to pure competition. When customers see few differences, they are less likely to be satisfied and will look for the lowest price. Businesses want to make their products different from the competition and more satisfying to customers. If that is accomplished, the market will be more like a monopoly.

Marketers understand that most products and services do not have to be just like those of their competitors. They realize there are many ways to change a product to make it unique and more appealing to consumers. Those differences occur through changes in the marketing mix. An effective marketer studies each of the mix elements to understand what can be changed and which changes will be most effective in a specific target market. We will first look at each mix element to identify possible changes that can be made. Then in the next section, we will show how marketers decide on the best choices for a market.

PRODUCT/SERVICE

The product or service as a marketing mix element includes anything offered to the customer by the business that will be used to satisfy needs. This element can be very complex. There are many choices businesses can make when developing the product element of the marketing mix. Figure 10-3 illustrates the major components of a product or service that can be used to create a product that is quite different from competitors' products and that responds to the specific needs of the target market.

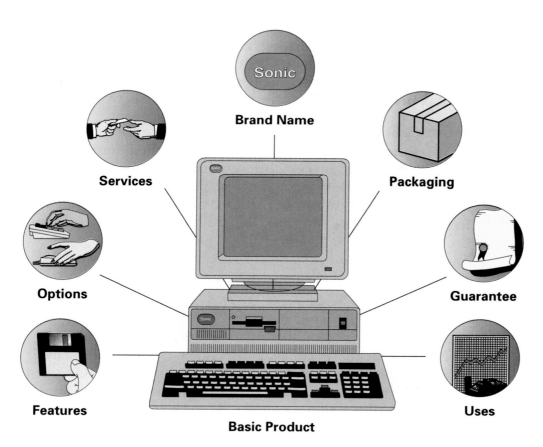

Brand Name

Services

Packaging

Options

Guarantee

Features

Uses

Basic Product

The Product Element of a Marketing Mix

FIGURE 10-3 ▪ The product mix element provides many ways to make a product different from competitors' products and satisfying to a target market.

Not all of the components listed will be used with every product or service. In some cases, all the target market wants is the basic product. At other times services and a guarantee are important. Both research and creativity are needed to develop an effective product. Marketers need to be familiar with all of the possible changes that can be made in a product and select the most satisfying combination to serve a target market.

Basic Product

The most important part of this mix element is the basic product offered. Whether the product is an automobile, a shirt, a telephone, or shampoo, it is the first factor considered by the consumer in deciding whether or not to purchase. If a product is not viewed as need satisfying, the consumer will not consider it as a reasonable alternative. Services can also be the basic part of a marketing mix. Movie theaters, child care, home cleaning, and tax preparation businesses all offer a basic service.

Product Features

After the basic product or service is identified, businesses can add features to make it different from and better than competitors' products and services. Most basic products are sold with a number of additional features. Consider the product offerings of automobile dealers. Every automobile today has hundreds of features. Some, such as seat belts, outside rearview mirrors, safety bumpers, and emission control equipment, are required by law. Others are included to satisfy the common needs of automobile purchasers like carpeting, reclining seats, locking gasoline filler covers, and stereo radios.

The same type of analysis will demonstrate the features offered on the other products. A shirt offers tailoring, easy-care fabric, double-sewn buttons, and multiple color choices. A telephone has push button dialing, ten-number memory, redial, and a volume control. Shampoo contains special moisturizers, a conditioner, and a pleasant scent. Many of these features are expected by consumers and they will not buy products that do not offer the features. It may be difficult to purchase the basic product without several additional features because manufacturers try to meet the expectations of most consumers.

Options

Features are added to improve the basic product. Some businesses make decisions about the features they offer to customers. Customers are not given choices; they must accept the features the company selects. Other companies, however, offer customers choices of the features to be included on the product they purchase. Those choices are known as options. When you order telephone service you are given choices such as call waiting, call forwarding, and three-way calling. Some customers choose one or more of those options while others choose just the basic services.

Associated Services

If your family has purchased a major appliance such as a washer or refrigerator, you were probably offered a maintenance contract by the salesperson. The maintenance contract is an associated service that will pay for repair work if the appliance fails to operate properly. There are many cases where services provided with a product make the product easier to use for consumers. If you purchase a computer system, you might want someone to set it up and test it to make sure it works properly.

Brand Name/Image

At first the brand name may not seem to be an important part of a product or service. However, you can probably identify products that you buy where the brand name is one of the most important factors in your decision. In fact, you may not be willing to buy a pair of jeans, athletic shoes, or a backpack if it is not a specific brand. The brand of certain products is an important factor in making a purchase decision for many people.

Your parents or other people may not always understand why you want to buy specific brands of certain products, but they are probably just as loyal to particular brands of automobiles, foods, athletic equipment, or magazines. Business people demonstrate brand loyalty for equipment, supplies, airlines, and hotels.

One of the important reasons for brand loyalty is the image of the brand. *The image is a unique, memorable quality of a brand.* Some brands have an image of quality, others of low price, and still others as innovative. The image of a product must match the important needs of the consumer to be effective.

Guarantee/Warranty

When customers purchase products or services they want to receive a good value. If they are concerned the product is poorly constructed, will not work properly, or may wear out quickly, they may be unwilling to purchase it. Companies offer guarantees or warranties with products to provide customers assurance that the product will be repaired or replaced if there are problems.

Packaging

An often overlooked part of the marketing mix is the package. Packaging provides protection and security for the product until the consumer can use it. However, packaging has other purposes as well. The package can provide information that helps the customer make a better purchasing decision. It can be useful in promoting the product by attracting attention, demonstrating uses of the product, and so forth. Packaging can even make the product more useful for the consumer. One producer of orange juice found that sales increased when a plastic spout with a cover that could be screwed on and off was added to their cardboard carton.

Uses

The final part of the product element of the marketing mix is the use of the product. It is possible that products and services can be more satisfying to customers or can appeal to new markets if other uses are found. A classic example of expanding markets through new product uses is baking soda. Very few con-

sumers bake their own bread today in the United States so a manufacturer of baking soda saw sales of the product declining. However, in a study of consumer behavior, it was discovered that consumers use the product for many purposes other than baking. Some use it to freshen refrigerators, garbage disposals, and litter boxes for pets. Others use it to brush their teeth. Through promoting those and other uses and actually creating some new products, the company has increased their sales dramatically.

DISTRIBUTION

The complete product or service that is offered by a company is certainly an important element of the marketing mix.

However, unless the consumers in the target market can locate the products, the company will not be successful. Distribution is the marketing mix element that facilitates the physical exchange of products and services between businesses and their customers.

Just as with product/service planning, there are many possible decisions about the locations and methods used to make products and services available to customers. Distribution planning will be discussed thoroughly in Chapter 15. Some important questions that should be answered in planning distribution include the following:

- Where will the customer be best able to obtain the product?

- Where will the customer use the product?

- Are there special requirements needed to handle the product, transport it, store it, display it, or prepare it for customer use?

- What types of distribution activities will the customer expect?

- When should distribution occur?

- Should the product be sold to the consumer directly by the manufacturer or should other businesses be involved?

- Who should be responsible for each type of distribution activity?

In addition to these general distribution decisions, many products require specific attention to physical distribution factors including the type of transportation, inventory control, product handling, protective packaging, order processing, and customer service.

PRICE

The economic foundations of marketing identify the importance of price as a marketing mix element. People have unlimited needs and limited resources to satisfy those needs. They will carefully evaluate products and services to determine if the price that must be paid is an appropriate amount.

It might appear that there is very little a marketer can do with this element of the marketing mix. A price must be set that is high enough so the business is able to make a profit, but not so high that customers will not want to purchase the product or service. There is more to pricing, however, than simply setting the price consumers will pay.

We know that price as a marketing mix element is defined as the actual cost and the methods of increasing the value of the product to the customers. There are several decisions about how to develop and present the price that can affect the customer's perception of value. They include the following issues:

■ Does the business want to increase sales, increase profits, or enhance the image of the product?

■ Will the company set a price to cover costs, set a price based on what customers are willing to pay, or set a price based on what competitors are charging for similar products?

■ Will there be one price that all customers are expected to pay? Will customers be allowed to negotiate the price? Will discounts or sales be used to change prices?

■ Will the price be clearly communicated through a price sticker or catalog?

■ Will the business emphasize the importance of other mix elements, such as a unique product or a convenient location, so customers will not consider price to be important?

■ Are there things that clearly satisfy the customer and make the product better and more valuable than alternatives?

PROMOTION

Consumers need information about product and service choices and assistance in making the best purchasing decisions. Businesses use the promotion element of the marketing mix to provide that information and assistance. Promotion includes the methods and information communicated to customers to encourage purchases and increase their satisfaction. Maybe more than any of the other mix elements, it is easy to see a variety of choices businesses have to change and improve the promotion mix element. Some of the following decisions need to be made when planning promotion:

■ Will the audience for the promotion be a general market or specific segments? Who is the decision-maker? Where are the customers in the decision-making process?

■ Is the specific goal of promotion to increase knowledge, to change attitudes, or to influence behavior? Does the business want to inform people of choices and product information, persuade them to make a decision, or remind them of the value of previous decisions?

■ What specific information does the audience need? Do they need to know more about the product, its location and availability, the price, how it satisfies needs or benefits the audience, or a combination of those messages?

■ Will promotion be most effective through advertising, personal selling, sales promotion, publicity, or some other form of communication?

■ Are customers most likely to expect information to be provided through mass media (television, radio, newspapers, magazines), or more personalized media (direct mail, telephone, individual contacts)? What image do consumers have of each of the media that could be used?

■ What is the total amount of money needed for effective promotion? When should the money be spent, on what activities, and for which media?

■ What information does the business need from consumers? When and how can feedback be obtained to make it most useful?

PLANNING AN EFFECTIVE MARKETING MIX

There are certainly a large number of choices available to change a marketing mix and to make it different from and better than competitors' mixes. However, it may seem that with all of those choices it will be difficult to determine the best combination of product, distribution, price, and promotion to use. Think of the two types of businesses we have discussed in this chapter. If you were helping the company selling graduation products or the furniture rental business plan their marketing mixes, how would you determine what mix they should use?

There are three factors to be considered each time a business plans its marketing mix. Those factors are (1) the type of competition, (2) the purchase behavior of consumers, and (3) the strengths and weaknesses of the business. There are two important tools available to marketers that can assist in understanding the factors and developing effective marketing mixes. Those tools are life cycle analysis and product/service purchase classifications.

LIFE CYCLE ANALYSIS

Products go through four stages in their life cycle, as shown in Figure 10-4. The stages of the life cycle are determined by changes in the type of competition the products face. By studying the competition, a business can determine the type of marketing mix needed in each stage of the life cycle.

Introduction

In the first stage of the product life cycle, a new product is introduced into the market. It is quite different from existing products so customers are not aware of it or realize how it can satisfy their needs. Because it is new, there are no other products that are direct competitors. It will be competing with older, established products.

As with many new things, few people will want to be the first to try the product. The business needs to identify those that are

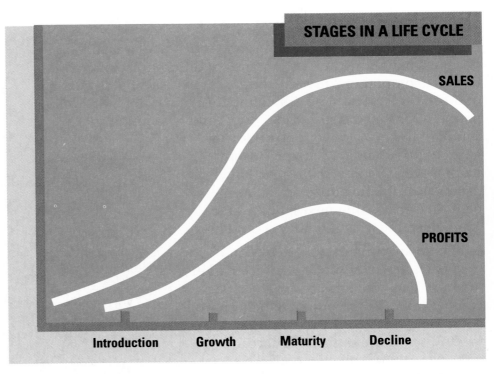

FIGURE 10-4 ■ Analysis of the stages of a product life cycle help businesses develop effective marketing mixes.

Unit 3 • Marketing Planning

very dissatisfied with current products and those who are most likely to want to experiment with something new. These people are the target market for the new product.

The product itself will be very basic since it has just been developed. There will not likely be many features or options. In fact, if the new product is too complicated, customers may not be willing to try it. To assure the customers of the quality of the new product, the company may offer a guarantee or warranty. A well-known brand name may also encourage people to buy the new product if the experience with that brand name has been successful in the past.

The product will not have to be widely distributed in the market since only a small number of customers will buy it initially. It would be too risky and too expensive for the company to try to get widespread distribution. The company will select those locations where the target market would be most likely to buy this type of product.

The price usually needs to be rather high at first since the company has many expenses in developing the product and expects fewer sales immediately. People who are the first to buy a new product or have needs that are unsatisfied will often pay a higher price. They also have no other similar products to use in comparing the price.

Promotion needs to be directed at the target market to inform them that a new product is available and show how it will satisfy their needs. The audience also needs to know where they can purchase the product. Often promotion in the introductory stage of the life cycle will emphasize that the product is new and exciting to encourage people who want to be the first to own something.

Growth

If a new product is successfully introduced, it attracts more customers and sales begin to grow rapidly. Competitors see that the new product offers opportunities for sales and profits so they enter the market with their own brands of the product as soon as they can. With this growing market and increasing competition, the marketing mix must change.

Competitors need to offer something different from the first brand in order to attract customers. They will try to add features and options that make their product better than the first mod-

els. They may also provide services that support the product. Brand name will be very important as each business tries to show consumers that its offering is best.

Because more consumers are now buying the product, it must be distributed more widely in the market. To be as efficient as possible, manufacturers may use many wholesalers and retailers to sell the product. Since customers have choices of brands, each business tries to be sure its brand is available where and when the customer wants it. They concentrate on improving their order processing and handling, transportation, and customer service activities.

Customers see a range of prices during the growth stage. They have many choices of brands, features, options, and services. Brands with a quality image charge higher prices. Those just entering the market or presenting an economy image have lower prices. Businesses emphasize the value customers receive from their brand.

Promotion in the growth stage becomes more competitive. It is focused on attracting more customers into the market. It also demonstrates the advantages of specific brands. More money is spent on promotion. Unique messages are directed at specific segments of the market. The messages aim to inform prospective customers, persuade those who are making decisions, and remind those who have already purchased about the effectiveness of their decision.

Maturity

During the maturity stage of the life cycle, sales peak and profits begin to decline. All of the customers who want the product and all of the companies who are offering this product are in the market. Therefore, the level of competition is very intense as companies compete for existing customers.

The products of competing companies are very similar in maturity. The features and options that were successful have been adopted by all of the companies, while those that were not successful have been eliminated. Customers are aware of brand names and images. Companies emphasize those that are successful and try to change those that are not. When possible, customer services are used to offer more value to customers.

Since customers view the products in this stage of the life cycle as very similar, they pay much more attention to price. Prices will be very competitive and businesses will regularly offer discounts or sale prices to encourage customers to purchase their brands.

Companies will increase the availability of products to make sure customers can easily obtain them. The products will be sold through many businesses and companies will compete for the best locations.

Promotion is very important in the maturity stage. Companies want to continually remind customers of their brand name and persuade them that their company's brand is better than other choices. Because of the large number of customers in the market, mass media and advertising will be emphasized. A great deal of money is spent on promotion in the maturity stage.

Decline

A market declines when consumers decide that a product is no longer satisfying or when they discover new and better products. Sales begin to drop rapidly and there is little or no profit available to companies with products still in the market. Businesses usually try to get out of the market as quickly as possible unless they have a group of loyal customers.

For products in the decline stage of the life cycle, there is little opportunity for product improvement. Because sales and profits are declining, companies are not willing to invest in product changes. Some companies may try to identify additional uses of the product to broaden the market and retain customers.

Distribution will be cut back to only the profitable locations. Companies may save money in distribution by keeping inventory levels low and cutting back on customer service.

Price is a difficult mix element to manage in this stage of the life cycle. Since profits are declining, businesses want to keep prices high. Only the most loyal customers will pay that price however. In most cases, prices have to be reduced to continue to sell the product and even that may not be enough to keep customers in the market.

Since promotion is expensive, companies reduce the amount of promotion. They are more selective in their media choices and promote much less frequently. Since there are fewer customers interested in this product, companies can use more direct methods of communication to keep their loyal customers as long as possible. The promotional message will remind those customers of the reasons they have purchased the product in the past.

CHALLENGES
PLANNING FOR A DECLINING MARKET

What large market has gone through the stages of the life cycle rapidly? Look at the video rental business. In just over ten years it went from a new product to one perched on the edge of decline. What started as a profitable opportunity for small business owners was soon taken over by large chains like Blockbuster. What caused the market to change so rapidly?

The advent of the video cassette recorder, coupled with increasing prices at movie theaters, changed America's movie viewing habits. For a rental price of under $3.00, a family and their friends could sit comfortably at home and watch recent movies. Video rental businesses opened in every shopping center. Soon the popularity of rental movies encouraged supermarkets and convenience stores to open rental centers. Seeing the growing demand, national chains in the form of rental superstores entered the market. With greater assortments and lower prices, the superstores started driving the small businesses out of the market. From introduction to growth and then maturity—the video rental business moved rapidly.

Are we seeing the decline stage of the product life cycle? Decline begins when customers have new and better alternatives to an existing product. What are the alternatives to video rentals? Movie theaters have decided to fight back with low cost movies—often under $1.00. Cable television offers recent movies on movie channels such as HBO and Showtime. Cable television companies are also competing with pay-per-view where you call the cable office and order a recent movie to be shown on your television for $3–$5. You don't even have to leave your home to go to the rental store.

Bell Atlantic Corporation has tested a system that allows its customers to access thousands of movie titles any time of the day or night through phone line transmission. Watching a movie costs about $3 and does not require a VCR or a trip to a video store. Do you believe the new technology from Bell Atlantic will mean the end of movie rental and cable television movie channels? If you were the marketing manager for a video rental store, what would you do to compete with cable channels and "dial-a-movie"?

Using Life Cycles as a Marketing Tool

Understanding the type of competition a business is facing is very helpful in developing a marketing mix. Initially, the product is most important. As competition increases, companies emphasize product improvement and distribution. Later price and promotion become most important. Finally, in the decline stage, the business reduces their marketing efforts and concentrates on the things that are important to loyal customers.

In each stage of the product life cycle, it is important for businesses to apply the marketing concept. If a target market is carefully identified and the needs of that market are used to help develop a marketing mix, a business may be even better at responding to the type of competition it is facing.

PRODUCT/SERVICE PURCHASE CLASSIFICATION SYSTEM

A second tool that can help marketers develop an effective marketing mix is the product/service purchase classification system. *The product/service purchase classification system is a description of the way consumers shop for products based on their needs and perception of products.* See Figure 10-5 on the next page for examples of each category of the classification system.

You do not purchase all products in the same way. For some purchases you are very careful, spending a great deal of time and comparing several brands before deciding on the one to buy. For others, you know what you want and will buy it as quickly and conveniently as possible. Finally, there are some products you would not consider buying. Through careful study of the ways consumers purchase products, marketers have developed the purchase classification system to help plan marketing strategies. The system is based on two important factors:

1. The importance of the purchase to the consumer

2. The willingness of the consumer to shop and compare products before making the purchase

Convenience Goods

There are many purchases that consumers want to make in the most convenient way possible. The reason for that decision de-

CONVENIENCE GOODS

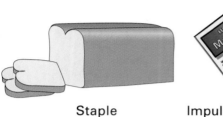
Staple

Impulse

Emergency

UNSOUGHT GOODS

SHOPPING GOODS

Attribute-based

Price-based

SPECIALTY GOODS

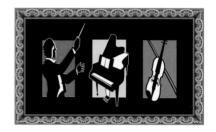

Product/Service Purchase Classifications

FIGURE 10-5 ▪ Marketing mixes can be planned using an understanding of how important a product or service is to consumers and their willingness to shop.

termines whether the product or service is a staple, impulse, or emergency good.

Staple convenience goods include the many products you buy that are regular, routine purchases. You know you need to buy them frequently, you are aware of the needs they satisfy, and you probably have a preference of brands for many of the purchases. These are products you routinely pick up when you go to a store. Staple goods include bread, milk, toothpaste, snack foods, and many other regularly purchased products.

The purchases are important because you use the products a lot. However since you know you need them you make regular purchases. Therefore you will typically purchase them at a convenient location or when you make a routine shopping trip. It is not likely you will shop around from store to store in order to buy a staple good. If the store you are in does not have your favorite brand you may be willing to buy another brand, or you may wait to buy it until the next time you go shopping.

How many times have you walked into a store to buy one or two items and left the store with several more purchases than you planned? These items that we purchase on the spur of the moment, without advance planning are *impulse goods.* Some examples of products that are impulse purchases for many people are candy, magazines, low-cost jewelry, unique items of clothing, and inexpensive new products. Impulse goods are often the items you see displayed near the aisles and check-out counters of supermarkets, department stores, and other retail businesses.

Consumers do not actively shop for impulse goods. They purchase them when they see the product displayed or advertised and identify an important need that they believe can be satisfied. Because of the strong need along with a belief there is no real value to be gained in shopping and comparing other products or brands, the consumer makes the purchase immediately.

You may have a favorite brand of gasoline or soft drink. When given a choice, you will probably select those brands and may even go out of your way to find them. However, when the fuel gauge on your car is on empty, you will probably pull into the most convenient gasoline station and buy that brand of gas. If you are very thirsty, you may be willing to buy another brand of soft drink or even a different beverage if your favorite is not available. Products or services that are purchased as a result of an urgent need are *emergency goods.* Common examples of emergency goods are automobile towing services, umbrellas, ambulance services, and plumbing repair services.

As with impulse goods, consumers do not actively shop for emergency goods. They decide to purchase only because the situation creates an urgent, important need. Because of the emergency, the consumer is unable or unwilling to shop and compare products before purchasing.

Shopping Goods

Most of the major purchases made by consumers are shopping goods. These products and services are typically more expensive than convenience goods. Consumers believe that the need is important, the amount of money to be spent on the purchase is significant, and that real differences exist among the choices of products and brands. Therefore they are willing to spend time shopping and comparing alternatives before making a final purchase decision. Examples of shopping goods for many people are clothing, cars, houses and apartments, stereo equipment, major appliances, colleges, dentists, and vacation locations.

For most shopping goods, consumers see a number of ways that choices are different. Each brand may have a different set of features or services. Prices may vary or some brands can be purchased on sale or using credit. When a variety of differences exist and the consumer considers a number of factors to determine the *best value*, the product is an *attribute-based shopping good*.

Some people evaluate major purchases and decide that several products or brands are basically alike. They will each provide the same level of satisfaction. However, the consumer believes the price is likely to be quite different among the choices. Because the need is important and the cost is high, it is worth the time needed to shop for the *best possible price*. Products that consumers believe are similar but have significant price differences are *price-based shopping goods*.

Specialty Goods

There are some products and services consumers purchase that are so satisfying that the consumer will not consider buying anything else as a substitute. Products that have this strong brand loyalty are known as *specialty goods*. We often think of very well known and expensive products as specialty goods. Automobiles such as Rolls Royce, Porsche, or Lamborghini fit the description. Lear jets and Rolex watches are certainly specialty goods. However, inexpensive and regularly purchased products are treated as specialty goods by some customers.

Do you have a favorite brand of blue jeans? Do you shop for tapes and CDs at the same store every time? Do you and your friends usually go to the same restaurant or other business after school activities? If you do and would not typically consider another choice, they would be specialty products and businesses.

Even such things as chewing gum and toothpaste can be specialty goods if the customer will not buy a different brand.

The two factors that determine if a product is a specialty good are its importance in satisfying an individual's need and

CLASSICS AND CONTEMPORARIES

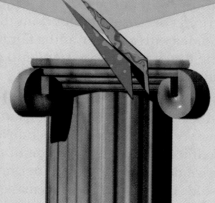

A REAL SPECIALTY PRODUCT

Do you have an extra $750,000 in the bank? If so, you may be able to purchase the car of your dreams. The Jaguar XJ220, the fastest car available to consumers, was in planning and development for over three years. When it was finally available in 1992, the entire production of 350 cars was already sold.

If the Jaguar is not what you want, maybe the McLaren F1 will meet your needs. However, be prepared to pay at least $1,000,000. If that is more than you can afford, there is the less expensive Lamborghini Diablo at just over $300,000. Each of these specialty cars is produced in very low quantities. It is estimated that worldwide sales of expensive sports cars is under 5,000 per year.

There are many luxury car manufacturers that produce unique cars for exotic car buffs. However, most direct their products at a different market than the people interested in the Jaguar, McLaren, or Lamborghini. Companies like Ferrari, Rolls Royce, and Aston Martin sell cars for $100,000–$300,000. Others, including Mercedes, Porsche, BMW, Lexus, and Infiniti, price their luxury automobiles between $50,000 and $100,000. Their customers also want a unique automobile with a quality repu-

tation, but are willing to buy a car that isn't limited to a few hundred people.

Uniqueness and image are factors that convince some people to spend large amounts of money on an automobile. Most people carefully consider two or three brands of automobiles and negotiate with dealers for the best price. Those people would not be part of the market for the top-of-the-line luxury automobiles. The customers for those cars know what they want and are willing to pay whatever it takes to own the car of their choice. Even if it means $750,000!

Source: "What Has Four Wheels, Costs $1 Million, and Goes 240 MPH?" Business Week, September 7, 1992.

the willingness of the customer to delay a purchase until the specific product or brand is located. In the case of specialty goods, consumers believe the brand is the only thing that will provide satisfaction. That belief is usually based on very positive past experiences with the chosen brand and less positive experiences with other brands. Because of the strong belief in the brand, customers will not compare brands when shopping. They will not make a purchase until they can find their choice. If that means waiting or traveling to another store, the customer is willing to do so. You can see that such customer loyalty is very valuable to businesses.

Unsought Goods

While consumers go to great lengths to find specialty goods, there are other products that consumers do not want to buy. They are known as *unsought goods.* If you were choosing things to purchase in the next year would the choices include life insurance or legal services to prepare a will? Those are typically not considered important needs for young people so they would currently be unsought goods in that market. However, when you get older with a career and a family, both of the items may become much more important and could become shopping goods or even specialty goods.

When a product or a specific brand of a product is first introduced into the market, consumers are not aware it exists. However, as soon as they become aware of the product, they decide if it is something that might meet a need. If a product or service does not fill a customer need, it remains unsought and unsold. Even if the business makes it easy to buy, through telephone or catalog sales or a salesperson visiting the person at home, consumers will not make the purchase.

USING PURCHASE CLASSIFICATIONS FOR MARKETING PLANNING

Just as life cycle stages provide important information about competition, purchase classifications help in the understanding of consumer behavior. That understanding is important in planning the best marketing mix. Each purchase classification requires a different mix in order to effectively respond to consumer needs.

Convenience Goods

Consumers want to purchase convenience goods as easily as possible. They do not see important differences among products and brands that make it worth their time to shop and compare. Therefore businesses need to emphasize product location (convenience) in the marketing mix. The product mix element will focus on brand, packaging, and image.

Price is important for staple goods. Prices cannot be set higher than similar products in the same location or the consumer will switch brands. For impulse goods, price is less important and for emergency goods price is only a minor consideration. Promotion is used to remind people of brand and image for staple goods, the need to be satisfied for impulse goods, and location and availability for emergency goods.

Shopping Goods

Because consumers are willing to shop and compare, the marketing mix for shopping goods is different from convenience goods. Products and services no longer have to be available in the most convenient locations. Promotion emphasizes the qualities of the product or service that consumers believe are most important. Promotion often helps consumers compare products or brands.

For attribute-based shopping goods, the product mix element is very important. Consumers are interested in the best combination of features, options, services, and uses. For price-based shopping goods, price is the most important. While customers want a quality product, they believe that several products are very similar. Therefore they do not evaluate differences in product features. They search for the best possible price. Businesses must demonstrate that they have the lowest price or the best possible financial terms. They also need to emphasize price in promotional activities.

Specialty Goods

Specialty goods are in some ways the easiest to market and in other ways they are somewhat difficult. The emphasis in the marketing mix will depend on why consumers believe the product or service is a specialty good. Typically, that status results from a unique or quality product. In that case, the business wants to emphasize the product in marketing planning to insure that the quality or uniqueness is maintained. Promotion reminds consumers of the reasons they prefer the product.

It is possible that consumers prefer a product or service because of its location. Some people select a bank, a physician, or even a college because of its location. They would not consider another choice because it would be inconvenient. Therefore, marketing activities for that product would emphasize the location more so than product features. There are some instances where price is the reason for specialty status. Consumers may buy only one brand because they believe it has the best price. Once again, marketing would maintain that price so consumers remain satisfied. Marketing would emphasize the price as a part of promotion.

Occasionally, products become specialty products because of effective promotion. Promotion that is able to create excitement, a unique image, or a belief that one product is far superior to others may result in the product being treated as a specialty good for at least a short time. This is often the case with items that are considered fads.

Unsought Goods

The marketing mix developed for unsought goods is particularly important. If the products are not well marketed, there will be no demand and the product will fail. If a product is new, the mix will emphasize promotion and distribution. Consumers must be aware of the product, how it satisfies needs, and where they can purchase it. If a business is successful with those two mix elements, the product will quickly become a convenience, shopping, or specialty good.

If customers are aware of the product or service and it remains unsought, the mix must be very carefully developed. The product is most important. The business must evaluate the product to determine why consumers do not want it. The product must be redesigned to make it more appealing to consumers and to relate to their important needs. Promotion can then be used to show consumers how the product will meet their needs.

Businesses must market unsought goods very carefully. Consumers may become quite upset if they believe a business is trying to sell them something they do not need. If consumers develop a negative attitude toward a product or a business, it will be difficult to sell them products in the future. Businesses that successfully sell unsought goods use a target market strategy. They identify the specific segments of the market who have needs related to the product or service. They then develop very personalized marketing mixes to work with those target markets at times and locations where there is a good chance to be successful. Some businesses are so effective with their marketing that a regularly unsought good becomes a specialty good for customers. For example, people who had never purchased life insurance may be impressed by the personal attention and knowledge of one insurance agent. They not only buy one insurance policy but continue to buy additional products from the same agent without considering other companies.

DEVELOPING SUCCESSFUL MARKETING STRATEGIES

The tools we have studied in this chapter can be very helpful in developing effective marketing mixes. If you can determine the stage of a product's life cycle, you will be able to develop the best marketing mix for that stage. If you can understand consumers' purchase behavior for a product of service, you can emphasize the mix elements that are most important to them. There are several criteria that will determine if you have done an effective job of planning a marketing strategy. Those criteria, as shown in Figure 10-6, are a valued product or service, satisfied customers, and a profitable business.

PROVIDING VALUE

In a competitive market there are many products and services available from which consumers can choose. They will select those that provide the greatest value for the money they plan to spend. Businesses must pay careful attention to other products and services in the market to be certain that their own

The Equation for Successful Marketing

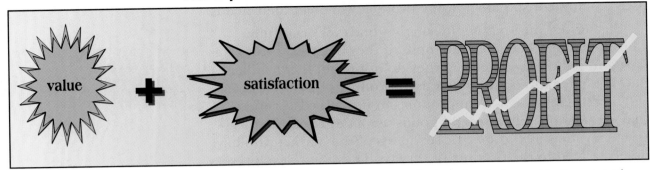

FIGURE 10-6 ▪ A marketing strategy results from developing and testing several marketing mixes. The best choice provides a valuable product that meets customer needs and company objectives.

products are competitive. One way of doing that is through an activity called positioning.

Positioning determines the attributes and qualities of the products and services competing with each other in a market. Some products have attributes that emphasize quality while others focus on value and convenience. Some attempt to create an exclusive image and others try to appeal to the broad market.

Companies that use the marketing orientation will study a target market to determine how customers perceive each of the products in the market. The company wants to know the *position* of each competing product. It uses that information to develop a marketing mix that best meets the needs of the target market. The marketing mix needs to emphasize attributes that are different from those of competitors and that consumers believe are most important. That type of positioning decision results in a marketing mix that offers the best value for the target market.

SATISFYING CUSTOMERS

Businesses will not be successful unless customers are satisfied. It is said that satisfied customers will seldom tell you, but a dissatisfied customer will tell many people. However, a business will know if customers are satisfied because complaints and problems will decrease and customers will return to buy again and again. Satisfied customers are those who believe the business is interested in them and their needs. They see the business developing a marketing mix that is different from and better than the mixes of competing products.

MAKING A PROFIT

Marketing activities will not be successful if they do not result in a profit for the business. A marketing mix needs to respond to customer needs but it also must use the resources of the business efficiently. If marketing is too expensive, the business will not be able to continue to offer the product or service.

Marketers need to consider several ways of implementing a marketing mix. Each mix can be evaluated to determine if it is different from competitors, how the target market will respond, and how profitable it will be. The one that results in the best match of satisfaction and profit should be selected.

REVIEW

The result of marketing planning is a marketing strategy. For a business that uses a marketing orientation, the strategy is developed through a two-step process. First, the business carefully studies the market to identify a target market. The target market must be a clearly identified group with unique needs the company wants to satisfy. Next, the business develops a marketing mix that is designed to satisfy the needs of the target market better than competitors.

Marketers know they have many choices in developing an effective marketing mix. Each mix element (product, distribution, price, and promotion) can be changed to provide the best combination of elements. Tools such as life cycle analysis and product/service purchase classifications are very helpful to marketers as they make mix decisions. The best marketing strategy will be the one that results in a valuable product or service, satisfied customers, and a profitable business.

MARKETING FOUNDATIONS

1. **MATCHING MIX ELEMENTS**

   Identify the marketing mix element described in each of the following items.

   a. The retail business that sells a product

   b. Using telemarketing to contact prospective customers

---

c. The message in an advertisement about the company's image

d. The material used in manufacturing the item

e. A new shape for the package

f. Accepting a credit card in payment for the service

g. Offering to exchange a product that was damaged by the consumer for a new product

h. Using air freight rather than trucks to get the product to the customer faster

i. A fall fashion show to inform important customers of the new apparel designs

j. A business that offers to meet or beat the price of any competitor if the customer brings in an advertisement showing the price

2. UNDERSTANDING MARKETING TOOLS

The following situations describe competitive situations faced by businesses and examples of customer purchase behavior. For each, identify the stage of the product life cycle or the product/service goods classification category being described.

a. There is little profit in the market and only the most loyal customers continue to buy.

b. The customer carefully compares product features and price at several stores before making a decision.

c. A telemarketer calls to describe a new product to a consumer. The consumer is not interested and hangs up the telephone.

d. Many companies offer a service that consumers view as quite similar. Because of the intense competition, the businesses emphasize promotion and often give customers price discounts.

e. As profits begin to increase in the market, several new companies decide to offer products for sale.

f. Driving home from work, Arthur remembers that he forgot to plan something to cook for the evening meal. Since his family will be home when he arrives, he quickly turns into the deli and purchases the evening's special to take home.

g. Franziene's tires on her automobile were almost worn out and she didn't have a lot of money to replace them. For two weeks she watched the advertisements for tires in the paper. When she saw one business offering a 20 percent discount for the purchase of four tires, she purchased them.

h. Jai needs to replace his lost calculator. He goes to several stores but cannot find the TD model 28 which he prefers. He finally locates one at the college book store and purchases it.

i. The Corway Company was test marketing a new transparent coating material for automobile windows that melts ice and snow at temperatures down to 10 degrees Fahrenheit. They learn that another company is developing a similar product, so they end their test market and begin selling the product in 20 northern states in order to beat the other business into the market.

j. Hector was walking through the mall when he saw an artist drawing charcoal portraits. Remembering his mother's birthday was in five days, Hector had his portrait drawn to give to his mother.

MARKETING RESEARCH

1. IDENTIFYING TARGET MARKETS

 If a business uses a target market strategy, it needs to clearly identify the market it wants to serve in order to attract those people to the business. That is often done through advertising. Review the advertisements for several businesses. Identify three businesses that appear to be appealing to specific target markets. You will want to study several advertisements for the same business to get detailed information about their target market. Using the information from the advertisements, prepare descriptions of the target market of each business. Include information for each of the following categories if possible: demographics, needs/wants, attitudes, and purchase behavior.

2. ANALYZING A PRODUCT LIFE CYCLE

A national association of home builders has collected data on the sales of various styles of manufactured windows for the past 30 years. One window style presents an interesting example of a product life cycle. It was introduced in 1971 and remained on the market until 1993. The following table summarizes its market performance during that time.

Year	Number of Manufac- turers	Total Units Sold	Total Sales in Dollars	Total Product Cost
1971	1	800	$ 36,000	$ 38,400
1972	3	2,800	123,200	126,000
1974	5	4,500	193,500	189,000
1976	6	5,700	245,100	228,000
1978	9	10,800	464,400	410,400
1980	15	22,500	945,000	787,500
1982	15	23,000	954,500	828,000
1984	13	23,000	943,000	851,000
1986	12	22,500	877,500	855,000
1988	8	18,000	684,000	693,000
1990	4	10,500	393,750	404,250
1992	2	4,800	177,600	182,400

a. Develop a table that illustrates the following information for each of the years listed:

   ■ average dollar sales per manufacturer
   ■ average sales price of each window
   ■ average cost of each window
   ■ total profit or loss for the industry

b. Construct a graph of the life cycle for the window illustrating total industry dollar sales and industry profit or loss.

MARKETING PLANNING

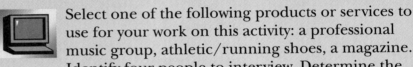

1. USING INTERVIEWS TO UNDERSTAND MARKETS

Select one of the following products or services to use for your work on this activity: a professional music group, athletic/running shoes, a magazine. Identify four people to interview. Determine the information you need to obtain from each person in order to develop a target market description and to classify their purchase behavior in the product/service purchase classification system. Conduct the interviews and complete the following activities:

a. Develop target market descriptions of each person.

b. Determine whether the four people would be part of one target market or more than one.

c. Identify the appropriate product/service purchase classification category for each person interviewed and provide a brief statement describing why you selected that classification.

2. A MARKETING MIX ILLUSTRATION

Identify a product that you own or would like to own that you consider to be a specialty good. Analyze the marketing mix of that product carefully. Using a large sheet of paper or a poster, create an illustration of the marketing mix used to sell the product. Label all parts of each mix element on the illustration.

MARKETING MANAGEMENT

1. ONE PRODUCT OR SERVICE—MANY CATEGORIES

People have different needs and different ways of shopping for products and services. Therefore it is likely that the same product or service can fit in several of the product/service purchase classification categories. For the following service and product, describe the consumer purchase behavior that would be used for each of the categories in the classification system.

■ Movie

■ Groceries

2. MANAGING MATURITY

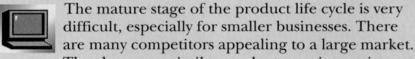

The mature stage of the product life cycle is very difficult, especially for smaller businesses. There are many competitors appealing to a large market. They have very similar products, are increasing their distribution and promotion, and many are starting to decrease their prices to encourage consumers to switch from one business to another. Since most businesses (and especially large businesses) are appealing to the large, mass market, smaller businesses may have the opportunity to be successful by using the marketing concept when planning a marketing strategy.

You are a marketing consultant for a small hotel. The business is finding it increasingly difficult to compete with the national chains that have large advertising budgets, can offer a variety of services, and are willing to cut their prices to attract business people and weekend travelers. Prepare a four-page report for the hotel owner that briefly describes the meaning of the marketing concept and why it can help the hotel develop a marketing strategy. Describe an example marketing strategy that could be implemented to help the hotel compete with the large chains. Provide a rationale to support the strategy.

CHAPTER 11

Writing a Marketing Plan

OBJECTIVES

1. Justify the need for a written marketing plan.
2. Outline the steps necessary for developing a marketing plan.
3. Describe the relationship between a marketing strategy and a marketing plan.
4. Explain the components of an effective marketing plan.
5. Identify the information needed to develop a marketing plan.
6. Write a simple marketing plan.
7. Explain how a marketing plan is implemented.

NEWSLINE

TARGET YOUR MARKET

Croemers department store opened in 1917. Over the years Croemers concentrated its marketing efforts on serving an upper middle class market. Croemers offered clothing, jewelry, appliances, furniture, linens, home accessories, and a full range of customer services. Croemers developed a loyal group of customers and achieved high sales and profits. However, Croemers almost went bankrupt learning about the importance of a marketing plan.

In 1989, two large discount stores entered the market. The discounters offered many of the same types of products as Croemers, but at very low prices. Croemers saw an immediate impact on sales and profits as customers seemed to be attracted by the low prices of the discount stores. In order to avoid losing additional customers, Croemers reduced prices, had regular sales, and ran more frequent promotions. Croemers' management also decided to reduce costs by eliminating some of the more unique and expensive items, reducing services, and purchasing lower quality merchandise.

Many new customers came into the store when the lower prices were advertised. However, most of the customers bought only the sale items. Croemers' image was changing: it was losing the customers who were willing to pay for quality, selection, and service.

Finally, the company turned to a marketing consultant who helped them complete a marketing study. Croemers learned that its primary customers viewed the store as their source of attribute-based shopping goods and specialty goods. These customers were willing to pay higher prices for important purchases because of the quality and service Croemers provided.

The marketing consultant helped

Croemers develop a marketing plan focused on its original target market. Croemers developed a smaller but more profitable line of quality products that were not carried in the discount stores. The employees increased their level of service. Finally, a new promotional program was developed to emphasize the needs of the target market for quality and service. This strategy was carefully developed, described

> **The marketing consultant helped Croemers develop a marketing plan focused on its original target market.**

in detail through the written marketing plan, and communicated clearly to all managers and employees.

Soon Croemers was able to reduce costs, increase profits on the items sold, and reestablish strong ties with its target market. Its new success was the result of careful planning and responding to customers' needs.

PLANNING FOR MARKETING

Developing a marketing plan is one of the most important steps businesses take to market their products and services. The marketing plan serves as a guide for coordinating many marketing activities. Today, almost all successful businesses have a written marketing plan. This chapter prepares you to describe a marketing plan. It presents the information typically included in a marketing plan. You will understand why a written plan is so important to a business. You will see how it is used to coordinate and manage the many marketing activities. If you study the information in this chapter carefully, you will be able to gather and evaluate information as part of a market analysis, develop major parts of a marketing strategy, and identify appropriate activities for an action plan. These are the same skills used in a business to create a marketing plan.

THE BENEFITS OF PLANNING

As you prepare to study for a test, you could just sit down, open your books and notes in front of you, and begin to go through them. Your hope is that if you look through everything, you will remember enough to do well on the test. However, there is probably a better way to study. Before you open your book, you could spend some time thinking about what is likely to be on the test. You could review the objectives for the course, what your teacher emphasized during the semester, what materials you have, and the time available to study. Using that evaluation you could develop a study plan that will focus on the most important materials and the best use of your time.

When a group of friends decides to take a one week travel vacation, they can simply start out driving and choose what to see as they go along. They might use their time effectively and have a good vacation or they might not. A better method may be for the group to agree on their destination, travel time, and activities. Then they can gather information about the planned destinations and activities. Using that information, they can develop a schedule to make the best use of their money and time.

A business person might try to get by without any planning before deciding what products to sell, how to promote them, what prices to charge, or how to respond to competition. In this case, each decision will be made when it seems important or when a problem occurs. The result might be that some decisions are made too late, without enough information, or without considering the impact on other parts of the business. To improve decision-making, the business person gathers information about customers and competition, decides on the profit and sales goals the business can achieve, and then carefully develops a specific plan to guide the purchase, distribution, pricing, and promotion of products and services (see Figure 11-1).

In all of the examples described in the preceding paragraphs, we compared a situation where little planning was done with one where a great deal of planning was done to prepare for an important activity. With careful planning, the student studying for a test, the group planning a trip, and the business person managing the sale of products has a much better idea of what they want to accomplish, the best ways to reach their objectives, and the likelihood that they will be able to accomplish what they planned.

WHAT IS A MARKETING PLAN?

Marketing in most businesses involves a large number of very complex activities. To be successful, the activities need to

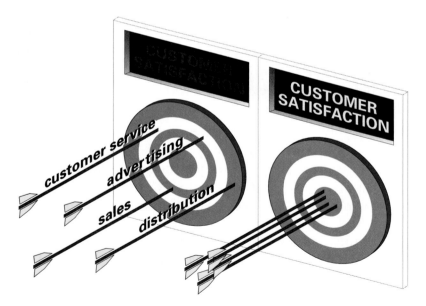

The Advantages of Planning

FIGURE 11-1 ▪ Without planning, the marketing efforts of a business will not be coordinated. With planning, all of those efforts can move in the same direction.

be coordinated with each other and with the activities occurring in other parts of the business. Many people are involved in carrying out the marketing activities. To make the best use of the time and work of those people, their activities should be coordinated as well.

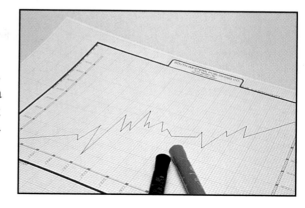

It often takes a very long time from when a product is developed or purchased until it is sold. A great many decisions must be made and often a large amount of money and other resources must be committed by the business during the time between production and the sale of the product. Careful planning and coordination of decisions and resources will be needed in order for the business to make a profit once the products have been sold.

To aid in decision-making and the coordination of the many people, activities, and resources involved in successful marketing, businesses usually develop a marketing plan. *A marketing plan is a clear written description of the marketing strategies of a business and the way the business will operate to accomplish each strategy.*

FROM STRATEGY TO A PLAN

In the previous chapter we studied the importance of developing a marketing strategy. In a marketing strategy the business identifies the target market to be served and develops a marketing mix. The marketing plan is based on a marketing strategy.

We know that marketing strategies must be developed very carefully. They need to be based on a complete study of a market and the possible ways the business can serve the market. If marketers are not careful in developing the strategy, they will be no better off than the companies that use a production orientation. They will likely make decisions based on their own opinions rather than the needs of the target market.

A marketing plan is an organized, objective method of identifying a marketing strategy and determining how the business should operate to make sure the strategy is successful (see Figure 11-2 on the next page). The process of developing a marketing plan encourages the marketer to gather and analyze information, consider alternatives, determine what competitors are likely to do, and study possible responses of customers.

From Strategy to a Plan

FIGURE 11-2 ▪ A marketing plan expands on a company's marketing strategy by gathering and studying information to determine actions needed to implement the strategy.

Based on that study, careful procedures can be planned for the best ways to achieve the marketing strategy. It is possible to determine in advance whether the strategy can be implemented as planned. If not, the strategy can be modified before mistakes are made. You can see that the marketing strategy describes what the business wants to do and the marketing plan provides the details on how the strategy will be implemented and evaluated.

PREPARING FOR MARKETING PLANNING

Just as when you plan to study for an important test or plan a vacation, marketing planning needs to be done carefully. It is a scientific process. A marketing plan is developed to solve a specific problem or accomplish an objective. Information is collected to help identify possible solutions. Alternative strategies are considered (and often tested) before deciding on the best one. Plans are developed so the marketing strategy selected will be implemented effectively. Finally, methods for evaluating the marketing plan are developed to insure that the marketing strategy is accomplishing the objectives or solving the problem.

Marketing planning is not easy. It requires time, information, and people who understand marketing planning procedures. Because of these requirements, some business people believe they do not need or cannot afford to develop marketing plans. They feel their past experience has prepared them to make marketing decisions. That attitude gives an advantage to the business people who carefully prepare marketing plans. They will know when changes are occurring in the market, how customers are likely to respond to new marketing strategies, and what competitors are likely to do. They will know in advance what needs to be done to accomplish their objectives rather than waiting for problems to occur.

PLANNING TO PLAN

Marketing plans are developed for a specific time period, often one year. Plans may be quite short for a small business, but can be very long and complex for a large business with a number of products and services in many markets. The marketing plan is usually developed by the top marketing executive in the business with input and assistance from many other people. In very large companies, there may be several people working throughout the year to gather and analyze the information needed to develop the marketing plan (see Figure 11-3). Even in small companies, it takes many hours of work and the accumulation of much information to prepare an effective marketing plan.

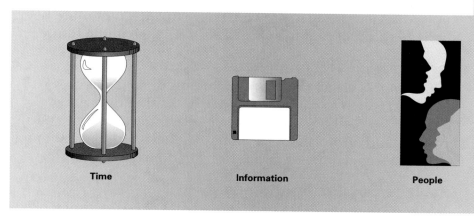

| Time | Information | People |

Resources for Effective Planning

FIGURE 11-3 ■ Businesses need to be sure they have the necessary resources for effective marketing planning.

PLANS ARE BUILT WITH INFORMATION

The work needed to develop a marketing plan begins long before the plan is actually written. A great deal of information is necessary to develop a good marketing plan. The people responsible for marketing planning must make sure needed information is collected and evaluated in order to begin the necessary planning.

Marketing plans developed without needed information or with limited information are likely to result in poor decisions and ineffective marketing. If the information is not available when needed and is not organized to make it easy to analyze, marketing planning will be delayed. Companies that develop marketing plans must carefully identify the information they need for those plans. Then they determine where and how the information can be obtained. They begin the data collection process long before the marketing plan is actually developed.

Each business uses different information for its own marketing plan. However, the following types of information are usually needed for effective marketing planning.

Performance of the Company

In order to plan for the future, marketers must know what has happened in the past and what is expected to happen in the future. Information on sales and profits, effective and ineffective marketing activities, and the company's strengths and weaknesses needs to be collected and reviewed. Marketers need to know what new products are being developed, if others are being eliminated, and if resources are likely to change in the future.

Performance of Competing Companies

Customers usually have several brands of products or services from which to choose. In order to develop marketing strategies that will be successful, marketers must evaluate the products and efforts of those competing businesses and attempt to predict what competitors are likely to do in the future.

Changes Outside the Company

Many things occur that affect the potential success of a product but are outside of the immediate control of the business or its competitors. The economy can decline or improve. Laws can be passed by state and local governments that affect business activities. Additional taxes or licenses can increase costs. Newly developed technology can result in improved products, or innovative production and marketing procedures. Businesses that regularly collect information to determine if changes are likely to occur are in a better position to respond to changes than businesses that do not pay attention to change.

Information about Current and Prospective Customers

Customer information is important to marketers. Understanding customers makes it possible for businesses to satisfy their needs. Through satisfying needs, businesses hope to make a profit. Businesses must continually study information about their customers. They must learn more about who their customers are and what their needs are. A business needs to know how customers perceive the business and its competitors. Are there changes or improvements in products and services the customers would like to see? It is also important for businesses to identify other prospective customer groups. The business can gain more customers by satisfying the needs of new groups.

GATHERING NEEDED INFORMATION

Companies that successfully prepare and use marketing plans have developed procedures to gather and analyze information. Many have sophisticated marketing information systems (which we will study in Chapter 22) that make it possible to quickly and objectively review large amounts of information.

Much of the information used in developing marketing plans is already available in the company (see Figure 11-4).

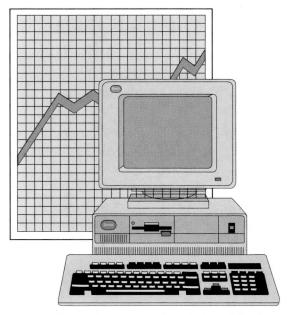

Improving Marketing Decision-Making

FIGURE 11-4 ▪ Marketers need accurate information to develop a marketing plan.

Records of production, operations, and sales are usually maintained. Detailed information on specific customers and their purchasing history is often available. In addition, many businesses regularly gather information about competitors, business trends, and the economy to use in planning.

If information is needed for marketing planning and is not currently available, procedures should be developed to obtain it. Again, some of the needed information may already be collected and available from a government agency, a trade association, or a company that specializes in market research. If those sources cannot provide the information, the business needs to complete the necessary research to obtain the information.

THE PLAN IS A TOOL

After a marketing plan is developed, it becomes a very important tool for the business. It can be viewed like a road map for a trip or like the directions for assembling a piece of equipment. The plan ensures that needed activities are performed in the correct order and at the proper time. It helps everyone involved in marketing understand what they must do and what others are doing to make sure that all marketing activities are accomplished as planned.

A MARKETING PLAN FORMAT

Marketing plans take many forms and can contain different types of information. They are developed to assist a specific business so they are written in a way that is most useful for the people in that business.

No matter what the actual form of a marketing plan or its length, all effective marketing plans contain common features:

■ An analysis of past, current, and future circumstances that can affect the business' performance.

■ The marketing goals and objectives of the business.

■ Descriptions of the target markets to be served.

■ Discussion of the marketing mixes the business plans to use.

■ Details on the activities, resources, and schedules needed to manage the marketing mixes.

■ Standards and procedures for evaluating the effectiveness of the marketing activities.

IN THE SPOTLIGHT

WHO IN THE WORLD IS BRØDERBUND?

Brøderbund Software is a company that understands the marketing concept and is willing to do things differently. A commitment to finding unique consumer needs for computer software and then developing products to meet those needs has allowed the small company to be very profitable.

Brøderbund started in the software business by developing personal computer versions of popular arcade games. But while other companies continued to produce games, Brøderbund recognized that people's needs were changing. As consumers got more comfortable with their personal computers, they began to look for other ways to use them. Those uses ranged from personal to home applications to education.

The first Brøderbund product developed for this market was Print Shop, a program that individuals could use to print banners, posters, letterhead, and personalized greeting cards. When Brøderbund saw that kids were using Print Shop, they began to explore other products for the younger market. They found a winner with the educational package *Where in the World is Carmen Sandiego?*

Recently Brøderbund adapted CD-ROM technology to produce a set of disks called Living Books. These are "books" developed to help very young children learn to read. Living Books seems destined to be another successful product for the company.

The managers at Brøderbund carefully develop marketing strategies that include reasonable prices. Brøderbund's promotion emphasizes the educational quality of the products as well as fun and entertainment. A commitment to the marketing orientation and carefully developed marketing strategies have keyed Brøderbund's success.

Source: "Identify a Need, Turn a Profit," Fortune, *November 30, 1992, pp. 78-79.*

A marketing plan is developed in three stages:

1. Gather and analyze information about the market.
2. Develop the marketing strategy.
3. Prepare a plan of action.

A format for a simple marketing plan is shown in Figure 11-5. It includes sections for each of the three stages of development.

Marketing Plan Outline

I. Market Analysis

A. Purpose and Mission of the Business
B. Description of Current Markets and Strategies
C. Primary Competitors and Their Strengths/Weaknesses
D. External Environment Analysis
    1. Economy   4. Competition
    2. Laws and Regulations   5. Technology
    3. Costs   6. Social Factors
E. Internal Analysis
    1. Strengths
    2. Weaknesses
    3. Anticipated Changes

II. Marketing Strategy

A. Marketing Goals/Expected Outcomes
B. Target Market Description
    1. Identifying Characteristics
    2. Unique Needs, Attitudes, Behaviors
C. Marketing Mix Description
    1. Product/Service
    2. Distribution
    3. Pricing
    4. Promotion
D. Positioning Statement

III. Action Plans

A. Activity
B. Responsibility
C. Schedule
D. Budget
E. Evaluation Procedures
    1. Evidence of Success
    2. Method of Collecting Evidence

FIGURE 11-5 ▪ A simple format for developing a marketing plan includes the three stages of development.

MARKET ANALYSIS

The first part of the marketing plan is an opportunity for the planners to review information to determine the most effective marketing strategy.

Purpose and Mission

The mission or purpose of the company identifies the nature of the business or the reasons the business exists. It is most often developed to describe broad categories of products or services the business provides (transportation, health care, legal services) or the types of customers the company wants to serve (business travelers, resorts in the sunbelt, single parents with children under 18). By identifying the mission or purpose, marketing planners concentrate their efforts in areas where the company is known and works best. An example of a mission statement for an auto dealership is "to offer automobiles at fair prices, to provide fast and effective service, and to treat all customers with courtesy and respect." A bank has a mission of "offering convenient and innovative financial services for the Southeast."

Description of Current Markets and Strategies

After identifying the mission, the planners briefly review the current marketing efforts of the company. The review includes an identification of the markets in which the company is operating and the marketing strategies currently being used to remind the planners of activities underway in the business. Determining the activities that are working well and those that are not helps in deciding to continue with the same strategies or to plan changes. A company might discover that its advertising costs are increasing at a rate much faster than its sales. In that case it needs to determine if the costs can be controlled or if the increased advertising might pay off later in faster sales growth.

Primary Competitors

An analysis of the competitors in the same product categories and serving similar customer groups is an important part of the marketing plan. In addition to identifying each competitor, an objective evaluation of the important strengths and weaknesses of each competitor is important. This evaluation helps the firm decide how to compete with each of those businesses. For example, if a competitor is known for keeping prices very low, it may be difficult for another company to develop a strategy that emphasizes price. On the other hand, if a competitor is having difficulty with providing repair services for the products it sells, another company may be able to attract new customers by emphasizing its customer service department.

External Environment Analysis

Another important part of the market analysis is to identify any factors outside of the company, the external environment, that can increase or decrease the effectiveness of its performance. Many of those factors were identified earlier in this chapter. They include the economy, competition, laws affecting the business, technology, changes in costs, and the expectations and needs of society. An example of the effect of technology on businesses is the introduction of the facsimile (fax) machine. With that technology, letters and other printed communications can be transferred almost instantly rather than waiting for delivery through the mail. It affected the way many companies communicate with their suppliers and their customers. Current or anticipated changes in the economy, technology, laws, the type of competition, as well as other areas, need to be identified and carefully considered when developing the company's marketing strategy.

Internal Analysis

The final part of the market analysis should be a very complete review of the current strengths and weaknesses of the company. This process is known as an internal analysis. The company's strengths and weaknesses are determined by reviewing current and past performance in existing markets. Analyzing products and production methods, marketing activities, personnel, and financial performance can point out areas where the company has advantages and disadvantages compared to competitors. If a company has a unique production process that competitors have been unable to duplicate, it should be emphasized. If customers believe the company has a better customer service record, it will be important to use it in the next marketing plan. On the other hand, if the company is having difficulty competing on the basis of price, strategies should be developed to avoid direct price competition.

MARKETING STRATEGY

The most important part of the marketing plan, in terms of the company's success, is the development of a marketing strategy. As discussed in Chapter 10, the marketing strategy is the description of the way marketing will be used to accomplish the company's objectives. The marketing strategy includes a complete description of the target market(s) to be served and the marketing mix designed for each target market.

Target Market Description

The marketing strategy will clearly identify the target market to be served. The target market will be defined completely so it can be located, so people in the business understand the market's characteristics and its needs and wants, and so it is clear that the marketing mix is appropriate for the market.

While each target market is unique, it is possible for an organization to serve several target markets at the same time. Very large businesses may work with dozens of target markets. When more than one market is identified, marketing planners must remember that each target market requires a specific marketing mix.

Developing a Positioning Statement

One of the most interesting parts of the marketing strategy is the positioning statement. *A positioning statement is a specific description of the unique qualities of the marketing mix that make it different from the competition and satisfying to the target market.* For example, a discount store suggests that it provides all of the products needed in the home for a family on a budget. A manufacturer of sporting goods positions itself to serve professional sports teams with products designed to meet the specific needs of each athlete. A home improvement service specializes in working with realtors and homeowners who are planning to sell their homes. Their positioning statement may be to increase the value of the home as a result of careful cleaning and repairs.

Specifying the Marketing Mix

A complete description of each mix element is included in the marketing plan. The discussion of marketing strategy in

Chapter 10 illustrates the type of information needed for each of the mix elements. Product, price, distribution, and promotion are described specifically and completely so everyone involved in implementing the mix understands what the company plans to do.

Determining Goals and Outcomes

The marketing strategy needs to include a specific statement of the goals the company plans to achieve or the expected outcomes of the marketing efforts. In this way the company is able to determine whether the marketing strategy is effective. Marketing goals include such things as increasing sales or profits for certain products, increasing the market share for a product in a particular geographic area or target market, increasing the effectiveness of particular parts of the marketing mix such as distribution or customer service, or other specific results.

ACTION PLANS

The marketing strategy will not be successful just because it is described in a marketing plan. Many people are responsible for implementing the strategy. Their activities must be planned and procedures set up to evaluate the activities. The final section of the marketing plan identifies the actions needed to accomplish and evaluate the marketing strategy.

Activity Schedule

Completing each part of the marketing strategy will require a series of activities. The needed activities must be determined along with a description of how and when the activities will be completed. Responsibility for completing each of the activities needs to be assigned.

Many people both inside and outside the company are involved in marketing. Their activities must be coordinated in order to be successful. For example, if a manufacturer is introducing a new notebook-size personal computer, the production schedule must be coordinated with distribution to retailers, the development of printed product information for the manufacturer's and retailers' salespeople, and the advertising schedule. If the computer is advertised to consumers before the retailer has a supply of the products or before salespeople are prepared to provide the necessary product information, both the consumer and retailer will be unhappy with the manufacturer.

Design Evaluation Procedures

To be able to determine if the action plan is effective, evaluation procedures should be developed. The evaluation procedures measure whether the marketing activities were completed on time and in the right way. They will also determine if the marketing objectives were accomplished.

Information on target markets can be collected to determine if they are responding to the marketing mix and if their needs are satisfied. Each of the mix elements can be studied to

CHALLENGES
CLEARLY CONFIDENTIAL?

Kelvin Gardner is a sales representative for Agri-Gro, an agriculture chemical producer. He sells to farm supply businesses in a four-state area: Illinois, Iowa, Missouri, and Kansas. For the past four years, Kelvin has been number one or two in total sales of all of the company's salespeople. However, this year has been quite different. The economy is suffering, companies are reducing or delaying purchases, and Kelvin is in tenth place in company sales.

One company in Kelvin's territory, Farmmore, has never purchased chemicals from Agri-Gro. It has businesses in three of the four states where Kelvin works and purchases 8 percent of all chemicals sold in those states. Kelvin has never received an order from Farmmore. Kelvin believes that if he can gain Farmmore's business, his sales will once again be near the top in the company.

Kelvin is meeting with Farmmore's vice-president when the vice-president is called to meet with the company president for fifteen minutes. While he waits, Kelvin notices a copy of Farmmore's marketing plan on the desk.

Kelvin knows that the marketing plan can provide important information on Farmmore's plans for the year. If Kelvin knows more about the company's marketing plan, he can show how Agri-Gro's products will help Farmmore be more effective.

Kelvin also knows that the marketing plan is a confidential document. Should Kelvin take the copy of the plan from the vice-president's desk? Should Kelvin quickly look at the marketing plan on the desk to learn as much as he can in a short time? Should Kelvin treat the marketing plan as a confidential document and not look at it?

identify whether it was developed as planned. Specific activities should be evaluated to determine if the quality is acceptable and if it was accomplished within the budget available.

Information collected in the evaluation is used to make improvements in marketing activities while the plan is being implemented. As soon as problems are identified, actions should be taken to correct those problems. Evaluation information is also useful in developing the next marketing plan.

DEVELOPING A SIMPLE MARKETING PLAN

A basic marketing plan can be developed based on the answers and descriptions in each section of the marketing plan outline. Those descriptions and answers should be based on a careful study of the market and analysis of the information resulting from that study. Figure 11-6, on pages 329 and 330, is a worksheet you can use to prepare a simple marketing plan. The worksheet provides questions that should be answered about each part of the marketing plan. Planning starts by identifying the broad market in which the business hopes to identify a target market and a general description of the basic product or service the business is planning to market. With that information, the worksheet can be completed.

IMPLEMENTING THE MARKETING PLAN

Once the marketing plan is developed it becomes a guide for all of the activities occurring in the business. Everyone involved in marketing must be familiar with the plan and be prepared to implement their parts of it. The top marketing executive in the business will develop procedures for presenting the plan to other managers and giving them the necessary information so they can train all marketing personnel to implement the plan.

A marketing plan is a very confidential document in a business. It describes specifically what the business plans to do to compete with other businesses in the same market. Therefore, the marketing plan must be carefully protected to be sure people outside the business do not obtain the information.

Worksheet for Developing a Marketing Plan

MARKET ANALYSIS

1. Developing a purpose or mission statement
   a. What is the reason this business exists?
   b. Who is the business most interested in serving?
   c. What are the important things the business is trying to accomplish?

2. Describing current markets and strategies
   a. Specifically, who are the businesses' current customers?
   b. What are the needs and wants of the current customers?
   c. How would the customers describe the important characteristics of the product, distribution, price, and promotion?

3. Analyzing the competition
   a. What other businesses do the customers consider when they buy this product?
   b. What are the things each of the businesses do that cause customers to choose the products of that business?
   c. What do customers dislike about each of the competing businesses?

4. Analyzing the business environment
   a. Is the economy strong, stable, or weak?
   b. What changes are experts predicting for the economy?
   c. Are there current or anticipated laws or regulations that will affect business operations, competition, any mix element, or the activities of consumers?
   d. Is inflation causing prices to rise?
   e. Are there costs to the business that are increasing or decreasing?
   f. Are competing businesses increasing or decreasing prices?
   g. Where is this product in the stages of the product life cycle?
   h. Is the level of competition increasing or decreasing?
   i. Does the business or competitors have any unique technology that changes the competition?
   j. Is there new technology available or being developed that will affect consumer behavior, business operations, or any of the mix elements?
   k. Are there social changes occurring that could affect consumer behavior in existing markets or in anticipated markets?

5. Analyzing the business
   a. What makes the business, its operations, and its marketing mix different from and better than the competition?
   b. What are the things that the business is not able to do as well as competitors?
   c. What plans are underway that may result in changes for elements that are currently strengths and weaknesses of the business?

MARKETING STRATEGY

1. Identifying the target market
   a. Will the target market be the same or different from the past marketing plan?
   b. What are the obvious identifying characteristics of the target market?
   c. Is the identified market a unique segment that requires a specific marketing mix?
   d. Is this market currently purchasing the company's product or a competing product?

e. What are the important needs and attitudes of the identified market that relate to the product to be provided?

f. How does this target market go about making a purchase decision for the product?

2. **Developing a positioning statement**

a. What is unique about the target market the business plans to serve?

b. What about the company or its marketing mix are the unique and identifying qualities that are important to the target market?

c. How can the unique qualities of the market and mix be clearly communicated in a brief statement?

3. **Describing the marketing mix**

a. What are the alternatives that could be developed for each of the mix elements?

b. Of the possible choices, what are the specific and important elements of product, distribution, price, and promotion that the target market would prefer?

c. Of the possible choices, what are the specific and important elements of product, distribution, price, and promotion that the business will be able to provide?

d. Which of the alternative marketing mixes best meets target market needs and can be implemented effectively by the business?

e. Who within and outside the company will need to be involved in implementing the marketing mix?

4. **Establishing goals and objectives**

a. What are the important results the company is expecting to achieve during the time of this plan?

b. What will be used to determine if marketing activities are successful?

ACTION PLANS

1. **Developing needed marketing activities**

a. What information is needed to complete marketing planning?

b. What activities must be completed in developing each of the mix elements?

c. What activities are needed to implement each of the mix elements?

d. Who will be responsible for each of the activities identified?

e. When will each activity be initiated?

f. When will each activity be completed?

g. How will activities be coordinated with each other?

h. What money and other resources will be needed for each of the activities?

i. How and where will the necessary money be obtained?

j. Who is responsible for preparing and managing the budget?

2. **Preparing to evaluate the marketing plan**

a. What specific evidence will show that each of the marketing activities is successful?

b. What evidence will demonstrate that goals and objectives have been accomplished?

c. How and when will the evidence be collected?

d. Who is responsible for collecting and analyzing the information?

e. Who will need to know the results of the evaluation?

FIGURE 11-6 ▪ Answering specific questions helps to provide the needed information for developing a marketing plan.

Only a few copies of the marketing plan are printed. The copies are distributed only to those people who need to have the complete information contained in the plan. Those people are usually the executives in the business and the top marketing managers.

A few people from outside the business may need to review the marketing plan. If the company is working with a bank or other financial institution to secure loans for operations, the marketing plan may be an important way of demonstrating the potential for success. An advertising agency usually needs to review the marketing plan to insure that advertising and promotion are coordinated with the other marketing activities.

Within the company, people involved in marketing are given general information about the entire marketing plan. They are then provided with detailed information about the part of the plan they are implementing. Whenever information from a marketing plan is shared, the people receiving the information must be very careful to protect that information.

The implementation of a new marketing plan is a very important time in a business. Often new activities are required as a part of that plan. People need to study the plan and determine what they need to do and what resources they will need to make the plan successful.

Perhaps a business develops a marketing plan for a new product. Perhaps the marketing plan involves a large number of people. The company may organize a large meeting for its employees. The company may also include the businesses that will be working with the company. The meeting may be very exciting. It may include entertainment, speeches, films, and demonstrations of new products. Examples of the support to be provided by the company may be given. The meeting will generate enthusiasm for the marketing plan. It will also begin preparing people for their work in carrying out the plan.

REVIEW

A marketing plan may be the most important document in a business for the people responsible for marketing activities. It is a written description of the marketing strategy for the business and the activities needed to carry out that strategy. Its purpose is to serve as a guide so that all of the activities are well planned and coordinated. While marketing plans can be very different, most contain the same basic information: a market analysis, the marketing strategy, and an action plan. If a marketing plan is successful, the goals and outcomes identified in the plan are achieved and the activities in the action plan are completed.

MARKETING FOUNDATIONS

1. **FIND THE CONCEPT**

   Each of the following questions is about a concept related to the development of a marketing plan. The concepts are presented in the chapter. Locate the concept in the chapter and use the information provided to answer the question.

   a. Why is planning useful to a business person who is managing the sale of products?

   b. Why do businesses usually develop a marketing plan?

   c. What is a marketing plan?

   d. What are the two parts of a marketing strategy?

   e. What is likely to happen if marketers are not careful in developing a marketing strategy?

   f. What is meant by the following statement: marketing planning is a scientific process?

g. Why do some business people believe they do not need to develop marketing plans?

h. Who is responsible for developing a marketing plan?

i. Why does the work needed to develop a marketing plan begin long before the plan is actually written?

j. What types of information are usually needed for effective marketing planning?

k. How do marketing information systems improve marketing planning?

l. Why are marketing plans often developed in many forms with different types of information?

m. What are the three stages of development for a marketing plan?

n. What is the mission or purpose of a company?

o. What is a positioning statement?

p. Why should evaluation procedures be included in a marketing plan?

q. Why should the marketing plan be carefully protected to be sure people outside the business do not obtain it?

2. HOW ARE THEY RELATED?

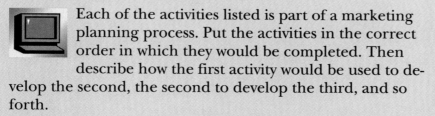 Each of the activities listed is part of a marketing planning process. Put the activities in the correct order in which they would be completed. Then describe how the first activity would be used to develop the second, the second to develop the third, and so forth.

▪ develop an action plan

▪ complete a market analysis

▪ design a marketing information system

▪ identify a target market

▪ write marketing goals and objectives

▪ prepare a positioning statement

▪ describe the marketing mix

MARKETING RESEARCH

1. TAKE A POSITION

Locate an advertisement or other type of consumer communication for one company or organization representing each of the categories in the following list. Based on the information collected, develop a positioning statement for each company or organization. The positioning statement should clearly identify the specific market the company/organization serves and the unique qualities of its marketing mix that make it different from and better than its competitors.

- lawyer or law firm
- college or university
- automobile dealership
- state (promoted for economic development or tourism)
- political candidate

- branch of the military
- food producer
- apparel retailer
- radio station
- supplier of gasoline for automobiles

2. USES OF MARKETING RESEARCH

Find and bring to class at least one example of a survey instrument used by a company or an organization in carrying out a marketing research activity. The example might be a questionnaire you or your family received in the mail or a survey that was included in a newspaper or magazine. It might be part of materials packaged with a new product you purchased. If you work for a company, they might have a copy of a survey.

Analyze the survey to determine the type of information being collected. Then prepare a brief oral report for your class that describes the survey and how you believe the results could be used by the company as part of marketing planning.

MARKETING PLANNING

1. ESTABLISHING RELATIONSHIPS

Data on the sales of one product often can be used to predict sales of another product. A company that markets patio furniture decided to try to find data that would help it establish sales projections. Data on five years of new home sales and annual expenditures for home remodeling were collected for the geographical area in which the company sells its products. Those data, as well as the company's annual sales for five consecutive years, are as follows:

Year	New Home Sales	Home Remodeling Expenditures	Patio Furniture Sales
1994	$10,320, 540	$620,800	$85,020
1993	11,550,860	600,250	83,800
1992	9,980,010	540,890	76,220
1991	10,500,800	510,400	73,010
1990	12,110,950	460,350	66,950

Calculate the dollar value and percentage of increase or decrease from year to year for each category. Then plot the percentage changes for each category on a scattergram. After analyzing the information, do you believe either new home sales or home remodeling expenditures can be helpful in predicting patio furniture sales? Support your answer.

2. RESPONDING TO UNCONTROLLABLE FACTORS

Businesses often have to respond to factors they cannot control. Their response often means a change in a part of their marketing mix. Review newspapers and magazines to identify examples of businesses that had to respond to the following list of uncontrollable factors. Find one business example for each factor.

Then identify the change the business made in responding to the factor. Write a brief summary of each example.

- change in a law
- change in technology
- new company enters the market
- change in the economy
- significant increase in a cost of doing business
- social or cultural change

MARKETING MANAGEMENT

1. WRITE YOUR OWN MARKETING CASE

Identify an experience you had with a business that demonstrated that the business did not have a carefully developed marketing plan. The experience would be one in which the target market was not clearly identified or the marketing mix was not well planned and implemented. Specific evidence could be mistreatment of the customer, poor communication, products or services that did not meet your needs, inappropriate pricing, offensive advertising, etc.

a. Write a 200+ word description of your experience in which you describe the business and its activities in detail. Make your description and explanation complete so others who read it will be able to understand the problem you experienced and some of the reasons why the problems occurred. Try to keep the description anonymous so others cannot easily identify the business you are describing. When you are finished, you will have written a case study about a business problem.

b. Exchange your case problem for one written by another student in your class. Using your knowledge of marketing planning, develop a solution to the case. Describe what the business should have done to avoid the problem using marketing planning. Organize your answer into three parts: market analysis, marketing strategy, and action plan.

2. COMPLETING A MARKETING PLAN

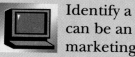 Identify a small business you would like to own. It can be an existing or fictional business. Use the marketing plan format and the planning worksheet from this chapter. Prepare a sample marketing plan by completing each section of the marketing plan format. Use the questions from the worksheet to guide your thinking as you develop the marketing plan. You will not have adequate information available to make objective decisions for each part of the plan. Make the best possible decisions with the information you have available and your understanding of marketing. This activity is designed to help you consider the types of decisions marketing managers make when completing a marketing plan.

PART

2

FUNCTIONS OF
MARKETING

UNIT

4

Creating the Mix: Product and Distribution

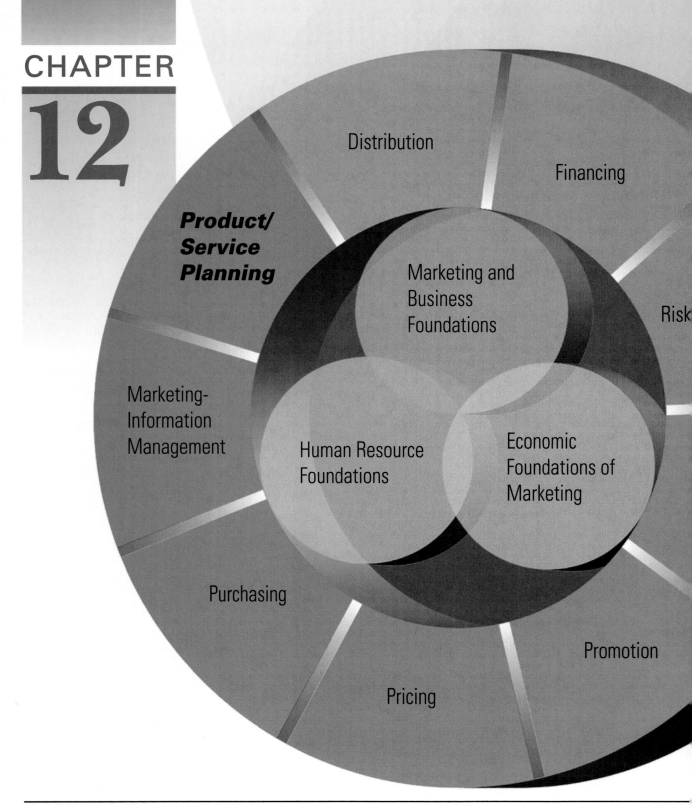

Distribution

Financing

Product/
Service
Planning

Marketing and
Business
Foundations

Risk

Marketing-
Information
Management

Human Resource
Foundations

Economic
Foundations of
Marketing

Purchasing

Promotion

Pricing

Develop a New Product

OBJECTIVES

1. Identify how consumers and business people define a product.

2. Describe the role of marketing in new product development.

3. List the factors that are part of the product mix element.

4. Make decisions about the product mix element based on market characteristics.

5. Understand the process businesses use to develop new products.

NEWSLINE

SALES OVER SUBSTANCE?

Light, high fiber, no cholesterol
What do these words mean? There is growing evidence that some companies have been more concerned about sales than about giving customers accurate information. For example, some products are labeled *light* to refer to their color rather than the amount of calories.

Nutrition Facts

Serving Size 1/2 cup (114g) • Servings Per Container 4

Amount Per Serving	
Calories 260	Calories from Fat 120
	% Daily Value*
	20%
Total Fat 13g	25%
Saturated Fat 5g	10%
Cholesterol 30mg	28%
Sodium 660mg	11%
Total Carbohydrate 31g	
Sugars 5g	0%
Dietary Fiber 0g	
Protein 5g	

Vitamin A 4% • Vitamin C 2% • Calcium 15% • Iron 4%

*Percents (%) of a Daily Value are based on a 2,000 calorie diet. Your Daily Values may vary higher or lower depending on your calorie needs:

Nutrient		2,000 Calories	2,500 Calories
Total Fat	Less than	65g	80g
Sat Fat	Less than	20g	25g
Cholesterol	Less than	300mg	300mg
Sodium	Less than	2,400mg	2,400mg
Total Carbohydrate		300g	375g
Fiber		25g	30g

1g Fat = 9 calories
1g Carbohydrates = 4 calories
1g Protein = 4 calories

AP

Source: FDA

Many business people, consumer groups, and government officials are concerned about misleading or false nutrition labeling.

Many business people, consumer groups, and government officials are concerned about misleading or false nutrition labeling. In December, 1992, the federal government issued food labeling rules that apply to every packaged food product sold to consumers. The rules require all food producers to use a standard label containing specific information that allows consumers to compare products and determine the impact of the product on their diets.

The information on each label must be based on a standard serving size and a daily consumption of 2,000 calories. The label must report the number of calories in each serving and the amount of fat, cholesterol, sodium, carbohydrates, and protein in both grams and percentage of the total daily diet requirements.

The use of terms is regulated as well. Specific meanings have been established for nutritional words like low-fat, high fiber, and light. For example, companies cannot label their products as *light* unless fat and calories are at least 50 percent lower than the original product.

Specific meanings have been established for nutritional words like *low-fat, high fiber,* and *light*.

The labeling requirements are not viewed positively by everyone. Some believe it will cost businesses as much as $2 billion to convert to the new system. Others think the rules will not be totally effective since they apply only to the information on product packages and not to advertising. The information is also not required on fresh foods or on restaurant menus.

STUDYING MARKETING FUNCTIONS

In Part 1 of this book, we learned about the foundations of marketing. We saw that marketing was an important part, but only a part, of a total business. Marketing will not be successful unless a business uses other functions well, such as production, finance, and operations. We also saw the importance of understanding economic concepts when planning marketing. Knowing the type of competition a business faces and understanding how economic principles influence the success of a business helps marketers make more effective decisions. Finally, we recognized that marketing is changing. It is very complex and scientific. Marketers needed to understand mathematics, communications, psychology, and international business as well as marketing principles to be successful. Recognizing the important relationship between consumers and business and using the marketing orientation results in a much different and much better approach to marketing planning than if traditional philosophies and practices are used.

As we finished Part 1, we studied the way businesses plan and prepare for marketing. We saw the importance of information in making effective marketing decisions. We saw how a marketing information system and marketing research provide that information. We learned about the two-step process used to develop a marketing strategy. The first step is identifying a target market. The second step is to develop a marketing mix that meets the needs of the target market. Marketing is complicated and involves a large number of activities and people. Therefore, we studied the importance of developing a written marketing plan. The plan provides a systematic way to gather and analyze important information, establish marketing goals, identify a marketing strategy and market position, and outline the procedures needed to implement and evaluate that strategy.

With that background, we are now ready to develop knowledge and skills in implementing the many marketing activities used by businesses. In Part 2 of this book, we will look at each function in detail (see Figure 12-1). Each of the func-

The Functions of Marketing

FIGURE 12-1 ■ All marketing activities are a part of the nine marketing functions. The functions must be carefully planned and coordinated with each other.

tions must be performed and performed well as a part of the marketing process.

Our study will identify the people and businesses involved in providing each function and the knowledge and skills you will need if you work in that part of marketing. We will begin by learning how to develop products that meet consumer needs.

WHAT IS A PRODUCT?

We have learned that a product is anything offered to a market by the business to satisfy needs. This definition can include both products and services. In this chapter, we will learn how businesses develop and manage products and in Chapter 13 we will study the development of services.

It is important for marketers to realize that a product is viewed differently by consumers than it is by business people. Business people often see their products as the first part of the definition—"anything offered to a market." Businesses focus on what they offer—the tangible products. Consumers have a different view of products. They see products as "anything...*that satisfies needs.*" They are concerned about their needs and view products as ways to satisfy those needs. Let's see how those two views can result in problems when businesses develop and market products.

What are your motives when you go to a store to purchase a product? While you may plan to purchase a pair of shoes, a hamburger, or a book, you have reasons for each purchase that go beyond simply owning the product. Shoes obviously are needed by people for protection of their feet. Beyond that, reasons for the purchase may be for style and image, to be able to play a sport, or to get durable footwear at a reasonable price. The purchase of a hamburger is typically a response to hunger. Additionally, taste, cost, and a social experience may be a part of your decision to buy the hamburger. When you purchase a book you are probably most interested in entertainment or education.

From those examples you can see that a product is more than a tangible item for consumers. It is a tangible item plus associated services that meet one or more important needs. The physical characteristics of the product are important. It must be durable, attractive, and safe. But beyond those qualities, the product must be useful to the consumer and meet the consumer's needs. If not, the consumer will be uninterested in buying the product no matter what its physical characteristics.

Business people make a mistake when they ignore consumer needs or believe the needs are so obvious that they are not particularly important to consumers when making purchase decisions. Some restaurant owners believe "food is food" and people will buy food when they are hungry. They fail to realize that hunger is a very basic need and few people who eat in restaurants are so hungry that it is the only factor they consider. Instead consumers decide on a restaurant on the basis of a large number of factors including menu, taste, speed and quality of service, atmosphere, location, and price. If restaurant owners are not aware of how consumers make choices on the basis of those needs, the business will probably not be successful. Few needs are really so obvious that business people can afford to ignore them.

A second mistake is to believe that business people are better able to define needs than consumers. U.S. automobile manufacturers made that mistake several years ago when they were convinced that consumers were much more interested in style and design than in safety and economy. They recognized their mistake only after automobiles from other countries were designed to respond to the most important consumer needs and took away a large part of the U.S. automobile market. The teenage market is one that is often misunderstood by businesses. You can probably identify many businesses that try to sell products to you but make mistakes in trying to match their products with your needs and interests.

PRODUCT DEVELOPMENT AS A MARKETING FUNCTION

Who should be responsible for product development in a business? When we think of new products, we often have an image of inventors, engineers, or scientists working in laboratories to create something new. Certainly those people are actively involved in most manufacturing businesses in developing new product ideas, but they can no longer afford to work alone.

The failure rate for new products is very high and very expensive. While the figures vary by the type of product, on average five of every ten new product ideas will not be successful. The cost to a company for the development and introduction of a new product is typically at least several hundred thousand dollars and could be as high as several million dollars. Those figures mean that the time and money spent on developing new products that fail are lost and can only be recovered from the successful products. Those successful products have to be very profitable in order to recover the large losses. The cost of a high rate of new product failure has to be passed on to the consumer in the form of higher prices on the successful products.

Why do products fail? We know from our study of economics and consumer behavior that products will be successful if they meet consumer needs better than other choices. Therefore, failed products are those that do not meet consumer needs or are not superior to competing products. Companies should be able to reduce the rate of product failure by improving their understanding of consumer needs and competition.

THE ROLE OF MARKETING

In the past, marketers were asked to sell the products that a business developed. That was an easy task if the product was needed by consumers, but very difficult if the product did not meet consumer needs well. Put yourself in the position of a salesperson of a product for which the consumer does not see a need or one that does not appear to be better than competing products. Yet, your success depends on selling the product.

You can see why salespeople sometimes have a poor image. In the situation described, the salesperson must try to convince the customer the product is needed or that it is better than the competitors even if it is not. That certainly is not easy and is probably not the right thing to do. The salesperson who successfully sells the product may still have problems. The customer may discover the product did not meet the needs described by the salesperson and return it for a refund. Even if the product is not returned, the consumer may be upset with the salesperson and the company and will not buy from them again.

To avoid that problem, the role of marketing has changed. We know that a company that believes in the marketing concept uses the needs of customers as the primary focus during the planning, production, distribution, and promotion of a product or service. With that philosophy, marketers should not be in the position of having to sell products that do not meet customer needs. Marketers should be actively involved with others in the business in the design and development of new products.

MARKETING ACTIVITIES IN PRODUCT DEVELOPMENT

It is said that marketing is the eyes, ears, and mouth of the customer in a business. Marketing is the direct link between a business and its customers. Marketers work with customers every day, whether in selling, promotion, product distribution, marketing research, or the many other marketing activities that occur in a business. Because of that close contact, marketers are in a good position to understand customers, what they like and do not like, how they view competing products, and whether they are satisfied with current products. Marketers must represent the consumer in the business as products are designed and developed.

There are three important roles for marketers in the product development process. Those roles are identified in Figure 12-2.

Marketing Supports Product Development

FIGURE 12-2 ▪ Marketers support product development in three important ways.

Gathering Information

The obvious role for marketers in product development is market research. Gathering market information, studying it, and using the results to assist in product planning keeps the focus on consumer needs and competition rather than the perceptions of the people involved in planning. Through research, marketers can study the competition, identify target markets, review alternative product designs and features, and analyze several marketing mix choices.

Information can be collected in many ways and from different sources to assist with product planning. Feedback from salespeople is very important in understanding both customers and competitors. Analysis of sales data will determine items that have sold well in the past and those that have not. It will identify the areas of customer complaints and product returns. The marketing department might maintain one or more consumer panels that meet regularly to discuss new product ideas and their experiences as customers. The results of those discussions can provide important information for product changes and improvements.

Marketing departments that are actively involved in product planning usually develop and use a marketing information system. It allows the information from many sources to be collected, stored, and analyzed when needed to improve new product decisions.

Designing Effective Marketing Strategies

A new product is developed to meet company objectives. It becomes a part of a marketing strategy. If the company's goal is to increase its share of a specific market, it might develop a different product than if the goal is to enter a market it has never competed in before. A new company that cannot risk failure with a new product may approach product development in a very different way than an experienced and profitable company.

A marketing strategy combines decisions about a target market and an appropriate marketing mix. The actual product is only one part of the strategy. Marketers participate in developing an effective strategy by helping identify possible target markets, determining company strengths and weaknesses, evaluating possible market positions, and suggesting alternatives for a marketing mix.

Testing Marketing Mixes

After a product and the remaining parts of the marketing mix have been designed, most companies conduct tests to determine if the new product will be successful. Testing is a way to reduce the number of product failures and to avoid spending money on products that will not be successful.

There are several ways to test a new marketing mix. In the past, many companies used test markets. Test marketing has become very expensive so other ways of testing are being tried. Companies use focus groups and other consumer panels to review product ideas and marketing mix choices. There are now very sophisticated computer programs that allow companies to simulate the marketing of products and determine expected levels of sales and profits. Personnel from marketing are usually responsible for market testing activities.

THE PRODUCT PLANNING FUNCTION

You can see that businesses using a marketing orientation involve marketing personnel in product planning. *Therefore an important marketing function is product/service planning—assisting in the design and development of products and services that will meet the needs of prospective customers.* The key parts of that definition are *assisting* meaning that marketers work cooperatively with others in product development, and *meet the needs,* meaning that the products of a company are designed to satisfy customers.

PARTS OF THE PRODUCT MIX ELEMENT

Even a product that seems very simple is made up of many parts. Think of the toothbrush you used this morning. Is it like every other toothbrush you could have purchased? What makes it unique? Why did you purchase it rather than one of the many other brands of toothbrushes available?

The basic product is easy to describe—a handle and head (usually plastic) and bristles (usually nylon). Even in that basic product, however, there are choices (see Figure 12-3). The handle may be long or short, contoured for an easier grip, bent to fit comfortably inside your mouth, and manufactured in several colors. It may have a hole drilled through it so you can hang the toothbrush when not using it, or it may have a rubber pick to massage your gums. The head also comes in various shapes and sizes. The bristles can be firm, medium, or soft. They can be short or long; some are even varied on the same toothbrush with shorter bristles in the middle. One manufacturer puts colored bristles in the middle to indicate when the toothbrush needs to be replaced. Bristles can be manufactured from several different materials.

Even with the variations described above, many people believe that all toothbrushes are quite similar. But we haven't explored all of the options. There are compact toothbrushes that collapse into a small case that you can carry with you. There are disposable toothbrushes that come with toothpaste already applied. And there are electric toothbrushes in many varieties.

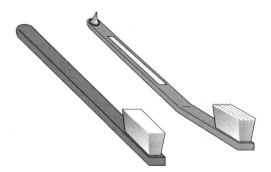

Analyzing a Common Product

FIGURE 12-3 ▪ Even common consumer products offer many choices of features to make them different from competitors' products and more appealing to consumers.

One electric toothbrush is part of a complete dental care system. The rechargeable handle can be used with the toothbrush, a tooth polisher, a water pic, and a flossing tool.

Most toothbrushes are sold with a brand name. Some of the brands are well-known brands under which many products are sold, such as Colgate. Others are brands specifically associated with tooth care, such as Oral-B.

Offering a guarantee is another way to give the product differences. Several toothbrush manufacturers offer replacements to dissatisfied customers. Others will refund the purchase price to consumers who are not satisfied. A testimonial is similar to a guarantee. This is a recommendation from a professional group, such as the American Dental Association, about the quality of the product.

The toothbrush example demonstrates that every product can be quite complex and unique. Businesses have many choices in the development of new products. Those choices were introduced in Chapter 10 and are reviewed in Figure 12-4.

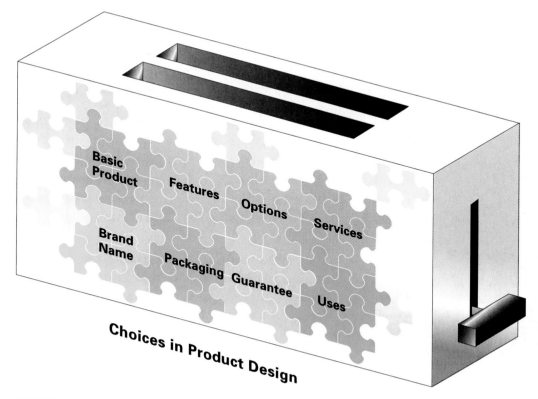

FIGURE 12-4 ■ Product planning involves the careful analysis of many factors in order to create the best possible product.

DESIGNING A PRODUCT

Product design moves through three steps. It begins with the basic product. Then the basic product is modified and improved. Finally services and complimentary products are developed to make it as useful as possible to consumers.

Basic Product

The most important part of the product is the basic physical product. It is a readily identifiable product in its simplest form. Consumers should be able to easily see the important need to which the product responds. The basic product is very much like that of competitors. Examples of basic products include a house, computer, shampoo, bicycle, microwave oven, or stereo.

Enhanced Product

The basic product responds to an important need of consumers. However, we know that consumers are usually trying to satisfy several needs with one purchase and evaluate products to see which one provides the best and most specific satisfaction. Companies add enhancements to their basic products to meet those needs. Enhancements include features and options. For example, a bicycle can be manufactured in several frame sizes, in models ranging from mountain bikes to racing bikes, and with 1 speed to 24 speeds. Choices of materials used in manufac-

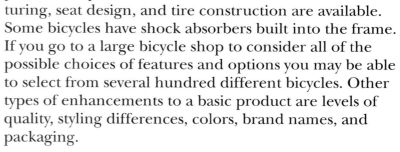

turing, seat design, and tire construction are available. Some bicycles have shock absorbers built into the frame. If you go to a large bicycle shop to consider all of the possible choices of features and options you may be able to select from several hundred different bicycles. Other types of enhancements to a basic product are levels of quality, styling differences, colors, brand names, and packaging.

Each type of enhancement changes the basic product. The change is likely to be viewed as an improvement by some customers, increasing the satisfaction they receive from the product. Other customers may view the change as unneeded or even dissatisfying. Enhanced products make it possible for companies to satisfy several target markets with one basic product. Different combinations of features, options, and even brand names are developed. Each alternative is designed with the specific needs of one target market in mind.

Extended Product

Businesses can improve the satisfaction provided by a product in other ways in addition to product enhancements. That improvement can occur as the business offers services, guarantees, information on effective use of the product, and even additional products that improve the use of the product.

Services are an effective way to meet additional customer needs beyond those directly related to the use of the product. Examples of important services for some customers that could influence product choice are credit, delivery, installation, repair services, and technical support.

Suggesting additional products that should be purchased so the primary product can be used more effectively is often an important method of improving customer satisfaction. Would you like to purchase a new camera only to find out when you wanted to use it that a tripod and flash attachment are needed for certain types of pictures? A skilled photography equipment salesperson will talk with you about the types of pictures you plan to take and the conditions in which most will be taken. Based on that information, a recommendation of additional products will be made so you can get the greatest enjoyment and value from your purchase.

IMPORTANT PRODUCT COMPONENTS

When consumers evaluate products to determine which will be the most satisfying, they are interested in more that just the physical product. Three important considerations in planning the product mix element are the product line, packaging, and brand development.

Planning a Product Line

New or small companies often offer only one product to a target market. However, with more experience and as a company grows, it is possible to expand into other markets and consider the development of a product line. *A product line is a group of similar products with slight variations in the marketing mix to satisfy different needs in a market.*

Product lines can be developed in several ways. Probably the easiest way to expand from one product into several is to vary the size of the product. The identical food item may be packaged in three sizes—single serving, servings for four, and servings for ten. Facial tissue may be sold in a pocket-sized cellophane wrapper, a box of 500 tissues, or a multi-box pack. Another variation of different sizes for the same basic product is demonstrated by the sizes of sheets for a bed. They are sold in twin, full, queen, or king size. In this case, the product is manufactured in varied sizes rather than just changing the quantity in a package.

Differences in quality can be used to develop a product line. Items such as paint brushes, carpenter or mechanic tools, lawn mowers, and even clothing often are sold in two or three quality levels. Consumers who use the products infrequently may not need the best possible quality and would prefer to save money in exchange for having a slightly lower quality. Adding features to the basic product may produce several levels of product choices for consumers. Automobile and appliance manufacturers often have a very basic model at a low price and several other models with selected features and options at higher prices.

As companies add items to their product line, they usually increase the satisfaction of individual consumers. However, the company is also adding to the costs of manufacturing, distribution, inventory control, and other related marketing activities. An expanded product line also requires additional display space for retailers. The retailer must make a decision whether to stock items from the complete product line or use the space for competing brands or entirely different products. If you visit a large supermarket and observe the displays of soft drinks, you will see an example of very extensive product lines and the competition brands have for display space.

In addition to product line decisions, companies plan product assortments. *A product assortment is the complete set of all products a business offers to its market.* Retail stores provide the best example of product assortments. Some specialty retailers, lawn and garden centers for example, have a very complete assortment of products homeowners need in one category. Other general merchandise retailers, such as discount and department stores, stock products in many different categories. They will probably not have as complete an assortment in one line as the specialty store, but they respond to a broader set of the customers' product needs.

Some manufacturers specialize in one product category and have a full assortment of products in that category. Other manufacturers may have a product assortment in many different product categories.

Packaging

Most products are sold in a package. The package serves the dual purpose of protection and promotion. In addition, some packaging improves the use of the product. Containers with pour spouts built into the package, resealable liners, and handles for carrying are developed to solve customer problems in the use of the product.

Manufacturers must carefully consider the ways customers use a product when designing the package. For example, if a cereal box is taller than the shelves in the customer's home, it will not be purchased. A manufacturer of a liquid cleaner found that people would not buy a large economy size because the container could not be lifted and poured with one hand in the way people were used to handling the product. Products that consumers use in a microwave oven must not have metal in the package.

Safety and protection are important concerns when planning the packaging of products. Products used by children certainly need to have safe packaging. A manufacturer of individual servings of puddings and fruits learned that children would lick the lid of the container when it was removed. The lid was changed from metal to plastic to prevent cuts. Glass and other fragile products need well-designed packages to insure they are not broken during shipment and display.

The promotional value of packaging is also important for many products. Impulse items are often purchased because of an attractive package that clearly shows the use of the product. Perfumes and colognes usually have very expensive and uniquely designed containers to convey an appropriate image.

Packaging can also be helpful in the display and security of products. In stores where products are displayed for customer self-service, the package may need to be designed to hang from a hook or to lay flat on a shelf. Small or expensive items are often packaged in large containers to reduce the chance of theft.

There is growing concern about the type and quantity of materials used for packaging. Manufacturers are increasingly using recycled materials for packaging and developing materials that are biodegradable. Many retailers are reducing the amount of packaging used or are helping consumers reuse or recycle packages.

Brand Development

Do you know the brand names of the shoes and clothing you are wearing? Do you have a favorite brand of pizza or automobile? In what stores do you prefer to shop? Each of these questions demonstrates that the brand of products can be very important to consumers as they make purchase decisions. *A brand is a name, symbol, word, or design that identifies a product, service, or company.* A brand is very important to a company because it provides a unique identification for it and its offerings. To insure that others cannot use a brand, a company obtains a trademark. *A trademark is legal protection of the words or symbols for the use of one company.*

Consider how difficult it would be to shop if there were no brand names. While some products are purchased without considering the brand (think of the paper you use for writing in school), in most cases consumers consider the brand as part of the purchase decision. Positive or negative experience with a brand will influence your future purchases. Business people know that brand recognition resulting from advertising often increases a product's sales.

The goal of a business in using branding is to gain customer recognition of the brand in order to increase the likelihood of a sale. There are several levels of consumer awareness of brands. Those levels are described in Figure 12-5.

Levels of Brand Recognition	
Nonrecognition:	Consumers are unable to identify the brand.
Rejection:	Consumers will not purchase the product because of the brand.
Recognition:	Consumers can recall the brand name but it has little influence on purchases.
Preference:	Consumers view the brand as valuable and will choose it if it is available.
Insistence:	Consumers value the brand to the extent that they reject other brands.

FIGURE 12-5 ▪ Businesses use brands to help consumers make choices. Branding is effective when consumers prefer or insist on a specific brand.

Brands can be developed by manufacturers or by retailers. Individual products can have their own brands or groups of products can carry a similar, or family brand. Some companies offer licensed brands to add prestige or a unique image to products. *A licensed brand is a well-known name or symbol established by one company and sold for use by another company to promote its products.* Disney and Sesame Street are examples of companies that license the use of character names and images for products ranging from toys to clothing. Professional and college sports teams license their names and mascot images for use on many products. Some people prefer to purchase products with those brands rather than similar products that do not carry the licensed brand.

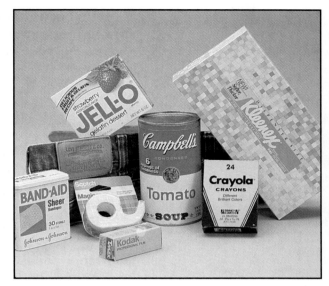

MARKET CLASSIFICATIONS

To be most effective, product planning should be based on an understanding of the market to which the product will be sold. Knowing who will use the product, the purpose for which it will be used, and the needs customers are attempting to satisfy with the product will result in a product designed for the consumer. Two broad market categories exist that have very different reasons for buying products. Those categories are consumer markets and business markets.

CONSUMER MARKETS

Consumer markets are made up of individuals or socially related groups who purchase products for personal consumption. When you, your family, or your friends buy products for your own use or for others to use, you are a part of the consumer market. You make purchase decisions on the basis of the satisfaction you receive from the use of the product. If you are buying the product for use by a friend or family member, you are interested in buying something that person will find to be satisfying. The demand for consumer products is known as direct demand. *Direct demand is the quantity of a product or service needed to meet the needs of the consumer.*

Final consumers purchase products that they or people with whom they have social relationships will use. Therefore they have a clear idea of the reasons to purchase products. They lo-

IN THE SPOTLIGHT

WHAT'S IN A BRAND NAME?

Does a company ever need to discourage the use of its brand name? Usually, the more popular a brand, the more successful the company. However a brand can become so successful that the company has to give up use of its name. Aspirin used to be a brand name as did cellophane, shredded wheat, and cola. Do the names *Jello, Kleenex,* and *Xerox* cause you to think of the product of one company or a whole group of products?

One product became so *hot* that it was in danger of losing its brand name. While Rollerblade is a dominant brand, it wants you to know that there are other brands of in-line skates. But many people refer to the sport as *rollerblading* and all brands of the product as *rollerblades.*

When a brand name becomes so popular that it is used to describe a group of products and activity, the company is faced with a real problem. Clearly Rollerblade wants people to remember the brand and to ask for it when they purchase the product. But Rollerblade also wants to make it clear that it is a brand. Therefore, in promotions, the company clearly and repeatedly uses *in-line skates* to describe the product category. Whenever the company sees the brand name being misused, it sends a letter describing the correct use of the brand and explaining why the misuse is a problem.

Rollerblade is expanding its product line so the brand becomes attached to products other than the skates. Rollerblade apparel, sun glasses, and head gear will help cus-tomers to associate the name with a company that sells many products. However, it is difficult to change behavior once consumers get comfortable with the language. Can you say *in-line skating*?

cate and purchase the products that best meet their important needs.

To develop appropriate products for the consumer market, business people must be aware of consumers' needs and how consumers choose products to satisfy those needs. We studied a system of classifying consumer products in Chapter 10 that will assist businesses in product planning. The product/service classification system is reviewed in Figure 12-6. You will recall that the system is based on two important factors:

1. The importance of the purchase to the consumer
2. The willingness of the consumer to shop and compare products before making the purchase

BUSINESS MARKETS

Business markets are the companies and organizations that purchase products for the operation of a business or the

CONVENIENCE GOODS

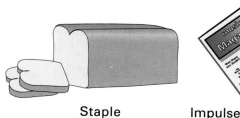

Staple Impulse

Emergency

UNSOUGHT GOODS

SHOPPING GOODS

Attribute-based

Price-based

SPECIALTY GOODS

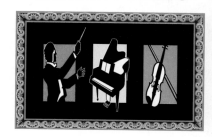

Classifying Products for the Consumer Market

FIGURE 12-6 ■ Marketers can develop effective products when they understand how consumers shop for those products.

completion of a business activity. Business markets include producers, manufacturers, retail businesses, nonprofit organizations, government offices and agencies, schools, and other types of groups that provide products or services for consumption by others. Business markets make purchase decisions on the basis of what is needed to effectively operate the business, to meet the needs of employees and customers of the business, and to produce the products and services of the business.

Businesses and organizations make purchase decisions on the basis of derived demand. *Derived demand is the quantity of a product or service needed by a business in order to operate at a level that will meet the demand of its customers.* A movie theater needs to buy enough popcorn, oil, and boxes to meet its customers' needs for popcorn during the showing of movies. If the theater purchases too much, some of the product will not be sold and money will be lost. If the theater purchases too little, customers will be dissatisfied and sales will be missed.

Developing products for the business market requires an understanding of how the products are used by the business. A business product classification system has been developed to aid in understanding the business market. The categories are shown in Figure 12-7.

Capital Equipment

The land, buildings, and major pieces of equipment are usually the most expensive products purchased by a business. They are also the most important. They must meet the specific needs of the business so it operates effectively. Often they are individually designed. They have little value to other businesses. Capital equipment can be very expensive. Costs range from thousands of dollars to hundreds of millions of dollars. A large office building, commercial airplane, or sophisticated computer system are examples of capital purchases. Most companies purchase the products using long-term loans from finance companies or the manufacturers. Some capital equipment is leased rather than purchased.

Operating Equipment

Smaller, less expensive equipment used in the operation of the business or in the production and sale of products and services is known as operating equipment. This type of equipment makes production or operations more efficient and effective.

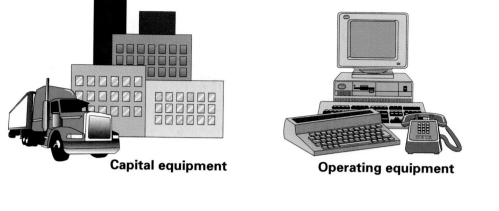

Capital equipment   **Operating equipment**

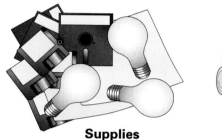
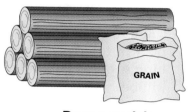
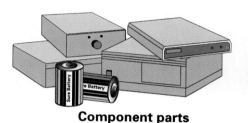

Supplies   **Raw materials**   **Component parts**

A Business Product Classification System

FIGURE 12-7 ■ There are many types of products purchased by businesses. Some are used in the operation of the business, while others become a part of the products and services the business sells to its customers.

Examples of operating equipment are tools, small machines, and furniture. They usually have a shorter life than capital equipment and must be replaced from time to time. They are more standardized, meaning that the same type of accessory equipment may be used in many different businesses.

Supplies

The products and materials consumed in the operation of the business are supplies. A business needs paper, pencils, and paper clips, as well as cleaning supplies, and parts for repairs to equipment. Some supplies are purchased and used in very small quantities and are quite inexpensive. Others, such as fuel, electricity, or lubricating oil, may be needed in large quantities and are a major expense for the company. Most supplies are quite standardized, meaning they are not uniquely developed for one business. They are available from many suppliers and are used in a large number of very different businesses.

Raw Materials

Producers and manufacturers buy many products that are incorporated into the products they make. Often they purchase raw materials, which are unprocessed products used as basic materials for the products to be produced. Logs are purchased by lumber producers, oil by plastics manufacturers, and grain by cereal processors.

It is important that purchasers of raw materials have an adequate supply and a standard quality of the raw materials they use to produce their products. The price of the raw materials is also important, since the cost has a big influence on what the company charges for their finished products. The purchasing company will want to sign a long-term contract with the supplier of the raw materials to insure they have a continuing supply and know what the cost of the materials will be.

Component Parts

Component parts are also incorporated into the products that a business makes. However, component parts have been either partially or totally processed by another company. For example, a computer manufacturer will buy computer chips from a chip manufacturer. These chips are already carefully developed and simply are installed as a part of the computer assembly. The same manufacturer buys parts for a disk drive from another company. Those parts must be assembled before the disk drive can be installed into the computer.

Component parts can be specifically designed for the needs of one company or they can be a standard product that is used by many companies. As with raw materials, the purchasing company is concerned that a dependable source of supply is available when needed, that the component parts meet the quality standards of the company, and that costs are reasonable.

PLANNING PRODUCTS FOR CONSUMER AND BUSINESS MARKETS

The classification systems for consumer and business markets are very useful to marketers as they complete product planning. Knowing whether the customer is a final consumer or a business consumer determines whether the product is being developed to meet a direct demand or a derived demand. For consumer markets, products treated as convenience goods require different planning than those treated as specialty goods. The product is less important than the location for convenience goods, so the company needs to develop a basic product at a reasonable cost. A specialty good is very important to the consumer, so care and attention must go into the product. It will probably require an enhanced and extended product to meet the consumer's needs.

For business customers, the type of product and its use are important factors to consider when planning products. Capital equipment is a major investment so the purchase is an important decision for the customer. The customer wants to work closely with the supplier in planning a product that will meet the company's needs, will have a long life, and that is affordable. Supplies, on the other hand, may be very routine purchases where little thought other than price is given by the customer as long as the supply is the type needed by the company.

Some products are sold to both consumer markets and business markets. Consumers buy automobile tires for replacements when the original tires on their car become worn. Automobile manufacturers purchase thousands of tires to mount on automobiles they produce. Consumers purchase bottles of shampoo for personal care. Hotels buy large quantities of shampoo packaged in small bottles or packets to place in rooms as a service to their guests. You can see with both examples that while the basic product is the same, the extended and enhanced products may be quite different. Also, the reasons and methods of purchasing will not be the same. Marketers need to understand the differences in purchases between the two types of markets in order to develop effective products and marketing mixes for each.

DEVELOPING A NEW PRODUCT

Businesses need new products. Consumer needs change, competitors introduce new products, products move through the stages of a life cycle, and technology offers new opportunities. Without new products, companies have a hard time keeping customers and maintaining a profit. However, we know that it is not easy to develop successful new products. The risk of failure is high and the costs of development and testing are great. A company needs to carefully plan the ways that new products are created to increase the likelihood they will be successful and to maintain control over costs.

WHAT IS A NEW PRODUCT?

Few products are really brand new in the sense that no other product like it has been available before. Many *new* products are changes and improvements to existing products or are just *new* to a specific market even though they have been sold in other markets in the past.

When personal computers were first designed in the 1970s they were completely new. Computers were not available to individuals before the development of the personal computer. People had to use a large *mainframe* computer. Today, there are many *new* personal computers as features are added and technology allows machines to be developed that are smaller, faster, and easier to use.

You are probably very familiar with companies that introduce products as new and improved. Brands of laundry detergent, toothpaste, diapers, and potato chips often use *new and improved* in their promotions. In many cases it is difficult to see what really is new or better about the product. Because some companies have misused the term *new* in order to attract customer attention, the Federal Trade Commission regulates how and when it can be used. A company can only use *new* for six months after the introduction of a product or a change in a product. To use the word, the product must be entirely new or changed in an important and noticeable way.

Fashions, music, ethnic foods, and other specialized products may be new in some markets but well known in others. Businesses often use that strategy when a market begins to get competitive. Much of the international trade in consumer products started by introducing products that were successful in one country into foreign markets.

THE STEPS IN NEW PRODUCT DEVELOPMENT

Most companies have designed a very careful process to identify and develop new products. The process is used to screen out products that are not likely to be successful before the company spends too much money for production and marketing. The process is used also to make sure that the products that are developed meet an important market need, can be produced well and at a reasonable price, and will be competitive with other products in the market. The steps illustrated in

CLASSICS AND CONTEMPORARIES

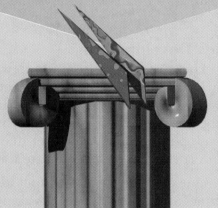

UH-HUH!

"You got the right one, Baby!" But which one is the right one? Two giant companies, Pepsi and Coke, share nearly half of the nearly $50 billion consumers spend each year on soft drinks. Most of those revenues have come from their main products—colas. But while they fought each other for the cola market, surprising changes have occurred. They are faced with a growing number of competitors marketing lower-priced brands of soft drinks. Also, the size of the cola market is declining while the sale of flavored teas, seltzers, flavored water, sports drinks, and fruit juices is increasing.

> **When the needs of the market are changing, Pepsi and Coke know they have to be ready to respond.**

Coke and Pepsi have responded with two distinct marketing strategies. First, the companies are working to strengthen sales of traditional soft drinks. They are trying to win back consumers with special promotions. They have also extended their cola product lines with diet colas, cherry colas, caffeine-free colas, and even clear colas.

There is an increased emphasis on their non-cola soft drinks, such as Mountain Dew and Sprite.

The second strategy is to develop a broader beverage assortment to appeal to the increasingly diverse tastes of consumers. Both companies are now marketing iced tea and each has introduced a sports drink to compete with Gatorade. Fruit juices and juice mixes are also a part of the companies' offerings. When the needs of the market are changing, Pepsi and Coke know they have to be ready to respond. Broadening product lines and product assortments is their answer.

Figure 12-8 are part of most companies' procedures for new product development.

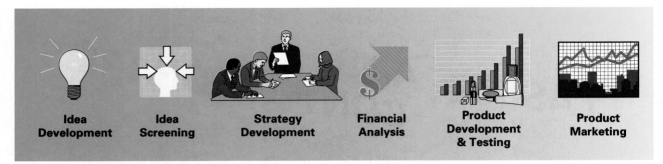

New Product Development

FIGURE 12-8 ▪ A carefully developed process for new product planning will increase the chances that the new product will be successful.

Idea Development

The most difficult step in new product development is usually finding ideas for new products. You may see a new product on the market and say, "I could have thought of that." But few people have successful new product ideas. Since products are developed to meet consumer needs, gathering information from consumers may generate ideas for new products.

One source of new product ideas is to identify problems customers are having, what they don't like about current products, or the complaints they make to the company. Often salespeople who work with customers every day have ideas for new products or product improvements. Many companies have consumer panels who meet regularly to discuss ideas for new products.

Developing new product ideas can be a very creative process. Some people seem to be more creative that others, and those people are often involved in the new product planning process. Tools such as brainstorming, creative thinking exercises, and problem-solving are used to identify product ideas for testing. Companies need an ongoing process to create and consider ideas for new products or product improvements.

Idea Screening

To encourage a large number of new product ideas, companies do not evaluate ideas in the first stage. However, the second step is to carefully review ideas to select those that have the greatest chance of being successful. Businesses develop a checklist of criteria that must be considered in deciding whether to proceed with product planning. Some of those criteria are listed below:

- Is there an identified market for the product?
- Is the competition in the market reasonable?
- Do we have or can we obtain the resources to produce the product?
- Is the product legal and safe?
- Can we produce a quality product at a reasonable cost?

Other criteria are not as straightforward and may be unique to a specific company. For example, some companies will not want to develop products that compete with their current products. Others will select products that can be developed with current equipment and personnel. Some companies are seeking opportunities to move into new markets so they want product ideas that meet the new market needs. The initial investment required to produce the new product may be an important factor for some companies and unimportant to others.

Strategy Development

After determining that the product idea seems reasonable, the business will create and test a sample marketing strategy. In this step, research is done to clearly identify an appropriate target market and insure that customers exist with the need and money for the product. Next, alternative marketing mixes are planned and analyzed to determine the possible combinations of product, distribution, price, and promotion. Again, each choice is carefully studied to determine if it is appropriate for the target market and if the company can effectively implement that mix. Often the study will involve presenting the product idea and mix alternative to a panel of appropriate consumers for their reactions. Based on that study, the best possible mix is selected. It is possible that the research in this step will determine that an effective mix cannot be developed so the product idea will be dropped.

Financial Analysis

If it is determined that a new product idea meets a market need and can be developed, the company will complete a financial analysis. Costs of production and marketing, sales projections for the target market, and resulting profits will be carefully calculated. Usually companies have computer models that help with the financial analysis. Several levels of analysis are completed to determine the best-case and worst-case possibilities. An understanding of the type of competition (pure competition to monopoly) and the level of demand is important in determining what prices can be charged and the amount of sales to expect. The results of the analysis are matched against company goals and profit objectives to determine if the product should be developed and marketed.

Product Development and Testing

After careful research and planning, the decision may be made to develop the product. For a manufacturer, that means designing the production process, obtaining the needed equipment and materials, and training the production personnel. For other companies such as a retailer, it involves identifying a producer or manufacturer that will supply the products and negotiating a contract for that production.

For very expensive or very risky products, the company may decide to develop a prototype, or sample, of the product. The prototype can be used to test quality and costs before beginning full-scale production. Another testing strategy in this step is a test market. A limited quantity of the new product is developed and the marketing mix is implemented in a small part of the market to determine if it will be successful. If the market test is not successful, the company can end production or change the product before a large amount of money is spent.

Product Marketing

The last step in product development is full-scale introduction into the target market. A great deal of preparation is needed for this step. All of the marketing mix elements must be planned. Cooperating companies such as wholesalers, retailers, transportation companies, and advertising agencies need to be involved. Production levels must be high enough to have an adequate supply of the product available to meet the target market needs. Marketing personnel need to be prepared for their responsibilities. All of the activities must be coordinated and controlled by managers.

If the all of the steps in the new product planning process have been carefully completed, the opportunity for success is very high. However, marketers still need to be cautious and continue to study the market carefully. It is possible that conditions have changed, competitors may have anticipated the new product, or consumers will not respond in exactly the way predicted. Adjustments in the marketing strategy may be needed as the market develops.

REVIEW

The product or service offered by a business is a key to customer satisfaction. However, it must be carefully planned as a part of a complete marketing strategy. In the past, marketers were asked to sell products after they had been designed and produced. That often led to poor relationships between the company and its customers.

A product is very complex. It is more than the physical product. Product planning involves the careful selection of features and options. It involves choosing services, a brand name, packaging, and other components. In some cases consumers want only a very basic product. Other consumers may want an extended or enhanced product.

In consumer markets, businesses respond to direct demand. Business markets have a derived demand based on the needs of their customers. Understanding the classification systems for consumer and business markets will help in planning appropriate products and marketing mixes.

Careful planning reduces the high level of new product failure. A step-by-step process starts with idea generation, evaluation, and testing, until the business is ready to produce and market the new product.

MARKETING FOUNDATIONS

1. SUPPORTING PRODUCT DEVELOPMENT

 You have been hired by the Izos Company as its new marketing manager. In the past, marketing has not been involved with new product planning but has been responsible for developing a marketing plan to sell the new products after they have been created. The company has seen its new product failure rate increase to nearly 60 percent. You have been asked to make suggestions to the company's CEO, Ms. Bair, on how marketing can help increase the success rate of new products. Using specific information from this chapter, prepare a one-page memo in which you respond to the following three questions:

a. Why is the new product failure rate so high?

b. Why should marketing be involved in product development?

c. What are specific marketing activities that will help Izos improve product development?

2. MATCHING CONSUMER AND BUSINESS PRODUCTS

Match the products listed in the column on the left with the correct category in the column on the right.

Product	Product Category
a. $10,000 diamond ring	1. Convenience good
b. Boeing 767 airplane	2. Shopping good
c. One car battery	3. Specialty good
d. 500 gallons of window cleaner	4. Capital equipment
e. Loaf of bread	5. Operating equipment
f. 50 automobile tires	6. Supplies
g. Railroad car full of wheat	7. Raw materials
h. Cash register	8. Component parts

MARKETING RESEARCH

1. USING CUSTOMER FEEDBACK

The Games & U company is planning to update the marketing strategy for its line of children's swing sets. The products are sold to families through toy stores and discount stores and to day care centers and community centers through the company's salespeople. To assist with planning, the company conducted a telephone survey of 360 previous purchasers of the swing sets. One-third of those surveyed were business customers and the remainder were final consumers. The survey asked the respondents to identify what they liked most and what they liked least about the product. The following results were obtained:

	Number of Responses	
	Business Customers	Final Consumers
Liked Most		
A. Rapid delivery	15	0
B. Durability	50	28
C. Salesperson's product knowledge	30	12
D. Optional equipment	0	50
E. Safety features	20	110
F. Price	5	40
Liked Least		
G. Difficulty of assembly	10	95
H. Lack of credit terms	45	0
I. Limited product information when buying	0	40
J. Cost of replacement parts	60	35
K. Customer service	5	70

a. Calculate the percentage of responses by business customers, final consumers, and total purchasers for each of the items listed. Prepare a bar graph that compares the responses in all three categories (business, final, and total).

b. Develop three specific recommendations for new product development based on the data. Make sure you apply the marketing concept when developing your recommendations.

2. WHAT'S NEW?

Study advertisements, product catalogs, and merchandise available for sale in stores in your community. Identify at least three products that fit into each of the following categories:

a. Products that are completely new

b. Products that have significant changes or improvements

c. Products that have been sold elsewhere but are new to this market

Using those products, create a poster or a display that illustrates the concept of *new* products.

MARKETING PLANNING

1. MATCHING PRODUCTS WITH NEEDS

Business people often describe their products in terms of the physical characteristics and features. Consumers evaluate products on the basis of the needs that can be satisfied. For each of the following product descriptions, identify a consumer need that can be satisfied or a benefit the consumer will receive as a result of using the product.

Product Description

a. cellular telephone

b. automatic bank teller machine

c. credit card

d. Headline News channel on cable television

e. computerized tax preparation software

f. rechargeable batteries

g. no calorie sugar substitute

h. shampoo with conditioner

i. digital audio tapes

j. stationary bicycle

Products are planned to respond to consumer needs. Those that best meet consumer needs are likely to be successful. For each of the common consumer needs listed below, identify a product that has been successful for several years because it meets the need very well.

Consumer Needs

a. health

b. economy

c. beauty

d. excitement

e. education

f. hunger

g. friendship

h. convenience

i. safety

j. status

2. **ANALYZING A CONSUMER PRODUCT OR A BUSINESS PRODUCT**

Identify any consumer product that has been on the market for at least five years. On a large sheet of paper or poster board, draw three circles that look like targets or bullseyes. Label the innermost circle—BASIC PRODUCT; label the middle circle—ENHANCED PRODUCT; label the outer circle—EXTENDED PRODUCT. Study several brands of the product you selected to identify the components that are basic, enhanced, and extended parts of the product. Based on that analysis, use words or drawings to illustrate each part of the product in the appropriate circle.

or

Identify a manufacturing, retail, or service business that you can study. Identify the major products purchased by the business. Divide a large sheet of paper or poster board into five sections. Label each section with one of the categories of business products. In each area on the paper, use words or drawings to illustrate examples of the products used by the company that fit that category of business products.

MARKETING MANAGEMENT

1. MANAGING PRODUCT LINES

Companies use product lines to be able to serve several target markets with the same basic product. Variations in the product's size, quality, features, etc. are used to meet specific needs of a market. Identify a consumer product that has a product line of at least four specific and different products. Prepare a chart that describes each of the specific products in the product line. For each one, identify the factors that make the specific product unique from the others in the product line. Then describe the characteristics of the target market to which you believe each product is designed to appeal.

2. DESIGNING A PACKAGE

A new company has started to take advantage of people's interest in nature and the environment. The company sells individual flowers that are no more that four inches tall and are planted in two-inch square plastic pots. The flowers are blooming and with proper care should live for several months or longer. They will be sold through supermarkets, gift shops, and even vending machines. You have been asked to help in the design of the package for the flowers. Create a package that will protect the flower, provide an appropriate display, and provide information on the care of the flower. Also develop a brand name for the product that will appear on the package.

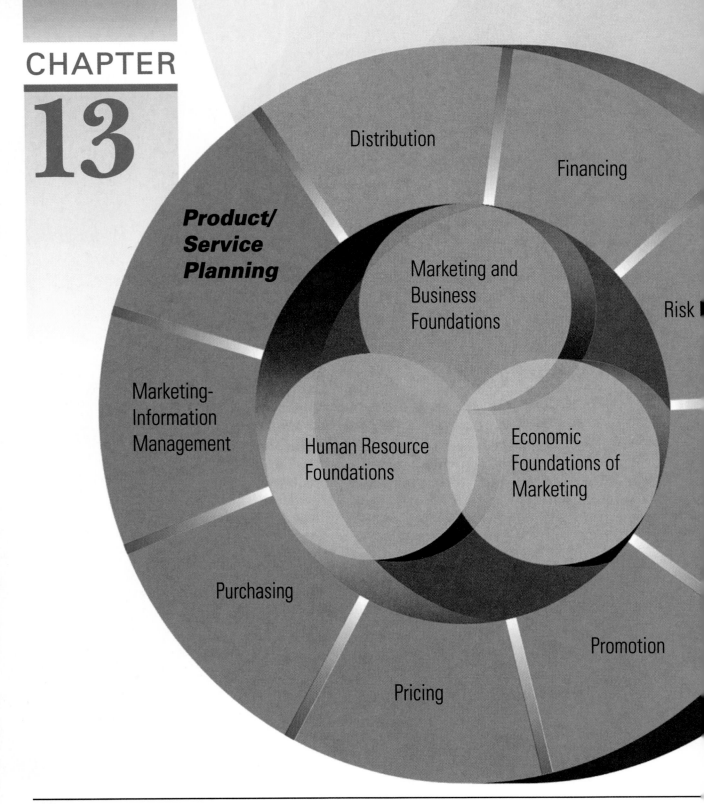

CHAPTER

13

Distribution

Financing

Product/
Service
Planning

Risk

Marketing and
Business
Foundations

Marketing-
Information
Management

Human Resource
Foundations

Economic
Foundations of
Marketing

Purchasing

Promotion

Pricing

Services Need Marketing

OBJECTIVES

1. Define the term *service*.

2. Understand the growth and importance of the service industry in the U.S. economy.

3. Identify the unique characteristics of services.

4. Classify service organizations by type of market, labor intensiveness, customer contact, level of skill, and goals of the organization.

5. Develop an appropriate marketing mix for a service organization.

6. Evaluate service quality based on competition, performance standards, and customer satisfaction.

NEWSLINE

PROMOTING LAWYERS

The legal profession has demonstrated the use of the marketing concept to some extent. Law firms target their markets, such as criminal law or business law, and then provide the services their customers need. They solicit feedback regarding the needs and wants of clients. Lawyers use various pricing methods depending on the market: some require large retainers (money in advance), some charge by the hour, some agree to accept a percentage of any award they are able to get for their client, and some use a combination of these methods. Attorneys adjust their hours to be more available to clients and have multiple office locations.

The legal profession hasn't done as much with the mix element of promotion. Various state and local laws, as well as professional guidelines, restricted or even eliminated advertising in the past. Until recently, the only advertising lawyers did was classified advertisements in telephone directories and newspapers. However, that has changed. Ads for attorneys can now be seen on billboards, television, and buses; in magazines, newspapers, and mailers; and almost anywhere else advertising takes place.

Lawyers are not free to do *any* type of advertising they want.

Baltimore, Maryland, has a law that restricts the content of lawyers' advertisements. Under this law, lawyers must warn clients if they will be responsible for legal costs and expenses if they lose their case. The Baltimore law also prohibits lawyers from boasting about their won-lost records without providing a disclaimer. That disclaimer must say that past performance does not guarantee future success.

The new guidelines have been approved by the Maryland Court of Appeals and are already in effect. They apply to television, radio, and print advertising. While some states allow almost unlimited advertising by lawyers, others still restrict the use of that marketing tool.

> **Law firms target their markets, such as criminal law or business law, and then provide the services their customers need.**

> **Ads for attorneys can now be seen on billboards, television, and buses; in magazines, newspapers, and mailers; and almost anywhere else advertising takes place.**

WHAT ARE SERVICES?

Marketing can be applied to both *products* and *services.* As we learned before, products are tangible objects that can be purchased or resold. They are usually easy to see and understand, such as cars, compact discs, or beds. Services are more difficult to define because the word *service* is used in different ways. We have used services to describe the support activities that are attached to the sale of a product, such as delivery, gift wrapping, and installation.

In marketing, however, there is a second definition and use of the term services. *Services are activities that are intangible, exchanged directly from producer to consumer, and consumed at the time of production.* Services range from banking to entertainment to auto repair. In this chapter, we will learn about marketing services and the growth of the service industry.

GROWTH AND IMPORTANCE OF SERVICES

The service sector of our economy is very important. By the year 2000, it is projected that over 70 percent of workers in the United States will be employed in service-producing industries. Employment in service-producing industries, such as transportation, communications, utilities, hotels, business services, and recreation, are expected to grow 1.6 percent every year through the year 2000 (see Figure 13-1). The service sector is responsible for generating more than 50 percent of the gross national product in the United States and that percentage continues to increase.[1]

There are many reasons for the growth of the service sector in our country. The first is the increased prosperity of our economy. Today, people have more discretionary income to spend on services such as lawn care, pet sitting and house painting.

A second reason why the service industry is growing faster than the goods-producing industry is that the goods-producing

---

[1]U.S. Department of Commerce, Bureau of the Census, *Statistical Abstract of the United States,* (Washington, D.C., Government Printing Office, 1991), pp. 401, 433.

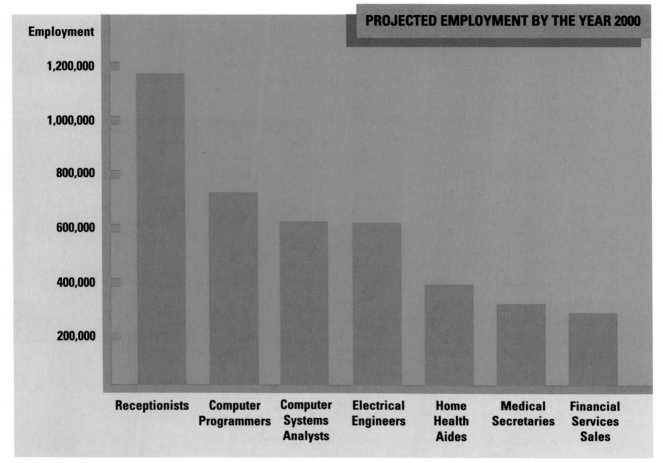

Source: U.S. Department of Commerce, Bureau of the Census, Statistical Abstract of the United States, (Washington D.C., Government Printing Office, 1991) p. 398.

FIGURE 13-1 ▪ These service occupations have the largest projected job growth of any occupations in the United States.

industry is becoming more automated and less labor intensive. That means that companies use fewer people to produce their goods because of the increasing use of technology. The former manufacturing workers turn to the service industry for continued employment.

A third reason that the service industry is growing is because many high technology products require complex installation, repair, and training. Entire new service areas have opened up around the computer industry. There are firms that specialize in training, consulting groups that specialize in applications, and companies that do nothing but equipment repair and service. These are all services that weren't around 30 years ago.

There are more services available today than ever before. People are willing to pay for plant care, image consultants, carpet cleaning, security services, and caterers. Businesses hire the services of architects, plant care experts, electricians, attorneys, and computer technicians. Services marketing is big business.

UNIQUE QUALITIES OF SERVICES

There are four important characteristics that distinguish services from products. Services are intangible, inseparable, perishable, and heterogeneous (see Figure 13-2).

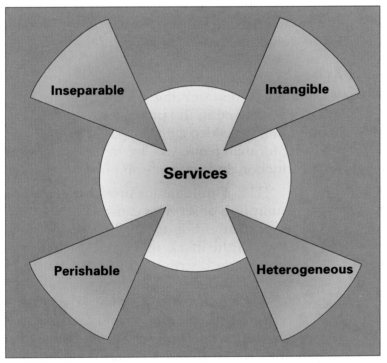

Unique Qualities of Services

FIGURE 13-2 ■ Services pose special challenges to marketers because they are intangible, perishable, heterogeneous, and inseparable.

INTANGIBLE

The most important difference between goods and services is that services are intangible. *Intangible means that the service cannot be touched, seen, tasted, heard, or felt.* Examples of intangible services include hair cuts, medical treatments, and legal services. They do not have a physical form, like products.

The intangibility of services presents special challenges for marketers. Because people cannot see or handle a service, it is important for the marketer to focus on the benefits customers will receive. Promotional activities need to be carefully conceived to develop mental pictures of benefits provided by services. Tourism, for example, relies heavily on photos, posters, videos, and travelogues to entice customers to select vacation destinations. The objective and challenge of tourism marketing is to get customers to imagine what it is like to be at a particular tourist location.

INSEPARABLE

A second characteristic of services is that the production and consumption of the service are inseparable. *Inseparable means that the service is produced and consumed at the same time.* Services such as a college class, a manicure, and a bicycle repair are produced and consumed simultaneously. In many cases, the customer is actually involved in the production of the service. When you drop money in a video game or pay an admission fee to watch your favorite football team, you are demonstrating the inseparability of production and consumption in a service business.

This simultaneous production and consumption of services causes marketers to pay special attention to the distribution component of the marketing mix. As you learned previously, distribution involves having the service available where and when it is needed or wanted by the consumer. An example of ineffective distribution would be to locate a lawn mower repair service in a downtown area. Because of its location, it probably would not attract many customers. On the other hand, a hotel limousine service located at the airport would be a good distribution strategy.

PERISHABLE

Another characteristic of services is their perishability. *Perishable means that services unused in one time period cannot be stored for use in the future.* An example of this is a lawn care service. You can not buy more than one grass cutting at a time. Though the person who cuts your grass might want to cut it 10 times in the spring when the weather is cool, services cannot be purchased that way.

Because of perishability, marketers are concerned about lost opportunity. An empty seat in a theater or an airplane cannot be sold later. After the movie has been shown or the plane has taken off, the revenue that could have been generated by a paying customer is lost forever.

Airlines work very hard to fill seats on every flight. They recognize that money is lost on each empty seat and can never be retrieved. That is why the airlines offer discounted fares and special promotions to people willing to fly when they know there will be empty seats. This is the airlines' attempt to overcome the perishability of their service.

The pricing component of the marketing mix is crucial in the sale of perishable services. Prices must be set to assure the business the greatest number of sales while covering expenses and allowing for a profit.

HETEROGENEOUS

Another characteristic of services is heterogeneity. *Heterogeneous means there are differences between services.* Services are usually performed by people. Since people differ in their skill level or even their enthusiasm for a job, the service is often not consistent. One baseball game, as a service, might be extremely different than another baseball game. The entertainment value of a baseball game in which your team wins would be different than a baseball game in which your team loses. People who use a tax preparation service or an auto repair business expect high quality service. If the type and quality of service changes, it is not likely that people will return.

Marketers involved in selling services need to pay particular attention to the marketing concept and satisfying the wants and needs of the consumer through the marketing mix. The heterogeneity of services allows marketers an opportunity to design services to meet the unique needs of a market segment. Training of service providers is needed to make sure the desired service is provided every time.

CLASSIFYING SERVICE ORGANIZATIONS

There are a variety of organizations and businesses providing services to the public. Such diverse organizations as schools, dry cleaners, roofing contractors, day care facilities, amusement parks, health clubs, medical clinics, banks, and financial advisors are all service providers. The development and marketing of services can be quite different for various types of services.

It is helpful for marketers to classify services in order to develop viable and appropriate marketing plans. Service organizations can be classified by type of market, labor intensiveness, contact with customers, level of skill required, and goals of the organization (see Figure 13-3).

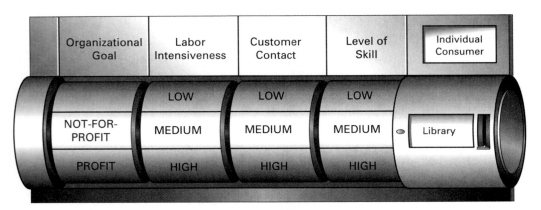

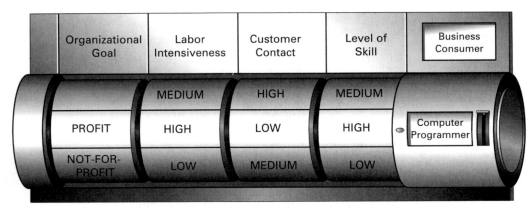

Service Organizations Satisfy Needs

FIGURE 13-3 ■ Service organizations satisfy the needs of individuals and businesses alike. The organizational goal, labor intensiveness, amount of customer contact, and level of skill of the service provider vary depending on the industry and organization.

TYPE OF MARKET

Just as with products, there are two types of markets for services: business consumers and individual consumers. A business consumer might employ a cleaning service, a grounds service, a maintenance service, and an equipment repair service. Businesses that provide these services to other businesses must offer services tailored to business needs that are available where and when the business wants them.

An individual consumer, like you or your parents, might also employ a cleaning service, a lawn service, a maintenance service, and an equipment repair service. However, you can see that the target market and marketing mix will be quite different.

A marketing mix that is designed to reach business customers might stress personal selling and quantity price discounts. A marketing mix that is designed to reach individual customers might stress individualized attention, advertising through print and broadcast media, and more standardized prices. As a marketer, you need to know your market and the specific wants and needs of that market in order to satisfy it.

LABOR INTENSIVENESS

Labor intensiveness refers to the amount of human effort required to deliver a service. Services range from extremely labor intensive to total reliance on equipment—and all combinations in between.

Equipment-based services are those that are provided with the use of machinery. These services require few people to provide the services. Examples of this are automated car washes, dry cleaning, and automated teller machines. People-based services are those that are provided through the work of people. Shoe shines, manicures, haircuts, and guided tours are examples of people-based services. These services are more labor intensive.

As a marketer, you will emphasize different parts of the mix depending on whether your service is labor or equip-

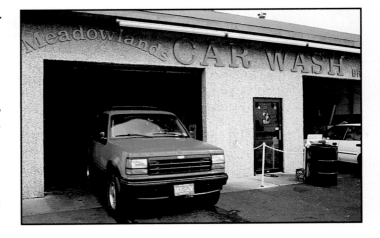

ment intensive. When marketing equipment-based services, you will pay special attention to the distribution or location of your services. Locating an automatic car wash on a busy street is more

IN THE SPOTLIGHT

DOCTOR BILL YOUNG MAKES CUSTOMER SERVICE A TOP PRIORITY

Dr. Bill Young, a physician at Cedar Sinai Hospital in Los Angeles, recognizes the importance of customer service. As an internist, Dr. Young believes that courtesy, availability, and ability are the three most important factors in success. He says, "I'm always available to my patients, 24 hours a day, 7 days a week."

Dr. Young doesn't consider his schedule too grueling. "I think many people have lost value for hard work. I could never be happy at a place where doctors put in their hours strictly from 8 a.m. to 5 p.m. and then leave, even if they're right in the middle of something."

Dr. Young's reputation has attracted many people to his practice. In an effort to satisfy their needs, he works very hard to respect the privacy of his patients. He does not have a sign-in list in his office. Also, when his staff calls clients with laboratory results, they do not leave a message on an answering machine. "You never know who might be listening to the message." Dr. Young is a good example of a professional who uses the marketing concept to deliver high-quality service.

appropriate than on a residential street. Placing an automatic bank teller machine in a safe, well-lighted place for a drive-through location gives customers a greater sense of security. You will also want to make sure the equipment is properly maintained.

With people-based services you will want to pay careful attention to the training of your personnel. You will train them in how to provide the service to satisfy your customers' wants and needs. A courteous and efficient waiter is a good example of well-trained personnel.

CUSTOMER CONTACT

The amount of customer contact a service provider has is another way to classify services. Some services have high customer contact. Examples of high-customer-contact services are hair cuts, doctors, schools, hotels, and restaurants. Other services, such as equipment repair, lawn maintenance, and movie theaters have low customer contact.

Recognizing and responding to the level of customer contact is important if you are a service marketer. In general, the higher the contact, the more you must rely on personal selling as a promotional activity. With low customer contact businesses, it is important to stress planning to provide maximum customer satisfaction since there is not much opportunity to interact with customers.

LEVEL OF SKILL

Another way to categorize services is by the level of skill the provider possesses. The most common way to categorize is to divide the providers into professional and non-professional groups. Professionals include providers whose services tend to be more complex and more highly regulated than non-professional services. The professional category would contain accountants, lawyers, teachers, physicians, therapists, and others who are required to have a combination of high-level skill, education, and a license to practice. The category of non-professional service skills would include service providers such as pet sitters, personal shoppers, hotel clerks, and image consultants who require limited preparation.

GOALS OF THE ORGANIZATION

The final method of classifying service providers is by their organizational goals. Some organizations have profit-making as a goal, while others operate as not-for-profit organizations. Most businesses that compete with each other in providing food, transportation, repairs and other services for which people pay are profit-making organizations.

There are many not-for-profit organizations that also deliver services. Examples of these types of organizations are universities, libraries, museums, government programs, churches, and social agencies. These organizations have goals and motives that are different from profit-making organizations. Their goals might be public service, public awareness of a message or idea, or knowledge. Money is not normally a significant motivating factor for not-for-profit service organizations. However, they are equally interested in delivering high-quality services that consumers need and want.

DEVELOPING A SERVICE MARKETING MIX

The unique characteristics of services make developing a marketing mix very challenging. A customer's ability to make a buying decision about a product is enhanced by the tangible nature of products. Because customers can see them, smell them, touch them, or taste them, the purchase decision for products is easier. Marketers of services must help their customers visualize their services. They do, however, apply the same principles of planning, pricing, promotion, and distribution to satisfy their customers.

PRODUCT/SERVICE PLANNING

When developing the service to be provided, service marketers must recognize that their services cannot be defined in terms of physical attributes. Instead, the services need to be developed by shaping the attributes of the service to meet the needs and wants of consumers in the most satisfactory way possible.

Federal Express sells a service and communicates the attributes of its service: fast delivery. Banks also sell their services: checking accounts, savings accounts, and loans. The attributes of bank services are dependability, convenience, low interest rates on loans, and high yields on savings. Both Federal Express and a bank must develop a favorable mental image of their services by communicating the benefits of their services.

Services are intangible, but businesses also recognize that customers pay attention to certain tangible elements associated with the service. The delivery trucks for Federal Express are brightly painted, clean, and in good repair. The bank is located in a building that reinforces its effort to say to the public, "We offer a safe place for you to deposit or borrow money." Imagine the mental image you would have of a bank if it was located in a building needing paint and repairs.

In an effort to recognize this idea of tangible products being important, many service organizations try to provide a physical item for customers to take along with them. Many times these items become a piece of specialty advertising as well. Dentists give toothbrushes, restaurants give mugs, and airlines may give duffel bags. Banks give checkbook covers, hospitals give T-shirts, and professional baseball teams give team hats. In each case, the service organization is attempting to provide a tangible symbol and reminder of the service it provides.

PROMOTION

Services are sometimes thought to be difficult to promote. Something that cannot be sensed is not as easily described in the promotional strategies available to marketers, such as advertising in print or broadcast media. Services are also difficult to promote through personal selling since they are difficult to demonstrate. It is important to remember, however, that whether you are promoting a product or a service, you need to appeal to the buying motives of the target market and stress the benefits derived by use of the service.

One promotional strategy that is effective in promoting services is to stress the tangible elements of the service. The well-dressed waiter, late-model rental automobiles, and high-quality furnishings in a lawyer's office are all tangible elements associated with intangible services.

Many services use endorsements as a promotional strategy. Satisfied users of a service describe their satisfaction with the service in a television, radio, or print advertisement. Sometimes the endorsers are well-known people and role-models for a target market. We are all familiar with celebrities being spokespeople for telephone services, airlines, and credit cards.

Service organizations also rely heavily on publicity and word-of-mouth promotion. People often consider information from friends to be very credible. Sellers of services encourage word-of-mouth promotion in several ways. They encourage satisfied customers to "tell a friend about us." They offer incentives to consumers if they bring someone with them the next time they return for service. They also develop publicity activities that are designed to encourage people to talk about their business.

Many marketers believe that personal selling is the most powerful promotional tool available. It is true that a well-trained sales staff can interact with customers to reduce their uncertainty, give reassurance, reduce doubts, and promote the reputation of the service provider. Careful training and management of customer-contact personnel is crucial to the success of a service organization.

The last part of the promotion strategy is the nature and the timing of the message. The nature of the message means that it must create a mental image of the performance of the service. It must also generate the idea of needs satisfaction in the customer. The timing of the promotional message must also be right. It must be close enough to the potential need and/or use for the service to be memorable and influence a decision.

PRICE

In the past, pricing was not viewed as particularly important among service providers. Services were perceived to be unique, much like a monopoly. With increased competition and government deregulation of many industries, businesses began to see pricing strategies as a way to improve their market positions and to differentiate themselves from their competition.

Service businesses are in a good position to alter their pricing strategies because they can change prices fairly easily. A hair salon in your neighborhood can change its pricing schedule to meet competition or to create a new image by simply printing a new price schedule. If needed, the services can be altered to reflect the new prices. The amount or complexity of a service can be increased or decreased with the pricing strategy. For example, the neighborhood hair salon can add styling specialists or additional hair services to justify price increases.

One interesting pricing strategy that many service providers use is called bundling. *Bundling is the practice of combining the price of several related services.* Imagine that you are planning to spend a week in Orlando, Florida. In this case, the airline would attempt to bundle the price of a ticket, a rental car, a hotel, and a four-day pass to the Magic Kingdom into one tour package for which you would pay one price. Another example of bundling is a college charging one price for a student's room, board, tuition, and fees covering library use, medical services, and insurance.

Bundling is a type of quantity discount. More services can be purchased for a lower price than if they were purchased individually. This has advantages for both the customers and the sellers of services. The customer pays a reduced price and has the advantage of one-stop shopping. The service marketer forms mutually beneficial relationships with other service marketers. The marketers are usually able to increase sales of their services using the bundling technique.

DISTRIBUTION

The distribution of services is primarily concerned with having the service in a location that is convenient for the consumer. Many services that we used to travel to are now provided in our home. Pet grooming, tire changing, car maintenance, and television repair are examples of services that will come directly to your home.

An important point to remember in marketing services is that for many services, production and consumption happen simultaneously. That is, the service is performed and you receive it at the same time. Therefore, the channels of distribution for a service are very short. In many cases, the channel is the producer and provider all rolled into one. A restaurant is a good example of this. The food is cooked and served at one site. Some types of services, however, make use of intermediaries.

For example, you might drop off your film for developing at a supermarket or drug store. The store then sends the film to a lab for actual developing.

CLASSICS AND CONTEMPORARIES

CONVENIENCE GIVES A COMPETITIVE EDGE

Americans are increasingly placing a premium on their time and seeking greater control over how it is used. In many service organizations convenience has emerged as a major marketing tool along with such stand-bys as quality and customer service. This trend opens market opportunities for businesses that sell convenience, such as self-service dry cleaners that stay open 24-hours-a-day, dentists who work evenings and weekends, and banks which offer credit approval over the telephone.

One of the most competitive responses to the convenience factor is automatic teller machines (ATMs). ATMs are now used by an estimated 140 million Americans who complete 300 million transactions each month. Originally ATMs only dispensed cash and deposited checks. Today they can issue monthly bus and rail passes, discount movie tickets, gift certificates, and store coupons.

ATMs are now used by an estimated 140 million Americans who complete 300 million transactions each month.

The merits of ATMs as a convenience tool are being realized by businesses other than banks. Increasing numbers of ATMs are being installed in McDonald's restaurants, Sears stores, and convenience marts.

At a county fair in San Diego, $1.25 million was dispensed through ATMs in just 20 days! The ATMs were installed in portable but secure trailers that could be moved to the most convenient customer locations. Do you think that convenience increased the amount of money spent by fair-goers?

In planning a distribution strategy for a service, the most important element of the strategy should be convenience for the consumers. Travel agents can usually bring the service of selling airline tickets closer to you than the airlines. Automatic teller machines bring the services of banks to more convenient locations and more convenient hours. Video stores rent movies so we can watch them at more convenient times in the comfort of our own homes.

EVALUATING SERVICE QUALITY

The United States is becoming a service-oriented country. We are continually finding new services to offer our customers, and consumers have more discretionary income to purchase these services.

With the large number of service businesses in the market today, a deciding factor for whether a company prospers or not is the quality of the service provided. *Service quality is defined as the degree to which the service meets customers' needs and expectations.*

Quality can be measured in a number of ways. Quality is controlled by the provider of the service. It might be in the qualifications of the provider or it might be in the speed of service. It might also be measured in cleanliness, efficiency, safety, comfort, or any number of variables.

To improve the quality of a service, an organization must first understand how customers decide which service they want and how they will judge the quality of the service. Three types of service standards can be used to evaluate service quality. They are competition, performance standards, and customer satisfaction.

COMPETITION

Marketers of services need to be aware of the nature and level of services their competitors are offering to customers. Organizations must provide services that are at least equal in quality to what their competitors offer for the same price. In addition, services must be positioned in a way that is unique and sets the business apart from its competition.

PERFORMANCE STANDARDS

A service organization should set its own service standards and communicate those standards to potential customers. Promotions used by airlines, car rental companies, delivery services, and telephone companies reinforce the commitment to quality service.

However, just saying the company is committed isn't enough. Each organization should have an actual list of standards that stands behind its advertising slogan. The standard should be measurable, such as the following: "Eighty-five percent of our arrivals will be on time," or "We will have no more than three customer complaints per month."

Once a standard is developed the service should be evaluated to see if it meets that standard. It is important to find out if the service offered meets the standards, and take corrective action if it doesn't.

CUSTOMER SATISFACTION

The real test of service quality is what customers think of it. Firms use many of the market research strategies you read about in Chapter 9 to find out exactly what customers think of their service. One of the most important and useful indicators of customer satisfaction is repeat business. Do customers continue to come back to buy the service? If they do, it is a strong indication that they are satisfied with the service offered and that the organization is achieving its service standards.

REVIEW

The service industry is growing in the United States. We are quickly becoming a nation of service providers and service users. Services differ from products because they are intangible, perishable, heterogeneous, and produced and consumed simultaneously. Because of these characteristics, marketers must emphasize specific elements of the marketing mix when preparing a marketing plan.

Services can be classified by the type of market they serve, the amount of labor necessary to perform the service, the amount of customer contact, the level of skill required to provide the service, and the service provider's goals. It is important to understand these classifications because they help marketers determine the most appropriate mix for their businesses.

Because there are so many services available for customers to choose from, it is important that marketers understand how to evaluate the quality of the service provided. Organizations evaluate quality based on their competition, their own performance standards, and the satisfaction of their customers.

MARKETING FOUNDATIONS

1. THE UNIQUENESS OF SERVICES

As you have learned in this chapter, services can be classified based on certain criteria: type of market, labor intensiveness, customer contact, level of skill, and organizational goals. Classify each of the following services by these criteria and develop a chart to illustrate their appropriate classification.

a. An insurance policy protecting a professional volleyball team from loss of the team's star player

b. A new paint job for an old car

c. Three empty horses on a circus carousel

d. A manicure while the customer's hair is styled

e. A heart bypass operation performed at Mayo Clinic

f. An opera performed by a local community group

g. Clean uniforms provided by the employer

h. A long-distance telephone call

i. Renting a motel room

j. A golf course

k. A high school education

l. Cable television installed in a new neighborhood

2. FILL IN THE BLANK

Read the following statements and supply the missing word or phrase.

a. _____ are tangible objects that can be purchased and resold.

b. _____ are intangible, perishable, and heterogeneous.

c. By the year 2000, it is projected that over _____ of workers in the United States will be employed in service-producing industries.

d. When a service is produced and consumed at the same time, it is said to be _____.

e. Services are performed by people, and since people differ in their abilities and skill level, services are said to be _____.

f. There are two types of markets for services: _____ _____ and _____ _____.

g. Automated car washes, teller machines, and telephone calling cards are examples of services that are _____ _____.

h. Whether you are promoting a product or service, you must remember to appeal to the _____ _____ of your target market.

i. With increased competition and government deregulation, businesses now use _____ _____ as a way to im-

prove their market positions and to differentiate themselves from their competitors.

j. _____ is the practice of combining the price of several
related services.

k. Services characteristically have _____ distribution
channels.

l. The degree to which the service conforms to customers'
specifications and expectations is called _____ _____ .

MARKETING RESEARCH

1. MARKETING TO BUSINESS CUSTOMERS AND FINAL CONSUMERS

On a separate sheet of paper make three columns.
Title the columns: *business consumer market, final
consumer market,* and *combination of both markets.* Use
the *Yellow Pages* from your local community to
identify service businesses that appeal to each of these markets. Write the names of the businesses in the appropriate
column. Try to locate at least three businesses for each column. Compare your results with your classmates.

2. CUSTOMER SATISFACTION

Though goods and services have many different
characteristics, one thing they both need to satisfy
is the wants and needs of the consumer. A dry
cleaning business handed out a questionnaire to
all customers who brought in or picked up clothes during
the month of October. Of the 1,435 questionnaires distributed, 705 were returned with the following results.

A. How often do you take items to a dry cleaning business?
At least once a week: 178; twice a month: 199; once a
month: 200; less than once a month: 128

B. Rate the following factors for this business:

	Very Satisfied	Satisfied	Not Satisfied
Location of the store	599	100	6
Hours of operation	200	300	205
Turnaround time	351	257	97
Friendliness of staff	264	254	187
Quality of service	532	101	72

Answer the following questions.

1. What percentage of the surveys were returned?

2. What percentage of the customers use dry cleaning services at least once a week? Twice a month? Once a month? Less than once a month?

3. Based on the rating of the store features and service quality, make three recommendations that the management can implement to improve customer service.

MARKETING PLANNING

1. PLANNING A SERVICE MARKETING MIX

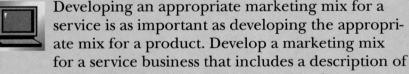

Developing an appropriate marketing mix for a service is as important as developing the appropriate mix for a product. Develop a marketing mix for a service business that includes a description of the service, the pricing strategy, the promotional strategy, and a plan for distribution. Choose from one of the following service businesses:

- Travel agency
- Video arcade
- Chimney cleaning service
- Hot air balloon rides
- Golf lessons
- Coin-operated laundry

2. BUNDLING

Bundling is an effort by service industries to sell related services in one location and for one price. Identify at least five services that can be bundled for each of the following service businesses:

- Evening entertainment
- Automobile upkeep
- Lawn maintenance
- Insurance
- Home appliance repair

MARKETING MANAGEMENT

1. EVALUATING SERVICE QUALITY

As the owner of a VCR repair shop, you have noticed that although the population of your community is growing, your business is not. You believe that you provide a quality service, but you are concerned about your business volume. After discussing your problem with a marketing specialist, you decide to evaluate your service quality. Using the service quality evaluation criteria, develop at least four specific things you can do to determine your level of quality.

2. MARKETING SERVICES

As a marketing specialist, you have been asked to speak to a group of service providers about the future of the service industry and how service providers can effectively market their services. In order to do this you have developed the following topics on which to speak:

1. Future of services
2. Differences between products and services
3. Different types of services
4. Importance of the marketing mix

Using these topics, prepare a speech describing each of the items. Use as many examples as possible.

Marketing-Information Management

Product/Service Planning

Purchasing

Marketing and Business Foundations

Pricing

Human Resource Foundations

Economic Foundations of Marketing

Promotion

Risk Management

Selling

Purchase Products for Resale

OBJECTIVES

1. Describe the business-to-business exchange process.
2. Identify the types of organizations involved in purchasing and the characteristics that make them different from final consumer markets.
3. Discuss the important factors in the purchasing process used by businesses.
4. Outline the steps followed by organizations when purchasing products.
5. Provide examples of ways businesses can improve their purchasing procedures.
6. List common purchasing records used by businesses.
7. Describe several unique factors involved in retail purchasing and international purchasing.

SIC CODES UNLOCK BUSINESS MARKETS

There is a market available that has over 16 million customers. Many of those customers spend millions of dollars each day on purchases. A few will budget several billion dollars each year to buy products and services. Is this the lifestyles of the rich and famous? No, it is the United States business market.

Businesses range in size from one-person, part-time enterprises to multinational corporations with hundreds of locations and thousands of employees. Most are producers and manufacturers, but the market also includes retailers, wholesalers, and service providers. They operate in such diverse areas as fishing, tourism, mineral extraction, and dentistry.

Sorting through all of the differences among businesses to find a

> **The federal government has developed a tool known as the Standard Industrial Classification System (SIC) that makes the task easier.**

target market can be difficult. But help is available. The federal government has developed a tool known as the Standard Industrial Classification System (SIC) that makes the task easier. The classification system was created to identify organizations in similar industries and to identify their primary activities, size, location, and other important descriptive information.

The SIC classification system begins with a two-digit code identifying 10 major industries. Then two additional digits are assigned to each industry code to describe subindustries. Additional numbers are added to identify the products that are produced (see Figure 14-1.)

Reports on industry information using the SIC codes are prepared by the Bureau of the Census, Department of Commerce, Department of Labor; business, trade, and professional associations; and commercial publications.

To target business customers, most companies start with SIC information. In that way they can identify businesses with similar purchasing needs. They can track

> **To target business customers, most companies start with SIC information.**

increases and decreases in the numbers of businesses, the volume of sales in the industry, and even changes in levels of employment. The Standard Industrial Classification system is an example of government assistance that is available to businesses and an important tool for marketing planning.

INDUSTRY DIVISION
Manufacturing (20-39)
  INDUSTRY NAME
  Fabricated metal (34)
    INDUSTRY GROUP
    Cutlery (342)
      INDUSTRY
      Hand tools (3423)
        PRODUCT CATEGORY
        Mechanics tools (34231)
          PRODUCT
          Pliers (34231.11)

FIGURE 14-1 ■ Example SIC codes for manufacturers

PURCHASING AS A PART OF THE EXCHANGE PROCESS

Any exchange of products and services involves a buyer and a seller. We most often think about businesses as sellers and individual consumers as buyers. However, you may be surprised to learn that the majority of exchanges do not involve the final consumer. They take place between businesses. One business buys products and services from another business. Business-to-business marketing is a very important part of our economy.

In Chapter 12, we studied a business product classification system. Those are the types of products that are bought and sold in business-to-business marketing. In addition, businesses purchase a variety of services as described in Chapter 13. The categories of business products and services are reviewed in Figure 14-2.

Categories of Business Products	
Capital Goods	The building and major equipment of business.
Operating Equipment	Equipment used in the daily operation of the business.
Supplies	Consumable materials used in the operation of the business.
Raw Materials	Unprocessed materials that are incorporated into the products produced by the business.
Component Parts	Partially or completely processed items that become a part of the products produced by the business.
Services	Tasks performed in the operation of the business or to support the production, sale, or maintenance of the products and services sold by the business.

FIGURE 14-2 ■ The business products classification system describes the types of products and services that are bought and sold in business-to-business marketing.

REASONS FOR BUSINESS PURCHASES

There are several reasons why businesses purchase products. A producer or manufacturer usually does not own everything it needs to develop the products it sells. Some companies do not have the raw materials used in production. Many of the component parts that are used in manufacturing products are often produced by other companies. Purchasing products to be incorporated into a production or manufacturing process is an important part of business-to-business marketing.

Some businesses purchase products for direct resale to other customers. It is not efficient to sell every product or service directly from the producer to the final consumer. Therefore, other businesses facilitate the marketing and sale of products. Typically, those businesses do not change the physical form of the product. They may repackage it. They may also provide a number of other marketing functions to meet customer needs.

A third reason for business purchasing is to obtain products and services needed to operate the business. Buildings and equipment are produced by one company for sale to others. Companies need a variety of supplies for their day-to-day operations. Many businesses purchase professional services from attorneys and accountants; business services from advertising agencies, employment offices, and cleaning services; and services that support the products they sell, such as repair services.

PURCHASING AS A MARKETING FUNCTION

Purchasing is an important function of marketing. You may recall that in Chapter 1 we defined purchasing as *determining the purchasing needs of an organization, identifying the best sources to obtain the needed products and services, and completing the activities necessary to obtain and use them.* Business must do an effective job of purchasing the products and services they use if they are to be successful. If they purchase the wrong products or products that are of poor quality; if they pay too much for the products they purchase; or if the company supplying the products is not able to deliver the products as promised; the company will be unable to operate effectively and serve its customers well.

To insure that purchasing is done correctly, procedures must be planned carefully. Many companies employ people who are purchasing specialists to ensure that the procedures are effective. Purchasing procedures and results are evaluated to be certain they meet company requirements. In this chapter we will study the types of businesses and organizations that purchase products and services, how businesses plan purchasing procedures, how they select the sources from which they will purchase, and how they manage the purchasing process.

PURCHASING BY ORGANIZATIONS

Do you think marketing to businesses and organizations should be done in a different way than marketing to final consumers? If you just picture the two types of customers in your mind you might believe the answer is yes. Consider selling radios to an automobile manufacturer as compared to selling a radio to a consumer to be installed in that person's car. You see a very large business purchasing hundreds and thousands of radios versus one person buying a single radio. You can expect that the business has very different reasons for purchasing the radios than does the individual. It is reasonable to believe that quite different procedures would be used to gather information and make a decision about the radio that will be purchased.

Even though those differences are great, the basic marketing process is not different. It is necessary to identify the target markets to be served, determine their characteristics and needs, and develop a marketing mix that meets their needs better than other companies are able to. Just as not all final consumers are the same, businesses also have important differences that require different marketing strategies.

TYPES OF BUSINESS PURCHASERS

One way of classifying business consumers is by the type of organization. The major categories of businesses are producers, resellers, service businesses, government, and nonprofit organizations. All businesses and other organizations purchase the products and services needed to operate including capital equipment, operating equipment, and supplies. In addition, they make purchases that are appropriate to the types of activities performed by the business.

Producers

Over six million businesses in the United States produce products for sale. Those types of businesses range from farms and ranches, mining companies, and oil drilling and refining businesses, to product manufacturers. They can be very small businesses that employ only a few people and spend less than ten thousand dollars a year on purchases to companies as large as General Motors or Procter and Gamble that each employ several hundred thousand people world-wide and may easily spend $10 million in one day on purchases. Producers are customers for raw materials and component parts as well as the other products and services needed for business operations.

Resellers

Wholesale and retail businesses are a part of the product distribution system connecting producers with consumers. They purchase products for resale. As a part of that process they maintain distribution and storage services, promote products through advertising and personal selling, extend credit to consumers, and complete a variety of other marketing activities designed to meet customer needs. More than 3 million businesses operate as resellers in the U.S. economy.

Service Businesses

There are more companies in the U.S. that produce services than produce products for resale. Nearly seven million service businesses were operating in the early 1990s and that number is growing faster than any other category of businesses. Most of the purchases made by service businesses are used in the operation of the business and the development of the services they sell. Some service businesses, such as rental firms, actually purchase products that are used by final consumers. Rather than selling the products to those consumers, however, they retain title and allow the consumer to use the product.

Some of the rental businesses are well known, like video stores, apartments, and stores that rent formal wear for proms and weddings. However, some types of rental businesses are less well known. Leasing automobiles for 1–3 years has been done by businesses for many years, but is now a popular option for individuals. When you go to an amusement park you can rent a video camera for the day. Investors build huge office buildings and then lease the space to companies rather than selling the building.

Government

Federal, state, and local government offices and agencies provide services to citizens, and develop and enforce laws and regulations. If you total all of the purchases made by the U.S.

government, it is the largest single customer in the world. However, from a purchasing standpoint, the government is made up of thousands of separate customers with very different needs and purchasing procedures. Government agencies and institutions purchase the full range of products from raw materials to supplies and services. Some government organizations such as city utility companies purchase raw materials and operate very much like privately owned producers. Part of the military operates like wholesalers and retailers when they purchase products for distribution and sale to military personnel and their families through commissaries and stores on military bases.

Nonprofit Organizations

Many organizations in our communities do not operate in the same way as private businesses. They have specific goals or clients that they are organized to serve and that service is the primary reason for operations. While they need an adequate budget to operate, profit is not the primary reason for their existence. In fact, most have a special "nonprofit" designation from the U.S. Department of Treasury so that they are tax exempt. The common examples of these organizations are schools, museums, churches, social service organizations such as shelters and community centers, colleges and universities, professional organizations, and some social clubs.

As with government agencies, nonprofit organizations operate to provide services to specific client groups. Therefore, they need to purchase those things necessary to offer the services. Those purchases could be only a limited number of operating supplies and products or they could be the full range of products and services in the business products classification system.

CHARACTERISTICS OF BUSINESS MARKETS

Businesses that sell to other businesses need to understand how those markets are different from final consumer markets. There are some common demographic characteristics and purchasing behavior that are typical of business markets.

Derived Demand

Businesses do not buy products for final consumption. Instead they make purchases to be used directly or indirectly in meeting the needs of final consumers. Therefore the types and quantity of products and services demanded by the business is based on the level of demand of their customers. In other words, the business demand is derived from their customers' demand.

Purchase Volume

Final consumers buy in a much smaller quantity than do business consumers. While final consumers may buy the same product again, their needs change much more frequently than business purchasers. Because businesses are making purchases to be incorporated into other products or for operations, they usually purchase large quantities of those products. However, they are less likely to make major changes in the items purchased unless their customers' needs change dramatically.

Similar Purchases

Businesses that produce or resell similar products and services usually have common purchasing needs. Consider two furniture stores serving the same target markets. They will likely purchase the same types of furniture and home accessories for resale and will buy similar capital and operating equipment for their stores. In most communities there will be several companies that mix concrete for use in construction projects. They need to purchase the same raw materials (cement, sand, stone), and similar equipment (storage and mixing facilities, trucks) to operate the business.

Number of Businesses

The number of business customers for specific products is usually smaller than the number of final consumers who will purchase a product. That is typically an advantage for those who sell to the business market. Fewer customers mean it should be easier to maintain contact with the customers and understand their needs. Because purchase volume for each customer is high, it should not restrict the amount of total sales a company can make in the business market.

Buyer/Seller Relationship

Businesses that produce products for sale to final consumers often have little contact with the customer. Because customers are located throughout the country and sometimes throughout the world, it would be difficult to distribute products directly from the buyer to the seller. Retailers and wholesalers are usually a part of the distribution system for consumer products. The retailer is responsible for selling the product and often for responding to customer problems with the product.

In business-to-business selling, direct distribution is used more frequently. The selling business is responsible for contacting prospective customers, selling the product, and providing follow-up support and service as well as solving customer problems. This is possible because of the lower number of customers. Also, in some business markets, the businesses that purchase similar products are in the same industry and may be located in the same geographic area of a country.

THE PURCHASING PROCESS IN BUSINESS

Effective marketing requires that the seller understand the buyer and how the buyer makes purchase decisions. When we studied individual consumers in Chapter 8 we learned that they go through a careful process of gathering information and evaluating choices before making a decision. Business consumers also use a careful decision-making procedure, but that procedure has some important differences from the one used by final consumers.

THE BUYING DECISION

The decision to buy is directly related to a business need. While the decisions of individual consumers are often guided by emotion, business purchasing is usually very rational. A purchase is not made unless the product or service is useful in the operation of the business or can be resold to customers. The product or service purchased will be the one that best meets the needs of the business at a reasonable price. If the purchase does not improve the business or cannot be sold to customers, the business will not be successful. If the business pays too much for a purchase, it will make it difficult to make a profit. Therefore, business purchasing is done very carefully.

Make or Buy

Businesses, especially manufacturers, do not always purchase the products and services they need. They may first decide if

IN THE SPOTLIGHT
TARGETING PRODUCTS THAT SELL

It is not an easy task to make sure every item is in stock in large retail stores that carry over 50,000 different products. Products take up space and lose money if they cannot be sold. Because retailers are fighting for profits, some have chosen to keep stock levels low and risk running out of products rather than spending money for higher inventories.

Target Stores is a Minneapolis-based discount retailer. It is one of the best in the industry at managing its merchandise. It achieved success by the use of technology. Employees use hand-held scanners and a computer system to track merchandise. The scanners track products from the time they are received from the supplier until they are sold to the customer.

The scanners gather information by reading unique bar code labels for each product. When the product is received in the stock room, information is collected and entered into the store's computer. The information identifies the quantity of the product and its location. Clerks on the store's selling floor can scan a bar code label on a display shelf and immediately identify the quantity of a product in storage and its location. When products are sold, the information from the scanner at the check-out is sent to the computer so employees can immediately be aware of sales volume for that product and remaining inventory.

Target has been able to reduce the percentage of items that are out of stock at any time to less than 2 percent. Some retail businesses have difficulty keeping that percentage below 10 percent. At the same time the total inventory carried in a Target store has been reduced by more than 25 percent, since most products are out of the stock room and on the shelves. Other benefits include faster customer service, more efficient purchasing and product handling procedures, and increased sales.

Source: New York Times News Service, *Dec. 25, 1992.*

they are able to make the product or provide the service with their own resources. For example, most businesses have a variety of printing needs. A company may want to send catalogs to customers or use direct mail advertising. They may use a large number of forms and other printed materials in their business. The business can find several printing companies to produce the materials needed. However, they may also be able to establish their own printing department within the company. If the volume of printing is large enough and printing is needed regularly, the company may save money by doing its own printing. There will be greater control over the quality and availability of printing services by owning the printing operation.

If a business decides to buy rather than make the products it needs, the company usually develops a specific procedure to follow. Three different types of purchasing situations determine the procedure that will be followed. Those situations are a new purchase, a modified purchase, and a repeat purchase.

New Purchase

The most difficult purchasing situation is when a business buys a product or service for the first time. Examples of new purchases for many companies are buildings, major pieces of equipment, and the raw materials and component parts needed when manufacturers develop a new product.

Because the product has never been purchased before, the business has no experience with it and probably has no experience with the companies that sell the product. The business must carefully determine what needs it must meet with the purchase, decide on the types of products that can meet those needs, and identify the companies that offer the products. Often the company takes a great deal of time planning for the purchase. The company may develop purchase specifications which the selling companies must meet. *Purchase specifications are detailed requirements for construction or performance of the product.* The buyer will also have expectations in terms of the supply needed; delivery methods and schedules; and technical support required for assembly, use, or repair of the product.

Modified Purchase

A company may find that the products purchased in the past do not totally meet current needs and so require changes. In this case, the company will identify the changes or improvements needed. The modifications will likely be communicated to the company that has been selling the original product and the opportunity provided for that company to meet the new requirements. Other companies may also be given the chance to sell the modified product, particularly if major changes are planned or if the buyer is not satisfied with products purchased in the past.

Retailers use modified purchasing when they have had success with a basic product and want to offer additional features and options to customers. Companies that have purchased computer systems may want to purchase additional computers, but want them upgraded with current technology. A company may have contracted with an accounting firm for bookkeeping services and now wants to extend the contract to include tax preparation.

Repeat Purchase

Most business purchases are very routine. The same products and services are purchased over and over. The buyer is very aware of the needs that are being met with the purchase and has identified the product that meets those needs. In many cases, the buyer has developed a good relationship with a seller and does not even consider buying from another company. When a new supply of the product is needed, the company simply reorders from the seller.

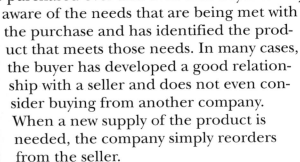

The purchasing process may become so routine that it is handled by a computer. The computer maintains the inventory level of the product. As the product is used or sold, the inventory level decreases until it reaches the reorder point. *The reorder point is the level of inventory needed to meet the usage needs of the business until the product can be resupplied.* When the reorder point is reached, the computer issues a purchase order to the supplier and the product is shipped.

When the product being purchased is not unique, with many companies offering the same product for sale, repeat purchasing becomes very competitive. Since the buyer realizes that the same product can be purchased from several sellers, price may become an important factor. The purchasing company may pressure the suppliers to reduce the price in order to make the sale. This happens regularly with companies that sell to large retailers and companies selling common operating equipment and supplies to businesses.

PURCHASING REQUIRES SPECIALISTS

Purchasing in businesses occurs continuously and involves thousands and even millions of dollars each day in many businesses. Many of the products purchased are unique and very complex and technical. The purchasing process involves arranging delivery and payment schedules. Often lengthy and complex contracts are prepared between the buyer and seller. Because the process is so important and complicated, many businesses have departments and personnel that specialize in purchasing. Job titles for people involved in purchasing include buyers, product managers, merchandise managers, and purchasing agents.

Usually several people are involved in the buying decision the first time a product or service is purchased. The types of people most often involved in business purchases are shown in Figure 14-3. The department using the product plays an important role in the purchase decision. An experienced employee or the manager from that department will help to identify the need and prepare specifications for the purchase. For a very technical product or a new product, engineers or other people

Typical Members of a Business Purchasing Team

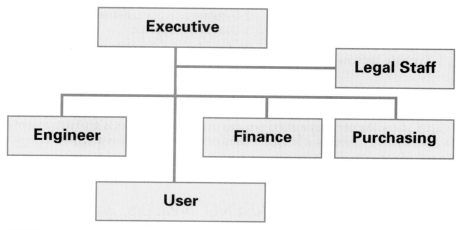

FIGURE 14-3 ■ Important purchase decisions in businesses are typically made by several people representing specific parts of the business.

with technical expertise may be involved to evaluate and test the product. Financial personnel participate in purchases when the purchase is very expensive or the prices of competing products are quite different. Lawyers may help develop contracts and review all of the documents involved in the purchase.

The person or persons responsible for managing the purchasing procedure will be members of the purchasing department. They identify possible suppliers, communicate needs and specifications, gather needed information, and manage the paper work. They are usually responsible for negotiating the price and terms of the sale. Finally, for very expensive or important purchases, one or more members of the top management will participate in the purchasing process.

STEPS IN BUSINESS PURCHASING

The general process that business customers use in making a purchasing decision looks very much like that used by final consumers. The steps in the process are shown on the right side of Figure 14-4. The business purchasing process will be more detailed and involve more people. You can see that the steps businesses use generally match the final consumer process, but are more specific.

Purchasing by Final Consumers and Business Consumers	
FINAL CONSUMERS	**BUSINESS CONSUMERS**
1. Identify needs	1. Identify purchasing needs
2. Gather information	2. Determine product alternatives
3. Evaluate alternatives	3. Search for suppliers
4. Make purchase decision	4. Select appropriate suppliers
5. Evaluate decision	5. Negotiate a purchase
	6. Make purchase decision
	7. Evaluate purchase

FIGURE 14-4 ■ The decision-making process used by businesses is similar to that of final consumers. However, it is usually more detailed and involves a number of people in the business.

IDENTIFY PURCHASING NEEDS

Even the first step, need identification, is complex. Remember that the demand for business products is derived from the needs of the business' customers. In addition, the needs of many parts of the business must be considered. Those needs may not always be the same and might even conflict with each other. For example, a conflict in a company whose sales are declining affects the purchase of training services. The sales department believes that additional training will help their salespeople serve customers more effectively and increase sales. At the same time, the human resource department needs to reduce expenses because of the lower sales volume, and wants to cut back on the amount spent for training. This conflict must be resolved before a purchase decision can be made.

DETERMINE PRODUCT ALTERNATIVES

In the second step, the business attempts to determine the types of products or services that will meet its needs. Here the business decides whether an existing product meets the needs best or whether a new product will be better. Money can probably be saved in the purchase if suppliers do not have to develop a unique product, but that product may not be the ideal product. The business will develop product specifications in order to clearly describe the product needed. In this step, the business also determines the procedures to be followed in purchasing and the people to be involved in the process.

SEARCH FOR SUPPLIERS

Next the business begins the search for suppliers. In some businesses, the purchasing department is responsible for maintaining lists of suppliers for various types of products and services. They may have catalogs or product lists which can be reviewed. Suppliers are selected for consideration based on a set of criteria established by the purchasing business. Those factors include availability of products, quality, reliability, delivery, service, and price.

SELECT APPROPRIATE SUPPLIERS

After possible suppliers have been identified, they are carefully evaluated. Often, several businesses offer acceptable products, but may vary on other factors important to the business. A decision will have to be made to determine what combination of supplier characteristics best meet the buyer's needs. A procedure called vendor analysis may be used to help with the decision. *Vendor analysis is an objective rating system used by buyers to compare potential suppliers on important purchasing criteria.* An example of a vendor analysis for the purchase of automobiles is shown in Figure 14-5.

NEGOTIATE A PURCHASE

The purchasing team will review the information available and determine which of the products and suppliers best meet the business' needs. One or two vendors will be selected and the purchasing agent will begin negotiations with them. Here is another difference from the process used by final consumers. Usually, retail businesses specify the conditions of the sale and the consumer decides whether to accept those conditions or not. In business-to-business marketing, the buyer often specifies the requirements the seller needs to meet. The buyer and seller may discuss those criteria and there may be changes before the final decision is made.

Negotiations are completed in several ways. If the company is buying a standard product or one that has been purchased in the past, the negotiations are very simple. The buyer and seller will discuss price, quantity, and delivery, and agree on the terms of the sale. If the buyer has not developed a complete set of criteria or selected a specific product to purchase, the company

Completing a Vendor Analysis

VENDOR ANALYSIS					
Vendor	**Purchase Criteria**				
	Specifications	Warranty	Service	Price	Availability
Dodge	10	8	5	6	4
Ford	9	9	6	4	5
GMC	7	7	9	8	7
Toyota	8	4	7	5	6
Scoring: 10 = high 1 = low					

FIGURE 14-5 ▪ If a company is planning to buy several new automobiles, it will usually analyze potential suppliers on important criteria in order to select the best vendor.

may develop a request for proposals. *A request for proposal contains a general description of the type of product or service needed and the criteria that are important to the buyer.* Suppliers then develop proposals for the buyer which contain detailed descriptions of the product or service they can supply and the way they can meet the buyer's criteria.

For the company that has carefully and completely determined its needs, product specifications are provided to the suppliers who then demonstrate how they can meet those specifications. Finally, the most restrictive type of negotiations is known as bidding. *In bidding, several suppliers develop specific prices at which they will meet detailed purchase specifications and other criteria prepared by the buyer.* The supplier that is able to respond to the buyer's requirements at the lowest price is usually selected to provide the product. A bidding process is a common practice in selling to government agencies.

MAKE A PURCHASE DECISION

After analyzing the information available, the buying team selects a supplier for the product. Because several people are involved in the decision, it may not always be easy to select a supplier. Each of the people has different needs to satisfy. Those will be both business needs (what is best for the department) and personal needs (what is best for the person's business career). Because of those differences, the final decisions may involve conflict and politics among the people involved. Businesses try to develop a purchasing procedure and specify criteria early in the process to avoid problems.

When a decision is made, the purchasing department prepares a purchase order or contract to be sent to the supplier. The purchase order will be very detailed to insure that the product is supplied in the form and quantity needed and at the correct time and price.

EVALUATE THE PURCHASE

When a purchase is made, the buyer determines if the product meets the needs as well as possible. That is also true for business customers. Businesses normally develop very detailed specifications for products. They use those specifications in evaluating purchases. The needs of the business' customers are also considered in the evaluation process. Sometimes, businesses complete the evaluation process before the products are actually used. When the product is received by the business it may be inspected to insure that it meets the requirements of the business. For products purchased in large quantities such as raw materials or component parts, it may not be feasible to inspect every product. In those cases, the purchaser may inspect by sampling a small quantity of the product and evaluating the samples.

When the purchases meet the buyer's needs, the buyer will usually continue to purchase from the same supplier unless needs change or unless the supplier is no longer able to meet the purchasing requirements of the buyer. In those cases, the procedure becomes a repeat purchase and reordering is managed by the purchasing department or the user department.

IMPROVING PURCHASING PROCEDURES

Companies know that effective purchasing does a great deal to improve the success of the business while poor purchasing causes serious problems. One company that manufactures instant breakfast drinks spent several million dollars on a new piece of equipment to seal the plastic liners that held the product inside the product's package. After using the machine for several months, the company found that the time needed to seal the packages slowed their production time by 20 percent. Because of that problem, the manufacturer's salespeople were unable to make commitments to customers about quantity and delivery schedules for the product. Because production was reduced, inventories of raw materials increased. The hours of work for many of the company's employees had to be reduced. So one purchase had a very big negative effect on the business.

An example of how purchasing improves business performance comes from a large retailer. The retailer found that some manufacturers gave significant price discounts for the purchase of very large quantities of certain products. The retailer usually purchased in those quantities believing that the low prices could be passed on to its customers resulting in increased sales. However, after several years of taking advantage of the price discounts, an evaluation of the purchases was completed. The retailer learned that the quantity purchases resulted in two problems. First, both transportation and inventory costs increased to

A GLOBAL VISION

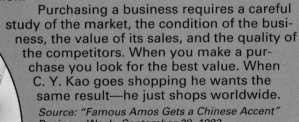

BUYING BIG

C.Y. Kao is the chief executive of President Enterprises, Inc., a snack food products company. The company is based in Taiwan but is expanding rapidly throughout the world with two of its biggest new markets in China and the United States. Mr. Kao has a goal to be one of the largest food companies in the world within twenty-five years. To do that, he and his managers have decided to purchase successful businesses as well as to expand their own product lines into other countries.

Probably President Enterprises is not a company whose name you readily recognize. But you have heard of Famous Amos cookies, which is one of President's recent purchases. President owns Wyndham Baking Co., one of the two U.S. companies that makes Girl Scout Cookies. It also sells Pepsi Cola and Kentucky Fried Chicken in Taiwan. Joint ventures in China have resulted in food processing facilities that manufacture basic food products such as noodles and flour.

Buying companies can be expensive. The Famous Amos purchase cost over $60 million. Wyndham cost more than five times that amount. But the benefits can be great as well. International sales for the company are estimated to be over $1,000,000,000, with nearly half of that coming from the United States. Profits in a recent year neared $100 million.

Purchasing a business requires a careful study of the market, the condition of the business, the value of its sales, and the quality of the competitors. When you make a purchase you look for the best value. When C. Y. Kao goes shopping he wants the same result—he just shops worldwide.

Source: "Famous Amos Gets a Chinese Accent" Business Week, *September 28, 1992.*

handle the large quantities of products. Also, the retailer had difficulty selling all of the products in a timely fashion. Some of the inventory had to be sold at very low prices just to get rid of it. And some of the products were never sold before they became out of date or spoiled. Therefore the total cost of the unsold products was lost.

After that analysis, the retailer put together a new purchasing plan. Purchase quantities were more closely matched with customer demand. Even though the cost of merchandise purchased was higher, the savings in inventory, transportation, and unsold products allowed the retailer to keep customer prices nearly as low as before while profits increased by almost 15 percent.

The examples show that there is more to effective purchasing than just the cost of the product. Identifying and monitoring the total costs of the business that are affected by a purchase is an important business activity.

Businesses are continually evaluating purchasing procedures and the products and services purchased to improve their purchasing performance. One of the management methods companies use to improve purchasing is known as just-in-time purchasing or JIT. *With just-in-time purchasing (JIT), a company develops a relationship with its suppliers to keep inventory levels low and to resupply inventory just as it is needed.*

Another new management tool that improves purchasing is total quality management (TQM). *Total quality management (TQM) establishes specific quality standards for all operations and develops employee teams who are responsible for planning and decision-making to improve business activities.* When TQM is used in purchasing, employees are involved in determining what needs to be purchased and how purchasing procedures can be improved to increase company performance.

PROCESSING PURCHASES

From the time decisions are made to order products until they are ready for use or resale in a business, a number of procedures must be completed. A variety of records must be maintained to make sure the purchasing procedures are completed correctly. Some of the most important records related to purchasing involve inventory and purchasing records.

INVENTORY RECORDS

Inventory is the assortment of products maintained by a business. Inventory includes the products and materials needed to produce other products and services, needed to operate the business, or to be sold to customers. Inventory management is needed so managers are aware of the supply of products on hand at any time. That information helps to control costs and to insure that operations can continue without interruption.

Inventory records are maintained to provide information about the products on hand in the business. That information can include the type of products, their source, age, condition, and value. It should also indicate how rapidly the inventory is used, when it is reordered, and the sources of supply.

Two types of inventory systems are typically used by businesses: physical inventory and perpetual inventory. *A physical inventory system determines the amount of product on hand by visually inspecting and counting the items.* A physical inventory count is conducted on a regular basis, often every few months or each half year.

A perpetual inventory system determines the amount of a product on hand by maintaining records on purchases and sales. Daily inventory levels determined through the perpetual system are often maintained on computers. Many businesses combine the use of physical and perpetual systems. There may be differences between the inventory level of each system. This can result from products that have been stolen or lost or from poorly maintained records.

PURCHASING RECORDS

A *purchase order*, a form describing all of the products ordered, is completed by the buyer and sent to the seller to begin the purchasing process. The seller fills the order and sends it to the buyer with a *packing list*, an itemized listing of all of the products included in the order. At the same time the seller sends an *invoice* to the buyer. The invoice is the bill for the merchandise. It lists all of the items purchased that are included in the order.

If the products are shipped by a transportation company, a *bill of lading* is sent with the merchandise identifying the products that are being shipped. When the merchandise is received by the purchasing company, it will be inspected and unpacked. A *receiving record* is completed, listing all of the merchandise in the shipment. The receiving record is sent to the accounting department where it is compared to the purchase order and invoice before payment is made.

Finally the products that have been received are entered into the *inventory records* of the company and the products are distributed to the departments where they will be used or sold. Some common purchasing records are identified in Figure 14-6.

Common Purchasing Records

FIGURE 14-6 ▪ The seller and buyer complete a number of forms in order to maintain accurate records of purchases.

RETAIL PURCHASING

Retail businesses purchase products for resale. Products sold by retailers change very rapidly. For example, a buyer for a large supermarket chain may review more than 200 new products each week for possible purchase. Also, many of the products sold in retail stores are seasonal. That means the products sell well during a particular time of the year but few customers want to buy them at other times. There is very little profit available to retailers on the sale of any one item in the store. Therefore if a product remains unsold, the business quickly loses money.

Customers and their needs are very important to retailers. Customers are studied carefully and their likes and dislikes considered when making purchase decisions. Retailing is also very competitive. If Company A offers a product that customers want and its competitors do not have that product, Company A has a real advantage. If a company is able to sell a similar product at a much lower price than competitors, it will usually sell a larger quantity. Retailers evaluate their competitors to determine what products are being sold and the prices charged in order to remain competitive.

DETERMINING RETAIL CUSTOMER NEEDS

Retailers use a great deal of marketing research to anticipate customer needs. Many have consumer panels and focus groups that meet regularly to evaluate new products. The business often contacts regular customers to determine what they like and dislike and to determine if the customers have needs that the business is not currently meeting.

Retail buyers and merchandise managers study market information including the economy, competition, and new product developments. They attend meetings and trade shows and talk with salespeople and other representatives of manufacturers and wholesalers.

Comparison shopping is used to study competitors. *In comparison shopping, people are sent to competitors' stores to determine products that are sold, prices charged, and services offered.* In some cases, products are purchased from competitors and then analyzed to determine their quality.

Retailers carefully track the sales of current products to determine which products sell rapidly and which do not. Computer technology aids in that process. Scanners at check-out counters are connected to computers that store inventory information. When a purchase is made by a customer, the scanner reads the bar code on each product purchased. The bar code is a distinct identifier for each product that provides information such as product name, product type, price, manufacturer, and the date the product was purchased by the business. That information is immediately analyzed by the computer. It is possible to identify sales levels by time of day and day of the week. Managers can determine if special displays, sales, or advertising programs affect sales volume of specific products.

Most retail store computer systems are connected to other computers in regional or national offices. Managers and buyers in those offices can monitor the performance of each store and each product in the store on a daily basis. With that information, purchasing decisions as well as marketing plans can be adjusted quickly to be sure that products are sold rapidly, products that do not sell are not reordered, and new purchases respond to customers' needs as demonstrated by past sales.

DEVELOPING A PURCHASING PLAN

Retail stores must offer an adequate assortment of products to meet the needs of their customers. Some stores, such as department stores, supermarkets, and discount stores, offer hundreds of different products in many merchandise categories. Specialty stores, such as apparel, office products, or sporting goods stores, offer less variety but a complete assortment in the specialty category.

A merchandise plan is developed by the business. *The merchandise plan identifies the type, price, and features of products that will be stocked by the business for a specific period of time.* The merchandise plan is like a budget in that it provides the basis for ordering merchandise and maintaining the store's inventory. The merchandise plan may be developed for a very short time period such as one or two months. It may also be developed for a specific season in which unique merchandise will be sold. While a general plan may be developed for a longer time period, few stores plan much longer than six months. Conditions can change dramatically in that time causing the merchandise plan to be out-of-date quickly.

The merchandise plan is developed from a basic stock list or a model stock list. *A basic stock list identifies the minimum amount of important products a store needs to have available to meet the needs of its target market.* The basic stock list will not change a great deal over time. *A model stock list describes the complete assortment of products a store would like to offer to customers.* The model stock list is more complete and is subject to change more frequently based on economic conditions, the financial resources of the business, and the changing need of customers.

LOCATING PRODUCTS FOR SALE

Retail buyers make purchases from many sources. Those purchases are made from both manufacturers and wholesalers. Many of the manufacturers and wholesalers have salespeople who contact managers at local stores. Or they may meet with regional or national buyers who make purchase decisions for several stores. Large retailers may have buying offices in major cities where many manufacturers are located. Some cities have trading centers for specific industries. For example, many furniture manufacturers open show rooms in High Point, North Carolina two times a year. Furniture retailers from all over the United States and the world come to the market to see the offerings of many manufacturers at one time and to order merchandise for the coming season.

Trade shows also offer an opportunity for many manufacturers to show their merchandise to large numbers of wholesalers and retailers at one time. A very large computer and electronics trade show is held each year in Las Vegas, Nevada. Companies spend hundreds of thousands of dollars on exhibit space, demonstrations, and advertising for the trade show because they know it is a time when retailers are looking for new product ideas.

A final method of purchasing is the use of catalogs distributed by wholesalers or manufacturers. Catalogs are used frequently by very small retailers who cannot afford to travel to trade centers or trade shows and who do not purchase in enough quantity to warrant frequent visits from salespeople. Catalogs are also used to sell standardized and frequently purchased items that are purchased primarily on the basis of price and availability. Some companies are now using telephones, computers, and facsimile machines to replace or supplement catalogs.

COMPLETING THE PURCHASE PROCESS

The retail buyer studies several sources of supply before selecting the one from which to order merchandise. Specific criteria are used based on the retailer's needs. Those criteria may vary for different products in the store's merchandise assortment. Some products may be unique and can only be obtained from one source. Others may be products that have been purchased for some time and customers are very loyal to that brand. Again, one supplier is used.

Still other products may be fast-selling, requiring the supplier to replace items in inventory rapidly. In that case, the retailer may want to purchase from a supplier who can guarantee rapid and reliable delivery. Some items sold by retailers may be very competitive products that can be purchased in many stores. The retailer's customers will shop for the lowest price, so a supplier must be located that will sell at competitive prices.

After the source of supply is determined, the order is placed. Most businesses have a standard procedure used to order merchandise. The order must be placed far enough in advance to be sure it is delivered before the current stock is completely sold or in time for the selling season for the product. The timing of orders is often a difficult problem for retailers. If the order is placed too soon, the merchandise arrives before it is needed, taking up space and adding to the storage and handling costs. If the order is late, the merchandise is not in stock when customers want it and sales are lost.

The seller ships the merchandise to the retailer's distribution center or store where it is unpacked and prepared for sale.

Again, each business has specific and careful procedures to be followed in receiving, unpacking, inspecting, and preparing products for sale. This is a very important part of the purchasing process. Large financial losses can occur in businesses that do not have effective procedures. Merchandise can be lost, stolen, or damaged during the receiving process. Because most retail businesses have very low margins of profit, any significant loss at this time can mean that the business will be unable to make a profit.

INTERNATIONAL PURCHASING PROCEDURES

As more companies become involved in international marketing, the importance of understanding the unique purchasing procedures of international trade increases. There can be advantages of purchasing products from international suppliers. They may offer unique products or manufacturing procedures, better availability, or quality. However, those advantages are lost if products are not supplied as expected or if costs are much higher than anticipated. Companies purchasing internationally must be aware of the unique customs and business practices of each country and develop effective relationships with their suppliers.

Locating products from international businesses is easier today than at any time in the past. Many businesses have foreign buying offices or purchasing representatives in other countries. Manufacturers wanting to sell to other countries will be represented at international trade shows or in foreign trading offices and trade directories. Most states and many large cities now have international trade centers where buyers and sellers can meet to exchange information and negotiate purchases.

Selecting products and suppliers from other countries is based on factors other than just the product to be purchased. The product and its characteristics are important and the purchaser must be assured of the product's quality. The purchaser should be able to inspect a sample of the product and talk to other businesses who have purchased or used the product.

The qualifications of the supplying company should also be considered. Problems can occur if the company is not reliable or financially stable. Often the purchaser's bank can help obtain financial information about the company. It is also important to consider the stability and economic conditions of the country in which the supplier is located. It can be risky to work with a business from a country that has a weak economy or is having political difficulties.

Two of the most important factors in international buying are negotiating price and transporting the products. Most countries have their own monetary system and it is sometimes difficult to accurately calculate rates of exchange. The exchange rate of money can change a great deal in the time it takes to negotiate a purchase and make delivery of a product. Also the countries of the supplier or buyer may impose tariffs or duties on the product which can drastically change the price.

One procedure some businesses use in international trade is reciprocal trading. *Reciprocal trading is a form of bartering in which products or services of one company are used as payment for the products of another company.* The practice of reciprocal trading is used when an unsatisfactory exchange rate exists between the two countries' currencies or when one of the companies does not have an adequate amount of cash to finance the purchase. As an example of a reciprocal trade agreement, a U.S. company that produces robots for use in automobile manufacturing sold a large order of equipment to a new company in Europe. Since the new company did not have enough cash to pay for the equipment, the companies negotiated a contract in which the U.S. business received a percentage of the sales of automobiles produced by the European company.

Banks that have experience in international business can provide a great deal of help in arranging financing of purchases. They can give advice on exchange rates, terms of payment, and methods of paying for purchases. Many banks that have experience in international finance have established working relationships with financial institutions in other countries. This makes it easier to gather financial information and complete financial transactions with businesses in those countries.

Transportation decisions include determining the method of shipment, selecting the transportation company, preparing the necessary transportation documents, and meeting each company's requirements for shipping, handling, and inspecting products. The time needed for transporting products between companies located in different countries may be no longer than shipments within a country in some cases. However, the timing and reliability of international shipments is a major concern for most purchasers. Careful study and planning for transportation should be done before a decision is made to purchase from an international supplier. Some companies make a small purchase or require a sample shipment before committing to a large order.

LREVIEW

A significant amount of all marketing activities occurs between businesses rather than between a business and a final consumer. When a business sells to another business, it must use the same careful process of identifying target markets and developing effective marketing mixes as it would in consumer markets. There are many types of business customers including producers, resellers, service businesses, government agencies, and nonprofit organizations.

Businesses purchase products for several reasons—to use in the production of other products and services, to use in the operation of the business, or for resale to other customers. The procedures used for business purchasing are somewhat different that those used by final consumers. Marketers need to learn as much as possible about reasons businesses buy and the procedures they use for various types of purchases. A very specific, step-by-step process is used by most businesses involving several people in the purchasing decision.

MARKETING FOUNDATIONS

1. KEY CONCEPTS

Read each of the following statements about business purchasing. Using information from the chapter, identify which of the statements are true and which are false.

a. The majority of exchanges in marketing are between businesses and final consumers.

b. Businesses that purchase products for resale to final consumers typically do not change the form of those products.

c. An example of a poor purchasing decision is selecting a supplier that is not able to deliver the product when promised.

d. The marketing process used for business-to-business marketing is very different from the one used to sell to final consumers.

e. The only types of companies classified as business consumers are producers.

f. The largest single customer of products and services in the world is the U.S. government.

g. The majority of products purchased by businesses are for final consumption.

h. Direct distribution from the producer to the customer is common in business-to-business marketing.

i. The most routine purchase for businesses is a repeat purchase.

j. In order to be as efficient as possible, businesses make one person responsible for all purchases.

k. The first step in the business purchasing process is to search for possible suppliers.

l. A vendor analysis is a procedure used to compare potential suppliers on important purchasing criteria.

m. In bidding, the buyer looks for the supplier who can meet product specifications and other criteria at the lowest price.

n. If a supplier can meet the needs of the buyer, it is likely that the buyer will continue to use the same supplier unless needs change.

o. Total Quality Management is a system in which the supplier resupplies a business' inventory just as the products are needed.

p. A physical inventory system determines the amount of product on hand at any time by continually maintaining records on purchases and sales.

q. It is illegal for retail businesses to send people into competitors' stores to determine what products are being sold and the prices charged.

r. A basic stock plan identifies the minimum amount of important products a store must stock to meet target market needs.

s. Companies wanting to purchase products from businesses in other countries find it increasingly difficult to obtain those products due to tariffs and quotas.

t. Reciprocal trading is a method of exchange that is very similar to the old practice of bartering.

2. HOW ARE THEY DIFFERENT?

 Business markets have several characteristics that make them different from final consumer markets. For each of the characteristics listed, provide a brief description that shows the difference.

a. Derived demand

b. Purchase volume

c. Similar purchases

d. Number of customers

e. Buyer/seller relationship

MARKETING RESEARCH

1. SIC INFORMATION

The Standard Industrial Classification System (SIC) is an important tool in helping companies collect information about business and organizational customers.

a. Using your school library or another information source, identify the SIC codes for the following:

- ▪ Major manufacturer in your city or state
- ▪ Product you purchased recently
- ▪ Type of service that businesses would typically use
- ▪ Government activity

b. Now locate and list four publications that use SIC codes to provide information about businesses, organizations, products, or services.

2. PURCHASER PREFERENCES

A vendor wanted to determine what factors were most important to its customers when they made purchase decisions. The company conducted a survey of purchasing agents and others involved in purchasing and asked them to assign a value from 0–5 for six factors they consider when purchasing products from the vendor. The meaning of the values ranged from 0 = not considered when making a purchase decision to 5 = most important factor in the purchase decision. The following results were obtained from 140 customers.

FACTORS	VALUE					
	5	4	3	2	1	0
Price	0	40	55	32	13	0
Delivery Schedule	45	38	36	20	1	0
Vendor Reputation	0	24	38	52	18	8
Past Experience with Vendor	7	10	68	55	0	0
Vendor Service after Sale	0	5	12	22	36	65
Product Quality	110	24	6	0	0	0

a. The vendor wanted to use the data to develop an average value for each of the factors. Calculate the mean value for each factor. The mean is determined by multiplying the value by the number of respondents selecting that value, totalling the result for all six value scores for the factor, and dividing the result by 140 (the total number of respondents). For example, the mean value of price is determined as follows: $(0 \times 5) + (40 \times 4) + (55 \times 3) + (32 \times 2) + (13 \times 1) + (0 \times 0) = 402; 402 \div 140 = 2.87$

b. The vendor asked a focus group to compare one of the vendor's products to similar products sold by two other competitors using the six factors from the research study. The focus group assigned each product a score of 1–10 for each of the six factors, with 1 being the lowest rating and 10 being the highest rating. The results of the focus groups ratings are shown in the table.

FACTORS	PRODUCT		
	Vendor	Competitor A	Competitor B
Price	6	8	10
Delivery Schedule	8	5	7
Vendor Reputation	7	7	5
Past Experience with Vendor	3	9	6
Vendor Service after Sale	8	4	6
Product Quality	10	7	8

The vendor then used the information from the original marketing research study to develop a product score for each company. The mean score for each factor (calculated from the research study results in Part a) was multiplied by the rating assigned to that factor by the focus group (from the table above). Then the result for each of the six factors were totaled, giving each company a final score. That procedure would predict that the company whose product received the highest score would be the one that best met the purchaser's needs.

Calculate the total product score for each company using the procedure described. Then be prepared to discuss the meaning of the results in terms of customer perceptions of the three companies' products.

MARKETING PLANNING

1. ANALYZING THE PURCHASING FUNCTION

 Develop a one or two paragraph written response to each of the following scenarios about purchasing. Apply the marketing orientation and your knowledge of purchasing procedures to develop your answers.

a. We learned in this chapter that final customers and business customers have different needs and characteristics. However some businesses are able to successfully serve both business and final consumers with the same marketing mix. One example is Sam's Clubs, a large mass merchandiser that sells a variety of products through a warehouse-type facility. Sam's Club is viewed as a wholesaler by many small businesses, but many customers are individual consumers buying for their personal and family needs. How does this fit the idea of target marketing and the marketing orientation?

b. There are many more final consumers than business and organizational consumers in the U.S. market. Also, business consumers involve more people in the decision-making process, take more time in making decisions, and carefully evaluate choices. Therefore, it would seem that marketing to business and organizational consumers is much more difficult than marketing to final consumers. Why would businesses choose to focus on the business and organizational markets?

c. Some retailers are trying to force the manufacturers from whom they buy products to reduce their prices, ship products more frequently, and take back merchandise that cannot be sold by the retailer. For those retailers who buy in very large volumes, manufacturers are likely to agree to many of the demands in order to be able to sell their products. However, they are finding it more difficult and less profitable to operate under the new requirements. Some have gone out of business and others have had to find ways to reduce the costs of operations, including reducing the quality of the products. Retailers say they have to require the changes or they will not be able to make a profit either. If you were the manager of a large retail business, how would you work with manufacturers?

d. When several people are involved in a purchasing decision in a business, there is often conflict because each person has different reasons for making the decision. Also it takes time for several people to gather information and make a decision. Some business people believe that a decision that everyone can agree on is not always the best decision but is a compromise. Would you recommend changing the procedure used by many businesses and have purchase decisions made by only one person?

e. Government purchasing is usually subject to close scrutiny by the public who are concerned that tax dollars are spent wisely. Therefore a bidding procedure is used for expensive purchases. Taxpayers expect that the people making the purchase decisions will select the lowest bid from among the suppliers who are able to meet the specifications established for the purchase. However, there are some situations where a higher bid seems to be a better alternative. For example, a police department purchasing several automobiles may want to select a higher bid from a local auto dealer than a lower one from an out-of-town dealer. A decision to buy rail cars for a mass transit system in California was protested when citizens learned the low bid was from a foreign rather than a U.S. supplier. What guidelines should government purchasers use when selecting bids?

f. A business that maintains both a physical inventory and a perpetual inventory regularly finds that the physical inventory count is much lower than the number of items in the perpetual inventory. That means that products are missing and there is no record of where they have gone. What are some possible explanations for the differences and what procedures can be developed to insure that the two inventory levels match more closely?

2. LEARNING MORE

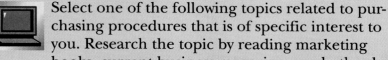 Select one of the following topics related to purchasing procedures that is of specific interest to you. Research the topic by reading marketing books, current business magazines, and other business resources. You might be able to identify a business person or other resource person in your community who is an expert on the topic to interview. Prepare a 3–5 page written report on the topic.

a. Census data related to businesses and organizations

b. Gathering information on international businesses

c. Using benchmarking to develop product specifications

d. Sources of information that aid in identifying vendors

e. Just In Time (JIT) inventory management

f. Total Quality Management (TQM)

g. Technology related to inventory management

h. Ethics of comparison shopping

i. Developing a model stock list for a retail business

j. Manufacturers' markets and trade shows

k. Exporting and importing procedures

MARKETING MANAGEMENT

1. DEVELOPING A PURCHASING PROCEDURE

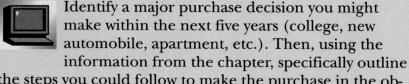 Identify a major purchase decision you might make within the next five years (college, new automobile, apartment, etc.). Then, using the information from the chapter, specifically outline the steps you could follow to make the purchase in the objective way followed by businesses. After you have outlined the steps, prepare a *vendor analysis* form. List the factors that you will consider when making the purchase. Develop nu-

merical values for each factor that reflect the relative importance of each factor to you. Create the form so it can be completed as you evaluate several companies or organizations that provide the product or service you plan to purchase.

2. ONE VENDOR OR MORE?

May Randall is the purchasing manager for Protective Insurance Company. The company has made a commitment to provide all employees who are involved with any type of information management or customer service and all company managers with a personal computer at their work station. The company currently has a large mainframe computer where all major company records are maintained. It is important that the computers purchased for employees are compatible with the mainframe.

Working with managers from each of the major divisions of the company, May has developed purchase specifications for the personal computers and has identified four manufacturers who can provide personal computers that meet the specifications. One of the manufacturers is the supplier of Protective's mainframe computer, but each of the other manufacturers has assured May that their personal computers are compatible.

May is now faced with two important decisions. First, should Protective Insurance buy all of the personal computers from one manufacturer or order from more than one. May is concerned that if only one is used, there may be difficulties with the prices charged for service. Also, real problems could develop if the manufacturer changes products or goes out of business in the future. On the other hand, using more than one supplier can create other types of service and support problems. The second problem is whether to purchase from the company who sold the mainframe since that product has worked well and the company has been very good about service and maintenance. However, that company has produced personal computers for only a short time while the other manufacturers are well known for manufacturing high-quality personal computers. What recommendations would you make to May to help her with the two decisions?

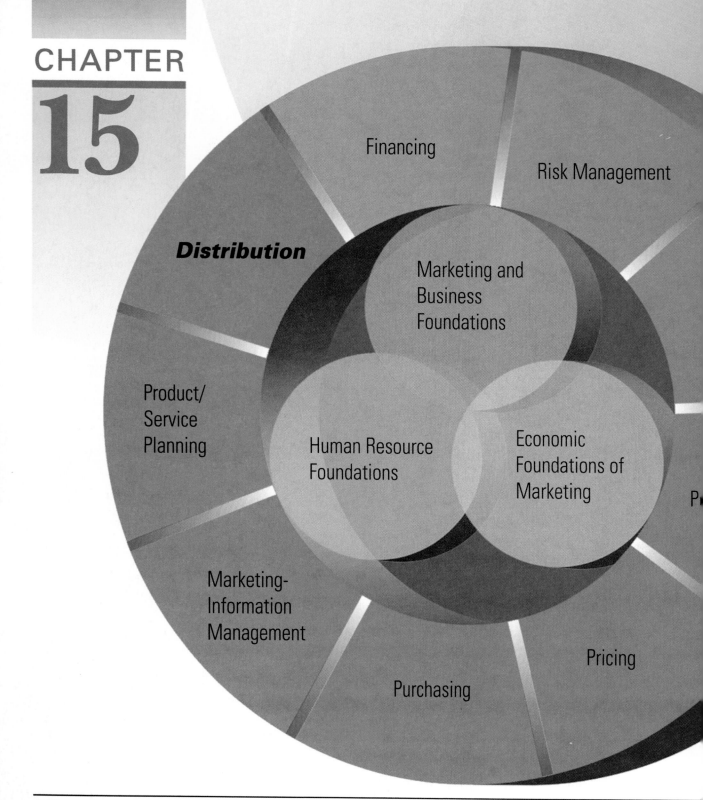

Financing

Risk Management

Distribution

Marketing and
Business
Foundations

Product/
Service
Planning

Human Resource
Foundations

Economic
Foundations of
Marketing

P

Marketing-
Information
Management

Pricing

Purchasing

Get the Product to Customers

OBJECTIVES

1. Discuss the importance of distribution as a marketing function.

2. Justify the need for an effective distribution system.

3. Explain how a channel of distribution is developed.

4. Describe the unique characteristics and roles of whole-salers and retailers.

5. Identify ways that physical distribution affects the success of a product.

NEWSLINE

THE SHIFT FROM IMAGE TO VALUE

People who did not want to be seen shopping at discount stores a few years ago are now bragging about the bargains they find in Kmart and Wal-Mart. After years of believing that "image means everything," many customers are shifting their thinking to "value means everything."

What has caused the change in attitudes? A long recession beginning in the last years of the 1980s and continuing well into the 1990s has shown many people that wealth is not guaranteed. A good job can disappear and savings can be used up. Many of the baby boomers now have children in college requiring large tuition payments, or they are considering whether they are financially prepared for retirement. Young people are wondering if they will have a lower standard of living than their parents as they struggle to find and keep a good job.

At the same time, customers are becoming more aware of similarities and differences in product choices. Many now realize that if they shop and compare before making a purchase, they can save from 25 percent to 50 percent on many purchases and still get the quality they want.

What does this significant change in shopping behavior mean to business? While many traditional department stores are struggling for survival, sales at discount department stores are increasing sharply. New leaders in retailing include factory outlets, off-price apparel stores, and warehouse clubs. Manufacturers who in the past have been able to command large markups and higher profits by promoting their national brands and restricting their distribution to exclusive stores now find that consumers are willing to accept off-brand and store-brand merchandise. Consumers are willing to forego the high level of services found at stores where they traditionally shopped when they see the savings they receive.

Will the trend continue toward low-price, high-value shopping? It is clear that there is still a part of the population with the resources to buy whatever they want and they are willing to pay for status and image. On the other hand, consumers have found that their changing behavior has not reduced their choices of products or their level of satisfaction. Even if they feel more financially secure with an improving economy, will they switch back from value to image? It is a gamble businesses must face.

THE IMPORTANCE OF DISTRIBUTION

Welcome to the world marketplace! U.S. consumers have access to hundreds of thousands of products. Products come from companies throughout the world. Any time of the day, and every day of the week, most people can locate a shopping center or store. Customers can find the products they need or a business that performs a desired service. If a shopping area isn't convenient, other choices are available. Purchases can be made from a catalog or a television shopping club using a telephone or even a computer.

The most complex and challenging part of marketing is distribution. With so many products and the convenience of shopping, this is difficult to imagine. Yet many people and companies are involved in the distribution of products and services from the producer to the consumer. Large percentages of marketing budgets are spent on the activities involved in distribution. For most products and services, over 50 percent of the cost of marketing is used for distribution activities.

Distribution is the oldest and most basic part of marketing. In fact, before the term *marketing* was even a part of business language, distribution was used to describe the activities that directed the flow of goods and services between producers and consumers. Today, because marketing activities have expanded, distribution is just one of the primary marketing functions. *As we learned earlier in this book, the distribution function involves determining the best methods and procedures to be used so prospective customers are able to locate, obtain, and use the products and services of an organization.*

When distribution works well, consumers are not really aware of its importance. Products and services are available where and when people want them and in a usable condition. However, when distribution does not work, it is very evident. Products are out of stock, back-ordered, available in the wrong styles or sizes, out-of-date, or damaged. Prices are incorrectly marked or missing, salespeople do not have adequate product information, or products advertised in the newspaper are not the ones carried by the store. Much of the dissatisfaction consumers have with businesses results from poor distribution.

DISTRIBUTION AS AN ECONOMIC CONCEPT

Distribution is an important activity for the effective operation of *any* economic system, but it is essential in a free enterprise economy. Free enterprise is based on the matching of production and consumption decisions. When a business person decides to produce a product, the product will not be successful unless it can be obtained by consumers. When consumers have a demand for a particular type of product or service, that demand will not be satisfied until they can locate the desired product. Distribution aids in the matching of supply and demand.

Another important concept studied in Chapter 4 was the principle of economic utility. Economic utility is *the amount of satisfaction a consumer receives from the consumption of a particular product or service.* Businesses can increase customer satisfaction by improving the form of a product or service, making it available at a more convenient time or place, or making it more affordable (possession utility). As you consider the four types of economic utility, you can see that distribution directly affects time and place. Distribution that is effective and efficient can insure that a product is available in a usable form at a reasonable price. So distribution is very important in increasing customer satisfaction.

DISTRIBUTION AS A MARKETING MIX ELEMENT

Another way of seeing the importance of distribution is to examine the marketing mix. *The marketing mix includes all of the tools or activities available to organizations to be used in meeting the needs of a target market.* Those activities are organized within the four mix elements—product, distribution, price, and promotion. *The definition of distribution as a part of the marketing mix is the locations and methods used to make the product available to customers.* When a marketer develops a marketing strategy and prepares a marketing plan, many alternatives for the best ways to distribute a product or service to a specific target market need to be considered. The choices made can determine whether the customer is able to easily locate and purchase the products and services needed.

DEVELOPING A DISTRIBUTION SYSTEM

Edu-Games was a new company that produced high-quality board games for children. The company carefully researched the market and identified a target market of parents aged 25–45 with 1–3 children under the age of 10. At least one parent had a college education and total family income was over $40,000. The families in the target market were concerned about the quality of their children's education and spent an average of $2,000 a year on education-related purchases for their children, including educational toys and games.

Based on the target market information, Edu-Games prepared a marketing plan for its board games. The games were constructed of finished wooden pieces and packaged in sturdy boxes. Package designs illustrated the games in use and descriptions of the educational value were clearly printed on the outside of each box. Prices were set high ($56 for each game) to match the quality image and prices were printed on the package so customers would be certain that they would pay the same price no matter where they purchased the game.

Edu-Games used distributors of games and toys to sell the product to retailers because Edu-Games was not large enough to have its own sales force. However, to help the distributors, the company identified the types of retail stores where the product should sell best. Those stores were primarily book stores with special children's collections and stores specializing in children's apparel. The company did not want the games sold through the large toy stores or discount stores because those stores did not fit the image of the product as high-quality and high-priced and the target market did not do most of their purchasing of education products in those types of stores. To help the retailer successfully sell the games, Edu-Games produced an easy-to-assemble display that provided adequate space for 300 games and contained information and pictures clearly describing the games, how they are played, and their educational value.

Three months after beginning distribution, sales were much lower than expected. An evaluation of marketing activities discovered that the mix was not being implemented as planned. Most of the games had been distributed to large toy stores because they were the traditional customers of the distributors and the distributors believed higher sales would result from those stores. The toy stores used a mass marketing strategy and cut the suggested price by 10 percent or more. Even with the discounts, the price was much higher than the average board game sold by the stores. The unique displays were not used by many of the stores because of space limitations. Instead the games were stacked on shelves along with many other products which did not allow the customers to see the unique packaging so they could understand the new products.

The experience of Edu-Games shows that the success of a product or a business is usually influenced by many other businesses. Even businesses that apply the marketing concept and try to respond to the needs of a target market can have problems if the businesses they use to distribute products do not have the same philosophy and do not follow the marketing plan. An important part of marketing is the design and management of an effective distribution system.

Any time a product or service is marketed to a customer, several decisions must be made in order for the exchange to occur. Those decisions include:

■ Where and when will the product be produced, exchanged, and used?

■ What are the characteristics of the product or service being exchanged that will affect distribution?

■ What services or activities must be provided in order for the product to be exchanged?

■ Is special physical handling needed?

■ Who will be responsible for the needed distribution activities?

■ When will each activity occur?

■ Who is responsible for planning and managing distribution?

THE NEED FOR CHANNELS OF DISTRIBUTION

When products and services are exchanged, they move through a channel of distribution. *A channel of distribution is made up of the organizations and individuals who participate in the movement and exchange of products and services from the producers to the final consumer.* The channel can be very simple, involving only the producer and the final consumer, or it can be very complex, involving many businesses.

If you buy a local newspaper, it is often edited, printed, and distributed by one company. However, if you buy a copy of *USA Today*, it is written and edited by one company in Washington D.C., printed by one of several other companies located in various parts of the country, then distributed and sold by other companies. There are several reasons that channels of distribution are needed in marketing.

ADJUSTING DIFFERENCES BETWEEN PRODUCERS AND CONSUMERS

There are many differences in what producers develop and what consumers need. Channels of distribution allow for adjustments to be made in those differences so the products available match the customers' needs. In Figure 15-1 on the next page you can see that consumers want to be able to buy products from many different companies. Adjustments are usually needed in the quantity and assortment of products, the location of the products, and the timing of production and consumption.

Differences in Quantity

Businesses usually sell their products to large numbers of customers. They produce thousands and even millions of those products in order to meet the total market demand. Individual consumers usually buy only a very small quantity of a product at any time. Therefore, a channel of distribution must be able to adjust the large quantity produced by the business to the small quantity needed by a consumer.

Differences in Assortment

A producer or a manufacturer often specializes in production. A company typically produces only a limited variety of products in one or a few product classifications. However, con-

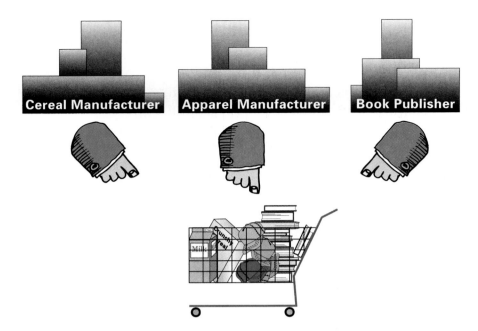

Adjusting Differences Between Producers and Consumers

FIGURE 15-1 ▪ Channels of distribution help to match supply and demand.

sumers have needs for a great variety of products. Another adjustment made through a channel of distribution is in the assortment of products. The channel will accumulate products from a number of manufacturers and make them available in one location to give consumers adequate choice and variety to meet their needs.

Differences in Location

Customers are usually not conveniently located next to the place where products are produced. They live throughout the country and throughout the world. It would be very difficult if not impossible for the manufacturer and final consumer to meet to complete an exchange. A channel of distribution is necessary to move the product from the place where it is produced to the place where it will be consumed.

Differences in Timing of Production and Consumption

In order to operate efficiently, most manufacturers operate year-round to produce an adequate supply of products. However, there are many products that consumers do not use year-round.

Snow blowers, swim wear, gardening equipment, and children's toys are all examples of products that are purchased in much higher quantities during certain times of the year.

Producers of agricultural products often have products for sale only at specific times of the year. However, consumers may want to consume those products, such as fresh fruits and vegetables, throughout the year. This presents a challenge to distributors to match seasonal agriculture production with year-round consumer demand. Making adjustments between the time of production and consumption is another responsibility of the channel of distribution.

Walk through a supermarket and study the adjustments made for the products sold in the store. Food has been accumulated from throughout the world. Some is fresh and some is processed. The wheat used in the bread and cereal may have been produced many months ago, processed into the products you see on the shelf, and distributed to many stores. The fruit and vegetables may have been rushed by airplane and refrigerated truck from fields in the United States or South America and arrived at the store only a few days after being harvested. Eggs and meat are evaluated and sorted so you can purchase them in different quantities and grades. Soft drinks have been accumulated from several bottlers so you can have a variety of choices. If the channels of distribution have worked well, the supermarket will be well stocked with all of the products you want to buy.

PROVIDING MARKETING FUNCTIONS

In any exchange between producer and consumer, all of the marketing functions must be performed. If no other organizations or individuals are involved in the exchange, the functions will need to be performed by either the producer or consumer. Often neither of those participants is willing or able to provide some of the functions. Other organizations or individuals then have the opportunity to become part of the channel of distribution and provide the needed functions.

Consider marketing activities such as transportation, financing, risk-taking, or promotion. Some businesses do not have the special equipment or the personnel to complete those functions, but the functions must be performed if the product is going to be sold to the consumer. Trucking companies, railroads, and airlines can provide transportation. Banks and finance companies provide credit to businesses and consumers. Wholesalers and retailers purchase products from manufacturers hoping to resell them at a profit. Advertising agencies, television and radio stations, magazines, and newspapers provide promotional assistance.

INCREASING MARKETING EFFICIENCY

If all exchanges of products and services occurred directly between producers and consumers, a great deal of time would be required for marketing. Consider the number of products that you and your family purchase during one week. What if you had to locate and contact each producer and manufacturer, agree on a price, and find a way to get the product from the business to your home? You would spend most of your time on those marketing activities.

When other businesses enter the channel of distribution, they take over many of the responsibilities, saving you both time and money. The business determines your needs and the needs of many customers like you. It then contacts the manufacturers of the needed products and has all of the products shipped to their location. You can then make one shopping trip to the business and purchase the needed products. In addition to saving you and the manufacturers time, the other businesses are very effective at locating and purchasing the needed products and finding the most efficient ways to ship them to their locations. Therefore, the cost of the marketing functions should be reduced compared to the cost if you had to complete them yourself. Figure 15-2 shows a simple illustration of the efficiency of exchange that can result from a channel of distribution.

PLANNING CHANNELS OF DISTRIBUTION

In order to have an effective distribution system, the channels of distribution must be carefully planned. Participants in the channel should be identified. Methods for developing and managing the channel should be considered. The channel of

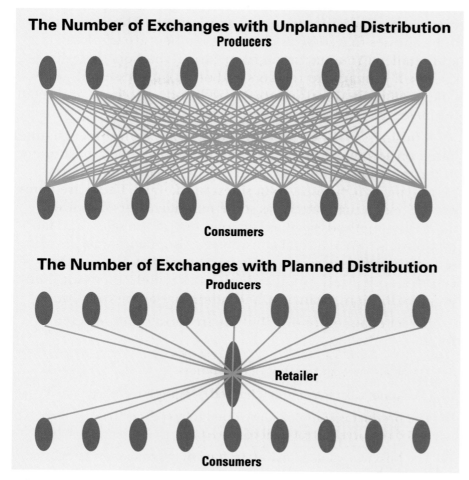

The Number of Exchanges with Unplanned Distribution

Producers

Consumers

The Number of Exchanges with Planned Distribution

Producers

Retailer

Consumers

FIGURE 15-2 ▪ Unplanned channels require that many exchanges occur before consumer needs are satisfied. A planned channel makes the exchange process much easier and more efficient.

distribution will be most effective if all participants believe in the marketing concept and direct their efforts at satisfying customer needs.

CHANNEL PARTICIPANTS

The businesses and other organizations that participate in a channel of distribution are known as channel members. Businesses use either direct or indirect channels of distribution. *In a direct channel, the product moves from the producer to the final consumer with no other organizations involved.* The producer or the consumer are responsible for providing or sharing all of the marketing functions. *An indirect channel includes other businesses between the producer and consumer that pro-*

vide one or more of the marketing functions. The typical types of businesses that serve as channel members are wholesalers and retailers. You may recall from earlier chapters that wholesalers sell primarily to retailers and other businesses, while retailers sell to final consumers. We will study wholesale and retail businesses later in this chapter.

A business chooses between a direct and an indirect channel based on several factors. Indirect channels are used most often in the sale of consumer products, while direct channels are more typical in business-to-business marketing. There are many exceptions to that pattern as some manufacturers use direct marketing methods such as catalogs, telephone sales, and factory outlets to reach final consumers. Also manufacturers who sell to businesses across large geographic areas and in other countries often rely on other businesses to help them with selling, distribution, financing, and other marketing functions.

Direct channels of distribution are most often selected when:

■ There are a small number of consumers.

■ Consumers are located in a limited geographic area.

■ The product is complex, developed to meet specific customer needs, or requires a great deal of service.

■ The business wants to maintain control over the marketing mix.

If the opposite market characteristics exist, an indirect channel of distribution will usually be developed.

Many manufacturers use multiple channels of distribution for the same product. This decision is consistent with the marketing orientation in that several target markets can exist for the same product. The needs and purchase behavior of each target market can be quite different.

Think of all of the different customers and needs that must be met by a carpet manufacturer. The same basic product may be sold directly to a contractor who is building several large office buildings. To reach a variety of final consumers, the carpet might be sold through furniture stores, home improvement centers, and discount and department stores. Some of those businesses will be contacted by the company's salespeople, while some very small retail businesses might buy from a wholesaler or another business that sells carpets for several manufacturers.

The possible channels of distribution for a carpet manufacturer are illustrated in Figure 15-3.

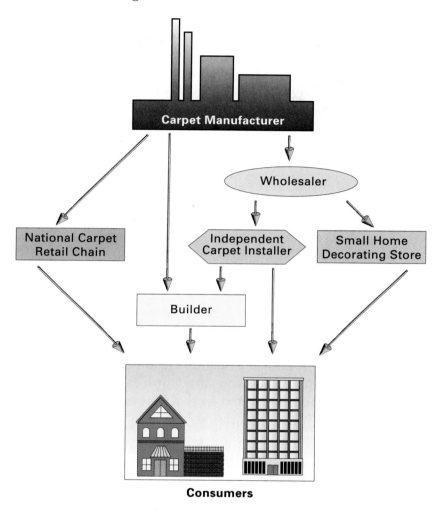

Multiple Channels of Distribution for Carpets

FIGURE 15-3 ▪ The same product may move through several channels of distribution before reaching the final consumer.

DEVELOPING AND MANAGING A CHANNEL SYSTEM

As we saw in the Edu-Games example, developing an effective channel of distribution is important if a marketing strategy is going to be successful. Few products can be distributed using a direct channel. Therefore channels must be developed carefully so that the product reaches the customers in the form they want, at the appropriate time and location, and at a price they can afford. Channel development and management is an important task for marketers.

Any business or individual can take responsibility for developing a channel of distribution. A manufacturer that develops a new product wants to find the best way to get the product to the target market. A retailer who discovers an important customer need will try to find a source of products that will satisfy that need. Even consumers can create channels of distribution by locating a supplier for a product they want that is not currently available in the market.

Channels of distribution are usually made up of independent businesses that treat each other as suppliers and customers as products move between them. They each have their own goals and customers and cooperate only when it is to their benefit. This often leads to problems and conflict. If a manufacturer has a very large inventory of one product and a limited supply of another, it is more likely to try to sell the first to retailers without being too concerned about what the retailer will do with the product. On the other hand, if a retailer is competing with another business that is cutting prices, it will try to force manufacturers and wholesalers it works with to cut the prices the retailer has to pay. The retailer will usually not worry whether those companies are able to make a profit.

When channel members do not cooperate, marketing problems may develop. Costs can increase, customer needs may not be met, and some marketing functions will not be performed well. Today, many businesses are concerned about the poor performance in channels of distribution and are developing ways to manage channels more effectively.

APPLYING THE MARKETING CONCEPT

Probably no situation provides a better example of the effectiveness of the marketing concept but is more difficult to implement than a channel of distribution. Businesses are used to competing with each other and working very independently. Manufacturers usually make their profits from the sale of products and services to wholesalers and retailers rather than to final consumers. Wholesalers are concerned about selling to retailers and retailers to final consumers. It is very difficult for all of the businesses in a channel of distribution to be concerned about satisfying the final consumer and how they must work cooperatively to meet consumers' needs. It is not easy to change a business' philosophy toward a belief that all of the businesses in the channel must be successful if the channel is going to work well. If indirect distribution is going to be used, businesses that believe in the marketing concept must look for ways to operate the channel so the goals of the marketing concept can be met.

WHOLESALING

As we learned earlier, many marketing functions must occur in the exchange process between a producer and consumer. They can be shifted and shared, but cannot be eliminated. In many cases, the producer or consumer are unwilling or unable to perform some of the functions. In other cases, they can and will perform the functions, but other individuals or organizations can perform some of the functions much more effectively, more quickly, or at a lower cost than either the producer or consumer. In those cases, the individuals or organizations are likely to become a part of the channel of distribution.

A traditional indirect channel of distribution would involve a producer, a retailer who accumulates the products from several producers, and the final consumers who make purchases from the retailer. However, the manufacturer may find that there are so many possible retailers that they cannot all be served effectively. Or the retailer may see the need to work with such a large number of producers that it is almost impossible to work well with each one. In those cases the traditional channel expands to include a wholesaler.

WHAT IS WHOLESALING?

Wholesalers are companies that assist with distribution activities between businesses. They do not work with final consumers in any significant way. Their role is to provide marketing functions as products and services move through the channel of distribution between producers and other businesses, including retailers.

Wholesalers provide very important marketing services to some organizations. Some businesses are unable to complete the large number of marketing tasks required. Others choose not to do some tasks. Wholesalers may provide one or more of the needed marketing activities better or at a lower cost than others. In that way, they participate in a channel of distribution. They contribute to the improvement of marketing. For example, a small retailer is not able to purchase most products in large quantities. Some manufacturers do not want to sell their products in small quantities. The shipping methods for small quantities often add considerably to the products' costs. A wholesaler combines the orders of several small retailers and purchases in efficient quantities. Shipments are made to several businesses in the same location. This allows less costly transportation methods to be chosen.

In the same way, a manufacturer usually tries to produce products on a regular basis throughout the year. Consumer demand for the products may be seasonal with most of the products being purchased during a few months. The manufacturer needs to have adequate facilities to store and maintain the products until they can be sold to retailers. If the manufacturer does not have the space, it may use wholesalers who specialize in storage and inventory management.

The typical wholesaling activities, as shown in Figure 15-4, include buying, selling, transporting, and storing products. Specifically wholesalers accumulate the products of many manufacturers, develop appropriate assortments for their customers, and distribute the products to them. Other more specialized activities that are provided by some wholesale businesses include financing the inventories of manufacturers until they can be sold and extending credit to retailers to enable them to make purchases.

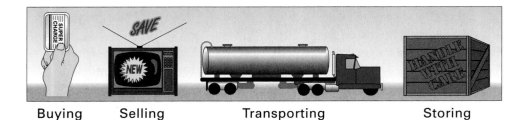

Buying   Selling   Transporting   Storing

Typical Activities of Wholesalers

FIGURE 15-4 ▪ While wholesalers can perform any of the marketing functions, the activities most often performed by those businesses in a channel of distribution are buying, selling, transporting, and storing.

Wholesalers can also be an effective source of information. They assist manufacturers in determining needs of retailers and final consumers and provide market and product information to retailers. Some support the promotional efforts of the manufacturers and retailers by promoting the products they sell.

There has been a recent increase in the popularity of a unique type of wholesaler. *Wholesale clubs are businesses that offer a variety of common consumer products for sale to selected members through a warehouse outlet.* Some of the well-known wholesale clubs are Sam's Club, PACE, and Costco Wholesale. Large quantities of products are available but often the variety of products and the choice of brands is very limited. Products are displayed in large warehouses with cartons stacked on the floor or on warehouse shelves. Customers search among the many products, select their purchases, pay cash, and are responsible for transportation.

The wholesale clubs primarily serve small businesses but most also offer memberships to the employees of large businesses and organizations. Because individuals as well as businesses buy products from wholesale clubs, these companies cross the line between retailing and wholesaling. However, the individual customer must be a member of the affiliated organization and must also pay an annual membership fee to the wholesale club. Most of the clubs also charge a higher price (often 5–10 percent) for products purchased for individual use rather than for use by a business.

HOW IS WHOLESALING CHANGING?

As many manufacturers and retailers get bigger and as distribution and communication methods improve, it would seem that the need for wholesalers would decrease. In fact, some large retailers refuse to deal with wholesalers, believing they can get better service and prices if they work directly with manufacturers. As the nature of marketing has changed, wholesalers have adjusted some of their business practices in order to continue to participate in channels of distribution.

There are still many more small- and medium-sized retailers and manufacturers than there are large businesses. Those smaller businesses need effective purchasing and distribution methods if they are going to compete with the large businesses. Wholesalers provide those functions because they specialize in evaluating the products of many manufacturers, buying and shipping in large quantities, assisting with financing, and many other important marketing activities. For those small businesses, wholesalers are more important today than ever before.

Also wholesalers provide access to new markets with less risk than if the retailer or manufacturer developed that market alone. Wholesalers help retailers become aware of new products and new manufacturers. They make products available from businesses that are located long distances away. For manufacturers who want to expand into new markets or sell to different types of businesses, wholesalers may already have experience in those markets. They can develop the new business opportunities much more quickly and effectively than if the manufacturer attempts it alone.

Export and import organizations are very important in building international business. They are informed of the conditions and customer needs, as well as business procedures and legal requirements, for operating in the international market. Without the help of wholesalers, many companies would not be successful in international business.

Of the recent changes in wholesaling, among the most important are better communications, information, improved technology, and broader customer service. Effective wholesalers believe in the marketing concept just as other businesses do. Therefore they work to identify their customers and understand their needs. They learn of the problems the customers are having with products and with marketing activities and help them to solve those problems.

Many wholesalers are adding marketing research and marketing information services. They help their customers gather information and provide them with data that will help the businesses improve their operations and decisions. Computer technology can process orders more rapidly and keep track of the quantity and location of products. New methods of storing and handling products reduce product damage, the cost of distribution, and the time needed to get products from the manufacturer to the customer. Wholesalers are providing additional services to their customers such as marketing and promotional planning, 24-hour ordering and emergency deliveries, specialized storage facilities, and individualized branding and packaging services.

RETAILING

Consumers purchase most of their products and services from retailers. While retailers do not develop the product, they are responsible for the marketing mix that the consumers will see. Retailers select the location where consumers will obtain the product, determine the price to be charged, and control much of the promotion for products and services. They often provide customer services during the sale and service for the product after the sale. Because retailers provide the consumer contact for all members in a channel of distribution, their role is very important.

WHAT IS RETAILING?

Retailing is the final business organization in an indirect channel of distribution for consumer products. While some large discount retailers sell products to other businesses, their primary customers are individual consumers purchasing to meet their own needs. Retailers accumulate the products their customers need by buying from manufacturers or wholesalers. They display the products and provide product information so customers can evaluate them. Many retail businesses help customers purchase products by accepting credit cards or providing other credit or financing choices. Additional services such as alterations, repairs, layaway, gift wrapping, and delivery are available in some stores.

Retailers also help wholesalers and manufacturers. In addition to purchasing products for resale, retailers provide many other marketing functions. They store much of the inventory of products until the customer buys them. Because of that, the retailers are assuming a great deal of the risk and are providing financing for the products. Promotion is an important marketing activity of retailers and increasingly, retailers are involved in marketing research and marketing information management. Some retailers even take responsibility for transporting products from the manufacturer to their stores.

WHAT ARE THE TYPES OF RETAILERS?

It is very difficult to define retailing because of the variety of businesses that sell to final consumers. Because there are so many consumers and their needs and purchasing behaviors are so different, retail businesses develop to respond to those differences.

Some consumers carefully plan their purchases, gather information in advance of shopping for products, and want to complete their shopping as quickly as possible. Other consumers use very little planning, gather information about products from information provided in the stores, and enjoy spending a great deal of time shopping. You probably know people who make frequent trips to stores and make a large number of small purchases. There are other consumers who shop very infrequently but spend large amounts of money and make many purchases when they do shop. Some people prefer to do their purchasing through catalogs or from television or computer-based shopping services rather than travel to the stores. Retail businesses are available that match each of these types of shopping behaviors. There are several ways to consider the types of retailing.

Product Mix of Retailers

One way of categorizing stores is by the types of products offered in the businesses. Some retailers specialize in one or a few product categories while others offer customers a wide range of products.

Single or limited-line stores offer products from one category of merchandise or closely related items. Examples include food, hardware, apparel, lawn and garden, or music. Some stores in this category offer a wide variety of types of products while others may be very specialized. For example, within the category of food, it is possible to find businesses that sell only coffee, cookies, or fresh fruits while other businesses offer many varieties of food in hundreds of product categories.

Mixed merchandise stores offer products from several different categories. Common examples of mixed merchandise retailers are supermarkets in which you can buy many products other than food; department stores that may offer 50 or more distinct departments of products; and large drug stores that sell everything from pet food, automotive products, and electronic equipment, to health-related products.

A relatively new concept in retailing is the superstore. *Superstores are very large stores that offer consumers wide choices of products.* Most superstores are mixed merchandise

IN THE SPOTLIGHT

CHANNEL FISHING

A fish processing company, Foley Fish, has improved the marketing of fish by carefully developing and managing the channel of distribution. Foley Fish is selective about the sources from which it purchases fish. It works with a select group of commercial fishers who catch their fish several hundred miles from shore where pollution and chemicals are not a problem. The company also trains its employees who purchase and process the fish so they can identify and discard those that are of poor quality. Foley is one of the few fish processors that ships and stores all of its fish in chipped ice from the time it is purchased throughout the processing until it is delivered to the retail stores. In addition, the temperature in the processing buildings is kept low to help maintain the quality of the product.

Foley's commitment to quality and effective marketing does not end when the fish leave the processing facility. The retailers keep fresh chipped ice under the fish and use small cards to identify the variety of fish and the Foley Fish brand name.

Until Foley's marketing program was developed, few people could identify the brand of fish they purchased. But the customers of Foley Fish are different. Foley has demonstrated that the effective management of a channel of distribution is an important marketing tool that can build strong customer loyalty.

Source: On the Menu *feature: Cable News Network*

businesses offering a variety of product categories so consumers can use the business for one-stop shopping. However, some superstores sell products in a limited category but offer consumers many choices of brands, product choices, and features within that category. Two of the most popular types of limited-line superstores today are computer stores and consumer electronics stores.

Location of the Retail Business

An important characteristic of retailing is the location of the store. The location can be studied in relation to the customer or to other businesses. *Convenience stores are stores located very close to their customers, offering a limited line of products that consumers use regularly.* Most convenience stores sell gasoline, food, and household products. However other convenience stores are becoming popular, including businesses that provide packing and mailing, photocopy and printing services, and video rental stores.

Shopping centers are a set of stores located together and planned as a unit to meet a range of customer needs. There are several types of shopping centers based on size and types of businesses. *Shopping strips* contain approximately 5–15 stores grouped together along a street. They offer a limited number of emergency and convenience products such as fast food, gasoline, laundry services and so forth. *Neighborhood centers* are 20–30 stores that offer a broader range of products meeting the regular and frequent shopping needs of consumers located within a few miles of the stores. *Regional shopping centers* contain 100 or more businesses. These large shopping centers attempt to meet most or all of consumers' shopping needs. The centers are developed around several large department or discount stores. They often attract customers from 10 or more miles away. The Mall of America in Minneapolis, Minnesota offers customers the opportunity to shop in over 300 businesses in one location. It attracts people regularly from 500–1,000 miles away and is designed as an international shopping location. It promotes its location to travel agents that arrange tours for groups from around the world.

Stand-alone stores are large businesses located in an area where there are no other retail businesses close by and offering either a large variety of products or unique products. Stand-alone businesses must have products that customers cannot easily find in more convenient locations or products so important or unique that consumers will make a special trip to the business. Examples of stand-alone businesses are some auto dealerships, superstores, and lawn and garden centers.

A unique category of retail businesses is non-store retailing. *Non-store retailing sells directly to the consumer's home rather than requiring the consumer to travel to a store.* Two of the oldest and most common forms of non-store retailing are door-to-door selling and catalog sales. Many years ago, traveling salespeople were used to sell many consumer products. The salespeople traveled to the customer's home because consumers took infrequent shopping trips. This method is used less frequently today because of cost and changing shopping behavior, but some companies such as Avon, Discovery Toys, and Tupperware, still use door-to-door selling. Catalog sales were also very popular in the past, but declined in popularity due to the time needed to order and ship a product by mail and the difficulty consumers had with product quality. Today, catalogs are regaining popularity in some product categories as a result of express delivery and a strong guarantee and warranty program by the businesses.

Other types of non-store retailing are vending machines, telephone sales, televised shopping clubs, direct mail selling, and even buying services that can be accessed using a computer. One supermarket now has a service available to its customers that own computers. The customer can place an order for groceries through the computer, pay by credit card, and the order will be delivered to the customer's home within 24 hours.

HOW IS RETAILING CHANGING?

Retailing has always been known for variety as well as rapid change. There is nothing to suggest that change will not continue. Retailing is likely to be very different in the next ten years than it is now. Also, because of the large number of retailers and the choices available to consumers, it will be increasingly difficult to compete in many types of retail businesses. Consumers expect variety, quality, service, and low price. Retailers will have to be very effective at purchasing, selling, and business operations. In addition they will have to find the most efficient ways to operate in order to keep costs low if they are to be profitable.

Changing Types of Retailers

It is likely that there will continue to be a need for both specialty and mixed merchandise stores. Some people predicted that specialty stores would disappear as people did more one-stop shopping. However, there are a large number of consumers who are willing to invest more time in shopping and are looking for a wider choice as well as unique or unusual items that are not widely available. The number of small specialty retail businesses has begun to increase again after a time when the numbers were declining. Also the very large specialty businesses continue to grow.

The Growth of Franchising

Franchising is becoming a very popular type of retail ownership (see Figure 15-5). In franchising, a company (the franchiser) develops a basic business plan and operating procedures. Other people (franchisees) purchase the rights to open and operate the businesses according to the standard plans and operating procedures. A franchise fee is paid to the franchiser for the business idea and assistance.

Franchises allow people with limited experience to enter a business. They are guided by the franchise plan which reduces the risk of failure. Franchise plans also increase customer awareness of the business because many businesses operate in different locations using the same franchise name and promotion. Examples of successful retail franchises include Dominos, Wicks 'N' Sticks, TCBY, Mail Boxes Etc. USA, Sir Speedy, and Midas. It is anticipated that franchises may account for nearly half of all retail sales by the year 2000.

FIGURE 15-5 ▪ Many successful businesses are operated as franchises including production, service, wholesale, and retail businesses.

Increased Use of Technology

Technology is having a big impact on retailers. Not only are most business operations managed using computers, but new types of equipment are being used in businesses to store, distribute, and display products. Display shelves and shopping carts are able to print coupons for customers as they shop to encourage the purchase of specific products. Customers can shop for products using a computer screen rather than walking around a store. When a product is selected from the description and picture on the screen, the consumer inserts a credit card into the computer. The product is selected, packaged, and available for pickup at the front of the store when the customer is finished shopping.

The Global Marketplace

Global retailing holds a great deal of promise for the future. While many manufacturers and wholesalers have been involved in international marketing for a number of years, retailers are often reluctant to expand into other countries. However, several types of retail businesses have successfully moved into Eastern and Western Europe and Asia. As countries of the former Soviet Union and Africa develop their economies, retail opportunities will expand there as well. Many of the U.S. fast food businesses have been quite successful in international marketing, as have businesses in the travel industry, including hotels and automobile rental agencies. U.S fashions have wide acceptance, so specialty stores are looking at other countries as likely places to expand their businesses.

PHYSICAL DISTRIBUTION

It is important to have the right combination of businesses in a channel of distribution. However, simply selecting the businesses does not insure that products will move effectively from the producer to the consumer. An important part of channel planning is physical distribution. *Physical distribution includes transportation, storage, and handling of products within a channel of distribution.*

Consider the number of activities that must be completed as a product moves through a channel. A great deal of paperwork is completed from the time the product is ordered until it is available and ready for sale to the final consumer. The product is usually handled many times as it moves from the manufacturing facility through several forms of transportation and many locations into the business where it will be consumed or sold. It is likely that the product will be grouped into large units for transportation and then divided into smaller units for display and sale. This requires further handling and packaging.

Usually products do not move continuously from one business to the next through the channel of distribution. They are often stored for some time as each business processes paperwork, sells to the next channel member, and determines the location of distribution. Storage facilities must be arranged to hold and protect the product, and inventory control procedures must be developed so the product does not become lost in the channel.

All parts of the physical distribution process must be carefully planned and controlled if a marketing strategy is going to be successful and products will be successfully exchanged. The primary physical distribution activities are transportation, storage and product handling, and information processing.

TRANSPORTATION

How will products be moved from producer to consumer? It seems like the answer to that question is not difficult. There are common transportation methods used to move most consumer products—railroad, truck, airplane, ship or boat, and pipeline. As you consider those alternatives, some are automatically eliminated because they are not available in certain locations or are not equipped to handle the type of product to be shipped. You clearly would not send small packages by rail car or ship, and iron ore and coal would not be moved by airplanes. Other factors such as the speed of delivery needed, whether the products need special handling, and cost enter into the choice of transportation methods.

Railroads

Railroads are particularly useful for carrying large quantities of heavy and bulky items. Raw materials, industrial equipment, and large shipments of consumer products from the factory to retailers often are moved by rail. The cost of this transportation method is relatively low if a large quantity of a product is moved, but the total cost to ship one or more carloads of a product is high. Products move quite slowly on trains compared to other methods of transportation.

Problems exist in using railroads for shipping products. Equipment is not always available where it is needed and it takes some time to move empty cars to new locations. Many areas of the country are not served by rail, meaning that other forms of transportation will be needed to and from the closest rail site. The time needed to load and unload freight from rail cars is long, particularly when a carload is made up of shipments from several companies or is intended for a large number of customers.

Railroads are responding to the need for improved service to customers. Railroad tracks and equipment are being upgraded and routes are being rescheduled to provide the services customers need. Newer methods of product handling are being developed, including packing products into large containers or even truck trailers which are then hauled on flatbed cars. To speed rail shipments to customers, it is now possible for a business to send several carloads of products from the production point and redirect them to customers while enroute as sales are made.

Trucks

Trucks are the most flexible of the major transportation methods. They can handle small or large shipments, goods that are very durable or require special handling, and products that are going across town or across the country. Trucks can reach almost any location and can provide relatively rapid service. Trucking costs are relatively low for short distances and easy-to-handle products but increase for longer or more difficult shipments.

Many companies own their own trucks. Small companies can often afford to own and maintain a delivery vehicle. Large manufacturers, wholesalers, and retailers often own fleets of trucks to be able to move products where and when needed. Trucking firms are important channel members. The firms provide the specialized service of transporting products to other channel members. They often have special product handling equipment, storage facilities, and well-trained drivers to insure that products are moved rapidly and safely.

Ships and Boats

A large amount of the products sold internationally are transported by water. While airlines move small shipments rapidly, ships can handle large quantities and large products very well at a much lower cost than air shipments. The major problem with this form of transportation is speed. Ships are relatively slow and it may take several weeks after a product is loaded on the ship before it is delivered to the customer. Also, as we have seen with accidents of ships carrying oil, there is a risk of large losses if a ship is damaged by weather or other conditions. Ships usually must be used in combination with trucks or railroads as they are limited to travel between shipping centers.

There is another type of water transportation used for shipping that is not as visible. That is the use of boats on inland waterways such as lakes and large rivers. Barges and large boats that haul cargo handle a number of products such as coal, grain, cement and other bulky and nonperishable items. Like ships they are also rather slow, but can handle large quantities at relatively low prices.

Air

If you want products delivered rapidly and can afford a higher cost, air transportation will often be the choice. Small parcels can be carried on commercial flights while large products or large quantities of a product can be moved using cargo planes.

Because of the high transportation costs, many companies do not consider air as a transportation choice. However, when other factors are considered, air transportation is not as expensive as it seems. For example, the speed of air delivery reduces the need for product storage. Products may need to be handled less and the speed of distribution reduces spoilage, damage, and theft. Companies that do not regularly use air transportation may choose that method for special or emergency deliveries.

Pipelines

While not used for many products, pipelines are still an important transportation method. Gas, oil, and water are moved in large quantities over long distances through pipelines. Even some products you would not think of move by pipe. Small coal and wood particles can be mixed with water into a *slurry* and sent through a pipeline between locations. Pipelines are expensive to construct and can be difficult to maintain. However once built, they can be a very inexpensive method to use when you consider the large volume of product that can move through the pipeline. It also may be the only choice to deliver products from some locations such as crude oil from oil fields.

Combining Methods

Products usually move through long channels among several businesses. It is likely that many will be transported using combinations of transportation methods. A shipment of appliances may be moved from a factory to a rail site by truck, moved across the country by rail, and then loaded on other trucks to be delivered to retailers. Shipments of grain from the midwest may move by train or truck to a grain terminal at a river. The grain is loaded onto barges for shipment to an ocean port. It is then loaded onto ships for transportation to another country.

Companies like Federal Express, United Parcel Service, and even the U.S. Postal Service combine their own fleets of cargo planes and delivery trucks to move small shipments between cities throughout the world overnight. Gasoline and other petroleum products are originally moved from a refinery to many locations across the country by pipeline. Then trucks are used to transport the products to wholesalers, retailers, and business consumers.

STORAGE AND PRODUCT HANDLING

Since production and consumption seldom occur at the same time, products must be held until they can be used. This means that methods and facilities for storage must be developed as a part of marketing. Effective storage allows channel members to balance supply and demand, but it adds to the costs of products and adds the risk that products may be damaged or stolen while being stored.

Storage of most products is usually done in warehouses. Warehouses can be privately owned by any of the companies in the channel of distribution. Private ownership allows the company to develop the specific type of facility needed for the products being handled at the locations where they are most needed. For companies who need limited storage space or need it less frequently, public warehouses are available. Public warehouses are often used for overflow storage or for products that are seasonal.

If you live in a medium- to large-sized city, you may have an area of town that was a warehouse district. Large, old, multistory buildings were used in the past by many wholesalers and manu-

A GLOBAL VISION

7-ELEVEN SHINES IN JAPAN

While much of the Japanese retail industry went through the same economic slump faced by U.S. businesses in the early 1990s, the over 4,000 stores that are a part of 7-Eleven Japan were able to grow at a rate of 10 percent a year in sales.

Two factors contribute to the remarkable performance. The stores' managers study customers and their needs in more detail than almost any other business. Also, the stores feature an up-to-date computer system that tracks sales of products so that only the items customers want to purchase are found on the shelves of each store.

For every sale, 7-Eleven employees enter customer information into the computer including gender, estimated age, and the variety and quantity of products bought. That information is analyzed immediately and the results shared with distributors and manufacturers. Each store ends up with its own special assortment of products designed for the customers who shop there.

Based on their success, the owners of 7-Eleven Japan have now purchased the U.S. company. They believe that many of the strategies they are using in Japan can turn the U.S. stores into profitable businesses. The idea is simple. Give customers what they want in well-run businesses and you will be successful. It's working in Japan.

Source: "Listening to Shoppers' Voices," Business Week/ Reinventing America 1992, *p. 69.*

facturers. They were often located near the center of town to be close to the retail businesses. Today, you will find storage facilities located at the edge of town near transportation facilities such as interstate highways or airports. The buildings are quite different from the old warehouses. They are still large but are usually only one story tall. If you enter the building you will likely see long conveyor belts or chains that move products through the building. There may even be computer-controlled trucks and carts that move products from area to area without drivers. Special storage shelves and equipment can move products in and out without the need for handling by people. Bar codes on the shelves, containers, and packages allow computers to keep track of the location of products and the length of time they are in storage.

The newest kind of storage facility is known as a distribution center. *A distribution center is a facility used to accumulate products from several sources, regroup, repackage, and send them as quickly as possible to the locations where they will be used.* A large retailer may have a number of distribution centers located throughout the country. Thousands of products are ordered from many manufacturers and shipped in huge quantities from the manufacturer to the distribution centers. The products are needed in various assortments and quantities in the hundreds of stores owned by the retailer. The costs of storage and transportation are quite high so the distribution centers must be very good at receiving the products from the manufacturers, combining the many different products into shipments for each store, and routing those shipments as quickly as possible so the merchandise can be sold. The goal of the distribution center is to reduce the costs of physical distribution while increasing the availability of products to customers. That can be done by careful and efficient product-handling methods and by reducing the amount of time products remain in the distribution center.

Another important part of product handling is packaging. We learned about packaging as a part of product development and saw that packaging aids in the effective use of the product as well as a tool for promotion. However, the primary purpose of packaging is to protect the product from the time it is produced until it can be consumed. A great deal of money is invested in products by manufacturers and other channel members that will be lost if the product is damaged or destroyed as it moves between companies.

Packaging materials need to be selected and packaging methods developed that protect the product and allow it to be shipped in appropriate quantities. The people planning the packaging need to consider the methods that will be used to handle the product and the method of transportation. A product that is handled with a fork lift and shipped in large containers using trucks and rail cars needs to be packaged differently than a product that is shipped in small quantities directly to the consumer using a parcel service. Products being sent across town require different packaging and packing than those that are being shipped around the world.

INFORMATION PROCESSING

Physical distribution systems match the supply of products with the demand for those products. First that requires that products are available. Then the inventory of products can be matched with the needs of consumers and channel members. An effective information system must be able to predict consumer demand (to be sure that adequate supply is available). The system must assure that the supply matches demand (not too much or too little of a product). Products must be routed to where they are needed as quickly as possible. The two important parts of the physical distribution information system are order processing and inventory control.

Order Processing

Order processing begins when a customer places an order. Typically the order is placed with a salesperson, but the order

may be called in by telephone, sent to the company by facsimile, or even processed through a computer using a modem from the customer's computer.

When the order is received by the supplier, a system must be in place so the order can be sent to the location in the business where it can be filled. At the same time, the order is being processed by the accounting department to determine the terms of the sale, method of payment, and cost of the products. Other people are determining the method, cost, and timing of transportation.

When the order is filled, it must be packaged and prepared for shipment. The order is checked to make sure it is complete and information is forwarded to accounting so an invoice can be prepared. The shipper is notified so transportation is available. The customer is informed that the order has been processed and shipped. This procedure is repeated at each stage of the channel of distribution until the product is delivered to the final consumer.

Inventory Control

The level of inventory affects the cost of marketing and the level of customer satisfaction. If too much inventory is maintained, the cost of storage will be much higher than necessary. There is also a risk that customer needs will change or the product will spoil or become out-of-date and will not be sold. If not enough inventory is available, customers will not be able to buy what they need and sales and goodwill will be lost.

An inventory control system needs to maintain several types of information. It is important to know what products are in inventory, what quantity of each product is available and how long each has been in inventory. Effective inventory control methods maintain information in a computer so it is not necessary to look at the inventory each time there is a question about it. We learned earlier about perpetual and physical inventory systems and how they help business people keep track of the products on hand.

A second important feature of an inventory system is a method to determine what products to order and what quantities to order. An inventory control system should identify how much of each product is being sold and how rapidly. The people responsible for maintaining adequate inventory levels should know how long it takes to process an order for each product so an adequate supply can be maintained. They should also be aware of products that are selling more rapidly or more slowly than planned. When sales are higher than expected, the company may want to order more to be able to meet customer needs. When sales are slow, reasons for the reduced level of sales should be determined and a decision made whether to re-order or not. The slow sales may indicate that consumer needs are not being met by the marketing mix for that product.

REVIEW

Distribution is one of the most important marketing functions. It is responsible for ensuring that products are available where and when consumers want them. If completed well, distribution can reduce costs so the product is more affordable and can help to make sure the product is available in the form consumers want.

Products move from producers to consumers through channels of distribution. Those channels can be direct with no other businesses involved, or they can be indirect involving several other businesses. The primary types of businesses involved in channels of distribution are wholesalers and retailers. Wholesalers sell to other businesses while retailers serve the final consumer. Each of the businesses in a channel of distribution is responsible for providing one or more of the marketing functions.

Physical distribution planning includes selecting the methods of transportation, determining how products will be packaged, handled, and stored, and developing systems for processing orders and maintaining needed information. When distribution is well planned, products move quickly through the channel, as inexpensively as possible so that the supply of products meets consumer needs for those products.

MARKETING FOUNDATIONS

1. SHOW THAT YOU KNOW

Each of the following concepts is an important part of distribution. Use this activity to demonstrate that you know what each means. Draw one or two pictures illustrating a product or service from the time it is developed until it is purchased and used by a consumer (final or business consumer). Include an example of each of the concepts in the pictures. Make sure you label the part of the picture that illustrates the concept and write a brief statement describing what is occurring in the picture.

Channel of distribution   Retailing

Direct channel   Physical distribution

Indirect channel   Distribution center

Wholesaling

2. IDENTIFY BUSINESSES

For each of the following categories, list as many businesses as you can from the areas you regularly shop. Use the *Yellow Pages* of your phone directory, a local business directory, newspaper advertisements, and your own personal knowledge to develop the lists.

Wholesale club   Shopping strip

Limited-line store   Neighborhood shopping center

Mixed merchandise store   Regional shopping center

Superstore   Stand-alone store

Convenience store   Non-store retailer

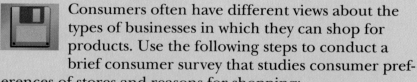

MARKETING RESEARCH

1. CHANNEL PREFERENCES

Consumers often have different views about the types of businesses in which they can shop for products. Use the following steps to conduct a brief consumer survey that studies consumer preferences of stores and reasons for shopping:

a. Using four note cards, write one of the following business categories on each card: factory outlet, specialty store, discount store, television shopping club.

b. Using four more note cards, write one of the following reasons for shopping at a specific type of store on each card: convenience, service, price, variety.

c. Use the following three products for your survey: jewelry, video cassette recorder, automobile tires.

d. Ask at least ten people to participate in the survey. For each of the products in Part c above, ask the respondent to choose from the first set of cards the store where they would most likely shop for that product. Then ask them to choose from the second set of cards the most important reason for their choice of a business.

e. Record each respondent's decisions for all three products. To help you with the recording, develop a chart for each product containing a list of the types of business and a list of the shopping reasons. Record the frequency with which each type of business was chosen and the frequency with which each reason was chosen.

f. Summarize the results by developing a table for each product that shows the respondent's preferences of businesses and reasons for shopping at those businesses. Prepare a one-half page written discussion of each table.

2. IDENTIFYING WHOLESALERS

There are many different types of wholesalers that provide a specific set of marketing functions or meet a particular marketing need. Several types of wholesalers that offer specific services are listed below. You will find that each one is very different from the others and provides marketing services in unique ways. Using resources in your library, locate information about each one and prepare a brief description (two or three sentences) of its activities.

Industrial distributor	Broker
Drop shipper	Truck wholesaler
Commission merchant	Manufacturer's agent
Rack jobber	Cash and carry wholesaler
Producer cooperative	

MARKETING PLANNING

1. FIND THE FUNCTIONS

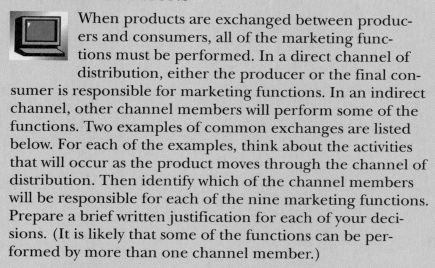

When products are exchanged between producers and consumers, all of the marketing functions must be performed. In a direct channel of distribution, either the producer or the final consumer is responsible for marketing functions. In an indirect channel, other channel members will perform some of the functions. Two examples of common exchanges are listed below. For each of the examples, think about the activities that will occur as the product moves through the channel of distribution. Then identify which of the channel members will be responsible for each of the nine marketing functions. Prepare a brief written justification for each of your decisions. (It is likely that some of the functions can be performed by more than one channel member.)

a. A consumer travels to a strawberry farm to pick and buy fresh fruit.

b. A home builder orders a truck load of plywood from a building supply wholesaler to be delivered to the job site by the supplier. The supplier fills the order from a shipment of plywood delivered last month by rail car from the plywood manufacturer.

2. FRANCHISE FACTS

The number of franchises is growing rapidly. There are franchise opportunities available in manufacturing and service development, wholesaling, and retailing. There are probably many franchises operating in your community. Identify a franchise you would like to study. Gather information about the franchise through library research, by writing to the company that sells the franchise, or by interviewing the owner of a local franchise. Gather the following information:

■ Is the franchise a manufacturing, wholesale, retail, or service business?

■ What are the primary products and services offered?

■ Who are the customers?

■ What other businesses does the franchise work with?

■ Where is the franchise located in the channel of distribution?

■ What marketing functions does the franchise perform?

■ What type of physical distribution activities are completed in the business?

Gather additional information you believe will help you understand the franchise business. Prepare a written or oral report from the information you collect.

MARKETING MANAGEMENT

1. LOCATION, LOCATION, LOCATION

The location of a retail business is very important to its success. Unless the product is extremely important to customers and they do not have choices of where to buy, they will not want to spend a long time and a great deal of effort looking for a place to purchase it. For each of the products listed, consider who the typical consumer would be and then determine whether the store that sells this product or service should be located in a.) a neighborhood shopping strip, b.) a regional shopping center, or c.) a stand-alone store. Develop a written justification for each decision.

   a. Homeowners and renters insurance

   b. Personal computers for home and business use

   c. New automobiles

2. DEVELOPING CHANNEL COOPERATION

 At the beginning of this chapter, we were introduced to a company, Edu-Games, that was trying to develop an effective channel of distribution for its unique product. The company was having difficulty because the distributors and retailers were not implementing the marketing mix the way it was planned. If a manufacturer is unable to get the necessary cooperation from other channel members, it is difficult to successfully market the products. To solve the problem, Edu-Games is considering three alternatives:

1. Selling the games directly to customers by mail.

2. Developing its own sales force to replace the distributors.

3. Finding ways to work more closely with its current distributors to implement the marketing plan that was already developed.

Prepare a written analysis of each of the three alternatives identifying advantages and disadvantages of each. Then select the alternative you believe is best and develop a rationale for your choice based on principles of marketing and distribution.

UNIT

5

Creating the Mix: Price and Promotion

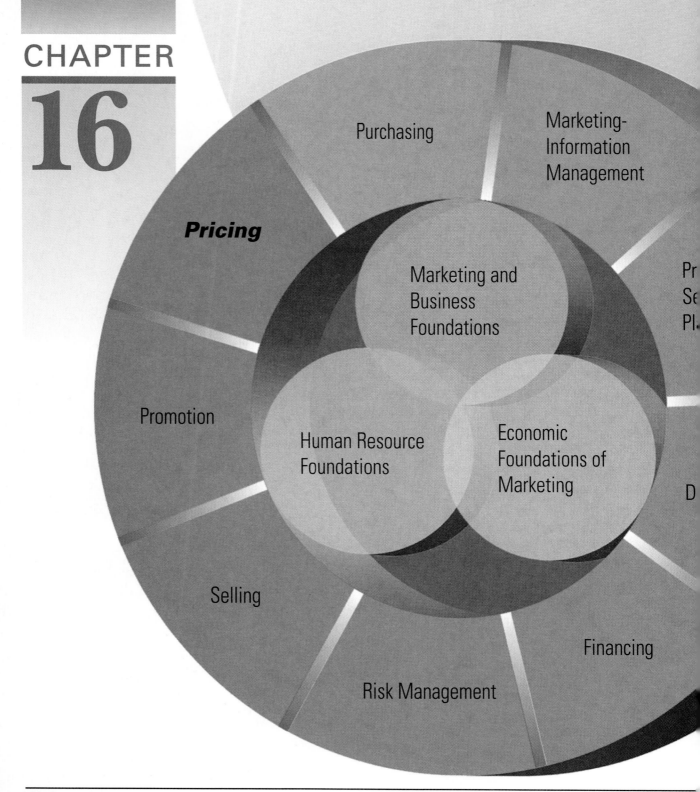

Purchasing

Marketing-Information Management

Pricing

Marketing and Business Foundations

Human Resource Foundations

Economic Foundations of Marketing

Pr
Se
Pl

D

Promotion

Selling

Risk Management

Financing

Determining the Best Prices

OBJECTIVES

1. Identify how prices influence customer satisfaction and business success.
2. Describe the relationship between economic concepts and price.
3. Compare price and non-price competition.
4. Examine the influence that governments have on pricing.
5. Discuss the elements of pricing procedures.
6. Demonstrate how a selling price is calculated.
7. Explain how credit can be used effectively in marketing.

NEWSLINE

ESTABLISHING VALUE AT HMOs

The rising cost of health care is one of the most serious problems facing the United States. The total cost of health care in the United States is nearing one trillion dollars each year.

Methods are being studied to make low-cost health services available to everyone. The use of preventive health care is having positive results. If people see health professionals regularly, problems can be identified and treated before they become serious.

Preventive health care is an important characteristic of health maintenance organizations (HMOs). HMOs offer alternative health care by providing complete medical services to subscribers. For a flat fee each subscriber has access to the medical personnel and facilities of the HMO.

A problem has developed as a result of the success of HMOs. In the past, people visited their physicians infrequently. Each visit was costly so people did not seek medical attention unless they were sick or injured. Now people go to HMOs to *prevent* problems rather than waiting for problems to occur. The re-

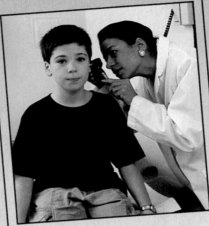

sult is subscribers come to the HMO even when there is no important need. This adds to the costs of operating the HMO. The costs that had been controlled by the HMO are now increasing again.

Studies of subscribers' attitudes identify two reasons for the increasing costs. First, since HMOs operate on the basis of a monthly charge, subscribers do not pay for specific services. Therefore, the subscribers view the services as "free." Second, HMO subscribers strongly believe in preventive health care. They visit the HMO

regularly to ensure that they remain healthy.

HMO managers needed to develop a way to increase the *value* of their services in the minds of subscribers while not changing the beliefs about the importance of prevention. A solution is the introduction of a small service fee for each HMO visit. Clients are charged a standard fee (usually $5–$15) each time they use the HMO. The fee is low enough that it does not discourage people who need to visit the HMO. However, it is high enough for subscribers to see the value of the services. They will not visit unless their problem is worth the amount they have to pay for the service fee.

Attitudes and perceptions are an important part of marketing. HMOs have shown that perceptions of people toward health care can be changed by the development of a unique service. However, it is also evident that the marketing personnel for HMOs need to be concerned about their customers' views of price and value if they are going to continue to reduce the cost of health care.

PRICE AFFECTS SATISFACTION

"That was a great value!"
"You didn't get your money's worth."
"Is that the lowest price available?"
"It can't be very good at that price."

We make many decisions about what to buy based on the prices we pay. Our satisfaction with our purchases is often based on the prices we pay. The lowest price is not always the best price for every customer. The Yugo was a very inexpensive automobile but did not offer most people the size, quality, or features they expected in a car. K-Mart was very successful in establishing an image of offering low cost merchandise, but had difficulty attracting customers that considered factors other than price when they made purchases. You can probably think of many products you buy that could be purchased at a lower price. Why do you decide to pay a higher price?

The prices charged for products and services are important to the businesses selling them as well as to consumers. The price determines how much money a business has to cover the costs of designing, producing, and marketing the product. If the price is not high enough to pay those costs and provide a profit, the business will be unable to continue to offer that product.

We know that effective marketing results in satisfaction for both the consumer and the business. A satisfactory price means that the consumer views the purchase as a value. It also means that the business makes a profit on the sale. In this chapter we will learn what price means as a part of the marketing mix and how businesses can determine an effective price.

WHAT IS PRICE?

Very simply, *price* is the money a customer must pay for a product or service. But price is much more complicated than that. Think of the various words used to identify the price of something. They include admission, membership, service charge, donation, fee, retainer, tuition, and monthly payment. You can probably identify other words used to communicate the price of a product, service, or activity. In some cases, money is not even used at all. In bartering, people must agree on the value of the items being exchanged rather than setting a monetary price.

THE IMPORTANCE OF PRICE IN MARKETING

Price is such an important part of marketing that it is one of the four elements of the marketing mix. We learned in Chapter One that **price** is the *actual cost and the methods of increasing the value of the product to the customers. As one of the nine functions of marketing, pricing is defined as establishing and communicating the value of products and services to prospective customers.* When planning any marketing activity, business people must consider the impact of the cost to the business, the price customers must pay, and the value that is added to the product or service as a result of the activity.

Price is an important tool for marketers because it can be changed much more quickly than other marketing decisions. Once a product is designed and produced, it is very difficult to change its form or features. A channel of distribution takes a great deal of time to develop. After the wholesalers and retailers are selected and the product is distributed it is not easy to change the locations where customers can purchase the product. Even promotion is not easy to adjust. Advertisements must be written and produced, time or space in media is purchased well in advance, and salespeople have to be hired and trained. It is difficult to quickly change the types of promotions for a product or service.

On the other hand, changing a price is often as simple as adding a new price sticker or marking out an old price. Even manufacturers can change the price charged by a retailer by offering a coupon or a rebate. Because prices can be changed more rapidly and easily than other marketing tools, marketers must be careful not to make mistakes with price changes.

ECONOMICS AND PRICE

Price is also an important economic concept. We know people have unlimited wants and needs that they try to satisfy with a limited set of resources. Price allocates those resources among people. If there is a small quantity of a product or service but a very large demand, the price will usually be quite high. On the other hand, if there is a very large supply of a product or if demand is low, the price will be low. Figure 16-1 illustrates how supply and demand affect price.

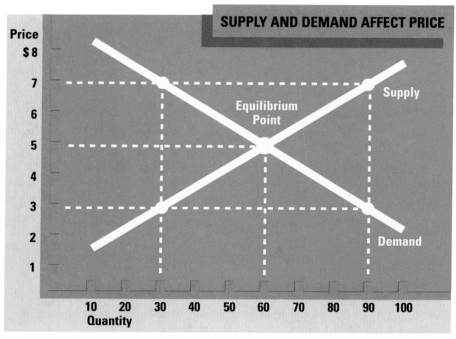

FIGURE 16-1 ▪ At a price of $3, demand (90) is greater than supply (30). At a price of $7, supply (90) is greater than demand (30). At a price of $5, supply equals demand (60) and the market is in equilibrium.

ECONOMIC UTILITY

The value customers receive from a purchase results from more than just the product or service itself. The concept of economic utility demonstrates that value is added through changes in form, time, place, or possession. Therefore, customers believe a product is a greater value (and will often pay a higher price) if the product is available at a better time or place than other choices or if it is more accessible or affordable. Figure 16-2 (on the next page) demonstrates how marketers can add to the value of a product by increasing the economic utility.

ELASTICITY OF DEMAND

It may seem that an easy way to get consumers to buy your product is to decrease the price. It seems logical that if the price

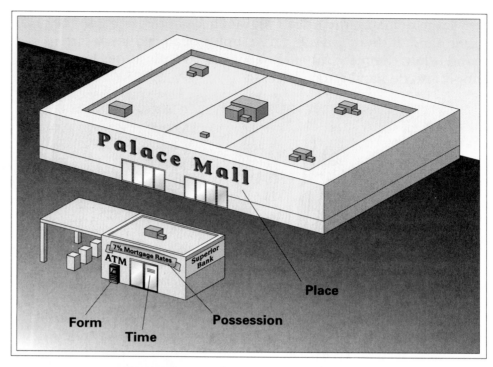

Economic Utility Adds to the Value of a Product

FIGURE 16-2 ■ A business can increase its economic utility for customers through improvements in form, time, place, and possession.

decreases, more products will be sold. Many people believe that if sales increase, profits will increase as well. However, that is not always the result. The table in Figure 16-3 shows several prices charged by a supermarket for one dozen eggs. The table also shows the quantity sold and the total revenue the store received from the sales. As you can see, the decrease in price does not result in enough additional sales to increase the total amount of money received. However, a very different result is shown in Figure 16-4. In this case, when the supermarket decreases the price of ice cream, the additional quantity sold increases total revenue.

The difference in the two examples shows the economic concept known as the elasticity of demand. *Elasticity of demand describes the relationship between changes in a product's price and the demand for that product.* The elasticity is based on the number of good substitutes for a product and the willingness of consumers to go without a product if the price

Inelastic Demand		
Price of One Dozen Eggs	Quantity Sold	Total Revenue
$.65	305	$198.25
.68	300	204.00
.71	292	207.32
.74	285	210.90
.77	277	213.29
.80	264	211.20

FIGURE 16-3 ▪ When the price is decreased for one dozen eggs, a larger quantity will be sold. However, the increase in quantity is not enough to increase the total revenue from the sales.

Elastic Demand		
Price of One Gallon of Ice Cream	Quantity Sold	Total Revenue
$3.65	180	$657.00
3.70	165	610.50
3.75	158	592.50
3.80	147	558.60
3.85	136	523.60
3.90	122	475.80

FIGURE 16-4 ▪ When the price is decreased for one gallon of ice cream, the quantity sold increases a great deal. The increase in quantity results in a higher total revenue from the sales.

gets too high. In Figure 16-3, the result occurs because consumers who purchase eggs have few substitutes for that product. When consumers need to purchase eggs, they will do so even if the price is increased. If the price decreases, they will not buy many more eggs than they would at the higher price. This is an example of inelastic demand. *In inelastic demand, a price decrease will decrease total revenue.*

Figure 16-4 illustrates elastic demand. *In elastic demand, a price decrease will increase total revenue.* This occurs when customers see several good substitutes for the product. Consumers view ice cream as one choice among several types of desserts. If

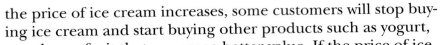

the price of ice cream increases, some customers will stop buying ice cream and start buying other products such as yogurt, cake, or fruit that are now a better value. If the price of ice cream is reduced, people who were buying other products may switch to the lower-priced ice cream that now seems more affordable.

If price changes are too great, the type of demand elasticity may change for a product. If eggs become extremely expensive, people will stop buying them. There is a limit to the amount of ice cream people will purchase and consume no matter how inexpensive it is. Therefore, marketers can use the concept of price elasticity only for price changes that consumers believe are reasonable.

COMPETITIVE ENVIRONMENT

When planning the prices of products and services, marketers need to be aware of the type of competition in the market. If customers see many good alternatives for the product being marketed, the prices of those products will remain very similar. However, if customers view a product as having few substitutes, the price of that product can be set at a different level than competing products.

There are certain types of market conditions where customers view products as very similar. Consider the difference between pure competition and monopoly. In pure competition, customers see all product choices as identical. Therefore, it is almost impossible for a business operating in pure competition to charge more for its products than other companies are charging. On the other hand, a business operating in a monopoly has the advantage that customers have no good substitutes. Therefore the company has much control over the price. That is why government often regulates monopoly markets.

In previous chapters, two marketing tools were introduced that aid businesses in the study of competition. They are life cycle analysis and consumer purchase classifications. Each of these tools is helpful in making pricing decisions.

Product Life Cycle

Throughout the stages of a product life cycle, the type of competition changes. This affects the prices that companies can charge. In the introductory stage, only one brand of a new product is available. This allows the business to control the price charged for the new product. Some companies enter the market with a skimming price. *A skimming price is a very high price designed to attract fewer customers but to emphasize the quality or uniqueness of the product.* Other companies use a penetration price in the introductory stage of the product life cycle. *A penetration price is a very low price designed to increase the quantity sold of a product by emphasizing the value.* A skimming strategy usually results in higher profits for the company and encourages other companies to enter the market. A penetration price may result in higher total revenues, but the initial level of profit is much lower. Companies use a penetration price to attract a large share of the market early and discourage other companies from entering the market.

In later stages of the life cycle, competition increases and there is an emphasis on price competition. In the maturity stage, customers see many choices that look very similar. Therefore a small price change might encourage them to switch from one brand to another.

Consumer Purchase Classifications

Consumer purchase classifications also provide an example of different levels of price competition. Staple convenience goods and price-based shopping goods illustrate intensive price competition. In each case, customers see few product differences. They often choose the lowest-priced product if they see a reasonable price difference. For products such as emergency or specialty goods, price is not as important to customers. Other factors cause them to purchase products at much higher prices than competing products.

Companies selling products with many similar competitors (common household products, basic clothing items, business supplies) have to be very careful of the prices they charge. They must pay close attention to the prices of competitors. On the other hand, companies with unique products (special jewelry or fashion designs, expensive automobiles, personal services) can be less concerned about the prices of competing products or services.

NON-PRICE COMPETITION

When businesses emphasize price as a reason for customers to buy a product or service, two problems can result. First, the emphasis on price may encourage customers to view price as the most important reason for buying. This causes them to see the other parts of the marketing mix as less important. Second, the emphasis on price means that businesses must keep prices as low as possible. With low prices, there is less profit available on each product sold. With lower profits, the company has less money to spend on marketing research, other marketing activities, or new product development.

To avoid those problems, some companies use non-price competition. *Non-price competition deemphasizes price by developing a unique offering that meets an important customer need.* Few people ask the price to be charged when they go to a physician with an illness. In the same way, price is not an important factor when purchasing a one-of-a-kind painting, applying for admission to an exclusive college, or planning a weekend getaway to celebrate a wedding anniversary.

Companies using non-price competition need to carefully study the needs of a target market. The products and services that people in the target market view as competitors must be examined. Market research can identify the things customers find dissatisfying about the competition. The company uses that information to develop a better marketing mix that is more satisfying to those customers. If the company is successful in developing a unique marketing mix that meets important customer needs, price will not be an important factor in the decision to purchase.

GOVERNMENT INFLUENCE ON PRICES

In private enterprise economies, businesses and consumers interact to determine what is bought and sold and what prices are paid. Governments play a role only when laws or regulations are needed to prevent unfair competition or to encourage activities that benefit society. When governments become involved in the economy they often have an effect on prices. The two most important ways governments influence prices are by regulating competition and taxation.

REGULATING COMPETITION

A foundation of private enterprise is that competition benefits both businesses and consumers. Whenever one business is large enough to control a market or when a few businesses cooperate to take advantage of smaller businesses or consumers, the government will regulate those businesses. Several years ago, the federal government believed that AT&T had too much control of the telephone communications industry. A court ruling required that the company divide itself into several smaller independent companies. This allowed other businesses, such as MCI and Sprint, a better chance to offer competing telephone services.

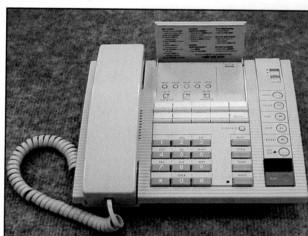

Another example of government regulation is the control of public-service monopolies, such as cable television and electrical and gas services. The government allows one company exclusive rights to serve a city because the monopoly is more efficient than if several companies each had their own electric, gas, and cable lines into every neighborhood. However, when the government grants a monopoly, it usually maintains control over the level of service provided and the prices charged by the company.

The government also wants to encourage the development of new products and services so consumers have additional choices to satisfy their needs. One way to help businesses is to protect new products from competition until they can become profitable. Patents are granted to inventors of unique products for a period of 17 years. During that time, no other business can market exactly the same thing unless permission is granted by the inventor or the patent is sold. In the same way, people who develop artistic works such as books, films, recordings, or art work can be protected by copyrights. If a company has a patent or copyright, it has greater control over the price it charges since there will be no product just like it for a period of time.

TAXATION

Taxes are another way governments affect the products and services marketed, the prices paid, and the level of competition. An increase in the tax on a product makes it less attractive to

consumers and reduces the level of sales. Taxes on products such as tobacco and liquor not only collect revenues for the government, but reduce the consumption of those products believed to be harmful. In the same way, import taxes increase the price of foreign products, making competing products produced in the country a better value for consumers. For products that are considered luxuries (furs or jewelry), a tax may not reduce the quantity of the products purchased but increases the taxes collected from people most able to pay.

Occasionally, the government wants to encourage a particular type of business or the development of certain products or services. Legislators use a reduction in taxes for that purpose. When businesses disappear from the central part of cities, city and state governments may reduce or eliminate taxes for several years if businesses will relocate in those areas. To encourage the use of alternative fuels, some states passed laws which reduced the tax on ethanol-based gasolines. When the price of ethanol-based gasoline dropped several cents per gallon lower than other gasoline, the consumption of it increased.

REGULATION OF PRICES

The federal government has specific legislation to regulate the pricing practices of business. Some of the most important areas regulated by laws include the following:

■ Price fixing: Competing companies at the same level in a channel of distribution (manufacturers, wholesalers, retailers) cannot cooperate in establishing prices.

■ Price discrimination: Businesses cannot discriminate in the prices they charge to other businesses in their channel of distribution. A manufacturer must offer equivalent prices, discounts, and quantities to all wholesalers or retailers rather than giving an unfair advantage to one or a few companies.

■ Price advertising: Businesses cannot mislead consumers through the advertising of prices. Examples of misleading advertising include using phony list prices (price at which the product is never sold), incorrect comparisons with competitors' prices, or continuous promotion of a *sale* price. Companies must clearly communicate the terms of credit offered to customers.

■ Bait-and-switch advertising: Companies cannot lure customers into a store with offers of extremely low prices and then tell the customer the low-priced product is not available or is of inferior quality.

■ Unit pricing: Many products that are sold in varying quantities or package sizes must carry a label that lists the price for a basic unit of measurement, such as a liter, ounce, or pound, to enable consumers to make price comparisons.

DEVELOPING PRICING PROCEDURES

It is not easy to determine the best prices to charge for products. Companies want prices that cover their costs and contribute a reasonable profit. Consumers are not particularly interested in what the company's costs are or whether the company makes a profit on the sale. Consumers want to get the best value and expect the product to be comparably priced to other similar products. Because it is not easy to determine the actual costs for marketing a product or what customers are willing to pay, many companies do not take enough care in setting prices. They may set their prices based on what competitors are charging. Or they may set their prices high believing they can reduce them if customers are unwilling to pay the original prices. Such practices are risky and may result in unsold products or loss of profits. Prices should be planned as carefully as the other mix elements.

SETTING PRICE OBJECTIVES

To begin price planning, marketers need to determine what objectives they want to accomplish with the product's price. Examples of possible objectives are to maximize profits, increase sales, or maintain a company image.

Maximize Profits

Companies that seek to maximize profits carefully study consumer demand and determine what customers in the target market are willing to pay for their products. The prices are set as high as possible while still satisfying customers. In this way, there is more money to cover the costs of production and marketing and return a profit. Companies that want to maximize profits usually select smaller target markets where unique products can be developed. Their products are quite different from competitors and meet important customer needs in those markets.

Increase Sales

Sales-based pricing objectives result in prices that achieve the highest possible sales volume. Companies that want a greater share of the market or have high levels of inventory may choose this objective. Prices will usually be quite low to encourage customers to buy. Companies using a sales-based objective need to set the price high enough to cover costs. Also they must have an adequate supply of the products to meet customer demand. They will usually sell their products in markets with a large number of available customers.

Maintain an Image

Companies can use the prices of products to create an image for the product or the company. Many consumers believe that price and quality are related—higher prices mean better quality while lower prices suggest poorer quality. Therefore companies that are building a quality image use higher prices than those on competing products. Companies trying to appeal to cost-conscious customers need to keep their prices as low or lower than competitors. Some companies advertise that they will "meet or beat" their competitors' prices. The intention of that strategy is to convince customers that the company will always have the lowest prices.

Have you shopped at a business where no prices were posted by the products? Have you eaten at a restaurant where the menu did not contain prices? These businesses are creating an image that price is unimportant in the purchase decision. They are using non-price competition to sell their products and services.

DETERMINING A PRICE RANGE

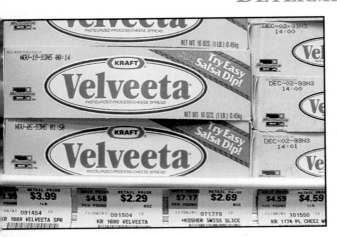

After a company determines the basic objective that will guide pricing, the next step is to determine the possible prices that can be charged for products and services. It is likely that there is more than one specific price that can be charged for a product. Study almost any product and you will see that it is sold at various prices depending on the brand, the store location, the time of year, and other factors. In order to set an effective price, the maximum and minimum prices for which the product can be sold must be determined. Those prices are the price range.

Maximum Price

The highest possible price that can be charged is determined by the target market. It is based on demand analysis. Marketing research is used to identify the customers in the target market and determine their needs. Then alternative products and services that the target market will consider in satisfying their needs are identified. Finally, the customers in the target market are asked to identify what they would be willing to pay for each of the alternatives. The highest price that results from this analysis of demand is the maximum price. Customers will not be willing to pay more than that amount as long as needs and alternatives do not change.

Minimum Price

The lowest price in the price range is determined by the costs of the seller. A company can sell a product at a loss for a short time or for a very few products. However, most prices must be set so that when all products are sold the company has covered its costs. In most cases, the minimum price must also contribute a profit to the company.

Determining the minimum price is completed by calculating all production, marketing, and administrative costs for the product. That is difficult because some costs cannot be directly related to specific products. Also, costs are often highest for new products and then go down as more products are sold.

One way companies determine the minimum price is through break-even analysis. *The break-even point (BEP) is the quantity of a product that must be sold for total revenues to match total costs at a specific price.* The break-even point is calculated using the following:

■ Fixed costs: The costs to the business that do not change no matter what quantity of the product is produced or sold

■ Variable costs: Those costs that are directly related to the quantity of the product produced or sold

■ Total costs: Fixed costs plus variable costs for a specific quantity of the product

■ Product price: Price at which the business plans to sell the product

■ Total revenue: The anticipated quantity that will be sold multiplied by the product price

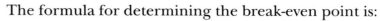

The formula for determining the break-even point is:

$$\text{Break-even point} = \frac{\text{total fixed costs}}{\text{price} - \text{variable costs per unit}}$$

Figure 16-5 illustrates a break-even analysis table for an Ascroe Garden Weeder. Let's use the information in Figure 16-5 to calculate the break-even point if the garden weeder sells for $14. The total fixed costs for the product are $85,000. The variable costs for each tool are $2.80. Ascroe wants to determine how many weeders must be sold to break even if the price is set at $14. Using the formula:

$$\text{Break-even point} = \frac{\$85,000}{\$14 - \$2.80} = \frac{\$85,000}{\$11.20} = 7,589 \text{ units}$$

Ascroe must determine if they will be able to sell this number of units. If so, they can set the price at $14.00. Additional calculations can be made at other possible prices to determine the relationships between prices, costs, and demand.

			Break-even Analysis for Ascroe Garden Weeder				
Units Sold	**Variable Costs per Unit**	**Fixed Costs**	**+ Total Variable Costs =**	**Total Costs**	**Price**	**Total Revenue**
5,522	$2.80	$85,000	$15,462	$100,462	$14	$ 77,308
6,054	2.80	85,000	16,951	101,951	14	84,756
6,998	2.80	85,000	19,594	104,594	14	97,972
7,589	2.80	85,000	21,249	106,249	14	106,246
8,225	2.80	85,000	23,030	108,030	14	115,150
9,110	2.80	85,000	25,508	110,508	14	127,540

FIGURE 16-5 ▪ The break-even point is the quantity where total costs equal total revenue. Using this chart, the company would have to sell about 7,589 units.

Price Range

Figure 16-6 shows a price range that was calculated for a pair of shoes. Using demand analysis, it was determined that customers in the target market would pay as much as $87.00 for the shoes when they are compared to all of the other choices. The company must charge at least $53.00 to cover fixed and variable

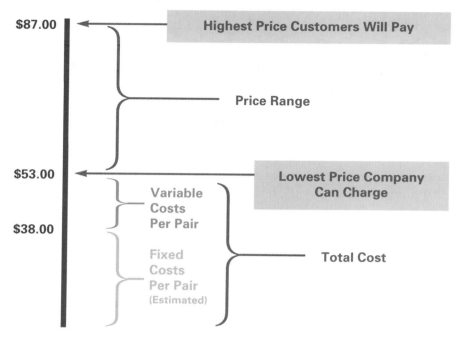

Price Range For a Pair of Tennis Shoes

$87.00 — Highest Price Customers Will Pay

Price Range

$53.00 — Lowest Price Company Can Charge

Variable Costs Per Pair

$38.00

Fixed Costs Per Pair (Estimated)

Total Cost

FIGURE 16-6 ▪ A company can price its product anywhere between its total cost (minimum price) and the amount customers are willing to pay (maximum price). All of the possible prices are known as the price range.

costs. The shoes can be sold at any price between the maximum and minimum. The company will select a price that meets its pricing objective and gives it the flexibility to increase or decrease the price as market conditions change.

If the goal is to sell the greatest quantity of shoes possible, the company will set the price near $53.00. If the goal is to establish a high-quality image and provide a higher level of customer service, the price will be closer to $87.00. A goal of being competitive with the price may result in a price that is close to the prices of other companies' brands.

PRICING POLICIES

Few people expect to pay the price that is listed on the window sticker of a new automobile. Yet, when you go bowling or play miniature golf, you pay the price set by the business. Companies develop policies to determine how the final prices paid by customers are established. Criteria companies use to determine pricing policies are described next.

Price Flexibility

Customers may not have a choice of the price they pay for a product. They either pay the price set by the business or they do not buy. *A one-price policy means that all customers pay the same price.* In other cases, such as the purchase of a new car, the price paid by customers is based on how effectively they negotiate with the salesperson. *A flexible pricing policy allows customers to negotiate the price within a price range.*

It may seem unfair to offer different prices for the same product. In some cases it is actually illegal to use flexible pricing. But consider a farmer selling fresh vegetables at a market. On days when there are a number of other farmers with the same products at the market, the farmer may need to lower the price in order to sell all of the products on hand. If the weather is bad and fewer customers come to the market, the price will likely be reduced. On the other hand, a high demand will result in higher prices.

Automobile dealers typically use flexible pricing to receive the highest price possible. However, they might reduce the price to sell a car to a specific customer. Some customers enjoy negotiating for a lower price while others do not. Recently some auto dealers have begun using a one-price policy. With this policy, a lower initial price is set and all customers are expected to pay the price listed for the automobile. The dealers believe they can reduce the costs of selling and that customers will believe they are being treated more fairly with the new policy. It will be interesting to see if the one-price policy becomes more popular in auto sales.

Price Lines

Many companies offer several choices of the same product to appeal to different customer groups. Appliance stores sell refrigerators, stoves, and dishwashers with several choices of features ranging from basic to full-featured. To make it easier to analyze the choices, the products are grouped into two or three price lines. *Price lines are distinct categories within which products are organized based on differences in price, quality, and features.* Companies must decide whether or not to offer price lines, the number of different lines to offer, and the difference in prices among those lines.

Geographic Pricing

Increasingly, companies sell products in different parts of the country and throughout the world. Costs of distribution and selling are quite different at various locations. Customer expectations of price, as well as the level of competition are often different. Companies must determine how prices will be set in each area.

IN THE SPOTLIGHT

MASTER CAR?

There was a great deal of surprise in 1992 when General Motors (GM) introduced its MasterCard. Why the surprise? The answer demonstrates how the marketing mix elements are related. In order to sell automobiles, manufacturers and dealers need to show customers that the products represent a real value. This is done with the product itself and the service provided by the dealership. But it is also done with price. In the past few years, price has become very important to customers as they compare brands of automobiles and decide whether to buy. To encourage purchases, the auto industry has been cutting prices and offering rebates. Those methods are used so much that customers now expect incentives before they will buy.

General Motors wants to establish its brand name in consumers' minds so they are more likely to buy a GM brand than another manufacturer's brand. GM management believes a credit card carrying the General Motors' name will help. People use credit cards regularly for purchases. If they use the GM MasterCard, the name GM will become a part of their buying process. When the customer receives a credit card bill each month, the name GM appears. The bill provides a regular opportunity for General Motors to include some promotional information for the customer.

A major incentive related to auto purchasing is also built into the use of the credit card. Each time the card is used, five percent of the purchase amount charged is credited toward a rebate on the purchase or lease of a GM automobile (up to $500 a year). Customers have a strong reason to purchase a GM product to take advantage of the rebate. GM believes this will keep customers focused on GM products for several years rather than just when they visit a showroom to purchase an automobile.

Source: "Can GM Sell Cars with a Credit Card?" Business Week, *September 21, 1992, p. 78.*

Some companies keep the product price the same but charge a different amount to cover transportation costs. A method for setting transportation costs based on geographic location is known as FOB pricing. *FOB (free on board) pricing identifies the location from which the buyer pays the transportation costs and takes title to the products purchased.* For example, "FOB factory" means the customer pays all transportation costs from the point where the product is manufactured. A seller can negotiate a lower price with the customer by agreeing to pay some or all of the transportation costs by identifying a selected city between the buyer's and seller's locations for the FOB designation. Another type of geographic pricing is zone pricing. *With zone pricing different product or transportation costs are set for specific areas of the seller's market.*

Discounts and Allowances

Sellers may choose to offer discounts and allowances to buyers. *Discounts and allowances are reductions in a price given to the customer in exchange for performing certain marketing activities or accepting something other than would normally be expected in the exchange.* Some common discounts and allowances include the following:

- Quantity discount: Offered to customers who buy large quantities of a product

- Seasonal discount: Offered to customers who buy during times of the year when sales are normally low

- Cash discount: Offered to customers who pay cash rather than using credit or who pay their credit accounts quickly

- Trade discount: Specific percentage reduction in price offered to businesses at various levels in a channel of distribution (wholesalers and retailers)

- Trade-in allowance: Reduction in price in exchange for the customer's old product when a new one is purchased

- Advertising allowance: Price reduction or specific amount of money given to channel members who participate in advertising the product

- Coupon: Specific price reduction offered by a channel member through a printed promotional certificate

- Rebate: Specific amount of money returned to the customer after a purchase is made

Added Values

The customer's perception of value can be changed by making additions to the purchase. This is typically done through services provided during and after the sale. Another way of adding value is to provide complementary products or a larger quantity for a reduced unit price such as, "buy two and get a third item free." Some businesses offer prizes and premiums for purchases or use incentives for regular purchasing. An example of incentives is the frequent flyer programs used by airlines. Customers are given *free* tickets after they have traveled a certain number of miles (such as 20,000) on one airline. Contests like the one sponsored by Publisher's Clearinghouse are used to encourage people to buy. In that particular contest, the company gives away money and prizes to a few people selected from the many who send in an entry form or order magazines during the year.

CALCULATING A SELLING PRICE

The price charged for a product or service is known as the selling price. The largest part of the selling price of most products is the cost of the product from the supplier. That cost should include transportation, insurance, and an amount for damaged, lost, or stolen products. *The difference between the cost of the product and the selling price is known as the gross margin.* The gross margin is the amount available to cover the business' expenses and provide a profit on the sale of the product.

The next component of the selling price is the operating expense. *Operating expenses are all costs associated with actual business operations.* The costs of buildings, equipment, utilities, salaries, taxes, and other business expenses need to be calculated and added to the product cost. Marketing costs are incorporated into the operating expenses or included as a separate amount.

The final component of the selling price is profit. *Net profit is the difference between the selling price and all costs and expenses associated with the product sold.* Profit is not guaranteed to businesses when they sell products. Often costs and expenses are higher than anticipated or the selling price has to be reduced to make the sale. In those cases, the business may not be able to make a profit or will actually lose money on the sale. Businesses try to set selling prices high enough that reasonable profits are possible even if some costs are higher than expected or the prices must be reduced. Figure 16-7 summarizes the components of the selling price.

Components of the Selling Price

FIGURE 16-7 ■ The selling price is made up of the cost of the product, operating expenses, and net profit.

To simplify the process of determining the selling prices for products, some businesses (especially retailers) use markups. *A markup is the amount added to the cost of a product to determine the selling price.* Markups are usually stated as a percentage rather than a dollar amount. Businesses determine the percentage needed to cover costs and provide a profit and use that percentage to determine the selling price.

Markups are usually determined as a percentage of the selling price but can be calculated as a percentage of the product cost. A box of 500 envelopes is sold at an office supply store for $3.50. The cost of the product to the store is $2.80. The markup as a percentage of the selling price is 20 percent ($.70 ÷ $3.50). However, the markup as a percentage of cost is 25 percent ($.70 ÷ $2.80).

A few businesses use a standard markup for most products. All products are originally marked up the same percentage, such as 45 percent, to determine the selling price. Other businesses determine the differences in operating and marketing costs or differences in the type of competition for various product categories. Then they develop a separate markup percentage for each product category.

High markups do not always mean that the business will make a larger profit on the product. Usually a high markup reduces the quantity sold or results in slower sales and higher costs to the business. On the other hand, business people must be careful in using very low markups. While the lower price may result in higher sales, the markup may not cover all expenses. In some cases, expenses increase because of the costs of handling a larger quantity of products. Marketers must carefully study the effects of different markup percentages before determining the one to be used.

Usually all products will not be sold at the original selling price. When products are not selling as rapidly as a business expects, a markdown will be used. *A markdown is a reduction from the original selling price.* Markdowns can be expressed as specific dollar amounts or as a percentage of the original selling price. Markdowns are usually viewed as *business mistakes* since the product did not sell at the planned price. The mistakes may be a result of poor product quality or from misunderstanding customer demand. They can also result from poor marketing mix decisions such as the location and promotion of the products or from changes made by competitors.

OFFERING CREDIT

A company marketing a very expensive product or service may have a difficult time selling it even if customers believe the price is fair. Few companies have the cash to pay for a $30 million building. Few individuals are able to pay the full amount for a new car whether it costs $7,000 or $70,000. Credit makes it possible for expensive purchases to be made. A company must determine if credit is necessary as a part of the price mix element.

TYPES OF CREDIT

Retail or consumer credit is credit extended by a retail business to the final consumer. The credit may be provided by the seller or may be offered by another business that is participating in the marketing process such as a bank, finance company, or a credit card company like VISA.

Most sales between businesses are made on credit. *Trade credit is offered by one business to another business.* This happens because of the time period between when a sale is negotiated and when the products are actually delivered to the business. Also, credit sales are a traditional business practice in many channels of distribution. Businesses rely on waiting 30 or 60 days or longer before making payment.

DEVELOPING CREDIT PROCEDURES

Credit provides a method for obtaining additional customers and sales than may be possible with cash sales only. However, if credit is poorly managed, costs may be very high and the money from the sale of products may never be collected from some customers. Business people responsible for credit sales must plan procedures carefully to be sure that credit is a successful part of a marketing strategy. The procedures include developing credit policies, approving credit customers, and developing effective collection procedures.

Credit Policies

The first decisions for a business are whether to offer credit and whether credit will be offered on all products and for every customer. Next the credit plan is developed. The business decides whether it will offer its own credit plan or rely on other companies to offer credit. Finally, the credit terms are developed. The terms include the amount of credit that will be extended, the rate of interest to be charged, and the length of time given to customers before payment is required.

Credit Approval

Not all customers are good credit customers. If a customer is unable to pay for purchases, the seller loses all of the money invested in producing and marketing the product as well as the cost of extending credit. Even if the product is recovered from the customer, it is not likely that it can be resold for an amount that will cover the costs.

A business that plans to offer credit must determine the characteristics and qualifications of the customers that will be able to make credit purchases. Those factors typically include customers' credit history, the resources they have that demonstrate their financial health, and the availability of the money with which they can make payments. Most businesses have a procedure through which customers apply for credit and provide financial references. These references include banks and other businesses from which they have obtained credit in the past. Credit services such as Dun & Bradstreet and TRW can be used to provide information on the credit history of businesses and consumers.

Collections

Effective collection procedures are an important part of a credit plan. The procedures are needed so that customers are billed at the appropriate time and pay their accounts when they are due. Because some customers are unable or unwilling to pay their accounts, procedures for collecting overdue accounts are an important part of a credit system. Most businesses that offer credit have a small percentage of their accounts that are never collected. Even a small percentage such as 2 to 3 percent can make a credit plan unsuccessful. This results in losses and the need to increase product or service prices to other customers.

A GLOBAL VISION

CLIP A COUPON, SAVE A BILLION

How does Mexico help U.S. consumers save almost $5 billion each year on their grocery bills? Not by providing low-cost food products. Instead, Mexico is the location of most of the companies known as *clearinghouses* which process more than eight billion manufacturers' coupons annually.

The coupon industry is a very large business and is not just a part of American shopping. While the United States still leads all other countries in the amount of coupons used, their use has become a part of the shopping experience in many countries. Yet, no matter where they are distributed, most of the coupons end up in Mexico. The clearinghouses are part of a complicated process to keep track of the coupons used and pay the retailers who accept the coupons from shoppers.

First, a manufacturer must decide to offer a coupon. The value of the coupon and any specific conditions the customer must meet are determined. Finally, the coupons are designed and incorporated into an advertisement or a mailing to customers. The design must be done carefully to avoid copying or counterfeiting of coupons.

Each year over 300 billion coupons are distributed. It is estimated that nearly three-fourths of all U.S. households regularly use coupons. Those coupons are given to retailers who send them to the manufacturers in order to receive payment for the value of the coupons. Handling coupons after they have been redeemed is as important as handling cash. If they are lost or misplaced, the retailer will not receive credit. If they are miscounted, the manufacturer may end up paying more to the retailer than the business should receive.

Most coupons are sorted by hand. That work is done in large warehouses in Mexico. The coupons are collected from stores throughout the world, accumulated by shipping companies, packed, and sent to the Mexican companies where workers sort and count the coupons and enter the totals on computers. Often the coupons are recounted for accuracy and security. Finally, the computer records are sent to the manufacturers or companies called *paying agents* where checks are issued to the retailers. All of the work must be done rapidly so retailers get their payments as quickly as possible.

Source: Los Angeles Times *News Service.*

REVIEW

The prices of products and services are very important to successful marketing. Customers must believe that prices are fair and offer a good value or they will not purchase the product. Businesses must receive enough money to be able to cover their costs and make a profit.

The needs customers are attempting to satisfy and their perceptions of choices are very important in determining a price. When customers see many similar choices, prices remain low. If there are few good choices, prices are usually higher. Laws and regulations also influence the prices of many products and services.

Businesses must be as careful in setting a product's price as they are in product development, distribution, or promotion. In planning prices, a basic pricing objective should be developed. Then research can be completed to determine a price range. Finally, specific pricing policies should be developed and a procedure for calculating the selling price developed.

Credit plans and procedures must be carefully developed. If they are well designed, credit procedures can increases sales and customer satisfaction. If not, they can result in uncollected accounts and increased costs causing losses rather than profits for the company.

MARKETING FOUNDATIONS

1. **UNDERSTANDING PRICING**

   The following definitions were presented in the chapter to describe specific pricing concepts. Identify the pricing concept that matches each of the definitions.

   a. The relationship between changes in a product's price and the demand for that product.

   b. A price decrease decreases total revenue.

   c. A price decrease increases total revenue.

d. A very high price designed to attract fewer customers but to emphasize the quality or uniqueness of the product.

e. A very low price designed to increase the quantity of a product sold by emphasizing the value.

f. Deemphasizing price by developing a unique offering that meets an important customer need.

g. The quantity of a product that must be sold for total revenues to match total costs at a specific price.

h. A policy in which all customers pay the same price.

i. A policy in which customers negotiate a price within a price range.

j. Distinct categories within which products are organized based on differences in price, quality, and features.

k. Identifying the locations from which the buyer pays the transportation costs and takes title to the products purchased.

l. Setting different product or transportation costs for specific areas of the seller's market.

m. Reductions in a price given to the customer in exchange for performing certain marketing activities or accepting something other than would normally be expected in the exchange.

n. Credit extended by a retail business to the final consumer.

o. Credit offered by one business to another business.

2. CALCULATING PRICE

 Using the information in the following chart, calculate the missing amounts.

Product Cost	Gross Margin	Operating Expenses	Selling Price	Net Profit	Markup (Selling Price)	Markup (Cost)
$120.00	$	$40.00	$	$15.00	%	%
	36.00	16.00	58.00			
.75	.30	.12				
865.00			995.00	27.50		
		12.75	38.50	5.25		
10.00				2.00		50
	25.00	25.00	80.00			
		27.00		64.00	70	

MARKETING RESEARCH

1. A VIEW OF PRICES

There are many terms used to present the price of products and services. Also, the price or value of a product or service can be represented in a variety of ways with numbers, graphics, and pictures. Look through newspapers, magazines, direct mail advertisements, and other print materials from businesses and organizations and find examples of the many ways prices are communicated to consumers. Cut out examples and create a collage of price and value on a sheet of poster board.

2. THE IMPORTANCE OF PRICE

Identify at least ten consumers who will participate in a study of the importance of price. Ask each person to respond to the following three items and record their answers:

1. Identify 5 products or services that you purchase regularly for which price is one of the most important factors in the decision.

2. Identify 5 products or services that you purchase regularly for which price is *not* one of the most important factors in your decision.

3. Compare the products from the two lists and identify up to three reasons why price is more important for the first list than for the second.

After you have collected the information, analyze the responses of the respondents and develop several conclusions about the importance of price in consumer purchase decisions.

MARKETING PLANNING

1. BREAKING EVEN

The goal of businesses when pricing products is to set a price that provides a reasonable profit after all products are sold. Calculating the break-even point identifies the minimum quantity that must be sold in order to cover the costs of the product. Using the following price and cost information for four products, determine the break-even quantity. Then construct a graph for each product that illustrates total fixed costs, total variable costs, total revenue, and total costs. Identify the break-even point on each graph.

Product	Price	Total Fixed Costs	Variable Costs Per Unit
A	$ 42.00	$ 20,000	$ 18.00
B	550.00	980,500	86.00
C	1.20	1,500	.90
D	150.50	75,250	102.00

2. UNDERSTANDING CREDIT POLICIES AND PROCEDURES

Identify one form of consumer credit to study. It can be a credit plan from a retail store, a credit card from a retailer or a manufacturer, a bank credit card such as MasterCard or VISA, installment credit, a loan plan from a bank or finance company, or other types of credit plans. Collect information by interviewing a credit manager or other person from the company who understands the credit system. Collect a copy of the credit application and other print information that explains the terms of credit. If possible, interview one or more people who use that particular form of credit. When you have finished your study, prepare a written report on the credit policies and procedures. Include the following information: who is offered credit, the application and approval procedure, the type of credit plan, the major credit terms, how billing is done, and the collection procedures for past due accounts.

MARKETING MANAGEMENT

1. OH, WHAT A DIFFERENCE

Jerry Englebrecht has operated a successful dog grooming service for ten years. Each year his number of customers has grown as satisfied customers have told others of his service. His expenses have always been quite low since he is the only employee and he operates the business from one-half of his garage that he remodeled into a small office and grooming area. For many years, the number of dog owners has increased in his town, but that growth has now almost stopped.

In the past two years, three other competing grooming services have started. One is being offered by a veterinarian, Dr. Humble, to serve primarily her customers. Another is part of a chain of pet grooming stores that is about three times as big as Jerry's business, and is located in a larger city 15 miles away. The newest competitor is a small partnership consisting of two people who are doing grooming on a part-time basis. They are only open two evenings a week and on Saturdays.

Until recently, Jerry has not been too concerned about the competition. He believed he had loyal customers and was regularly getting inquiries from new pet owners. However, recently he has noticed few new people calling to ask about grooming and some of his regular customers have not returned for their regular grooming appointments. In talking to some of his current customers, he learns that the chain store and the partnership are both offering grooming services at a much lower price than Jerry.

Jerry does not want to lower his price because that will decrease his profits. His goal has always been to use the profits to buy a building and expand his business. Also he believes his service is better than that offered by competitors.

a. How can Jerry decide whether he should lower his price?

b. If Jerry wants to emphasize non-price competition, what are some recommendations you would make to him in the areas of product, place, and promotion that could help him increase customer satisfaction?

2. PERSONAL GREETINGS

A small company has just created a new type of greeting card. It looks the same as the typical greeting card you can buy in most retail stores. However, the unique feature is a microchip in the card on which the sender can record a 30-second personalized message. Initially, the cards are being produced in two categories—Valentine cards and New Year's cards—for times when people may want to send more unique and personalized messages. If these cards are successful, the company may choose to expand into other holidays, seasons, and categories of cards.

Because of the computer technology and special envelopes needed to protect the card, the company's cost before distribution is higher than other cards—$3.40 each. It has been decided that the cards will be sold to a select set of specialty retailers throughout the world. A few wholesalers may be used for distribution if they follow a carefully developed marketing plan. The cards will also be sold to individual consumers who purchase in quantities of at least 50 cards. Those cards will be distributed by a parcel delivery service.

Your task is to develop a proposed set of pricing policies for the company. Develop a specific policy for each of the following items that is consistent with the product, its image, the type of competition that will exist, and the marketing strategies described: price objective, price range, price flexibility, price lines, geographic pricing, discounts and allowances, and added value.

Pricing

Purchasing

Promotion

Marketing and Business Foundations

Ma
Inf
Ma

Selling

Human Resource Foundations

Economic Foundations of Marketing

P
S
P

Risk Management

Distribution

Financing

Promotion Means Effective Communication

OBJECTIVES

1. Understand how promotion informs, persuades, and reminds consumers.
2. Identify the various elements in the communication process.
3. Explain the different roles played by interpersonal communication and mass communication.
4. Describe the four types of promotion and their advantages and disadvantages.
5. Discuss how marketers develop a promotional mix.
6. Outline the steps of the promotional planning process.

NEWSLINE

INFLUENCING WHAT YOU EAT

"Buy me!"
"Try me!"
"Take me home for dinner."
Do you ever get the feeling that the supermarket shelves are talking to you? Companies go to great lengths to convince you to buy their brands. Promotion is the tool they use and the payoff can be big. Some estimates suggest that as much as 80 percent of the purchases made by the average supermarket shopper are unplanned.

> **Some estimates suggest that as much as 80 percent of the purchases made by the average supermarket shopper are unplanned.**

Businesses use a variety of new promotional tools to make sure their products are the ones selected by consumers. Large screen television monitors located above the checkout aisles broadcast a news channel with plenty of ads thrown in. The goal is to get consumers away from reading *People* magazine or *The National Enquirer* and get them to watch the advertisements while waiting in line. Electronic bulletin boards above each aisle display the advertised specials and other information with moving messages that encourage you to walk down that aisle. Flashing buttons located on the shelves under featured products can be pushed to play a 10-second commercial and dispense a coupon.

One company has developed a video shopping cart. The monitor on the cart can display a map of the store, identify locations of specific products, print recipes, compare prices, and provide product information. The cart needs to be effective; it costs $100,000 per store to install the system.

Why the interest and investment in unique methods of promotion? Competition among products and brands in supermarkets is intense. Customers make many spur-of-the-moment deci-sions. The new types of point-of-purchase promotions are much more effective than an advertisement in the morning paper or a radio commercial.

> **The cart needs to be effective; it costs $100,000 per store to install the system.**

Source: "Big Brother Is Grocery Shopping with You." Business Week, March 29, 1993, p. 60.

THE ROLE OF PROMOTION IN MARKETING

It is estimated that the average person is exposed to over 3,000 promotional messages every week. These messages occur through such media as television, radio, direct mail, personal selling, coupons, and rebates. Their purpose is to tell the consumer about products and services that are available and to encourage exchanges in the marketplace. Not all of the messages are received. However, consumers remember the messages that have meaning for them.

Promotion is any form of communication used to inform, persuade, or remind consumers about an organization's goods or services. Because of its high visibility, promotion is the mix element that often comes to mind when a person thinks of marketing. It is a powerful element that can be strategically combined with product/service development, pricing, and distribution to satisfy the overall marketing objectives of the organization (see Figure 17-1).

As a vital component in the marketing mix, promotion has three different roles in marketing: to inform, to persuade, and to remind.

FIGURE 17-1 ▪ Promotion, when carefully planned to support the other mix elements, contributes to an effective marketing strategy.

INFORM

The first task of promotion is to inform potential and current customers of a new product or service or of an improvement to an existing product. The information task of promotion is often used when a product is in the introduction stage of the product life cycle. During this stage, a great deal of emphasis is placed on providing information to the customer. Usually, people will not purchase a good or service until they know its characteristics and benefits. The expectation is that the information provided through promotion will help consumers make more intelligent purchasing decisions.

Some products and services require complex and detailed promotion. For instance, the promotions for automobiles, electronic equipment, hospital services, and bundled vacation packages is more lengthy and complex than promotion for simpler items, such as books or candy.

Promotions that inform are not used just for new products and services. Current brands that are in the later stages of the product life cycle can be improved or reformulated. Promotional messages are used to inform consumers about changes to these products. Also, new uses for old products are common. For example, Johnson's and Johnson's created a promotional campaign to reach a new segment of users—adults—for its baby shampoo. Arm & Hammer baking soda created an informational campaign to get consumers to put baking soda in refrigerators and on carpets. These are examples of promotion in its role of informing consumers.

PERSUADE

Persuasion attempts to encourage a customer to take a specific action, such as purchasing a product. It is designed to stimulate action. This term has a negative meaning for some people, but it should not be seen as negative. An example of persuasion is encouragement to buy healthier bread products.

Persuasion is often an important task of promotion during the growth stage of the product life cycle. At this point, customers should have a general awareness and some knowledge of how a product can fulfill their needs. The promotional task moves from informing the customer about a product to persuading the customer to buy. The marketer emphasizes the product's advantages over the competitors' products. Persuasive promotions often use coupons, rebates, or free samples to provide additional incentives to buy.

Persuasion is used throughout the life cycle for products that are very competitive and similar to other brands. For example, marketers of soft drinks and toothpastes flood their markets with promotional activities which are designed to persuade people to switch brands. For these products, the need for new product information is not particularly strong.

REMIND

The final role of promotional activities is to remind customers about existing products on the market. Marketers remind consumers of how good their products taste, how attractive their products look, or how their companies have satisfied customers' needs and wants in the past. Promotion that reminds is frequently used during the maturity stage of the product life cycle. Kellogg's campaign to "taste them again, for the first time," is an attempt to remind adults of the good taste of their childhood cereals. Another popular promotional strategy is to package current products in old-fashioned boxes or bottles that remind people of their use of the product in the past.

PROMOTION IS A COMMUNICATION PROCESS

In order for marketers to communicate with their target market, it is important that they understand the communication process. *The communication process is the transfer of a message from a sender to a receiver.* In marketing, communication begins when someone has a thought or idea and wants to communicate it to another person to facilitate an exchange. The sender is usually someone with a promotional idea and the receivers are the customers, clients, or potential consumers of a product or service. Figure 17-2 illustrates the communication process.

SENDER

The sender is the source or originator of the message in the communication process. The sender may be an organization or a person. The sender usually has a message to share with another person or group. For example, Pepsi Cola sends messages to cola drinkers suggesting that Pepsi drinkers are members of the "Pepsi Generation." Pepsi wants to convey the message that people who drink Pepsi feel and behave as though they are young at heart.

ENCODING BY THE SENDER

The next part of the communication process is encoding. *Encoding is putting the message into language or symbols that are familiar to the intended receiver.* It is important that the sender encode the message with the proper language and with the appropriate symbols. For example, when Pepsi creates television advertisements, it often uses popular music, loud colors, and young people doing exciting things to capture the attention of the target audience.

MESSAGE CHANNEL

In order for the encoded message to be transmitted to the ultimate receiver, the sender must select and use a message channel. *A message channel is the medium the sender chooses*

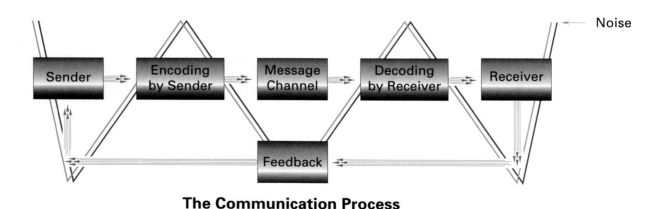

The Communication Process

FIGURE 17-2 ■ Promotion uses the communication process to send messages from the seller to the buyer.

to transmit the message. Media used in marketing include television, radio, magazines, direct mail, sales presentations, or billboards. When Pepsi decides to create a television advertisement to appeal to teenagers, it might place its advertisement on a cable television channel like MTV. This message channel has a good chance of reaching one of Pepsi's important target audiences.

RECEIVER

The receiver is the person or persons to whom the encoded message is directed. Receivers normally consist of the target audience for a product, service, or idea. Receivers can be young children, bicycle riders, college professors, high school automobile owners, or any one of a number of target groups. The receivers for Pepsi Cola's messages are selected from a broad group of people identified as cola drinkers.

DECODING BY THE RECEIVER

Decoding means interpreting the message or symbols and converting them into concepts and ideas. Even though the message is received, it will not necessarily be decoded correctly. When people receive a message they tend to manipulate, alter, and modify the message to reflect their own needs, biases, knowledge, and culture. It is a constant challenge for the sender and encoder of messages to assure that their messages are appropriately decoded.

NOISE

Though the communication process seems to be a direct path between the sender and the receiver, not all messages are clearly communicated. One of the major problems is called noise. *Noise is interference that can cause the message to be interpreted by the receiver incorrectly.* Noise occurs in all stages of the communication process. Examples of noise are competing messages, misinterpretation, radio static, poor quality printing, or the use of ambiguous or unfamiliar words. Marketers are continually working at identifying sources of noise and attempting to reduce and eliminate them.

FEEDBACK

The last concept associated with the communication process is feedback. *Feedback is the receiver's reaction or response to*

the source's message. The concept of feedback is extremely important to the implementation of the marketing concept. Feedback, or the responses to the promotional message, is how marketers measure the effectiveness of their promotional strategies.

Feedback may not take place immediately. For example, Pepsi Cola may choose to send a message through the newspaper that includes a coupon to be redeemed for 50 cents off the purchase of a six-pack of Pepsi Crystal Light. The feedback going from the receiver back to the sender does not take place until the receiver uses the coupon to purchase the product. Feedback or lack of feedback is used to modify or change promotional messages.

TYPES OF COMMUNICATION

Marketers study the communication process to determine the types of communication necessary for their products or services. The type of communication used depends on the product or service and the intended target market characteristics. There are two kinds of communications that are important to marketers: interpersonal communication and mass communication.

INTERPERSONAL COMMUNICATION

The first type of communication is interpersonal. *Interpersonal communication involves two or more people in some kind of person-to-person exchange.* This type of communication is usually two-way, with the communicators having the ability to respond to each other. An example of this type of communication is personal selling. When you walk into a department store and a salesperson assists you in selecting your purchase, interpersonal communication is occurring. The salesperson is asking questions and is receiving immediate answers from you.

Interpersonal communication is frequently used in business-to-business marketing. Many businesses have a professional sales staff to provide customers with information about available products and services. The salesperson's job is to meet the wants and needs of the customers by working one-on-one with each customer. This type of communication keeps the sales personnel in close contact with their customers and in a position to receive immediate feedback, both positive and negative, about their products or services.

MASS COMMUNICATION

Mass communication involves communicating to huge audiences, usually through mass media such as magazines, radio, television, or newspapers. Mass communication is one-way. It does not provide the audience with a method of directly communicating with the sender.

An advertisement in a newspaper is an example of mass communication. A department store might place an advertisement in the local newspaper to inform customers of an upcoming sale. In this case, the senders do not know exactly who will and who will not read the advertisement. There is little opportunity for the readers of the ad to ask direct questions about the sale or express pleasure or displeasure with it.

In an effort to overcome this lack of direct feedback, many businesses use other techniques to gauge the effectiveness of their promotions. They use coupons or directives to the consumer, such as "tell them Joe sent you," to gauge the effectiveness of their mass communications. Marketing research is also used to track consumer reactions to advertising and other mass communication techniques.

TYPES OF PROMOTION

Marketers understand the communication process and the types of communication available to them. To relay their messages to their target audiences, businesses and other organizations use several types of promotion. There are four common types of promotion available to marketers: advertising, personal selling, publicity, and sales promotion.

Each promotional technique has advantages and disadvantages. It is important that marketers understand the characteristics of each type of promotion.

ADVERTISING

Advertising is a word often used synonymously with promotion. However, that is not really accurate. *Advertising is any paid form of nonpersonal communication sent through a mass*

medium by an organization about its products or services.
Examples of these mass media are television, radio, direct mail, outdoor advertising, transit (vehicle) advertising, magazines, and newspapers (see Figure 17-3). These media carry well over $100 billion worth of advertising every year.

Forms of Mass Media Used by Advertisers

FIGURE 17-3 ■ Advertisers use mass media to send messages to consumers about organizations, products, services, and ideas.

Advertising is the most common type of promotion. It gives marketers flexibility and can be used to reach extremely large audiences. Marketers can also reach narrow target markets through a direct mail campaign or by televising an advertisement on a specialty cable channel such as ESPN.

Besides the usual forms of advertising, marketers are continually seeking new ways to capture the attention of consumers. Advertising is placed on hot air balloons, on public rest room walls, and most recently, on a rocket destined for space.

Advantages of Advertising

Advertising has many advantages. The first advantage is that it reaches millions of people at a relatively low cost per person.

For example, a 30-second McDonald's commercial shown on television at 8 pm on a Tuesday night might cost McDonald's $500,000. It is seen by approximately 36 million people. The cost to McDonald's is about $.14 per viewer.

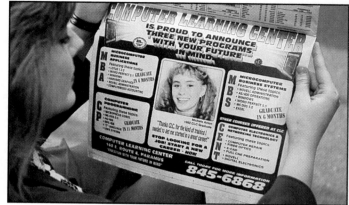

The second advantage is that advertisements can reach geographically diverse people at the same time. That means that people in Bangor, Maine, can receive the same message at approximately the same time as people in Phoenix, Arizona.

The third advantage of advertising is that the combination of color, print, sound, and motion can make us cry, laugh, nostalgic, or even angry. Advertising is a very expressive form of promotion.

Finally, advertising can repeat the message to us many times. McDonald's tells us about its quick, friendly service at 8:00 at night while we watch television, in the morning as we pass outdoor signs while driving to work, and even in magazines or newspapers that we read. The message can be repeated and reinforced as many times as McDonald's chooses.

Disadvantages of Advertising

For all the advantages of advertising, there are also many disadvantages. The first disadvantage is cost. Though the cost per viewer might be low, there is no escaping the fact that McDonald's pays millions of dollars to send its messages to us through advertising.

The second disadvantage is that the target audience might not be in the right place to receive the message. Consumers might decide to watch a video tape instead of television, turn off the radio, or switch to a different station. What if the intended audience doesn't read a specific issue of the magazine or the newspaper on the day the advertisement appears? The advertiser cannot control consumers' viewing or reading habits. They can only predict consumers' tendencies. If they are wrong, the money is wasted.

The final disadvantage is advertising's impersonal nature. It communicates to us, but we cannot respond immediately. We cannot tell McDonald's that we like or dislike the advertisements or the product or service mentioned. Feedback returns to the advertiser very slowly, in terms of increased or decreased sales or other consumer actions.

IN THE SPOTLIGHT

GETTING COLLEGE CREDIT

A credit card company does not make a sale just because someone carries its card. Most consumers choose among several cards every time they make a purchase. Each credit card company looks for ways to encourage the use of *its* card.

MasterCard targets college students with a comprehensive promotional program. Called College MasterValues, the program starts with a series of seminars held on college campuses to help students with their financial problems and questions. Many students are budgeting and handling their own money for the first time. They often want help with learning how to pay bills, applying for loans, and managing credit. In addition, the seminars offer tips on applying for scholarships and other methods of financing college expenses. The company also offers discounts to students on merchandise purchased with its credit card.

Another part of the promotional plan includes a scholarship competition for college chapters of the American Marketing Association. The chapters are asked to develop marketing plans (often focused on the college-student market) which are judged in a nationwide competition. Scholarships are awarded at the annual AMA Collegiate Conference.

The most visible promotional activity is a College Music Tour sponsored by MasterCard. The company helps pay the expenses of well-known music groups to appear on college campuses. Of course, MasterCard is very visible in the promotion of the tour.

The College MasterValues program is developed to combine education, involvement, and fun. That is an image that is appealing to college students and one that the credit card company believes will build loyalty well beyond college graduation for 13 million potential credit card users.

Source: "College MasterValues Program Targets 13 Million 'Independents'." Marketing News, *March 15, 1993, p. 5.*

PERSONAL SELLING

The second major type of promotion is personal selling. *Personal selling is person-to-person communication with potential customers in an effort to inform, persuade, or remind them to purchase an organization's products or services.* Personal selling is commonly used in industry, where vendors meet with clients to inform them of potential products or services. This type of selling, professional selling, usually requires a large amount of information about the product or service and the customer's needs. It also requires a lot of follow-up even after a sale is made to insure that the client is satisfied with the product or service and will place a reorder.

Telephone companies have salespeople whose job is to call on large businesses to sell complete telephone systems. To sell a telephone system is a complex, time-consuming process that works best on a person-to-person basis. Another type of personal selling that you might be more familiar with is retail sales. As you walk into a sporting goods store, you are approached by a salesperson to assist you with your purchase. It is this person's job to question you about your needs and suggest a product that will satisfy them. As with professional selling, this salesperson can provide immediate feedback to your questions and concerns.

Advantages of Personal Selling

The first advantage of personal selling is the personal contact. It can be much more informative and persuasive than advertising because of the person-to-person interaction. The salesperson in the sporting goods store can attempt to satisfy your needs immediately.

The second advantage is that through this person-to-person contact, feedback from the customer is immediate. That means positive responses can be acted on immediately, and hopefully a sale can be made. It also means that negative reactions can be responded to with additional questions, or alternative suggestions.

Disadvantages of Personal Selling

There are also disadvantages to personal selling. The major disadvantage is the per-person cost. Though the cost of advertising is high, advertising reaches millions of people. Personal selling, on the other hand, reaches one customer at a time, one sale at a time. The cost per customer can be extremely high. In professional sales, it might take several months of planning and sales calls involving many people before a company decides on a telephone system. Every sales encounter doesn't actually result in a sale. There are many meetings, calls, and interactions with customers that do not result in a sale.

PUBLICITY

The third type of promotion, and one that is often overlooked, is publicity. *Publicity is a nonpaid form of communication about a business or organization, or its products and services, that is transmitted through a mass medium.* Publicity is often a news story about an organization or its products or services.

Though the company receiving the publicity does not pay directly for the cost of the media used, there are still costs associated with publicity. A company often has a publicity or a public relations department with staff that work on developing the news stories and identifying opportunities for publicity. Those people will work closely with the media to try to get free coverage of the important information.

Advantages of Publicity

The major advantage of publicity is the goodwill it can create for an organization, product, or service. *Goodwill is defined as the customer's positive feelings about an organization, product, or service.* One example is the Disney Company. Disney works very hard to maintain a positive image as a good, wholesome source for family entertainment. As a result, Disney enjoys the goodwill of the public.

When the public hears or reads about the latest safety innovations developed by an auto manufacturer, that is also an example of positive publicity. All organizations are eager to receive good publicity. It keeps their names, products, services, or ideas in front of the public in a positive way.

Disadvantages of Publicity

The major disadvantage of publicity is that the organization has little control over it. Since it is generated by the media, the organization cannot cancel or change the reports. The same automobile manufacturer that enjoys publicity when the media reports new safety features does not welcome a report about the high incidence of accidents with its cars.

SALES PROMOTION

The last type of promotion available to marketers is called sales promotion. *Sales promotions are activities or materials that offer consumers a direct incentive to buy a good or service.* Examples of sales promotions are coupons, sweepstakes, contests, free samples, and rebates. The chapter on services discussed products that are given away with services, such as a toothbrush from your dentist or a refrigerator magnet with a dry cleaning service. These are examples of sales promotions.

It is important not to confuse the term *sales promotion* with *promotion.* Sales promotion is only one aspect of the larger area of promotion, which includes advertising, publicity, and personal selling.

Advantages of Sales Promotion

There are more advantages than disadvantages to the use of sales promotion. The first advantage is it generates immediate, short-term sales. The offer of a free product, or a cents-off coupon is often enough incentive to the customer to purchase a product. Fast food restaurants such as Hardee's and McDonald's, have continued success with their toy promotions.

The second advantage of sales promotion is its use to support other parts of the promotional campaign. For example, a television advertisement introduces a new fat-free ice cream. Later that week, the consumer receives a coupon in the mail for the new ice cream. On Saturday, when the potential customer is doing the weekly shopping, a representative of the ice cream company is offering free samples at the supermarket. The potential customer tastes it, puts a gallon in the shopping cart, and uses the coupon at the register. A product is sold with the help of sales promotion.

Disadvantages of Sales Promotion

The main disadvantage of sales promotion is the cost. It is estimated that over $90 billion is spent every year on sales promotion activities. If the promotion does not result in a significant sales increase, the business will lose money on the product or service.

THE PROMOTIONAL MIX

Marketers combine promotional tools to develop a promotional mix (see Figure 17-4). *The promotional mix is a blend of the promotional elements of advertising, personal selling, pub-*

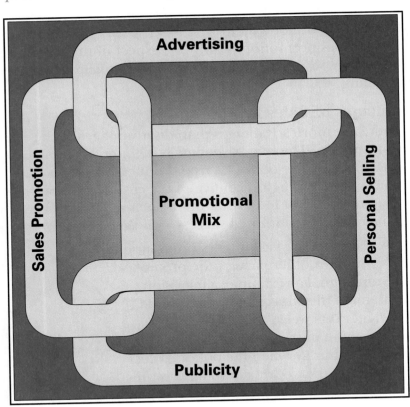

Elements of a Promotional Mix

FIGURE 17-4 ■ Advertising, personal selling, publicity, and sales promotion work together to create a promotional mix.

licity, and sales promotion into a strategy for delivering a message to the target market.

It would be very unusual for an organization to rely only on one type of promotion. For example, it is not likely that an airline would rely only on advertising, a university only on personal selling, a lawn mower manufacturer only on publicity, or a restaurant only on sales promotion. However, it does happen. In a highly unusual one-medium campaign, Motel 6 reached millions of consumers. With one announcer, radio spots that promised to "leave the light on" were very successful.

In most cases, businesses rely on a mix of all four elements to bring their products or services to the attention of the target market. How firms blend these activities and which elements they use depends on several factors (see Figure 17-5).

MARKETING MIX

First, the promotional mix depends on the characteristics of the marketing mix that was developed for the product or ser-

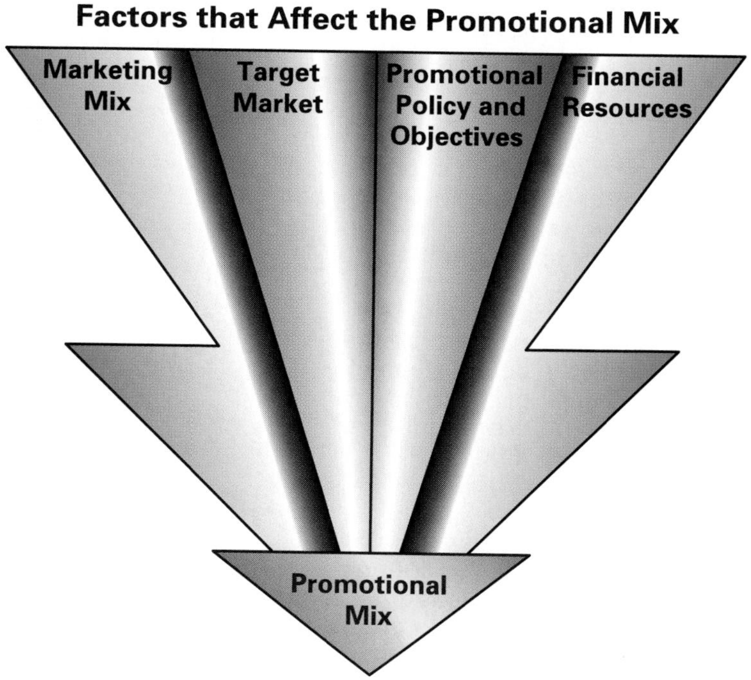

Factors that Affect the Promotional Mix

FIGURE 17-5 ■ Developing a promotional mix is a major responsibility of marketers. Many factors affect the choices they make about the blend of advertising, sales promotion, personal selling, and publicity.

vice. As we learned earlier, the stage of the product life cycle might dictate the best promotional strategy. The price of a product also determines the type of promotional mix. A very expensive product might need more personal selling and less television advertising. Also, if the product is seasonal, it changes the characteristics of the promotional mix. Consumers do not hear very much about snow blowers until winter. Then there is often a media blitz to inform consumers about them and to encourage them to buy. Advertising may be accompanied by a coupon or rebate. There will usually be a salesperson in the store to help the customer. The company will try to get publicity to support the other types of promotion.

TARGET MARKET

The second factor in determining an appropriate promotional mix is the target market. It is critical to remember the

CHALLENGES
COUNTERFEIT COUPONS

One of the sales promotion activities that many marketers use is coupons. Coupons are designed to encourage people to buy goods and services by giving them a discount. Some of the most widely used coupons are those found in the Sunday newspaper for cereal, health and beauty aids, and other convenience items. A typical coupon might offer 35 cents off the purchase of deodorant or 25 cents off the price of toothpaste.

One of the challenges associated with providing coupons as a sales promotion tool is counterfeiting. Coupon counterfeiters make color photocopies of coupons and take the counterfeits to businesses in an effort to redeem them for cash or merchandise. In fact, counterfeit coupons are now so prevalent that many marketing businesses are training their employees to detect them. Coupon fraud is costing marketers approximately one billion dollars per year.

One technique used to stop coupon fraud involves using special ink that makes the word *void* invisible until the coupon is photocopied. There are also check-out scanning devices that catch fake coupons for cashiers. Some marketers have made the time span to redeem their coupons so short that counterfeiters won't have time to make counterfeits.

Source: Adapted from Business Week, *June 15, 1992.*

characteristics of the target market so that the promotional campaign can be focused on them and their needs. It would be inappropriate to advertise a furniture sale on MTV, because the viewers of MTV are not the primary target market for furniture. The marketer needs to develop a specific promotional mix that reaches each target market.

COMPANY PROMOTION POLICY AND OBJECTIVES

The third factor in determining a promotional mix is the company's policy and objectives for promotional activities. Some companies have specific promotional guidelines. The Hershey Company did not advertise its product at all until after 1950. Hershey's position was that the unique product and its quality reduced the need to promote the product. More recently, Ryan's Family Steakhouse, a chain of restaurants that is growing in popularity, advertises only on billboards. Ryan's company philosophy is that a good product and word-of-mouth from satisfied customers reduce the need for promotion.

COMPANY RESOURCES

A fourth factor to consider is the company's financial situation. Promotion can be expensive. It is the marketer's job to determine which elements should be used for the greatest impact and which have the best chance of meeting the company objectives. National companies with products or services appealing to a wide range of people may have enough money to engage in national advertising campaigns. Small local firms might find many forms of advertising to be too costly. However, that small firm might profit from the use of a few well-trained direct salespeople.

PROMOTIONAL PLANNING

As you think about the concept of a promotional mix, it is important to remember that each type of promotion serves a different function and should be used to complement the other methods of promotion. Advertisements, for example, appeal to large audiences and create awareness. Without them the personal sales effort would be much more difficult, time consuming, and expensive. Publicity, on the other hand, provides information to a wide audience but is more difficult to control. Personal selling offers credible, face-to-face contact and is quite flexible. It carries with it the ability to close a sale. Without personal selling, the initial interest generated by advertising might be wasted. Sales promotion supplements the other three promotional mix methods by stimulating short-term sales efforts.

PROMOTIONAL PLAN

The development of the promotional mix is not something that occurs easily or automatically. It must be planned in a logical way. *The promotional plan is a carefully arranged sequence of promotions designed around a common theme responsive to specific objectives.*

THE STEPS IN PROMOTIONAL PLANNING

Marketers should use a carefully developed planning process to prepare a promotional plan. The promotional planning process will assure the marketer that planning is thorough and focused. The promotional planning process involves analyzing the market, identifying the target market, developing promotional objectives, developing the promotional budget, selecting the promotional mix, implementing the promotional plan, and evaluating results (see Figure 17-6).

Analyze the Market
The most common method of analyzing the market is to conduct market research. As explained in Chapter 9, either primary or secondary research methods can be used.

Identify the Target Market
Information obtained from the market analysis enables the marketer to determine the target market or markets. The segmentation characteristics of the market are identified so the marketer can begin to identify promotional strategies to reach each group of consumers.

Develop Promotional Objectives
Promotional objectives identify the purpose or expected result of promotion. The objectives should be written and based on the market research that was completed. They should be

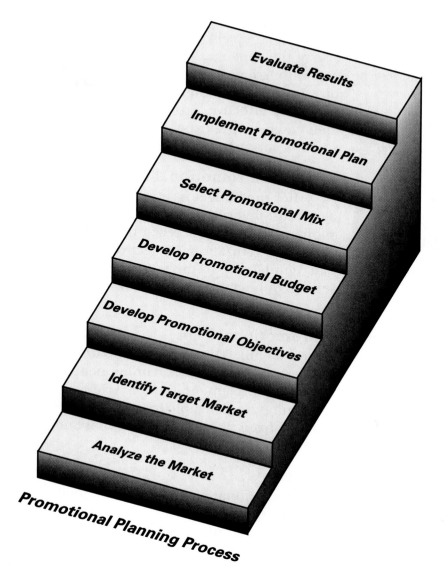

Evaluate Results

Implement Promotional Plan

Select Promotional Mix

Develop Promotional Budget

Develop Promotional Objectives

Identify Target Market

Analyze the Market

Promotional Planning Process

FIGURE 17-6 ▪ Effective promotion requires a successful promotion plan. By using the promotional planning process, marketers follow a step-by-step model to arrive at a promotional plan that is focused, consumer-driven, and based on achievable goals.

achievable and measurable and fit into the overall marketing plan. They should be flexible and reviewed periodically to determine if they still meet the organizational objectives.

Develop a Promotional Budget

After the objectives are determined, the next step is to plan the promotional budget. In order to be effective, it is important to determine the budget after the objectives are set. If the budget is determined first, the objectives might be scaled down or eliminated because of the expense. Promotional financing should not be done with "whatever money is left over." It requires careful planning and managerial commitment to be effective. Promotional budgets are often based on the expenditures for the previous year or a certain percentage of expected sales.

Select the Promotional Mix

After the budget is set, the marketing manager must determine the most appropriate promotional strategies to reach the target market, achieve organizational objectives, and remain within the budgetary guidelines. In this stage the mix of advertising, personal selling, publicity, and sales promotion will be decided.

Implement the Promotional Plan

After the promotional mix is determined, the implementation schedule must be set. This includes naming people or departments responsible for implementation of various parts of the plan and determining the timetable for each promotional strategy. Specific dollars from the total promotional budget will be allocated to each activity.

Evaluate the Results

The final step in promotional planning is to evaluate the plan against the objectives that were set. Marketing managers must carefully evaluate their strategies to determine if they should be continued, altered, or changed completely. Each promotional activity will be measured against the promotional plan. Research will be used to gather information about consumer perceptions and actions before and after the promotion has occurred.

REVIEW

Promotion is a very visible element of the marketing mix. Many people think only of promotion when they think of marketing. Promotion, however, is only one element. It must be blended with the decisions made about product, price, and distribution if it is to be used effectively.

Promotion is designed to inform, persuade, and remind consumers. Types of promotion include advertising, publicity, personal selling, and sales promotion. These are all forms of either interpersonal or mass communication. It is critical that marketers understand the communication process and the roles of the sender, the message, and the receiver.

Skillful marketers combine the various types of promotion into a promotional mix. The ingredients of the mix are dependent on the objectives of the marketer. The promotional mix is determined through a carefully developed planning process.

MARKETING FOUNDATIONS

1. CLASSIFYING THE PROMOTIONAL METHOD

There are four types of promotional activities within marketing: advertising, personal selling, publicity, and sales promotion. On a piece of paper, draw four columns with one type of promotional activity named at the top of each column. Read the following activities and decide what type of promotional activity is involved. Then write each of the activities under the appropriate column.

1. A press conference announcing a new automobile safety feature.

2. A coupon for 50 cents off the purchase of toothpaste.

3. A shoe salesperson suggesting the purchase of shoelaces to a customer.

4. Skywriting over a football stadium.

5. A full-page ad in a newspaper devoted to the sale of seafood products.

6. A hospital inviting people to visit its new pediatric wing.

7. An end-of-aisle display offering a free cooler with the purchase of a case of bottled water.

8. A telemarketing call encouraging you to buy a magazine subscription.

9. A lobbyist encouraging a legislator to vote for a particular bill.

10. The offer of a chance to win a free trip to purchasers of a new automobile.

11. A school sending its drama troupe to entertain in a retirement home.

12. A billboard depicting a new golf course.

2. **MATCHING**

Match each of the following sales promotion terms with the statement that best describes it.

a. Advertising	g. Message Channel
b. Decoding	h. Noise
c. Encoding	i. Publicity
d. Feedback	j. Receiver
e. Interpersonal Communication	k. Sales Promotion
f. Mass Communication	l. Sender

1. The person or persons to whom the message is directed.

2. The process of interpreting the message or symbols by converting it into concepts or ideas.

3. Interference that causes messages to be interpreted incorrectly.

4. Any paid form of nonpersonal communication by an identified sponsor.

5. The receiver's reaction or response to the source's message.

6. The originator of the message.

7. Putting a promotional message in language or symbols that is familiar to the target audience.

8. The vehicle that the sender uses to transmit the message.

9. Usually involves two people in a person-to-person transaction.

10. Communication to huge audiences.

11. Nonpaid form of nonpersonal communication transmitted through a mass medium.

12. Activity or material that offers purchasers a direct inducement to buy.

MARKETING RESEARCH

1. THE IMPACT OF ADVERTISING

 Four magazines that direct their messages at a similar target audience are *Vogue, Harper's Bazaar, Elle,* and *Mirabella.* The following chart shows the number of ad pages sold between January and June for each of these publications in 1991–1993.

The Impact of Advertising			
Magazine	1991 Ad Pages	1992 Ad Pages	1993 Ad Pages
Vogue	885.13	906.26	832.43
Harper's Bazaar	376.90	301.14	499.19
Elle	553.58	490.06	367.96
Mirabella	323.12	264.83	268.27

a. Calculate the total number of pages sold every year.

b. Calculate the percentage share each magazine has for each time period.

c. Create a bar graph comparing 1991, 1992, and 1993 and the four publications, based on total pages sold.

2. INVESTIGATING A CAMPAIGN

Marketers use a variety of media when creating a campaign for a product. Pick one product that you are familiar with and track its campaign for one week. Write down all television and radio commercials that relate to the product. Check the newspapers for coupons, print advertisements, or publicity pieces about your product. After one week, determine the target market and the theme of the campaign. Be prepared to report your findings to the class.

MARKETING PLANNING

1. A REAL ESTATE PROMOTION

Every community has residential real estate marketing activity occurring in it. Real estate marketers all use some form of promotion. Those forms of promotion cover the whole range of promotional methods. For this activity, you are a residential real estate marketer. You must decide what percentage of your promotional effort should be expended on each of the methods for your community. You have 100 percent of your money and effort available for promotion. It is your task to divide that 100 percent among advertising, publicity, personal selling, and sales promotion efforts. Tell how you would divide your budget and effort and give reasons for your decisions.

2. ORGANIZATIONS AND PROMOTION

Promotional techniques are not just for businesses that are selling products and services and hoping to make a profit. Many organizations, such as the

American Lung Association, the Red Cross, and political parties, use promotional techniques to communicate their messages and ideas.

Choose a not-for-profit organization with which you are familiar. Demonstrate how you believe they use each of the promotional techniques by preparing a written or oral report.

MARKETING MANAGEMENT

1. THE OBJECTIVES OF PROMOTION

Marketing managers and planners understand that a good management plan that includes promotional activities requires well-written objectives. Objectives help focus the campaign and allow the results to be measured and analyzed.

The following list contains several products and services. It is your task in this activity to develop two promotional objectives that are appropriate for these products or services. Make certain the objectives are achievable through promotion. You may want to focus on a specific role of promotion: to inform, persuade, or remind.

a. General Motors four-wheel drive vehicles

b. Gourmet jelly beans

c. Wooden step ladders

d. Guided tours of South American Mayan ruins

e. Artificial tanning lotion

2. PRESCRIBING PROMOTIONAL APPLICATIONS

A marketing or promotional manager can demonstrate talent, skill, and intuition by developing promotional strategies to achieve promotional objectives. For each one of the objectives you developed in the previous activity, suggest one promotional strategy that you think would be most effective in helping to achieve the objective. Explain why you think it would be most effective.

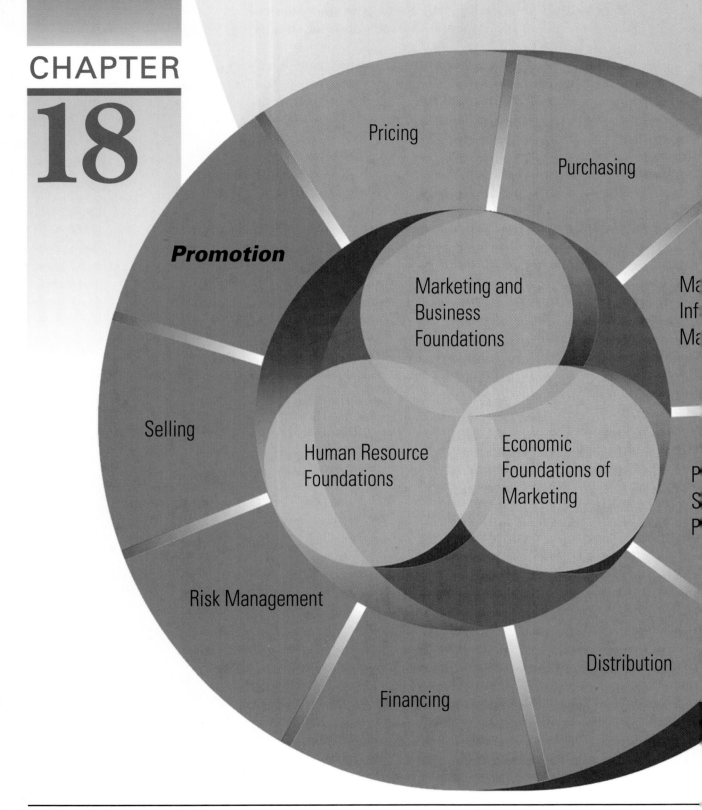

Pricing

Purchasing

Promotion

Marketing and
Business
Foundations

Ma
Inf
Ma

Selling

Human Resource
Foundations

Economic
Foundations of
Marketing

P
S
P

Risk Management

Distribution

Financing

Be Creative with Advertising

OBJECTIVES

1. Describe the role of advertising within the marketing mix.
2. Differentiate between organizational advertising and product advertising.
3. Identify the steps in developing an effective advertising plan.
4. Explain the responsibilities of advertising agencies.
5. Discuss self-regulation and the impact of government regulation on the advertising industry.
6. Investigate alternative approaches to advertising.

NEWSLINE

WHERE'S THE CONSUMER?

The New York Department of Consumer Affairs analyzed over 2,000 advertisements in 10 magazines to determine minority representation. The results of the analysis show that more minority group members are being included in magazine advertisements. That's the good news. The percentage of minority group models used in advertisements rose from 3.4 percent in one year to 5.2 percent the following year.

The New York Department of Consumer Affairs analyzed over 2,000 advertisements in 10 magazines to determine minority representation.

The bad news is that advertisers presented minority models in stereotypical roles. They were often shown as musicians, athletes, or objects of pity in corporate philanthropy advertisements. Minority models were seldom portrayed as consumers. One car

The percentage of minority group models used in advertisements rose from 3.4 percent in one year to 5.2 percent the following year.

company showed minority group members in 24 of its 134 ads. However, only one of those ads showed a minority group member as a car buyer. That buyer was a professional basketball player.

The bad news is that advertisers presented minority models in stereotypical roles.

A separate study of 14 of the most frequent advertisers in the magazines showed that half included no minority group members in their advertisements at all. Finally, two of the magazines that have over 25 percent minority readership had less than 6 percent

A separate study of 14 of the most frequent advertisers in the magazines showed that half included no minority group members in their advertisements at all.

of their advertisements containing minority group members.

Source: Adapted from USA Today, January 28, 1993.

WHAT IS ADVERTISING?

Ask someone how wave theory applies to acoustical engineering and you will probably get a blank stare. Ask someone how the writings of Montaigne apply to modern-day problems and you will probably get another blank stare. But ask someone what makes effective advertising and it's a good bet that you will get a lengthy response. People may tell you what they believe and do not believe in the ads they have seen. They will often have an opinion about the amount of advertising they are exposed to and the quality of the ads. Even though advertising is very technical and complex, most people believe they know a great deal about it.

Advertising is any form of nonpersonal promotional communication by an identified sponsor. The distinguishing characteristics of advertising are that the organization pays for the message that it sends to an audience through a mass medium. The name of the sponsor of the advertising is clearly stated and that sponsor controls the message that is sent.

Advertising is very big business. The expenditures for advertising in the United States are almost $150 billion per year. For the last 30 years the leading advertising medium has been newspapers. However, television advertising dollars have almost doubled during this same time. Direct mail is growing in importance, while outdoor advertising is declining. Radio remains relatively constant as an advertising medium.

Billions of dollars are spent on advertising every year, with some industries advertising more than others. For example, businesses that sell games and toys spend a large percentage of their sales dollars on advertising. Businesses that sell beverages also spend a lot of money on advertising. Pepsi Cola, Coca-Cola, and the many coffee producers, for example, all have extensive advertising plans and budgets.

Businesses are not the only organizations that use advertising. Churches, educational institutions, political organizations, and government agencies advertise.

THE ADVANTAGES OF ADVERTISING

There are many advantages to advertising as a method of promotion. Advertising can be used to communicate to a large audience in various geographic locations. A single television ad might reach 30 million viewers or more. Several large city news-

papers reach over one million readers every day. In the case of magazine ads, the audience reached is increased when the magazine is read by more than one reader. For example, one copy of *Time* in a dentist's office may be read by several dozen people. Each of those people is exposed to advertisements contained in the magazine.

A second advantage is that the cost *per viewer* for advertising is relatively low. A television ad that costs $300,000 to produce and broadcast may reach as many as 30 million viewers. That results in a cost per 1,000 viewers of only $10.

A third advantage is that the advertiser can target the ad to a specific audience. The organization can customize the words, medium, graphics, timing, size, or length of the advertisement based on the target market. For example, if an advertiser wants to reach Spanish-speaking women in Tucson, Arizona, the ad can be placed on a Spanish radio station, a Spanish-language television channel, or in a Spanish-language newspaper.

DISADVANTAGES OF ADVERTISING

Advertising also has some drawbacks. First, the communication is one-way; advertiser to consumer. If a customer asks a salesperson a question, there is an opportunity for a discussion. A customer seeing an advertisement on television is unable to ask questions about the product or service being advertised.

A second drawback is that advertisers have no control over who might be watching, reading, or listening to their advertisements. Though they work very hard to make sure the ad is directed at the appropriate target market, whether consumers see or hear the ad is another question. Television commercials are often a good time to get something to eat, have a conversation, or start the laundry. Another barrier to reaching the target audience is the use of VCRs to delete commercials from prerecorded shows. This is bad news for advertisers who have spent millions of dollars trying to attract the viewers' attention.

A third disadvantage is the total cost of placing advertisements. Although the cost per viewer is quite low for a $200,000 ad on national television, the advertiser must have the $200,000. This sometimes eliminates the small or local business person from many types of mass media advertising.

TYPES OF ADVERTISING

We learned in Chapter 17 that the three purposes of advertising are to inform, persuade, and remind customers. The message can communicate information about products and services or about the businesses that sell the products and services. These objectives are accomplished by using two types of advertising: organizational advertising or product advertising.

ORGANIZATIONAL ADVERTISING

The first type of advertising is called organizational advertising. *Organizational advertising is designed to promote ideas, images, and issues associated with a company or organization.* The most prominent characteristic of organizational advertising is that specific products, services, or prices are not featured in the advertisement. Instead, the benefits of the business or organization to customers or society are the main themes of the advertisement.

For years, the DuPont Chemical Company used the slogan, "Better things for better living through chemistry." This advertising slogan was used to promote and strengthen the image of DuPont. BASF promotes its business with advertisements that say, "We don't make the product, we make the product better." During the half-time of televised college football games, the colleges represented show a promotional message about their schools. This video, a form of organizational advertising, is designed to promote the image of the particular university.

PRODUCT ADVERTISING

The second type of advertising is product advertising. *Product advertising is used by organizations to sell specific products.* A product advertisement can be identified by the identification of a specific product, service, or price in the advertisement. The U.S. Postal Service sells stamps. Soft drink companies sell colas. The Schwinn bicycle company sells bicycles. The Sierra Club invites you to go on one of its tours. In each case, the organization is promoting a product or service in its advertisements and not just its organizational image.

DEVELOPING AN ADVERTISING PLAN

When a company decides to include advertising as part of its promotional mix, the first step is to develop an advertising plan. *An advertising plan describes the activities and resources needed to prepare and present a series of related advertisements focusing on a common objective.* It is usually part of a larger overall promotional plan that includes several promotional mix elements.

The advertising plan centers around a specific product, service, or group of products and services. Since advertising involves huge sums of money, plans are carefully developed. As depicted in Figure 18-1, developing an advertising plan requires

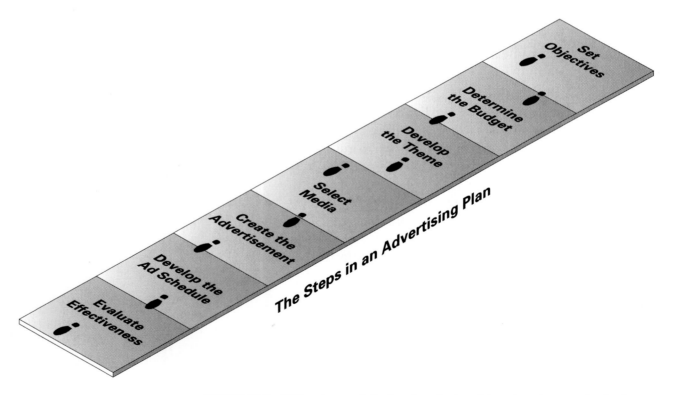

FIGURE 18-1 ■ Without a carefully developed advertising plan, the organization's advertising dollars can be wasted.

setting objectives, determining the budget, developing the theme, selecting media, creating the advertisements, developing an advertising schedule, and evaluating the plan's effectiveness.

SETTING OBJECTIVES

The first step in the development of an advertising plan is to determine the advertising objectives. *Objectives are the desired results to be accomplished within a certain time period.* The advertising objectives should support the marketing mix. The advertising objectives state what specific message the plan should communicate, to what target audience, and in what specific period of time. Objectives should be very specific and they should be measurable.

Objectives for a specific advertising plan will vary from organization to organization and from product to service. For example, an advertising plan for a municipal library might have as its objective to attract 1,000 new library card holders between the ages of five and ten during the next month. An advertising plan for the Mazda Miata might have as its objective the sale of 3,000 new Miatas to Spanish-speaking residents of Texas and Arizona in the months of June, July, and August.

It has been said that without objectives you will never know when you have arrived at where you are going. This cliché is certainly true in advertising. Figure 18-2 presents objectives for the advertising plan of Seaside Resorts.

Setting Objectives	
Elements of Objectives	**Plan for Seaside Resorts**
Desire or needed results	Increase reserved summer rentals by 10 percent by February 15
Advertising message to be communicated	Make reservations early to assure availability and save $100 off the weekly rate
Target market	Families who spend one week or more at the beach every year

FIGURE 18-2 ▪ Objectives are the results to be attained by the advertising plan.

DETERMINING THE ADVERTISING BUDGET

Once the advertising objectives are defined, the budget should be developed. It is usually good to identify a total advertising budget early in the planning process. Then a more detailed budget is prepared as planning is completed. There are four common methods of determining the amount of money that will be allocated for advertising (see Figure 18-3).

What You Can Afford

One method of determining the ad budget is called the *what you can afford* approach. In this system, organizations account for all of their other expenses and whatever is left over is budgeted for advertising. This method does not properly support the advertising objectives.

Percentage of Sales

A second method used to determine an advertising budget is called the *percentage of sales* approach. The percentage of sales approach budgets a percentage of past, current, or projected future sales for advertising. For example, a firm that sold $50 million of tractors last year and allocated five percent of sales to advertising would budget $2.5 million for advertising.

One drawback of this method is that advertising varies directly with sales. If sales are low, advertising expenditures will be limited. However, when sales are low, advertising expenditures might need to be increased, not decreased in order to help improve sales volume.

Firms need to be very cautious about using *past* sales to determine the *current* or *future* budget. What has happened in the past will not necessarily be repeated in the future. For example, an independent video store might be facing a more difficult year because a large chain has just

Four Methods of Budgeting for Advertising

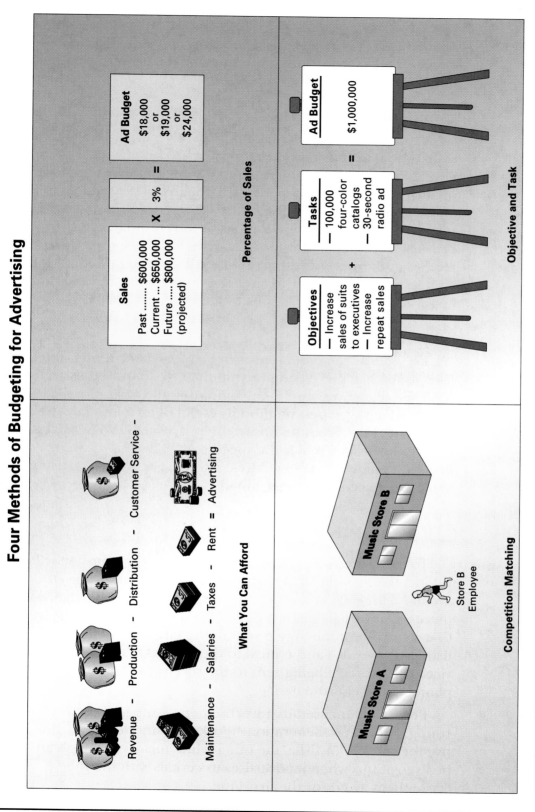

Percentage of Sales

Sales
Past $600,000
Current ... $650,000
Future $800,000
(projected)

× 3% =

Ad Budget
$18,000
or
$19,000
or
$24,000

Objectives
— Increase sales of suits to executives
— Increase repeat sales

+

Tasks
— 100,000 four-color catalogs
— 30-second radio ad

=

Ad Budget
$1,000,000

Objective and Task

What You Can Afford

Revenue – Production – Distribution – Customer Service –
Maintenance – Salaries – Taxes – Rent = Advertising

Competition Matching

Music Store A   Music Store B

Store B Employee

FIGURE 18-3 ▪ Without a budget, it is hard to develop a theme, select the media, or create the advertisement.

opened nearby. The advertising budget should be determined based on the current and future situation, taking into consideration any new competitive challenges.

Competition Matching

A third method of determining an advertising budget is called the *competition matching* approach. This approach suggests that an organization should spend a similar amount of money on advertising as its competitors. Though it is reasonable to be aware of what your competitors are doing in terms of advertising, this method of budgeting has serious drawbacks. One drawback is that competitors may have different advertising objectives and different resources. Also, it is difficult to determine competitor's budgets until after the fact. Therefore, using this approach can result in serious mistakes.

Objective and Task

The *objective and task* approach involves determining the objectives to be achieved, identifying the tasks required to accomplish the objectives, and then computing the costs of each task. This is usually the best method to use in determining an advertising budget, if accurate information is available. The advertising manager determines the specific objectives and strategies needed to meet those objectives. Then the cost of advertising to meet the objectives is determined.

DEVELOPING THE THEME

To provide a focus for its advertising, an organization will develop a theme next. *A theme is one idea, appeal, or benefit around which all advertising messages in a plan revolve.* All pieces of advertising in the plan should feature the theme so that a consistent message is sent to the target audience. Advertising is expensive and critical to the success of a product or service. The message being sent to the receiver must be carefully planned and coordinated.

Pepsi Cola focused its advertisements on people who think young: "the Pepsi Generation." Pork is positioned as an alternative for chicken or fish: "the other white meat." Kellogg's appeals to adults when it advertises its cereals with the theme "taste them again for the first time."

SELECTING MEDIA

After the necessary decisions surrounding objectives, budget, and theme are made, the media plan is developed. The media plan consists of two important components: the type of media and the actual media in which advertising will be placed.

Media types are the various categories of media that carry advertising. The major media are television, radio, newspapers, magazines, outdoor signs, and direct mail. Figure 18-4 summarizes the advantages and disadvantages of using these major

CHALLENGES
MEASURING ADS WITHOUT A RULER

John Wanamaker, founder of the Wanamaker Department Stores, once said, "half of all the money I spend on advertising is wasted. The problem is, I don't know which half." In an era of belt tightening among marketers, no one can afford to waste any of the advertising budget. Unfortunately, sometimes marketers do not put much effort into evaluating advertising. An account executive for a telephone directory suggests that an overwhelming percentage of business owners have no idea if the money they are spending on advertising is improving their sales. They sometimes spend thousands of dollars not knowing if their money is well spent.

This doesn't have to be the case. Richard A. Gagne, owner of Dental Horizons in Oxnard, California, was unable to tell which of the many media in which he advertised was bringing in the most clients. Then he began listing different phone numbers in advertisements that ran simultaneously. Now he is able to track which ads are drawing phone calls by comparing response rates to ads in various publications. He then allocates his advertising budget accordingly.

Coupons provide another method for measuring customer response to advertising. In many areas business owners participate in Val-Pak direct mail coupon packages. These coupon packages are sent to thousands of households in a community. Val-Pak lets a business choose the area or district it wants to cover. They help design and print the coupons as part of their service. Their subscribers know exactly how much business the coupons generate by keeping track of coupon redemption.

One simple way to determine which advertising is effective and which is not is to ask customers how they heard about the business. Regardless of the method used, it is important to determine whether advertising money is wasted as Mr. Wanamaker suggests. How would you try to determine the effectiveness of an advertisement?

Advantages and Disadvantages of Advertising Media		
Media	**Advantages**	**Disadvantages**
Television	Reaches large audiences Low cost per viewer Combination of sight, sound, and motion Highly segmented markets	High total cost Long lead time Strong potential for interference
Radio	Highly mobile Relatively low cost Short lead time High segmentation	Message limited to audio Often do not have listener's full attention
Outdoor signs	Low cost Can repeat message High visibility Short lead time	Increasingly regulated Message is short Seldom have viewer's complete attention
Direct mail	Highly segmented Easy to measure effectiveness Stimulates action Hidden from competition	Often considered junk mail Expensive
Magazines	Long life span Excellent print quality Can carry response vehicles High pass-along rate Highly segmented	High cost Long lead time
Newspapers	Short lead time Large circulation Can carry response vehicles (coupons)	Lower print quality Short life Limited segmentation Competes with many other advertisements

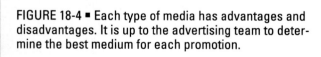

FIGURE 18-4 ▪ Each type of media has advantages and disadvantages. It is up to the advertising team to determine the best medium for each promotion.

types of media for advertising. After identifying the types of media to be used, businesses make *specific* choices within each category. The exact newspapers, radio programs, television stations, or outdoor sign locations that will reach the target audience best within the available budget are selected.

Each type of media has characteristics that should be analyzed before a choice is made (see Figure 18-5). The advertising manager should consider the costs, reach, frequency, and lead time of each category to determine the best choice.

<table>
<tr><td colspan="1">Questions to Consider When Selecting Media</td></tr>
</table>

Cost
- What is the total cost of the medium?
- What is the cost per viewer?
- Does the cost fit into the advertising budget?
- Is it the most effective use of advertising dollars?

Reach
- What is the circulation?
- What is the viewership?
- Will it reach the target audience?
- Is there a strong pass-along rate?

Frequency
- How often will the target audience receive the advertising message?
- How many times will the ad run?

Lead Time
- How quickly can the audience be reached?
- How flexible is this medium?
- How close to print or air time can the ad be changed?

FIGURE 18-5 ▪ Media vary in terms of cost, reach, frequency, and lead time. All of these factors should be considered before deciding on a medium.

Cost

The costs of advertising media depend on the media chosen, the length of time the message runs, and the complexity or length of the message. Costs are measured in two ways. First, the total cost of the advertisement is calculated. Second, the per-reader or per-viewer cost is computed.

The total cost of an ad in a national magazine might be $50,000. The per-reader cost of magazines is expressed on a cost per thousand (CPM) reader basis. The CPM for an ad that costs $50,000 and reaches 500,000 people is $100 ($50,000 ÷ 500 = $100).

Reach

The advertiser needs to know the total number of people who have seen the advertisement. Reach refers to the number of readers or viewers in a medium's audience. The number of

copies of a magazine or newspaper that are sold or distributed is the circulation. In broadcast and outdoor media, advertisers need to know the coverage area or regions where the message can be received as well as the size of the potential audience. Advertisers want the largest reach possible within their target markets for their advertising dollars.

Pass-along rate is also of interest to advertisers. The pass-along rate is the number of times a copy is read by another person. Magazines have the greatest potential for pass-along rate. It is said that a copy of *Newsweek* is read by about six people. Therefore, its reach is much higher then its actual circulation.

Frequency

Frequency is another characteristic of media that an advertiser must analyze. Frequency refers to the number of times a member of the target audience is exposed to the advertising message. Radio, television, and newspapers can be used quite frequently. In fact, advertisers can run the same message daily or even hourly in these media.

Lead Time

Finally, lead time is an important consideration when selecting media. Lead time is the amount of time required to place an advertisement. Lead time for placing an advertisement varies tremendously among media types. The lead time for a newspaper ad might only be a day or two. The lead time for a national magazine can be several months. The lead time for radio and television can be less than one month, but production time may make it much longer. In general, the longer the lead time, the more difficult it is to use advertising to respond to unexpected situations.

CREATING THE ADVERTISEMENTS

After the media decisions are made the creative work begins. This is where the advertisement is actually created. The advertisement must reach the target audience, be consistent with company objectives, reflect the chosen theme, and fit within the budget.

Advertisers can choose from a number of different formats when creating ads. The format chosen should take into account all of the decisions made so far in the planning process: the objectives, theme, and media.

Slice-of-life

This format shows people using the product or service in an everyday setting. The people look and act like typical consumers. An example is children eating cereal at the breakfast table.

Fantasy

This format creates a fantasy about using the product or service. Calvin Klein is well noted for creating fantasy ads involving its products.

Musical

This format revolves around the use of people or characters singing a song or jingle about the product. The Diet Pepsi ad in which Ray Charles sings, "You got the right one baby, uh-huh" is an example of a musical theme.

Technical Expertise

This format involves the manufacturer or producer explaining how its product is made. Often car companies explain the technical components of their manufacturing process to show the consumers the quality of their products.

Testimonial

This format uses either celebrities or everyday people endorsing a product. Sports figures are often used in testimonials. Everyday people might also be used because they appear to be believable. Excedrin uses ordinary people to talk about the benefits of its products.

Lifestyle

This format shows a product or service in relation to a specific lifestyle. Automobile manufacturers often use this theme when advertising sports models, vans, or pickups.

Mood or Image

This format portrays a specific emotion. Hallmark and AT&T are good examples of mood or emotion creators.

Character

This format uses a fictitious character, often in a cartoon format, to represent the product or service. Cap'n Crunch, the Jolly Green Giant, and the Keebler Elves are all examples of characters that companies have created to establish a memorable image.

Scientific Evidence

This format uses rational reasoning and scientific information to tell the consumer why products are superior. Advertisers use scientific evidence and statistics to prove their claims. Often these advertisements begin with "Clinical evidence shows...."

DEVELOPING THE ADVERTISING SCHEDULE

The work of the advertising manager is not finished after the ad is created. The next step in the advertising plan is to schedule the timing of the advertisements. Timing refers to the schedule on which advertisements will appear in each medium.

There are two common ways to schedule advertisements. One is called continuity. *Continuity means that the ad will be scheduled regularly throughout the year.* This is the common timing technique for products that do not have seasonal swings. For these products, steady, continuous advertising is often the best schedule to use.

A second scheduling technique is called pulsing. *Pulsing means that advertisers increase their advertising efforts during a specific period of time and decrease or even withdraw their advertising during another period of time.* Pulsing is very common for seasonal goods. For example, toy manufacturers increase their advertising prior to Christmas. Companies who sell heating and air conditioning units pulse their sales to coincide with the beginning of winter and summer.

Pulsing allows advertisers to be more focused with their advertising messages. Advertisers direct their messages at their target audience when the audience is in a mood to buy. Pulsing

CLASSICS AND CONTEMPORARIES

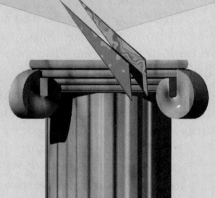

TALKING BACK TO ADS

Interactive television is slowly making its way into American homes. With the backing of telecommunication giants, such as Tele-Communications Co., Gannett Co., A.C. Nielson, and NBC, the new Interactive Network is already operating. Interactive Network allows viewers in three markets to respond instantly to game shows, sports events, dramas, and news shows. Now, when Vanna White turns a letter on the Wheel of Fortune, viewers at home actually play along and compete with other at-home players for prizes.

The wireless, laptop device that controls the interaction is available for about $200. To be a member of the network costs about $15 per month. NBC plans to identify programs provided by the Interactive Network with a small IN logo on the screen.

Marketers have been doing their research to find out just how many consumers are interested in interacting with their television sets. In a recent survey, 56 percent of the 500 adults surveyed said they would be interested in interactive TV. The service is especially appealing to people aged 18–30, who have outgrown their Nintendos and are looking for more sophisticated toys.

Advertisers are also interested in interactive television. A group of advertisers are cooperating in a variety of interactive media tests via Interactive Network. The group will look at how

consumers interact with the medium, when and how to tell the viewer that the ad is interactive, and how to provide incentives for viewer participation.

A Chrysler spokesperson said "It's a way to break through the clutter of the usual ad format. We hope to have people take a few test drives using interactive television."

One thing is certain: a whole new advertising format is not far off. And just when you thought television was getting boring.

Source: Adapted from "Interactive TV Finally Plugged In," Marketing News, January 3, 1994, pp. 10–12.

can save advertisers money if they limit their advertising expenditures to specific times.

EVALUATING THE PLAN'S EFFECTIVENESS

The final step in advertising planning is to measure effectiveness. *Evaluation is measuring how well the advertising plan achieves its original objectives.* Advertising activity is difficult to evaluate. However, this step should not be avoided just because it is difficult. The type of evaluation procedures depends on the objectives. When advertising objectives are described in terms of changing attitudes, or increasing awareness, for example, then the evaluation should attempt to measure whether these changes have occurred.

If the advertising has a built-in evaluator, like a redeemable coupon, a rebate offer, or a two-for-one offer, then the advertisement's effectiveness can be determined from the usage rate for these promotional items. Many advertisements, however, do not have built-in measures. They need to be evaluated using other techniques.

Advertisements should be evaluated throughout the development and use of the ad. Pretesting occurs before an advertisement is run. Advertisers might evaluate advertising using pretesting to determine the best choice among several preliminary designs. Posttesting occurs after an advertisement is run. Advertisers are interested in finding out the strengths and weaknesses of advertisements in various media.

There are several different methods used to posttest ads. Focus groups are structured discussions with groups of potential customers lead by a facilitator. Advertisers use focus groups to obtain information about advertisements that have just been run. Some of the things that advertisers can learn from focus groups are whether the advertisement appeals to the target audience, whether the message is clear, and ways to make the ads more effective.

Recall testing can be conducted on a sample of consumers from the target market. They are asked to recall certain parts of an advertisement. Often recall tests are done at different time intervals to determine how long recall lasts.

Recognition testing is another evaluation method. Individuals are shown the actual ad and asked if they recognize it. If they can recognize the ad they are asked additional questions about it.

However advertising is measured, it is important to evaluate all parts of an advertising plan. Evaluation shows advertisers what they did well and what they did not do well. It provides information that can aid in future decision making.

USING ADVERTISING AGENCIES

Advertising plans are often the responsibility of advertising agencies hired by the business. These agencies can handle all or part of the advertising function. Almost all advertising agencies coordinate their work with the company's marketers when preparing an advertising plan.

Each advertising agency has account executives. These are individuals who work directly with the business' marketing department. Advertising agencies typically provide creative services and purchase space or time for the company's advertising in the various media. Advertising agencies also do research to help determine the effectiveness of the advertising plan. Agencies are often compensated by a percentage of the cost of media purchases. However, agencies may also bill the client for the cost of their time and other expenses.

REGULATING ADVERTISING

Advertisers must be honest and ethical in their professional activities. Almost all advertisers follow regulations established by federal, state, and local government agencies, as well as their own professional code of ethics. The rules are designed to protect consumers and competitors from unfair and inappropriate promotional practices.

The Federal Trade Commission and the Federal Communications Commission use several approaches to guard against inappropriate advertising practices. These approaches include the requirements of full disclosure, substantiation, cease and desist orders, corrective advertising, and fines.

FULL DISCLOSURE

The requirement of full disclosure demands that all information necessary for a customer to make a safe and informed

decision be provided in a promotional message. For example, if a product is promoted as being a diet product, the label must tell the number of calories and the amount of fat contained in the product.

SUBSTANTIATION

Substantiation requires that an organization be required to prove all of the claims it makes in its promotional messages. If an audio tape is promoted as suitable for recording music, then the advertiser must be able to prove that it has tested the tape for that purpose.

CEASE AND DESIST ORDERS

Cease and desist orders require firms to discontinue a promotional activity that is considered deceptive. The organization may not be forced to admit guilt or pay fines, as long as it obeys the cease and desist order.

CORRECTIVE ADVERTISING

Corrective advertising demands that an organization run a new advertisement to correct any false impressions left by previous ones. For example, Listerine was told to spend $10.2 million in advertising to correct prior messages claiming that the product was a cold remedy. Listerine ran ads with the following phrase: "Listerine will not help prevent colds or sore throats or lessen their severity."

FINES

The final remedy to inappropriate promotion is fines. Fines are monetary penalties imposed on an organization for deceptive promotion. A company may be required to pay a large sum of money to the government if it is found guilty of engaging in deceptive promotions.

SELF-REGULATION

In addition to government restrictions, media have developed voluntary standards for advertising practices. For example, the National Association of Broadcasters monitors the ads placed on television and radio for truth in advertising. Other groups, such as the Better Business Bureau and the American Association of Advertising Agencies, also participate in the self-regulation of advertising.

ALTERNATIVE ADVERTISING

The study of advertising is not complete without considering alternative advertising. While most advertisers use the traditional types of media, they are often concerned about the amount of advertising each consumer is exposed to every day. This leads consumers to ignore many advertisements. Advertisers are seeking new and innovative approaches to reach their target markets and attract attention and interest with advertising.

One such innovation is the infomercial. An infomercial is usually a half-hour television program that looks like a talk show. In reality, it is a 30-minute commercial.

Another alternative advertising technique is the use of television monitors in supermarket check-out lines and in airports that show commercials while you wait. Posting advertisements on the walls and doors in public restrooms is also a popular way to creatively attract consumer attention.

ℝEVIEW

Advertising is a very important and visible element of marketing. Expenditures for advertising approach $150 billion each year. Advertising is used to promote organizations and products. It is also used to create awareness and stimulate sales by informing, persuading, and reminding consumers of products and services that are available to meet their needs.

The steps in developing an advertising plan are to set objectives, determine the budget, identify the theme, select media, create the ads, determine the timing for advertising, and develop appropriate evaluation procedures. The advertising function often is handled by an outside advertising agency that works with marketing personnel in the business.

Advertisements must be truthful and ethical. Advertisers are regulated by many government agencies, as well as their own professional organizations.

MARKETING FOUNDATIONS

1. ORGANIZATIONAL AND PRODUCT ADVERTISING

Select five advertisements from a newspaper or magazine that are examples of organizational advertising and five advertisements that are examples of product advertising. Cut and mount each advertisement on a sheet of paper. Write a sentence telling why it is organizational or product advertising and why the company will benefit from this type of advertising.

2. UNDERSTANDING THE ADVERTISING PLAN

Each of the following statements represents a different step in the advertising plan. Match each statement with the correct step.

STEPS IN ADVERTISING PLAN

Set objectives   Create the advertisement

Determine the budget   Schedule the plan

Develop the theme   Evaluate the plan

Select the media

STATEMENTS

1. Inviting potential customers to view the advertisement and discuss the ad's effectiveness.

2. The manufacturer of a flea and tick spray wants to increase its market share by 10 percent.

3. The media specialist of a large department store determines that the potential customers of a back-to-school sale should be reached by a direct mail advertisement.

4. A manufacturer of a cough syrup advertises only during the flu-and-cold season.

5. A national soft drink company uses a sports star to promote its products.

6. A producer of cake mixes centers its advertising efforts around the concept, "Our cakes are just like mom's."

7. The managers of a local grocery store increase spending by 5 percent because of the holiday season.

MARKETING RESEARCH

1. THE COSTS OF ADVERTISING

Annual advertising costs in the United States are approaching $150 billion. Clearly, marketers spend a great deal of money on advertising. Your task in this activity is to become acquainted with advertising costs in a local market. Select an advertising medium used by marketers in your community, such as a radio station, a newspaper, a shopper's guide, an outdoor advertising agency, or a television station.

Contact the organization or use reference materials to obtain information regarding its advertising rates. Be prepared to report to your class regarding the cost of advertising per minute, per inch, per week, per day, or whatever measurement is used.

2. CUSTOMER FEEDBACK

One of the major concerns of organizations that advertise is the effective use of their advertising dollars. A recent survey of 259 successful companies asked what type of evaluation techniques they use. The responses are summarized in the following table. (Respondents could select more than one type of approach.)

Type of Approach	Number of Respondents
Coupon redemption	179
Toll-free customer line	114
Focus groups	114
Customer survey	44
Rebate redemption	41
Recognition tests	26

a. Calculate the percentage of each of the response types and create a bar graph to illustrate the results.

b. Based on these results, how have the companies decided to allocate evaluation dollars? Do you think this is the best approach for all companies? Explain your answer.

MARKETING PLANNING

1. A COMPETITIVE PROBLEM

You are the owner of a taxi company in a city of 100,000 people. Until recently you were the only cab company in town. You have been able to reduce your promotional efforts because of the lack of competition.

Recently, a new cab company with five taxis has acquired a license to operate in your city. Describe your marketing response in terms of price, product, distribution, and promotion. Emphasize the type of advertising planning you would do.

2. SMOOTHING OUT THE BUMPS

Many businesses experience seasonal fluctuations in sales. Listed below are three products or services that often experience high and low sale periods. Suggest two advertising strategies for each product/service that could help reduce these sales fluctuations.

a. Lawn maintenance

b. Pet grooming

c. Toy manufacturer

MARKETING MANAGEMENT

1. QUESTIONING THE PLAN

You are the chief executive officer of a company that manufactures golf equipment. Your marketing research determines that there is a large market for an oversized driver golf club. Your company invests heavily in designing and manufacturing this new driver.

The advertising agency you have hired is developing an advertising plan for the new golf club. As CEO, develop one good question you will ask the account executive for each step of the advertising plan. An example for the "set objectives" step might be "What audience are you targeting with the advertisements?"

2. THE LEGALITIES OF ADVERTISING

 Research one of the laws or agencies that deal with illegal advertising and prepare a 200-word report. Be prepared to present your findings to the class.

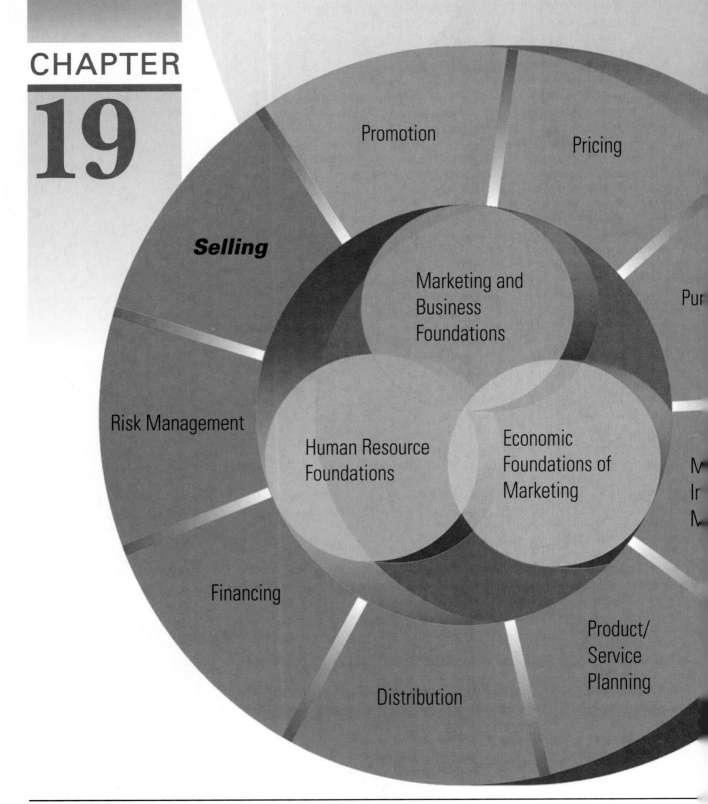

Promotion

Pricing

Selling

Marketing and Business Foundations

Pur

Risk Management

Human Resource Foundations

Economic Foundations of Marketing

M
Ir
M

Financing

Product/ Service Planning

Distribution

Selling Satisfies the Customer

OBJECTIVES

1. Describe the value of personal selling as a part of the marketing mix.

2. Identify why salespeople need to understand their customers, products, and competitors.

3. Demonstrate the steps in the selling process.

4. Provide examples of activities that support personal selling.

5. Explain how salespeople effectively manage their work.

NEWSLINE

SELLING WITH TECHNOLOGY

Several hundred thousand dollars are at stake as the salesperson for a truck manufacturer sits in an office with clients from a trucking company. The customer will place an order for three trucks but only if the manufacturer meets some very specific requirements.

Copies of the order are faxed immediately to the sales manager, the accounting department, and the factory.

The salesperson uses her laptop computer. She selects a design menu on the screen and an outline of a truck appears. As she asks questions of the purchasing team,

she adds features to the truck design that meet the company's requirements. The price of the truck is displayed on the screen. Each time a feature is added, the price is adjusted. The customer sees the cost of each change. The salesperson compares several alternate designs for the customer.

When the design is completed, the salesperson uses the modem on the computer to contact the factory for production schedules. Information is sent to the production scheduler who determines that the trucks will take six weeks to build if the order is placed this week.

The customer makes an offer that is five percent below the list price for the trucks. The salesperson uses the modem and electronic mail to check the offer with her manager. The manager agrees on the price if three trucks are ordered. The salesperson confirms the order with the customer and prints out a personalized contract. Copies of the order are faxed immediately to the sales manager, the accounting department, and the factory.

In her hotel that evening, the salesperson prepares for the next

day's customers. From her hotel room she plugs into the company's database. She requests the records for two companies she plans to visit the next day. She receives reports on their purchases, records of previous sales calls, past two years of sales, profits, and market share. Before going to sleep, she checks on the progress of two orders that she placed last month.

Laptop computers, modems, fax machines, and other technology reduce the time needed for each of those activities and makes information instantly available to salespeople.

Salespeople rely on information and communications. Laptop computers, modems, fax machines, and other technology reduce the time needed for each of those activities and makes information instantly available to salespeople.

Source: "Taking a Laptop on a Call," Business Week, October 25, 1993.

THE VALUE OF SELLING

Salespeople provide the link between the customer and the business. To many customers, the salesperson *is* the business. Customers sometimes have no personal contact with the business other than through the salesperson. It is the responsibility of the salesperson to sell the products of the business. As one business person said, "Nothing happens in business until someone sells something."

The ultimate goal of any business is to sell its products and services profitably. The resources of a business are wasted and the efforts of the employees are of no value if the products remain unsold. Those resources and efforts often rest on the shoulders of one group of people—the salespeople. The selling process involves people who work for or represent the company. These people communicate directly with customers in order to persuade them to purchase the company's products and services.

Successful sales occur when customers are able to purchase the products and services they need. The business is then able to make a profit on the money invested in developing and marketing those products and services. As shown in Figure 19-1, for businesses that understand the marketing concept, all marketing efforts are directed toward the sale of products and the customer's satisfaction.

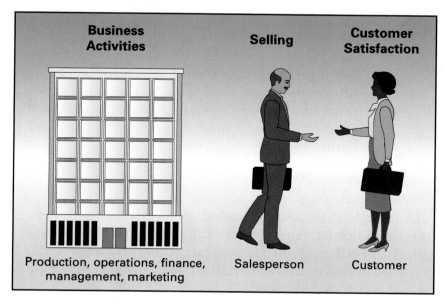

Business Activities

Selling

Customer Satisfaction

Production, operations, finance, management, marketing

Salesperson

Customer

The Important Role of Selling

FIGURE 19-1 ▪ Selling directs the efforts of a company toward customer satisfaction.

UNDERSTANDING PERSONAL SELLING

Selling is a part of the promotion element of the marketing mix. Promotion includes the methods and information communicated to customers to encourage purchases and increase their satisfaction. As we learned in Chapter 19, there are a variety of promotional methods that businesses use. Each has a specific purpose. The definition of selling describes its purpose and value. *Selling is direct, personal communications with prospective customers in order to assess needs and satisfy those needs with appropriate products and services.*

Direct and Personal Communications

All promotional methods involve communication with customers. Most are directed at large groups of customers. The methods must be quite general to appeal to the common needs of the audience. Personal selling, however, is used to communicate with one or a very few customers. Salespeople work directly with customers. They tailor the information to meet the individual needs of each person.

Direct communication (usually face-to-face) means that the salesperson can meet and talk with the customer. Based on the discussions, the salesperson provides additional, specific information if needed. If a customer has concerns or asks questions, the salesperson is able to respond. By listening to the tone of voice or observing body language, the salesperson may determine that the customer is still uncertain about a decision. Based on that feedback, the salesperson personalizes the communication to address the customer's doubts.

Assess and Satisfy Needs

Effective marketing responds to customer needs in order to provide the most satisfaction possible. Determining customer needs is often done through marketing research. Customers with similar needs are grouped into target markets. Even with those common needs, however, individual customers may have additional, more specific needs. Some people may be ready to make a purchase while others need additional information. Concern about payment methods may prevent some customers from committing to buy a product. Other customers may want to understand the warranty that is offered by the company. A salesperson can discuss the purchase decision with each customer to determine specific needs and concerns. The salesperson offers each customer the best possible solution the company can provide to meet those needs.

USING PERSONAL SELLING

There are advantages and disadvantages to personal selling. Those advantages and disadvantages are summarized in Figure 19-2. Business people need to understand when personal selling is needed and when it may not be the most effective promotional tool.

When to Use Personal Selling	
Advantages of Personal Selling	Disadvantages of Personal Selling
More Information	Cost Per Customer
Flexible	Time Required
Uses Feedback	Less Control
Persuasive	Skilled Personnel
Follow-up	

FIGURE 19-2 ▪ Personal selling is not appropriate for all exchanges. Organizations need to consider the advantages and disadvantages of personal selling when deciding whether to use it.

Advantages

When a business provides information through an advertisement, there is a limited amount of information that can be included. An outdoor billboard or electronic display is usually restricted to under ten words because viewers pass by very quickly. Television and radio commercials last no more than one minute with most fitting into even shorter time slots. While newspaper and magazine advertisements can be longer, few people will spend more than a minute or two reading a print advertisement.

Salespeople spend considerably more *time* with customers. Even in the very shortest sales presentation to a customer, the conversation may last for several minutes. Effective salespeople often meet with customers several times. Each meeting may last from ten minutes to one hour. With that amount of time, a great deal of information can be provided.

Personal selling is *very flexible*. The sales presentation is typically scheduled at a time and place that is convenient for the customer. During the meeting, if it is clear that a customer understands certain information or if that information is not important to the customer, the salesperson moves on to another topic.

Because personal selling is two-way communication, the customer provides *feedback*. An effective salesperson asks questions, listens to customers' concerns, and determines if additional information is needed. That feedback is used to make the information even more specific to the individual needs of the customer. In addition to obtaining feedback from the customer, the salesperson provides feedback to the company. If the customer is dissatisfied with any part of the marketing mix or if competing products appear to meet customer needs better, the salesperson can inform the company.

Selling is typically used near the end of the consumer decision-making process. At that time the customer is deciding whether or not to make the purchase. The customer may be comparing one or two very similar products before making a final decision. A salesperson is able to be *persuasive* at that time. By knowing the important needs of the customer, those needs can be matched with the qualities of the company's product and compared to those of competitors. The salesperson needs to be sure the product will satisfy the customer. If it does, the salesperson is in a position to help the customer make the decision to purchase.

A sale is not completed at the time the customer makes a purchase. The customer must use the product and decide if it meets the needs for which it was intended. If the customer is dissatisfied with the product, it will probably be returned. The customer may not want to buy other products from the company. An important responsibility of a salesperson is to follow up with the customer after the sale. The *follow up* provides an opportunity to insure that the customer is able to use the product correctly, has everything needed, and is satisfied.

Disadvantages

While there are many advantages of personal selling, there are also some disadvantages. One of the most important disadvantages is *cost*. We often hear of the high cost of advertising. A magazine ad can cost tens of thousands of dollars and a nationwide television advertisement on a popular show can cost hundreds of thousands. It doesn't seem possible that personal sales could be more expensive. However, businesses are concerned about the cost per customer as well as the total cost.

IN THE SPOTLIGHT

SMART. VERY SMART.

What is the future of retailing? Do customers have to trade service for low prices and a large product assortment? While many retailers seem to be answering *yes,* there are some exceptions. One exception is Home Depot, a rapidly growing chain of building and supply stores. Home Depot employs knowledgeable salespeople who can assist both homeowners beginning their first remodeling project and experienced carpenters.

The initial emphasis is on training. Home Depot starts each new employee with five days of training. Even though many of its salespeople have previously worked as carpenters and electricians, they go through training that includes company information, product information, and how to greet a customer. Salespeople are encouraged to ask "What project are you working on?" rather than "What product are you looking for?"

The salesperson is then assigned to a manager. For three weeks, the new employee learns all parts of the operation of a department and works on selling skills. Employees are expected to learn the locations of all of the 30,000 items carried by the store. If a customer asks for a product that is not in that person's department, the salesperson takes the customer to the location and finds another salesperson to help.

Training is not the only part of Home Depot's strategy. There are regular information sessions led by the CEO and President that are televised to all stores. Salespeople are never paid commissions. The emphasis is on selling what the customer needs, not what makes the salesperson the most money. However, after one year employees can participate in a program where they own shares of stock. The better the company, the greater the value of the employee's stock.

Home Depot seems to have discovered the new approach to retailing—size, sales, and service. Its success is built on customer-oriented selling done by well-trained and motivated salespeople.

Source: "Cheerleading, and Clerks Who Know Awls from Augers," Business Week, August 3, 1992.

If an advertisement reaches thousands of potential customers, the cost per person might be as low as one dollar or less. A salesperson's expenses can include the cost of salary, travel, time spent with a customer, equipment and materials needed for sales presentations, and so forth. A salesperson may only talk to a few customers each day. Therefore, the cost per customer can be very expensive. For sales of products to businesses, the cost is often more than a hundred dollars. Occasionally costs are as high as a few thousand dollars per customer before a sale is made.

Because a salesperson meets with customers one or a very few at a time, it takes a great deal of time for a large number of customers to be contacted. Compare that to an advertisement that reaches millions of people at the same time. The length of time needed to reach a large number of customers is a disadvantage of personal selling. A company can solve that problem by employing a large number of salespeople, but that adds to the costs of selling.

The salesperson is responsible for deciding what information to provide as well as how and when activities are completed. Therefore, the company's managers have limited control over the sales process. Salespeople often work alone or in small selling teams. During the time they are with a customer, they provide the information they believe is needed to help the customers decide to buy. When salespeople are not meeting with customers, they can plan additional sales calls, follow up on previous sales, and complete a variety of record-keeping tasks.

The last disadvantage involves the knowledge and skill required to be an effective salesperson and the difficulty of the selling job. Salespeople need to understand selling procedures, communications, psychology, accounting, and management. In addition, they need a great deal of knowledge about their products and services and those of their competitors. The selling process requires people who are outgoing, creative, able to adjust to different people and situations, and good at solving problems. The job often requires long work hours and travel. Because of the complex and difficult job, it is not easy for companies to find and hire skilled salespeople.

Choosing Personal Selling

Personal selling should be used when it improves the marketing efforts. It can be the only method of promotion used by a company. Usually it is combined with other methods as a part of a promotional plan. Characteristics of products and markets that indicate the need for personal selling include:

- complex or expensive products

- markets made up of a few large customers

- new or very unique products with which customers are unfamiliar

- customers located in a limited area

- a complicated or long decision-making process

- customers who expect personal attention and help with decision-making

PREPARING FOR EFFECTIVE SELLING

The success of a salesperson is typically measured by the sales that are made and the satisfaction of the customers. However, that success is often determined well before the salesperson meets with the customer. Figure 19-3 on the next page illustrates that effective selling requires a great deal of preparation. Many salespeople spend more time preparing for sales than they do in actual contact with customers. Of course a critical part of that preparation is skill in selling. We will study that process in the next section. In addition to developing effective selling skills, three areas are important: understanding the customer; understanding the product; and understanding the competition.

UNDERSTANDING THE CUSTOMER

Marketing is responsible for creating satisfying exchanges. Because salespeople negotiate the sale of products and services with the customer, they need to ensure that the customer is satisfied with the purchase. Understanding the customer helps organize the sales presentation to meet the customer's needs.

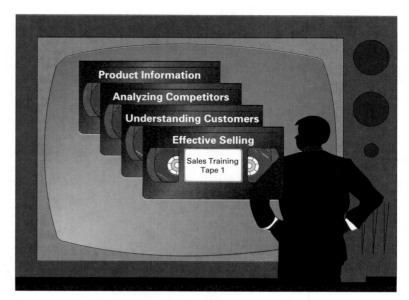

Requirements for Effective Selling

FIGURE 19-3 ▪ A salesperson needs to understand effective selling as well as customers, competitors, and the products and services being sold.

Identifying Customers

Salespeople need to identify appropriate customers. Information is needed about who the customers are and where they are located. A great deal of time is wasted if the salesperson is talking to people who are not interested in the company's product or are not able to buy them.

Some salespeople use a process called cold calling. *With cold calling, a salesperson contacts a large number of people who are conveniently located without knowing a great deal about each person contacted.* A business products salesperson may call on every business listed in a city business directory with annual sales over $1,000,000. A telemarketer may use a computer dialing system programmed to randomly call all residential numbers in a telephone directory. A door-to-door salesperson stops at every home on a block to try to locate customers for a carpet-cleaning business.

You can imagine that using cold calling is difficult and discouraging. A large number of customers may have to be contacted before finding someone who is interested in the salesperson's products. Also, the salesperson has a difficult time beginning the selling process when little is known about the prospective customer whom the salesperson has just met. Most importantly, people contacted by the salesperson may be quite upset if they are not interested in the products being sold. They may not want to be bothered by a salesperson at that time. The salesperson is wasting the time of people who have no current needs related to those products. Also wasted are the resources of the company that could be better spent on interested consumers.

A marketing-oriented business does not use cold calling. Salespeople gather information on possible customers and determine if they fit the characteristics of the company's target market. Often, through the company's marketing information system or marketing research, information is already available to assist the salesperson. Also, other promotional or marketing efforts such as coupons and product registration cards are used to identify customers and gather other information. If the salesperson knows who prospective customers are, where they are located, some of their important needs, and when and how to contact each customer, the selling process is much more productive.

Qualifying Prospective Customers

Not all people in a target market are prepared or able to purchase a product at a particular time. A salesperson will complete a procedure known as qualifying a customer. *Qualifying involves gathering information to determine which people are most likely to buy.* Three characteristics qualify a person as a prospective customer. Without all three characteristics, the person will not purchase the product. The characteristics include:

1. A *need* for the product.
2. The *resources* to purchase the product.
3. The *authority* to make a decision to purchase.

While everyone in a target market has a general need for the product being marketed, that need may not be as important as other needs. The customer may have already purchased another product to meet the need. Salespeople identify customers who have the strongest need and who are ready to make a purchasing decision.

We know that most people have many more needs than they can satisfy at a given time. Often a limitation on purchasing is the resources (money) to buy the product. It is possible that a customer does not have the money or adequate financing cannot be arranged through the use of credit. No matter how hard the salesperson works or how effective the sales presentation is, a sale is not possible if the customer is unable to afford the product. Part of the information-gathering process of salespeople is determining if the customer has adequate resources.

Many times people want to buy a product but do not have the authority to make the decision. A child may have to ask a parent, a manager may need to get approval from the purchasing department, or a partner in a business may need to have the agreement of the other partners. Salespeople often need to work with several people before a purchase decision is made. It is important to determine which person or people will make the final decision and make sure they are included in the selling process.

Understanding Customer Decisions

We learned earlier that consumers go through a series of steps when they make a decision. Those steps include identifying a problem or need, gathering information, evaluating alternatives, making a decision, and evaluating the decision. Consumers need specific types of information as they move through each step. If the consumer is gathering information on possible products to satisfy a need, information on financing alternatives will not be helpful. On the other hand, if the customer has narrowed the choice to two products and is comparing them, general information on the needs a product satisfies will not help.

Salespeople often translate the consumer decision-making steps into a series of mental stages that lead to a sale. Those mental stages are summarized with the letters AIDCA. The meaning of each letter is shown in Figure 19-4.

A salesperson knows that the customer must first focus *attention* on the salesperson and the sales presentation. It is important to get the customer's *interest* in the product early in the

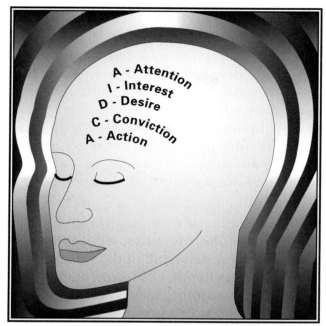

Mental Stages of Consumer Decision-Making

FIGURE 19-4 ■ Consumers complete a series of mental decisions as they decide whether to make purchases. Salespeople who understand the mental stages can use the information to plan their sales presentations.

presentation. A customer moves from interest to *desire* when it is clear that the product meets important needs. The desire turns to *conviction* when the customer determines the product is a good value and the best choice. That leads to *action*, or the purchase of the product.

A salesperson who understands consumer decision-making and is able to determine which of the AIDCA stages each customer is in will be able to provide the specific information that each customer needs. An important advantage of personal selling is the capability of providing specific information to each customer.

UNDERSTANDING THE PRODUCT

As the representative of the company to the customer, the salesperson is responsible for providing the information needed for the customer to make a good decision. There are two parts to that responsibility. The salesperson must have adequate product knowledge. Also, the salesperson must be able to communicate the information effectively to the customer.

Product Knowledge

Choosing the best product to satisfy a customer's needs is often not an easy task. Customers may not be able to determine by examining a product, or even by reviewing the information that accompanies a product, whether it is the one they should buy. Salespeople need to know a great deal about the products they represent. They need access to additional information so they can answer customers' questions and demonstrate the product effectively.

Salespeople must be familiar with all parts of the marketing mix. Customers are concerned not only about the product but also about price, availability, and promotion. While an individual customer is not interested in all of the information, the salesperson must be able to tailor the presentation to the needs of each customer. One customer may want to know about the construction and durability of a product. Another may be concerned about the warranty and repair services. Still another needs to know about financing. A salesperson who does not know that information or who is unable to obtain it quickly will not be able to satisfy potential customers. The saleperson will lose sales to salespeople who can provide the information each customer needs.

A variety of sources of product information are available. Companies prepare information sheets and product manuals. Advertisements and other types of promotion often contain valuable information including price changes, special promotions, and so on. The product's marketing plan and marketing research reports are sources of useful information as are other salespeople and company personnel.

Many companies offer training for salespeople that emphasizes important product information. They also prepare sales aids and other materials for salespeople to use. Effective salespeople regularly read business publications, attend conferences and trade shows, and study other information sources to keep up-to-date on the products and services they sell.

Communicating Product Information

Which of the following statements is more effective as a part of a sales presentation?

"The standard engine in this vehicle is a 4.3 liter V6."

"Our standard engine offers the best combination of efficiency and power. You will average 26 miles per gallon. You will also have enough acceleration so you won't have trouble merging into the faster traffic when entering the freeway."

The statements provide examples of features and benefits. Figure 19-5 illustrates this difference. *A feature is a description of a product characteristic.* The first statement describes a feature—the standard engine. *A benefit is the advantage provided to a customer as a result of the feature.* The second statement describes how the customer will benefit from the engine—efficiency and acceleration. Salespeople communicate most effectively when they can describe the benefits of a product for a customer.

Feature-Benefit Comparison

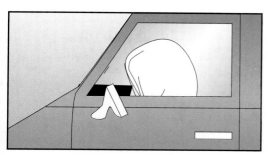 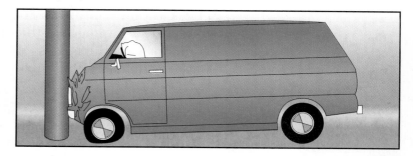

Feature: a driver's side airbag   **Benefit:** allows a person to walk away unhurt from an accident

FIGURE 19-5 ▪ Features have little meaning to customers until they understand how each feature provides a benefit. Salespeople need to be able to understand customer needs in order to communicate the benefits of the product.

Many of a product's features are similar to those of competitors. Other features are different and a few may be unique. Customers want to know how various products and brands are similar and different. They also want to know how the features will meet their needs. The salesperson needs to understand the features, translate them into customer benefits, and communicate the important benefits in an understandable way to each customer.

UNDERSTANDING THE COMPETITION

Seldom will a customer make a purchase without considering several choices. The consumer wants to buy the most satisfying product and the best value. However, it is not always easy to make the best choice. With products that are very similar, quite complex, or for which little information is available, consumers may have a difficult time determining which is best. It is not unusual for a customer to buy one product only to realize later that another choice would have been better.

Salespeople want to sell the products and services they represent, but they will be more successful in the long run if the customer is satisfied with the purchase. The salesperson who is familiar with competitors' products can help the customer understand differences among the choices. This salesperson will be viewed quite differently by customers than the salespeople who can only describe the products of one company. It is not unusual for customers to study several brands or similar products before making a decision. A knowledgeable salesperson can explain important differences to customers to assist them with the comparison. The customer will often look at those differences when examining a competitor's product and will be able to see the advantages of the original brand. Just as with their company's products, it is important that salespeople study all parts of the marketing mix for competitors' products.

THE SELLING PROCESS

Nothing demonstrates the marketing concept better than the selling process when it is completed effectively. A salesperson carefully assesses the needs of a customer and uses the resources of the company to design an effective marketing mix. The salesperson then presents that mix to the customer and describes how it meets the customer's needs. The salesperson asks questions to determine if the mix satisfies the customer or if adjustments must be made. The salesperson helps the customer make the best decision.

The selling process just described may not fit your perception of selling. Remember that not all companies and salespeople understand or believe in the marketing concept. It is not unusual to find salespeople who believe their responsibility is to convince the customer to buy their company's products. They look at the selling process as a type of contest between the customer and the salesperson. Each tries to negotiate the best deal possible. The salesperson uses information and the resources of the business to persuade the customer to buy.

Effective selling is a very demanding profession. People who are skilled at selling are in high demand in business. They are well compensated for their abilities. The skills needed by sales-people can be summarized in the six steps of the selling process. Those steps are listed in Figure 19-6.

Steps in the Selling Process	
Step	**Purpose**
Preapproach	Studying the customer and his/her needs
Approach	Contacting the customer to determine information needs and establish a helping relationship
Demonstration	Presenting the marketing mix in an interesting way that emphasizes customer benefits
Answering Questions	Helping the customer resolve concerns and ensure the marketing mix meets the customer's needs
Closing the Sale	Obtaining a decision to purchase from the customer and suggesting other products and services the customer may see as valuable products
Follow-up	Continuing contact with the customer to determine if the mix was provided as promised, if the needs were satisfied, and if the customer has additional needs

FIGURE 19-6 ▪ Effective salespeople follow a specific procedure to match customer needs with the company's products and services.

PREAPPROACH

We are often told that time spent in preparation leads to successful performance. Whether it involves studying for a test, practicing for a musical performance, or training for an athletic event, people who spend time learning and perfecting their skills are usually more successful. Salespeople are no different. Preparation during the preapproach improves the chances for a successful sale.

The preapproach includes gathering needed information and preparing for the sales presentation before contacting the customer. Salespeople study target market information and any other information available on the specific customer they are meeting. They also review and organize all of the information about the company, its products and services, and the other parts of the marketing mix. Based on customer information, the salesperson prepares for the first meeting with the customer.

Most good salespeople outline and practice their sales presentation before meeting with the customer. The intention is not to memorize the information. Instead, the salesperson organizes the presentation to lead the customer effectively to a decision. Practice makes the salesperson more comfortable. It allows the salesperson to concentrate on the customer during the sales presentation.

CHALLENGES
HOW THINGS CHANGE

Sears, Roebuck and Co. was in trouble. For more than a century it was respected as a company that went out of its way to serve customers. It was now facing charges of customer fraud in California and several other states. Sears Auto Centers were accused of selling unnecessary parts and services to customers who brought their cars in for repair. When the word quickly spread that customers could not trust the advice of the service personnel at Sears, sales began to drop.

How did a company move from a position of trust among its customers to one where customers had lost their confidence? It started with a change in philosophy about selling. For many years, Sears viewed its sales personnel in the Auto Centers as customer advisors. They diagnosed the problems of customers' cars and recommended the necessary repairs. They were paid by salary that was not dependent on the amount of sales they made to a customer.

The auto repair industry became more competitive. Sears management decided that salespeople would be more aggressive if they were rewarded for the quantity of services and parts sold. The compensation system for salespeople was changed from salary to straight commission.

Salespeople saw that the way to make money was to increase their sales. They began to find every possible service and repair needed. As sales increased, so did the commissions paid to salespeople. The company raised sales quotas so additional sales were required for salespeople to maintain their incomes. Under those pressures, many of the salespeople began to recommend services and repairs that customers did not actually need.

The change in compensation changed the philosophy of the salespeople. Their first concern was no longer the satisfaction of customers. It was now selling as much as possible. A management idea that ignored the importance of the customer/salesperson relationship brought the company the worst kind of publicity and the loss of customer confidence.

Source: "Smart Selling." Business Week, August 3, 1992.

APPROACH

The approach is the first contact with the customer when the salesperson gets the customer's attention and creates a favorable impression. The approach might be initiated by the customer or by the salesperson. In either case, the salesperson is responsible for the result. The approach provides the opportunity for the salesperson to attract the customer's attention and create an interest in the product or service.

Consider the situation in which a customer enters a retail store. The salesperson must decide whether to approach and greet the customer or whether to allow the customer to look around the store. Some customers have a particular product in mind. Others are simply spending time in the store without any real interest in making a purchase. A salesperson who approaches the customer in a pleasant and courteous way can quickly determine if the customer wants assistance. The salesperson can also determine where the person is in the mental stages of decision-making.

For the customer who is just beginning to search for a product, the salesperson provides information on the basic characteristics of products that might meet the customer's needs. The salesperson allows the customer to examine several choices. If the customer is nearing a decision, the salesperson might review payment methods, advantages of certain product features, or any final important factors that will help the customer decide to buy.

Salespeople who call on business customers have different factors to consider when planning an approach. Since several people may be involved in making a purchasing decision, the salesperson must decide whom to contact. A method of contacting the person must be developed that will result in the opportunity to meet with the customer for the sales presentation. Business people have frequent contacts from many salespeople. They do not have time to meet with all of them and select only those that they believe can be of help. Telephone calls, letters of introduction, or special promotional materials sent to the prospective customer can be used to make the customer aware of the salesperson, the company, and its products.

DEMONSTRATION

The major part of the sales presentation is the demonstration. *The demonstration is a personalized presentation of the features of the marketing mix in a way that emphasizes the benefits and value to the customer.* The real value of personal selling is shown in the demonstration. The salesperson tailors the product information directly to the customer and emphasizes the parts of the mix that best meet the customer's needs. The demonstration is designed to turn the customer's interest into desire.

As the salesperson moves from the approach to the demonstration, the needs of the target market should have been determined. The salesperson confirms those needs and determines the information that will help the customer make a decision. The salesperson does this by asking questions and listening carefully to the customer.

The most effective demonstrations are based on a feature-benefit presentation. The salesperson must identify the features of the marketing mix that are most important to customer needs. The salesperson clearly describes how the customer will benefit from each of the important features.

Characteristics of an effective demonstration include the following:

■ Use active, descriptive language that is understandable and meaningful to the customer.

■ Direct the customer's attention to a specific feature and explain the benefit.

■ Observe reactions and listen to comments to keep the demonstration focused on the customer's needs.

■ Demonstrate the feature rather than just describing it, when possible.

■ Involve the customer. Let the customer handle and test the product.

■ Make the presentation dramatic so the customer will remember important features.

■ Use sales aids such as pictures, charts, computer demonstrations, and such to enhance understanding.

■ Review the benefits that are most important to the customer.

ANSWERING QUESTIONS

A salesperson resolves concerns and provides additional information needed by a customer when answering questions. As a salesperson responds to a customer's questions, the customer is mentally moving from desire to conviction.

In the past, this step in the selling process was known as *handling objections*. It was believed that customers resisted making a purchase decision and would raise objections to avoid that decision. Salespeople had to overcome that resistance by handling the objection. When the salesperson has the interests of the consumer in mind and is presenting a product or service that meets customer needs, there is less resistance. Customers want to be certain they are making the correct decision and ask questions to clarify their understanding.

A salesperson should welcome and encourage questions. Questions will often help the salesperson identify the most important needs of the customer. They indicate the parts of the marketing mix the customer does not understand. By answering the questions well, the salesperson demonstrates how the product meets important needs. Answering customer's questions provides more specific information, and gains the confidence of the customer. An effective procedure for answering questions is shown in Figure 19-7.

Answering a Customer's Questions

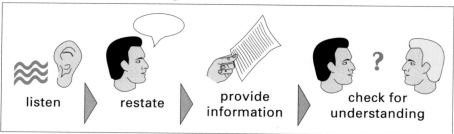

listen   restate   provide information   check for understanding

FIGURE 19-7 ▪ Salespeople should listen carefully before answering a customer's questions. It is important to make sure that the customer understands the information before continuing.

CLOSING THE SALE

A salesperson closes the sale when the customer makes a decision to purchase. A well-planned sales presentation helps the customer move from attention to interest, to desire, and then to conviction. A customer must be convinced that a product or service offers the best value. At that point, the final step in the decision-making process can be completed—action.

It is not easy for the customer to make a decision to buy. This is especially true for an expensive product or one that the customer has not purchased before. A salesperson needs to be skillful in closing the sale. A customer that feels pressured will resist buying the product. On the other hand, some customers need encouragement. They do not want to appear eager to buy. If the salesperson does not ask for the order, the customer may postpone the decision and buy something else later. The salesperson must provide easy opportunities for the customer to purchase the product. The salesperson must also be willing to continue the sales presentation if the customer is not ready to buy.

The salesperson should look for opportunities to close the sale. *Providing the customer with the opportunity to buy during the sales presentation is known as a trial close.* A customer that repeatedly handles the product, appears satisfied with answers to questions, or responds favorably to a feature-benefit description or demonstration may be ready to buy. The salesperson should take that opportunity to ask for the order.

There are several ways a salesperson can close a sale. The goal is to make the decision easy for the customer. Methods of closing a sale include:

Close on an important benefit.
"You obviously are concerned about safety for your family. This automobile not only has dual air bags in the front but also has built-in child safety seats in the rear. You can't find a safer family automobile on the market today."

Offer the customer a choice.
"Would you prefer the green or the blue trim?"

Provide an extra value.
"This month we are offering a 3 percent discount for orders of 500 units or more."

Ask about the method of payment.
"Will you pay cash, or would you like to use our easy payment plan?"

Emphasize availability.
"If you place the order today, it will be delivered by next Tuesday."

Guarantee satisfaction.
"You can try it for two weeks. If you are not satisfied for any reason, we will gladly replace it or offer a full refund."

As soon as the customer makes the decision to buy, the salesperson should take the opportunity to reinforce that decision.

Customers want to believe they made the right choice but often have concerns about the decision after it is made. The salesperson can emphasize the value and summarize the benefits the customer will receive from using the product or service.

One of the responsibilities of the salesperson at the completion of a sale is to be certain the customer's needs are satisfied. It is possible that the product can be used more effectively if the customer purchases related merchandise. A bicycle helmet is needed by a bicycle rider. Sheets and blankets may be useful for someone who just purchased a bedroom suite. When a pet is purchased, the family may need food, grooming supplies, and so on. If customers go home without all of the things needed to use the product, they will probably be dissatisfied. *Offering additional products and services after an initial sale in order to increase customer satisfaction is known as suggestion selling.*

FOLLOW-UP

Customers who purchase products and services from a company and are satisfied with their purchases are likely to buy from that company again. *Making contact with the customer after the sale to ensure satisfaction is known as follow-up.* It is the responsibility of the salesperson to follow up with each customer to ensure that the customer is satisfied. Follow up also provides another opportunity to reinforce the customer's decision as well as to determine if the customer has additional needs that the business can meet.

Part of the follow-up responsibility may include checking on delivery schedules, making sure warranty or product registration information is accurate, scheduling product installation and maintenance, or completing paperwork for financing. If the customer has any problems, the salesperson can arrange to resolve them quickly. When the customer sees the salesperson completing the follow-up activities, it will be clear that the customer is important to the business.

PROVIDING SALES SUPPORT

Selling is one of many business and marketing functions. For selling to be effective, the salesperson must receive support from many parts of the business including other marketing personnel. In order to meet customer needs, the salesperson must have products and services that are well designed, readily available, and priced competitively. People in production, finance, and management need to coordinate their work with the salespeople to match the supply of products with sales. Order processing, customer service, and many other business activities are needed in order for the selling process to be successful.

An analysis of each of the marketing functions demonstrates how salespeople depend on other marketing activities for support.

1. **Product/Service Planning:** Salespeople can provide information on customer needs and customer's reactions to the current products and services offered by the business. That information can be used to improve existing products and develop new products so the salesperson can meet customer needs.

2. **Purchasing:** Salespeople must have an adequate supply and variety of products to offer to their customers. Buyers working for wholesale and retail businesses identify sources of the needed products and negotiate the necessary purchases.

3. **Financing:** Many customers need to finance their purchases. Salespeople must have access to credit services that they can offer to their customers. Salespeople may also need assistance in explaining financing and completing the necessary paperwork.

4. **Distribution:** Products and services often need to be delivered to customers. Salespeople rely on transportation services to get the products delivered at the time the customers want them. Salespeople need to have information on transportation schedules and costs when they work with their customers.

5. **Pricing:** Many prices are not set but can be negotiated by the customer working with the salesperson. Offering discounts, accepting trade-ins, and other methods can be used to adjust the price. A salesperson must have the authority to negotiate the price or must be able to get pricing information quickly.

6. **Risk Management:** Insurance is needed when some products are sold. Buying and selling some products involves a great deal of risk (agriculture products, securities, travel services, and so on). Salespeople must be able to discuss the types of risk with customers and, in some cases, provide insurance or use other methods to reduce the risk.

7. **Marketing Information Management:** Salespeople need access to a wide variety of information throughout the selling process. In the preapproach, the salesperson needs information on customers

and their needs. During the sales presentation, the salesperson may need to gather additional information about products and their availability, pricing, or other matters to answer customer questions.

8. **Promotion:** Usually customers obtain information from sources other than the salesperson to aid in making a buying decision. Other types of promotion, including advertising and publicity, can create interest, inform potential customers of product choices, or reinforce a purchase decision after the sale is completed.

PERSONAL MANAGEMENT FOR SALESPEOPLE

Personal selling is a very demanding career. Most salespeople are responsible for their own time and activities with limited direction from their managers. Often they are paid on commission. This means they are not paid unless they sell something.

A sales career can also be very rewarding. Professional salespeople who do their jobs well are paid more than many other business people. Because salespeople are responsible for a sales presentation, there is a great deal of satisfaction when a sale is made and the customer is satisfied.

Successful professional salespeople are good managers. The important areas of management are self-management, customer management, and information management.

SELF-MANAGEMENT

Selling requires motivation and an effective use of time. It is difficult to call on another customer at the end of a long day. It is demanding to complete the necessary research needed to plan a sales presentation. Much of a salesperson's time is spent on non-selling activities—paperwork, research, solving customer problems. A salesperson must be able to determine what needs to be done, set a work schedule, and devote the necessary time to complete all of the work.

Salespeople need to be emotionally and physically healthy. A great deal of stress is involved in the job. Salespeople may feel stress because success depends on customers deciding what to purchase and when they will purchase. Long hours of work leave little time for exercise and relaxation.

Finally, an important part of self-management is personal development. Salespeople must be well-educated and informed. They need to continue to learn about new selling procedures, the use of technology such as computers, and information about products, customers, and competitors.

CUSTOMER MANAGEMENT

Selecting and scheduling customers is a difficult challenge for salespeople. Some customers offer a greater potential for sales because they purchase more frequently or in larger quantities. Certain customers require a greater amount of time from salespeople because they are at an earlier stage in decision-making. Some customers require more time because their needs are not well identified or they ask for a great deal of information. Salespeople must be able to decide how much time to spend with each customer to maximize their sales.

When salespeople travel to meet customers, they have to carefully schedule their time. They need to limit the amount of time they are traveling in order to spend more time selling. Also they need to keep their travel costs as low as possible to increase profits.

INFORMATION MANAGEMENT

The *Newsline* at the beginning of the chapter describes how today's salespeople manage information using a laptop computer. It illustrates the importance of information to salespeople. Consider the salesperson who does not have access to information about specific customers and attempts to develop a sales presentation. That presentation will be very general and based on the salesperson's assumptions. In the same way, if the

salesperson does not have immediate access to updated product information, price changes, distribution schedules, service records, and the like, it will be difficult to respond to customer needs and answer customer questions.

Salespeople must be able to identify needed information, develop effective record-keeping systems, and use the company's information system. In addition, salespeople must complete orders and other sales records carefully and completely.

REVIEW

Professional, personalized communications are an effective promotional tool for many businesses. Personal selling allows a company to respond to the unique needs of customers with specific messages designed to help customers make purchasing decisions.

Personal selling involves a series of steps. Those steps match the consumer decision-making process. The selling process includes preapproach, approach, demonstration, answering questions, closing the sale, and follow-up.

Selling will not be effective unless it is supported by other business and marketing functions. Salespeople can assist the company in designing products and services to meet customer needs. In the same way, the salesperson needs support from all parts of the business to design and deliver an effective marketing mix for each customer.

Management skills are important to salespeople because of the difficult job they must perform. Salespeople need to develop skills in self-management, customer management, and information management.

MARKETING FOUNDATIONS

1. CONCEPT MATCHING

The following concepts are examples of personal selling.
Match each example with the correct selling concept.

assess and satisfy needs

benefit

customer decision-making process

feature

feedback

flexibility

follow-up

product knowledge

qualifying customers

time

a. During a sales presentation, the salesperson has the advantage of responding to the customer's questions or determining if specific information is needed.

b. In personal selling, salespeople can adjust their sales presentations to include information that is most useful to the customer.

c. Effective salespeople often meet frequently with their customers to provide information and support for products and services they have sold.

d. Lin Chung estimates that she spends about one-third of her time with customers who have previously purchased her products.

e. "The excellent print capability of this machine will make your correspondence look professional at half the cost of a printing service."

f. Rosa Garcia likes to make sure her customers get the best products possible to solve their problems.

g. Using marketing research information to determine the appropriate customers who are interested in and able to buy the company's products or services.

h. Fred March works closely with his customers so he can understand when they are ready to make decisions to purchase.

i. Sales publications, manuals, promotional pieces, conferences, trade shows, and trade publications are studied and used by effective salespeople.

j. "This telephone system has a 200-call capacity."

2. SHORT ANSWER

Read each of the following questions and write the answers in complete sentences.

a. Why is the job of the salesperson important to an organization?

b. What should an effective salesperson do to prepare for selling?

c. Why is effective selling considered a perfect example of the marketing concept?

d. List and define the steps of a sale.

e. Why is sales support critical to the success of an organization?

MARKETING RESEARCH

1. SALES EFFECTIVENESS

Sales people are often paid bonuses or commissions on their total sales. Each of the following salespeople earn $60,000 per year and earn 2 percent commission on all sales over $250,000 per year.

Salesperson	Total Sales	Number of Sales Calls Per Year	Number of Sales Per Year
Chin Mueller	$2,345,200	250	107
Jane Brown	3,395,200	350	120
Marcus Gonzalez	2,930,400	400	99

a. What is each salesperson's total salary for the year?

b. What is the average amount of each salesperson's sale?

c. What percentage of calls resulted in a sale for each salesperson?

2. KNOWLEDGE IS NEEDED

Before making a sales call, the salesperson should be armed with information about the customer, the product, and the competition. Assume you are a salesperson for an industrial firm. List three pieces of information that would be helpful to know about your customer, your product, and the competition. List three ways that you can find the necessary information.

MARKETING PLANNING

1. FEATURE-BENEFIT ORGANIZATION

It is important to remember that effective salespeople solve customer problems by explaining how a product or service will benefit the consumer. In preparing for a sales call, it is best to prepare a feature-benefit chart for the product. Assume you are a salesperson selling a video camera. For each of the following features, describe a customer benefit.

Features:

a. automatic focus

b. date and event imprinter

c. soft-sided case with strap and handle

d. lightweight

e. three-hour battery

 f. fade-in and fade-out

g. detachable microphone

h. lens cover

 i. tripod attachment

 j. zoom-in capabilities

2. AIDCA AND SELLING

AIDCA is a series of mental stages that customers go through in the decision-making process. Draw a diagram of the steps of a sale and add the AIDCA model to the steps to show how the selling process can aid customer decision-making.

MARKETING MANAGEMENT

1. SALES PRESENTATION

Choose a product or service of your choice and prepare a sales presentation. Use a classmate as a customer. Be prepared to role-play your presentation to the class.

2. SALES SUPPORT

As the CEO of a computer technical support company, you understand how important it is to provide sales support to your sales staff. For each of the marketing functions, specify one activity that each area can do to provide the necessary support for your sales staff.

UNIT
6

Managing Risks, Finances, and Information

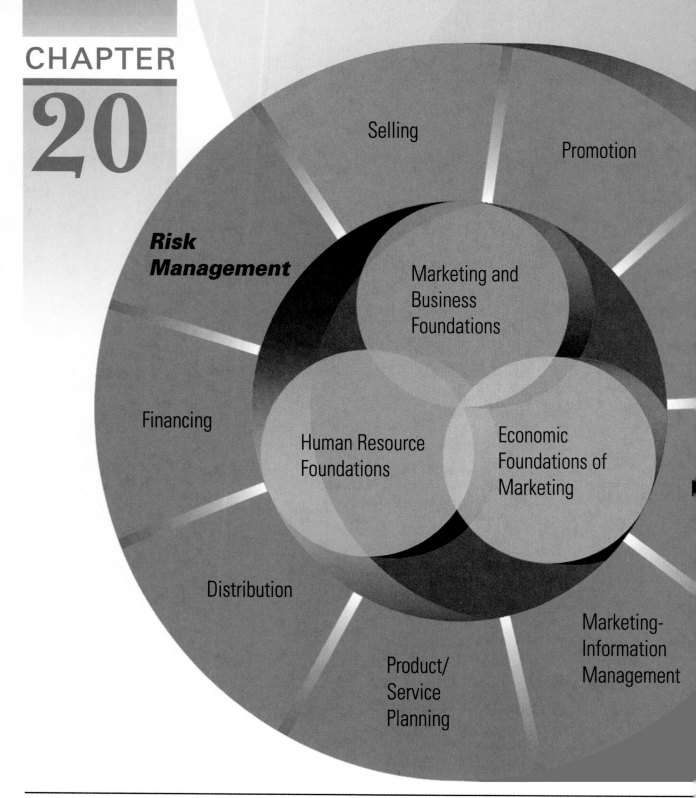

Selling

Promotion

Risk Management

Marketing and Business Foundations

Financing

Human Resource Foundations

Economic Foundations of Marketing

Distribution

Product/ Service Planning

Marketing-Information Management

Be Aware
of Risks

OBJECTIVES

1. Discuss risk and the classifications of risk.
2. Identify four methods of dealing with risk.
3. Describe the types of risk faced in the marketing environment and in the marketing mix.
4. Develop a plan for managing marketing risk.

NEWSLINE

PRODUCING SUCCESS

The startling results of a recent survey indicate that businesses find it harder than ever to develop new products. Managers from America's top retail and manufacturing businesses were asked about the success rate of their new products in recent years. While the typical success rate has been reported at between 10 and 20 percent in the past, the managers responding to the survey indicated that only 8 percent of their new product ideas ever reach the market. Of those few that are introduced to consumers, less than 20 percent succeed. Simple analysis of those results show that nearly 99 percent of product ideas developed by businesses today, fail.

Why does it appear that new product results are moving in the wrong direction? The managers participating in the survey believe

Why does it appear that new product results are moving in the wrong direction?

it is because the costs of new product development are too high and it takes too long to see a profit. Therefore, companies are not willing to spend the time and money needed to develop new products. Another problem reported is the tendency for company managers to change new products to fit their own ideas rather than relying on research gathered from the target markets for the new products. When managers think they know more than customers about what will work and what will not work, the result may be a product that customers will not buy.

Managers report that their new product development process is much faster than it was in the past. New products can be developed and moved to the market quickly. However, managers believe that is one of the biggest weaknesses of the process. When a company needs to move fast, it is more likely to make mistakes.

Some companies seem to have overcome problems with new product development. Three companies were voted as the best in developing profitable new products. Con-

When a company needs to move fast, it is more likely to make mistakes.

Agra gets the greatest sales growth from new products. Procter and Gamble was seen as the company with the greatest profitability for new products introduced in the United States. Sony received the same recognition for worldwide new product development.

Source: "Survey: New Product Failure is Top Management's Fault," Marketing News, February 1, 1993, p. 2.

BUSINESSES TAKE RISKS

Every year thousands of people decide to open their own businesses. Most entrepreneurs will use all of the money they have saved. They will borrow thousands of additional dollars. They may quit their current jobs to devote all their time to the

new business. Each believes he or she has an idea that will attract customers, earn a living, and maybe even make the owner very wealthy.

At the same time that thousands of entrepreneurs are opening new businesses, many others are closing their doors. Their dreams did not come true. They are disappointed and discouraged. Most lost the money they invested in the business. Many will never attempt a new business again.

RISK OR OPPORTUNITY?

When a person decides to open a business or a company decides to develop a new product, there is a chance for success and a chance for failure (see Figure 20-1). *The possibility that a loss can occur as the result of a decision or activity is known as risk.* Why do people invest a great deal of time and money in new businesses or products when there is a risk of loss? The typical answer is that while there is a chance of loss, there is also an opportunity. *An opportunity is the possibility for success.*

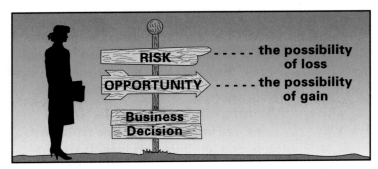

The Outcomes of a Business Decision

FIGURE 20-1 ■ A business is willing to take risks because of the potential opportunities. It may lose money if the decision is not successful. On the other hand, the business has the chance of making a profit.

Success takes many forms. For both individuals and businesses, it can mean recognition, being viewed as a leader, or providing personal satisfaction and satisfaction for others. An important measure of

---

success in business is profit. The private enterprise economy is organized to encourage risk-taking. People invest money and take risks in business in order to make a profit.

Each of us takes risks every day. You might decide whether to speak to a new person you meet. The risk is that the person might not respond in a positive way. The opportunity is that you will establish a new friendship. You may have spent a great deal of time and effort in the past few years selecting difficult courses, completing homework, and preparing yourself for college. There is a risk that all of the effort will not pay off. Your grades might not be high enough, or you may not have the money needed to attend the college you have chosen. However, you are willing to take the risk for the opportunities provided by a college education.

CLASSIFICATION OF RISK

Marketers need to understand the risks involved in order to deal with them. There are three classifications of risk. The classifications are based on the result of the risk, control of the risk, and insurability of the risk.

Result of the Risk

Some risks, known as pure risks, present the chance of loss but no opportunity for gain. When you are driving, you are at risk of being in an accident. If you have an accident you will

likely suffer a loss. You could be injured, you could injure others, or there could be damage to the vehicles. If you avoid an accident you do not have an opportunity for gain.

The result is different for other risks. *If you have the chance to gain as well as lose from the risk, it is known as a speculative risk.* If you invest money in the stock market, it is possible you could lose a great deal of money if the value of the stock goes down. On the other hand, there is an opportunity for making money if the stock price increases.

Control of the Risk

Controllable risks can be reduced or even avoided by actions you take. If you are concerned about losing jewelry or cash, you might decide to put it in a safe or a safety deposit box in a bank. If the roads are slippery, you can avoid driving or drive very carefully to reduce the chance of an accident.

If your actions do not affect the result of a risk, it is an uncontrollable risk. The weather cannot be controlled. However, the type of weather has a big impact on some businesses, such as farms. If the weather is favorable, farmers have the opportunity to grow and harvest crops. With poor weather, crops will not develop.

Insurability of the Risk

If a risk is faced by a large number of people, if the risk is pure rather than speculative, and the amount of the loss can be predicted, it is an insurable risk. Many people who own homes or buildings face the risk that their property could be destroyed by fire. Insurance companies look at the amount of losses from fires in past years and sell insurance that would pay for the buildings that could be damaged from fire.

For noninsurable risks, it is not possible to predict if a loss will occur or the amount of any loss. Speculative risks are not insurable. A business is not able to buy insurance that will pay for losses suffered because customers did not buy a new product. The person who invests in the stock market has to accept any losses or gains because it is not possible to accurately predict the result of the investment.

DEALING WITH RISK

Clearly, people prefer success rather than failure. Marketing activities are subject to a great many risks. Every activity performed has the chance of success or failure. Each target market may provide a profit or loss for the company. Marketers need to be familiar with ways to deal with risks.

People responsible for risk management go through a careful process to decide the best way to deal with each risk faced by the business. There are four methods that can be considered (see Figure 20-2 on the next page).

Dealing with Risk	
Management Strategy	**Result**
Avoid the Risk	Business chooses to pursue a different strategy that doesn't involve the risk
Transfer the Risk	Business lets another business complete the risky activity
Insure the Risk	Business pays an insurer to reimburse the amount of any losses from the risk
Assume the Risk	Business goes ahead with the decision and takes full responsibility for the result

FIGURE 20-2 ▪ When facing a risk, managers have several choices of how to respond.

AVOID THE RISK

It is possible to avoid some risks. If there is evidence that it will be very difficult to enter a market to compete with several larger businesses, that market can be avoided. Some shipping methods are more likely to result in lost or damaged products. To avoid that risk, the marketer would choose another shipping method.

TRANSFER THE RISK

A common method of dealing with risk in marketing is to transfer the risk to others. A business that believes it will have difficulty collecting money from credit customers doesn't offer its own credit. Instead it accepts several national credit cards. The credit card companies accept the risk for the opportunity to make a profit.

INSURE THE RISK

If a financial loss is possible from the risk and that loss can be predicted, the risk can be insured. The company facing the risk pays a small amount of the potential loss to an insurer. If the loss occurs, the insurer guarantees payment to the company. The company is willing to accept a small, certain loss (the cost of insurance) for protection from a larger, uncertain loss. Remember that many risks are not insurable because they are speculative.

ASSUME THE RISK

A company that assumes a risk faces the risk and deals with the result. Some risks are quite unlikely to occur. Other risks have relatively small losses compared to the opportunities. There are risks that are a normal part of business. In each case, it may be best to assume the risk, because it will not have a serious negative effect on the business.

There are other risks that a business has to assume because they cannot be avoided, transferred, or insured. Once a product is in the market, many things can happen that may result in much lower sales than expected. The business accepts that possibility and attempts to make the product as successful as possible. Occasionally, conditions change rapidly and the business faces a risk that was not anticipated. There is not enough time to make changes so the business must assume the risk.

MARKETING RISKS

Business people, including marketers, face a variety of risks. An important marketing function is risk management. *Risk management in marketing includes providing security and safety for products, personnel, and customers, and reducing the risk associated with marketing decisions and activities.* It is possible to analyze the marketing environment and marketing mix to identify the areas where risks are likely to occur.

THE MARKETING ENVIRONMENT

Many factors combine to determine whether a business is successful or not. Those factors include the type of competition, the economy, laws and regulations, technology, and customer demand. Each factor poses risks but also offers opportunities. Marketers are always looking for profitable new opportunities. They are willing to take a risk if there is a real possibility of success. They evaluate opportunities to determine which provide the greatest opportunities with the least risk.

Businesses regularly face the risk of a change in the economy. Sales may be high and customers value the product until faced with a recession. Suddenly, the business is unable to main-

IN THE SPOTLIGHT

IT'S ALL A GAME

Some people take risks when there is little chance for success. Others seldom take risks even when everything seems to be in their favor. Analyzing risks and opportunities is an important skill for business people and consumers alike. Brian Wiersema believes everyone should know how to take financial risks. As a former teacher, he knows that games can be an important teaching tool. He developed *The Reward Game*.

The game helps players understand the influence the economy has on investments. That is certainly not an easy concept. However, Wiersema found that using The Reward Game, even elementary school students could understand it. After playing the game, younger students could do as well as many adults including some stockbrokers.

The Reward Game is played on a board much like Monopoly. Every player starts with cash, stocks, and bonds. During the game inflation can increase the value of those assets or downturns in the economy can reduce their value. As each player moves around the board, there are opportunities to make purchases and investments, or increase savings. Some decisions will be profitable while others will not. Money can be borrowed when needed but players might be surprised by a sudden jump in interest rates.

People who have played The Reward Game come away with a new appreciation for how the economy works. They see that the best decisions can be ruined or poor decisions improved by changes in the economy. However, they also learn that it is possible to understand the factors that can influence the success or failure of investment decisions. Learning through a game is not as risky as spending your own money for the lesson.

Source: New York Times *News Service*

tain sales and profits fall. The same result occurs because of a government action. Increases in taxes, implementation of new laws, or a judgment from a court ruling can require a major change in operations.

New technology and products can enter the market at any time. Those changes can have an immediate effect on a business. Consider how quickly a new video game or a new version of computer software makes existing products out of date. When a few supermarkets and other retail stores converted to scanner technology to speed customer check-outs, other stores had to quickly install the equipment or risk losing customers.

Customer needs can change with little notice. Marketing responds to customers' needs, so such a change will cause a loss of business. Product life cycles illustrate how demand changes for products. Some life cycle stages last only a very short time and require the business to make changes to maintain sales and profits.

THE MARKETING MIX

When selecting from among several target markets, a company reduces its risk if it works with markets that can be clearly identified and located. The company should choose a market for which adequate information is available. A group of customers that has purchased a company's products before and has been very satisfied presents a better opportunity for introducing a new product than a group that has no previous experience with the company. When a company has choices of marketing mixes, the company will often select the one that emphasizes its strengths and that can be completed successfully.

Each of the marketing mix elements is subject to some risks. Those risks should be considered by marketers when planning and implementing marketing decisions.

Product

The product itself faces several risks. Probably the most obvious is the risk of damage before the product is sold or used. The product needs to be designed so it is sturdy and durable. Packaging needs to protect the product while it is transported and stored. You have probably purchased products that were damaged or bro-

ken when you opened them. Perhaps they did not perform the way you expected when you used them. It is likely that you returned the product for a refund. You may have lost confidence in that product and others with the same brand name. A company risks a great deal with a poorly designed product.

Businesses must study how the consumer will use the product. They must be sure it is designed to meet consumer expectations for use. Also if the product will not be consumed immediately, it must not spoil or deteriorate before it is used. Many food products are dated to tell consumers when they were processed or when they should be used. Restaurants that prepare foods in advance have to discard food if it sits too long before being ordered.

The product design must be up-to-date. If competing products have improvements or incorporate new technology, customers will quickly see the differences and switch to those brands. There are many examples of businesses that failed because their products did not change with the times. Even the most loyal customers will not continue to buy the same product when they see that a superior design is available.

The product risk that concerns most businesses is liability. *Liability is a legal responsibility for loss or damage.* We frequently hear or read of a company that has to pay millions of dollars to a person who was injured while using the company's products. Companies are responsible for the design and use of their products. When injury, death, or financial loss occurs that involves a company's product in any way, the company may be held legally liable. Even services are subject to that risk. One of the highest expenses for physicians is the cost of malpractice insurance. The insurance is needed for protection from the cost of lawsuits brought by patients who believe they were mistreated or injured while under the doctor's care.

Distribution

When planning for the distribution of products, businesses need to be concerned about safety, security, and performance of distribution activities. Safety risks include the safety of products, buildings, and equipment; the people involved in distribution activities; and customer safety. Whenever products are moved from one location to another, there are opportunities for damage or injury. Procedures for product handling, storage, and transportation are planned carefully to reduce that possibility. People are trained in proper handling procedures. Safety standards are used in the design of facilities and equipment.

As products move through a channel of distribution, there are many opportunities for theft. Products can be stolen by burglars, by customers who shoplift, and by employees. Security equipment and procedures and security personnel are used to protect against theft. You can see the importance that is placed on security when you visit most retail stores. Well-designed merchandise displays, security tags, video monitors, security personnel, and electronic sensors at all exits are used to reduce shoplifting and employee theft. Even with the thousands of dollars invested in security, shoplifting in many businesses is as much as 10 percent of sales. That loss adds tremendously to the price of products. It also requires special product handling procedures that are an inconvenience to customers and an extra expense to the business.

The final area of business risk related to distribution is the performance of the distribution system. Products need to be available to the customer at the place and time they are needed. If the product is not there, a sale is missed. Products must move through the distribution system efficiently. Ordering and order processing, inventory control, materials handling, and transportation must all work effectively. If an order is misplaced, a shipment is sent to the wrong location, or inventory levels are not maintained at the correct level, customers cannot purchase the products they want. Product damage is another concern in the distribution system. Procedures and equipment are used that protect the products while they move through the channel of distribution.

It is even possible for factors outside the control of a business to interfere with distribution. Poor weather conditions can slow transportation or damage or destroy buildings, equipment, and inventory.

Price

Customers must see the product price as a value. They also must be able to afford the product. Companies face two risks when pricing products and services. The price can be set too

high. This reduces demand causing products to remain unsold. On the other extreme, if products are priced too low, the company is unable to make a profit.

As we learned earlier, setting a product price is very difficult. A number of factors enter into the price including the costs of production, marketing, and operations. Any services offered, discounts, markdowns, and the cost of credit must be figured into the price in order for a profit to be earned. Every business in a channel of distribution must be able to make a profit after paying its costs. Finally, customers will usually compare the cost of a product with those of competitors. You can see why pricing decisions are risky for businesses.

Promotion

What are the risks involved in promoting products and services? The goal of promotion is to communicate with consumers to influence them to purchase the company's products. Anything that interferes with that goal is a business risk. The media need to perform as planned. If a radio or television commercial is not aired as planned or if a newspaper or magazine is not distributed on schedule, the promotional plan is less effective. If a salesperson cannot meet with a customer or does not communicate effectively, sales are lost.

Just as companies are subject to product liability, there are legal responsibilities related to promotion. Information must be honest and accurate or the company may be liable for the harm caused by inappropriate or illegal promotion.

Another area of risk is the damage that can result from the promotion of other businesses or information communicated by other organizations. Sometimes other companies' promotions contain misleading or incorrect information about a competitor's products. While it may be possible to get the company to stop using those promotions, damage may already be done. It is difficult to correct misinformation. Customers who have had a negative experience with a product will often tell many other people about their experiences. That word-of-mouth publicity can be very damaging.

MANAGING MARKETING RISKS

With the large number of risks in marketing, businesses must find ways that prevent those risks from interfering with the marketing plans. The first goal should be to prevent risks. If it is not possible to prevent a risk, plans should be made to reduce the negative effects of a risk on the business and its customers. You will remember that there are four ways to deal with risks. They are to avoid the risk, transfer the risk, assume the risk, or insure the risk. No matter which method is used, careful planning is needed. Risk management is so important to the success of a business that it should be incorporated into the company's marketing plan. In addition to planning, most businesses implement specific security and safety plans, purchase insurance to protect against financial loss, and regularly review marketing activities and operations to identify and reduce risks.

MARKETING PLANNING

Developing a marketing plan provides an ideal opportunity for a business to identify potential risks and make plans to avoid or reduce those risks. Each of the three sections of a marketing plan provides opportunities to identify and develop plans for managing risks (see Figure 20-3).

Reducing Risk with the Marketing Plan

FIGURE 20-3 ■ The marketing plan is a tool that can be used to reduce and manage risk. Risk management should be a part of each section of the marketing plan.

When completing a market analysis, information is gathered on current marketing strategies, competitors, the marketing environment, and strengths and weaknesses of the company. Each of those areas can be studied to determine risks and opportunities. Changes in the economy, new technology, and competitors' actions that can affect a business should be identified as part of the market analysis.

The second section of the marketing plan is used to develop the marketing strategy. Target markets are identified and the marketing mix needed for each market is described. The analysis of market segments to select target markets should include an analysis of the risks that exist in each market. The study of marketing mix alternatives also should review the possible risks. Likely, the business will have choices of mix alternatives. Some will be more risky than others.

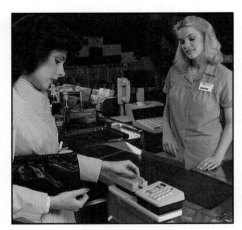

For example, many supermarkets are currently deciding whether to accept credit and debit cards as a method of payment. The alternative is to accept only the traditional choices of cash or check. Credit cards add an additional expense for the business and some additional risk. However, accepting credit cards may keep customers who otherwise would switch to another store. This choice may add customers from stores not accepting credit cards. The business will not always choose the mix with the least risk. However, the business will analyze the risks and compare them to the opportunities presented with each choice.

The final section of the marketing plan is the action plan. In this section the activities and responsibilities for the marketing strategy are identified. Some of the activities and responsibilities will relate to risk reduction. For example, people are given responsibility for quality control, scheduling and coordinating distribution activities, checking promotional plans to make sure they meet all legal requirements, and the many other activities that deal with the risks in marketing. A responsibility of the marketing manager is to carefully review each part of the action plan to determine if risks are adequately addressed.

PROVIDING SECURITY AND SAFETY

The importance of security and safety to businesses has already been identified. Because of its importance, security and safety planning is often a responsibility of people specifically trained in that area. In many businesses, security and safety management is part of the operations area. However, it must be

A GLOBAL VISION

KEEPING DISTRIBUTION ON TRACK

A shipment of oil drilling equipment is loaded on a truck at a factory in Denver, Colorado. It is headed for an oil field in Saudi Arabia. The equipment will travel by train to the coast where it will be transferred to a ship. Once it arrives in the Middle East, it will be transported by truck to its final destination. It will take approximately six weeks and the efforts of four transportation companies for the $200,000 shipment to move through the distribution system. There are many opportunities for the shipment to be lost, stolen, or damaged.

Keeping track of products and ensuring their delivery is a difficult challenge facing marketers. Estimates of losses suffered by the United States trucking industry alone are as high as $5 billion dollars. That figure is low when compared to similar losses in other countries. Improving the record of product distribution presents an obvious business opportunity.

Integrated Cargo Management Systems (ICMS) from San Antonio, Texas, offers a high-tech answer. It has designed a "suitcase" of electronics that is enclosed in the shipping container of a company's products. The suitcase contains a temperature and humidity gauge, a device that measures shocks if the container is dropped or involved in an accident, an instrument that records whether the container is opened, and a camera that records anyone who handles the shipment. The most important part of the product is a radio transmitter. It sends information at any time through a worldwide satellite system that identifies the location of the shipment and its condition. ICMS monitors the signals and informs the shipper, customer, and insurance company whenever there is a problem.

The cost is high ($2,500 for each container plus a $450 per month monitoring fee). But companies with important and expensive shipments are willing to pay the price to help ensure that their products will be delivered safely.

Source: "Cargo that Phones Home," Fortune, November 15, 1993, p. 143.

coordinated throughout the business including marketing activities. Marketers will work with security and safety experts to identify areas needing attention and procedures to use that will reduce those problems.

All marketing personnel should receive special training in safety and security procedures (see Figure 20-4). They should know how to recognize problems and prevent accidents and injuries. They should be aware of company policies regarding security, shoplifting, and theft prevention. Salespeople and customer service personnel need to discuss risks and safety concerns related to product use with customers. Products and packaging should be analyzed to insure that they meet all safety and health requirements. Information should be supplied with all products informing customers about safe handling and use of the products.

1. Know how to recognize problems
2. Know how to prevent accidents and injuries
3. Be aware of company policies

Employee Training in Security and Safety

FIGURE 20-4 ▪ It is important that all employees of a business receive training in safety and security. Well-trained employees can be very effective in reducing the losses suffered by a business.

PURCHASING INSURANCE

One method of transferring risk is to purchase insurance. The payment of insurance premiums transfers some or all of the financial loss for the insured risk to the insurance company. There are some common areas of marketing in which businesses purchase insurance. Those areas are shown in Figure 20-5.

Insurance on marketing personnel includes health and life insurance as well as surety bonds. *A surety bond provides insurance for the failure of a person to perform his or her duties or for losses resulting from employee theft or dishonesty.*

Property insurance protects the buildings, equipment, and in some cases, the inventory of the business. Liability insurance

Common Types of Insurance for Marketing Risks

FIGURE 20-5 ▪ Purchasing insurance is an important way of reducing risk in marketing. There are a variety of specialized policies that insure against common marketing risks.

pays for damage caused to other people or their property. Theft insurance also provides property protection. There are several types of insurance available to protect against damaged and lost merchandise while it is being transported. *Another important type of insurance is product liability insurance which provides protection from claims by people resulting from the use of the company's products.* Similar insurance is available for service businesses. An example is the malpractice insurance for physicians discussed earlier.

REDUCING RISKS

Marketers are constantly searching for opportunities. Those opportunities include new target markets and improved marketing mixes. With every opportunity comes a certain amount of risk. Risks can never be eliminated entirely in marketing. However, careful planning and effective marketing management can avoid some risks and reduce the negative effects of others.

The most important way to reduce risks is with careful planning. The marketing plan provides a useful structure to identify risks and develop ways to deal with them. Another important method of reducing risk is with the careful selection and training of marketing personnel. Employees should be selected who are concerned about customers and their needs. Employees should want to perform their jobs effectively. Then they should be trained to follow safety and security procedures. Finally, all marketing employees should constantly be alert to possible risks that can cause problems for the business or harm to customers or other people. When problems are identified, changes should be made to reduce the risk and avoid damage or loss.

REVIEW

People who open a new business or develop a new product without considering the risks involved face a high probability of failure. On the other hand, those who carefully study markets, competitors, and alternatives increase the chance of discovering very profitable opportunities. Being able to identify risks and develop strategies for dealing with those risks is a critical marketing skill.

Risks can be classified as pure or speculative, controllable or uncontrollable, and insurable or noninsurable. Once a risk is identified, businesses have several choices of ways to deal with the risk. Those methods include transferring the risk, insuring the risk, or assuming the risk.

Marketers work with other people in the business and in the channel of distribution to develop effective plans for managing risks. An important part of risk management is gathering and studying information. Information is needed about the marketing environment and the marketing strategy in order to identify the types of risks that are likely to occur.

The marketing plan provides an excellent tool for developing risk management strategies. Each of the three sections of the plan includes elements related to risk management. It is important that the action plan identifies activities and responsibilities for controlling and reducing risks.

MARKETING FOUNDATIONS

1. **REVIEW TO LEARN**

   Answer the following questions.

   a. Define risk.

   b. Why is it important that business people understand business risks?

   c. Describe the types of risk.

d. Describe the four methods marketers use to deal with risk.

e. Describe how security and safety relate to risk management.

2. LISTS OF FIVE

List five marketing risks, five human risks, and five natural risks faced by a business.

MARKETING RESEARCH

1. RISK IN THE REAL WORLD

Interview a local business person concerning the types of risk faced by her or his business. Use the following questions as a guide for your discussion, but do not limit yourself to these questions.

▪ What industry is your business in?

▪ What types of risk does your business face?

▪ How can you prevent, reduce, or avoid these risks?

After you have completed your interview, bring your results to class and share them with your classmates. Tabulate the class results and answer the following questions.

a. List the types of risks named by each business.

b. Are there similarities and/or differences in the types of risks faced by various businesses?

c. What types of solutions or remedies did the businesses employ to prevent, reduce, or avoid their risks?

2. SHOPLIFTING

The management of a local department store has just received the monthly figures for gross sales and losses due to shoplifting for the past year:

Month	Gross Sales	Dollar Losses Due to Shoplifting
January	$200,356	$ 2,003.56
February	237,595	4,039.11
March	377,920	7,558.40
April	394,395	9,859.75
May	420,400	4,204.00
June	310,497	7,762.42
July	292,304	2,923.04
August	230,422	5,760.55
September	379,295	11,378.85
October	599,395	29,969.75
November	735,284	40,440.62
December	923,502	55,410.12

a. Calculate the percentage of gross sales lost to shoplifting each month.

b. Calculate the total gross sales and the total dollars and percentage of sales lost to shoplifting for the year.

c. Develop a bar graph by month showing the dollar amount lost to shoplifting.

MARKETING PLANNING

1. RISK MANAGEMENT

The best method of reducing risk is to be an informed marketer. The information needed by a marketer is usually gained by maintaining a marketing information system and doing specific market research. Marketers cannot make good decisions without knowing as much as possible about all internal and external influences on their products or services. Using your knowledge of marketing information, describe a marketing risk associated with each of the following areas. Explain how a marketing information system can reduce the risk.

a. New tax laws

b. Increased cost of raw materials needed to manufacture your product

c. Possible strike of transportation workers

d. Price cutting tactic of a major competitor

2. RISK AND POSITIONING

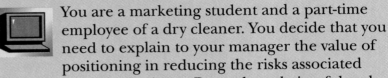

You are a marketing student and a part-time employee of a dry cleaner. You decide that you need to explain to your manager the value of positioning in reducing the risks associated with operating the business. Recently, a chain of dry cleaners has opened in your town. They have taken many of your customers away. Your manager is unsure of how to respond to these problems. In your discussion, remember to explain problems versus opportunities, positioning, and repositioning.

MARKETING MANAGEMENT

1. RISK MANAGEMENT AND NEW PRODUCT DEVELOPMENT

Interactive television/computer systems for the home are currently in the introductory stage. It is predicted that in the near future, these systems will be widely available. Millions of dollars have been invested in the research and development of these interactive systems. Using your knowledge of new product development and risk management, answer the following questions:

a. What type of risk is involved in the development of this revolutionary product?

b. How can a company attempt to minimize the risks? Can they avoid these risks completely?

c. Explain how the steps in the new product development process help minimize risk.

Unit 6 • Managing Risks, Finances, and Information

2. RISK MANAGEMENT AND PRICING STRATEGIES

Utilizing correct pricing strategies is an effective way of managing risk. Explain how the following pricing strategies are used in effective risk management:

a. Penetration pricing

b. Price skimming

c. Non-price competition

d. Discounts

e. Price lining

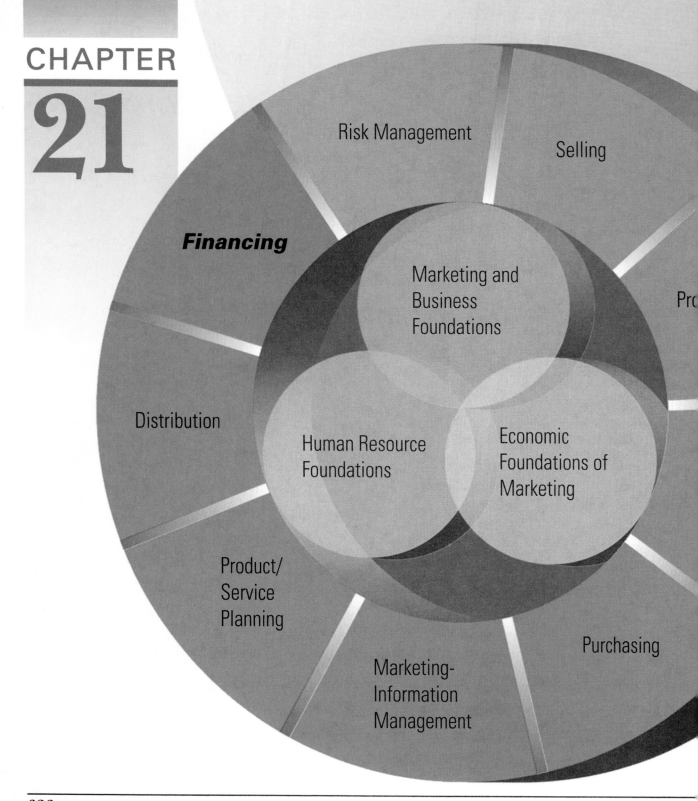

Risk Management

Selling

Financing

Marketing and Business Foundations

Pro

Distribution

Human Resource Foundations

Economic Foundations of Marketing

Product/ Service Planning

Purchasing

Marketing- Information Management

Marketing Requires Money

OBJECTIVES

1. Identify reasons that financial planning is important in marketing.
2. Describe the tools used in financial planning and operations.
3. Demonstrate how revenues and expenses are affected by marketing activities.
4. Analyze marketing revenues and costs to improve financial performance.
5. List sources of financing for capital expenses, inventory, and marketing operations.

NEWSLINE

FRITO-LAY FOCUSES ON FINANCE

If your company was one of the top financial performers in the world, would you be worried? Many companies would be satisfied, but not PepsiCo. Most people know PepsiCo for its major products—Pepsi and the related soft drink brands. But PepsiCo is an international company with products as diverse as Lay's Potato Chips, Pizza Hut pizza, and Crystal Pepsi. PepsiCo owns other businesses including Carts of Colorado, a food cart business that sells food in airports, schools, and shopping malls.

> **Most people know PepsiCo for its major products—Pepsi and the related soft drink brands.**

PepsiCo's Frito-Lay division is the top company in the U.S. salty-snack market, capturing 45 percent of the $9 billion market in 1992. But in the late 1980s, several competitors of Frito-Lay became very aggressive in trying to switch consumer choices. Eagle Snacks made a big push into the consumer market with new prod-

ucts, low prices, and extensive promotion. At the same time, Frito-Lay was increasing its prices and continuing with traditional marketing strategies. The efforts of competitors were noticed by PepsiCo's managers and they decided to act.

The new chairman of Frito-Lay, Roger Enrico, analyzed the company's performance. Market research showed that competing chips were beating Frito-Lay products in taste tests. Cost analysis of company operations demonstrated that money being spent on administration and management cut into the funds available for marketing. Enrico knew that marketing, not administration, had the greatest impact on sales. He decided to make major changes before the competition cut heavily into the company's market share and profits.

New strategies were put in place. Product research was completed resulting in improved texture and taste for existing products. New types and flavors of chips were created and tested. Manufacturing and distribution operations were streamlined. Products were produced faster and at less cost and moved quickly to retailers. The number of managers in

company factories was reduced by 40 percent with many of the employees shifted into selling jobs. Those salespeople worked much more closely with retail outlets. Advertising was designed to create an exciting, fast-paced image for the company. Prices were evaluated and set at more competitive levels when possible.

Profits from snack foods account for almost 40 percent of PepsiCo's profits. It is expected that the streamlined company will increase its profits by 15 percent each year. Attention to competition, marketing strategy, and financial performance should keep the company ahead of the competition.

Source: "If it Ain't Broke, Fix it Anyway," Fortune, Dec. 28, 1992, pp. 49–50.

MARKETING COSTS AFFECT BUSINESS SUCCESS

Marketing costs money. On average, 50 percent or more of the retail price of products and services is needed to pay the cost of marketing activities. Therefore, managing marketing costs is important to the profitability of a business. If marketing costs are carefully controlled, there is more money available to use for important activities such as marketing research, product improvement, and customer services. The result should be greater customer satisfaction. On the other hand, if marketing costs are not well managed, the company does not have the money to improve the marketing mix.

Production costs may need to be reduced, marketing activities cut back, or prices increased to customers. The result is a product or service that is less satisfying to customers and not as competitive with other brands. There will be reduced profits for the company. This makes financial management an important marketing skill.

FINANCIAL PLANNING

One of the results of effective marketing is revenue—the money received from the sale of products and services. In order to sell products, money must be spent to pay for the products and services to be sold. The cost of operating and managing the business must be covered. The expenses of the marketing activities needed to facilitate the exchanges between the business and its customers must be paid. When all of those costs are subtracted from the revenue the result is a profit or loss for the business. This basic financial equation is illustrated in Figure 21-1.

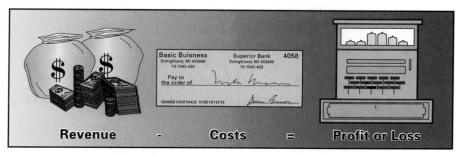

Revenue - **Costs** = **Profit or Loss**

The Basic Financial Equation

FIGURE 21-1 ▪ Businesses must be able to balance the income received with the costs of operating the business. If revenue is higher than expenses, the business makes a profit. If costs are greater than income, the business loses money.

Even in non-profit businesses or other organizations, finances are important. If the expenses of those organizations are higher than the funds available, they cannot operate at the level they would prefer. If expenses exceed revenue they cannot offer the products and services their clients need or expect.

For example, a day-care center might operate as a non-profit organization. However, the center is still involved in marketing. The center must offer the appropriate services in a safe and comfortable facility. It must be open when clients need day-care services, and offer affordable prices. The organization needs to communicate with current and prospective clients about the center's services. If the revenue collected from the clients is not adequate to support the marketing mix, the center will not be able to continue to operate. Therefore, it is important that the manager of the day-care center carefully plans and controls the finances in order to keep the center open and available to families in the community.

THE ROLE OF MARKETING IN FINANCIAL PLANNING

We know that most large organizations have a part of their organization that deals specifically with financial planning and management. Experts in finance and accounting are responsible for maintaining the best possible financial position for their company. These experts assist other managers with planning. They maintain the financial resources and records and they provide information on revenue and expenses.

Even small businesses and other organizations usually have assistance to help managers with financial planning and record keeping. A business may employ an accountant full- or part-time, use an accounting service, or consult a financial planner. There are easy-to-use computer software programs that can help even the newest and smallest organizations with financial decisions.

While marketers may have people and other resources to help them with financial planning, they are still responsible for the revenue and expenses related to marketing activities. Marketers need to identify ways to increase revenues while controlling the costs of marketing. They must decide which markets present the most profitable opportunities and which choices in a marketing mix are the most cost effective.

Let's look at some examples of decisions marketers make that affect the financial performance of a company. One decision is the choice of target markets. A company may have a choice between two markets. One market has a smaller number of potential customers than the second. However, the consumers in the first market spend a higher percentage of their incomes on the product and there are fewer competitors. In another situation, a new international market seems very risky. It may be difficult and expensive for the business to enter a market that is far from their location and with which they have no experience. If the business is not successful in the market a great deal of money will be lost. However, successful entry could mean a very profitable market for many years to come and the opportunity to enter markets in other countries. In each of these examples, the decisions about the target markets determine the amount of sales and revenue that can be obtained.

In the same way, decisions about the marketing mix have an important impact on the company's financial resources. As the product element of the marketing mix is developed, marketers may decide that additional customer services or improved packaging to prevent product damage are needed. Each of those choices increases the cost of the product. However, the changes may also result in increased sales or customers who are willing to pay more because of the improvements.

Distribution decisions can also increase expenses. Examples include using several channels for distribution or operating regional warehouses to reduce the time needed to get products to customers. Expenses involved with the pricing element include offering credit, coupons, or rebates. Expenses associated with the promotion mix element are more frequent advertising, direct marketing efforts such as telemarketing, or additional training for salespeople. Each time marketers consider changes in the marketing mix, they need to study the costs of those changes and predict the effect of the change on sales.

Tools for Financial Planning

Figure 21-1 identifies the three factors that contribute to the financial performance of a business. They are revenue, costs, and results (profit or loss). Managers are responsible for operating the business so that customers are satisfied and the business makes a profit. Several financial tools help managers meet that responsibility. Those tools can be classified as planning tools and operating tools.

Planning Tools

Businesses operate from plans. Plans identify the goals of the business and determine the best ways to achieve those goals. Business plans guide the activities of employees. Plans are used to evaluate the progress of the business in meeting its goals. Two important types of financial plans are forecasts and budgets.

Forecasts

Plans are based on estimates of future events. Managers want those estimates to be as accurate as possible. They prepare forecasts to aid in planning. *Financial forecasts are numerical predictions of future performance related to revenue and expenses.* Forecasts are usually made for a period of at least a year or more into the future. Some companies develop forecasts for as long as five years. However, those forecasts are usually not as accurate as shorter forecasts. Conditions can change that cause long-range forecasts to become inaccurate.

The most important financial forecasts for marketing are sales, market share, and marketing expenses. Sales forecasts predict the quantity of sales or the dollar volume of sales for a product or a specific market. For example, a sales forecast may predict the sales of a product to increase by 5 percent for each of the next two years and then by 3 percent for the third year. Forecasts of market share anticipate the percentage of sales in a market that will be made by each of the major competitors. A furniture store that currently has 13 percent of the market in a city will need to determine how to respond to a forecast that projects its share dropping to 11 percent in two years. Expense forecasts project changes in the amount a company will need to spend for specific operations or activities. A forecast for a wholesale company that uses trucks to distribute products projects transportation costs to increase by 18 percent in five years due to an anticipated gasoline shortage.

Budgets

When planning for a shorter time period, managers use budgets. *Budgets are detailed projections of financial performance for a specific time period (usually one year or less).* When managers identify the activities that must be completed to accomplish the goals of the business, they develop budgets to anticipate the costs of the activities and the revenue that can be expected. Two common examples of budgets used in marketing are sales and advertising budgets. However, budgets are usually developed for each product, market, and major marketing activity.

OPERATING TOOLS

Managers use several financial tools to determine the effectiveness of operations. Those tools are known as financial statements. *Financial statements are detailed summaries of the specific financial performance for a business or a part of the business.* The important financial statements for marketers are income statements and balance sheets.

An income statement reports on the amount and source of revenue and the amount and type of expenses for a specific period of time. The purpose of an income statement is to determine if the business earned a profit or loss on its operations. A sample income statement is shown in Figure 21-2 on the next page.

An income statement can be developed to analyze the profitability of the entire company or just one operating unit of the company. For example, Toys "R" Us operates stores in many different countries. They can develop an income statement for the entire corporation which includes the income and expenses of all stores in every country. They can also analyze the performance of all of the stores operating in a specific country or region of a country. Finally, each store will also have its own income statements. Managers may also want to determine the profitability of specific parts of the business operations. An income statement can be developed for a specific market, category of customers, product, or product category. The income statement in Figure 21-2 analyzes the profitability of sales of a product from four different regions of the country.

Sample Income Statement

Dendum Products, Inc.
Income Statement
For the Period Ending June 30, 19—

Revenues:
  Gross Sales:
      NE region $123,528
      NW region 195,426
      SE region 232,965
      SW region 148,258
          Total Gross Sales $700,177
  Less Sales Returns:
      NE region ....$ 6,123
      NW region 5,896
      SE region 8,344
      SW region 7,421
          Total Sales Returns 27,784
  Net Sales...$672,393

  Cost of Products Sold:
      Inventory, January 1, 19— ....$ 86,593
      Purchases $583,226
      Less: Purchase Returns ....– 6,048
            Purchase Discounts ....– 3,582
      Net Purchases 573,596
    Total Cost of Products For Sale $660,189
      Inventory, June 30, 19— ....– 78,190
      Net Cost of Products Sold 581,999
Gross Margin ....$ 90,394

  Operating Expenses:
      Rent Expense ....$ 8,225
      Bad Debts Expense 695
      Credit Card Fee Expense 1,200
      Transportation Expense 10,150
      Equipment Purchases 860
      Equipment Depreciation 620
      Insurance Expense 1,050
      Salaries and Wages 12,845
      Payroll Taxes 1,926
      Supplies Expense 734
      Advertising Expense 18,040
          Total Operating Expenses 56,345
Net Income Before Taxes ....$ 34,049

FIGURE 21-2 ▪ An income statement is an important financial tool for marketers. It shows the relationship between sales and expenses in order to determine if operations are profitable.

A balance sheet describes the type and amount of assets, liabilities, and capital in a business on a specific date. Assets include the things the business owns. Liabilities are the amounts the business owes. The difference between the amount of assets and the amount of liabilities is the actual value of the business, or capital. Managers must be able to identify changes in those amounts to determine if the financial condition of the business is improving or declining. Figure 21-3 shows an example of a balance sheet.

Marketers use income statements to determine if marketing activities are resulting in an adequate volume of sales. They are also used to identify the costs of the activities needed to achieve

Sample Balance Sheet

Froerich Fundamentals
Balance Sheet
December 31, 19—

ASSETS

Current Assets:
Cash	$ 95,436	
Accounts Receivable	42,827	
Product Inventory	135,673	
Supplies	21,128	
Prepaid Insurance	2,442	
Total Current Assets		$ 297,506

Capital Assets:
Buildings	$647,545	
Vehicles	97,221	
Equipment	228,322	
Capital Assets	$973,088	
Less: Depreciation of Capital Assets	13,286	
Total Capital Assets		959,802
Total Assets		$1,257,308

LIABILITIES

Current Liabilities:
Accounts Payable	$ 92,286	
Mortgage Payable	296,243	
Notes Payable	63,552	
Payroll Taxes Payable	71,074	
Insurance Payable	6,995	
Total Liabilities		$ 530,150

CAPITAL

Retained Earnings	$286,680	
Owners' Equity	440,478	
Total Capital		727,158
Total Liabilities and Capital		$1,257,308

FIGURE 21-3 ▪ A balance sheet shows the relationship between the assets and liabilities of a business.

that sales volume. Important information that marketers obtain from balance sheets includes the value of assets used for marketing activities, the levels of inventory of products for sale, and the amount owed by customers who have been offered credit. A balance sheet also identifies if the company has money available to spend on such things as new product development, buildings, equipment, and other resources needed to improve marketing activities.

USING FINANCIAL TOOLS

Marketers work with finance and accounting experts to develop and use financial tools. Some of the information used to prepare forecasts, budgets, and financial statements comes from the marketing department and its operations. Marketers help to collect and report the necessary information. When the reports are prepared in accounting and finance, they are distributed to marketing personnel for use in decision-making. Marketers must be able to understand and interpret financial statements. Marketers use the information to develop marketing plans and to improve marketing operations.

Developing Forecasts and Budgets

Financial plans are not helpful unless they are reasonably accurate. Planners use several methods to develop good forecasts and budgets. The most common planning method to use is past performance. By comparing the forecasts and budgets from previous years with the actual results, planners can see which ones were accurate and which were not. Using that past experience makes planning more accurate.

A second method is to use information from comparable businesses and markets to develop plans. Often trade associations or information services collect and report on the financial performance of businesses in a particular industry. Some government agencies, including the Department of Commerce, also gather and report financial information on businesses.

Additionally, planners can look for related figures that help to predict performance. For example, the number of tires that an auto service business might sell can be based on the number of cars in a market and the age of those cars. The original tires on a car will normally need to be replaced between two and three years after the car is sold.

Identifying the number of those cars in the shopping area of the business will help in developing a forecast for tire sales.

The most effective way to develop a budget for marketing expenses is to calculate the costs of performing the necessary marketing tasks. Here again, the marketing plan is an effective tool. A marketing plan describes the marketing activities necessary to implement the marketing mix. The marketing manager analyzes each of the planned activities to determine what personnel and resources will be needed. Then the wages, costs of resources, and the amounts of all other expenses are matched with each activity. When all of those items are totaled, the marketing manager has a specific estimate of the amount that needs to be budgeted for that activity. An example of that type of budget development is shown in Figure 21-4.

Developing a Budget for a Marketing Activity	
Planned Monthly Customer Service Department Expenses	
Management Salary	$ 4,028
Personnel Wages	18,840
Facility Expense (space and utilities)	3,526
Office Equipment	305
Telephone Expense	498
Computer Expense	295
Postage	86
Supplies	175
Travel Expense	830
Product Returns and Replacements	644
Total Budgeted Expenses	$29,227

FIGURE 21-4 ▪ A budget is a tool that a marketing manager can use to anticipate the expenses of implementing a part of a marketing mix. In this example, the manager can analyze the costs and benefits of operating a customer service department.

Gathering Information for Financial Statements

The information needed to prepare income statements and balance sheets is the actual financial performance of the business. Therefore, the marketing department is responsible for maintaining accurate records on sales, expenses, inventory levels, customer accounts, and equipment. This information is then available to prepare the statements.

Traditionally, employees were asked to record information while completing a marketing activity or after the activity was completed. For example, when a sale was made, information

about the customer, product, and terms of the sale would be recorded on a purchase order, invoice, or sales receipt. In retail businesses, the information may have been recorded by punching keys on a cash register or a point-of-purchase computer.

Today, much of the information is captured through electronic scanners and bar codes on products. As products move through a manufacturing and distribution process, the bar codes are scanned automatically or by employees using scanning equipment. Additional information can be entered along with the bar code data using a keyboard, touch-screen, or even an electronic pen.

Federal Express, United Parcel Service, and other delivery companies track each item they handle using this technology. From the time packages are received to the time they are delivered information on each item is maintained in computers. Reports on numbers of items delivered, speed of delivery, costs, and location can be obtained at any time.

BUDGETING FOR MARKETING ACTIVITIES

Every activity in a business costs money. Businesses have limited amounts of money to use in financing their operations. Decisions need to be made on the most effective use of that money. Those decisions often start with the top executives of the company who develop a general budget. The budget will contain an amount for marketing. Marketing managers then decide the best way to use the marketing budget. They will do that by analyzing the expenses involved in marketing.

A marketing strategy provides the basis for developing the marketing budget. The marketing strategy identifies the target markets that the business intends to serve and the marketing mixes to be used for each market. As we learned earlier in the book, a written marketing plan is prepared to show how the business will implement the marketing strategy. The plan describes the activities to be completed and the resources needed.

The people involved in developing a marketing plan often find they do not have adequate resources to develop the most effective marketing mix. For example, research might show that customers prefer a product with several options that is sold through a large number of outlets. Yet the company cannot afford to spend money on both product improvements and more

CLASSICS AND CONTEMPORARIES

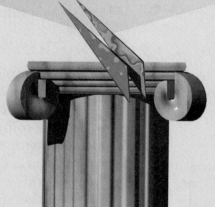

GOODBYE SEARS CATALOG

Ask anyone who lived in the United States between 1885 and 1993 and they will remember the Sears catalog. It was the store at home offering access to thousands of products through the convenience of the telephone or mailbox. However, for future generations, the *Big Book* will only be a memory. Sears decided to get out of the catalog business, and 1993 was the last year the catalog was published.

How can a company decide to abandon a product that was successful for 97 years and was the market leader for most of that time? Even in its last full year of operations, it earned the company $3.3 billion in sales. However, even with that much income, the catalog continued to lose more and more money.

Industry experts suggest that the catalog concept has not died; Sears just could not adjust to the changing conditions of the market. Customers no longer have to rely on catalog sales as in the first half of the century. At that time, access to the latest consumer products was restricted to large cities. Customers in rural areas and small towns used the Sears catalog to see what was new and to have a full range of products to purchase. Today, most people are less than 15 minutes from a major department or discount store, or they can use a television shopping channel 24-hours-a-day.

Sears has always appealed to the broad shopping needs of the middle class, and the Sears catalog followed the same strategy. They sold some of everything but were neither top-of-the-line nor lowest cost. Even into the 1990s, Sears' huge catalog offered everything from tires and batteries, appliances and lawn care products, to family fashions, all with little visual appeal. At the same time, other catalog businesses were moving to limited lines of specialty items with a very high-quality visual presentation. In fact, even though Sears was losing money, the catalog sales industry was growing an average of 10 percent in new sales each year. This was much better than the 2–3 percent growth rate in other parts of the retail industry. By 1992, the total volume of catalog sales in the United States had reached almost $60 billion.

In catalog sales the new emphasis is on niche marketing, low-cost operations, quick customer response, and high levels of service. Sears decided it could not respond and gave up the $3 billion dollar business. Other retailers cannot wait to jump into the big gap left by the death of the *Big Book*.

Source: "It Was the Worst of Times," Marketing News, *March 15, 1993, pp. 1–2.*

extensive distribution. A decision needs to be made whether to put more money into the product or into distribution. That decision is often based on which of the mix elements is most important to the customer, the type of mix offered by the competition, and the actual costs of each choice to the company.

The marketing mix and budget are also affected by the way the company has spent money in the past. If the company was responsible for the transportation of its products, it may have invested in trucks or other equipment needed to move products from the business to customers. Warehouses or distribution centers may have been built to handle the inventory. If the company has already made those investments, it will typically try to use marketing mixes that take advantage of those resources. However, if a company has relied on other businesses to store and transport products in the past, it may be very expensive for the company to change and provide those marketing activities now.

EFFECTS OF MARKETING ON REVENUE

Marketing activities are completed to generate revenue. Most of the revenue for a business results from the sale of products and services. The marketing plan identifies the markets that the company plans to serve. Marketing activities are developed to meet the needs of customers in the market so they will purchase the products or services offered by the company. There are several parts of the marketing mix that can affect the amount of revenue. Sources of revenue affected by mix elements are shown in Figure 21-5.

Sales of Products and Services

The primary objective of a marketing strategy is for the business to obtain the most profitable level of sales possible while satisfying a target market. The marketing mix is developed to increase customer satisfaction by offering a product or service that is different from and better than those offered by competitors. It is possible for a company to improve a product by offering additional features and options, better packaging, or customer services. The product can be made available in a more convenient or more appropriate location. Credit can be offered to make the product more affordable.

Revenue Sources from Marketing Activities

FIGURE 21-5 ■ Most of the revenue a business receives is the result of sales of its primary products and services. However, there are other ways that income can be earned.

Promotion and other types of communication can clearly show the customer the value of the product and how it can be used most effectively. Marketers need to study the impact of each mix choice on sales and profits and select the mix that achieves the best combination for the company. The most important source of revenue for an organization is the sale of its primary products and services.

Several factors can reduce the level of sales. Customers may not be satisfied with a product because it is damaged, is not what the seller promised, or does not meet the customers' needs. In those cases customers will return the product to the seller and expect a replacement or a refund. Returned and replacement products reduce the level of sales and add to the seller's costs.

After-Sale and Related Revenue

It has been said that a current customer is more profitable than a prospective customer. There are ways to increase sales to existing customers while satisfying their needs. Automobile dealers and movie theaters provide two examples of this marketing strategy. Selling automobiles today is a very competitive business. Customers carefully shop for the best price so dealerships often have to cut prices so low they make little profit on the sale of the automobiles. Profit for the business comes from activities that occur after the sale. A very important source of revenue and profit for automobile dealers comes from servicing and repairing automobiles they have sold. They work very hard to encourage customers to return to the dealership for service.

In the same way, many movie theaters rely on the sale of other products to operate profitably. Most movies are shown several times a day for many weeks. The first few times the movie is shown, the theater may be full of customers and the sale of tickets by itself will make a profit. Later on, however, the movie is shown to fewer customers at a time. The sale of concession items (popcorn, soft drinks, candy, posters) provides the opportunity for the theater to make a profit when ticket

sales alone do not. Think of the number of businesses that have a variety of products they sell that complement the original purchase.

Sometimes businesses identify other ways of generating revenues in addition to the sale of the primary products and services. Restaurants may sell T-shirts, coffee mugs, or packaged popular food items (salad dressings, seasonings). Those sales are both effective promotional tools as well as another source of revenue. In the northern states, construction businesses often see their profits reduced during winter months because of poor weather. If there is a great deal of snow, the businesses may not be able to maintain their normal work schedules. Some of those businesses that own trucks or other construction equipment may contract with cities or large businesses to clean the snow from streets and parking lots. This provides some revenue during a time when they otherwise would not be able to operate.

Credit and Interest

Many purchases are made with cash. As soon as the sale is made, the seller receives payment. However, when credit is offered to customers, the sale is not complete. Financial statements often include an item called accounts receivable. Accounts receivable are sales for which the company has not yet been paid. Credit is often offered to increase sales beyond the amount that is possible if customers have to pay cash.

Many businesses use credit services offered by other companies rather than developing and managing a credit department. For example, a retail store may accept credit cards such as MasterCard, VISA, or Discover. The credit card company pays the retailer who accepted the customer's credit card for the amount of the purchase. It is then the credit card company's responsibility to collect the account from the customer who made the credit purchase. In return for using the credit card company, the retail business is charged a fee which usually amounts to 2–6 percent of the total amount of their credit sales.

Some companies have their own credit systems or even their own credit cards which can be used only for the purchase of products from their business. There are several costs for the companies who choose to manage their own credit services. The company needs to design the credit system and determine the terms that will be offered to customers. Then personnel must be hired and trained to manage the credit system. Computers and other equipment are needed to maintain the credit records, billing, payments, and other information. Since credit customers do not pay for their purchases for a month or more after the sale is made, additional money is needed to finance the expenses of the company until payment is received.

Even with the most careful and effective credit system, some customers do not pay their accounts when billed. Businesses offering credit usually charge interest to their customers to pay for the credit services. If all accounts are paid on time, it is possible that the interest charges will even provide a profit for the company. However, a percentage of credit accounts may remain uncollected. Even a small amount that is unpaid eliminates any profit the company makes on credit sales and actually reduces the total dollar amount of sales. Companies offering credit to customers work to develop effective credit procedures to reduce the amount of unpaid accounts. They carefully track the age of the unpaid accounts. If an account remains unpaid for several months beyond its due date, it will likely never be paid.

No matter how carefully credit accounts are managed by a company, it is not unusual to have 1–2 percent of credit sales that are uncollectable. Those uncollected accounts and the cost of collection activities are an important business expense. While credit may appear to be an important service to offer customers, businesses must carefully study whether the increases in sales resulting from credit actually adds to or reduces the amount of profit.

Companies that offer credit need to be aware of laws that regulate credit activity. Among the important federal laws are the Equal Credit Opportunity Law that prevents companies from discriminating among the people to whom they offer credit. The Truth-in-Lending Act identifies the type of information businesses must provide to credit customers. The Fair Credit Reporting Act regulates the use of the credit information that businesses gather about individual customers. Also, the methods companies use to collect money owed by customers are controlled under the Fair Debt Collection Practices Act.

The seller may offer the customer a discount on the price charged if the customer is not satisfied or receives less than promised. Again, the amount of discounts reduces the sales volume. If the company offers a rebate to customers, the amount of the rebates must be subtracted from the total sales.

EXPENSES ASSOCIATED WITH THE MARKETING MIX

Just as the sale of products and services by marketers results in income for a business, the completion of marketing activities adds to the business' expenses. There are expenses associated with each of the marketing mix elements. The following sections review the common marketing expenses for each part of the marketing mix.

Product Expenses

The majority of expenses related to product development for manufacturers is a part of the production budget. Those expenses include the cost of materials, equipment, and personnel needed to produce the product. Also, the cost of packaging is considered a production cost. For wholesale and retail businesses, products must be purchased from other companies so their costs are determined by the prices paid for the merchandise.

There are other expenses related to the product mix element. The expenses associated with offering a guarantee or warranty as well as the costs of repairing items that are damaged or fail must be included. In addition, many businesses offer customer services, some of which can be very expensive. Some services are offered as part of the actual sale such as delivery and set up or training. Other services are provided for a long time after the sale while the customer is using the product. For example, many computer software companies have technicians who will work with a customer if they are having problems with a product. General Electric has a toll-free telephone number that customers can call to get information about the use of any product the company manufactures ranging from small appliances to large industrial equipment. Several automobile manufacturers offer a 24-hour-a-day roadside repair service for their customers.

Distribution Expenses

Distribution costs are a major area of marketing expenses. Companies have the costs of transportation, storage, and display for their products. These costs include long-term expenses, such as buildings and equipment, and short-term expenses, such as wages and supplies. Even service businesses have expenses associated with delivering the services to customers or operating the location where customers come to purchase the services. In addition to the obvious costs of distribution, other expenses for most businesses include the costs of developing and managing the channels of distribution, inventory control costs, materials handling expenses, and the costs of order processing.

Price Expenses

The major expense related to the price mix element is the cost of offering credit, discussed earlier. Another price expense item is the cost of communicating prices to customers. This may seem like an unimportant item. However, consider the thousands of items that a business stocks and sells during one year. If each item has to have the price identified on it, the cost of printing the stickers or tags and the expense of placing the price on the item can be high. Then if a price change has to be made, the cost increases. Many retail businesses, such as supermarkets, found the time and expense of pricing products so great that they have introduced other methods. The products no longer carry price stickers. Instead the price is posted on the display shelf. The price is stored in the company's computer and is identified through the bar code on the product package. A price change is made by changing the amount in the computer and updating the price on the product display.

Promotion Expenses

There are many costs associated with promotion. Few inexpensive ways are available for companies to communicate with customers. Each type of promotion has its own set of expenses.

Advertising is the most common type of promotion. The major cost of advertising is the expense of purchasing space in newspapers or magazines or buying time on television or radio. However, it is also expensive to create and produce the advertisements. Those expenses include the salaries of a variety of creative people as well as the equipment and materials they need for their work.

Selling is also an expensive promotional method. An important cost of selling is the salaries of salespeople. However, additional costs include training and management as well as the equipment, materials, and product samples salespeople use. Salespeople for manufacturers often travel regularly to meet with customers. Their sales territories can cover several states or even several countries. The costs of operating an automobile, airplane tickets, hotel rooms, meals, and other related expenses can be several hundred dollars each day. You can see that salespeople need to be very effective in order to make enough sales just to cover their expenses.

It is said that the most inexpensive form of promotion is word of mouth. But companies that want customers to help sell their products often spend money to insure that it is done well. When a customer buys a product, the company may make a follow-up telephone call to make sure the customer is satisfied. Letters and gifts may be sent to show that the company appreciates the customer's business. Some companies offer satisfied customers money or other incentives if they identify a prospective customer who ends up buying a product.

CLASSIFYING MARKETING EXPENSES

To determine the amount of money needed in a budget, marketing expenses need to be classified as either long term or short term. Long-term expenses are items that the company can use for several years. Short-term expenses are for current activities or items used within a short time, typically less than a year. Long-term expenses are usually paid for over an extended period of time. They are often financed by borrowing money from a bank or other financial institution. Normally, short-term expenses must be paid for when they are purchased. Sometimes they are financed with credit from the seller that will be paid within one or a few months. Figure 21-6 illustrates examples of long-term and short-term marketing expenses.

Long-Term Marketing Expenses

Most of the long-term costs to a business are used for production or operations rather than marketing. The costs of land, buildings, and equipment are the typical expenses in this category. Some marketing plans identify land and building needs. In the earlier example, a company that distributes products may need buildings, vehicles, and equipment for product storage

Long-Term Marketing Expenses

Short-Term Marketing Expenses

Classifying Marketing Expenses

FIGURE 21-6 ▪ Marketing expenses are both long-term and short-term. Long-term expenses are paid for over a number of years while short-term expenses are usually paid for in less than one year.

and handling. Manufacturers using direct sales to customers through factory outlet stores need to build or rent facilities and equipment for retail operations. The increased use of technology in other parts of marketing will require investments in special equipment. For example, computers are essential for effective marketing research and marketing information management. Companies that use telemarketing or provide customer information and service often invest in telephone systems, computers, and other office equipment. Advertising and other types of promotion require sophisticated audio, video, and print production equipment and facilities. While most companies hire advertising agencies and production companies to develop their advertising and promotional materials, some larger companies maintain their own facilities, equipment, and personnel for those tasks.

Short-Term Marketing Expenses

Most marketing expenses result from performing specific marketing activities that are completed in a short period of time. Those types of expenses depend on the marketing mix, but there are a common set of short-term expenses that most businesses have. They include the cost of salaries and wages, administrative costs, operating expenses, order processing, customer services, advertising and promotion, and transportation costs. Examples of short-term marketing expenses are shown in the income statement in Figure 21-2.

ANALYZING FINANCIAL INFORMATION

Information available from financial tools can be very valuable in improving marketing decisions. Forecasts and budgets are evaluated to determine their accuracy. The projections are compared with actual performance. When differences are found, they are studied to determine why the differences occurred and what can be done to reduce the amount of difference in the future. It is possible that the projections were not accurate so methods used to develop the forecasts and budgets need to be modified. On the other hand, marketing activities may have been less effective than anticipated and must be improved.

TYPES OF FINANCIAL ANALYSIS

Financial statements are evaluated to determine the changes that occur from one period of operations to the next. A marketing manager studies a specific market to determine if sales are increasing or decreasing. Inventory levels can be compared from year to year, as can the amount owed by customers. If the information shows that the financial performance is improving, the marketing manager will want to continue with the same activities. On the other hand if sales are decreasing or inventories and customer accounts are increasing, marketing activities need to be changed to correct the problems.

Another type of analysis is to compare one type of financial performance to another. For example, sales volume can be compared to advertising expenses. If expenses are going up at a faster rate than sales, a problem may be developing. Other important comparisons in marketing are the level of inventory to sales, costs of transportation compared to costs of product handling and storage, and comparing the cost of the product to marketing expenses.

USING FINANCIAL INFORMATION

We know that information is essential for effective market-ing. Marketing research provides information to aid in the un-derstanding of customers. Financial information is needed to be able to determine what marketing activities the organization can afford to complete and the impact of those activities on profits. Some people do not consider that marketers need to understand accounting and finance. However, you can see that financial planning is an important marketing skill.

Marketers use financial information to identify how to in-crease revenue and reduce costs. As shown in Figure 21-7, if a greater volume of sales can be achieved while controlling ex-penses, profits will increase. In the same way if sales can be maintained while reducing the costs of marketing, the company will also be able to increase profits.

Increasing Revenues

Increased revenue results from selling more products and services. Financial information is analyzed to determine the products that sell the best and the customer groups who buy the most products. Efforts are directed at the best products and markets. Poor performing products and markets are ei-ther improved or dropped. Each time a new marketing plan is

Marketing Strategies to Increase Profits

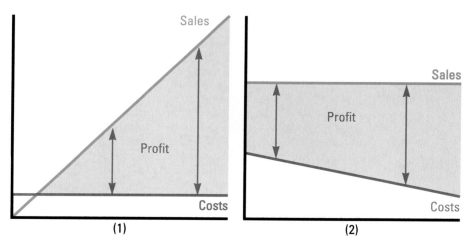

FIGURE 21-7 ▪ When the goal of a business is increased profits, marketers have two ways of accomplishing the goal. (1) They can work to achieve a higher level of sales while holding costs steady. (2) If sales are not increasing, marketers can reduce the cost of achieving that sales level.

A GLOBAL VISION

THE WORLD BANK

Where does the world go to do its banking? In the 60s and 70s, U.S. banks led the world in assets and loans. They regularly loaned money and provided other banking services to businesses throughout the world. Today, the top commercial banks in the world are very different. Of the top ten banks, eight are Japanese banks and two are headquartered in France. The largest U.S. bank in international banking is Citicorp, which ranks 25th.

Several reasons led to the change in leadership. Many of the loans U.S. banks made to foreign governments and businesses were not repaid when the world economy experienced a downturn in the 1970s. Not only was a great deal of money lost, but the banks became much more cautious about international lending. U.S. banking operates under very different rules and regulations than banks in other countries. When the U.S economy entered a deep recession in the 1980s, regulators required banks to cut down on high-risk loans. At the same time, they had to pay more for the funds they borrowed than did banks in many other countries. This provided the opportunity for foreign banks to improve their market position.

Today's banks are facing a new type of competition, however. It is not just banks from other countries, but financial services businesses that are positioned to better meet the needs of international business. Diversified financial service firms offer a wide range of products, including securities, insurance, financing, investment banking, brokerage services, and a variety of information and management services. These firms provide complete financial assistance worldwide to meet the specific needs of each business. With this new type of product, U.S. businesses compete quite well. Five of the top ten international diversified financial services companies are headquartered in the United States.

Just as in any market, businesses must be able to change and respond to customer needs, economic conditions, and competition. While U.S. banks have had difficulty in the international financial markets, the emerging full-service financial firms are meeting the challenge.

Source: "The Global Service 500," Fortune, August 24, 1992, pp. 213, 215.

developed, the marketing manager will identify the most important products and markets for that planning period.

Marketers are also concerned that an effective price for a product is maintained. It is possible that more products can be sold to customers if discounts are offered or the price is reduced. Some salespeople who have control over price are quick to reduce the price believing that is the only way the customer will buy. However, the lower price may reduce revenue to the point where a profit cannot be made. Salespeople who understand customer needs make an effective presentation of the entire marketing mix in response to those needs. They know that customers look for the best value, not the lowest price.

Reducing and Controlling Costs

Marketing managers are very concerned about reducing and controlling the costs of marketing activities. When businesses are in very competitive markets, it is often the company that operates efficiently that makes a profit. Businesses that are concerned about satisfying customer needs must be very careful in cutting costs. Marketing activities that are important to customers cannot be eliminated without considering the impact on customer satisfaction. However, it is often possible to find ways to perform marketing activities in a less costly way while keeping the same level of customer service. For example, an insurance company provided its salespeople with personal computers to reduce the number of forms to be completed. The company also wanted to cut the time it took for information to be exchanged between the salesperson and the company. The company found that the use of computers not only reduced expenses by over 15 percent but also cut the number of errors on insurance applications by nearly 5 percent.

Another example of reducing marketing expenses comes from a large supermarket in the Southeast. They operate a very large fleet of trucks to deliver products from their warehouses to their stores. The trucks would deliver the products and return to the warehouse empty. The transportation manager started to identify suppliers of products that were located in the towns where the supermarket had stores. When a truck was delivering a load from the warehouse to a store, the manager would determine if a nearby supplier had an order to be sent to the warehouse. If so, the supermarket's truck would pick up the order and bring it back rather than driving back empty. This procedure saved the company several thousands of dollars each month in transportation costs.

Marketing employees as well as managers need to be aware of the costs of marketing activities and identify ways to reduce expenses. It is often possible to identify ways that marketing activities can be performed more efficiently, the amount of supplies or materials can be reduced, or waste can be eliminated. Many companies provide incentives for employees who can identify important cost savings.

FINANCING MARKETING ACTIVITIES

An important part of financial planning is identifying the sources of money needed to pay for marketing activities and expenses. Marketers work with the executives and financial managers of a business to identify financial needs. They must also identify the methods that will be used to obtain the needed money. The three main types of financial needs as shown in Figure 21-8 are capital expenses, inventory expenses, and operating expenses.

CAPITAL EXPENSES

Capital expenses are long-term investments in land, buildings, and equipment. They are usually financed by money borrowed from a financial institution such as a bank or insurance company. Some manufacturers participate in long-term loans to

Financing Marketing Activities

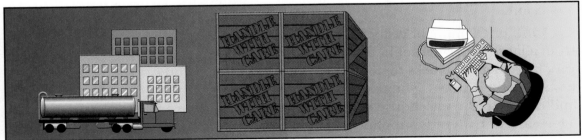

Capital Expenses   Inventory Expenses   Operating Expenses

FIGURE 21-8 ▪ Money is needed to finance marketing activities. Marketing managers must work with finance personnel and other managers in a business to determine the amount and sources of funds necessary for effective marketing operations.

their customers to help finance a major equipment purchase. It is also possible to lease equipment and buildings rather than buying them. The financial personnel of an organization are usually responsible for arranging for financing of capital purchases.

INVENTORY EXPENSES

Inventory is the assortment and quantities of products the company maintains for sale to customers. Inventories for manufacturers are produced with the anticipation that they will be sold to customers. For other channel members, inventories are purchased and then resold to their customers. The cost of the inventory is not recovered until the products are sold and the customer pays for the purchase.

Financing of inventory is usually done in one of two ways. Short-term loans may be obtained from financial institutions. However, most banks will not loan the full value of the inventory since it may not be sold. The other common method of financing inventory is through credit extended by the seller. Since most sellers will only finance the sale for a very short period of time (often 30–60 days), the purchasing company must be able to sell the inventory quickly in order to pay for the order on time. In both cases, the purchaser pays interest on the money borrowed and includes the cost of financing in the price of the products.

OPERATING EXPENSES

The final category of marketing expenses are operating expenses. These are the costs of the day-to-day activities of marketing. They include salaries and wages, materials and supplies, advertising and special promotions, and offering customer services. Marketing expenses include the variety of other marketing activities completed regularly to sell products and services and to meet customer needs. The operating costs are normally paid as they are incurred or shortly after. The money for payment of operating expenses comes from the cash on hand in the business and the income from sales. Monthly and weekly budgets and financial reports monitor operating expenses and income to insure that money is available to pay the expenses. Marketing managers pay careful attention to operating budgets and make changes rapidly if it appears that operating expenses are too high or revenues are too low.

REVIEW

The financing function of marketing involves planning for the effective use of resources, collecting and analyzing information, and improving marketing activities in order to increase revenue and decrease costs. Because marketing activities cost a great deal of money, it is important that the money is spent effectively.

There are several tools that aid marketers with financial planning. Forecasts are used for long-range planning, while budgets are used for short-term planning. After planning is completed, financial statements, including income statements and balance sheets, are used by managers to make operating decisions. Marketing managers must know how to develop forecasts and budgets. They must know how to analyze financial statements and use the information in planning marketing strategies.

Marketing activities affect the revenue of a company as well as its expenses. Target markets and marketing mixes should be studied to identify ways to increase revenue and control costs. The result should be increased profits for the company.

Marketing can be very expensive. There are several important categories of marketing costs including capital expenses, inventory costs, and operating costs. Sources of financing need to be developed for each category of costs. Those sources include financial institutions, credit offered by sellers, cash available in the business, and money obtained from the sale of products and services.

MARKETING FOUNDATIONS

1. OBTAINING FINANCIAL ASSISTANCE

 You are the marketing manager for EnviroSaf, a company that has developed a new type of lawn care product that controls weeds and insects without chemicals. The product is currently sold through garden centers in eight states in the northwestern United States. You are responsible for all distribution and promotion activities, and for completing marketing research. You work with other managers to set product prices, to develop and provide customer services, and to complete new product planning. You believe that 0-you can make the most effective decisions if you have financial information available related to the marketing activities you control.

Develop a one-page memo to Mr. Francis Payton, Chief Financial Officer of EnviroSaf. In the memo, identify the types of financial information you need, the financial tools that will help you with planning and operations, and why it is important for the marketing manager to be involved in financial planning for the business. Use information from the chapter to help you prepare the memo.

2. **LIST TWO**

From information provided in the chapter, list two examples for each of the following:

a. Parts of the basic financial equation that determine whether a company makes a profit or not

b. Types of financial plans

c. Types of financial statements

d. Methods used to develop good forecasts and budgets

e. Ways that marketing personnel can gather financial information

f. Sources of revenue resulting from marketing activities

g. Categories of marketing expenses based on length of time

h. Types of financial analysis that will be helpful in marketing decision making

i. Ways that an understanding of financial information can be used by marketing managers in order to increase profits

j. Main types of financial needs in marketing

MARKETING RESEARCH

1. SOURCES OF FINANCIAL INFORMATION

 Two important methods of planning and analyzing financial information are (1) comparable information from similar businesses and (2) the costs of performing specific marketing tasks and activities. There are a number of reference books published by the federal government, trade and professional associations, and private businesses that contain this information. Using the library in your school, a business information encyclopedia, other business reference books, or the resources of a business person you know, identify at least two sources of specific financial information available to marketers. After you have identified the sources, review one and prepare a written summary of the information that is contained in the reference. Provide examples of the specific information.

2. COSTS VERSUS BENEFITS

Business people are sometimes reluctant to use marketing research because of its cost. Marketing research is a marketing expense item and does not directly contribute to revenue. Therefore some people believe that the use of marketing research reduces profits. Marketing managers must be able to develop a budget for marketing research and be able to justify the expenses.

Assume you are the marketing manager for the franchiser of a chain of family haircutting centers that are located in major shopping malls in ten states. You want to complete a marketing research project to determine if the company's pricing strategy should change. Currently the price of haircuts is $18, but coupons are frequently distributed through newspaper ads and direct mail offering $5 discounts. You believe customers may be more satisfied with a one-price policy in which haircuts are always $15 with no coupons. You plan to survey customers in the ten states using mall intercepts done by employees from the franchises. People would be stopped in malls and asked to complete a five-item questionnaire. The questionnaires would be returned to your office for analysis.

a. Using Figure 21-4 as a model, make a list of the items you believe should be included in a budget for the marketing research project. Think of all of the types of expenses that would be involved from the time the project is started until you have a report on the results of the research.

b. You do not have to develop estimates of the amount of money you would budget for each item in the budget. Instead, for each item identify the method you would use to determine the amount to budget for each item. Write a one- or two-sentence explanation of the method you would use beside the item.

c. Now, prepare a brief oral presentation to give to the president of the franchise. Explain the purpose of the research, how you will develop the budget, and why the expense for the marketing research is justified even though it does not contribute directly to revenue. Be prepared to make your oral presentation to your instructor and other class members. You may want to develop some visual aids to support your presentation.

MARKETING PLANNING

1. ANALYZING MARKETING PERFORMANCE

The income statement in Figure 21-2 shows a company's financial information for the first six months of the year. The following income statement shows financial information for the comparable six months in the previous year. Calculate the percentage increase or decrease from the first to the second year for each of the figures on the income statement ([second year − first year] ÷ first year). Based on those calculations, develop three questions you would want to answer as a marketing manager about the financial performance of the company that led to the decrease in profits.

Sample Income Statement

Dendum Products, Inc.
Income Statement
For the Period Ending June 30, 19—

Revenues:
    Gross Sales:
        NE region $120,442
        NW region 198,665
        SE region 232,400
        SW region 153,868
            Total Gross Sales $705,375
    Less Sales Returns:
        NE region .... $ 6,435
        NW region 5,112
        SE region 7,890
        SW region 6,975
            Total Sales Returns 26,412
    Net Sales.. $678,963

    Cost of Products Sold:
        Inventory, January 1, 19— .... $ 87,105
        Purchases $540,906
        Less: Purchase Returns .... − 6,400
            Purchase Discounts .... − 3,050
        Net Purchases 544,256
    Total Cost of Products For Sale $631,361
        Inventory, June 30, 19— .... − 82,910
        Net Cost of Products Sold 548,451
Gross Margin $130,512

Operating Expenses:
    Rent Expense .... $ 8,050
    Bad Debts Expense 950
    Credit Card Fee Expense 2,200
    Transportation Expense 9,400
    Equipment Purchases 450
    Equipment Depreciation 800
    Insurance Expense 1,050
    Salaries and Wages 9,870
    Payroll Taxes 1,200
    Supplies Expense 445
    Advertising Expense 16,880
        Total Operating Expenses 51,295
Net Income Before Taxes .... $ 79,217

2. I PREDICT

One of the methods of forecasting sales for products and services is to identify relationships between two products or services. In the chapter, it was suggested that the volume of automobile sales can be used to predict the sale of automobile tires. If business people can identify similar relationships among products and services, they can increase the effectiveness of their forecasts. List at least ten other product/service relationships where you believe the sale of one affects the sale of the other. Two more examples are given to help you.

The sale of	Is related to the sale of
computers..	....computer software
winter coats	.....gloves and hats

MARKETING MANAGEMENT

1. SELECTING FINANCING

A hardware store decides to add free delivery as a service for customers who purchase over $250 of merchandise in one order. Delivery will also be available to other customers but a delivery fee will be charged. The store can purchase a delivery van for $18,000. Three methods of financing the van are being considered.

a. The store's bank will provide a one-year capital improvement loan at 9 percent interest. To qualify for the loan, the company must maintain 120 percent of the value of the vehicle in checking or savings accounts with the bank.

b. A finance company will purchase all of the company's accounts receivable for 86 percent of their value. The store's accounts receivable currently are valued at $26,500.

c. The store can use cash on hand to make the purchase. The current balance sheet for the store shows the cash balance is $31,800. The cash budget for the coming twelve months shows that the highest projected cash total during that time is $38,000 and the lowest projected cash total is $12,200.

Analyze the three sources of financing to determine the direct cost of each to the business and the possible advantages and disadvantages of each method. Prepare a written recommendation of the method you believe the store should use to finance the delivery van.

2. IT'S A CELEBRATION

 One of the school clubs to which you belong needs to raise funds to pay for a trip to a state conference. The members are tired of the old ways of fund raising and want to do something that will be fun, provide a community service, and result in a reasonable profit for the club. The idea being considered is an Ethnic Food Celebration. Your club would be responsible for contacting community groups who would agree to staff a booth in which a specific type of ethnic food would be prepared and sold. The group would also develop a display representing the ethnic culture or provide a short presentation (dance, historical story, and so on) about the culture. The ethnic celebration would be held on a Saturday afternoon for three hours in the school's gymnasium. People would come to sample the food and to enjoy the presentations going on throughout the afternoon.

For financial planning, some of the anticipated costs are:

Rental of the gymnasium............. $300

Table rental for booths................ $3 per table
(minimum of 50 tables)

Security... $45 per hour

Insurance...................................... $80

Cost of possible promotional materials:

Flyers.. $.08 each

Posters... $.45 each

Envelopes and postage .... $.32 each

<pre>
30-second radio ad.................... $58 each
                                  (10 for $500)
                                  +$80 production
                                  costs (fixed)
</pre>

Salesperson commission.................. $8 per booth sold

Labor costs
    (set up, tear down, cleaning) ...... $6 per hour

The plan is to sell booths for the celebration. There is space for up to 40 booths in the gymnasium if three tables are used per booth. The groups would be able to sell their foods and keep all revenues from the sale after paying the booth fee. Also, an admission could be charged to the celebration. Other products could be sold as a part of the celebration as well (T-shirts, souvenir cups, and so on).

Develop a plan of activities to be followed by your class in planning and managing the celebration. Include all aspects of a marketing mix (product development, distribution, pricing, promotion). Based on the plan of activities, prepare a budget for the celebration using the income statement format illustrated in the chapter. Include projections of all types of revenues and reasonable expenses. Estimate those expenses for which no costs are given. Develop at least three projections of revenues using alternative prices charged for the booths, varying admission prices, or different attendance levels. Calculate the impact of the change on the profit or loss from the celebration.

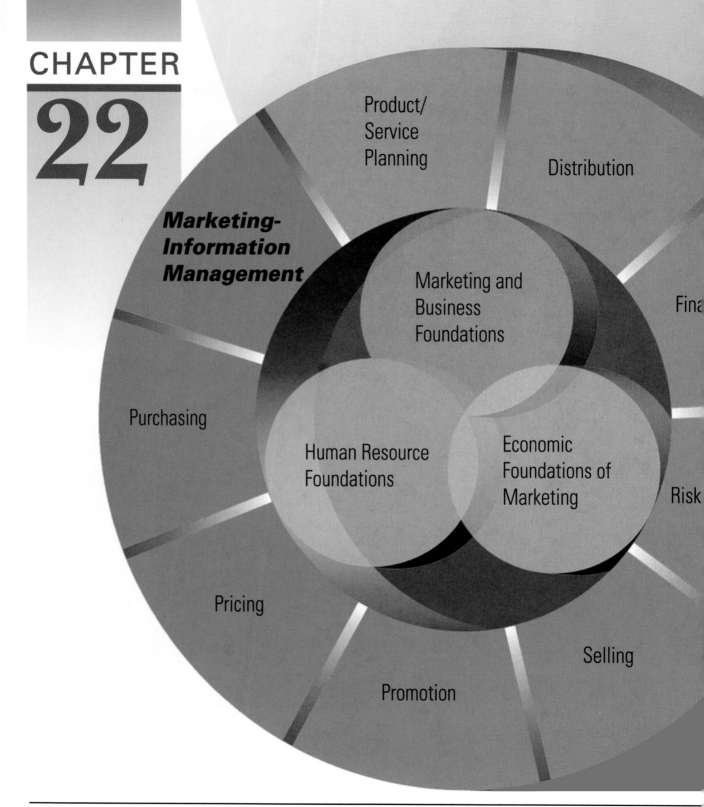

CHAPTER
22

**Marketing-
Information
Management**

Product/
Service
Planning

Distribution

Marketing and
Business
Foundations

Fina

Purchasing

Human Resource
Foundations

Economic
Foundations of
Marketing

Risk

Pricing

Selling

Promotion

Marketers Need Information

OBJECTIVES

1. Discuss why it is important to manage information.
2. Outline the characteristics of a well-designed marketing-information system.
3. Provide examples of the uses of marketing information.
4. Identify internal and external sources of market information.
5. Describe the value of marketing intelligence to individuals and organizations.

nt

NEWSLINE

TO TEST OR NOT TO TEST

Test marketing is an important marketing tool. Before spending the money to produce and distribute products to the entire market, a company introduces the product and the marketing strategy in selected markets. It studies customer and competitor reactions carefully before making a decision to broaden its markets. Recently, some businesses have begun to question whether test marketing is useful or whether it results in poor marketing decisions.

Marketing moves very rapidly and test marketing takes time. When testing a new type of shampoo, a company must wait until customers purchase, use, and then repurchase the product. That requires more than a month. In that time period another company can introduce a similar product in the market so the company loses its advantage.

Competing companies watch for test markets and try to disrupt the market. If a competitor can change the conditions of the market during the test, the results will not reflect how the product will actually perform in a normal market. For

example, when one company introduces a new brand of soap in a test market, a competitor runs a "two for the price of one" coupon for its brand. The coupon has a major effect on sales during the test.

Consumers respond to products that are new and different in ways they will not act when they become accustomed to the product. Businesses have to be careful that the customer response in the test market is based on a real belief in the value of the product rather than its novelty. A fast-food restaurant introduced a low-fat hamburger. Sales were very high at first but then dropped. Consumers tried it for the novelty but decided they preferred the original hamburger.

Test marketing is expensive. It's not unusual for a business to invest $2–$5 million (and often a great deal more) in a test of a new product.

Some businesses believe that test markets are no longer the best information sources. With reliable

methods to gather information and with greater use of technology,

> **Some businesses believe that test markets are no longer the best information sources.**

less expensive and faster methods can be selected. However, other businesses continue to emphasize test marketing as an important part of their information system. They believe that nothing is better than experience in determining what will work and what will not work.

THE NEED FOR INFORMATION

We have been told that we are in the information age, and it is easy to see why. Information is around us all of the time. Consider the resources you can access for communication, information, and entertainment. Newspapers, magazines, books, newsletters, dozens of radio and television channels, and telephone services are easily available to most people. Personal computers have opened up additional sources of information. With a computer and modem you can access libraries, airline schedules, stock markets, and banking services. You can communicate with friends or people with similar interests through E-mail or computer bulletin boards.

Just like consumers, business people have access to vast amounts of information. Stacks of reports move across the desks of managers. Businesses gather information from customers, channel members, and competitors. Government agencies, trade associations, and independent businesses gather and distribute information ranging from economic trends to industry performance.

It would seem that consumer and business decisions would improve with all of the information that is available. However, the amount of information can contribute to poor business decisions. Reasons include:

1. Not all information is good information.

2. It takes too long to study and analyze the information.

3. People believe the information provides solutions to problems rather than help in developing solutions.

As we saw in the Newsline at the beginning of the chapter, some businesses are not using test markets as much as in the past. Each of the reasons listed describes problems those businesses have had with test markets.

MANAGING INFORMATION

As businesses increase access to information, they need to be able to use the information effectively. This need creates an important new function in business known as information management. *Information management is the systematic collection and organization of information so that it can be quickly and easily used in decision-making.*

Information management is used in all parts of a business. Production managers, finance managers, and human resource managers all need immediate access to a variety of information. This information is needed in order to make effective decisions. Marketing managers need this information also. To respond to the needs of all parts of the business, information systems are developed and personnel are hired to manage them. *An information system is the organized procedures (often using computer technology) for obtaining, storing, processing, and retrieving information needed in the operation and management of a business.*

MANAGING INFORMATION IN MARKETING

Effective marketing depends on information. A long time ago marketing involved fewer activities. Marketing was used to sell whatever product was produced by a business. In those times, marketing managers might have been able to use their best judgement to make decisions. Today, each target market is different. Many other businesses are involved in implementing a marketing strategy. A variety of activities must be coordinated to insure that the entire marketing mix works as planned. It is not possible for one person to know enough to manage marketing without additional information. Therefore, one of the key marketing functions that improves decision-making is marketing-information management. *Marketing-information management is the process of obtaining, managing, and using market information to improve decision-making and the performance of marketing activities.*

Marketers are aware of the importance of information (see Figure 22-1). Marketers identify the information they need. They find the best sources of that information. They determine how the information will be obtained and used. Then they develop procedures to make sure it is available when planning and implementing marketing activities. Those procedures are organized into an information system.

It is important for marketers to have an information system that will help them use important information to make decisions. The system must be able to provide needed information quickly and accurately. Most marketing departments today either use the company's information system or develop a specific marketing-information system. *A marketing-information system (MkIS) is an organized method of collecting, storing, retrieving, and analyzing information to improve marketing decisions.*

DESIGNING A MARKETING-INFORMATION SYSTEM

There are several characteristics of a good information system:

- provides needed information
- accurate
- easy-to-use
- provides information rapidly
- not too expensive

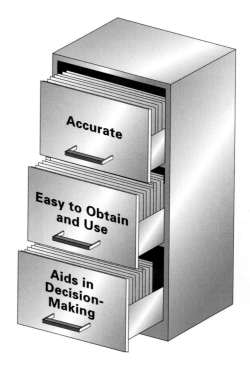

Qualities of Effective Information

FIGURE 22-1 ▪ Information can be an important tool for marketers.

Planning a marketing-information system requires that several questions be answered. The answers to those questions result in the five elements of an effective information system: input, storage, analysis, output, and decision-making. The questions and their results are shown in Figure 22-2 on the next page.

INPUT

How do you make decisions? If you want to be as objective as possible and make good decisions, you must gather information. *Input is the information needed for decision-making.*

A great deal of information results from the regular operations of a business. It is known as routine information. Routine information about customers, competitors, and business operations is used for marketing decisions. Marketers need to know what customers purchase, in what quantities, and at what prices. They must know where customers buy their products and what factors influence them.

Designing an MkIS	
Question	**MkIS Element**
What information is needed to develop and implement the marketing strategy?	Input
How should the information be maintained so it is in a usable form and is easy to access when needed?	Storage
What methods should be used to organize and study the information in order to make effective marketing decisions?	Analysis
How and when should the information be made available for most effective use?	Output
What ways should the information be used to improve marketing?	Decision-Making

FIGURE 22-2 ▪ A marketing-information system (MkIS) is designed to help marketers obtain, store, organize, and use information to improve decisions.

Marketing is influenced by the activities of competitors. Information is needed on which businesses are competing in specific markets, the marketing mixes they use, their strengths and weaknesses, their market share, and their profitability. Marketers can use information about business operations to determine what activities are effective or ineffective.

Occasionally, additional information that is not routinely collected by the business is needed for a decision. In that situation, a marketing research procedure is used to collect the information. Marketing research data provides important input for a marketing-information system.

STORAGE

Have you ever rushed to a class only to discover that your assignment was not in your notebook? Many of us are very good at collecting information. We may not be as good at storing it where we can locate it when needed. *Storage includes the equipment and procedures used to hold information until needed.* A storage system in an MkIS has several characteristics. Most importantly, it must protect the information. If information is lost or damaged it is not useful when a decision must be made. Some business information is very confidential. The storage system should be designed so it can only be accessed by the people who are authorized to use the information. Finally, the storage system should be organized so information is easy to locate when needed.

Most of the storage of information in businesses today is done using computer technology. After data is entered into the computer, it is maintained on a hard or floppy disk, a CD-ROM, or on other type of storage media. Careful planning is done to make sure that back-up copies of all data are maintained and that information is secure. More traditional methods of information storage continue to be used, such as keeping documents in filing cabinets or using micro-photography to make copies of information that can be stored and retrieved on microfilm or microfiche.

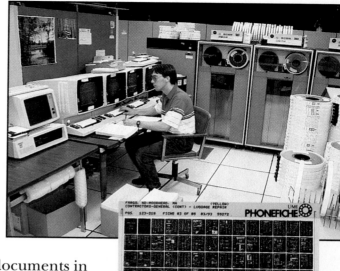

ANALYSIS

Information in an MkIS is maintained in order to improve decision-making. Usually the information by itself has little meaning. *Through analysis, information is summarized, combined, or compared with other information.* In order to plan a promotional budget, a manager may examine the budgets for other products or for past years. The effectiveness of one retailer in a channel of distribution may not be apparent until that company's sales are compared with those of similar companies. The costs of marketing activities for national and international activities need to be combined to determine the total marketing costs of the company.

The type of analysis needed is usually determined when planning the marketing-information system. Procedures are developed to obtain needed information from storage, to organize it for analysis, and to complete the needed analysis. Today, with computer technology, specific programs are available that assist with those procedures. For example, database and spreadsheet programs have specific procedures for analysis of the information. If statistical analysis is needed, the formulas are developed within the program or a specific statistical package is used to analyze the data quickly and accurately.

Companies that complete a large amount of data analysis usually employ people skilled in organizing and analyzing data. Most finance and accounting departments, as well as marketing research and operations units, have specialists in data analysis. These specialists develop and manage computer programs or work with the information if it is stored in another form.

OUTPUT

From the viewpoint of managers and other decision-makers, the most important part of an MkIS is the output. Many people never see the information when it is being collected, stored, or analyzed. They are given data summaries or reports to use in making decisions. *The information given to the decision-makers is the output.*

Output is usually written information or graphics. It is provided in print form or accessed through the monitor of a computer system. Some computers now have audio output capabilities. Output must be useful to the people receiving the information. If it is not well organized or uses language or data that is difficult to understand, it may be misused or not used at all.

DECISION-MAKING

The purpose of a marketing-information system is to improve decision-making. Decisions should be better and should be made more quickly if the MkIS is well designed. The types of decisions and the process for decision-making should be planned as carefully as the other parts of the system. The decision-making process includes who is involved in the decision, when decisions need to be made, any policies or procedures that should be considered, and the information needed by the decision-makers.

Some decisions are routine and the result of the analysis will determine the decision that should be made. For example, information in the MkIS of an office supply store shows that inventory levels of computer paper have dropped to a level where it needs to be reordered. The analysis program in the computer determines that 200 cases of paper are needed. It searches the vendor list to determine which of the approved vendors has the lowest current price for that quantity. The vendor is selected from the list, the re-order quantity identified, and a purchase order is printed and faxed to the vendor. No management attention to this decision was required and the inventory was resupplied (see Figure 22-3).

Routine and Unique Decisions

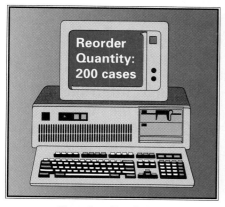

Routine Decision

Unique Decision

FIGURE 22-3 ■ An effective marketing-information system removes routine decisions from managers and lets them concentrate on the unique decisions.

Other decisions are unique and very important to many people inside and outside of the business. A major credit card company considers whether to offer a money-back guarantee on all products consumers purchase using the card. The guarantee is viewed as an important service that will encourage people to use the credit card and could attract many more customers. However, the results will affect the company, the businesses that accept the credit card, and competing credit card companies. The decision to add the guarantee means important changes in the entire marketing mix used by the company. Once the company announces the new service, it will be difficult to end the service even if it proves to be too expensive to maintain. The decision requires a great deal of time and information, and many people, including most of the company's managers, will be involved in making the decision.

WHAT INFORMATION IS NEEDED?

To build an effective information system, a company must identify the information needed by marketing personnel. One way to identify the information needed is to consider the marketing decisions that will be made. We know that organizations using the marketing concept make two important decisions. They first identify the target markets to be served. Then they develop the marketing mix that will be used to serve each market. Marketers identify the information they need for each of those decisions.

Another, more specific way of determining the information needed is to examine each of the marketing functions. The marketing functions describe the activities that occur as products and services are exchanged in a channel of distribution. Marketing information is used to plan each of the marketing functions (see Figure 22-4). Some examples of the important information for each of the functions are described in the following sections.

PRODUCT/SERVICE PLANNING

Businesses regularly evaluate their current products and services to determine whether the product should be maintained, improved, or dropped. They also decide if new products or ser-

FIGURE 22-4 ■ Each marketing decision should be carefully studied to determine the information needed.

vices should be added. To make those decisions, the company needs information from customers about the level of satisfaction with the product. They need to know how customers' needs could be satisfied even better with product modifications. Competitors' products must be studied and compared to the company's products. Product research, information from consumers and company personnel, and attention to new technologies aid in identifying new product ideas.

PURCHASING

What information do you need when you decide to make a purchase? Certainly, it depends on the type of purchase you are making, the importance and cost of the purchase, and your experience with that product or service. A large amount of information is used to make the decision even though you may not specifically identify the information each time.

When businesses make purchases, they too need a great deal of information. If it is a new purchase or a very expensive purchase, the information will be very important. For routine or inexpensive purchases, the company may spend less time or effort in identifying and analyzing the information, but information is still used. Factors considered when making purchasing decisions include sources of supply, availability, quality of the product or service, reliability of the vendor, delivery schedule, guarantees, and services provided. Price and credit information is usually important as well.

FINANCING

Financing as a marketing function includes budgeting for marketing activities, obtaining the necessary finances, and providing financial assistance to customers. Information is needed on the company's financial performance. Specific sales and cost figures are used to develop marketing budgets. As new marketing activities are planned, information on projected costs and revenues must be obtained. This information is gathered from the results of test markets, using computer simulations of market conditions, or by comparisons to similar products.

If the company requires financial support from a bank or a vendor, those organizations usually ask for financial information and business or marketing plans. When the company offers credit to a customer, information is gathered to determine if the customer has a good credit history.

DISTRIBUTION

Getting the product or service to customers at the right place and time is a key to successful marketing. Not only does it increase customer satisfaction, but distribution is a difficult decision to change quickly. Therefore, businesses approach distribution planning carefully.

Where do customers prefer to buy the product? What type of atmosphere and services do they expect? Selecting a direct or indirect channel of distribution is based on information about the time and cost of getting products to customers, choices of channel members, and the company's ability to complete distribution activities.

Business customers in a channel, as well as final consumers, have high expectations for service. They want orders processed rapidly but accurately. They want products available very close to the time that they will be used. Materials handling is important to make sure products arrive undamaged. Customers may need follow-up service or technical information.

PRICING

An effective price is a careful balance between customers' perceptions and the business' costs. Pricing too high means products go unsold. A low price may not allow for a profit. Information is needed on all costs of production, marketing, and operations. Demand must be studied, as well as competitors' prices and pricing strategies. Pricing may be affected by laws and regulations.

RISK MANAGEMENT

How does an insurance company decide whether to insure a particular risk? How much should be charged for the insurance so the company will be able to pay the loss if necessary? It relies on a careful study of the risk, factors that could affect the risk, and the history of losses for the type of risk. For example, if the insurance company writes policies to insure the cargos of ships, it would study the types of risks the ships could encounter, events and activities that could increase or decrease the chances of loss, and the number of times ships have had losses in the past.

Some marketing risks are big and difficult to predict, such as a major change in the economy or the development of new technology by a competitor that results in major market changes. More typical examples include ways to reduce shoplifting and employee theft or the amount of merchandise returned by customers in order to control costs.

CHALLENGES
STEP RIGHT UP

How do consumers get information while shopping? In the past, they would ask a salesperson. But now they are able to ask a machine. Information kiosks may become the primary information source for consumers in the future.

You are already familiar with simple versions of information kiosks. Automatic teller machines in banks provide basic services and information about your accounts so you do not have to go to a teller. Shopping centers have introduced touch-screen computers that provide brief announcements and descriptions of stores and products.

Most of the new kiosks have large color screens, voices, and music. You can step up to a computer screen and find out about area tourist attractions, job openings, medical services, or voter registration locations. Many of the kiosks are equipped to take orders for products and services. They can accept payment with a credit card and arrange delivery to most locations throughout the world.

Marketing research companies predict the number of information kiosks and their applications will grow rapidly as technology improves and as customers become comfortable using them. Less than 50,000 kiosks were in use in the United States in 1990. That number expanded to nearly 2 million by the middle of the decade. There will be many opportunities for businesses to use kiosks in the future. Allstate Insurance sells insurance policies in supermarkets and department stores using information kiosks. Some deli counters in New England installed kiosks so customers can easily select made-to-order sandwiches. What types of applications do you predict for the machines?

Source: "The Kiosks Are Coming, The Kiosks Are Coming," Business Week, *June 22, 1992, p. 122.*

MARKETING-INFORMATION MANAGEMENT

This function is the information gathering and analysis activities of marketing. To effectively manage information in marketing, it is important for managers to learn about the newest and best methods and technology used to collect and analyze information. Marketing-information management is usually a part of a larger management information system in an organization. Therefore, marketers have access to information from other parts of the business. That information is important for cooperative planning and coordination of the business' activities.

PROMOTION

One of the most important types of information needed for promotional planning is an understanding of the consumer and the decision-making process. Also, information on competitors' products and services is needed in order to clearly position the company's products. Promotional methods, media, and costs are studied. Companies carefully evaluate each promotion for future planning.

SELLING

The most effective salespeople carefully gather information about the customer and then provide specific information about the product and its benefits. The types of information that are important in the selling function are a thorough understanding of the customer, the product, other elements of the marketing mix, and competing products and services.

Companies that use salespeople as an important part of their marketing strategy collect information about the potential of various market segments. This information is used to assign salespeople and establish sales quotas and sales budgets. The performance of each salesperson, as well as that of customers, is carefully studied to determine effectiveness and to plan how to improve sales performance.

SOURCES OF INFORMATION

Where do you go to find the titles of the most recent movies available on video tape? What is a good source of information to help you learn about careers or college choices? If you want to find out how much to pay for a particular model of automobile, where do you turn for help? Each of these decisions requires information. For most there may be more than one information source. You would select from the sources which are familiar and accessible. Factors that influence your selection of an information source may include whether it is available, how quickly it can be accessed, how complete or accurate you believe it to be, and your past experience with the source.

As business people identify data sources for their marketing-information systems, they go through a similar process. The process is summarized in the following steps:

1. Identify the types of information needed.

2. Determine the available sources of each type of information.

3. Evaluate each information source to determine if it meets the organization's needs (accuracy, time, detail, cost).

4. Select the sources that best meet the identified needs.

5. Enter the information into the marketing-information system.

There are three categories of marketing-information sources: internal sources, external sources, and marketing research. Chapter 9 discusses marketing research. In the following sections, internal and external sources are described.

INTERNAL INFORMATION SOURCES

Internal information is information developed from activities that occur within the organization. A great deal of information flows through a business. Much of it is valuable for marketing decision-making. Often, however, the information is not recorded or is not available to the right people or at the time when it would be useful for decisions. For example, salespeople learn a great deal from current and prospective customers. They get information about needs, perceptions of price, satisfaction with services, or requested changes in products. That information may never be communicated back to the company. Even if it is, it may not be a part of the information reviewed when marketing plans are being developed.

Most businesses keep detailed records on production schedules and inventory levels. That information should be reviewed by the people planning special promotions if the result of the promotion will increase demand for some products. Examples of important types of internal information are shown in Figure 22-5.

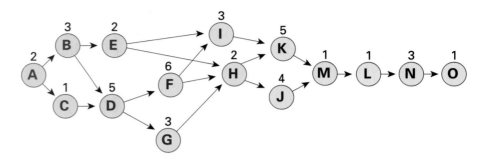

Production and Operations Reports

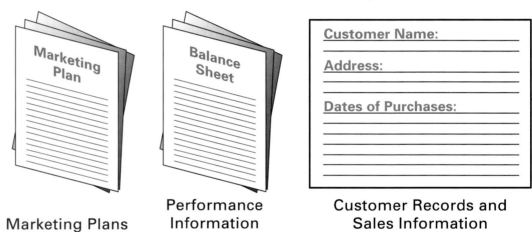

Marketing Plans

Performance Information

Customer Records and Sales Information

Internal Information Sources

FIGURE 22-5 ■ A great deal of information that is helpful when making marketing decisions is available inside a business.

Customer Records and Sales Information

Customer information is important for effective marketing planning. Therefore customer records are an important information source. Many companies keep a complete record of all transactions they have with a customer. They record what is purchased, the date, and quantity purchased. If the customer purchases accessory or related products, at that time or a later time, the information is also recorded and matched with the original purchase. Detailed information on the form of payment and the history of credit payments is also maintained. If the customer requires service, a service record is prepared.

In order to effectively target products and marketing activities at specific customers, information more detailed than sales records is very useful. We learned in our study of consumer behavior that businesses need to have demographic information such as age, family size, income, and address. They need an understanding of consumer needs, interests, and attitudes. Businesses need information regarding how the consumer makes buying decisions such as where they gather information, what choices are considered, where they decide to purchase, and so on. That information can be gathered through market research, but some businesses have discovered other ways to gather customer information.

Often detailed profiles are completed on a customer by the salesperson as a part of the selling process. Many realtors ask prospective buyers a great deal of information in order to locate the best possible home. Salespeople who work in clothing and apparel stores develop complete information on their regular customers' needs and preferences.

A relatively new information tool used by businesses is a customer club. Prospec-tive and current customers are provided with special incentives to join the club. In order to join, the consumer completes a detailed profile form. Based on that profile, each consumer is sent regular mailings providing new product information, special purchase opportunities and discounts, and promotional information for products and services the company believes the customer will want to buy. Some companies have used the consumer club to develop a consumer database of millions of people.

Production and Operations Reports

Production and operations activities are important to marketing. Products and services must be available when customers want them. Quality standards need to be met. Expenses need to be controlled in order to price the products and services competitively. Information about production and operations activities is collected but might not be shared regularly with the people planning marketing activities.

When a business is a part of a channel system working with a manufacturer, it is even more difficult to get needed information about production and operations. Often manufacturers do not believe channel members need that information or are unwilling to share it, believing it is confidential.

When companies that make up a channel of distribution work closely together and share operating information they can meet customer needs much better and operate more efficiently. In that way all members of the channel benefit. Those companies have developed information systems where they can quickly share information about sales, costs, inventory levels, and production and delivery schedules.

Marketing Plans

Everything that happens in marketing should be based on the marketing plan. When we studied the development of a marketing plan in Chapter 11, we saw that a great deal of information was needed. Once completed, the marketing plan should become a part of the information available in the company. As marketers make decisions and complete activities, they can refer to the marketing plan to be sure it is being followed.

Performance Information

The success of a business is judged by its performance. Some people believe the only important performance measure is the amount of profit a business makes. Managers must pay attention to profitability. However, there are other performance measures that need to be watched as well. The types of performance measures important to most businesses are sales, costs, quality, and customer satisfaction.

Performance is typically measured in one of three ways. For companies that have operated for a number of years, there are records of past performance. The current sales or costs can be compared to those of a previous month or year to determine if performance is improving.

A second method is to compare performance with that of similar businesses. Information on other businesses is available from external information sources (see next section) and is not always easy to obtain. Trade associations and some private information bureaus, such as A.C. Nielsen Company and Dun & Bradstreet, provide performance data on companies within the same industry that can be used for comparison.

The most important performance measure is the comparison of actual performance with expected performance. When managers plan marketing activities, they develop goals, performance standards, and budgets. Those tools identify what the expected level of sales should be, the planned expenses, and the activities that will be needed to accomplish the marketing plan. Planning tools should be used regularly to check current performance.

EXTERNAL INFORMATION SOURCES

Marketing regularly involves other people and businesses. It is important to understand and effectively work with those outside the organization. *External information provides an understanding of factors outside of the organization.* In addition to the information gathered through marketing research, there are several valuable sources of external information that businesses can use. Those sources are reviewed in Figure 22-6.

External Information Sources

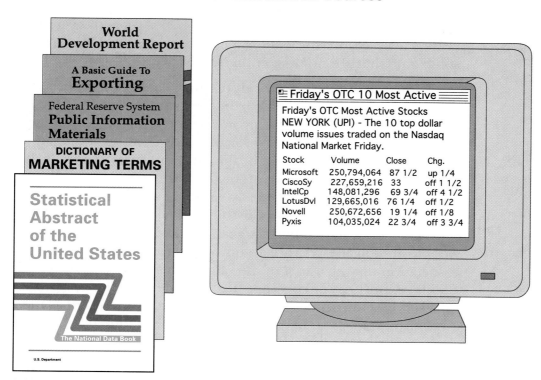

FIGURE 22-6 ▪ Government reports, commercial data services, business publications, and trade and professional associations are all external sources of information.

Government Reports

We often think of regulation and taxation as the major roles of government in business. However, another important activity of federal, state, and local governments is to supply information that can be used by businesses and consumers. There are a large number of agencies that regularly collect information that can help businesses improve their marketing decisions.

Probably the best known data collection agency is the U.S. Bureau of the Census. Every ten years, the Census Bureau conducts a complete census of the country's population. The report of that census is very detailed and specific. It provides an excellent source to learn about the number of people and important characteristics of individuals and households in specific areas of the country. The Census of Population data is available on computer disks for easier analysis. Some companies analyze census data and sell reports to businesses.

The population of the United States is not the only census completed by the federal government. Others include the Census of Manufacturers, Retail Trade, Wholesale Trade, Transportation, and County Business Patterns. Many of the studies are completed in full either every five years or every ten years. However, the Bureau of Census provides yearly updates of some data that are not as comprehensive.

There are literally thousands of other databases, reports, and information sources available from government offices. One of the most difficult parts of using government information is determining what is available. Information is developed on agriculture, education, housing, health, and international trade as well as many other areas of interest to businesses.

Trade and Professional Associations

Trade and professional associations are organized to serve people and businesses with common interests. Members of the association may be a part of the same industry such as travel, retailing, exporting, or corn producers. Other associations provide services for people in particular job categories such as the American Management Association and the National Association of Market Developers.

Most associations provide information specific to the needs of their members. That information may be disseminated through journals, newsletters, or more detailed research reports. Some associations have research services, libraries, or data services that can be used by members.

A GLOBAL VISION

WORLDWIDE COMMUNICATIONS

Many businesses have developed effective information systems for the markets in which they have worked for many years. As they consider markets in other countries, they realize they do not have the information needed to plan effectively. An online information service is available to provide that information.

International Strategies is a Boston company that has developed the Export Hotline in cooperation with AT&T and several other companies. Information about 58 industries in over 50 countries is available to businesses who use the information service. Companies can obtain information about the country, purchasers and suppliers located in the country, specific laws and regulations that could affect the sale of specific products, and shipping requirements. After locating a report that the customer needs, it can be ordered while on the telephone and will be faxed immediately.

How does International Strategies develop all of the information on the hotline? It relies on the United States government. The Department of Commerce and U.S. embassy personnel in other countries gather information and prepare reports that help businesses sell products and services in that country. International Strategies collects the reports, enters them into its database, and makes them available through the hotline.

Companies that have used the Export Hotline report that the information makes it much easier to begin the export process. The only limitation is the amount of information available. Many countries and product categories are not currently included. Based on initial demand, that problem may be solved. With experience and additional revenues, International Strategies is prepared to add more countries, industries, and information to the hotline.

Source: "An Export Service of 'Great Import,'" Business Week, *September 28, 1992, p.138.*

Business Publications

Magazines and journals provide useful information for business people. Those publications include general information newspapers and magazines such as *The Wall Street Journal, Forbes,* and *Business Week,* as well as more specialized publications including *Black Enterprise, Advertising Age,* or *American Demographics.* Business publications are useful sources of current information on the economy, legislation, new technology, or business ideas. Often the publications devote specific issues or sections to analysis of business performance. For example the *Fortune 500* analyzes the largest corporations in the United States each year. *Fortune* also provides information on major international businesses and U.S. corporations in a number of industries. *Sales & Marketing Management* publishes the annual *Survey of Buying Power* that analyzes consumer purchasing in all major U.S. markets.

Commercial Data and Information Services

There are a number of businesses that collect, analyze, and sell data. Dun & Bradstreet and Equifax provide credit information on consumers and businesses. A.C. Nielsen conducts research on a number of topics and sells the information to business customers. One of the best known of their services is the Nielsen ratings for television viewing. Other well-known information service companies are SRI International, Burke, SAMI, and Dow Jones.

MARKETING INTELLIGENCE

Much of the information described in this chapter is gathered in order to develop marketing plans and make major marketing decisions. But marketing decision-making goes on every day and all marketing personnel are involved in those decisions. Because markets and marketing change so quickly, it is important to keep up to date with those changes. *Information on day-to-day changes in marketing and the marketing environment is known as marketing intelligence.*

PERSONAL MARKETING INTELLIGENCE

Professional marketers continually increase their knowledge of marketing and of their company and industry. Personal marketing intelligence is developed by reading, attending conferences and meetings, and talking to people who can provide important information. It is not unusual for marketing managers to read one or more newspapers each day, to read several magazines and books regularly, and to study business reports and other information. Many attend conferences, visit trade shows, and meet with colleagues in professional organization meetings. Continuing professional development activities provide them with important information needed to be effective in their jobs.

MARKETING INTELLIGENCE FOR ORGANIZATIONS

Organizations need to continuously gather and analyze information in order to identify changes that affect marketing plans. Being aware of competitors' activities, proposed laws or regulations, new technology, and consumer trends will allow adjustments to be made before the changes have a negative effect on business.

There are many ways businesses gather marketing intelligence. Large organizations have personnel that study publications, government reports, and other information sources. They may have product testing departments that analyze competitors' products. Test marketing and other types of research are important parts of a marketing intelligence system. Employees provide information gathered from meetings, conventions, visits with vendors, and other regular activities.

Businesses also have some unique methods of gathering marketing intelligence. They include "bird dogs," "ghost shoppers," and employee reports. Bird dogs are people not employed by the organization who watch for and report important changes in the market. Bird dogs may include important customers, former employees, channel members, or other people who have an interest in the company and have access to useful information.

Ghost shoppers are usually company employees who visit competitors' businesses or meet with salespeople to study the products, services, and marketing procedures of those companies. They often purchase competing products so they can be studied by the company. There are companies that provide ghost shoppers for other companies to avoid using the company's own personnel. Ghost shopping is used frequently by retailers, but it is also used by other types of businesses to study their competitors.

One of the best sources of marketing intelligence is a company's employees. Employees have regular contacts with customers, channel members, and even competitors. They have access to important information but often do not believe the information is important or do not know how to share the information. One of the oldest methods of obtaining information from employees is a suggestion box. However, to encourage employees to gather and report information, many companies have now developed short, easy-to-complete forms. They provide employee training and even incentives for completing the forms. When employees see that the information is used to make changes, they are usually very willing to complete the forms.

ONLINE DATABASES

A relatively new source of marketing intelligence is online databases. There are many companies that offer important information to businesses through a computerized database. Information is gathered and stored in data files on computers and updated regularly. Businesses can purchase access to these databases.

Because there are literally thousands of databases available, it is not easy for a business to know what information is available or how to easily access the information. When a need exists in a market, new businesses usually develop to meet that need. In this case, the businesses are known as online vendors. *Online vendors are wholesalers of computerized databases.* Online vendors contract with the companies that have created specific databases. They have contracts with many independent companies representing a variety of types of information. The vendor organizes the databases so they are easy to use. The service is then sold to users who can access all information through one source. They receive only one bill for the information they purchase. If they have any problems with the databases, they can get technical assistance from the online vendor rather than working with many different companies.

Some of the best known online vendors are PRODIGY, America Online, CompuServe, The Source, Dow Jones News/Retrieval Services, and Dialog Information Services. These companies are popular with consumers as well as businesses. Many online vendors not only provide information, but also allow users to purchase products, make payments, and complete other business activities through the service.

REVIEW

Effective marketing requires information. Consumers need information in order to make effective purchasing decisions. Businesses need information in order to understand the market, customers, and competitors. Most organizations have developed marketing-information systems so that information can be collected, stored, and analyzed. Information is used to identify target markets and to develop marketing mixes. Specific information is needed to plan activities for each of the marketing functions.

Two major categories of information are important to businesses: internal information and external information. Internal information is developed from activities that occur within the organization. External information provides an understanding of factors outside of the organization. Marketers need to identify the internal and external information needed and the sources of that information in order to incorporate it into the marketing-information system.

Information on day-to-day changes in marketing is known as marketing intelligence. Because markets and marketing change so rapidly, it is important to have effective methods for gathering marketing intelligence. Online vendors are new types of businesses that provide access to marketing intelligence contained in computer databases.

MARKETING FOUNDATIONS

1. **ANSWERS PLEASE**

   Answer these questions using information from the chapter.

   a. How can information actually contribute to poor business decisions?

   b. What is an information system?

   c. What is marketing-information management?

d. What are the characteristics of a good information system?

e. What are two ways to identify the information that will be needed by marketing personnel?

f. What are the steps business people go through in identifying information sources for their marketing-information systems?

g. What are the three categories of marketing-information sources?

h. How is internal information different from external information?

i. How is marketing intelligence different from other types of marketing information?

j. What are online vendors?

2. **DETERMINE THE DIFFERENCES**

Marketing information comes from many sources. Three different categories of information sources are internal sources, external sources, and marketing intelligence. Sources of marketing information are listed below. Identify each source by selecting the correct letter:

  I = internal information

  E = external information

  M = marketing intelligence

1. Customer records

2. Government reports

3. Commercial data services

4. Online vendors

5. Trade associations

6. Customer clubs

7. Ghost shoppers

8. Forms completed by employees

9. Marketing plans

10. Bird dogs

MARKETING RESEARCH

1. THE EFFECTIVENESS OF A DOLLAR

J&G Distributors is concerned about the effectiveness of its marketing activities. In its MkIS are data on marketing expenditures and sales for the past three years. Using the information supplied by a trade association, J&G has been able to estimate the marketing expenditures and sales of its competitors for those same years. Those data are shown in the following table:

Comparison of Marketing Expenditures to Sales						
	Three Years Ago		Two Years Ago		One Year Ago	
	J&G	Competitors	J&G	Competitors	J&G	Competitors
Marketing Expenditures	$582,600	$3,657,900	$605,280	$3,725,820	$645,860	$3,810,260
Total Sales	$1,256,920	$6,125,825	$1,496,040	$6,205,060	$1,765,900	$6,430,195

a. Calculate the total marketing expenditures and total sales for each year.

b. Determine J&G's percentage of total marketing expenditures and its market share for each year.

c. Use the total investment in marketing during the three-year period to answer the following questions?:

   ▪ For each dollar spent by J&G Distributors on marketing, how many dollars of sales resulted?

   ▪ For each dollar spent by competitors on marketing, how many dollars of sales resulted?

   ▪ For each dollar spent by the entire industry on marketing, how many dollars of sales resulted?

d. Use the information in the table to make at least two other comparisons that you believe would be important for J&G to study. Write a short statement for each comparison identifying why you think it is important information for marketing decision-making.

2. **CUSTOMER COLLECTIONS**

Businesses use a variety of methods to gather information from customers that can be used to improve marketing. Two common methods include comment cards and warranty registration forms. Many other types of data-gathering forms are used regularly. Locate three different examples of questionnaires, coupons, or other forms businesses use to gather consumer information. For each example, identify the specific information that the business obtains and describe the ways the information might be used in marketing planning. (Bring a copy of each of the examples to class, if possible.)

MARKETING PLANNING

1. **INFORMATION SYSTEMS IN USE**

Find three examples of information systems currently in use in your school, your home, or your community. Look carefully and you are likely to find many information systems in use. (Each system does not have to be computer-based.) Develop a poster that illustrates each of the information systems you found. On each poster, clearly label each of the five components of an information system. Write brief descriptions of each information system discussing its purpose, information sources, and how the system is managed.

2. **IMPROVING YOUR MARKETING INTELLIGENCE**

As we learned in this chapter, professional marketers continually increase their knowledge of marketing and of the company and industry in which they work. Prepare a plan for improving your marketing intelligence by completing the following steps:

1. Identify a marketing occupation in which you are interested. Identify the industry in which you might work if you entered that occupation. Choose a company you could work for.

2. Prepare a list of information you should collect if you are to be as informed as possible about the career, the industry, and the company.

3. Identify the primary sources of information you would use regularly to increase your marketing intelligence. While many sources can be a part of a personal marketing-information system, the list should include one each of the following:

   - daily newspaper

   - general-interest magazine

   - business publication

   - government agency or report

   - person who can serve as an information source

   - professional or trade association related to the career or industry

   - relevant commercial database or information service

   - related college major or other education program for the career

After you have developed the list, prepare a three column chart with the following headings:

Type of Marketing

Intelligence	**Information Source**	**Use**

Complete the chart for each of the information sources you identified. Make sure you identify the occupation, industry, and business on your chart.

MARKETING MANAGEMENT

1. DESIGNING A DATABASE

 Customer records are important resources for marketers. If they can develop detailed profiles of their customers, they will be able to tailor marketing mixes specifically to meet the customers' needs. Many schools have school stores that sell products such as school supplies, school-related apparel, gifts, and other items to students.

Design a sample database that could be used to plan a marketing strategy for a school store. If you have access to a computer and a database software program, use it to design the database. If not, use a note card that is large enough to record the information that will be collected. The characteristics of the database should include at least ten separate types of data on each person. Information in the database should describe consumer demographics, needs, attitudes, and purchasing behavior. The database, when analyzed, should provide information that will help the managers of the school store make specific decisions about target markets and marketing mixes.

Print one copy of the database format that does not have any information included. Then prepare another copy filling in all items of the database with information about yourself.

2. MARKETING DECISIONS FROM MARKETING INFORMATION

 The database formats developed in the previous activity will be used for this project. With the other students in your class, review the sample formats prepared. Select one that your class agrees fits the characteristics of a good information system. Make enough copies of the format so each student in the class can complete the form. When they are all completed, enter the data for each class member into the computer to develop a class database. Using the database, prepare a report that summarizes the class characteristics. In the report, provide examples of how the information would be helpful in (a) identifying target market characteristics and (b) developing each marketing mix element for a school store.

UNIT

7

Managing and Improving Marketing

CHAPTER

23

Product/
Service
Planning

Distribution

Marketing-
Information
Management

Human Resource
Foundations

Purchasing

Economic
Foundations of
Marketing

Marketing and
Business
Foundations

Pricing

Selling

Promotion

Take Control with Management

OBJECTIVES

1. Describe the role of managers in effective marketing.

2. Define the five management functions and list activities managers perform for each function.

3. Explain how a marketing plan improves the management of marketing.

4. Demonstrate how marketing managers plan, organize, staff, lead, and control.

5. Identify ways to determine the effectiveness of marketing.

NEWSLINE

QUALIFY WITH QUALITY

One of the most important responsibilities of a retail manager is maintaining quality. Even the lowest prices will not attract customers to a store if they are not satisfied with the shopping experience. What are the factors that indicate quality?

A recent survey asked almost 1,000 shoppers about their shopping experiences. Respondents were asked to rate 21 specific factors that influenced their attitudes about a store. The most important quality feature to consumers is time. Time was rated twice as important as any other category. Time includes how long it takes to check out, total time to complete shopping, and how quickly the store processes credit cards and checks. Second in importance was customer treatment. Consumers want to feel that the store is concerned about their needs and that each employee is helpful, friendly, and courteous. If customers want help or need information, they expect it to be available. They also want employees to treat their purchases with care.

Efficiency, including the number of check-out lanes or registers and the ease of locating merchandise, was rated third. Price and the physical environment were tied for fourth place. Customers are concerned that prices are clearly marked and specials are easy to locate. They want to shop in a pleasant, roomy atmosphere. Finally, consumers are concerned about technology. They want stores to use modern technology. They also want employees to know how to use the cash registers quickly and accurately.

Managers can rate their own stores against these quality factors. Areas where ratings are high should be maintained while managers work to improve the lower-rated factors. Improving quality is one of the best ways to ensure customer satisfaction.

> **Areas where ratings are high should be maintained while managers work to improve the lower-rated factors.**

Source: Adapted from "Retailers Who Keep Score Know What Their Shoppers Value," Marketing News, May 24, 1993, p. 9.

> **Respondents were asked to rate 21 specific factors that influenced their attitudes about a store.**

COORDINATING PEOPLE AND RESOURCES

The work of an organization consists of thousands and thousands of activities. Those activities often seem unrelated to each other. Many employees in a business and most customers are totally unaware of the variety of activities that go on every day in many different locations. However, all of that work is necessary for products and services to be produced and distributed and for customer orders to be received and processed. Each activity needs to be completed on time and accurately. Each activity must be coordinated with other related activities.

What makes a company successful? A quality product? satisfied customers? well-trained and motivated employees? efficient operations? profit? Each of these is an important ingredient in success. Successful organizations have another important factor—management.

Effective managers are able to organize the resources and work of a company in ways that result in success. Companies with effective managers usually have good products, employees, and operations resulting in satisfied customers.

MANAGEMENT WORKS

Management is one of the most important functions of a business. *Very simply, managing is getting the work of an organization done through other people and resources.* How can businesses make sure the resources and people work as well as possible so that they are successful? If the resources available are not the ones needed for a task, that work cannot be performed. If employees are dissatisfied with their jobs or are not well trained, they will not work effectively. If customer service is not performed well, salespeople may receive complaints. If someone in order processing is not careful in calculating prices on an invoice, someone in accounting will face the problem of explaining an overcharge or the need for an additional payment to a customer. These are the types of challenges facing managers (see Figure 23-1).

The Work of Management

Without Management   With Management

FIGURE 23-1 ▪ Without management, there would be little coordination of the work in an organization.

MARKETING MANAGEMENT

Consider the many resources and people involved in marketing. Products need to be planned, priced, distributed, and promoted. Each of the mix elements must be coordinated with the others. If a product is not distributed in the time or the way that is expected by salespeople or advertisers, customers may be promised a product that cannot be delivered. If product development costs much more than budgeted, pricing decisions will need to be changed. *Marketing management is the process of coordinating people and resources to plan and implement an effective marketing strategy.*

The work of more than one company usually needs to be coordinated as products move through a channel of distribution.

The channel may include a manufacturer, transportation company, finance company, wholesaler, retailer, advertising agency, and others. The work of marketing managers can be very complex.

Now that you understand what a marketing strategy is, you are able to describe the work of marketing managers. Marketing managers are responsible for identifying markets and planning marketing mixes. You also know how to determine if marketing managers are doing a good job. According to the marketing concept, effective marketing results in satisfying exchanges. Marketing managers are successful when customers in the target markets are satisfied and the company is profitable.

MANAGEMENT FUNCTIONS AND ACTIVITIES

The definition of managing provided earlier is quite general. It is hard to determine specifically what managers do from that definition. A better understanding of management comes from examining the five functions of management. Those functions are illustrated in Figure 23-2.

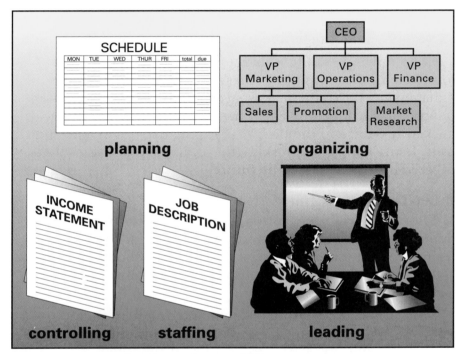

The Functions of Management

FIGURE 23-2 ▪ Five functions are common to all managers. This is true whether or not managers work in small or large businesses; whether they are a company president or a beginning supervisor.

PLANNING

Planning involves analyzing information, setting goals, and determining how to achieve them. The president of a company is responsible for determining the direction of the business and making sure that plans are in place to move forward. Supervisors determine what their work groups need to accomplish each day and assign duties to each person. Even though the two managers work at different levels in the organization, both have planning responsibilities as a part of their jobs. There are two types of planning that managers complete—long-range planning and short-term planning.

Long-Range Planning

Long-range planning analyzes information that can affect the business over a long period of time (typically one year or more). Long-range planning includes setting broad goals and direction. Examples of long-range planning in a business are the strategic plan and business plan. In marketing, the marketing plan is a long-range plan because it sets direction and goals for all marketing functions and personnel.

Long-range planning is difficult because it relies on information from a variety of sources that may not be totally accurate. Managers need to anticipate what might occur over the time that the plan will be in place. They must use their experience, marketing data, and the help of planning experts to make decisions. Using management skills, they will make decisions that will guide the business in the future.

Short-Term Planning

Short-term planning (often known as operational planning) identifies specific objectives and activities for each part of the business. Short-term planning is based on the long-range plan, so that all of the areas of the business are coordinated with each other.

Think of the marketing plan that we studied in Chapter 11. The marketing plan identifies the target markets that the business plans to serve. It identifies the marketing mix that must be developed to meet the needs of each market. It also sets goals that the company will use to evaluate whether the plan is successful.

The managers of each specific area of marketing (research, distribution, sales, customer service) use the information from the marketing plan to determine the objectives and activities for their areas. They will meet regularly to coordinate their plans and activities. In this way, each of the short-term plans will coordinate to meet the long-range goals.

Research managers determine the information needed to make good decisions in each part of marketing. They plan the studies or collect the data at the appropriate time so it is available to managers who are making the decisions. The distribution managers determine what products need to be moved to specific locations in what quantities.

Sales managers provide training and product information to salespeople. They help identify target markets and prepare the salesperson to work with those customers. They provide appropriate information about the marketing mix to meet the customers' needs. Customer service managers insure that personnel and resources are available to respond to customer needs after a product purchase. They make sure problems are solved and the customer is satisfied with the purchase.

ORGANIZING

Managers organize resources so work can be accomplished effectively and efficiently. Organization charts in a business divide work into divisions or departments and show the relationships among those work units. There are many ways to divide up the work in a business. Managers organize by assigning responsibility and authority to others to get work done. Managers must develop effective working relationships within the work group and with other work groups. Later in this chapter, different ways of organizing marketing activities are discussed.

STAFFING

The activities needed to match individuals with the work to be done are known as staffing. Managers prepare job descriptions, recruit and select employees, determine how personnel will be compensated, and provide the necessary training so employees can complete their work well.

Staffing is often considered the most difficult of the management functions. There are a number of activities involved in staffing, and the need to work with a variety of people. It may be difficult to find people with the skills that match the jobs in a company. Effective training requires time and money. Some companies are not willing to invest in good training programs. Managers are also responsible for evaluating the performance of each employee. They can reward those who are doing well but may need to terminate employees who cannot meet the requirements of their jobs.

LEADING

Is there a difference in being a manager and being a leader? Who do you identify as leaders—in your class, school, community, or country? What are the characteristics of an effective leader? Today in business, leadership is identified as one of the most important qualities of effective management. *Leading is the ability to communicate the direction of the business and to influence others to successfully carry out the needed work.* Effective leadership includes commitment and motivation, effective communications, establishing good working relationships, and recognizing and rewarding effective performance.

CONTROLLING

When controlling, managers measure performance, compare it with goals and objectives, and make corrections when necessary. A company establishes a goal that 95 percent of all customer orders are delivered within 24 hours. The manager tracks the orders to be certain that the goal is met. When the manager sees that fewer than 95 percent of the orders are being delivered on time, quick action must be taken. The manager must determine why orders are late and take steps to improve performance.

Specific controlling activities include setting standards, collecting and analyzing information, considering methods of improving performance, changing plans when necessary, solving problems, and resolving conflicts. Several common tools are used by managers to control operations including plans, budgets, evaluation forms, financial reports, and management information systems.

IMPROVING MANAGEMENT WITH A MARKETING PLAN

Studies have been done that compare successful companies with unsuccessful companies. While there are many things that affect success, one of the most important differences typically seen is that successful companies develop written plans, while unsuccessful ones do not. Marketing plans are developed to help marketing managers complete each of the management functions (see Figure 23-3).

Marketing Plan Outline

I. Market Analysis

A. Purpose and Mission of the Business

B. Description of Current Markets and Strategies

C. Primary Competitors and Their Strengths/Weaknesses

D. External Environment Analysis

    1. Economy   4. Competition

    2. Laws and Regulations   5. Technology

    3. Costs   6. Social Factors

E. Internal Analysis

    1. Strengths

    2. Weaknesses

    3. Anticipated Changes

II. Marketing Strategy

A. Marketing Goals/Expected Outcomes

B. Target Market Description

    1. Identifying Characteristics

    2. Unique Needs, Attitudes, Behaviors

C. Marketing Mix Description

    1. Product/Service

    2. Distribution

    3. Pricing

    4. Promotion

D. Positioning Statement

III. Action Plan

A. Activity

B. Responsibility

C. Schedule

D. Budget

E. Evaluation Procedures

    1. Evidence of Success

    2. Method of Collecting Evidence

FIGURE 23-3 ▪ Each section of a marketing plan is important to a marketing manager in completing the five functions of management.

INFORMATION FOR PLANNING

It is easy to see how the marketing plan is related to the planning function. It is a long-range plan that sets goals and direction for the company for the length of time that the plan is in effect. The first part of the plan, *Market Analysis*, reviews internal and external information that affects marketing. By studying that part of the plan, managers learn about the competition, the economy, and other important factors that can affect the success of their plans. They are made aware of strengths and weaknesses so weaknesses can be improved and strengths can be emphasized.

CLASSICS AND CONTEMPORARIES

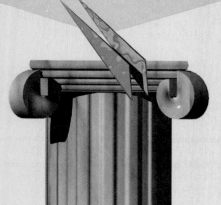

THE MANAGER AS MARKETER

What is your image of bank executives—gray suits, large offices, conservative attitudes? A work schedule that includes meetings in plush conference rooms or on the golf course with top business leaders? You may be surprised to meet the managers of Fifth Third Bank in Cincinnati. You may even have difficulty meeting them. It certainly won't be on the golf course. It will more likely be in their cars as they travel to meet with current or potential customers.

Fifth Third Bank has discovered the value of marketing and involving managers as salespeople for the bank. Each manager is assigned a number of area businesses. The managers don't wait for the businesses to call and inquire about banking services. They don't even rely on telephone calls to the business. Instead, each manager has a daily "call book." Armed with information about Fifth Third's products and services, the managers visit each customer. They discuss the customer's business and financial needs and determine the level of satisfaction with the customer's current bank.

Often prospective customers will meet with them simply because they are surprised and impressed with the personal contact from the manager of a bank. If they switch to Fifth Third, they continue to receive the same personal attention and a variety of financial services particularly tailored to small- and medium-sized businesses.

The results of this personalized, marketing approach to banking have been effective. While Fifth Third Bank is small compared to many other banks, it has a higher performance rating than banks that are over 100 times its size. Their rating is significantly higher than the industry average. In addition to adding customers, it is growing by purchasing other small, regional banks. One of the first strategies in each of the new banks is to teach marketing and selling skills to the managers.

Source: Adapted from "A Bank That's Putting on the Blitz," Business Week, August 3, 1992, p. 50.

The second section of the marketing plan is the *Marketing Strategy*. In this section the target markets are identified and the marketing mix is described. Most importantly, the goals and outcomes that will be used to measure the success of the marketing plan are described. Every manager who has marketing responsibilities needs to be very familiar with this section of the plan. Every planning activity in the company is directed at implementing that strategy and achieving those goals and objectives. The managers responsible for each marketing function must determine how their function supports the marketing strategy. The goals and objectives they develop for their part of the business must also support the goals identified in the marketing plan.

In the final section, *the Action Plan,* specific activities and responsibilities are identified to guide short-term operations. All of the managers of marketing activities contribute to the development of this section. It identifies the work needed in their part of the business and guides them in planning day-to-day activities, including schedules and budgets. Most companies require each manager to prepare written operational plans and to show how their plans support the marketing plan.

DIRECTION FOR ORGANIZING

Much of the organizing work in a company is done before a marketing plan is developed. A company decides which marketing functions and activities it will perform and which will be left to other companies. It develops a structure that organizes marketing personnel and activities into departments. It identifies the responsibilities of managers for the various departments and activities. Those decisions usually will not change a great deal even though many marketing plans will be written. If a company is successful with its target markets and makes only minor adjustments in the marketing mixes, it will not want to change its basic organizational structure unless it sees ways to improve performance or save money with the change.

SUPPORT FOR STAFFING DECISIONS

Effective marketing requires people with the skills necessary to perform the required marketing activities. Again, the marketing plan provides a useful tool for managers to determine staffing needs. The Action Plan is particularly important since specific activities and responsibilities are described in that section.

Managers match those activities with the current marketing employees. If the employees do not have the necessary skills to perform the activities, managers need to develop training programs. If there are not adequate numbers of employees to perform the necessary work, new employees need to be hired or other businesses can be brought into the marketing channel to perform those activities. In some instances the current employees may not be needed for new marketing activities. If they cannot be retrained to perform other needed work, they may need to be terminated.

Using the marketing plan to evaluate staffing needs is an important way for managers to determine where problems are likely to occur. You are probably familiar with businesses that had problems because they did not have adequate numbers of employees or the employees did not have the needed skills or were not motivated to serve customers well. Managers who pay careful attention to staffing needs, training, and employee motivation often have a decided advantage over their competitors.

MANAGERS AS LEADERS

Many marketing efforts fail because the people responsible for the activities do not perform them well. Poor performance does not always occur because people do not have the skills to do the work. It may be due to a lack of leadership. Even though a manager has developed an effective plan and has the people and resources needed to carry out the plan, another ingredient is necessary—leadership.

Employees need to be a part of the business. They want to be involved and understand why the work they do is important. A marketing manager that is a leader involves employees in developing the plan. The manager discusses the marketing plan with employees when it is completed. In that way, the employees see why the plan is important. They understand how it can lead to success for the business and the people who work for the business.

The marketing manager also determines the working relationships that are necessary to implement the plan. Those relationships may be among people in the same department, in different departments in the company, and even among people in other businesses. A good leader develops effective working relationships. The manager also finds ways to recognize and reward the people who do their work well. When activities are completed that are an important part of the marketing plan, the people who are responsible need to know that they are doing the right things and that their manager and co-workers appreciate the good work.

GAINING CONTROL OF MARKETING

An old proverb says, "if you don't know where you're going, you will never know when you get there." A marketing plan states clearly who the business wants to serve, what marketing activities are required, and the goals the business expects to achieve. Each of those decisions is used to measure the effectiveness of marketing.

Evaluating Effectiveness

Marketing managers study how well they are reaching and serving each target market. They determine the market potential, the company's market share, and the share held by each competitor. Most businesses evaluate customer satisfaction with the products and services as well as with other parts of the marketing mix. They want to see high satisfaction levels. A business becomes concerned if satisfaction begins to decline or if competitors are rated higher by customers.

The marketing mix is identified in the marketing plan. The activities needed to implement each mix element are specifically described. Schedules, budgets and other planning tools are prepared. Most businesses develop standards of performance for marketing activities and evaluate each to see if the performance standards are being met. Whenever managers receive information that shows activities are not being performed as expected, they must take immediate action to correct problems.

Responding to Environmental Change

There is another valuable way that the marketing plan helps managers with the controlling process. The first part of the marketing plan carefully describes the internal and external environment on which the plan is based. A change in any part of that environment could affect the success of the marketing plan. Managers read research reports, magazines, and newspapers. They attend conferences, talk to colleagues, and review other information so they will be up-to-date and prepared to respond to changes.

The types of environmental factors that often change are the economy, technology, competition, and laws and regulations. For example, during 1993, many economic signs indicated that consumers were changing their spending patterns. Manufacturers and retailers began to produce and stock more novelty and luxury consumer products for the end-of-year holiday period.

MARKETING MANAGEMENT

This section discusses some of the specific activities that marketing managers perform. Dyang Chen is the executive vice-president of marketing for an international automobile manufacturer. James Swathmore is a field sales manager for a food products wholesaler. He supervises five salespeople in a large northeastern state. The partial organization charts in Figure 23-4 illustrate the differences between Chen's and Swathmore's positions.

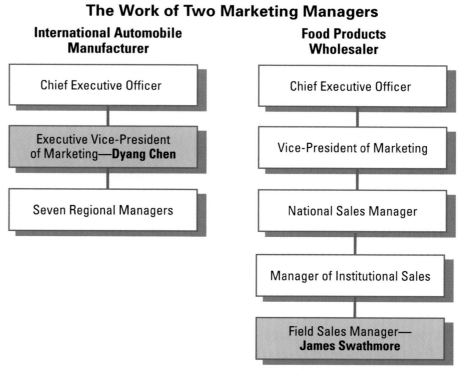

The Work of Two Marketing Managers

International Automobile Manufacturer	Food Products Wholesaler
Chief Executive Officer	Chief Executive Officer
Executive Vice-President of Marketing—**Dyang Chen**	Vice-President of Marketing
Seven Regional Managers	National Sales Manager
	Manager of Institutional Sales
	Field Sales Manager— **James Swathmore**

FIGURE 23-4 ▪ Dyang Chen and James Swathmore hold very different positions within their companies. However, both must be effective at planning, organizing, staffing, leading, and controlling.

PLANNING

Ms. Chen spends most of her time planning with four other top executives and the CEO to set direction for the company. She is involved in strategic planning, which identifies how the company must change over the next five to ten years. Ms. Chen studies consumer purchasing trends throughout the world and how the economies of various countries are developing. She is very concerned about international trade agreements, increases and decreases of quotas, and changes in tariffs among several countries that have a major impact on the international automobile industry. Energy sources and prices, inflation, and the values of world currencies are also concerns for Ms. Chen.

The major responsibility of Ms. Chen's office is to prepare the company's marketing plan. The plan is developed for a five-year period, with specific plans for each of the five years. The marketing plan is used by seven regional managers to prepare more specific plans for their regions of the global market.

Mr. Swathmore is also involved in planning but he concentrates on short-term plans. He develops quarterly plans, but implements monthly and weekly plans. While Mr. Swathmore must be familiar with the entire company's marketing plan, he is most concerned with the promotional mix element and the selling responsibilities.

Mr. Swathmore spends most of his planning time identifying customers, assigning them to salespeople, developing schedules and budgets for each person, and helping salespeople to develop specific sales strategies for major customers.

ORGANIZING

Mr. Swathmore and Ms. Chen have very different organizing responsibilities. The overall marketing structure of each company is already set. The automobile manufacturer is organized into seven worldwide regions. The food wholesaler is organized by customer type and geographically by state. Several common ways that companies organize their marketing operations are shown in Figure 23-5 (on page 712).

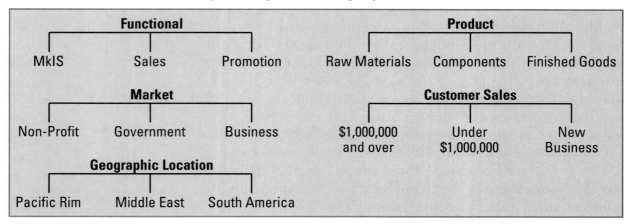

Organizing Marketing Operations

Functional		
MkIS	Sales	Promotion

Product		
Raw Materials	Components	Finished Goods

Market		
Non-Profit	Government	Business

Customer Sales		
$1,000,000 and over	Under $1,000,000	New Business

Geographic Location		
Pacific Rim	Middle East	South America

FIGURE 23-5 ▪ Marketing activities can be organized by function, product, market, sales, or geography. Managers' responsibilities will vary depending on the organization of their businesses.

Ms. Chen's organizing activities focus on developing company-wide policies and procedures. Those policies and procedures will determine the organizational structure for marketing, the functions that are performed, and the types of companies that will participate in marketing the automobiles.

Mr. Swathmore must work within the policies and procedures established by his manager. He is responsible for determining what activities need to be performed and assigning those duties to the salespeople. He delegates authority and responsibility to each salesperson to complete the necessary selling tasks.

STAFFING

Each of the managers is responsible for getting the work of the organization done through other people. Therefore they need to identify the needs for personnel and fill those positions with the most qualified people. Ms. Chen will hire a few people to be her assistants. However, her main responsibilities for staffing are to develop policies and procedures. She makes decisions about the percentage of the marketing budget that will be allocated to employee salaries, benefits, and expenses.

Mr. Swathmore is directly responsible for the salespeople who work in the territory he manages. He may not have total responsibility for hiring each person, but he identifies when an opening exists and describes the requirements for any open position. He helps with recruiting, interviewing, and selecting the person to fill the position. Most sales managers are very active in training new salespeople and helping to improve the selling skills of experienced employees.

LEADING

Leading is an important responsibility for each of the managers. Some people would expect that Ms. Chen has more leadership responsibilities because she is the top marketing executive in the company. However, Mr. Swathmore must be an effective leader if the selling team is to be successful in its territory. Each manager must be able to involve people in planning, communicate expectations, and build effective teams to accomplish the work. They need to be able to recognize performance that contributes to the goals of their company and provide rewards that encourage people to continue to perform well.

CONTROLLING

Controlling is another area of marketing where both managers have similar responsibilities. Each prepares objectives and specific plans to guide their work. They have developed standards for performance of the various marketing activities for which they are responsible. The major controlling activity is to gather and review information to determine if the objectives, plans, and standards are being met.

An effective marketing information system is important to each manager. The marketing information system gathers and analyzes information. It identifies when problems are occurring. Both Mr. Swathmore and Ms. Chen spend a great deal of time studying reports. They must identify the part of their plans that are working well and the areas where problems may be developing. Ms. Chen concentrates on products or regions that have high and low performance. Mr. Swathmore is concerned about individual customers and salespeople.

When a specific problem is identified, each manager works quickly to correct it. They review budgets, schedules, and activities from their plans to see if some are not being performed in the way that was expected. They may have to revise the plans if it is clear that the original plans will not work.

IN THE SPOTLIGHT

CREATING OPPORTUNITY

A special skill of effective managers and entrepreneurs is recognizing which unmet needs suggest business opportunities. Gaynell and Elias Henricks created a business that many others felt could not succeed. They did it because they understood the major elements of successful marketing and management.

Wee Care Academy, Inc., is a unique type of child-care facility. Located in an older low-income neighborhood in Birmingham, Alabama, it is not just a place for parents to drop off their children while they work. It is a learning center where children from six weeks to six years of age are introduced to reading, mathematics, and language skills. Because most of the center's clients are African Americans, Wee Care emphasizes African-American culture to build a strong self-concept and identity in each child.

The business idea grew out of the experience and needs of Mr. and Mrs. Henricks. Gaynell and Elias both had successful careers: Gaynell at IBM and Elias with AT&T. Both had completed their MBA degrees before their triplets were born. Finding adequate day care was a problem, so Gaynell stayed home to care for the babies. However, the Henricks realized that other families faced the same child-care problems they did. The Henricks believed they could create a successful day care center, even though others had tried and failed.

Banks were unwilling to invest in their idea, so they started the center in an old school house with the savings the family had accumulated. They knew that most parents preferred an academic center, so Wee Care emphasized a strong curriculum of art, music, and history.

Careful product development and marketing expanded the enrollment in the Wee Care Academy from 6 to 40 children in just six months. The idea has been so successful that the fourth Academy is about ready to open. The Henricks are earning revenues of nearly $2 million a year from their business. That is a profitable reward for two people who recognized an opportunity and had the management skills to take advantage of it.

Source: Adapted from "Wee Academy: The Challenges and Triumphs of Launching Birmingham's First Afrocentric Day-care Centers," Harold Jackson, Black Enterprise, November, 1993, pp. 78–81.

DETERMINING MARKETING EFFECTIVENESS

Remember that managers are responsible for getting the work of the business done through other people and resources. If the work is not done well, the manager has not been successful. An important management responsibility is determining the effectiveness of marketing.

How can managers decide if marketing is effective? Is it based on the highest sales, largest market share, or most profit? Is the company with the best products or the products that have been on the market longest the most effective?

Managers may not be able to agree on what is effective marketing (see Figure 23-6). However, the definition of marketing that we learned at the beginning of the book states that effective marketing results in satisfying exchanges. That means that both the customer and the business must be satisfied. If we believe in that definition, then we need to be able to determine when the customer and business are satisfied.

Measures of Marketing Effectiveness

Sales, Profits, Costs, Employee Performance, Channel Effectiveness, Customer Satisfaction

FIGURE 23-6 ▪ If you were the marketing manager of a company, what would you use to determine the effectiveness of marketing?

MEASURING CUSTOMER SATISFACTION

Customers are satisfied when they select a company's product or service to meet a need, use it, and choose it again when they have the same need. Because of this process, an increasing level of sales is usually a good indication of customer satisfaction. However, companies should be careful to gather information on repeat purchase and use. They should be able to identify the level of sales for specific target markets.

Many companies spend a great deal of time and money studying customer satisfaction. They telephone customers or ask them to complete surveys. Some companies develop customer service centers to make sure they identify and solve customer problems. It is important to keep records of customer questions, problems, and complaints. Positive responses from customers

should also be recorded. You are probably familiar with businesses that have customer suggestions cards and other methods of regularly gathering consumer information.

Companies should not ignore the satisfaction of other businesses in the channel of distribution. Retailers and wholesalers are customers of manufacturers. If they are not satisfied with the products and services provided by the manufacturer, they may decide to work with a competitor. Retailers and wholesalers need to inform manufacturers of any problems customers have with their products so the problems can be resolved. Many businesses now involve other channel members in planning. They regularly check with those businesses to make sure they are receiving the support needed to be effective.

MEASURING BUSINESS SATISFACTION

Every business operates for a purpose. For many businesses, the purpose is to make a profit for the owners. For some businesses, however, profit is not the most important purpose. Some people start and operate a business because they enjoy the work. Some organizations are developed because of the contribution they make to the community. The success of schools, churches, city missions, public health centers, and other similar organizations is usually not measured by the level of profit. They certainly need enough money to operate. These organizations have to operate very efficiently, but profit is not the primary reason for existing. They determine their success by looking for improvements in the community or society that result from their work.

Analyzing Goals

The success of a business is determined by its goals. If the goal of a business is to increase sales or market share, it will not be successful if sales and market share decline. If a business sets a goal to achieve a profit of 4 percent of all sales or an 11 percent return on the money the owners have invested, it will be successful when it achieves that goal. Even if the goal of an organization is to change the attitudes or behavior of a group of people (stop smoking, stay in school), it will be successful only if the people it works with have changed.

Most goals of businesses and organizations are quite specific and can be measured. Businesses gather information on sales, costs, market share, and profits to determine their success. Non-profit organizations gather information on increases in attendance, use of services, changes in behavior, or differences in attitudes and beliefs.

Financial Analysis

When people think of marketing, they often fail to recognize the importance of budgets and financial performance. However, marketing managers must pay careful attention to those factors. They need to understand financial information and use it to determine the success of marketing activities. Sales of products in various markets can be compared from one year to the next. Costs associated with specific activities can be analyzed. Profits from one target market can be compared with those from another. The profitability of a specific marketing strategy can be analyzed.

Employee Satisfaction

Managers also need to be concerned about the satisfaction of the people who work for the business. There is a great deal of evidence that employees who enjoy their work are more productive. They want to contribute to the success of their employer. When employees are not happy, they will often find reasons not to do as well as they could.

Marketing managers need to determine the level of employee satisfaction. Some companies ask their employees to complete surveys. Others hold regular meetings where employees can discuss problems and make suggestions. Today, many companies form work teams. The teams have a great deal of responsibility for setting goals. They may determine the ways that work should be completed or how to solve customer problems. They may even be responsible for hiring other members of the work team and determining how bonus money should be distributed. Involving employees in important decisions usually increases their satisfaction.

REVIEW

Marketing is a very complex combination of functions and activities. If the activities are not well planned and coordinated, it is likely that problems will occur, customers will be dissatisfied, and the company will be unable to make a profit.

Managers have the responsibility to accomplish the work of an organization through the use of people and other resources. While each manager in a business performs very different activities from other managers, all managers are responsible for the same five management functions: planning, organizing, staffing, leading, and controlling.

The marketing plan is a guide for marketing management. It is used to gather and analyze information, determine goals, develop a marketing strategy, and describe action steps for implementing the plan. Managers must be familiar with the marketing plan and use the information in it as a basis for their own planning. In this way, the many marketing activities and management decisions will be coordinated with each other.

Marketing managers are responsible for determining the effectiveness of marketing. Each business and organization will identify the factors used to measure effectiveness. Both customer satisfaction and business satisfaction are important to successful marketing.

MARKETING FOUNDATIONS

1. NAME THE MANAGEMENT FUNCTION

Read each of the following statements and determine if it is a planning, organizing, leading, controlling, or staffing function.

a. The home office of a drug store chain sends directions on how merchandise should be displayed on the shelves.

b. The owner of Norma's Hardware surveys her customers

regarding the hours she should be open and decides to open her shop one hour earlier.

c. Aries Stavros holds a staff meeting every week to make sure that the staff understands their job assignments and to hear any complaints and questions they may have.

d. The owners of a dog grooming service decide to offer training classes to their employees in customer service.

e. Su Lee Han finds it necessary to review the budget allocations for her department once a week.

2. MAKING EFFECTIVE EXCHANGES

A business will thrive if satisfactory exchanges are made. Both the company and the customer must be satisfied that they have received the most value for their money. List five ways a marketer can measure customer satisfaction and five ways a marketer can measure business satisfaction.

MARKETING RESEARCH

1. CUSTOMER CLUES

A lumber yard recently decided to survey its final and business consumers to determine if they were satisfied with the type of service they were receiving. The following results were obtained:

	Final Consumers		Business Consumers	
	% Yes	% No	% Yes	% No
Are sale items usually available?	45	55	75	25
Do you wait more than two minutes to be helped?	15	85	37	63
Is sales staff knowledgeable?	95	5	83	17
Are prices competitive?	50	50	94	6
Is sales staff courteous?	82	18	85	15

a. Develop a bar graph comparing the responses of business and final consumers.

b. Identify three problems that company managers can address and write three measurable objectives to correct the problems.

2. QUALITIES OF A GOOD MANAGER

Look at the classified ads in your local newspaper. Cut out at least five ads for managers. Paste each ad to a piece of paper and list the qualifications for each job. Is there one qualification that is predominant in all of the ads? If so, which one?

MARKETING PLANNING

1. ORGANIZING FOR GROWTH

 Mark Peters is the owner/manager of a wholesale electrical supply house. He has 40 employees and until recently has managed the entire operation himself. Lately, his business is growing. He has decided he needs to reorganize the business and have a layer of management that reports to him.

Eighteen people work in the warehouse. They are responsible for shipping, receiving, and inventory. The supply house has five employees who work the counter, maintain inventory records, and handle some of the more routine paper work. There are ten truck drivers who deliver and pick up merchandise. And finally, seven people work in the office handling budgets, accounts receivable, and order-taking.

Develop a complete organizational chart for the business, adding the layer of management. Indicate levels and areas of responsibility.

2. LEADING YOUR EMPLOYEES

Managers realize that a good product or service will go unsold unless the employees do the best job possible in dealing with customers. Managers spend a great deal of time motivating and encouraging employees to do their very best. From your personal experience, describe five ways that managers can support their employees through positive motivation.

MARKETING MANAGEMENT

1. INVESTIGATING NEW IDEAS

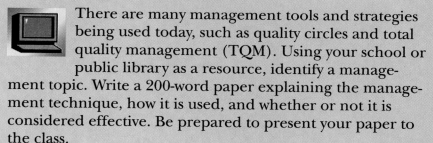

There are many management tools and strategies being used today, such as quality circles and total quality management (TQM). Using your school or public library as a resource, identify a management topic. Write a 200-word paper explaining the management technique, how it is used, and whether or not it is considered effective. Be prepared to present your paper to the class.

2. USING THE MARKETING PLAN AS A GUIDE

Identify a specific business and the product or service it markets. Explain how each section of the marketing plan can be used as a guide for each of the management functions within the organization. Describe the function and the management activities that would be completed to market the product or service.

There Is Room for Improvement

OBJECTIVES

1. Discuss the contributions of marketing.
2. Examine areas where marketing can be improved.
3. Analyze ethical issues facing marketers.
4. Describe the impact of technology on marketing.
5. Identify factors that are expected to affect marketing in the future.
6. Explain why professional development is important in marketing.

NEWSLINE

DOES SCENT SELL?

Would people use an automatic teller machine more often if the money dispensed has a mint smell? If consumers receive advertisements for automobile loans that smell like a new car, are they more likely to apply for loans? Are movies more realistic when scents are sprayed into theaters? Can hospitals, dentist offices, or banks become less intimidating through the use of pleasant scents?

Fragrance is one new marketing tool being tested by a variety of companies. Some people believe it is a tool that will not work. Others suggest it is unethical to provide a stimulus that consumers are not aware of in order to encourage them to buy.

Scents are not really new in marketing. The smell of popcorn in movie theaters and cookies in bakeries have attracted customer interest and increased sales for years.

Fragrance is one new marketing tool being tested by a variety of companies.

However, introducing odors where they don't naturally occur is relatively new. The method was first used in magazine and direct mail advertising with "scratch-and-sniff" patches. Advertisers of perfumes, laundry detergents, and other products that have a distinctive fragrance were able to add that fragrance to the page on which the ad was printed.

The newest application of fragrance marketing is to continuously pump a small amount of fragrance into a retail store. Those who use the marketing tool see it as an extension of clean floors, fresh paint, and good lighting.

Information on the effectiveness of using fragrances to sell products is not extensive. Studies have shown that some scents seem to result in increased numbers of customers,

while other scents actually result in reduced sales. Consumer surveys also have mixed results. Many consumers are upset about the possibility of businesses using fragrances to influence purchases. Others believe that pleasant fragrances can make shopping more enjoyable and that the scent of some products is an important part of the purchase decision.

Many companies are looking carefully at the new marketing tool. Is it just a fad or a gimmick, being promoted by the very companies that sell the equipment to add fragrances to the air, to packaging, and to advertising? Or is it a method that can increase customer satisfaction with a company and its products? Is it ethical to use fragrances to market products without the customers' knowledge? Will the cost of the technology increase the price of products with no real customer benefit? As with most new ideas, there are benefits and risks. Marketers and customers will ultimately determine the success of fragrance marketing.

Source: Adapted from "Scent as a Marketing Tool," Marketing News, January 18, 1993, pp. 1–2.

MARKETING IMPACTS OUR LIVES

How has marketing changed our lives? When you began your study of marketing, you might have had a difficult time answering that question. Now you can identify many ways that marketing affects your life every day. Let's examine a few of the ways our lives are different because of marketing.

MARKETING GIVES US CHOICES

We often take for granted the variety of products and services available. However, our lives would be quite different without them. Not only can we obtain almost any type of product or service, but we usually have choices of brands, prices, and features for each of those products and services. The best way to see how marketing improves choices is to compare countries that have market-driven economies with those that have controlled economies.

Consumers in controlled economies often find that products and services are expensive and difficult to obtain. When they can find a product, they usually have to buy the only one available rather than choosing one that best meets their needs.

MARKETING REDUCES COSTS

An understanding of economics demonstrates that prices are highest when there are few good alternatives in controlled markets. As choices increase and as markets expand, prices decrease. Look at almost any new product and you will see that prices are highest when the product is first introduced. As the company finds more customers and as competitors enter the market, prices come down.

Marketing influences prices in many ways. Products can be widely distributed. Customers and competitors alike receive information so decisions are better. Marketers also make products easier to obtain and afford.

MARKETING CREATES A WORLDWIDE MARKETPLACE

The U.S. consumer market is the envy of many other countries because of the variety

of products that are available and affordable to average consumers. U.S. products are distributed throughout the world because of that consumer demand. Not only are U.S. products exported to meet international demand; marketing makes foreign-produced goods and services readily available in the United States.

MARKETING OFFERS REWARDING CAREERS

It is often said that one of every three jobs in the United States is a marketing job or one that requires a significant number of marketing skills. Marketing is one of the best routes to the top management positions in many companies. Most organizations now value marketing. They train many of their employees to understand and use marketing in their jobs.

Marketing careers also offer variety. Marketing jobs are found from the lowest to the highest levels in business. Some require little education beyond high school. Others require many years of advanced education and experience. Marketing careers provide opportunities in all types and sizes of organizations throughout the world.

MARKETING IMPROVES BUSINESS PRACTICES

In the past many companies produced the products they wanted to make. They sold them in the ways they believed were best. This was known as the production orientation. As marketers learned more and more about consumers, companies began to understand their needs. They began to respond to those needs and provide the products and services that consumers wanted.

An understanding of the marketing mix improved the locations where products were sold. It improved pricing strategies and communications and promotion efforts of businesses. Today, using the marketing orientation, all parts of the business work together to satisfy customers and make a profit.

MARKETING IMPROVES THE STANDARD OF LIVING

Marketing increases economic activity. Product choices, reduced prices, and jobs result from marketing activities. When people have jobs, they have money to spend on products and services. The businesses that sell to those consumers use the money received in a number of ways. They purchase from other companies, expand their operations, and pay employees. All of this economic activity leads to direct benefits for society.

In addition to more product choices and jobs, the consumers and businesses pay taxes. Those taxes allow government to provide the variety of services that citizens request. Look at times of recession or depression to see the results of a weak economy. Because of marketing, economies are stronger and peoples' lives are improved.

MARKETING CAN BE IMPROVED

Marketing is very different today than it was even 15 years ago. We know that when companies perform marketing activities better and more efficiently, they are at an advantage in the marketplace. There is also evidence that responding to consumer needs and working to be socially responsible contributes to company success. Business people are constantly studying marketing activities and identifying ways to improve them. But just because marketing is changing does not always mean that it is better. Several areas are of particular concern among marketing professionals.

DO MARKETERS KEEP THE BEST INTERESTS OF CONSUMERS IN MIND?

Marketers gather detailed information about consumers. They understand consumer decision-making much more than in the past. It is possible to misuse that information to manipulate consumers. If the goal of marketers is simply to make a sale, the consumer may be very dissatisfied after the purchase. On the other hand, if marketers focus on long-term customer satisfaction, they are likely to be very careful in their use of information and marketing activities.

DOES MARKETING SUPPORT THE PURPOSE OF THE BUSINESS?

In the past, the sole purpose of marketing was to sell the products and services of the business. Today, as marketers conduct market research and identify marketing opportunities, there may be pressures on businesses to respond to that information.

Some businesses that have tried to respond to opportunities identified by marketers have not been very successful. Franchises have expanded too rapidly and been unable to keep a high level of customer service. Manufacturers have developed new types of products based on consumer surveys. Then they found they did not have the needed technology to produce and service the new products in the quantities necessary to be profitable. Retailers have tried to change their product mixes to attract new customers only to find they no longer meet the needs of their existing customers.

New opportunities need to be carefully studied to be sure they are appropriate for the business. The business must be able to successfully respond to new opportunities.

ARE MARKETING DECISIONS ETHICAL?

In the 1980s, a number of business people received publicity for their unethical business practices. Their work in the savings and loan industry and in investment banking resulted in a large number of business failures and losses of millions of dollars. The life savings of many people were lost. The business activities were illegal as well as unethical.

Those affected were customers, other people in the business, and competitors. Unethical marketing practices harm people directly and indirectly. The next section examines marketing ethics in more detail.

ARE MARKETING ACTIVITIES SOCIALLY RESPONSIBLE?

Environmental concerns, quality of life, community improvement, international relations—all of these are current issues that can be affected by marketing. What is the responsibility of marketers in these areas?

The marketing orientation that guides most marketing decisions is based on meeting the needs of customers. However, it is possible to satisfy customers while not being socially responsible. For example, fast-food restaurants found that the packaging used to keep products hot contributes to the amount of litter and takes up space in landfills. Manufacturers and retailers of tobacco and alcohol products know that there is a demand, but also a social cost, for the use of their products.

Some people suggest that marketing needs to expand beyond a marketing orientation to a social responsibility orientation. Decisions would be made by considering the needs of society and the impact on society, as well as the needs of the customer. The difficulty presented by the social responsibility orientation is that there is seldom agreement on the needs of society. It may also be very difficult to determine how marketing decisions will affect society until long after the decisions are made.

MARKETERS MUST BE ETHICAL

As we learned in Chapter 3, ethics refers to decisions and behavior based on honest and fair standards. In more specific terms, ethics means that you do the right thing and that you do things right. Marketers are regularly faced with choices when making decisions. When marketers have choices, those choices should be evaluated to determine if the decisions involve ethics. If there is a possibility that actions may not be honest and fair, marketers must carefully consider their actions. When companies and individuals are viewed as unethical, the level of trust decreases. People seldom want to work with companies and people who are unethical.

ETHICAL DECISION-MAKING

Ethical decision-making is not always easy. What is right and wrong? There are many concepts on which most people agree. Often we are guided by laws, business policies, and professional codes of ethics. But ethics are based on values, and values can differ among groups of people.

Cultures and societies have specific values. Marketers often find differences in beliefs as they work with a variety of target markets. Those differences in values and beliefs sometimes result in embarrassments and mistakes by companies marketing products, particularly in international markets.

Because the United States is made up of many cultures and values, marketers cannot expect that everyone they work with will view marketing decisions in the same way. They must find ways to hold to their personal values and ethics, those of the company they work for, and those of the consumers.

The process of ethical decision-making is somewhat like the scientific process. However, rather than identifying facts on which to base decisions, the ethical process identifies important values and expectations. The steps in ethical decision-making are:

1. Identify situations that present an ethical choice.

2. List possible decisions that can be made.

3. Identify individuals and groups that will be affected by the decisions and their important values and beliefs.

4. Study the impact of each possible decision to determine if it would be viewed as ethical or unethical by those affected.

5. Select the decision that meets the ethical standards of all those affected by the choice.

Completing an ethical decision-making process provides several benefits. First, it causes decision-makers to be more careful and thoughtful. Often when we make a decision quickly, the decision results in problems. As we reconsider the decision, we see that had we taken more time, gathered information, and thought about the consequences, we might have made another choice. Second, the process encourages the identification of several possible decisions. It might result in solutions that would not have otherwise been considered. Third, the process requires that the values and beliefs of several individuals and groups be studied. In doing that, the marketer learns about the organization and specific groups of customers. A better understanding of the market helps the marketer make the best marketing decisions.

Can you think of companies, products and services, or marketing activities that have been criticized because they were viewed by some consumers as inappropriate, in poor taste, or inconsiderate of their beliefs? Consumer values are an important part of decision-making for many purchases.

ETHICAL ISSUES IN MARKETING

There are many specific ethical issues that marketers face. Some of those issues have been important for many years. Other issues develop because of changing technology or emerging social issues. For example, businesses have always faced the issue of how much information to share with potential customers. Should customers be told about potential problems or defects of a product even if they are not obvious? Should a product that does not meet the safety standards of one country be sold in another country where the standards, that are lower, are met? What if the company knows that use of the product, although legal, may result in harm to customers?

There are two broad areas where ethical issues are of concern to marketers: product issues and process issues. Some marketers argue that their only ethical concerns are with the process of marketing. However, we know that marketers need to be involved in product issues if marketing is to be effective. The product is one of the four mix elements. Product/service planning is a marketing function. Marketers are often in the best position in the company to anticipate customer reactions to products and services. Marketers need to carefully analyze the features, brand name, guarantees, and customer services of their products to insure they meet ethical standards. Product-related ethical issues that companies have recently faced are described in Figure 24-1 (on page 732).

Product-Related Ethical Issues

FIGURE 24-1 ■ Some ethical issues result from products that do not meet the claims of the company. Marketers share the responsibility to be sure that information provided about products is accurate.

Each marketing activity should also be carefully evaluated. As each mix element is planned, the ethical decision-making process should be used. In addition, as marketers complete marketing research, identify target markets, and evaluate the competition, ethical issues may be encountered. Figure 24-2 lists several ethical issues related to the process of marketing.

MARKETING USES TECHNOLOGY

Is technology an important part of marketing? Some people who are not familiar with the range of marketing activities or who have not kept up to date with today's marketing practices may not be aware of how marketing has been changed by technology. It does not take long, however, to see that there is no area of marketing today that has not been influenced by technology. Marketers need to be aware of the applications of technology in their businesses and its use in their specific jobs. Technological knowledge and skills are becoming an important requirement for all marketing occupations. The people and the businesses who are comfortable with technology and apply it effectively have real advantages compared to those who do not.

Ethical Issues Related to the Marketing Process

FIGURE 24-2 ▪ Promotion, pricing, and distribution are the direct responsibility of marketers. Unethical decisions result in the loss of customers and the possibility of legal action.

TECHNOLOGY IN THE PLANNING PROCESS

Information is very important. Governments, as well as businesses, collect and analyze information that is useful for marketing planning. Several types of technology make it easier to collect and report information. Information, stored in large databases, is often accessible to business people who are studying markets, competition, and business conditions. The marketing information management function is very important to organizations. Technology makes that function much more effective.

There are many interesting applications of technology being used in marketing research. Video and audio monitoring equipment are used to observe consumer behavior, record focus

CHALLENGES

CRITICISM CHANGES
A COMPANY

Why should a company that has been a leader in its business since 1907 completely change its target market and marketing mix? When customers complain, it gets the attention of the company. When those customers start switching to competitors, it causes the company to change.

United Parcel Service (UPS) has been known for most of this century as the leading private package delivery service for consumers. We have all seen the brown trucks parked in front of houses as the driver rushes a package to the door. UPS was very good at distributing individual packages to individual customers. But it was not as good at delivering packages to businesses. The company held a traditional view that all customers were the same. UPS prided itself in saying that all customers, no matter how big or small, paid the same price for package delivery. Drivers held to a pickup and delivery schedule that did not change even if a customer had a large package or emergency delivery.

The fastest growing segment of the package delivery market in the past several years has been the business market. While UPS developed its procedures to meet the requirements of final consumers, other companies responded to business needs. Quick response to customer questions, varying prices based on volume shipped, and special schedules to meet business needs allowed competitors to quickly take business from UPS. When business customers first complained about the level of UPS service, the company ignored them. UPS believed it was the expert in package delivery. But when market share and profits declined, the company took action.

For many years, UPS ignored marketing, employing less than ten people as marketers. The marketing staff has now grown to 175 people. Marketing research included personal interviews with thousands of customers. This resulted in the development of service standards. Standards included guaranteed dates of delivery, rapid delivery at a higher cost, and price discounts for large volume customers. Customer service representatives were assigned to specific customers so they could understand each business and respond quickly to customer needs. New technology, costing nearly $2 billion, was purchased to speed product handling and to allow employees to identify at any time where each package is located.

Maybe the most important change, however, was a commitment to a new target market. UPS recognized that the business market was unique from final consumers with a much greater sales potential. A much greater profit was possible from delivering a large volume of packages to a single customer. At the same time they saw intense competition from companies such as Federal Express, Airborne, and Roadway. To meet that competition, UPS has to understand and respond to the needs of the business market. The entire mix of services, distribution, pricing, and promotion has been redesigned to fit those needs. Marketing and customer service have become the new focus of the company.

Source: Adapted from "After a U-Turn, UPS Really Delivers," Business Week, *May 31, 1993, pp. 92–93.*

groups, and test product usage. Data can easily be captured using laser technology, touch-screens on computers, or computer-based writing pads.

TECHNOLOGY IN THE PRODUCT MIX ELEMENT

Many products now have features and options that are available only because of technology. Packaging has become lighter, more durable, and biodegradable. Some of the most noticeable changes in the product mix element are seen in service businesses. Look at the technology used in banks, libraries, and parcel delivery services. Technology created whole new businesses including desktop publishing, facsimile services, and satellite telecommunications.

TECHNOLOGY IN DISTRIBUTION

Distribution uses technology for storage, product handling, inventory control, and order processing. Technology allows for just-in-time inventory management and continuous product monitoring from design to sale. Channel members are able to coordinate marketing efforts because they can easily share information through common databases and computer systems. Buyers and managers in a central office can have instantaneous reports on product sales from throughout the world. This makes ordering and distribution extremely accurate. Traffic monitoring equipment can help determine the best locations for stores as well as the ideal locations for products within a store. A variety of technologies have been combined to increase direct marketing through cable television, telemarketing, or computer access.

TECHNOLOGY IN PRICING

You can see examples of technology in pricing every day in the marketplace. The use of credit and debit cards has been a part of marketing for many years. Now new equipment is used to create the cards and make them more secure from misuse. Businesses can quickly verify a credit or debit sale by entering the card number into the computer using scanning technology at the check-out counter. The methods used to price products, display the prices of the products, and make price changes have been simplified. Applying for and approving credit is very quick and accurate because businesses record information and check credit histories and references using computers.

TECHNOLOGY IN PROMOTION

Finally, promotion has seen exciting technological applications. Many of those applications are in the creation of advertising. New processes, higher quality, more efficient development, and even new media are the results. There are also interesting uses of technology in sales promotion, displays, and publicity. Even personal selling has benefitted. Most business-to-business salespeople now carry computers to track customer accounts, check inventory levels and delivery schedules, process orders, and even to help with sales presentations.

WHAT WILL THE FUTURE BRING?

How many times have you been asked what you will be doing five years from now? Sometimes it is hard to know what we will be doing next week much less a year or more from now. However, just as we each need to plan for the future, marketers and other business people must be prepared for the future.

You may be considering a career in marketing or you may have a job in which marketing skills are very important. If so, the future of marketing is important to you. Even as a consumer, you will be affected every day by marketing. How marketing changes and responds to your needs will be important to you in that role.

We cannot be certain about changes that will affect marketing. However, businesses are regularly planning for five to ten years into the future. Experts, called futurists, study a variety of factors that can affect businesses and other organizations and predict changes that we can expect. It will be interesting to look back in the next century to see how accurate those predictions were. Here are some of the predictions that will affect marketing in the future.

A GLOBAL MARKETPLACE

This may be the easiest factor to predict since we already live in a worldwide economy. However, much of international trade is completed by a very small percentage of larger businesses. Few businesses are truly multinational. In the future almost all businesses will find it possible and profitable to participate in international business. In fact, it may be difficult to be competitive if a business limits itself to customers and channel members in only one country.

CHANGING DEMOGRAPHICS

Again, there are few people who are not aware that the demographics in the marketplace are changing. Figure 24-3 on the next page presents an interesting illustration of the world's population. In the United States, the population is increasing and growing more diverse. The growth and change results primarily from immigration rather than an increasing birthrate. Not only is the racial and ethnic composition of the United States changing, the diversity of cultures, beliefs, and values is also increasing. Worldwide, there are great differences in population growth rates, education levels, economic conditions, and natural resources. These differences are challenging but they present opportunities for marketers who understand and can effectively respond to the differences.

INCREASING CONSUMER SOPHISTICATION

Consumers are one-half of the exchange process. They try to make the best possible decisions to satisfy needs and use resources as efficiently as possible. Many consumers are becoming much more informed about products and services as well as about business activities. With additional information, consumer expectations increase. In the future, businesses will not find it easy to meet the needs of educated consumers. However, if businesses treat consumers with respect and help them make good purchase decisions, they will likely have much better relationships with consumers than have existed in the past.

The World Population Distribution

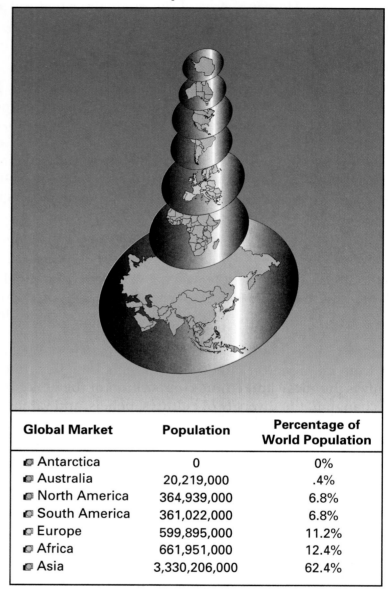

Global Market	Population	Percentage of World Population
Antarctica	0	0%
Australia	20,219,000	.4%
North America	364,939,000	6.8%
South America	361,022,000	6.8%
Europe	599,895,000	11.2%
Africa	661,951,000	12.4%
Asia	3,330,206,000	62.4%

FIGURE 24-3 ▪ When working in a global market, marketers need to be aware that population is unevenly distributed throughout the world.

MARKET SEGMENTATION

The days of mass marketing are gone for most businesses. Consumers do not want what everyone else is buying. They have specific needs. They know that some business will respond to those needs. Consumers reward those businesses by becoming loyal customers. In the future, organizations will need to be very sophisticated at market segmentation. They will need to tailor marketing mixes to several very narrow segments of a market.

CHANGING COMPETITION

Global competition is a reality. It opens opportunities but increases the numbers of businesses competing in each market. Many countries today are adopting market driven economies. They recognize that competition and private enterprise increase choices for consumers, create jobs, and improve the economic condition of the country. Laws and regulations in the United States and many other countries are now encouraging competition and removing restrictions to competition.

In some markets a limited number of large firms seem to dominate and drive out small businesses. At the same time, however, new small businesses are being created in record numbers. Many of those small businesses find market niches and operate successfully. There is room for all types and sizes of businesses whose managers are skilled at responding to market needs and are not afraid of stiff competition.

SCIENTIFIC MARKETING

Some people argue that marketing is more of an art than a science. Even if that is somewhat true today, it will not be true in the future. Marketers use research to learn what works and what does not. Companies cannot afford to invest large sums of money in marketing activities that may not work. While it is expensive to complete research, it is even more expensive to use trial and error. The top managers of a company will expect marketing personnel to carefully plan marketing and select the strategies that will result in profitable sales and satisfied customers.

BROADER MARKETING APPLICATIONS

Marketing is now recognized as one of the most important functions in a business. Businesses devote a large part of their budgets to marketing activities because they recognize the value of marketing to their success. Other types of organizations are starting to use marketing as well. Those organizations range from museums to schools to community organizations. They are finding out that marketing is not as easy as they expected. They are learning that marketing is more than advertising and selling. They are finding out that effective marketing requires an adequate budget and people who are skilled in marketing.

IN THE SPOTLIGHT

YOU CAN BET IT'S BLACK!

Competition often gets the attention of a business. The successful 1980 launching of BET (Black Entertainment Television), a new cable channel, caught the attention of the market leader in cable music channels, MTV. Starting with $15,000 and two hours of air time, Robert Johnson built BET into a 24-hour a day cable channel reaching over half of all African American households. When the success was evident, MTV responded by offering a half-hour program called "Yo! MTV Raps." That program was so successful, MTV continued to expand its programming aimed at the black audience.

Most U.S. businesses and advertisers have ignored markets composed of ethnic and racial minorities. But it is apparent that the African American market potential is bigger than most of the international markets companies pursue. Nearly 15 percent of the U.S. population is African American and this market spends $300 billion each year.

The characteristics of the African American market may surprise some. For example, fewer black consumers than white consumers live below the poverty level. Over 60 percent of high-school-aged African Americans graduate from high school. That graduation rate is increasing faster than any other group. Over one-fourth of all African American households earn more than $35,000 a year.

Not just MTV and BET are competing for the black entertainment dollar. Most movie studios are now producing films developed by black writers and directors. Time Warner, a major magazine publisher, has plans for a black culture magazine. It takes companies like BET to break the barriers.

Sources: Adapted from "Many Marketers Still Consider Blacks 'Dark-Skinned Whites,'" Marketing News, January 18, 1993, pp. 1, 13. "Where Black Is Gold," Newsweek, December 2, 1991, pp. 42–43.

DEVELOPING PROFESSIONAL MARKETING SKILLS

Because marketing is more important in organizations today, the people who perform marketing activities are more important to the organizations as well. Businesses hire people for a variety of marketing jobs. They have high expectations of the people they hire.

MARKETING EDUCATION IS A MUST

Marketing is becoming more complex. The people hired for marketing jobs must have a much higher level of knowledge and skills than ever before. While in the past people could learn how to perform marketing on the job, that is seldom possible today. Most marketing jobs require some amount of marketing education. That education can be obtained from high school and college marketing classes and through training programs provided by companies.

Entry-level jobs are available in some companies for people who have not studied marketing and who have little or no work experience. However, those jobs are often low-paying and have few opportunities for advancement. In order to advance, the employee will have to work in the company for many years. The employee will learn a great deal on his or her own or through company training opportunities. Many companies expect their employees to complete a college degree in order to move up in the marketing organization. For more and more companies, completion of a college degree is a minimum requirement for employment.

A PROFESSIONAL DEVELOPMENT PLAN

If you are planning a career in marketing, you should prepare for your professional devel-

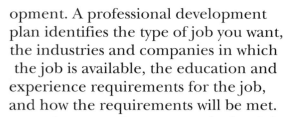

opment. A professional development plan identifies the type of job you want, the industries and companies in which the job is available, the education and experience requirements for the job, and how the requirements will be met. The minimum requirements for most marketing jobs include strong basic and academic skills, computer literacy, an understanding of business and marketing principles, effective work habits, self-management, and interpersonal and communication skills. Some marketing jobs also require specific technical knowledge of products, services, or marketing procedures.

It will usually take many years to prepare for your ideal marketing job. That time can include several years of high school and college. It may include a number of years of experience in a sequence of marketing jobs leading to your career goal. Many people today combine work experience and education by working part time while going to school.

You can plan your employment carefully starting with the jobs you hold while in high school and college. Through planning, you can have both the education and experience needed for an advanced-level marketing job when you complete your formal education. Many colleges offer internship programs that place you in exciting marketing jobs while you are in school.

In addition to formal education and work experience, other activities are an important part of your professional development. Many people work on personal development to improve self-confidence, speaking, listening, and writing skills. They may do that through reading, participating in professional or social organizations, or taking adult-education classes. One of the best strategies for professional development is to work with a mentor. A mentor is an experienced person in an area of your career interest. A mentor gives you advice, help, and support with your professional development plan.

SUPPORTING THE PROFESSIONAL DEVELOPMENT OF OTHERS

After you have worked for a company for some time, you will probably have the opportunity to train new employees. That training is very important. Think of your first few days on a new job. You wanted to do a good job but you were not always certain of the correct procedures. As a new employee, you did not know the other employees, so you may have been uncomfortable asking them for help. Many new employees quit their jobs in the first two weeks because they make too many errors or do not feel that they fit in. You can help new employees by making them feel comfortable and providing an orientation for the work they will be doing.

When you become a supervisor or manager, you will be responsible for a number of people and their work. You will not be successful in your job unless the people you supervise can do their jobs well. Part of your responsibility will be to serve as a coach for the people who work in your area. As a coach you will identify the skills each person needs. You will help each employee identify the best ways to develop those skills. As employees practice the skills you will need to observe them from time-to-time. You will encourage them to perform the skills accurately, praise them when they do a good job, and help them when they have problems. Finally, you will want to help each person with his or her own career development plan. You should encourage employees to continue their education so they can achieve their career goals.

REVIEW

Today's marketing is quite different from the marketing of several years ago. There are new marketing activities, technology is more important, and it is a much more important function in most businesses. Marketers need to study both the strengths and weaknesses of marketing to improve marketing.

Marketers are faced with many ethical issues. When companies are viewed as unethical, consumers will be reluctant to do business with them. Some ethical issues are created as a result of differences in values and beliefs among people from different cultures.

Change will be a part of marketing in the future. Studying predictions and trends helps marketers plan for the future. Some of the expected changes include the growing importance of global markets, changing demographics, more educated consumers, greater competition, and the use of marketing in a broader set of organizations.

People planning careers in marketing need to recognize the value of education and training. A career development plan will help you to achieve the marketing career you want. As a marketer, you will want to help new employees and people you supervise to develop their skills. Successful companies have well-trained employees.

MARKETING FOUNDATIONS

1. MARKETING IN YOUR LIFE

Marketing has improved our lives, but also has areas in which it can be improved. The chapter identifies several contributions of marketing and several concerns about the practices of marketing. For each of the following contributions, develop a specific example from your life (you or your family, friends, community) that illustrates the value of marketing to you. Then for each of the concerns, identify a marketing activity you have seen or been a part of that illustrates how poor marketing practices can result in problems.

Contributions

- Marketing gives us choices.
- Marketing reduces costs.
- Marketing creates a worldwide marketplace.
- Marketing offers rewarding careers.
- Marketing improves business practices.
- Marketing improves the standard of living.

Concerns

- Do marketers keep the best interests of consumers in mind?
- Does marketing support the purpose of the business?
- Are marketing decisions ethical?
- Are marketing activities socially responsible?

2. MARKETING FOR THE FUTURE

 The following predictions of changes in the future were discussed in this chapter: a global marketplace, changing demographics, increasing consumer sophistication, market segmentation, changing competition, scientific marketing, and broader marketing applications. Identify a business that you might like to own or manage. Write a one-paragraph description of the business—type of business, products or services offered, location, size, typical customers, and so on. Then select any three of the changes listed. Prepare a two-page essay describing how your business will respond to those changes and why you believe the response will make your business successful.

MARKETING RESEARCH

1. A GROWING AND CHANGING MARKET

The demographics of the United States are changing. Even U.S. Census Bureau projections have been revised. Those revised projections reflect a higher birth rate, longer life spans, and more immigrants. The percentage of population in various ethnic groups is also predicted to change because each of these factors is not changing at the same rate for all groups.

The following data show projections made by the Census Bureau in 1989, projections made in 1992, and recent projections by ethnic group for the years 1992 and 2050.

U.S. Population Projections (in millions)		
Projection For this Year	Projection Made in 1989	Projection Made in 1992
1995	260	263
2000	270	275
2005	275	285
2010	280	300
2020	295	325
2030	300	350
2040	305	365
2050	300	385

U.S. Population Projections by Ethnic Group (in millions)		
Ethnic Group	1992	2050
Asian/Pacific	7.65	42.10
African American	35.70	63.20
Hispanic	22.95	76.60
Native American	2.55	5.75
White	186.15	199.16
Total	255.00	386.81

Using the information from the tables:

a. Calculate the difference between the 1989 and 1992 projections of total population for each of the years listed. Then determine the percentage by which the 1992 projections exceed the 1989 projections for each of the years.

b. Prepare a bar graph that illustrates the total population projections made in 1989 and 1992 for each of the years listed in the table.

c. Determine the percentage of total population represented by each of the ethnic groups for 1992 and 2050.

d. Prepare a pie chart for each of the years showing the projected composition of the U.S. population by ethnic group.

2. WHAT ABOUT TECHNOLOGY?

 There are many reports on new types of technology. Much of that technology will be used in marketing. New technology can result in important changes in the way marketing activities are performed. Look at several recent issues of newspapers and magazines to find a detailed article on a new type of technology. After reading the article, think of ways the technology can be used in marketing. Consider each of the marketing mix elements and the nine marketing functions.

Prepare a three-page typed report that clearly describes the technology. Be sure to identify who is developing it, where it is being developed, and when it will be available for use by businesses. Also discuss the marketing applications you believe can result from the use of the technology and how those applications could improve the marketing process. Make sure you reference the sources of the information in your report.

MARKETING PLANNING

1. ACTING ETHICALLY

The ethical decision-making process consists of five steps:

1. Identify a situation that presents an ethical choice.
2. List possible decisions that can be made.
3. Identify individuals and groups that will be affected by the decisions and their important values and beliefs.
4. Study the impact of each possible decision to determine if it would be viewed as ethical or unethical by those affected.
5. Select the decision that meets the ethical standards of all those affected by the choice.

Figures 24-1 and 24-2 list several ethical issues faced by marketers. Select one of those issues. Complete the ethical decision-making process by developing a written response to each of the steps in the process. Prepare a short rationale to support the decision you select in Step five.

2. PROFESSIONAL PLANNING

You have learned enough about marketing to determine how it can be useful to you in your career plans. You may be considering a career in marketing. You may be planning for a career in another area where marketing knowledge and skills will be useful. This activity will help you plan for your career goal.

Complete the following steps to begin a professional development plan. You will probably need to use several career resources from your library or guidance office to complete the plan. If possible, identify and talk to a person who currently works in the career area you select.

a. Identify the job you would like to have ten years from now. Describe that job as completely as possible.

b. Identify an industry in which the job is performed and several companies or organizations in which that job is found.

c. List in as much detail as possible the knowledge and skills needed to perform the job. Make sure to describe how marketing knowledge and skills can be used. List any technical requirements.

d. Identify the type and amount of education and experience needed to obtain the job. List the jobs you would typically hold as you prepare for this job.

e. Describe other activities you will use, in addition to education and work experience, to prepare yourself for the job.

MARKETING MANAGEMENT

1. MEET THE PRESS

Health food stores are popular with the consumer market segment that wants to purchase specialty food products for special dietary needs. An important part of the product line in the stores is a variety of vitamin and mineral supplements. The sale of those products has come under attack by some medical and consumer groups. The groups claim that many of the supplements are not needed by people who have a normal diet. They claim the prices charged are often excessive and that some customers consume the products in quantities that are large enough to be harmful.

Representatives of the health food industry argue that the products are wanted by consumers. They believe that consumers know if they need supplements for their diets and what those supplements are worth. Representatives say that most people who shop in health food stores are very well educated about the amount of each vitamin or mineral supplement they should consume.

Your class is going to hold a press conference to question representatives of the health food industry about the ethics of selling vitamin and mineral supplements. You will be assigned the role of either an industry representative or a member of the press by your teacher. If you are a member of the press, prepare several questions for the industry representatives that identify their beliefs about marketing, social responsibility, and ethics. If you are a representative of the industry, prepare information that will help you answer those questions from the press. Demonstrate your understanding of marketing and the marketing concept in your answers.

2. VIVA LA DIFFERENCE

For many years the unique differences and needs of ethnic and racial groups, those in the United States and in other countries, were ignored or misunderstood by many businesses. Today, those markets are identified as very important. Businesses are working to develop effective marketing mixes that respond to each market's needs.

Select one racial or ethnic group that you would like to study. The group selected can be a U.S. market or an international market. Gather information on the market and prepare a two-page report that includes the following:

a. Develop a detailed description of the market including demographic information; unique elements of culture, values, and beliefs; decision-making process; and buyer behavior unique to the market.

b. Recommend marketing strategies that are responsive to the needs of the market, including desired characteristics of products and services; appropriate distribution strategies; recommended pricing strategies and methods of enhancing value; and effective promotional strategies.

Make sure your report is factual. It should be based on accurate information about the selected market and not on the biases or stereotypes of others.

PHOTO CREDITS

GLOSSARY

A

accounting function • maintains the records and information related to the business' finance.

administration function • involves developing, implementing, and evaluating the plans and activities of a business.

advertising • any paid form of non-personal communication sent through a mass medium by an organization about its products or services.

advertising plan • the activities and resources needed to prepare and present a series of related advertisements focusing on a common objective.

analysis • the way in which information from an MkIS is summarized, combined, or compared with other information so decisions can be made; element of a marketing-information system.

answering questions • fourth step of the selling process in which the salesperson resolves concerns and provides additional information needed by a customer when answering questions.

approach • the first contact with the customer when the salesperson gets the customer's attention and creates a favorable impression; second step of the selling process.

attribute-based shopping goods • consumer goods for which customers believe there are significant differences among the features of the competing brands and customers make their purchasing decisions based on the best value.

B

balance of trade • difference between the amount of a country's imports and exports.

balance sheet • financial statement describing the type and amount of assets, liabilities, and capital in a business on a specific date.

bartering • exchanging products or services with others by agreeing on their values.

basic stock list • identifies the minimum amount of important products a store needs to have available to meet the needs of its target market.

benefit • the advantage provided to a customer as a result of the feature.

benefits derived • segmentation technique that divides the population into groups depending on the value they receive from the product or service.

bidding • negotiation type where several suppliers develop specific prices at which they will meet detailed purchase specifications and other criteria prepared by the buyer.

bill of lading • document sent with the merchandise identifying the products that are being shipped.

boycott • organized effort to influence a company by refusing to purchase its products.

brand • name, symbol, word, or design that identifies a product, service, or company.

break-even point (BEP) • quantity of a product that must be sold for total revenues to match total costs at a specific price.

budgets • detailed projections of financial performance for a specific time period of one year or less.

bundling • practice of combining the price of several related services.

business consumer • consumer who buys goods and services to produce other goods and services or for resale.

business markets • companies and organizations that purchase products for the operation of a business or the completion of a business activity.

buying behavior • the decision processes and actions of consumers as they buy and use services and products.

buying motives • reasons that people buy.

C

central market • a location where products are brought to be exchanged conveniently.

channel members • businesses and other organizations that participate in a channel of distribution.

channel of distribution • organizations and individuals who participate in the movement and exchange of products and services from the producer to the final consumer.

closed-ended questions • questions offering two or more choices from which respondents can select one answer.

closing the sale • fifth step in the selling process in which the customer makes a decision to purchase.

code of ethics • statement of responsibilities for honest and proper conduct.

cold calling • process in which a salesperson contacts a large number of people who are conveniently located without knowing a great deal about each person contacted.

communication process • transfer of a message from a sender to a receiver.

comparison shopping • competitive study technique where people are sent to competitors' stores to determine the products sold, prices charged, and services offered.

competition matching approach • method of determining an advertising budget in which an organization attempts to spend a similar amount of money on advertising as its competitors.

consumer behavior • study of consumers and how they make decisions.

consumer credit • credit extended by a retail business to the final consumer.

consumer decision-making process • process by which consumers collect information and make choices among alternatives.

consumer markets • markets made up of individuals or socially related groups who purchase products for personal consumption.

consumerism • organized actions of groups of consumers seeking to increase their influence on business practices.

continuity • scheduling advertisements regularly throughout the course of a year.

controllable risk • risk which can be reduced or even avoided by actions taken.

controlled economy • government attempts to own and control important resources and to make the decisions about what will be produced and consumed.

controlling • function of management involving establishing standards for each of the company's goals, measuring and comparing performance with the established standards to see if the goals are being met, and taking corrective action when problems are identified.

convenience goods • consumer goods and services that are purchased frequently with little thought or effort spent on the buying process.

convenience stores • stores located very close to their customers offering a limited line of products that consumers use regularly.

culture • common beliefs and behaviors of a group of people who have a similar heritage and experience; the sum of people's values, attitudes, beliefs, and habits; set of beliefs or attitudes passed on from generation to generation.

D

decline stage of life cycle • fourth stage of the product life cycle, during which sales drop rapidly and little or no profit is generated.

decoding • interpreting a message or symbols and converting it into concepts and ideas.

demand • quantity of a product consumers are willing and able to purchase at a specific price.

demand curve • graph of the relationship between price and quantity demanded.

demographics • descriptive characteristics of a market such as age, gender, race, income, and educational level.

demography • study of the characteristics of human populations, such as age, income, and ethnic background.

demonstration • personalized presentation of the features of the marketing mix in a way that emphasizes the benefits and value to the customer; third step of the selling process.

derived demand • quantity of a product or service needed by a business in order to operate at a level that will meet the demand of its customers.

direct channel • distribution channel where the product moves from the producer to the final consumer with no other organizations involved.

direct competition • competition in a market segment with businesses that offer the same product or service.

direct demand • quantity of a product or service needed to meet the needs of the consumer.

direct exporting • process in which businesses take complete responsibility for marketing their products in other countries.

discounts and allowances • reductions in a price given to the customer in exchange for performing certain marketing activities or accepting something other than would normally be expected in the exchange.

distribution • locations and methods used to make the product available to customers.

distribution center • facility used to accumulate products from several sources, regroup, repackage, and send them as quickly as possible to the locations where they will be used.

E

economic market • all of the consumers who will purchase a particular product or service.

economic resources • resources classified as natural resources, capital, equipment, and labor.

economic utility • amount of satisfaction a consumer receives from the consumption of a particular product or service.

elastic demand • economic concept describing the situation when a price decrease will increase total revenue.

elasticity of demand • relationship between changes in a product's price and the demand for that product.

emergency goods • products or services that are purchased as conveniently as possible as a result of an urgent need.

emotional motives • forces of love, affection, guilt, fear, or passion that compel consumers to buy.

encoding • putting a message into the language or symbols that are familiar to the intended receiver.

ethics • decisions and behavior based on honest and fair standards.

evaluation • final step in the advertising plan which measures how well the advertising plan achieves its original objectives.

experiments • tightly controlled situations in which all important factors are the same except the one being studied for marketing research.

exports • products and services that are sold to another country.

F

feature • a description of a product characteristic.

feedback • receiver's reaction or response to the source's message.

final consumer • consumer who buys a product or service for personal use.

finance function • plans and manages financial resources related to the business' finance.

financial forecasts • numerical predictions of future performance related to revenue and expenses.

financial statements • detailed summaries of the specific financial performance for a business or a part of the business.

financing • budgeting for marketing activities, obtaining the necessary financing, and providing financial assistance to customers to assist them with purchasing the organization's products and services.

flexible pricing policy • pricing policy that allows customers to negotiate the price within a price range.

focus group • small number of people brought together to discuss identified elements of an issue or problem.

follow-up • making contact with the customer after the sale to insure satisfaction; the sixth and final step of a sale.

foreign investment • owning all or part of an existing business in another country.

foreign production • a company's production facilities owned and operated in another country.

form utility • satisfaction resulting from changes in the tangible parts of a product or service.

free economy • all resources are owned by individuals rather than the government, and decisions are made independently with no attempt at regulation or control by the government.

free on board (FOB) pricing • geographic pricing policy which identifies the location from which the buyer pays the transportation costs and takes title to the products purchased.

G

geographic segmentation • dividing consumers into markets based on where they live.

goodwill • customer's positive feelings about an organization, product, or service.

gross margin • difference between the cost of the product and the selling price.

growth stage of life cycle • second stage of the product life cycle, during which sales are increasing rapidly and competitors enter the market.

H

heterogeneous • characteristic of a service, meaning there are differences between services.

I

imports • products or services purchased from another country.

impulse goods • items that are purchased on the spur of the moment, without advanced planning.

income statement • financial statement reporting on the amount and source of revenue and the amount and type of expenses for a specific period of time.

indirect channel • distribution channel that includes other businesses between the producer and consumer that provide one or more of the marketing functions.

indirect competition • when a business competes with a product that is outside its product classification group.

indirect exporting • process in which marketing businesses with exporting experience serve as agents for a business and arrange for the sale of its products in other countries.

industrial economy • economy where the primary business activity is the manufacturing of products.

inelastic demand • economic concept describing the situation when a price decrease will decrease total revenue.

inflation • when prices increase faster than the value of the goods and services.

information management • systematic collection and organization of information so that it can be quickly and easily used in decision-making.

information system • organized procedures (often using computer technology) for obtaining, storing, processing, and retrieving information needed in the operation and management of a business.

input • information needed for decision-making; an element of a marketing-information system.

inseparable • characteristic of a service meaning the service is produced and consumed at the same time.

insurable risk • risk faced by a large number of people, risk that is pure rather than speculative, and risk in which the amount of the loss can be predicted.

intangible • characteristic of a service meaning it cannot be touched, seen, tasted, heard, or felt.

internal information • information developed from activities that occur within the organization.

international trade • sale of products and services to people in other countries.

interpersonal communication • communication involving two or more people in some kind of person-to-person exchange.

introduction stage of life cycle • first stage of the product life cycle, during which the new product enters the market.

inventory • assortment of products maintained by a business.

inventory records • records where the purchasing company enters information on products that have been received.

invoice • bill for merchandise purchased.

J

joint venture • independent companies develop a relationship to participate in common business activities.

just-in-time purchasing (JIT) • procedure where a company develops a relationship with its suppliers to keep inventory levels low and to resupply inventory just as it is needed.

L

labor intensiveness • amount of human effort required to deliver a service.

law of demand • relationship characterized when the price of a product is increased, less will be demanded; when the price is decreased, more will be demanded.

law of supply • relationship characterized when the price of a product is increased, more will be produced; when the price is decreased, less will be produced.

leading • the ability to communicate the direction of the business and to influence others to successfully carry out the needed work.

liability • legal responsibility for loss or damage.

licensed brand • well-known name or symbol established by one company and sold for use by another company to promote its products.

life cycle • the four stages that a product goes through, including introduction, growth, maturity, and decline.

limited-line stores • stores offering products from one category of merchandise or closely related items.

M

macroeconomics • study of the economic behavior and relationships for the entire society.

management function • developing, implementing, and evaluating the plans and activities of a business.

managers • employees who organize resources so work can be accomplished effectively and efficiently.

managing • getting the work of an organization done through other people and resources.

markdown • reduction from the original selling price.

market • description of the prospective customers a business wants to serve and the location of those customers.

market opportunity analysis • studying and prioritizing market segments to locate the best potential based on demand and competition.

market position • unique image of a product or service in a consumer's mind relative to competitive offerings.

market potential • total revenue that can be obtained from the market segment.

market price • point where supply and demand for a product are equal.

market segment • group of individuals or organizations within a larger market that share one or more important characteristics.

market share • portion of the total market potential that each company expects to get in relation to its competitors.

marketing • process of planning and executing the conception, pricing, promotion, and distribution of ideas, good, and services to create exchanges that satisfy individual and organizational objectives; the creation and maintenance of satisfying exchange relationships.

marketing concept • using the needs of customers as the primary focus during the planning, production, distribution, and promotion of a product or service.

marketing-information management • obtaining, managing, and using market information to improve decision-making and the performance of marketing activities.

marketing-information system (MkIS) • organized method of collecting, storing, analyzing, and retrieving information to improve the effectiveness and efficiency of marketing decisions.

marketing intelligence • process of gaining competitive market information; information on day-to-day changes in marketing and marketing environment.

marketing management • process of coordinating people and resources to plan and implement an effective marketing strategy.

marketing mix • blending of four marketing elements (product, distribution, price, and promotion) by the business; all of the tools or activities available to organizations to be used in meeting the needs of a target market.

marketing plan • clear written description of the marketing strategies of a business and the way the business will operate to accomplish each strategy.

marketing research • procedure to identify solutions to a specific marketing problem through the use of scientific problem-solving.

marketing strategy • the way marketing activities are planned and coordinated to achieve the goals of an organization.

markup • amount added to the cost of a product to determine the selling price.

mass communication • communicating to huge audiences, usually through mass media such as magazines, radio, television, or newspapers.

maturity stage of life cycle • third stage of the product life cycle, during which sales level off and profits begin to decline.

merchandise plan • identifies the type, price, and features of products that will be stocked by the business for a specific period of time.

merchandising • offering products produced or manufactured by others for sale to customers.

message channel • medium the sender chooses to transmit a message.

microeconomics • study of the relationship

between individual consumers and producers.

mixed merchandise stores • stores offering products from several different categories.

model stock list • describes the complete assortment of products a store would like to offer to customers.

monopolistic competition • market condition where there are many firms competing with products that are somewhat different.

monopoly • market condition in which there is one supplier offering a unique product.

multinational companies • businesses that have operations throughout the world and that conduct planning for worldwide markets.

N

need • anything you require to live.

neighborhood centers • type of shopping center with 20-30 stores that offers a broad range of products meeting regular and frequent shopping needs of consumers located within a few miles of the stores.

net profit • difference between the selling price and all costs and expenses associated with the product sold.

noise • interference that can cause the message to be interpreted incorrectly by the receiver.

non-insurable risk • type of risk for which it is not possible to predict if a loss will occur or the amount of any loss.

non-price competition • competition occurring when businesses decide to emphasize factors of their marketing mix other than price, such as quality, brand, location, or service; deemphasizes price by developing a unique offering that meets an important customer need.

non-store retailing • retail business that sells directly to the consumer's home rather than requiring the consumer to travel to a store.

O

objective and task approach • method of determining an advertising budget in which an organization determines the objectives to be achieved, identifies the tasks required to accomplish the objectives, and then computes the costs of each task.

objectives • the first step in the development of an advertising plan; the desired results to be accomplished within a certain time period.

observation • method of gathering research information by recording actions without interacting or communicating with the participant.

oligopoly • market condition where a few businesses offer very similar products or services.

one-price policy • pricing policy where all customers pay the same price.

online vendors • wholesalers of computerized databases.

open-ended questions • questions which allow respondents to develop their own answers without information about possible choices.

operating expenses • all costs associated with actual business operations.

operations • ongoing activities designed to support the primary function of a business and to keep a business operating efficiently.

opportunity • the possibility for success

organizational advertising • advertising designed to promote ideas, images, and issues associated with a company or organization.

organizing • arranging resources and relationships between departments and employees and defining the responsibility each has for accomplishing the job.

output • results of analysis; the way in which information is given to decision-makers; an element of a marketing-information system.

P

packing list • itemized listing of all of the products included in the order.

patronage motives • consumer motive that encourages consumers to purchase at a particular store or to buy a particular brand.

penetration price • a very low price designed to increase the quantity of a product sold by emphasizing the value.

percentage of sales approach • method of budgeting in which the organization budgets a percentage of past, current, or future sales for advertising.

perishable • characteristic of a service meaning the service unused in one time period cannot be stored for use in the future.

perpetual inventory system • inventory system that determines the amount of a product on hand by maintaining records on purchases and sales.

personal selling • person-to-person communication with potential customers in an effort to inform, persuade, or remind them to purchase an organization's products or services.

personality • well-defined, enduring patterns of behavior.

physical distribution • channel planning that includes the transportation, storage, and handling of products within a channel of distribution.

physical inventory system • inventory system that determines the amount of product on hand by visually inspecting and counting the items.

place utility • making products and services available where the consumer wants them.

planning • function of management involving analyzing information, setting goals, and determining how to achieve them.

population • all of the people in a group a company is interested in studying for marketing research.

positioning statement • specific description of the unique qualities of the marketing mix that make it different from the competition and satisfying to the target market.

possession utility • satisfaction resulting from the affordability of the product or service.

postindustrial economy • economy based on a mix of industrial and consumer products and services produced and marketed using high-technology equipment and methods that are purchased and sold in the global marketplace.

preapproach • gathering needed information and preparing for the sales presentation before contacting the customer; first step of the selling process.

preindustrial economy • economy based on agriculture and the development of raw materials (mining, oil production, lumber, and so on).

price • actual amount customers pay and the methods of increasing the value of the product to the customers.

price-based shopping goods • consumer goods for which customers believe there is little difference among the features of competing brands and customers make their purchasing decisions based on price.

price competition • rivalry among firms on the basis of price and value.

price lines • distinct categories within which products are organized based on differences in price, quality, and features.

pricing • establishing and communicating the value of products and services to prospective customers.

primary data • information collected for the first

time to solve the problem being studied.

private enterprise • economy based on independent decisions by businesses and consumers with only a limited government role regulating those relationships.

product • anything offered to a market by the business to satisfy needs, including physical products, services, and ideas.

product advertising • advertising used by organizations to sell specific products.

product assortment • complete set of all products a business offers to its market.

product liability insurance • insurance providing protection from claims by people, resulting from the use of the company's products.

product line • group of similar products with slight variations in the marketing mix to satisfy different needs in a market.

product/service planning • assisting in the design and development of products and services that will meet the needs of prospective customers.

product/service purchase classification system • description of the way consumers shop for products based on their needs and perception of products.

product usage • dividing a market based on the frequency that a consumer uses a product.

production • creating or obtaining products or services for sale.

profit motive • decision to use resources in a way that results in the greatest profit for the organization.

promotion • methods and information communicated to customers to encourage purchases and increase their satisfaction; any form of communication used to inform, persuade, or remind consumers about an organization's goods or services.

promotional mix • blend of the promotional elements of advertising, personal selling, publicity, and sales promotion into a strategy for delivering a message to the target market.

promotional plan • carefully arranged sequence of promotions designed around a common theme responsive to specific objectives.

psychographics • dividing a market based on people's interests and values.

publicity • non-paid form of non-personal communication about a business or organization, or its products and services, that is transmitted through a mass medium.

pulsing • scheduling advertisements so that advertising efforts are increased during a specific period of time and decreased or even withdrawn during another period of time.

purchase order • form describing all of the products ordered; completed by the buyer and sent to the seller to begin the purchasing process.

purchase specifications • detailed requirements for construction or performance of the product that are provided to potential vendors.

purchasing • determining the purchasing needs of an organization, identifying the best sources to obtain the needed products and services, and completing the activities necessary to obtain and use them.

purchasing power • amount of goods and services that can be obtained with a specific amount of money.

pure competition • market condition with a large number of suppliers offering very similar products.

pure risk • risk which presents the chance of loss but no opportunity for gain.

Q

qualifying • gathering information to determine which people are most likely to buy a product or service.

quota • limit on the numbers of specific types of products foreign companies can sell in the country.

R

random sampling • procedure in which everyone in the population has an equal chance of being selected in the sample for marketing research.

rational motives • functional benefits to be derived from a product or service.

receiver • person or persons to whom the encoded message is directed.

receiving record • document completed by the purchasing company listing all of the merchandise in a shipment.

recession • period of time in which production, employment, and income are declining.

reciprocal trading • form of bartering in which products or services of one company are used as payment for those of another company.

reference groups • groups or organizations from which you take your values and attitudes.

regional shopping centers • shopping centers containing 100 or more businesses that draw customers from a wide geographical area.

regulated economy • resources and decisions are shared between the government and other groups or individuals.

reorder point • level of inventory needed to meet the usage needs of the business until the product can be resupplied.

request for proposal • general description of the type of product or service needed and the criteria that are important to the buyer.

retail credit • credit extended by a retail business to the final consumer.

retailing • final business organization in an indirect channel of distribution for consumer products.

revenue • money received from the sale of products and services.

risk • possibility that a loss can occur as the result of a decision or activity.

risk management • providing security and safety for products, personnel, and customers, and reducing the risk associated with marketing decisions and activities.

S

sales promotion • activity or material that offers purchasers a direct inducement for buying a good or service.

sample • smaller group selected from the population for marketing research purposes.

scarcity • unlimited wants and needs combined with limited resources.

secondary data • information already collected for another purpose that can be used to solve the current problem.

segments • components of a market in which people have one or more similar characteristics.

self-regulation • taking personal responsibility for actions.

self-sufficient • not relying on others for the things needed to survive.

selling • direct, personal communications with prospective customers in order to assess needs and satisfy those needs with appropriate products and services.

sender • source or originator of the message in the communication process.

service quality • degree to which the service meets customers' needs and expectations.

services • activities that are intangible, exchanged directly from producer to consumer, and consumed at the time of production.

shopping goods • consumer products and services for which the customer is willing to spend considerable thought and effort on the buying process.

shopping centers • set of stores located together and planned as a unit to meet a range of customer needs.

shopping strips • type of shopping center containing approximately 5-15 stores grouped together along a street.

simulations • experiments operated in laboratories where researchers create the situation to be studied.

single-line stores • see definition of limited-line stores.

skimming price • a very high price designed to attract fewer customers but to emphasize the quality or uniqueness of the product.

social class • lifestyle, values, and beliefs that are common to a group of people.

social responsibility • concern about the consequences of actions on others.

specialization of labor • concentrating on one or a few related activities so that they can be completed very well.

specialty goods • products with strong brand loyalty.

speculative risk • risk which presents the chance to gain as well as lose from the risk.

staffing • management activity needed to match individuals with the work to be done.

stand-alone stores • large businesses located in an area where there are no other retail businesses close by and offering either a large variety of products or unique products.

standard of living • average value of resources produced by a country based on its total population.

staple convenience goods • products that are regular, routine purchases.

storage • equipment and procedures used to hold information until needed; an element of a marketing-information system.

strategy • planning that identifies how a company expects to achieve its goals.

subsidy • money provided to a business to assist in the development and sale of its products.

suggestion selling • offering additional products and services after an initial sale in order to increase customer satisfaction.

superstores • large stores that offer consumers wide choices of products.

supply • quantity of a product that producers are willing and able to provide at a specific price.

supply curve • graph of the relationship between price and quantity supplied.

surety bond • insurance for the failure of a person to perform his or her duties or for losses resulting from employee theft or dishonesty.

survey • planned set of questions to which individuals or groups of people respond.

T

tariff • tax placed on imported products to increase the price for which they are sold.

target market • a clearly identified segment of the market to which a company wants to appeal.

test market • specific city or geographic area in which marketing experiments are conducted.

theme • one idea, appeal, or benefit around which all advertising messages in a plan revolve.

time utility • satisfaction resulting from making the product or service available when the customer wants it.

total quality management (TQM) • management tool that establishes specific quality standards for all operations and develops employee teams who are responsible for planning and decision-making to improve business activities.

trade credit • credit offered by one business to another business.

trademark • legally protected words or symbols for the use of one company.

trial close • providing the customer with the opportunity to buy during the sales presentation.

U

uncontrollable risk • risk that is not affected by any actions taken.

unsought goods • products that consumers do not want to buy or do not consider important at a particular time.

V

value • decision to use resources in a way that results in the greatest satisfaction of wants and needs.

vendor analysis • objective rating system used by buyers to compare potential suppliers on important purchasing criteria.

W

want • an unfulfilled desire.

what you can afford approach • method of determining the advertising budget in which the organization accounts for all of its expenses and whatever is left over is budgeted for advertising.

wholesale clubs • businesses that offer a variety of common consumer products for sale to selected members through a warehouse outlet.

wholesalers • companies that assist with distribution activities between businesses.

Z

zone pricing • geographic pricing policy in which different product or transportation costs are set for specific areas of the seller's market.

INDEX

ket in, **20**; implementing, **19–22**; in international markets, **131–132**; in monopolistic competition, **176**; in monopoly, **174**; planning offering in, **164–170**; satisfying customer needs in, **16–17, 163–164**

Marketing costs, effect of, on business success, **628–631**

Marketing departments: emphasis on, in marketing, **43–44**; in product planning, **350**

Marketing efficiency, increasing, **450**

Marketing environment, risks in, **609–611**

Marketing functions, **11–13, 344–346**; channels of distribution in, **449–450**; company use of, **13–14**; distribution in, **11, 12, 142**; financing in, **11, 12, 141**; information management in, **12, 13, 143**; pricing in, **12, 13, 142**; product development in, **348–349**; product/service planning in, **11, 12, 140–141**; promotion in, **12, 13–14, 143**; purchasing in, **11, 12, 141, 406–407**; risk management in, **12, 13**; selling in, **12, 14, 143–144**

Marketing-information: gathering, **138–140**; management of, **246–247**; in marketing plan, **317–320**; need for, **664–667**; reasons for business' need of, **240–244**; sources of, **676–684**; visual summaries of, **252**. *See also* Information

Marketing-information management, **592–593, 676**; in international marketing, **143**; as marketing function, **12, 13**

Marketing-information system, **246, 667**; analysis of, **669–670**; decision-making in, **670–671**; information needed for, **671–676**; input in, **667–668**; output of, **670**;

storage of, **668–669**; in tracking customer wants, **57**

Marketing intelligence, **204–206**; definition of, **204, 684**; for organizations, **685–686**; personal, **684–685**

Marketing management, **700, 710–711**; controlling in, **704, 713–714**; definition of, **700**; leading in, **704, 713**; organizing in, **703, 711–712**; planning in, **701–703, 711**; staffing in, **703, 712–713**

Marketing mix: brand name/image in, **283**; decisions in, **164–165**; definition of, **20–21, 164**; developing, **20–22, 278–280**; distribution in, **284–285, 444**; effect of, on promotional mix, **531–532**; expenses associated with, **644–646**; guarantee in, **284**; identification of, in marketing plan, **709**; identifying alternatives in, **280–287**; in marketing risks, **611–614**; packaging in, **284**; planning effective, **287–298**; price in, **285–286**; product in, **281–283**; product/service purchase classification system for, **293–297**; promotion in, **286–287**; service in, **281–283, 390–395**; specifying, in marketing strategy, **325–326**; testing, **351**; uses in, **284**; warranty in, **284**

Marketing plan, **312–313, 328, 329–330**; action plan in, **326–328, 707**; benefits of, **313–314**; controlling in, **709–710**; definition of, **314–315, 315**; and environmental change, **709–710**; format for, **320, 322–328**; gathering marketing-information in, **319–320**; identification of marketing mix in, **709**; identification of target markets in, **702**; implementing, **328–331**; improving management with, **704–710**; as information source, **680**;

leading in, **708–709**; in managing marketing risks, **615–616**; market analysis in, **705–707**; marketing-information in, **317–319**; as marketing tool, **320**; organizing in, **707**; preparation of, **316–320**; staffing in, **707–708**; strategy in, **315–316, 707**; using purchase classifications for, **298–301**

Marketing research: effect of, on planning, **243–244**; in global marketing, **255**; primary data collection in, **256–261**; in problem solving, **247–255**; in product development, **350**; proper use of, **262**; questionable practices in, **258**; in tracking customer wants, **57**

Marketing research reports, **253–255**

Marketing risks, **609**; environment in, **609–611**; managing, **615–620**; marketing mix in, **611–614**; reducing, **619–620**

Marketing strategy, **325**; customer needs in, **162–164**; definition of, **274–275**; designing effective, **351**; developing, **274–280**; developing successful, **301–303**; distribution decisions in, **166–167**; in marketing plan, **315–316**; planning in, **160–170**; positioning statement in, **325**; pricing products and services in, **167–169**; product development in, **166**; specifying marketing mix in, **325–326**; target market description in, **325**

Marketing tool: economic utility as, **109**; life cycles as, **293**; marketing plan as, **320**

Market opportunity: analysis of, **164**; and cultural diversity, **139**

Marketplace, changing,

Property insurance, **618**

Psychographics in market segmentation, **188**

Public awareness, role of marketing on increasing, **65**

Publicity: advantages of, **528**; definition of, **528**; disadvantages of, **529**

Public-service monopolies, government control of, **493**

Pulsing, **558–560**

Purchase behavior, impact of marketing in, **61–63**

Purchase classifications, using, for marketing planning, **298–301**

Purchase in consumer decision-making process, **226**

Purchase order, **423**

Purchase specifications, **413**

Purchase volume, **410**

Purchasing, **592**; definition of, **406**; improving procedures in, **420–422**; information needed for, **673**; in international marketing, **141, 429–430**; as marketing function, **11, 12, 406–407**; need for specialists in, **415–416**; by organizations, **407–411**; as part of the exchange process, **404–407**

Purchasing needs, identifying, in business purchasing, **416–417**

Purchasing power, **137**

Purchasing process in business, **411–416**

Purchasing records, **423–424**

Pure competition, **99–100, 173**

Pure risks, **606**

Purpose, in market analysis, **323**

management responsibility for, **698**

Quantity discount, **502**

Questions: answering, in selling process, **588–589**; closed-ended, in surveys, **256**; open-ended, in surveys, **256–257**

Quotas, **137–138**

changes in, **463–465**; definition of, **459**; location of retail businesses, **462–463**; product mix of retailers, **460–464**; types of retailers in, **460–463**

Retail purchasing, **424–425**; completing process, **428**; determining retail customer needs in, **425–426**; developing plan, **426–427**; locating products for sale, **427**

Retail Trade, **682**

Revenue: definition of, **629**; effects of marketing on, **640–643**; increasing, **649, 651**

Reward Game, **610**

Rhino Records, **70**

Risk: assuming, **609**; avoiding, **608**; classification of, **606–607**; control of, **606–607**; dealing with, **607–609**; definition of, **605**; insuring, **608–609**; result of, **606**; transferring, **608**

Risk management, **142–143, 592**; definition of, **609**; information needed for, **674–675**; as marketing function, **12, 13**; risks taken by businesses, **604–607**

Robinson-Patman Act (1936), **69**

Rollerblade, **360**

Rome, Treaty of, **120**

Routine decision-making, **229–230**

Ryan's Family Steakhouse, **533**